THE NAVAL CHRONICLE

VOLUME IV

THE NAVAL CHRONICLE

The Contemporary Record of the Royal Navy at War

Volume IV 1807 – 1810

Consolidated Edition
containing a

GENERAL AND BIOGRAPHICAL HISTORY

of

THE ROYAL NAVY

of the

UNITED KINGDOM

During the War with the French Empire

War Reports, Commanding Officers' Gazette Letters of Naval Actions, Narratives taken from Foreign Sources, Intelligence Reports on the Fleets of Europe and of the American Republic, Letters from Serving Officers on Naval Strategy, Tactics, Gunnery, Ship Design, and Professional Concerns, and With a Variety of Original Papers on Nautical Subjects.

*

Under the Guidance of Several Literary and Professional Men, and Prepared for General Use by:

NICHOLAS TRACY

CHATHAM PUBLISHING

LONDON

First published in Great Britain in 1999 by
Chatham Publishing,
61 Frith Street,
London W1V 5TA

Chatham Publishing is an imprint of Gerald Duckworth & Co Ltd

British Library Cataloguing in Publication Data
A catalogue record for this book is available from the British Library

ISBN 1 86176 094 9

Typeset by Linda Jones
Printed and bound in Great Britain by Bookcraft (Bath) Limited

Contents

Introduction to Volume IV

Much of the action during the years between Trafalgar and the end of the decade was directed to the elimination of the fleets of French vassal states, preferably by negotiation, and reassurance, but if necessary by violence. The vacillating policy of Russia was of central interest. Shortly before his death in 1806 Pitt had succeeded in drawing Tsar Alexander into the Third Coalition against the French. To accommodate the Russian ally, a naval expedition under the questionable leadership of Vice-Admiral Duckworth was sent in 1807 through the Dardanelles to Constantinople to catalyse a settlement between Russia and Turkey, but the only consequence was a break with Turkey. The abortive Dardanelles expedition, and the assault on Copenhagen in 1807 to eliminate any possibility that the Danish fleet would serve French purposes, were typical of Royal Navy operations following Trafalgar, against fortified positions ashore. The Copenhagen expedition was operationally highly successful, but strategically questionable as its brutality alienated Russia. Under pressure from the French army, the Tsar made an accommodation with Napoleon. As a consequence, the British Mediterranean fleet had to take on the task of blockading the Russian squadron which had been operating in the Aegean, but which, on the diplomatic break between Britain and Russia, found shelter in Lisbon. The Russian 'War', however, was a formality which London was careful to minimise, and the Portuguese themselves were eventually persuaded to trust to British assistance, and to withdraw their fleet and court to Brazil to avoid subjugation by a French army.

Spain had been drawn into the war against Britain early in 1805, but following Trafalgar the Spaniards played little part in the naval war, and the Spanish revolt against their French overlords in 1808 created the context for much of the naval and military action of the second half of this volume. Transport of soldiers to the Iberian theatre, and close support of Spanish regular, and irregular, forces operating near the coast became stock in trade of the Royal Navy. Cadiz became an allied town under French siege. British assistance to Spain suffered a major setback when, following the successful army action under General Wellesley at Vimeiro, General Dalrymple agreed to a convention at Cintra which permitted the French to withdraw to France with all their booty, and even provided them with British transport, but did not prohibit their immediate return to the Spanish theatre across the French frontier. One of the terms of the convention permitted the Russian squadron in the Tagus to be interned at Spithead, rather than surrender as prizes of war. That disgraceful convention was followed in early 1809 by the retreat of the British Army under Sir John Moore, before overwhelming French superiority and without the support from the Spanish which had been promised. At Corunna it fought a masterful rearguard action while awaiting the arrival of the naval transports.

Apart from a minor mopping-up operation in the West Indies, and the continued support of British and Spanish forces in Spain, the navy's work in 1809 focused on the main French battlefleets. In April an ambitious, and contentious, effort was made, using fireships and explosive devices, to destroy the squadron sheltering in Basque Roads. In July the largest operation carried out by British combined forces during the war sailed to destroy the French controlled fleet in the Scheldt. A landing was successfully made on Walcheren island, and the navy worked its way up the defended river to assist in the final assault on Antwerp, but the Commander-in-Chief, the Earl of Chatham, was so dilatory that the French were able to reinforce their positions. He decided to withdraw, retaining only Walcheren, which was held until the end of the year, but at such a cost in sickness that it had to be abandoned without a fight.

The least satisfactory development during this period was the increasing tension with the United States over the exercise of British control of maritime commerce. In the wake of Trafalgar, Napoleon had put in place a system of trade embargo known as the 'Continental System', intended to destroy the British economy by denying Britain the ability to sell its produce and manufactures to continental Europe. This was a very real threat, although it involved the French in such expense and diplomatic conflict that it eventually backfired on them. The British method of resisting the French embargo was to establish a comprehensive control of all maritime trade so that Europeans had no alternative but to connive at smuggling British goods into their harbours. The Americans vigorously resisted this control, and Washington increasingly found itself preferring the Buonapartist police-state over Britain. This conflict was to lead to war between Britain and the United States in 1812 but, fortunately for the British, was also a contributing factor in the Spanish revolt against Napoleon, and was to lead to a renewal of war between France and Russia.

1807 – Naval News, Spring

1807 STARTED WELL FOR THE BRITISH when Captain Brisbane, under the orders of Vice-Admiral Dacres, arrived at the Dutch settlement of Curaçao. Its defences were massive, but surprise was complete and Brisbane employed it well. In three-quarters of an hour the place was his, and half an hour later the Dutch governor formally surrendered.

The year, however, was to be a hard one. The political direction of Britain continued to be unstable following the death of Pitt. In March 1807 the Grenville administration collapsed following its attempt to permit Catholics to hold commissions in the armed forces. The Duke of Portland formed the new government, and replaced Lord Howick at the Admiralty with General Lord Mulgrave, who soon turned out to be a very unpopular choice in the fleet. Portland's foreign policy decisions were all but disastrous.

The dominant strategic consideration continued to be the need to react to Emperor Napoleon's efforts to exploit his continental victories to reverse his naval defeat at Trafalgar, by employing his capacity to control the trade of most of the European continent, and to control its resources of shipping. The Berlin decree had set out to deny Britain access to continental markets for its own produce and manufactures, and for its re-exports. The British response was to extend a 'paper' blockade around the entire coast of French-dominated Europe and to seize any ship trying to enter or leave which was not sailing to or from a British port. The objective was to force Europeans to 'buy British'. Because of the attractiveness of British goods and of their prices, it was to succeed admirably, and ensured Britain the economic resources needed to support the continental campaigns which ultimately defeated Buonapartism. However, it also caused tremendous resentment amongst neutral trading nations, and was to lead to war with the United States in 1812.

Napoleon's Continental System caused him no less grief. In an effort to oblige Portugal to break off its trade with Britain, a French army crossed the border from Spain and occupied Lisbon, but the Prince Regent and all the Portuguese court were persuaded to accept a British escort,

1

commanded by Sir Sidney Smith, to establish a court in exile in Brazil. The attempt to ensure French control of Spain was to lead to the Spanish revolt in 1808, and Napoleon's efforts to control Russian trade was later to lead to the invasion of Russia in 1812. That campaign, conducted with inadequate resources because of the number of his men employed in enforcing the customs barrier in northern Germany, was to be the destruction of the Grand Army.

On behalf of the Russians, against whom the Turks had declared war, a British fleet under Sir John Duckworth was sent through the Dardanelles to persuade the Turks to break their new connection with France, but this operation was a diplomatic disaster, and a costly naval one as well. Following the battle of Friedland in June 1807, the Russians and Prussians were obliged to conclude the Treaty of Tilsit with the French (4-6 July).

The attempt to supplant Spanish colonial power at Buenos Aires had been a consistent part of the mercantilist strategy of trade domination, but the British military commitment to that theatre was entirely inadequate to contain the nationalist ardour of the colonial population, who not only drove out the British but acquired their independence from Spain at the same time. The year's campaign opened well with the capture of Montevideo, but in June an attempt to recapture Buenos Aires led to the surrender of the British army, and its return to Britain.

Napoleon's control of the Spanish, Dutch and Venitian fleets made the possibility that he might also acquire control of the Danish, Swedish and Russian fleets a continuing matter of concern. In August 1807 the British navy was sent back to Copenhagen, under the command of Admiral Gambier, and this time an army of 20,000 was landed to besiege the city from landward. After a stubborn battle, it surrendered, and the Danish fleet was taken to Britain. Unfortunately, this *coup de main* seriously affected relations with Russia. It was a dark moment in British history, and of questionable utility. Russia followed Denmark in declaring war, and a Russian squadron was sent to Lisbon to co-operate with the French. It became a matter of importance to London to ensure that it was not used against them, but it was believed that Russia was playing as little a part as it could and care was taken not to goad the Tzar into a more active hostility.

Given the small size of the American navy, and the invulnerability of the United States to French bullying, there was no danger perceived to British naval dominance from that quarter, except from the willingness of Americans to facilitate desertion from the British navy. Efforts to stop the haemorrhaging of British manpower led to a brief engagement between HMS *Leopard* and the USS *Chesapeake*, and to a major diplomatic crisis which became one of the stepping stones to war in 1812.

A View of the Outer Harbour of Messina, with the Light-house, Sicily. Engraved by Baily, from a Drawing by Bennet.

The harbour of Messina is of an oval form, large, and towards the Fare' inclosed by a crooked neck of land; on the broadest part of which, to the east, stands the citadel: towards the west end, is a fort, called St. Salvador, which defends the narrow entrance to the harbour. Near this neck of land is the Lazaretto, built upon a rock which projects out of the sea. Plate 317

An Account Showing the Number of Ships Composing His Majesty's Navy on 1 January 1807

From the 'Naval History of the Present Year,' 1807, May-June. XVII 507-509

Ships of the 1st Rate,		Sloops, ship-rigged	127
From 120 to 100 guns	13	ditto, brig-rigged	99
Second Rate, 98 ditto	20	ditto, the nature of their	
Third Rate, 84 to 80 ditto	15	rigging not yet ascertained	5
73 to 72 ditto	119	Yachts	11
64 ditto	4	Brigs	20
Fourth Rate, 60 ditto	1	Advice Boats	3
Fifth Rate, 44 guns	15	Surveying Vessel	1
40 ditto	4	Bomb Vessels	18
38 ditto	62	Mortar Vessel	1
36 ditto	49	Fire Ships and	
34 to 32 ditto	23	Vessels	27
Sixth Rate, 28 to 24 ditto	23	Store Ships	10
22 guns	17	Armed Brigs	3
20 ditto.	7	Armed Vessels	8

The above engraving by Nesbit, from a drawing by Pocock, represents the *Royal Charlotte* yacht, built at Deptford in the year 1749. Her dimensions are as follows: - Length of gun-deck, 90 feet, 1 inch. Keel for tonnage, 72 feet 2 inches and a half. Breadth, 24 feet 7 inches. Depth, 11 feet. Tons, 232. Light draft of water afore, 5 feet 10 inches; abaft, 8 feet 8 inches. Headpiece Plate

Armed Galliot	1	Receiving Ships	14
Armed Tenders	2	Hulks	11
Cutters	32	Other small Vessels,	
Luggers	2	Transports, &c.	65
Prison Ships	5	Ships & Vessels under	
Hospital Ships	6	the Line	821
Gun-brigs	123	Ships of the Line	211
		Total of the RN	1,032

[See also: Ships Building and Ordered to be Built, in his Majesty's and Merchant's Yards.]

Capture of Curaçoa

From the 'Memoir of the Public Services of Sir Charles Brisbane, Knt.' XX 98-101

The *Pomona* having been completely secured, Captain Brisbane took her in tow, and carried her into Jamaica; after which he was despatched, by the commander-in-chief, with a squadron of frigates, consisting of the *Arethusa, Latona, Anson*, and *Fisgard*, to reconnoitre the island of Curaçoa and to ascertain, if possible, whether the inhabitants were disposed towards an alliance with this country.

It was on the 1st of January, 1807, that this little squadron arrived off Curaçoa. No orders whatever had been given to attack the island; but, having perfectly ascertained the situation of the place, Captain Brisbane formed a plan for carrying it by a *coup de main*; and, imparting his intention to the respective captains under him, with a zeal for the service, which would have done honour to the character of a Nelson, taking the sole responsibility of the act upon himself, he led his squadron into the harbour, in close order of battle, passing the formidable line of sea batteries, by which its entrance was protected, and came to an anchor. It is well deserving of remark, that, previously to this, and unknown to their officers, the men, participating in the spirit of their gallant leader, had arranged themselves for attack; and, when beat to quarters, they were found with the words, "*Victory or Death*", chalked upon their caps! As an additional stimulus,

Captain Brisbane instantly put on his dress uniform, and proceeded as we have already stated. "The harbour," as Captain Brisbane describes it, in his official letter, "was defended by regular fortifications, of two tiers of guns, Fort Amsterdam alone consisting of sixty-six pieces of cannon; the entrance only fifty yards wide, athwart which was the Dutch frigate *Hatslar*, of 36 guns, and *Surinam*, of 22, with two large schooners of war, one commanded by a Dutch commodore; a chain of forts was on Misleburg commanding height; and that almost impregnable fortress, Fort Republique, within the distance of grape shot, enfilading the whole harbour."[1]

The enemy, as we have observed in our Memoir of Captain Lydiard, were panic-struck at such unexpected gallantry, and all was confusion.[2] The pacific notification of Captain Brisbane - that the British squadron was there to protect, not to conquer; to preserve to the inhabitants their lives, liberty, and property - not being attended to, a severe and destructive cannonade commenced; the frigate, sloop, and schooners were carried by boarding; and the lower forts, and the citadel and town of Amsterdam, were taken by storm. All this was accomplished in only three quarters of an hour. In the progress of this service, Captain Brisbane, the hero of the scene, seemed to "ride upon the whirlwind - to direct the storm." He was the first man who boarded the *Hatslar* frigate, that lay athwart the harbour. He pulled the Dutch colours down with his own hands; and then, followed by about four-and-twenty men, he instantly proceeded to the shore, where he also was the first man, at the storming of Fort Amsterdam, the colours of which he likewise struck with his own hand. The latter achievement will appear the more extraordinary, when it is stated, that the fort was garrisoned by two hundred and seventy-five regular troops - As soon as he had got possession, Captain Brisbane made his way to the governor, and told him, that precisely five minutes were allowed for him to decide upon surrendering. The governor requested half an hour; alleging, that *a shorter time would not save his head in Holland*. Captain Brisbane pulled out his watch, and assented to the time required. At the expiration of the half hour, he entered the council-chamber, where the governor and council were assembled, and inquired whether they had made up their minds to surrender the island and its dependencies to the crown of Britain. The governor immediately presented a paper, containing preliminary articles of capitulation, placing the island in the possession of his majesty; to the whole of which, with one exception,[3] Captain Brisbane agreed.

By ten o'clock, the British flag was hoisted on Fort Republique; the whole of the island, defended by 1,200 militia, besides a considerable number of regular troops, having been reduced, and brought into the quiet possession of the English, by a force not exceeding 800 effective men, in less than four hours.

The splendour of the achievement might well excite the astonishment of the commander-in-chief; who, it is said, had calculated, that no less a force than ten sail of the line, and 10,000 land forces, would be necessary for the capture of the island which had been thus subdued by a mere handful of men.[4] . . .

Immediately after the capture, Captain Brisbane proceeded to disarm the militia -

1 *Vide* Naval Chronicle, Vol. XVII page 168.
2 Vide Naval Chronicle, Vol. XIX page 450. - Some additional particulars, of considerable interest, respecting the capture of Curaçoa, will be also found in our Memoir of Captain Lydiard.
3 "Article VI. All the merchants' vessels, with their cargoes in the harbour, of whatsoever nation they belong to, shall be in the possession of their proper owners. - Answer - Not granted."
4 The entire loss of the British was only three seamen killed, and fourteen wounded. Two of the former, and five of the latter, belonged to the *Arethusa*.

a most politic measure, considering the very slender state of the British force - and to administer to the inhabitants of the island the oath of allegiance to his Britannic majesty. The Dutch governor having refused to take that oath, Captain Brisbane constituted himself his successor, *pro tempore,* and assumed the functions of government accordingly.

Under the idea of retaining the government of Curaçoa, Vice-Admiral Dacres having very warmly recommended him to that post, and anxious, as his majesty's representative, to make a favourable impression upon the minds of the inhabitants, Captain Brisbane furnished the government house anew, in a style suitable to his office and dignity. In a short time, however, his majesty's ministers thought proper to nominate Sir James Cockburn, Bart. as his successor; a circumstance by which Captain Brisbane sustained a very heavy pecuniary loss.

But his services were not overlooked by his sovereign, who was graciously pleased to present him with a gold medal, and to confer upon him the order of knighthood, in honour of the professional gallantry which he had displayed. . . .

[Captain Sir Charles Brisbane's memorial detailing his service and applying for a pension is printed in Vol. xx, pp103-108.]

From the 'Naval History of the Present Year,' 1807,
February-March. XVII 251-263

Catholics May Hold Commissions

A subject of the utmost national importance was discussed in the House of Commons, March the 5th, on the Motion of Lord Howick, that

CATHOLICS MIGHT BE ENABLED TO HOLD COMMISSIONS IN THE NAVY AND ARMY.

We do not presume to give our crude and jejune ideas on so bold an innovation; but give it a preference to any other event in our concise history. It requires the heads of the most cool and experienced statesmen, and was admirably answered by Mr. Percival; who in the course of his speech observed: - It was not so much to the individual measure that he objected, but to the system of which it formed a part, which was growing day after day, and threatening to expand into the most alarming magnitude. If it was desirable to preserve any of our ancient and venerable establishment, it could only be effected by making a stand against every fresh attempt at innovation. He had as great a regard for true toleration as any man. . . .

Blockade of the Dardanelles

Letters received at Plymouth, dated in December last, from our fleet in the Dardanelles, state the following interesting particulars of the state of affairs at that period in Turkey: The *Canopus*, 84 guns, Rear-Admiral Louis, the *Endymion*, 44 guns, and another frigate, are stationed directly opposite the Grand Signior's [sic] seraglio, or palace. The *Thunderer*, 74 guns, and *Standard*, 64 guns, and two frigates, are anchored to command the passage of the Dardanelles. A few days before these letters came away, a Russian frigate from the Mediterranean passed the Dardanelles without molestation from the Turkish batteries; but Sebastiani, the intriguing ambassador from France to the Ottoman Porte, made a violent remonstrance at this frigate passing the Dardanelles; but could get no redress, as our Envoy, Mr. Arbuthnot, gave in a representation of the business, and placed it in its proper point of view, to the satisfaction of the Turkish Government.

There are twenty sail of the line and fifteen frigates in the arsenal, but not five of them are half manned. Our ships are all in high order and discipline. The Turks treat our people with the greatest civility and attention. Refreshment of all kinds are sent on board our men of war. Our gallant admiral and his officers, and the captain and officers of the other British men of war, frequently dine on shore with Mr. Arbuthnot, whose good sense and manly conduct are much admired.

Order of Council Sequestering Captured Hamburg Ships Except Those Trading to Britain

At the Court at the Queen's Palace, 26th March 1807, present, the King's Most Excellent Majesty in Council

It is this day ordered by His Majesty in Council, that all ships and goods belonging to the inhabitants of Hamburg, and other places and countries in the North of Germany, now in the possession, or under the control of France and her allies, which have been detained prior to the 1st of January last, shall be restored, upon being pronounced by the High Court of Admiralty to belong to the inhabitants aforesaid; and that the ships and goods shall be permitted to proceed to any neutral port; and all such ships and goods captured on or after the said first of January, and pronounced in like manner, shall be detained (save and except ships and goods engaged in a trade to or from the ports of this country) until farther orders; and the goods shall be sold by the claimants thereof, under a commission from the Court of Admiralty, to be granted, upon notice given to His Majesty's Procurator-General; and the proceeds, after deducting the claimant's advances in respect thereto, shall be paid into the Registry of the said Court, and shall be invested in Government Securities, until His Majesty's further pleasure shall be signified thereon: and the Right Honourable the Lords Commissioners of His Majesty's Treasury, the Lords Commissioners of the Admiralty, and the Judge of the High Court of Admiralty, are to give the necessary directions herein, as to them may respectively appertain.

(Signed) STEPHEN COTTRELL

Imperial Parliament
Monday, March 2 1807

Message From His Majesty: Peace With Prussia

Lord Howick presented a Message from the King, which was read by the Speaker, and which was as follows:

"G.R. His Majesty thinks proper to acquaint the House of Commons, that a Treaty of Peace has been concluded between His Majesty and the King of Prussia; a copy of which, as soon as the ratification have been exchanged, shall be communicated to the House; and His Majesty also thinks fit further to apprise the House, that His Majesty's Minister, by whom the Treaty was signed, in consequence of authority from His Majesty, and the urgency of affairs on the Continent, has taken on himself to advance to the Prussian Government a sum of money amounting to about £30,000, which advance His Majesty has been pleased to approve; and His Majesty trusts, that the House will enable him to make good the same."

On the motion of Lord Howick, His Majesty's Message was ordered to be referred to the Committee of Supply.

Tuesday, March 5 1807

Catholics Bill

Lord Howick brought in a bill, the object of which was, to allow all persons who profess the Roman Catholic Religion to serve His Majesty in the Navy and Army, with the free exercise of that religion.

Vestal's Gale

From the 'Naval Biography of Captain Edwards Lloyd Graham.' XXIX 359-360

The *Vestal* continued under the orders of Commodore Owen, during the remainder of the year 1806, and the beginning of the ensuing one, 1807. In February, during the severe gale of wind, when so many of our ships and brave mariners were lost, Captain Graham experienced a most miraculous deliverance. On the 18th of that month, when at his station off Dungeness, about four A.M. whilst the weather which had been previously serene, was extremely severe from cold wind at N.N.E. and a very heavy snow; a most tremendous gale came on. The cold was so intense, that several of the crew, who had been sent up aloft to furl the topsails, became benumbed, and were obliged to be lowered down, in that state, by ropes. After repeated efforts, the sails of the *Vestal* were at length furled, except the main-top-sail which was blown to atoms. The *Vestal* was then brought to; and such continued the violence of the gale, that at eight P.M. finding they could not weather the French shore, no alternative was left to save their lives, but to risk their immediately anchoring the ship within only three miles of the town of Dieppe. The gale afterwards continued with unabated fury during all the night; and the ensuing break of day displayed one of the most awful and tremendous sights, that was ever beheld by those "who go down to the sea in ships, and see the works of the Lord and his wonders on the deep." As the morning broke, around the *Vestal* were at first indistinctly discerned through the haze, between 20 and 30 sail of British merchant ships, which had been blown out of the Downs. Some already wrecked on the enemy's shore, others driving bodily on the French coast, with signals of distress flying; many without masts, and the greater part with their sails split. The humane efforts and utmost skill of the captain and officers of the *Vestal*, could only save one merchant vessel, which drove close by them. Immediately, notwithstanding the tremendous sea that was then running, as landsmen would term it, "mountains high," one of the *Vestal*'s boats was hoisted out, and actually succeeded in bringing the said vessel to an anchor; the gale afterwards gradually abated.

Female Tom Bowling

From 'Naval Anecdotes.' XVII 309

At the Public Office, Queen Square, an old woman, generally known by the name of Tom Bowling, was lately brought before the magistrate, for sleeping all night in the street; and was committed as a rogue and vagabond, and passed to her parish. She served as boatswain's mate on board a man of war for upwards of 20 years, and has a pension from Chatham Chest. When waked at midnight by the watchman in the street, covered with snow, she cried, "*Where the devil would you have me sleep?*" She has generally slept in this way, and dresses like a man; and is so hardy at a very advanced age, that she never catches cold.

From the 'Naval History of the Present Year,' 1807,
March-April. XVII 329-352

New Admiralty Administration, Lord Mulgrave First Lord

There is an old proverb in the Spanish language, that Three Changes are equal to a Fire. Another, and a most sudden change, has again taken place at the Admiralty; and the plans which the cool judgment of Mr. Grenville had begun to mature, must give way to new men, and other projects. We have often lamented the injury which the best interests of the state must sustain, from the uncertain tenure by which the station of the First Lord is held: and anxiously wish, that an equal degree of stability was given to this situation, as appears in the War Department: but every thing belonging to our naval interests does not seem to rest on so secure and fixed a basis as our military.

In our last, we early marked our astonishment at the bill which Lord Howick deemed it right to bring forward: but though we dreaded the consequences of such a measure, little did we expect, that so complete a revolution would thus be brought about in the political world.

The ingenious Mr. Barrow, who is well and universally respected, has been re-appointed to the situation of Second Secretary to the Admiralty.

Lord Mulgrave, who at present presides at the Board, is the brother of the celebrated navigator, who, in 1773, sailed to explore the North Polar Seas, and who, on the 4th of December, 1777, was appointed one of the Lords Commissioners of the Admiralty. He was an early and steady patron of the late Lord Nelson. The present Lord, who was Secretary of State for the Foreign Department in 1796, is a Lieutenant-General, and colonel of the 91st regiment of foot: and particularly distinguished himself at the siege of Toulon. The Right Honourable George Rose, who succeeded Mr. Sheridan as Treasurer of the Navy, has been long known and respected for his abilities and experience, particularly in every thing that relates to the trade and commerce of his country. It is but doing justice to the humanity of Mr. Sheridan to remark, that before he left the situation of Treasurer, the sole request that he made, was a petition to His Majesty, which secured a very old man, who had been fifty-seven years in the Navy Office, a considerable independence for life.

London 'Gazette Extraordinary,' April 12 1807

Capture of Montevideo

[A relief force under General Sir Samuel Auchmuty and Rear-Admiral Sir Charles Sterling arrived at Maldonado on 5 January 1807, on the 18th an attack was commenced on Montevideo, and on 2 February that town was taken by assault.]

Captain Donelly [sic], of His Majesty's ship *Ardent*, arrived this morning with dispatches from Rear-Admiral Stirling, commanding a squadron of His Majesty's ships in the Rio de la Plata, of which the following are copies.

Diadem, off Monte Video, 8th February 1807
I have peculiar satisfaction in congratulating my Lords Commissioners of the Admiralty on the capture of Monte Video [sic], as well from the importance of the conquest, as from the honour which has thereby been acquired by His Majesty's arms.

Immediately on the arrival of Brigadier-General Sir Samuel Auchmuty, at
Maldonado, it was determined to invest this place, and having assembled our force off
the Island of Flores, a descent was effected on the 16th ult. near Carreta Point, which is
about seven miles to the eastward of the town. The enemy had assembled in considerable
numbers, and with several pieces of artillery seemed determined to oppose our progress.

The navigation of the Rio de la Plata, with the strong breezes which we have
experienced for several weeks, rendered the landing of troops, and assisting their
operations, very difficult, but the place chosen was happily adapted to allow the covering
vessels, under the direction of Captain Hardyman, to approach so close as to command
the beach, and notwithstanding the weather threatened, and was unfavourable, the
soldiers got all on shore without a single accident of any kind, and were in possession of
the heights before six o'clock, with such things as the General wanted.

On the 19th the army moved forwards, and as an attempt to harass the rear was
expected, I directed boats to proceed close along shore to look out for and bring off any
wounded men, whilst the covering vessels were placed to prevent the enemy from giving
annoyance, and I had the happiness to hear that all the sufferers were brought off, in
despite of well directed efforts to destroy them. In the evening I dropped, with the
fleet, off Chico Bay, near which the army encamped, within two miles of the city.

I had landed about eight hundred seamen and royal marines, under the orders of
Captain Donnelly, to act with the troops; and, as I saw no advantage could result from
any effort of ships against a strong fortress, well defended at all points, and which, from
the shallowness of the water, could not be approached within a distance to allow shot to
be of any use, I disposed the squadron so as to prevent any escape from the harbour, as
well as to impede a communication between Colonna and Buenos Ayres, and confined
my whole attention to give every possible assistance in forwarding the siege, by landing
guns from the line of battle ships, with ammunition, stores, provisions, and every thing
required by the commander of the forces.

The distance which the ships lay from the shore, with the almost constant high
winds and swell we had, and the great way every thing was to be dragged by the seamen,
up a heavy sandy road, made the duty excessively laborious. The squadron had almost
daily fourteen hundred men on shore, and this ship was often left with only thirty men
on board.

The defence made by the enemy protracted the siege longer than was expected,
and reduced our stock of powder so low, that the King's ships, with all the transports,
and what a fleet of merchantmen had for sale, could not have furnished a further
consumption for more than two days, when a practicable breach was fortunately made,
and on the 3d instant, early in the morning, the town and citadel were most gallantly
carried by storm.

In a conversation with the General on the preceding day, I had made such disposition
of the smaller vessels and armed boats, as appeared most likely to answer a desired
purpose; and so soon as Fort Saint Philip was in possession of the British troops,
Lieutenant William Milne, with the armed launches, took possession of the island of
Rattones, mounting ten guns and garrisoned by seventy men, which surrendered without
any resistance, although it is well adapted for defence, and might have given considerable
annoyance. A very fine frigate mounting twenty-eight guns was set fire to by her crew,
and blew up with an awful explosion; as also three gun-boats, but the other vessels in
the harbour were saved by the exertion of our people.

It has been much the custom to speak slightingly of the resistance to be expected from the Spaniards in this country; and with confidence of the facility which has been given to naval operations, by a prior knowledge of the river; but the battles lately fought prove the former opinion to be erroneous; and experience evinces that all the information hitherto acquired has not prevented the most formidable difficulties. ...

Discovery of a Communication Between the Mississippi and the Pacific Ocean

From 'Naval Anecdotes.' XVII 369-374

In the year 1805, after the cession of Louisiana to America, an expedition was fitted out by the American Government, for exploring the countries west of the Mississippi, and endeavouring to discover a passage by the Missouri, and some of the streams, which it was conjectured might be found running westward, near the source of that river, into the Pacific Ocean. The command of the expedition was entrusted to Captain Lewis; and it will be seen by the following interesting letter from Captain Clark (who was second in command,) to his brother General Clark, that they completely succeeded in penetrating through that vast continent; and after wintering on the shores of the Pacific Ocean, returned in safety to the Mississippi.
[It has been impossible to include the text of Captain Clark's letter.]

1807 – Vice-Admiral Duckworth's Action at the Dardanelles and in the Sea of Marmora, and the Occupation of Alexandria

TOWARDS THE END OF 1806 the Porte, which historically had strong ties with France and enmity with Russia, was persuaded by the French Ambassador, General Sebastiani, that, despite the recent French occupation of Egypt, it had most to fear from Russian expansion in the Mediterranean, Crimea and Georgia. The passage of the Dardanelles was closed by a Turkish squadron. The Russians responded by sending an army through the Balkans, and Vice-Admiral Collingwood deployed British squadrons to the Levant. On 19 February, Sir John Duckworth passed under the guns of the Dardanelles forts, which opened fire, and passed the Turkish squadron, which were attacked by Rear-Admiral Sir Sidney Smith. From an anchorage near Constantinople the British Ambassador, the Right Honourable Charles Arbuthnot, tried to negotiate an accommodation between the Turks and Russians. However, the position of the British squadron became increasingly untenable. Duckworth was unable to attack the arsenal because of a protracted calm and difficult currents, the defences of the capital were rapidly strengthened, and it became evident that it was essential to repass the Dardanelles forts without further delay. The second passage proved far more deadly than the first. All that had been achieved was to add Turkey to the list of Britain's enemies.

On 6 March, before the outcome of events at the Dardanelles was known, General Fraser with 5000 men had embarked in 49 transports under the command of Benjamin Hallowell at Messina to take possession of Alexandria. The British could still find friends there, and the after landing the troops and taking advanced positions with little loss, a capitulation was agreed to. A sortie to Rosetta, however, was ambushed in the streets and only withdrew with great loss. A second attempt to secure Rosetta to save Alexandria from famine was driven back with loss, and finally the British garrison at Alexandria agreed to a convention proposed by the Governor of Egypt who had arrived with massive forces. On 22 September they re-embarked.

Although not published until 1812, *The Naval Chronicle*'s account of the Dardanelles expedition really begins with its biographical memoir of Captain John Stewart. In it was inserted a letter from Mr Adair, in 1808-09 British Minister Plenipotentiary at the Porte, to the author describing the collapse of British influence at the Porte, and Arbuthnot's flight in *Endymion*. Collingwood's orders to Duckworth, and Duckworth's despatches, which were printed by order of the House of Commons, were supported by other eye-witness accounts. The author of the biography of Captain Richard Daches, which was published in 1811, strongly questioned why Sir Sidney Smith, with all his experience in Turkish diplomatic and naval affairs, had only been given a subordinate command. A correspondent supplied a copy of Smith's report on his action with the Turkish fleet, and another, a journal of *Endymion*'s escape. In *The Naval Chronicle*'s collection of reports of shipwreck is an account of the fire which destroyed HMS *Ajax* a few days before the first passage of the Dardanelles. Although *The Naval Chronicle* was careful about criticising the actions of government and senior officers, in its biographical memoir of Sir John Duckworth, it pointed out that the failure of the expedition could to some extent be attributed to the fact that no soldiers had been provided to make it possible for the Dardanelles forts to be occupied. The experience of 1915 underlines the importance of that consideration.

Crisis in Turkish Affairs

From the 'Naval Biography of the Late Captain John Stewart, R.N.'
XXVIII 37-40

[Letter to the author on Turkish affairs by Mr Adair, in 1808-09 British Minister Plenipotentiary at the Porte.]

Queen Street, May Fair, April 3d, 1812
Sir, ... That war [between Great Britain and Turkey commencing in 1806] was produced by the adherence on our part to our engagements with Russia. Turkey, influenced by France, had in many instances infringed the treaty of triple alliance, entered into by Great Britain, Russia, and herself, to protect her against the French power during the war of the Revolution. These infractions happened during the summer and autumn of 1806, and were of a nature to provoke, and almost to invite, acts of hostility on the part of Russia. In the mean time, Buonaparté, after destroying the Prussian monarchy at Jena, had established himself on the Vistula, and was preparing to penetrate into the heart of the Russian empire. The English government, aware of the temptations which

a Turkish war had at all times presented to Russia, in the easy conquest of Moldavia and Walachia, and anxious to avert the mischief which they saw must inevitably result to the common cause, if any part of the Russian force were diverted from the Vistula to the Danube, exerted their utmost endeavours, both at St. Petersburg and Constantinople, to bring about an accommodation. Their representations at St. Petersburg were successful; and they soon obtained from that Court, not only the unequivocal renunciation of all views of conquest and aggrandizement on the side of Turkey, but the manifestation of a strong desire to restore peace on any reasonable conditions. On the other hand, acting in the spirit of good faith towards Russia, and guided by a public policy, which was rendered indispensable by the then circumstances of Europe, they instructed Mr. Arbuthnot, their Ambassador at Constantinople, to insist firmly on the re-establishment of the treaty of triple alliance; and they sent a squadron to the Dardanelles, with orders to co-operate with him, and to support his negotiations.

In giving effect to this policy, they were well seconded by Mr. Arbuthnot; for although, during this time, the French influence at the Porte was at its height, so prudently did he conduct himself, and such was the real deference of Turkey towards Great Britain, that he had actually obtained the consent of the Divan to restore the treaty in its principal points; when the entry of the Russian troops into Moldavia, in consequence of the first orders from St. Petersburg, destroyed in one moment the whole effect of his exertions. This false step of the Russian Cabinet, enabled General Sebastiani to complete the rupture, and as a necessary consequence, to ruin irrecoverably the influence of Great Britain at the Porte.

Every thing, indeed, conspired just then to favour the views of France. In consequence of our interference at the Court of St. Petersburg, and the dispositions produced by it, despatches of a pacific nature were prepared by the Russian government, and forwarded to their Ambassador, Count Kalinsky, both by the usual road, and by the Black Sea. The first set of these despatches was intercepted on the frontiers; and the corvette containing the duplicates, was detained at the entrance of the Bosphorus, on the ground of her being a ship of war. Count Kalinsky, it is true, had by this time quitted Constantinople; but Mr. Arbuthnot remained there, availing himself of every opportunity to promote a reconciliation. Had he gotten possession of these papers, there is scarcely a doubt that, in consequence of his preceding arrangements, peace would then have been restored; but they never were delivered to him, and their contents consequently remained unexecuted.

Sebastiani availed himself of these advantages with so much industry, that the British Ambassador in a short time became a sort of prisoner in his palace; and was even deprived of the means of communicating either with his government, or with the dependencies of his embassy.

In this situation, Mr. Arbuthnot took the resolution of embarking on board the *Endymion*, then at anchor in the port of Constantinople, and of joining the fleet under Admiral Duckworth. With this fleet he shortly afterwards passed the Dardanelles; intending to proceed straight up to the walls of the Seraglio, and to propose his terms of accommodation, under the auspices of the British flag. The circumstances which prevented the full execution of this intention, are not matter for inquiry in this place. Suffice it to say, that the squadron came to an anchor at the Prince's islands, that a negotiation was begun with the Turkish government, that it failed, and that war ensued.

Journal of Endymion's Escape From Constantinople
From 'Correspondence.' *XVIII 133-139*

Mr. Editor, The enclosed Journal has accidentally come into my possession: I am not acquainted with the writer of it, but it bears evident marks of being a genuine account of the passing and repassing the Dardanelles: as such I transmit it for insertion in the *Naval Chronicle.*

A SUBSCRIBER

We sailed from Constantinople on the 29th of January, 1807, between the hours of ten and eleven o'clock at night, in his Majesty's ship the *Endymion*, Captain Capel; and such was the hurry in which we went off, that both her cables were cut: we carried easy sail all the night, and anchored the following evening at Gallipoli: on the morning of the 31st, we sailed for the Dardanelles, and passing Point Pesquies, where the Turkish fleet was anchored, we saluted the Captain Pacha, whose flag was flying on a frigate of 36 guns, and which returned our salute gun for gun. Soon after we passed the Straits of Sestos and Abydos, where we saluted the castles according to custom, and had the salute returned. We anchored about two or three miles below Abidos, when we joined Sir Thomas Louis, in the *Canopus*, together with the *Thunderer* and *Standard* line of battle ships: here all the British subjects, who were brought away from Constantinople, by the ambassador, were distributed on board the several ships of war, and I was embarked in the *Standard*, Captain Thomas Harvey. About four o'clock, P.M. of the same day, the squadron weighed, and dropt [*sic*] to the entrance of the Hellespont, and remained there until the following morning, 1st February, when we weighted again, and anchored off the island of Tenedos soon after.

On the 6th February the *Active* frigate arrived from Malta, with the intelligence of the arrival at that place of Sir John Duckworth, having the command of five sail of the line and two bombs, and of their intending speedily to join us. On the 8th February the *Glatton* man of war arrived from Smyrna, having on board the English Gentlemen and their families, who had left that place by order of the ambassador. On the 10th February, in the forenoon, the squadron under the orders of Sir John Duckworth joined us, consisting of the *Royal George* and *Windsor Castle*, three deckers, the *Pompée*, Admiral Sir Sidney Smith, the *Repulse* and *Ajax*, two deckers, and the *Lucifer* and *Meteor* bombs. On the 11th February, in the morning, the whole fleet weighed, and stood for the entrance of the Dardanelles, but the wind not being fair, we were obliged to anchor off Cape Janissary. The *Glatton*, with a convoy of merchant ships, which she brought from Smyrna, remained at anchor off Tenedos. Nothing of any consequence transpired in the fleet till on the night of the 14th of February, when signals of distress were made by the *Ajax*, and presently after she was perceived to be on fire. . . .

Sir John Duckworth's Orders; Dated 13 January 1807
From 'Naval Anecdotes.' *XIX 273-276*

(Most Secret)

Vice-Admiral Collingwood's Orders to Sir John Duckworth
Some late proceedings on the part of the Turkish government, indicating the increasing influence of the French in their councils, and a disposition in the Porte to abandon the alliance which has happily subsisted between that government and his Majesty, inducing

a conduct on their part which it would be inconsistent with the dignity of his Majesty's crown to submit to, have determined the king to adopt such prompt and decisive measures as are suitable to the occasion.

On the other hand, the last accounts, of date the 13th October last, from his Majesty's ambassador at Constantinople, stated the matters of difference to have been amicably adjusted; yet, as recent events may have an effect unfavourable to his Majesty's interests, it is necessary that a squadron, under the command of a judicious and skilful officer, should proceed to Constantinople, to be ready to act with vigour and promptitude, as circumstances and the state of affairs on his arrival may make necessary.

You are hereby required and directed to take under your orders the ships named in the margin,[1] which you are to collect as you arrive at the stations and ports where they are, and having completed the provisions and water to four months at Gibraltar, proceed as expeditiously as possible to the Straits of Constantinople, and there take such a position as will enable you to execute the following instructions:

On your arrival at Constantinople, you are to communicate with his Majesty's ambassador as soon as possible, sending him the accompanying despatches, and consulting with him on the measures necessary to be taken.

Should the subject of difference have been amicably settled between the Turkish court and the British ambassador, as was stated in the last accounts from him, the relations of amity are to be maintained; should, however, the reverse be the case, or should the representations which Mr. Arbuthnot is instructed to make to the Turkish government fail of their effect, you are to act offensively against Constantinople. But as from a barbarous practice of the Turkish government, it may happen, that the ambassador, and the persons of his suite, are forcibly detained, in such case, before you proceed to any actual hostility, you are to demand and insist on the release of that minister and his suite, together with all those who belong to and compose part of the British factory; and in the event of the demand not being complied with, you are to proceed to measures of hostility against the town. If Mr. Arbuthnot shall not have been forcibly detained, or, having been detained, should be released in consequence of your requisition, you are then to communicate and consult with that minister on the measures proper to be pursued, and govern yourself in your further proceedings by such communications.

Should the result of your communications with Mr. Arbuthnot determine, and he inform you it is his opinion that hostilities should commence, having previously taken all possible precaution for the safety of that minister, and the persons attached to his mission, and having disposed the squadron under your orders in such stations as may compel compliance, you are to demand the surrender of the Turkish fleet, together with a supply of naval stores from the arsenal, sufficient for its complete equipment, which demand you are to accompany with a menace of immediate destruction of the town.

At this crisis, should any negotiation on the subject be proposed by the Turkish government, as such proposition will probably be to gain time for preparing their resistance, or securing their ships, I would recommend that no negotiation should be continued more than half an hour; and, in the event of an absolute refusal, you are either to cannonade the town, or attack the fleet where ever it may be, holding it in

1 At Sicily, Palermo; *Pompée*, Rear-Admiral Sir S. Smith. In the Archipelago, under the orders of Rear-Admiral Sir T. Louis, *Canopus, Thunderer, Standard, Endymion, Active, Nautilus, Delight, Royal George, Windsor Castle, Repulse*, and *Ajax*.

mind that the getting the possession, and, next to that, the destruction of the Turkish fleet, is the object of the first consideration. On the adoption of hostilities, the communication of that decision to the commander in chief of the British army in Sicily, and the officers commanding the squadron on the coast of that island, must be as prompt and immediate as possible, sent by a fast sailing vessel; and the more to insure this important communication, a duplicate should follow in a very few days, orders having been sent to General Fox to detach 5,000 men for the purpose of taking possession of Alexandria, as soon as he is informed that hostilities have commenced; which armament you must regard as acting within the sphere of your co-operation, and be prepared to give all the assistance to it that is in your power.

When hostilities have been entered upon in that quarter, it will be of the first importance to possess a naval station in the Archipelago. The island of Milo, from its situation and the excellence of its harbour, presents itself as best calculated for preserving the communication in the Archipelago, and such as will certainly be necessary in the Morea. In proceeding up the Archipelago, pilots are procured at Milo, and when you are there for that purpose it will be a favourable opportunity for you to examine how far the possessing yourself of it is practicable, and what force will be necessary to maintain it, and make such communications to General Fox on this subject, and request for troops, as may be wanted to possess it.

His Majesty's ship *Glatton* is stationed in the bay of Smyrna, for the purpose of receiving on board the persons and property of the factory resident there, whenever circumstances make it necessary for them to embark; and as this will depend upon the operations at Constantinople, you will give Captain Seccombe and the factors timely notice for their security.

Having thus detailed particularly the situation of affairs at the Porte, and what are the instructions of his Majesty in the event of a war with Turkey, yet in a service of this nature many circumstances will doubtless occur which cannot be foreseen, and can only be provided for by an intelligent mind upon the spot; in your ability a resource will be found for every contingency; and in your zeal for his Majesty's service, a security that for the full execution of these instructions whatever is practicable will be done.

The force which is appointed for this service is greater than the original intention, as it was expected the Russians from Corfu would be ready to co-operate with you; but as its success depends upon the promptness with which it is executed, I have judged it proper (that no delay may arise from their squadron not joining) to increase your force by two ships. I have, however, written to Vice-Admiral Sercovin to request him to detach four ships with orders to put themselves under your command; and that you may be possessed of all the force that can be applied to the important service under your immediate direction, you are hereby authorized to call from the coast of Sicily whatever can be spared from the perfect security of that island, as well as the despatch vessels at Malta; but as little more naval force is at Sicily than is absolutely necessary for its defence, and the convoy which may be wanted for the troops, a strict regard must be had that that island is not left in a weak state of defence; while employed on this service, you must take every opportunity of communicating to me your proceedings in as full detail as possible, transmitting to me by such opportunities the general return and state of the squadron.

In the event of your finding a pacific and friendly disposition in the Porte, so that the squadron under your orders is not required in hostile operations there, you are to detach a flag officer with such number of ships as are not wanted, which detachment being made up of five ships of the line from those at Sicily, [whom] you will direct to proceed off Toulon, endeavouring to fall in with any squadron of ships the enemy may have put to sea thence; not finding the enemy at sea, those ships attached to the service of Sicily are to return to their stations, and the flag officer with the others are to proceed and join me at this rendezvous.

I enclose for your information copies of the orders delivered to Rear-Admiral Sir Thomas Louis, and Captain Seccombe of the *Glatton*. Given on board the *Ocean*, off Cadiz.

Sir Sidney Smith's Subordinate Command

From the 'Naval Biography of Captain Richard Daches, R.N.' XXVI *367-368*

As impartial observers, it seems to us, that there were several circumstances, which ought to have pointed out Sir Sidney Smith, as the most proper officer that could be selected, for the conduct of an expedition against Constantinople. His local knowledge of the country, it is thought, might have been an object of some consideration; he spoke the language; he had proved himself the saviour of the Othman [sic] empire, at St. John of Acre; and he had been accredited as a joint minister plenipotentiary to the then reigning Sultan, Selim III. Yet, palpably absurd as it must appear, he was taken from the active station of Sicily, where he commanded,[2] and placed, not *first, not second,* but THIRD, in command of an expedition, of which he alone was competent to be the commander-in-chief! and, as an aggravation of this absurdity, when on the spot, he was not employed in the only diplomatic part of the proceedings, which Sir John Duckworth entrusted out of his own hands! At the very time that the commander-in-chief was complimenting Sir Sidney Smith, Sir T. Louis was officiating, as his deputed diplomatic agent! . . .

[The *NC* quoted a letter, dated 12 February 1807, from Sir Sidney to the Sultan, which he made available to Admiral Duckworth and the British envoy, Mr Arbuthnot, but of which they preferred not to avail themselves.]

Sir Sidney Smith's opinion of the expedition, and of the manner in which it had been conducted, will best be seen, by the following passage of a letter from him, addressed to a near relative in England:

Pompée, off the Island of Tenedos, March 11, 1807
. . . 'Tis painful to look back, and our ascendancy in these countries lost, by the political experiment of sending new diplomatic men, who (whatever their talents) had to buy their local experience, and, during their novitiate, were totally in the hands of a *dragoman* [official linguist], who, if not in the French interest, was in that of the Turks; which becoming blinded latterly by the march of the Russians into Moldavia and Wallakia [sic], enabled Buonaparté to induce the Turks to see their safety in the success of the French arms, and not to listen to the counsel of the British ambassador, who could no longer speak as an ally, after the expiration of our treaty, which was, as you know, signed by S____ and me on the 6th January, 1799. The Turks are wrong in their calculations after all, for they have more to fear from French pretended friendship, than from the passage of Russian troops through two provinces that hardly belonged to them. I am quite sure I could have made them see this, if I had been allowed to open a collateral intercourse with those who could have overruled the cry of the fanatic *junta* and mob,

2 [The fulsome letter of thanks from Queen Charlotte, of the Two Sicilies, cannot be reproduced here.]

by our aid. These latter will be the victims in the end. *Quem Deus vult perdere prius dementat*, you will have said on the first knowledge you had of this rupture; the Sultan knows better, but the ecclesiastical and juridical bodies being in one, and having a *veto* in every thing, he cannot act as sound policy dictates. S____ can explain this to you, and will agree with me in the advice I sent the poor Sultan, by his confidential messenger, Isaak Bey; *viz.* to employ the three fleets combined, to chastise his rabble, and guard his capital against the French. I am convinced he personally was sorry to see us go. . . .

Loss of the Ajax

From the 'Correct Relation of Shipwrecks.' XVII 319-323

In the absence of official accounts, respecting the unfortunate loss of His Majesty's ship *Ajax*, by fire, we submit the following extract of a letter from an officer in the squadron under Sir J.T. Duckworth, as containing some interesting particulars:

"Our force has lately experienced a diminution from an event which I now with grief relate to you. Valentine's day was, indeed, a sad one for the unfortunate *Ajax*. At half past nine on the evening of that day, the *Ajax* took fire in the bread-room, and in ten minutes she was in a general blaze from stem to stern; the wind blew fresh from the N.E. which prevented the boats of the ships to leeward from rendering any assistance; but from those to windward, and near her, she was well enough supplied to save upwards of 400 of her people! and those may consider themselves as most providentially preserved; as it had blown a gale all the day, and for two or three days before, and fell moderate towards the evening - a continuance of the gale would paobably have rendered all assistance impossible. The fire, it appears, had been for some time (comparatively speaking,) alight in the bread room before the alarm was given; for when the first Lieutenant, and many others, broke open the door of the Surgeon's cabin, the after bulk-head was burst down by the accumulated flames and smoke abaft it, and so rapidly made its progress through the cockpit, that it was with difficulty he could regain the ladder, and most of those who accompanied him were suffocated in the attempt. On reaching the quarter-deck he found the fire had out-run him, and Captain Blackwood agreeing with him that she was past all remedy, they both ran forward where the majority of the people were assembled, calling most piteously on their God for that help they despaired of getting, although many boats were approaching them, so rapidly did the fire work its way forward, and leapt from the sprit-sail-yard, when the *Canopus*'s boat fortunately picked them up. At this time the boats were assembling under the ship's bows, and saved most who still clung to them; though many, naked, benumbed with cold, and pressed on by others, let go their hold and perished, as did every one who imprudently on the first alarm jumped overboard. The boats, however, cleared her bows, though many of them were in imminent danger of swamping, from the number of the poor creatures who were clinging to the gunwales, and who were obliged to be forced off, and left to perish, for the safety of the rest. The ship burnt all night, and drifted on the island of Tenedos, where she blew up at five next morning, with a most awful explosion.

The unhappy sufferers of her ward-room are Lieutenant Rowe, Lieutenant Sibthorpe, Captain Boyd, of the Royal Marines; Mr. Owen, Surgeon; and Mr. Donaldson, Master. The Gunner, unhappy father! had thrown one child overboard, which was saved; but, going down for another, perished in the flames. Of forty-five midshipmen of every description, about twenty are saved; a son and a nephew of the late Captain Duff, and who were with him in the *Mars* when he gloriously fell in the action off Trafalgar, are among the survivors. Three merchants of Constantinople were on board, two perished; also a Greek pilot. One woman, out of three, saved herself by following her husband with a child in his arms down a rope from the jib-boom-end. The Purser's Steward and his Mate and the Cooper, are missing. The occasion of the accident cannot, indeed, be exactly ascertained; but that there was a light in the bread-room when there ought not to have been one, is certain. Several of the people died after they were got on board the different ships, the rest are distributed among the squadron."

[Vice-Admiral Sir Thomas Duckworth had not been authorised to hold courts martial on ships lost, but in order to enable him to continue in active service during the campaign, Captain Blackwood requested a board of enquiry, which exonerated him. A subsequent court martial ordered by Lord Collingwood confirmed that judgement (Vol. XVII, pp378-381).]

Naval State Papers XIX 408-412

Papers, presented to the House of Commons, relative to the Expedition to the Dardanelles. Ordered to be printed 23d March, 1808

No. 3, dated off the Dardanelles, on the 14th of February, 1807, is a copy of a letter from Sir J.T. Duckworth to Lord Collingwood, detailing his proceedings, and the difficulties which he expected to encounter in passing that strait. Sir John says:

"I think it a duty I owe to his Majesty, and my own honour, to observe to your lordship, that our minister having left Constantinople sixteen days since, and the Turks employed French engineers to erect batteries to flank every turn in our passage through the Dardanelles, I conceive the service pointed out in my instructions *as completely altered*; and viewed in whatever manner it may, has become *the most arduous and doubtful that has ever been undertaken*; for as I am instructed by your lordship to communicate and consult with his Majesty's ambassador, and to be guided in my proceedings by such communication, it is on that principle that the resolution has been adopted, for the honour and character of the nation appear pledged, and in our hands they never can be tarnished.

Of the hazard that attends such an enterprize I am most fully aware. We are to enter a sea environed with enemies, without a possible resource but in ourselves; and when we are to return, there cannot remain a doubt but that the passage will be rendered as formidable as the efforts of the Turkish empire, directed and assisted by their allies the French, can make it."

In his postscript, Sir John Duckworth says:

"Having thought it right to read Mr. Arbuthnot this letter to your lordship, his observation was, that he should with pleasure place his signature by the side of mine; he said, however, that the fortifications of the Dardanelles, and in the canal of the Bosphorus, had not been undertaken merely from the time of his own departure from Constantinople, but that Frenchmen had been desired to assist in their construction the very instant that a war broke out between the Porte and Russia; and, that when the *Endymion* passed down, the workmen were seen driving in piles, &c. and that the batteries were already advanced far towards their completion."

No. 4 is a letter from Sir Thomas Louis to Lord Collingwood, dated from the anchorage off Tenedos, on the 5th of February, 1807; in which Sir Thomas says:

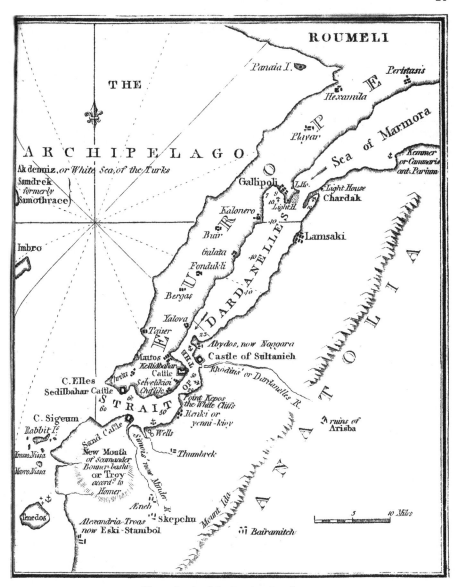

Chart. Strait of the Dardanelles. Plate 350

"I beg leave to take this opportunity of stating my opinion to your lordship, of the number and kind of force which I judge will be absolutely necessary to fully perform the service of forcing our passage to Constantinople, destroying the forts in our way, reducing the capital to subjection, and capturing or destroying all their navy; and, in consequence, obliging them to accept the offers proposed by our government.

The naval force I apprehend, to carry these measures into effect, should consist of at least ten sail of the line, two of the number three-deckers, a proportion of frigates and small vessels, with some bombs *and some troops*, for the purpose of an occasional *coup-de-main* where necessary, or to garrison one of the castles at the Dardanelles

(Abydos) while the other (Sestos) which is neither tenable nor necessary to possess, might be destroyed, as well as any other points that might occur in conducting the general service."

[This was not published until the summer of 1808, at which point *The Naval Chronicle* commented:]

This, our readers will do us the justice to recollect, is precisely what we insisted, in our memoir of Sir J. T. Duckworth, ought to have been attended to [see below]. Sir Thomas Louis observed: "Both the bombs and the troops might with great facility and expedition be sent us from Sicily, from whence, as there is so large a force stationed, I apprehend this number of men might be spared without inconvenience or risk, as also the bombs." Why they were not sent, or why they were not provided, in the first instance, we have yet to learn. (Sir Thomas does not mention the requisite number of men.)

Duckworth's Dispatches

From the 'Naval History of the Present Year,' 1807,
April-May. XVII 425-440

Letters On Service, Admiralty Office, May 4, 1807

Extracts of a Letter and its Enclosures, which have been received at this Office from Vice-Admiral Lord Collingwood, Commander in Chief of His Majesty's Ships and Vessels in the Mediterranean, addressed to William Marsden, Esq.; dated on board His Majesty's Ship Ocean, off Cadiz, the 8th of April, 1807

Sir, His Majesty's sloop *l'Espoir* has joined me to-day, bringing dispatches from Vice-Admiral Sir John T. Duckworth and Mr. Arbuthnot. Copies of the Vice-Admiral's letters to me, detailing the proceedings of the squadron in passing and repassing the Dardanelles, the burning of the Turkish ships which lay off Point Pesquies, with lists of the killed and wounded on the 19th and 27th February, and 3d March, are herewith transmitted.

COLLINGWOOD. . . .

Royal George, off Constantinople, February 24, 1807

My Lord, I had the honour of transmitting to your Lordship, by the late first Lieutenant of the *Ajax*, the various details relating to the transactions of the squadron till the 17th ultimo. Your Lordship will from thence have been informed of my resolution of passing the Dardanelles the first fair wind. A fine wind from the southward permitted me to carry it into effect on the morning of the 19th.

Information had been given me by His Majesty's Minister, Mr. Arbuthnot, and Sir Thomas Louis, that the Turkish squadron, consisting of a sixty-four gun ship, four frigates, and several corvettes, had been for some time at anchor within the Inner Castle; and conceiving it possible they might have remained there, I had given orders to Rear-Admiral Sir Sidney Smith to bring up with the *Thunderer, Standard,* and *Active,* and destroy them, should our passage be opposed.

At a quarter before nine o'clock the whole of the squadron had passed the outer castles, without having returned a shot to their fire (which occasioned but little injury). This forbearance was produced by the desire of His Majesty's Minister, expressed to preserve every appearance of amity, that he might negotiate with the strongest proof of

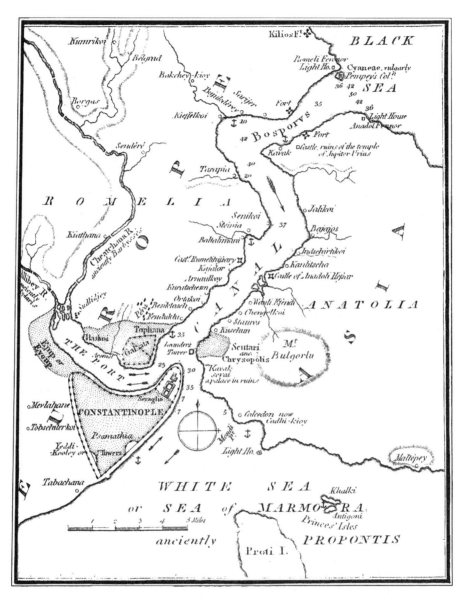

Chart. The Port and Canal of Constantinople. Drawn and engraved by Luffman.
Plate 352

the pacific disposition of our Sovereign towards the Porte: a second battery, on the European side, fired also with as little effect. At half past nine o'clock, the *Canopus*, which, on account of Sir Thomas Louis's knowledge of the channel, joined to the steady gallantry which I had before experienced, had been appointed to lead, entered the narrow passage of Sestos and Abydos, and sustained a very heavy cannonade from both castles, within point-blank shot of each. They opened their fire upon our ships as they continued to pass in succession, although I was happy in observing that the very spirited return it met with had so considerably diminished its force, that the effect on the sternmost ships could not have been so severe.

Immediately to the N.E. of the castles, and between them and Point Pesquies, in which a formidable battery had been newly erected, the small squadron which I have already alluded to were at anchor. The van division of our squadron gave them their broadsides as they passed, and Sir Sidney Smith, with his division, closed into the midst, and the effect of the fire was such that in half an hour the Turks had cut their cables to run on shore. The object of the Rear-Admiral was then to destroy them, which was most rapidly effected; as in less than four hours the whole of them had exploded, except a small corvette and a gun-boat, which it was thought proper to preserve. I enclose to your Lordship a statement of their number; and when I add also an account of the loss His Majesty's ships have sustained, I cannot help expressing my satisfaction that we have suffered so slightly; as, had any of their stone shot, some of which exceed eight hundred weight, made such a breach between wind and water, as they have done in our sides, the ship must have sunk; or had they struck a lower mast in the centre, it must evidently have been cut in two; in the rigging too, no accident occurred that was not perfectly arranged in the course of the next day. The sprit-sail-yard of the *Royal George*, the gaff of the *Canopus*, and the maintop-sail-yard of the standard, are the only spars that were injured.

It is with peculiar pleasure that I embrace the opportunity, which has been at this time afforded, of bearing testimony to the zeal and distinguished ability of Sir Sidney Smith; the manner in which he executed the service entrusted to him was worthy of the reputation which he has long since so justly and generally established. The terms of approbation in which the Rear-Admiral relates the conduct of Captain Dacres, Talbot, Harvey, and Moubray, which, from my being under the necessity of passing the Point of Pesquies before the van could anchor, he had a greater opportunity of observing than I could, cannot but be highly flattering; but I was a more immediate witness to the able and officer-like conduct which Captain Moubray displayed in obedience to my signal, by destroying a frigate with which he had been more particularly engaged, having driven her on shore on the European side, after she had been forced to cut her cables, from under the fire of the *Pompée* and *Thunderer*. The sixty-four having run on shore on Pesquies Point, I ordered the *Repulse* to work up and destroy her; which Captain Legge, in conjunction with the boats of the *Pompée*, executed with great promptitude and judgment. The battery on the point, of more than thirty guns, which, had it been completely finished, was in a position to have annoyed the squadron most severely in passing, was taken possession of by the Royal Marines and boats' crews of the rear division, the Turks having retired at their approach, and the guns were immediately spiked. This service was performed under the direction of Captain Nicholls, of the *Standard*'s marines, whose spirit and enterprise can never be doubted; but as circumstances rendered it impracticable to effect the entire destruction of the redoubt, orders were given by Sir Sidney Smith to Captain Moubray, which I fully approved, to remain at anchor near the Pesquies, and to employ Lieutenants Carrol and Arabin, of the *Pompée*, and Lieutenant Lawrie, of the marines, to complete the demolition of the redoubt and guns, which when performed, the *Active* was to continue in the passage of the Dardanelles till further orders.

At a quarter past five P.M. the squadron was enabled to make sail; and on the evening of the next day, the 20th, came to an anchor, at ten o'clock, near the Prince's Islands, about eight miles from Constantinople, when I dispatched Captain Capel, in the *Endymion*, to anchor near the town, if the wind, which was light, would permit the ship to stem the current, to convey the Ambassador's dispatches to the Sublime Porte in the morning by a flag of truce; but he found it impracticable to get within four miles, and consequently anchored at half past eleven P.M. . . .

I have the honour to be, &c.

J.T. DUCKWORTH

Right Honourable Lord Collingwood, &c. &c.

[*Pompée*'s signal log for 19 February 1807 was published in Vol. XXIV, p42.]

The Dardanelles Fortifications

From 'Naval Anecdotes.' XVIII 36-40

As an illustration of our memoir of Vice-Admiral Sir J.T. Duckworth, we present the following *description of the approaches to Constantinople, by water, from the Archipelago*:

The strait of the Dardanelles, as the whole passage is usually called, unites the Archipelago with the little sea of Marmora. It is about twelve leagues in length. It separates Europe from Asia; but is in some places not wider than 3 or 400 fathoms. In other places it is 1,500 or 2,000 fathoms. At what may be considered as the mouth of it, next the Archipelago, are two forts on the opposite shores, distant about 1,500 fathoms; so that they can hardly be said to protect the passage. But, about three leagues within the strait is a kind of promontory projecting into the passage, and narrowing it to about 400 fathoms. On each side of this narrow stands a castle. These are the Dardanelles: their cannon completely command the opposite shores: and very heavy pieces are mounted in them. These were for a long time the only defences of Constantinople by water. Above this narrow, the passage winds, and shortly forms another constriction, hardly so wide as the former. This is also now defended by forts. This being passed, the strait widens; but is again contracted before it enters the sea of Marmora, which is of considerable width, and at the bottom of which Constantinople is situated, without any other impediment to the approach of vessels.

It may easily be conceived that the batteries and forts mentioned, if well served, would be sufficient to defend a passage, which, whatever ship should attempt to force it, would be exposed to their fire when advancing, when alongside, and when passed; in fact, in all directions. Nevertheless, we must add the mention of another impediment of the greatest consideration, to those who attempt to enter from the Archipelago; for the waters of the Black Sea pouring through this narrow gullet into the Mediterranean, form a current so powerful and so steady, that ships, without a favourable wind, can hardly stem it with all their sails set: and even with the wind in their favour, the pilotage requires skilful management. This is a grand obstacle to the navigation of this strait, as the currents must regulate the steerage of the vessel sailing against them; but this inevitably exposes the vessel to the fire of the forts. And it needs no remark, that a vessel with all her sails set, is an object not easily missed in such a contracted space.

The Dardanelles are ancient fortifications; but the batteries on the headland called the Barber's Point, and those on the opposite shore, were constructed by Baron de Tott, in the year 1770. He also built others on another headland, called the Mill Point, nearer to the Dardanelles, on the European shore. These were visited and augmented by Major (now Sir Charles) Holloway, and Major Hope, the engineers who accompanied General Koehler on the mission sent to assist the Turks against the French, when they were in possession of Egypt. Having been favoured with the perusal of private journals kept during the whole of that mission, we have had an opportunity of knowing that the British officers did not think de Tott's constructions were very capital works; for they made several alterations in them, enlarged them, and added very considerably to their strength and importance. They mounted a number of heavy guns, and directed a general course of repairs, which, after all, however, were only executed *à la Turque*. The Baron, indeed, tells us that he made his batteries twenty-two feet thick: but he also informs us that the plague sometimes carried off twenty of his labourers in a day - is it surprising that his works were imperfectly executed? The battery at Mill Point was finished by a private Turk, whose patriotic spirit considered his expenses and labour as a work of merit. - The whole of the works opposed to an enemy an uninterrupted fire for the entire space of seven leagues.

The Baron gives the following account of a part of the defence:

"On the side of the castle the Turks had placed an enormous piece of ordnance, which would carry a marble ball of eleven hundred pounds weight. This piece, cast in brass, in the reign of Amurath, was composed of two parts, joined together by a screw, where the charge is contained, after the manner of an English pistol. It may be supposed that, as its breech rested against a massy stone work, it had been placed, by the means of large levers, under a small arch, which served as an embrasure. I could not make use of this enormous cannon in the outworks; and, as they were disposed in such a manner as to prevent its being fired, the Turks murmured at my paying so little regard to a piece of artillery, which, no doubt, had not its equal in the universe.

The Pacha made some remonstrances to me on that head. He agreed, with me, that the difficulty of charging it would not allow, in case of an attack, to fire it more than once; but, he urged this single discharge would be so destructive, and reach so far, that no one entertained a doubt but it would be alone sufficient to destroy the whole fleet of the enemy. It was easier for me to give way to this prejudice than overthrow it, and, without changing my plan of defence, I could, by cutting through the epaulment, in the direction of this piece, allow it room to be fired; but I was willing first to judge of its effect.

The crowd about me trembled at this proposal . . .

Never certainly had any cannon so formidable a reputation. Friends and enemies were alike to suffer from its fury. A month had now elapsed since it was determined to load this piece of artillery, which required no less than three hundred and thirty pounds weight of powder; and I sent to the head engineer to prepare a priming. All who heard me give this order immediately disappeared, to avoid the predicted danger. The Pacha himself was about to retreat, and it was with the utmost difficulty I persuaded him that he ran no risk, in a small kiosk, near the corner of the castle; from whence he might, notwithstanding, observe the effects of the ball.

Having succeeded in this, nothing remained but to inspire the engineer with courage; who, though he was the only one who had not fled, shewed no great resolution in the remonstrances he made to excite my pity; I at last rather silenced than animated him, by promising to expose myself to the same danger. I took my station on the stone work, behind the cannon, and felt a shock like that of an earthquake. At the distance of three hundred fathoms I saw the ball divide into three pieces, and these fragments of a rock crossed the strait, rebounded on the opposite mountain, and left the surface of the sea all in a foam through the whole breadth of the Channel. This experiment, by dissipating the chimerical fears of the people, the Pacha, and the engineers, proved to me likewise the terrible effects of such a ball; and I cut through the epaulment in the direction of the piece. . . ."

Sir Sidney Smith's Engagement
From 'Correspondence.' XIX 292-296

Chatham, March 31, 1808
Mr. Editor, My attention, in common with that of the rest of the public, having been attracted to transactions in the Levant, by the motions lately made in the House of Commons by the member for Barnstaple, tending to promote an inquiry into the causes of our late failure at Constantinople, I have naturally referred to all the papers already published connected with those operations; and I have been surprised to find that so interesting and important a document as Rear-Admiral Sir Sidney Smith's report to Vice-Admiral Sir John Duckworth, concerning the rear-admiral's successful attack on the Ottoman squadron, should have been withheld from the public. My intercourse with the Mediterranean squadron having put me in possession of a genuine copy of the documents in question, I offer it to your valuable work, as likely to gratify your naval readers, and more particularly as an act of justice to those individuals whose merits seem to have been overlooked by the higher powers, although so properly noticed and recommended by their immediate and heroic chief, who it is surprising to see yet undecorated with any *British* [3] honourific distinction, marked as he is with the admiration of the world at large.
Your humble servant,

NAUTICUS

[Rear-Admiral Sir W Sidney Smith to Vice-Admiral Lord Collingwood:]
His Majesty's Ship Pompée, within the Dardanelles, February 20, 1807
Sir, In reporting to you the entire completion of the service you were pleased to order should be executed by the rear division under my immediate direction, I need not inform you that the ships were anchored in the thick of the Turkish squadron, and in close action with them, as you must have observed it; but as the intervention of the land after you passed the point, prevent your seeing the subsequent operations, it is my duty to acquaint you therewith.
    The Turks fought desperately, like men determined to defend themselves and their ships as long as they could; but the superiority of our fire, within musket-shot, obliged them in half an hour to run on shore on Point Pesquies, or Nagara Burun. As the redoubt on the point continued to fire, also as the ships kept their colours up, and the part of their crews which had deserted them remained armed on the beach, while a considerable body of Asiatic troops, both horse and foot, appeared on the hills, it was necessary to make an arrangement for boarding them, with some precaution; at the same time, that it was of consequence to press them closely before they recovered from the impression and effect of our cannonade. A few shells from the *Pompée* dispersed the Asiatics, and convinced them that we commanded the ground within our reach, and

3 Sir Sidney is knight of the Swedish order of the Sword, conferred on him upon the field of battle in Finland, by the late king, Gustavus III, and of the Sicilian order of St. Ferdinand and of Merit, which he received two years ago from the present king, Ferdinand IV, but he is not even an English baronet, after 33 years' arduous service.

that they could not protect the green standard they had hoisted, which I caused to be brought off by Lieutenant Oates, of the *Pompée* marines, that they might not rally there again. The *Standard*'s guns bearing best on the frigates on shore, I sent the *Thunderer*'s boats to that ship, to be employed with her own, under the direction of Captain Harvey, making the signal to him to destroy the enemy's ships in the N.E. The *Active*'s having been previously made to follow and destroy a frigate, which had cut her cable to get from under the *Thunderer*'s and *Pompée*'s fire, and ran on shore on the European side in the N.W. At the same time Lieutenant Beecroft, of the *Pompée*, was detached to take possession of the line of battle ship, on which the *Thunderer*'s and *Pompée*'s guns could still bear, under the protection likewise of the *Repulse*, which you had considerably sent to my aid; that officer brought me the captain and second captain, the latter of whom was wounded, also the flag of the rear-admiral who had escaped on shore, which I shall have the honour of presenting to you. The whole of the Turks were landed, in pursuance of your orders, including the wounded, with due attention to the sufferings of our misguided opponents, as I must call them, for the term enemy does not seem applicable, considering their evident good disposition towards us nationally. The ship was then set on fire by the *Repulse*'s and *Pompée*'s boats, and completely destroyed.

Captain Harvey, in making his report to me of the conduct of the boats' crews under the command of Lieutenants Carter, Waller, and Colby, of his Majesty's ship *Thunderer*, and of the marines employed with them to board and burn the frigates and corvettes, under the command of Captain Nicolls, speaks in strong terms of the gallantry and ability of them all. The latter, whom I have long known to be an intelligent and enterprising officer, after destroying the frigate bearing the flag of the Captain Pasha, which is preserved to be presented to you, Sir, landed, and, profiting by the consternation of the Turks from the explosions on all sides of them, the effects of which occasioned no small risk to him, Lieutenants Fynmore, Boileau, and the party, he entered the redoubt (the Turks retreating as he approached), set fire to the gabions, and spiked the guns, thirty-one in number, eight of which are brass, carrying immensely large marble balls. As, however, the expected explosion of the line of battle ship made it impossible for the boats to stay long enough to destroy them effectually with their carriages, or to level the parapets, the wicker of the gabions being too green to burn, I have directed Lieutenants Carrol and Arabin, of his Majesty's ship *Pompée*, and Lieutenant Lawrie, of the marines, to continue on that service, with the Turkish corvette, and one gun-boat, which you will observe by the return were not destroyed, and to act under the protection and direction of Captain Moubray, of his Majesty's ship *Active*, whose name I cannot mention without expressing how highly satisfied I am with the able and gallant manner in which he executed my orders to stick to the frigate with which he was more particularly engaged, and to destroy her. Captain Talbot placed his ship admirably well, in support of the *Pompée*, thereby raking the line of battle ship and the frigate we were engaged with, when I made his signal to anchor, as the *Pompée* had previously done, under the directions I gave for that purpose to Captain Dacres, which were promptly and ably executed; Mr. Ives, the master, applying his local knowledge and experience, as I had a right to expect from his long tried abilities, while Lieutenant Smith made my signals to the squadron in rapid succession, and with precision. Captain Harvey merits my entire approbation, for placing the *Standard* in the manner in which he did, and for completing the destruction of the others. Much as I must regret the loss of the *Ajax*, as a most efficient ship in my division, I have felt that loss to be in a great degree balanced, by the presence of my gallant friend, Captain Blackwood, and the surviving officers and men, whose zeal in their voluntary exertions on this occasion does them the highest credit: in short, all the captains, officers, and men concerned, merit that I should mention them in high terms to you, Sir, as their leader, whose example we humbly endeavour to follow. The signal success that has attended the general exertion under your direction speaks more forcibly than words.

I have the honour to be, &c.

W. SIDNEY SMITH

Vice Admiral Sir Thomas Duckworth, K.B.
[Attached is a list of killed and wounded.]

Duckworth's Despatches

From the 'Naval History of the Present Year,' 1807
April-May - cont. $^{XVII\ 426-440}$

Letters on Service, Admiralty Office, May 4 1807

Royal George, at anchor off Prince's Islands, February 28, 1807

My Lord, I have to inform your Lordship, that it was perceived at nine o'clock yesterday morning, that the Turks had landed on the island of Prota, near which the squadron was anchored, and were erecting a battery in a position to annoy us: I immediately ordered the marines of the squadron to be prepared for landing, and the boats to be manned and armed; and the *Repulse*, with the *Lucifer*, having been directed to cover them, they proceeded towards the island. The Turks, on the ships firing a few grape to scour the beach, quitted the island in their boats, when all but one boat with eleven men escaped; at which, with two guns they had intended to mount, fell into our possession.

At half after two o'clock in the afternoon Sir Thomas Louis sent to inform me, that he had received intelligence of a small number of Turks being still on the island, and requesting permission to send marines to take them; my reply was, that no risk whatever must be run, but if it could be effected without hazarding the people, it might; and a party of the *Canopus*'s marines was immediately sent on shore in consequence, with the most positive orders to Captain Kent, from Sir Thomas Louis, not to pursue the object if he found it attended with any hazard. At four o'clock the party on shore made the signal for assistance, and the marines and boats manned and armed were directly ordered away from the *Royal George, Windsor Castle*, and *Standard*, with particular directions to bring off the *Canopus*'s people, but to avoid being drawn into danger. A little before sun-set an officer was dispatched with orders for the whole to return on board.

On the return of the boats, which was not till after dark, I heard with the deepest regret of the loss we had sustained; a list of which I herewith transmit, and do most particularly lament Lieutenant Belli, a young officer of the fairest promise, who had never served but with myself. To account in some degree for this unlucky affair, it appears that the information of a few Turks only having remained on the island was entirely false, as nearly an hundred of them had retired to an old convent, from loop-holes in the walls of which, they defended themselves with musketry. The people of the *Canopus* had in the first instance advanced close under the walls, and in endeavouring to relieve them from their unpleasant situation, the others suffered.

In order, if possible, to prevent the retreat of the Turks from this island, the launches of the squadron, armed with their carronades, were ordered to row guard during the night, under the direction of Captain Elliot, of the *Lucifer*; but notwithstanding every possible vigilance, they are supposed to have escaped in the night, as the next morning it was represented to me that only seven Greek inhabitants of the place were remaining.

I have the honour to be, &c

J.T. DUCKWORTH

Royal George, without the Dardanelles, March 6, 1807
My Lord, Together with this letter, I transmit to your Lordship two letters of the 21st and 28th ultimo; the former of which will have informed you of my arrival with the squadron near Constantinople; and the latter of an unlucky attempt, in which the marines and boats' crews of the *Canopus, Royal George, Windsor Castle,* and *Standard,* had been engaged.

It is now my duty to acquaint your Lordship with the result of the resolution which, for the reasons I have already detailed, I had adopted of forcing the passage of the Dardanelles. My letter of the 21st is dated at an anchor eight miles from Constantinople, with wind not admitting of a nearer approach; but the *Endymion*, which had been sent a-head with a flag of truce, at the request of the Ambassador, was enabled to anchor within four miles. Had it been then in our power we should have then taken our station off the town immediately, but as that could not be done from the rapidity of the current, I was rather pleased than otherwise with the position we had been forced to take, for in the conferences between His Majesty's Minister, Mr. Arbuthnot, and the Captain Pacha, of the particulars of which your Lordship is in possession, it was promised by Mr. Arbuthnot, that even when the squadron had arrived before Constantinople, the door to pacification should remain open, and that he would be willing to negotiate on terms of equality and justice. In consideration of this promise, and as it would convince the Porte of His Majesty's earnest desire to preserve peace, as well as possess her ministers with a confidence of the sincerity of our professions, it was the opinion of Mr. Arbuthnot, in which I concurred, that it was fortunate we had anchored at a little distance from the capital, as a nearer approach might have given cause for suspicion and alarm, and have cut off the prospect of an amicable adjustment of the differences which had arisen.

At noon of the 21st, Ysak Bey, a minister of the Porte, came off; from whose expressions Mr. Arbuthnot thought it impossible not to believe that, in the head of the Government (for in the present instance every circumstance proved, that between him and the armed populace a great distinction is to be made) there really existed a sincere desire for peace; and the negotiation was carried on, as will appear by the documents transmitted to your Lordship, till the 27th; but from the moment of our anchorage till we weighed, on the morning of the 1st of March, such was the unfortunate state of the weather, that it was not at any time in our power to have occupied a situation which would have enabled the squadron to commence offensive operations against Constantinople. On Sunday the 22d alone, for a few hours, the breeze was sufficient to have stemmed the current where we were placed; but such was the rapidity on shore where the *Endymion* was at anchor, that Captain Capel thought it very doubtful whether the squadron could have obtained an anchorage, though it had been held in preparative readiness, by signal, from day-break; but the peculiarly unsettled state of the weather, and the Minister's desire that I should give a few hours for an answer to his letter, through Ysak Bey, prevented me from trying. Before five o'clock P.M. it was nearly calm; and in the evening the wind was entirely from the eastward, and continued light airs or calm till the evening of the 28th, when it blew fresh from the N.E. and rendered it impossible to change our position.

Two days after our arrival near Constantinople, the Ambassador found himself indisposed, and has been ever since confined with a fit of illness, so severe as to prevent him from attending to business. Under these circumstances he had delivered on the 22d to the Turkish Minister a project, as the basis on which peace might be preserved, and at his desire the subsequent part of the negotiation was carried on in my name, with his advice and assistance; and while I lament most deeply that it has not ended in the re-establishment of peace, I derive consolation from the reflection, that no effort has been wanting on the part of Mr. Arbuthnot and myself to obtain such a result, which was soon seen from the state of the preparations at Constantinople could be effected by negotiation only, as the strength of the current from the Bosphorus, with the circuitous eddies of the port, rendered it impracticable to place ships for an attack without a commanding breeze; which, during the ten days I was off the town, it was not my good fortune to meet with.

I now come to the point of explaining to your Lordship the motives which fixed me to decide in repassing the channel of the Dardanelles, and relinquishing every idea of attacking the capital, and I feel confident it will require no argument to convince your Lordship of the utter impracticability of our force having made any impression, as at this time the whole line of the coast presented a chain of batteries; that twelve Turkish line of battle ships, two of them three deckers, with nine frigates, were with their sails bent, and apparently in readiness, filled with troops: add to this, near two hundred thousand were said to be in Constantinople, to march against the Russians; besides, there were an innumerable quantity of small craft, with boats; and fire vessels had been prepared to act against us. With the batteries alone we might have coped, or with the ships, could we have got them out of their strong hold; but your Lordship will be aware, that after combating the opposition which the resources of an empire had been many weeks employed in preparing, we should have been in no state to have defended ourselves against them as described, and then repass the Dardanelles. I know it was my duty, in obedience to your Lordship's orders, to attempt every thing (governed by the opinion of the Ambassador) that appeared within the compass of possibility; but when the unavoidable sacrifice of the squadron committed to my charge (which must have arisen, had I waited for a wind to have enabled me to cannonade the town, unattended by the remotest chance of obtaining any advantage for His Majesty's service) must have been the consequence of pursuing that object, it at once became my positive duty, however wounded in pride and ambition, to relinquish it: and if I had not been already satisfied on the subject, the increased opposition in the Dardanelles would have convinced me I had done right, when I resolved on the measure as indispensably necessary. I therefore weighed with the squadron on the morning of the first; and as it had been reported that the Turkish fleet designed to make an effort against us; to give them an opportunity, if such was really their intention, I continued to stand on and off during the day, but they showed no disposition to move.

I therefore, as every hour was of importance, bore up at dusk with the squadron; we arrived off Point Pesquies towards the evening of the 2d instant, but the daylight would not admit of our attempting to pass the castles, and the squadron came to anchor for the night; we weighed in the morning; and when I add, that every ship was in safety outside of the passage about noon, it is not without the most lively sense of the good fortune that has attended us.

The Turks had been occupied unceasingly in adding to the number of their forts; some had been already completed, and others were in a forward state. The fire of the two inner castles had, on our going up, been severe, but, I am sorry to say, the effects they have had on our ships returning, has proved them to be doubly formidable: in short, had they been allowed another week to complete their defences throughout the channel, it would have been a very doubtful point, whether a return lay open to us at all. The manner in which they employed the interval of our absence has proved their assiduity. I transmit your Lordship an account of the damages sustained by the respective ships; as also their loss in killed and wounded, which your Lordship will perceive is far from trifling. The main-mast of the *Windsor Castle* being more than three quarters cut through by a granite shot of eight hundred weight, we have found great difficulty in saving it.

I have the honour to be, &c.

J.T. DUCKWORTH

P.S. I am sorry to observe that, in the course of this letter to your Lordship, I have omitted to mention, that having placed the Honourable Captain Capel in the *Endymion*, which had been advanced in the stream of the Bosphorus, for the purpose of ascertaining when the squadron could stem the current, and for a watchful observation of the movements of the Turks, as well as to facilitate communication with the Porte, I feel myself indebted to that officer for his zealous attention and assiduity during the time he was placed in that arduous situation.

[Total killed and wounded: 42 killed, 235 wounded, and 4 missing.]

The Need for Land Forces to Secure the Forts

From the 'Biographical Memoir of Sir John Thomas Duckworth, K.B.'
XVIII 22-25

The failure of this expedition has been the subject of much conversation; and it was at one time generally understood, either that Sir John Duckworth would be brought to a court martial by government, or that he would himself demand a trial of that nature, in order that his conduct might be exhibited through a correct medium.

Whether any state reasons may have intervened, to render such an investigation impolitic; whether His Majesty's present Ministers may have approved of Sir John Duckworth's conduct; and whether Sir John may rest satisfied with such approbation, if it have been given, are points to which we are wholly incompetent to speak. His conduct was never before impeached by any party or set of men; but certain it is, that the friends of the late ministers still most vociferously insist, that their orders, respecting the proceedings of the squadron before Constantinople, were not obeyed. . . .

There is a circumstance relating to this expedition, which must attract the notice of every person. *There were no land forces on board.* How is this to be accounted for? Was it an oversight, or was it expected that the Turks would accede to the terms of the English, immediately that they should be proposed? - If there had been a sufficient number of troops on board of the squadron, they might have been landed, in detachments; and, as the forts of the Dardanelles were unprotected on the land side, they might thus have been speedily demolished, or at least have been rendered incapable of injuring any ship which might attempt the passage. The castles of Sestos and Abydos were particularly deserving of attention in this respect. The advantages which would have resulted from such a mode of proceeding must be obvious to every one. Had the forts which protect the passage of the Dardanelles been dismantled, Sir John Duckworth's squadron might have remained in the sea of Marmora as long as he had pleased; and might also have been in the constant and regular receipt of such supplies and reinforcements as it should have been deemed expedient to send. Thus, the expedition *must*, ultimately, have experienced a favourable termination.

Passage of the Dardanelles

From 'Naval Anecdotes.' XVII 463-467

The following extracts of letters will be found to throw some additional light upon the late passage of the Dardanelles, by Sir J.T. Duckworth's squadron. Such articles are worthy of preservation, as tending materially to assist the labours of the future historian.

The first of the succeeding communications is transcribed from a letter, by an officer of the *Canopus*; which, after giving an account of the *Ajax*, Captain Blackwood, previously to passing the Dardanelles, proceeds as follows:-

"This unfortunate accident threw a damp upon the spirits of the whole squadron: at any time the loss of such a ship, and such a number of brave fellows, would have been severely felt; but it was doubly distressing to our little squadron at such a time, as it weakened us greatly. To add to our chagrin, the wind was against us, which prevented us getting up the Dardanelles, and gave the Turks an opportunity of getting additional guns to their forts and batteries, and erecting new ones. It was not until the 19th we had a wind to go up. We then had a fine breeze, and got under weigh at day-light. The *Canopus* led the van, and, as the sailors called it, took off the fiery edge: the entrance is pretty wide, therefore the shots from the first forts, which are very strong ones, did little or no execution; and in passing, the [British] bombs threw in a few shells, which we have reason to imagine did a good deal of mischief. These forts are, one on the Asiatic side, and one on the European; but still we had to pass two tremendous ones at a very narrow part, exactly opposite to each other, that on the Asiatic side called Abydos, and on the European Sestos, besides several small mud batteries, and one Turkish two-decker, five frigates, four corvettes, two gun-boats, and other small craft, that were moored a little above the Castles. It is said that we did not mean to commence hostilities. As our Ambassador went up in the *Royal George*, we wished to bring them to the terms he had formerly proposed to them, but they fired at us, and compelled us to act on the defensive; the fire from the forts was very heavy, and very much cut us up in the rigging-way; but, thank God, not half so bad as we expected. The shipping also kept up a very good fire, but we soon silenced them; and Sir Sidney Smith, with the sternmost ships, set fire to them, and destroyed the whole, but one corvette, which we kept possession of, but left behind when we came down. In this affair we had but three killed, and nineteen wounded, some badly; this we considered as trifling, considering what we had to contend with. You will be astonished, my dear Mary, to hear what unmerciful stone shot they fire from their forts; had I not witnessed it myself, I could not have given credit to it. We received one shot, which is now in my storeroom, that weighs 546 lbs., is 23 inches diameter, or five feet nine inches in circumference. Another of the same size broke in the forecastle; we have got some others something smaller; and some of the ships have got those of a larger size. In coming down, the *Windsor Castle* received one which has wounded her main-mast so badly, that it will cause her to leave this place; it is better than seven feet round, and weighs, I am told, upwards of 800lbs.

I forgot to tell you the *Glatton* remained at Tenedos to protect some vessels that came with the factory from Smyrna, and also we suppose to give intelligence of our proceedings to any English vessel that might arrive.

On the 20th, we anchored close to a group of islands, within four miles of Constantinople; the next day flags of truce passed from Constantinople to the Admiral, and we were led to imagine that matters would be amicably settled; but the wind setting out right against us, gave them another opportunity of increasing their fortifications, and throwing up works in every direction; so that in five or six days the entrance of the harbour was so very formidably fortified, that, in my opinion, it would have been madness to attempt to enter it. - Their shipping were also not to be despised. It is said, that 14 sail of the line were completely ready to come out, with nine frigates, six fire-ships, and near 200 sail of small vessels, manned with volunteers, to board us during the action. Had this been the case, it would have been a dreadful scene; for the Turks are not accustomed to give or take quarter: still our lads were in as good spirits as if they were in Hamoaze.

On the 26th, we perceived they were making some movements on the island close to us, called Prote. Boats were coming from the Main frequently with numbers of men; and, to all appearance, they were going to fortify the island. As they would have annoyed us greatly had they been suffered to proceed, on the 27th the Admiral ordered the *Repulse* and a bomb, with the boats of the squadron, manned and armed, to go and scour the island: they sent a few shot and shells on shore, took two small field pieces, and stopped a couple of boats with some Turks and Greeks, who voluntarily came on board. [They reported?] that a number of Turks were yet on the island, and had taken refuge in a monastery - a large square stone building. Our own boats were sent to dislodge them, but they soon found they were not in force sufficient to effect it: their position was very strong, and they had a much greater number of men than we were told of. They fired at our poor fellows out of loop-holes and windows, as they ascended the hill, and some were killed and wounded in a very few minutes; still our people were not dismayed, but boldly pushed up to the door, and set it on fire. The boats from the other ships were then sent to assist. Their people likewise suffered a good deal on first going up; but night coming on, they had orders to leave the island, and get on board their respective ships, without effecting any thing. Captain Kent, of the marines, one seaman, and two marines, were killed; ten badly wounded, two of whom are since dead; and I am truly sorry to say, that James Reiley, my Mate, was one of those two: he had a dreadful wound in the belly, but remained perfectly sensible. He expired the following evening, much lamented by every body, as he was a very valuable man. I don't exactly know the number of killed and wounded of the other ships - this you will see by the public accounts. - Mr. Rouse, of the *Royal George*, son to Mr. Rouse, the rope-maker, is amongst the latter; but I am happy to add, it is only a flesh wound in the leg, and he is now doing well. . . .

As all negotiation was at an end, I suppose the Admiral thought it imprudent to remain any longer with the small force we had, as, had any ship been disabled or driven on shore, the consequences would have been very serious. On the 1st inst. we got under weigh, and on the 3d we once more passed the castle and batteries, and found them, I think, much warmer than they were before. We again led the van - we had many more shot struck us than we had in going up."

Naval State Papers XIX 410-411

Papers, presented to the House of Commons, relative to the Expedition to the Dardanelles. Ordered to be printed 23d March, 1808

No. 8, from [Sir J.T. Duckworth to Lord Collingwood], is dated on board the *Royal George*, near the Dardanelles, March 7, 1807. It is as follows:

"My Lord, Having in my letter of the 9th of February, acquainted your lordship of my having signified to General Fox, that as the ambassador had left Constantinople, he might with propriety send the troops to take possession of Alexandria; and the general having in a letter of the 18th ultimo acquainted me that they were embarking, and would sail without delay on that service, I therefore, having been so unfortunate as to fail of success off Constantinople, shall direct my attention to this armament, as being within the sphere of my co-operation; and as Milo is not deemed a healthy island, I shall endeavour to find out some island contiguous to the entrance of the Dardanelles which does not labour under that disadvantage, to make a naval station of; but I have to observe that General Fox, in his letter of the 2d February, in reply to mine of the 29th and 31st of January, specifying that a small proportion of troops would be required to take post and keep possession of Milo or some other island, says that 5,000 men are the utmost his instructions go to, and indeed that can possibly be spared from the defence of Sicily, and these troops are expressly ordered to garrison Alexandria, [therefore] the detaching any part for the occupation of Milo, or any other island or place on the coast of the Archipelago, must rest solely at the direction of the general officer commanding this corps; for if they go, I do not conceive myself at liberty to allow of any detachment being made so as to endanger the defence of Alexandria.

Thus, my lord, you will see I can have no expectation of any military aid, but I beg you to believe no endeavours of mine shall be wanting to do what will most promote his Majesty's service, and meet your lordship's wishes.

J.T. DUCKWORTH"

Occupation of Alexandria

From the 'Naval History of the Present Year,' 1807 April-May. XVII 433-434

Letters on Service, Admiralty Office, May 9 1807

Extract of a Letter from Vice-Admiral Lord Collingwood, Commander in Chief of His Majesty's Ships and Vessels in the Mediterranean, to William Marsden, Esq.; dated on board the Ocean, off Cadiz, the 27th of April, 1807

The *Delight* sloop joined me last night, having left Alexandria on the 28th last, and brought an account of the surrender of that city and its fortresses, to His majesty's forces, by capitulation, on the 20th ult. A copy of Captain Hallowell's letter, relating the circumstances of this capture, I enclose for the information of the Lords Commissioners of the Admiralty, in which their Lordships will find an example of great zeal and ability in conducting this enterprize, by the commanders of the sea and land forces, where they acted with a promptitude and judgment which prevented resistance. Two frigates and a corvette were found in the western harbour, and surrendered by the capitulation.

His Majesty's Ship Tigre, off Alexandria, March 24, 1807
Sir, I have the honour to acquaint you, that, in obedience to your orders, addressed to
the senior officer at Sicily, I sailed from Messina, on the 6th instant, with the troops
under the command of Major-General Fraser, destined to take possession of Alexandria.

On the 15th we reached the Arabs' tower with fourteen sail of the convoy, nineteen
having parted on the night of the 7th in a heavy squall and thick weather. With so small
a proportion of the army the General did not think it prudent to show the transports,
until he had received some information of the enemy's force. I therefore stood in with
the *Tigre* on the 16th, having Major-General Fraser on board, (leaving the convoy in
the offing,) hoping to ascertain from Major Misset, the British Resident, and Mr. Briggs,
the Vice-Consul, (whom we expected to find in the *Wizard* brig, which had been
previously detached to receive them on board,) the strength and disposition of the
garrison and inhabitants of the place. On the evening of the same day, having received
most satisfactory accounts from Major Misset and Mr. Briggs, of the friendly disposition
of the inhabitants towards us, and the little prospect there was of meeting any opposition
on our landing, the transports were called in, and we all anchored off the western harbour.
A summons was immediately sent, demanding possession of the fortresses, and promising
protection in the persons and private property of every individual; but, contrary to
our expectations, the officers who had been sent with the summons returned the morning
after, with a declaration from the Governor that he would defend the place to the
last extremity.

As our intentions were now known to the enemy, every delay on our part would
have afforded them an opportunity of strengthening their position. The General therefore
determined on landing immediately with the force he had with him, and on the evening
of the 17th, between six and seven hundred troops, with five field pieces, and fifty-six
seamen under Lieutenant Boxer, were put on shore near the Ravine, from lake Mariotis
to the sea, without opposition; but from the heavy surf which got up during the night,
it was late in the afternoon of the following day, before the remainder could be got on
shore. As soon as the whole were collected and formed, they moved forward and attacked
the enemy's advanced works, which were carried with little loss. And as we had been
informed that a number of Albanians were expected from Rosetta and Chiro [Cairo?],
to reinforce the garrison, the army took up a position to the eastward of Alexandria,
occupying the cut on the canal, by which all communication was cut off between
Alexandria and Rosetta.

On the 19th the *Apollo* and remainder of the convoy appeared in the offing, and
having joined, she proceeded with all the transports to Aboukir Bay, where they began
on the 20th to land their troops, (the castle of Aboukir having been previously occupied
by us previous to their anchoring). The appearance of such a reinforcement induced
the Governor to offer terms of capitulation, similar to those which we at first proposed;
which were accepted on the 20th in the afternoon, and possession taken of the heights
of Caffarillie and Cretin, at two o'clock on the morning of the twenty-first. . . .

BEN. HALLOWELL

[See also below, pp60-62; 148-150.]

1807 – Naval News, Summer

IN THE SUMMER OF 1807, the most important events were the defeat of Russia and Prussia at the battle of Friedland in June, which led to the Treaty of Tilsit with France in July, and the British expedition in August to seize the Danish fleet to ensure that it did not fall under the control of France. *The Naval Chronicle* reported Lord Selkirk's speech in the Lords on 10 August in which he warned of the growing naval threat from France. Fear that Denmark would become a French vassal was made all the more urgent by the importance of the Baltic in the economic war. The resolution to revisit Copenhagen came in the context of the extension of the French ban on British trade, which led to the issue of new British 'Orders in Council' controlling trade with the continent. That of 19 August respecting the traders of four north German towns was to be one of many to be promulgated later in the year. *The Naval Chronicle* reported on the debate in Parliament on trade policy and, in its law reports, reported Sir William Scott's decision in the High Court of Admiralty that an American ship which the French had captured, and which had then been recovered by a British cruiser, had to pay prize salvage even though the American ought to have been released by the French as a neutral. Elimination of any possibility of the Danes blocking British trade to the Baltic was considered justified on the plea of necessity.

Neither the operation at Copenhagen nor British trade control were approved of in Russia. *The Naval Chronicle* reported that war with Russia was apprehended. For Britain, there was also growing trouble across the Atlantic. Relations with the United States became unusually difficult when HMS *Leopard* opened fire on the USS *Chesapeake* to arrest British deserters who had signed on her crew.

Of service interest was the debate on naval victualling, and the news of new uniform regulations for naval officers.

Other news included a report that the Turks were unable to drive the Russians out of Tenedos, and that Napoleon was demanding that the Portuguese make available a naval force to operate against Britain. In consequence, it was reported, an expedition had been sailed from Cork to ensure that the Portuguese court understood the implictions. It was also reported that British forces were to be evacuated from South America, with the expectation of courts martial to follow.

The initial reports dealing with the crisis with the United States, with British and Russian operations in the Aegean, with the evacuation of British forces from South America, and with the expedition to Copenhagen, have been reproduced in this chapter. Subsequent, and more detailed, reports have been collected into separate chapters in the *Consolidated Edition.*

From the 'Naval History of the Present Year,' 1807
June-July. [XVIII 62–88]

Battle of Friedland,
Russia and Prussia Forced to Make Peace With France

By the disastrous result of the battle of Friedland, on the 14th of June (the anniversary of the battle of Marengo), the combined powers have again been humbled before the military genius of Buonaparté. The consequence is, that separate treaties of peace have been entered into between France and Russia, and France and Prussia; so that, with the exception of the noble-minded monarch of Sweden, we have now no ally, and scarcely a friend, upon the Continent. - On the termination of an armistice, which had been entered into between Sweden and France, hostilities have been recommenced by the latter; and in all probability Sweden will ultimately be compelled to submit to such terms as may be proposed by the general subjugator of Europe. We have Mr. Canning's authority for stating, that there is a force of 14,000 men in British pay, for the defence of Stralsund and Pomerania. Four thousand more were to be added to that number; but whether, under existing circumstances, it will be deemed prudent to send them, we are not prepared to say.

Two Operations in Preparation Against the Enemy

Thus, it appears likely that we shall again have to support a "single-handed" contest with France. This prospect has aroused all our wonted energies. A strict embargo has been laid on all the ports; an unusually hot impress has taken place; troops have been collected from all quarters of the United Kingdom; and preparations, offensive and defensive, are every where making, with almost unprecedented vigour and alacrity. Two expeditions are in great forwardness. One of them, it is generally believed, is destined to act against the town and flotilla of Boulogne. The attack, it is supposed, will be on a much larger scale than has been hitherto attempted.

1 This gave birth to a circumstance of rather a ludicrous nature: It may be necessary to observe, that on hoisting in or out of a man of war, the boatswain's pipe is used. Many ladies visited us, who, as we had not an accommodation ladder, were of course *hoisted* on board in a chair. From the continual *piping* of the boatswain's mate on the gangway, a parrot in a cage under the half-deck, imitated the pipe so very well, that the men who were lowering a corpulent lady over the side, on the parrot piping *let go,* but too readily obeyed it, sousing our visitor thoroughly: nor was it observed until she had remained some time in this cold and comfortless situation. - However "fondlie fashioned her limbes" might have been, she had not, like our fair countrywomen at present, "scorned all the draperies of arte," and to this perhaps she was indebted for not suffering more.

View near Bergen, on the coast of Norway. Engraved by Hall, from a drawing by
G.T.

August 28, 1804

Sir, The enclosed sketch may serve to give some idea of the navigation on the coast
of Norway. It was taken in the month of January, when the barren aspect of the
country was only relieved by a few firs, and the distant mountains being clothed in
snow. In many parts of the passage towards Bergen, the ship passed within a very
few yards of the rocks; yet was the lead unthought of by our Norwegian pilots
(whose little yawl was hoisted on the booms). On the eye alone they depended,
while one on the fore-yard conned to his comrade at the helm. Though it blew in
severe gusts at times, we were so sheltered by the mountains as to experience no
motion but from the pressure of the wind.

A few habitations, sheltered in some degree by the evergreens of the north, opened
on us as we rounded the different projecting points; yet not without the watchful
dog giving warning to their tenants of our near approach. On several of these
points, as well as on detached rocks, some scarcely above the surface of the water,
were rings fastened to secure vessels by, in adverse winds.

We passed vast abundance of wild fowl, and the eagle was frequently seen perched
on a rock, or soaring high in air, with watchful eye below in search of prey.

At Bergen we remained some days, not without an apprehension of being detained
by the ice. So large a man of war (a 38-gun frigate) had not been there for many
years, and the novelty brought great numbers of the inhabitants of both sexes on
board to visit us.[1]

I am your humble servant,

G.T. Plate 257

The other expedition, which is evidently designed for a descent on the enemy's coast, is of a most formidable description. No fewer than 86 ships are to be employed; and the naval part of the service is to be under Admiral Gambier, Vice-Admiral Stanhope, Rear-Admiral Essington, Sir Home Popham (captain of the fleet), Commodore Sir Samuel Hood, and Commodore Keats. The following ships, forming a part of this force, were assembled at Yarmouth, on Saturday, the 25th of July:

Prince of Wales	98	Franchise	36
Pompée	80	Leda	38
Minotaur	74	Surveillante	36
Resolution	74	Solebay	32
Orion	74	Comos	22
Majestic	74	Cambrian	33
Goliath	74	Leveret	18
Valiant	74	Goshawk	16
Vanguard	74	Alacrity	16
Thunderer	74	Orestes	16
Nassau	64	Fearless	14
Ruby	64	Minx	14
Dictator	64	Safeguard	14
Centaur	74	Ariel	18
Alfred	74	Hyacinth	18
Agamemnon	64	Halcyon	16
Agincourt	64	Archer	14
Brunswick	74	Urgent	14
Maida	74	Cayenne	22
Ganges	74	Fury	12
Spencer	74	Acute	14
Mars	74	Alert	16
Defence	74	Pincher	14
Captain	74	Tigress	12
Hercule	74	Zebra	16
Hussar	36	Princess of Wales cutter	
Sybille	38	Thunder	8
Nymphe	36	Forward	14

On Sunday, the 26th, in the evening, the first division of the fleet, consisting of the following ships, sailed, with a fine wind at S.S.E. - Prince of Wales, Admiral Gambier; Pompée, Vice-Admiral Stanhope; Centaur, Commodore Sir S. Hood; Ganges, Commodore Keats; Alfred, Spencer, Captain, Brunswick, Orion, Maida, Goliath, Nassau, Hercule, Vanguard, Dictator, Ruby, Surveillante, Cambrian, Nymph, Leda, Sybille, and Franchise; Comus, Alert, Mosquito, Leveret, Cayenne, Goshawk, Turbulent, Pincher, Forward, Tigress, Urgent, Acute, Alacrity, Fury, Zebra, and Thunder.

Sir Samuel Hood led the van, and Commodore Keats the rear.

The second division, under Rear-Admiral Essington, was to sail on Wednesday the 29th. The following are some of the ships of which it was to be composed: Minotaur, Resolution, Mars, Agamemnon, Agincourt, Valiant, Defence, Caesar, Hussar, Richmond, Safeguard, Minx, and Vesuvius.

All the ships have as many flat-bottomed boats on board as they can stow; and the number of troops is stated to amount to 20,000. General Lord Cathcart is the military commander in chief. There are three lieutenant-generals; - the Earl of Rosslyn, Sir George Ludlow, and another; and ten major-generals.

The Baltic is mentioned by some, and Holland by others, as the probable destination of this force; but so laudable a secrecy has been preserved on the part of government, that no statement can go beyond the length of conjecture.

Action Between Leopard and USS Chesapeake

Another circumstance, which has made a considerable impression on the public mind, is an action which has been fought between his Majesty's ship *Leopard* of 50 guns, Captain Humphreys, and the American frigate *Chesapeake* of 44 guns, Commodore Barron, off the Capes of Virginia. Government received the intelligence of this event (which took place on the 23d of June) on the 26th of July. The official particulars have not transpired: the circumstances, as far as we have been able to learn, were as follow: - The American frigate was known to have several deserters from our ships, lying off Norfolk, on board. Representations of this fact were made to the Secretary of the American Navy, but without receiving any satisfactory answer. As it was known that the *Chesapeake* was about to sail for the Mediterranean, Captain Humphreys received orders to cruise off the Capes, and examine her for the deserters. Accordingly, when he came up with her, he sent a boat on board, with advice of the information he had of the deserters, and his orders to search for them; Commodore Barron refusing the search, Captain Humphreys fired several shots, which the other paying no attention to, he at length fired a broadside into the *Chesapeake*, which she returned by six or seven scattering guns; and on receiving a second broadside, struck her colours. On examination, the deserters, to the number of five or six, were found, the very men who had been demanded. In this short recounter the *Chesapeake* had six men killed, and twenty-one wounded: she returned into port very much shattered.

The inhabitants of Norfolk [Virginia] are said to have entered into some violent resolutions, and have prohibited all intercourse with our ships, and all supplies of water and provisions. It is added, that great riots have taken place at Norfolk; and that the mob burnt upwards of 200 water-casks belonging to the *Melampus* frigate.

The affair has been mentioned in both Houses of Parliament. His Majesty's servants expressed their readiness, should it be found necessary, to give all the information which they possessed, on the subject; but they entertained a hope, that the character of the transaction would not be found to require such a communication. Had there been any impropriety on the part of the British officer, the fullest satisfaction would be given.

Debate on Navy Victualling
Imperial Parliament, House of Commons, July 10 1807

Admiral *Harvey* and Admiral *Markham* both spoke on the same side of the question. [Replying to a harangue by Lord Cochrane calling for papers showing the poor victualling and repair of ships, the improper economies ordered by Lord St Vincent in the naval hospital, and the orders prohibiting leave for officers while the Channel Fleet commander actually lived ashore,] no redress, said the latter, had ever been applied for to the Admiralty, upon any of the grounds stated by the noble lord; and in what condition, he would ask, was the navy to be placed, if an inferior officer could bring his commander in chief to the bar of that House? As to the supply of the ships with fresh beef, more had been done in the administration of Lord St. Vincent than under any former administration. There were two modes formerly adopted: the one was to send bullocks out alive, the other to kill them before sending them out. Both these practices were subject to inconvenience; in rough weather it was hard to get them on board, and many died on their passage; if they were killed and the wind were unfavourable, the meat was often spoiled before it could arrive. The course which was now taken to remedy these inconveniences, was, to parboil the fresh beef on shore, and when it arrived at the fleet it made most excellent soup.[2] As to surgeon's stores, they were supplied, he said, under the administration of Lord St. Vincent, precisely according to the plan which had been originated, either by Lord Melville or Lord Barham; and this was the first time that he had ever heard any thing of their scarcity. The honourable member also entered into an explanation respecting the difficulty of sending men to the hospital. While officers, he observed, could send men to the hospital on the mere certificate of their own surgeon, they, naturally anxious for a good crew, were too apt to make use of their influence with the surgeon, to send any man to the hospital whom they did not happen to like. The allusion to the residence of the commander in chief in London, could derive no influence but from delusion. The Channel fleet was in different divisions, and the fact was, that for the purpose of communicating with each, the noble lord had better be ashore than at sea. Indeed, unless he took the station of junior admiral, he could not consistently join any of the divisions.

The *Chancellor of the Exchequer* Mr. *Windham*, Mr. *Sheridan*, and others, opposed the motion of Lord Cochrane; considering that, if the alleged grievances had existed, an application ought, in the first instance, to have been made to the Admiralty.

Lord *Cochrane* disclaimed any motives whatever on this occasion, except a regard to the good of the service. One of the gentlemen who had spoken in reply to him [Rear-Admiral John Markham], belonged to the Admiralty in the late administration; and the services of that gentleman were better known ashore than afloat.

From the 'Naval History of the Present Year,' 1807
July-August. XVIII 148-176

Baltic Operation

The principal objects of attention to the naval historian continue nearly the same - the operations of the powerful fleet which has been sent to the Baltic, and the conduct of the Americans. Respecting the first, the following is the latest and most correct information we have been enabled to collect from a variety of sources. In an interview with the Prince Royal of Denmark, Mr. Jackson requested to be informed, whether the Danish Government intended to declare for, or against England: because in the present system of violent measures adopted on the Continent, the neutrality of Denmark could no longer be acknowledged. His Royal Highness made this reply: "I shall consider any power as my enemy, which shall endeavour to make me depart from my neutrality." And having thus delivered his sentiments, the Prince immediately set off from Kiel for Copenhagen where he arrived on the 11th of August. It appears that our admiral waited

2 It is deserving of notice, that, on the very morning after these observations were delivered, a letter was received in town, from Plymouth, stating, "that the sending out beef half boiled to the fleet *is given up, and live bullocks are to be sent out* for the use of the seamen, as usual, which will be a considerable saving *to government*, and *much better for the health of the men*." Editor

the result of Mr. Jackson's mission before he commenced his operations. According to a private letter, August 14th, the British men of war, with the troop ships, form a complete line of circumvallation round the island of Zealand, some divisions have also entered the great and little Belts. That excellent officer, Commodore Keats, with four sail of the line, and some frigates, passed the Belts on the 4th. - Between Copenhagen and Elsinor there were, on the 8th, eighteen sail of the line, besides frigates. The English fleet formed a telegraphic line from Copenhagen to Kiel. Such was the state of our naval proceedings in the Baltic at the beginning of the month of August. The first great object which our ministers had in view was to secure the Danish fleet from becoming a powerful weapon in the hands of our inveterate enemy; and in the accomplishment of this, they have certainly shewn a laudable promptness of decision accompanied with a dignified forbearance. Our admiral has 90 pendants under his command, with near thirty thousand troops. An expedition more formidable in point of force, and fitted out with more activity, never sailed from a British port. - We trust, that having secured the Danish fleet, it will afterwards be directed against the Russian navy.

Buonaparté has placed us, as it were, under the ban of the Continent - he has endeavoured to set all the Continent against us, and we are justified in taking such measures, as our safety may render necessary, against all those nations which he can control. He will not permit any nation to be neutral towards us. Switzerland, whom we have never injured, is not to receive our merchandize. Portugal who bribed him to let her remain neutral, is forbidden to open her ports to us. Our property is to be seized on neutral ground, and yet Buonaparté cries out for the freedom of the seas, and the abandonment of our maritime rights. - We are placed in a situation in which we must use the same weapons which he does. - The necessity is to be lamented, but the necessity is our justification. . . .

America

The latest accounts from America are of a pacific nature; and the probability is, that the fermentation of the people will subside, and that the affair will be amicably adjusted between the respective governments. An American vessel, which has since reached England, passed through Commodore Douglas's squadron on the night of the 17th of July, without experiencing the slightest interruptions. Commodore Douglas arrived at Halifax, in Nova Scotia, on the 28th of July.

The observations of Mr. Canning, with respect to America, a few days before the breaking up of Parliament, are particularly deserving of notice. He expressly stated, that the misunderstanding had in no degree arisen from the views or conduct of his Majesty's present ministers; that on coming into office they had conceived it to be their duty to act up to the spirit of the treaty which had been framed by their predecessors; and that no new instructions whatever had been sent out, either to his Majesty's representative in America, or to the naval commanders on the station. . . .

Proclamation Controlling Trade

At the Court at the Queen's Palace the 19th of August, 1807
Present: The King's Most Excellent Majesty in Council

His Majesty, taking into consideration the measures recently resorted to by the enemy for distressing the commerce of the United Kingdom, is pleased, by and with the advice of his Privy Council, to order, and it is hereby ordered, that all vessels under the flag of Mecklenburgh, Oldenburgh, Papenburgh, or Kniphausen, shall trade in future at any hostile port, unless such vessels shall be going from or coming to a port of the United Kingdom; and in case any such vessel, after having been so warned, shall be found trading, or to have traded, after such warning; or in case any vessel or goods belonging to the inhabitants of such countries, after the expiration of six weeks from the date of this order, shall be found trading, or to have traded, after six weeks have expired, at any hostile port, such vessel and goods, unless going from or coming to a port of the United Kingdom, shall be seized and brought in for legal adjudication, and shall be condemned as lawful prize to his Majesty: - And his Majesty's principal secretaries of state, the Lords Commissioners of the Admiralty, and the judge of the High Court of Admiralty, and judges of the Courts of Vice-Admiralty, are to take the necessary measures herein as to them shall respectively appertain.

New Uniform Regulations
Admiralty Office, August 7, 1807

The King having signified to my Lords Commissioners of the Admiralty his royal pleasure that the following uniform clothing shall in future be worn by the masters and pursers in his royal navy, their lordships do hereby give notice thereof to all masters and pursers in his Majesty's royal navy accordingly, and require and direct them to conform strictly thereto.

Full Dress
"Blue cloth coat, with blue lapels, cuffs, and collar, collar to stand up, three buttons on pockets and cuffs, white lining; white cloth waistcoat and breeches; plain hat."

Undress
"Blue cloth coat, blue lapels and round cuffs, fall down blue collar; waistcoat and breeches of white or blue cloth as may be convenient. - The buttons worn by the masters to bear the arms of the Navy Office, and by the pursers those of the Victualling Office."

Debate on Mercantilist Strategy
Imperial Parliament, House of Lords, Thursday August 13 1807

Lord *Stanhope* moved a resolution, importing that "equality and complete reciprocity ought to form the invariable rule of conduct of the government, with regard to states at peace with this country." - His lordship observed, that if any man wished to complete the ruin of our commerce; if he wished to add to the already nearly insupportable weight of taxes; if he wished to increase bloodshed, and to second the views of Buonaparté, he would, as the most likely means of accomplishing his purpose, be eager to involve this country in a war with America. Within the last fifteen years, upwards of £40,000,000 had gone out of this country for the purchase of corn. Poland had hitherto been our granary; but in the present state of Europe, where, in future, could we look to for a supply, but America. It was the same with respect to naval stores. He wished their lordships also to be aware, that the man who had offered his secret to government for destroying ships of war, by a speedy and infallible method [Robert Fulton], was at this moment in America and employed in extensive preparations for carrying his plan into execution. The American government had rewarded him with a sum of £15,000. He was assured that a ship of the largest size could be destroyed on the principle of the invention alluded to, at an expense not exceeding £20.

The *Lord Chancellor* moved the previous question, which was put and carried; consequently Lord Stanhope's motion was lost.

[See Appendix 8, p388.]

Buonaparte's Blockading Decree Justifies British Claim to Prize Salvage

Law Intelligence, Court of Admiralty, August 18 1807

An interesting question was decided by Sir William Scott, which arose out of the decree of Buonaparté, for placing this country in a state of blockade, and thus aiming an ineffectual blow at the commerce of neutral nations with this country. Under the decree of blockade issued by Buonaparté, an American ship, the *Sanson*, had been captured by a French cruiser, and was afterwards recaptured by a British ship of war. In consequence of the recapture, a demand of salvage was made, which was resisted by the American, on the ground that the decree of blockade was not to be carried into effect against Americans, and that the vessel would have been restored to the owners by the French Tribunal.

On this question Sir William Scott was clearly of opinion, that the owners having received real benefit by the recapture, were clearly bound to pay salvage. The decree of France was declared to form a solemn and fundamental law of the empire, till such time as England chose to relax her claims, and recognize certain terms more compatible with the rights of other nations. The meaning of the word blockade in this decree must necessarily be the same as when applied to the blocking up of a single port or harbour, and therefore the decree must be clearly understood as extending to prevent all intercourse of the subjects of neutral states with this country. Such being the state of things, it was impossible not to say, that, *prima facie*, great service had been done to the American owners by the recapture. There was nothing in the decree to distinguish the Americans from other nations, or to exempt them from its effects.

Sir William Scott therefore pronounced a decree granting salvage to the re-captors.

The Brig Friendship, August 19th

The owners of the vessel in question were subjects of the United States of America, and the ship sailed from Baltimore for Bourdeaux [Bordeaux], laden with staves, empty barrels, &c and having on board the master (a native of France), five French merchants, seven French marine officers, and eleven French mariners, with a number of boys and other persons. She was captured on her voyage to Bourdeaux by his Majesty's ship *Emerald*, and carried into Plymouth.

The learned advocates, Drs. Arnold and Robinson, on the part of the captors, contended that this was an illegal hiring of a neutral vessel for the purpose of carrying persons of a naval and military character, subjects of a country with whom we were at war, contrary to the law of nations, and by which the ship and cargo became confiscated to the captors. The captain of the ship had been by birth a Frenchman, although now a naturalized subject of the United States; the officers were all Frenchmen, belonging to French ships of war, in the service (as appeared from the documents before the Court), of "his royal and imperial Majesty;" the eleven mariners were also French subjects, serving a-board ships of war, in the service of France; all of whom were shipped on board by an officer in the French service (a consul), resident at Baltimore, and authorised to provide a passage home for all subjects of France; and all of whom were victualled and provided for at the expense of the French Government, while on board; they were all under the command of one particular officer, and returning to their own country, probably for the purpose of being employed against this. From the nature and amount of the cargo, it was further argued, that this vessel was purposely fitted out as a transport, to carry enemy's troops. Under all these circumstances, both ship and cargo were liable to confiscation.

Doctors Lawrence and Swabey, on behalf of the claimants, contended, on the other side, that this ship was fitted out, chartered, freighted, &c. for the sole purpose of mercantile transactions, and none other. The persons found on board were neither in a military nor naval character at the time. They were shipped by a person authorised to provide for and protect the subjects of his own country, but who was not armed with any military or naval authority, and acted merely in his character of a commercial agent. These passengers were provided for by the master of the vessel in the usual board, nor any thing which could be construed into an intention of hostility against this or any other nation. With respect to the cargo, they contended it was exactly the cargo fitting for such a voyage; it was the usual cargo from that part of the United States to Bourdeaux, and in return for which the ship was to have carried home wines and other commodities, chiefly dealt in at that place. - Judgment deferred.

French Naval Resources

From 'Naval Anecdotes.' XVIII 276-278

Lord Selkirk, in the speech which he delivered in the House of Lords on the defence of the country, August 10, 1807, and which has since been published separately, observed:

"When we look at the vast extension of the resources of France, at the means of recruiting her navy, which she has acquired by her continental conquests, it would be blindness not to perceive, that her naval power must soon become far more formidable than it has ever yet been. France is now in possession of the finest forests in Europe, and of countries capable of affording ample supplies of every naval store: she may command the services of all the seamen which the continent can afford, from Memel to Cadiz, and from Cadiz to Constantinople. We may look too to the certain prospect, that the whole energy of the French government will now be directed to this object: we know in fact that during all the pressure of their continental wars, the most active exertions in ship-building have never been discontinued in their naval arsenals: they have now no other object to divide their attention; and we may be well assured that all the ability of the ruler of France will now be turned to naval affairs. The same genius, which has created such an astonishing change in the discipline and tactics of the French army, will now be unremittingly employed in the improvement of their navy. We have therefore, my lords, every reason to believe, that the naval superiority of England must ere long be exposed to a more severe contest, than any which it has recently had to maintain. Whatever confidence we may entertain in the valour and skill of our seamen, it is not the part of a prudent politician, under such circumstances, to overlook the possibility of our navy being worsted. This, my lords, is an event for which we ought to be prepared; and fortunately there is room to hope that we shall have sufficient time to prepare against it. But any one who considers well what the state of this country would be, if the French should obtain a superiority at sea, will certainly not be disposed to think that we can begin too soon to provide against such an emergency.

But, my Lords, this is not all - we have dangers more closely pressing upon us, dangers which, if we are to meet, we have not a moment to lose. An invasion is certainly no impracticable undertaking for the French, even at this moment, notwithstanding all our actual superiority at sea. The ablest and most experienced naval officers have given their opinion of the practicability of the enemy landing in force on our shores. Repeated experience has proved the impossibility of effectually blockading the ports of the enemy, notwithstanding the greatest naval superiority; and when we consider the vast range of coast that is now under their influence - a range which ere long may have no other limits than those of Europe itself, it is evident that we may be threatened at the same moment from so many different points, that it will be more difficult than ever to watch them all, and that thus the chances are greatly increased, of the enemy being able to convey an armament to the most vulnerable points of our empire. Our ablest admirals have repeatedly seen the French fleets escape from them, even when their whole vigilance was directed to the single port of Brest. But what would be the case, if armaments were ready at the same time in Cadiz, in Ferrol, in Rochefort, in Brest, in Cherburg, in Flushing, in the Texel, in the Elbe, and perhaps even in Norway? What rational hope could be entertained that some one or other of them would not escape, and land either in England or in Ireland a force sufficient to put the existence of our empire on the hazard of the die?"

From the 'Naval History of the Present Year,' 1807
August-September. ^{XVIII 221-268}

Copenhagen Taken and Danish Fleet Seized

An expedition more adequate to its object has seldom been equipped, than that which has just effected the reduction of Copenhagen, and the capture of the Danish fleet. By this grand *coup de main* of the British government - a stroke by which Buonaparte has been completely outwitted - we have wrested from the grasp of the enemy eighteen Danish ships of the line, mounting from 64 to 96 guns each; three ships of the line, upon the stocks; fifteen fine frigates; six brigs; twenty-five gun-boats; and an immense quantity of naval stores and ammunition.

We confess ourselves to be amongst those who regard the *necessity* of the case as a sufficient apology for our conduct. Britain has acted on that first principle of our nature - *self-preservation*. The question was simply this: Whether Buonaparte should be permitted to seize upon the Danish fleet, and to employ it in hostile purposes against England (as we have been assured, from unquestionable authority, was his intention): or whether, by securing that fleet ourselves, we should deprive him of the means of annoying us, and ensure our own safety? - His Majesty's ministers wisely preferred the latter. Yet we intended no injury to the Danes. Disclaiming all ideas of *capture*, we solicited only a *deposit*. The proposal was even merciful to the Danes; as, had they acceded to it, their fleet and naval stores would have eluded the rapacious grasp of Buonaparte, and have been safely restored to them at the conclusion of a general peace. Whether, under the circumstances by which they have now fallen into our possession, this will be the case, must, we conceive, depend upon future contingencies.

Government, we are assured, had received the most positive intelligence, that Buonaparte had formed a plan for occupying Zealand, and that, having possessed himself of the Danish navy, it was his intention immediately to invade Ireland. In this intention he is happily frustrated. We fear, too, that, viewing our maritime ascendancy with a jealous eye, the Danes would rather have facilitated than thwarted his views. We have a right to infer this, from their former conduct at the period of the Northern Confederacy: and from the uncommon abundance of stores which were found in their arsenals - stores which could not have been amassed but from hostile aims. There was something determined, also, in their opposition. They extinguished the lights of Anholt, Skagen, Pakkeberg, and Langeland: and it has been said, that the Crown Prince gave orders for the burning of the fleet, rather than that it should be suffered to fall into the hands of the English. It has been reported also - and we believe it was accredited at the Admiralty - that, when we took possession of the Danish ships, holes were discovered to have been cut in all their bottoms: the object of which must have been, that they should sink on their passage to this country. Another statement, however, insists, that the holes, instead of being artfully concealed, were plainly perceptible; and that the intention of the Danes was, instead of burning their ships, to sink them in the harbour. Time will discover which of these two accounts is the more correct.

Deeply do we regret the effusion of innocent blood. The Danes, it is said, have sustained a loss of from five to six thousand in killed and wounded; the steeple of the great church, in Copenhagen, fell in with a tremendous crash; eighteen hundred houses were destroyed; and the conflagration of the town was terrific almost beyond description. In the absence of all accounts which can be depended on, as to the injury incurred by the Danes, we present the following from a foreign paper: - "Besides the principal church, several streets in the northern quarter of the town are mostly in ashes; there is scarcely a house that is not damaged. According to report, the bombs, grenades, and rockets thrown into the town, exclusive of the cannon shot, exceeded 2,000 in number. Fifteen hundred burgers and inhabitants have lost their lives; and four hundred wounded persons, of both sexes, have been carried to Frederick's Hospital. Notwithstanding this dreadful devastation, the courage and valour of the garrison, supported by their burgers, can scarcely be described. The King's life guard, mostly composed of students, under Count Hauch, distinguished themselves to such a degree, that the English called them 'The Corps of Officers.' Their loss consisted of sixty killed and wounded. The artillery, and the officers of every description, have done all that could be expected of brave men. - The commandant, Major-General Peyman, was wounded by a musket-ball, in the attack upon the Classen Garden. Several officers are dead of their wounds." - Our loss has been but slight; though Sir David Baird had a very narrow escape.

Nothing, however, can prove the moderation of the English character more decidedly than the conduct which has been pursued by our commanders at Copenhagen. From the first moment of our landing, the most efficient measures were adopted for preventing the oppression or injury of individuals; and, no sooner had our object, in acquiring possession of the fleet and arsenals, been accomplished, than affairs were suffered, as much as possible, to revert to their former channels. Were not comparisons odious, we would exultingly exclaim: Look at the conduct of the British, in the conquest of Copenhagen, and at that of the French, in the subjugated territories of the continent!

Vice-Admiral Stanhope and Sir Home Popham, we understand, are the superintending officers to whom the equipment of the Danish fleet for sea has been entrusted. By their exertions, it was expected, when the last despatches left Copenhagen, that the ships and stores would be ready to proceed for England about the 22d or 23d of September.

Immediately after the intelligence of the capture had arrived, directions were sent to Chatham and Sheerness, for receiving the Danish fleet at those places; the Trinity Houses, at London, Hull, and Leith were ordered to furnish a certain number of masters and pilots, well acquainted with the navigation of the North Sea, to pilot them to England; and a proclamation was issued by government, offering an allowance of £2 10s and able seamen's pay, to the crews of the Greenlandmen lately arrived, and to other sailors employed in the British fisheries, &c to induce them to proceed to Copenhagen, and to assist in navigating the ships to this country. From the advantages holden out to them – such as having a protection from the impress, and the assurance of being sent back, on their return, free of expense, to the respective ports where they might have entered – upwards of 2,000 have already volunteered in the river, and in the eastern ports; and it is conjectured, that many more will be collected for this purpose.

From the circumstance of Admiral Gambier not having been able to spare a sufficient number of men from the fleet, to navigate the Danish ships across the water, it has been inferred, that the expedition has yet an ulterior object. Probably the Russian fleet, at Cronstadt.

Our countrymen will, of course, be pleased to learn, that the commanding officers at Copenhagen are to be invested with honourary rewards. Admiral Gambier is to be raised to the dignity of a Baron; Vice-Admiral Stanhope and Sir Home Popham are to be created Baronets; and Lord Cathcart, the military commander in chief, is to be advanced from the rank of a Scotch Baron to that of an English Viscount. Captain Collier, of his Majesty's ship *Surveillante*, who brought over Admiral Gambier's despatches, announcing the surrender of Copenhagen, has received the honour of knighthood; and Lieutenant Cathcart, the son of Lord Cathcart, who brought home the military despatches relative to the same event, has been promoted to the command of a company.

Heligoland Captured

Under the present aspect of affairs, the capture of Heligoland will prove a great advantage to this country. As its captor, Admiral Russell, observes, "with a small expense this island may be made a *little Gibraltar*, and a safe haven for small craft, even in the winter: it is a key to the rivers Ems, Weser, Jade, Elbe, and Eyder, the *only* asylum at present for our cruisers in those seas."

War With Russia Apprehended

Serious apprehensions are entertained of a war with Russia. Since the Emperor Alexander put his hand to the disgraceful peace of Tilsit he has appeared to be in a mood to concede every thing to France. Already has he surrendered the passes of Cattaro, and the republic of the Seven Islands [Corfu], to Buonaparte; and, should that marauder take possession of Trieste and Fiume, he will have the complete command of the Adriatic.

According to recent advices from St. Petersburg, batteries for red hot shot were preparing at Reval and at Cronstadt. A letter from Stockholm also mentions, that the Russian ambassador had delivered a note to the Swedish government, declaring, that if assistance were rendered to the British fleet, or if any part of it were admitted into the ports of Sweden, it would be considered as a declaration of war, and a Russian army would be marched into Finland. This statement is corroborated by the fact, that the King of Sweden, after having been compelled to evacuate Stralsund, and to retire to Rugen, has left the command of his troops in that island to Baron Toll, proceeded to

Carlscrona, and there *ordered the whole Swedish fleet to be equipped for service*; a measure which, we conceive, he would not have thought it necessary to adopt, but for the threats of Russia. In contemplating these circumstances, it is impossible not to suppose, that a naval confederacy had been planned, and was making rapid advances to maturity. The vigour and promptitude of our government have at least checked its progress.

Turks Fail to Drive Russians out of Tenedos

An event which may perhaps heighten the naval confidence of Russia has recently occurred. Three successive attempts of the Turkish admiral upon the island of Tenedos were frustrated; and, in a general engagement with the Russian fleet, on the 1st of July, he sustained a complete and signal defeat. The slaughter was immense. The famous Bekir Pacha, six captains, and twelve Tschiaoux, were killed; the grand admiral himself narrowly escaping, in his dismasted three-decker, to the canal of Constantinople. - At the latter end of June, a Russian squadron also appeared before Sinope and Trebisond, in the Black Sea.

Lord Collingwood, we understand, arrived off Tenedos, with seven sail of the line, about the latter end of August; a circumstance which excited much alarm in Constantinople. Sir Arthur Paget, who is with his lordship, is reported to have demanded, that Egypt should be put under the protection of Britain, till the conclusion of general peace.

Buonaparte Decrees Ban on Trade With Britain

Buonaparte maintains all his accustomed inveteracy against this country - an inveteracy which is not likely to be mollified by our late proceedings at Copenhagen. From Leghorn, we learn, that the regulations for preventing any communication with England are to be carried into execution with increased rigour and activity in all the territories of the allies of France. On the 29th of August, the French General Miolis [Miollis] entered the town of Leghorn at the head of 4,000 men. These troops immediately took possession of the harbour and the forts, and a proclamation was issued, ordering the discovery of all English goods within the period of twenty-four hours. Meanwhile an embargo was laid on all the shipping in the port. - Similar regulations are likewise enforced with peculiar rigour in Holland. A ship laden with coffee and sugar, which was supposed to have come from this country, was seized on the 18th of September, at Catwyck, and the captain thrown into prison. It is said, that no less than forty ships, with their cargoes, all insured at Lloyd's, have in this manner been confiscated. A considerable number of French troops, both infantry and cavalry, line the coast of Holland, for the purpose of cutting off all intercourse with this country. The Dutch merchants are in a state of the greatest alarm.

Buonaparte Demands Aid From Portugal

As a part of his plan of operations against England, Buonaparté is said to have made a demand upon Portugal, for ten sail of the line, with a proportionate number of smaller ships; in consequence of which the Portuguese government has given orders for the equipment of the following vessels: - Ships of the line - *Alfonzo d'Albuquerque, Meduza, Conde Don Henrique.* Cherreus *S.Godo Magno Principe* (going to Bania) *Princeza Real.* Frigates *Minerva, Princeza, Carlotta.* Brigs *Gavio* (under orders) *Condeca de Refeada*, ditto.

Expedition Sails From Cork

Another expedition has been fitted out by the British government, at Cork, and has probably sailed. It has about 8,000 troops on board, under the command of General Beresford. It has been conjectured, that the object of this armament is, to obtain possession of the Portuguese shipping, until the period of peace. Nothing, however, is known upon the subject.

French West Indian Islands to be Blockaded

It is expected that government will shortly declare all the French West India Islands in a state of blockade.

Settlement of Disputes With the United States?

It is believed that the negotiations between the British and American ministers are drawing towards a close; the result of which it is supposed will be of an amicable nature. Mr. Monroe, the American ambassador, aspiring to the presidentship of the United States, has taken his passage for New York, leaving Mr. Pinckney in England to manage the diplomatic relations between the respective governments.

Evacuation of South America, Courts Martial Expected

The most distressing intelligence which has for a long time reached England, is that of our failure in the attempt upon Buenos Ayres, and our consequent evacuation of Monte Video, and the whole of Spanish South America. Nothing is known respecting the business, beyond what the gazette furnishes; but it is generally understood, that the military commanders in that unfortunate and disgraceful affair will be brought to a court martial.

Admiralty and Navy Boards Active

The zeal and activity of the present Admiralty and Navy Boards are truly great. The influence of their spirited conduct is evident where ever it can operate, particularly in all the merchants and the king's dock-yards in the river. Ten sail of the line are ordered to be built in the former, in addition to several now on the stocks, while, from the latter, within these few weeks, the following have been launched, equipped, and are now lying at North Fleet ready for sea, viz. the *Elizabeth*, of 74 guns, Honourable Captain Curzon; the *York*, of 74, Captain Barton; the *Marlborough*, of 74, Captain G. Moore; and the *Cumberland* of 74, Captain ____. The *Bombay*, of 74 guns, from Deptford; the *Invincible* of 74, and *Undaunted* of 40 guns, from Woolwich, will be launched on the 15th and 16th of October. Two frigates of 40 guns each, that have undergone a thorough repair, are also to be undocked, and immediately equipped. The utmost care and diligence appear to be exerted in the king's yards at Woolwich and Deptford, to prevent the admission of improper persons: boards are stuck up at various parts of these yards, signed by Commissioner Cunningham, intimating that no persons but those upon business are allowed to land or enter therein; measures, we presume, adopted in consequence of the late fire at Chatham.

1807 – Conflict With The United States

AMERICAN RESISTANCE TO British exercise of trade control was less hypocritical than was that of the Baltic states, which had long histories of trade exploitation of their own, but the importance of the issue to British survival made confrontation unavoidable. The size of the American merchant marine made it a significant factor in the ability of Napoleon to implement his Continental Strategy, and of Britain's ability to resist it. The willingness of the United States to favour the despotism of the French police state, understandable if it is considered that British sea power had the potential for stifling American economic growth, cooled sympathy. The ease with which British deserters could obtain naturalisation in the United States added to the necessity for the British to confront the United States if their naval and economic power was not to be fatally undermined.

The Naval Chronicle was certain that war with the United States was to be avoided if at all possible, but had little sympathy with the Americans. In June 1807, however, a very serious event took place when sailors from the North American squadron operating out of Norfolk, Virginia, were seduced to desert, and then to sign on the American warship, the USS *Chesapeake*. Captain Humphreys of HMS *Leopard*, acting under orders from Admiral Berkeley, encountered her at sea and demanded a right to search her for deserters. When the demand was refused, *Leopard* opened fire on the American warship, forced her to lower her colours, and then removed the deserters by force. At a court martial at Halifax one of them was condemned to death, and hanged. In retaliation, the United States government closed its ports to British warships, and forbade the sale to them of supplies.

The Chesapeake and the Leopard

From the 'Naval Biography of Salusbury Pryce Humphreys, Esq.' XXVIII 354-367

From the official orders of Admiral Berkeley, dated June 1, 1807, it appears that, while the British squadron were at anchor in the Chesapeake, many of their men, subjects of

52

View of the high land of Never-Sink and Sandy-Hook Light-House. Engraved by
Baily, from a drawing by J.E.
    This is a cruizing ground for the national pilots, and also a customary station of
warlike cruizers, of which too, a line of battle ship and a frigate are represented in
the plate, as employed in the service of blockade. [Plate 413]

his Britannic Majesty, "deserted and entered on board the U.S. frigate called the
Chesapeake, and openly paraded the streets of Norfolk, in sight of their officers, under
the American flag, protected by the magistrates of the town, and the recruiting officer
belonging to the above-mentioned American frigate, which magistrates and naval officer
refused giving them up, although demanded by his Britannic Majesty's consul, as well
as the captains of the ships from which the said men had deserted. The captains and
commanders of his Majesty's ships and vessels under my command (says Admiral
Berkeley, in the official document to which we have alluded) are therefore hereby required
and directed, in case of meeting with the American frigate, the *Chesapeake*, at sea, and
without the limits of the United States, to shew to the captain of her this order, and to
require to search his ship for the deserters from the before-mentioned ships (*Belleisle,
Bellona, Triumph, Chichester, Halifax*, and *Zenobia*), and to proceed and search for the
same; and if a similar demand should be made by the American, he is to be permitted to
search for any deserters from their service, according to the customs and usage of civilized
nations, on terms of peace and amity with each other."[1]
    Captain Humphreys proceeded in strict conformity to these orders. On the morning
of June 22, in obedience to a signal from Captain Douglas, of H.M.S. *Bellona*, the
senior officer of the squadron, he weighed and reconnoitred; and, having arrived off
Cape Henry, to the distance of about four or five leagues, he bore up towards the
Chesapeake frigate, which had been descried by the *Bellona*. On arriving within hail, he
despatched an officer with Admiral Berkeley's order, and also with a polite note from
himself, to the captain of the *Chesapeake*, expressing a hope, that every circumstance

1 N.C. XVIII 117.

might be adjusted in such a manner, that the harmony subsisting between the two countries might remain undisturbed. - After an absence of three quarters of an hour, the boat returned, with an answer from Commodore Barron, of the *Chesapeake*, stating, that he knew of no such men as were described; that the officers, on the recruiting service for the *Chesapeake*, had been particularly instructed, not to enter any deserters from his Britannic Majesty's ships; and that he had been instructed, never to permit the crew of any ship that he might command, to be mustered by any but her own officers.

On the receipt of Commodore Barron's letter, Captain Humphreys, from motives of humanity, and a desire to prevent blood-shed, endeavoured to make the search, without recurring to more serious measures, by repeatedly hailing, and remonstrating, but without effect. He then directed a shot to be fired across her bow; after which he again hailed, without obtaining a satisfactory answer. He consequently felt himself under the necessity of enforcing his orders, by firing into the *Chesapeake*: a few shots were returned, none of which struck the *Leopard*. At the expiration of ten minutes from the first shot being fired, the pendant and ensign of the *Chesapeake* were lowered, when Captain Humphreys gave the necessary directions for her being searched. Jenkin Ratford, a deserter from the *Halifax* (afterwards tried, found guilty, and executed), and three deserters from the *Melampus*, were found on board the *Chesapeake*. Several other English subjects composed part of her crew; but, as they did not claim the protection of the British flag, and did not fall within the limits of Admiral Berkeley's orders, Captain Humphreys allowed them to remain. - After the search had been made, Commodore Barron wrote a note to Captain Humphreys, stating, that he considered the *Chesapeake* as his prize, and that he was ready to deliver her to any officer who should be authorized to receive her. Captain Humphreys observed, in answer, that, having, to the utmost of his power, fulfilled his instructions, he had nothing more to desire; repeating, that he was ready to give every assistance in his power, to the *Chesapeake*; and deploring that any lives should have been lost in the execution of a service, which might have been adjusted more amicably. . . .

Into the detail of the voluminous correspondence which ensued between the respective governments of Great Britain and America it is here impossible for us to enter. The most conciliatory conduct, however, was, from the first, adopted on the part of his Majesty's ministers; Mr. Secretary Canning explicitly disclaiming the "right to search ships in the national service of any state for deserters;" thereby virtually declaring, that the issuing of orders for that purpose by Admiral Berkeley, was an illegal and unauthorized act. Still farther to conciliate the American government, the offending admiral was recalled.

The refusal, however, of the United States, to revoke Mr. Jefferson's Proclamation of the 2d of July, 1807, (by which the British navy was interdicted from entering the ports of America) and the attempt to blend other subjects with the matter immediately in question, rendered it impossible to bring the negotiation to an amicable close, in London. At the close of the year 1807, Mr. Rose was, in consequence, despatched, on a special mission to the American government. His exertions were not more successful. By his instructions, he was expressly precluded from entering upon any negotiation for the adjustment of the difference arising from the encounter of the *Leopard* and *Chesapeake*, as long as the Proclamation alluded to, remained in force. The American minister on the other hand, contended, that before the Proclamation should become a subject of discussion, satisfaction should be made for the acknowledged aggression by which it had been preceded - the attack of the *Chesapeake* by the *Leopard* - and also for numerous irregularities, alleged to have taken place prior to that event.

New York Meeting

From 'Naval Anecdotes.' $^{XVIII\ 114-131}$

At a general Meeting of the Citizens of New York, held in the Park, on Thursday, July 2, 1807, the Hon. DE WITT CLINTON *was unanimously called to the Chair, and General Jacob Morton was unanimously appointed Secretary to the Meeting*
Having received, with the most lively indignation, authentic information that on the 22d ult. an attack, unwarranted by the known usages of nations, and in violation of our national rights, was made off the Capes of Virginia, on the United States frigate *Chesapeake . . .[etc.]*
    [See also: correspondence between Michael Kalteisen, Captain Commanding *Charleston*, and Captain William Love, of His Britannic Majesty's sloop *Driver*, 2 and 3 May 1807; and 'Correspondence between Captain Douglas, of His Majesty's Ship *Bellona*, and the Mayor of Norfolk in America' , Vol. XVIII, pp29-31 and 122-130.]

Proclamation, by Thomas Jefferson, President of the United States of America

During the wars which, for some time, have unhappily prevailed among the powers of Europe, the United States of America, firm in their principles of peace, have endeavoured by justice, by a regular discharge of all their national and social duties, and by every friendly office their situation has admitted, to maintain, with all the belligerents, their accustomed relations of friendship, hospitality, and commercial intercourse. Taking no part in the questions which animate these powers against each other, nor permitting themselves to entertain a wish but for the general restoration of peace, they have observed, with good faith, the neutrality they assumed, and they believed that no instance of a departure from its duties can be justly imputed to them by any nation. A free use of their harbours and waters, the means of refitting and refreshment, of succour to their sick and suffering, have, at all times, and on equal principles, been extended to all, and this too amidst a constant recurrence of acts of insubordination to the laws, of violence to the persons, and of trespasses on the property of our citizens, committed by officers of one of the belligerent parties received among us. In truth these abuses of the laws of hospitality have, with few exceptions, become habitual to the commanders of the British armed vessels hovering on our coasts and frequenting our harbours. They have been the subject of repeated representations to their government. Assurances have been given that proper orders should restrain them within the limit of the rights and of the respect due to a friendly nation; but those orders and assurances have been without effect; and no instance of punishment for past wrongs has taken place. At length, a deed, transcending all we have hitherto seen, or suffered, brings the public sensibility to a serious crisis, and our forbearance to a necessary pause. A frigate of the United States, trusting to a state of peace, and leaving her harbour on a distant service, has been surprised and attacked by a British vessel of superior force, one of a squadron then lying in our waters and covering the transaction, and has been disabled from service, with the loss of a number of men killed and wounded.
    This enormity was not only without provocation or justifiable cause, but was committed with the avowed purpose of taking by force, from a ship of war of the United States, a part of her crew, and that no circumstance might be wanting to mark its character, it had been previously ascertained that the seamen demanded were natives of the United

States. Having effected his purpose, he returned to anchor with his squadron within our jurisdiction. Hospitality under such circumstances, ceases to be a duty; and a continuance of it, with such uncontrolled abuses, would tend only, by multiplying injuries and irritations, to bring on a rupture between the two nations. This extreme resort is equally opposed to the interests of both, as it is to assurances of the most friendly dispositions on the part of the British government, in the midst of which this outrage has been committed. In this light the subject cannot but present itself to that government, and strengthen the motives to an honourable reparation of the wrong which has been done, and to that effectual control of its naval commanders, which alone can justify the government of the United States in the exercise of these hospitalities it is now constrained to discontinue.

In consideration of these circumstances, and of the right of every nation to regulate its own police, to provide for its peace and for the safety of its citizens, and consequently to refuse the admission of armed vessels into its harbours or waters, either in such numbers, or of such description, as are inconsistent with these, or with the maintenance of the authority of the laws, I have thought proper, in pursuance of the authorities specially given by law, to issue this my PROCLAMATION, hereby requiring all armed vessels bearing commissions under the government of Great Britain, now within the harbours or waters of the United States, immediately and without any delay to depart from the same, and interdicting the entrance of all the said harbours and waters to the said armed vessels, and to all others bearing commissions under the authority of the British government.

And if the said vessels, or any of them, shall fail to depart as aforesaid, or if they or any others, so interdicted, shall hereafter enter the harbours or waters aforesaid, I do in that case forbid all intercourse with them or any of them, their officers or crews, and do prohibit all supplies and aid from being furnished to them or any of them.

And I do declare and make known, that if any person from, or within the jurisdictional limits of the United States, shall afford any aid to any such vessel, contrary to the prohibition contained in this proclamation, either in repairing any such vessel, or in furnishing her, her officers or crew, with supplies of any kind, or in any manner whatsoever, or if any pilot shall assist in navigating any of the said armed vessels, unless it be for the purpose of carrying them, in the first instance, beyond the limits and jurisdiction of the United States, or unless it be in the case of a vessel forced by distress, or charged with public despatches, as hereinafter provided for, such person or persons shall, on conviction, suffer all the pains and penalties by the laws provided for in such offences. . . .

Statement of the American Navy

Ships of 44 guns
United States, Chesapeake, Constitution, Philadelphia, President.
Ships of 36 guns
Constellation, New York, Congress, Insurgent.
Ships of 32 guns
Boston, General Greene, Essex, Adams, George Washington, John Adams.

Estimate of the number of persons composing the crews of the navy of the United States
5 frigates   of   44 guns and 400 men   2000

4 frigates	of	36 guns and	360 men	1440
2 ditto		32	265	530
4 ditto, smaller		32	214	1356
8 ships, of		20 to 26	180	1440
3 sloops of war		18	140	420
2 brigs		16 to 18	100	200
5 ditto schooners		12 to 14	70	350
7 galleys			28	196
Total, including marines				7532

Present State of the American Navy

From 'Naval Anecdotes.' *XVIII 279-280*

Mr. Hanson, the author of a new work, called, "The Stranger in America," gives the following account of the very *formidable* navy of the United States:

"On my last visit to the navy yard, I found six frigates, dismantled and laid up in ordinary, and one nearly equipped for sea, for the purpose of carrying back the Tunisian embassy to Barbary. A small vessel of war, pierced for 20 guns, had just been launched. Mr. Jefferson, two years ago, adopted an idea of his own, in order to raise the credit of the American navy, and for the destruction of the powers of Barbary. This is, to build a number of small vessels of about 100 tons burden, to be called gun-boats, each of which is provided with two heavy pieces of ordnance, one at the stem, and the other at the stern. Though the inutility of these mockeries of men of war has been manifested on many occasions, yet the president persists in riding his naval hobby-horse, even in Kentucky, where several gun-boats are building on the river Ohio. One of them is nearly lost on a voyage to the Mediterranean - being, the whole voyage, to use a sea phrase, "wet and under water." Another *gun-boat*, No. 1, (thus they are named to No. 8) in a hurricane in South Carolina, was driven nearly a mile into the woods . . . Added to these, the Americans have a frigate and two or three small vessels of war in the Mediterranean, which constitute the whole of their navy."

Annual Expenses of the American Navy

The following appropriations were made by the government of the United States for the navy for 1805, a year when they were at war with Tripoli:

Pay and subsistence of officers, and pay of seamen	$ 415,587
Provisions	227,086.40
Medicines, instruments, hospital stores	10,750
Repairs of Vessels[2]	411,951.20
The corps of marines	82,593.60
Clothing for the marines	16,536
Military stores for the marines	1,635
Medicine and hospital stores	1,250
Contingent expenses	8,419
Navy yards, docks, clerks, &c.	60,000
	$1,235,799.20

2 Though the American navy is scarcely twelve years old, yet the reader will perceive, by this charge, that the repairs are nearly equal to the "*pay and subsistence of the officers, and the pay of the seamen.*"

Paine's System of National Defence

From 'Correspondence' - 1809. *XXI 116-121*

Mr. Editor, If the name of Paine should not operate as a repellent, some useful ideas may be derived from a perusal of the following recent production of that writer. He does not appear fully to comprehend the subject in all its points; but several of his remarks are deserving of notice; and the information which he gives, relative to the expenses of ship-building in America, will, I doubt not, prove acceptable to many of your readers.

I am, &c.

"H.L."

"Natural defence, by men, is common to all nations; but artificial defence, as an auxiliary to human strength, must be adapted to the local conditions and circumstances of a country.

What may be suitable to one country, or in one state of circumstances, may not be so in another.

The United States have a long line of coast, of more than two thousand miles, every part of which requires defence, because every part is approachable by water.

The right principle for the United States to go upon, as a defence for the coast, is that of combining the greatest practical power with the least possible bulk, that the whole quantity of power may be better distributed through the several parts of such an extensive coast. . . .

The ship *United States* cost 300,000 dollars, gun-boats cost 4,000 dollars each, consequently the 300,000 dollars expended on the ship, for the purpose of getting the use of 44 guns, and those most [*not?*] heavy metal, would have built *seventy-five* gun-boats, each carrying a cannon of the same weight of metal that a ship of 100 guns can carry. . . .

The difference also in point of repairs, between ships of war and gun-boats, is not only great, but it is greater in proportion than in their first cost. The repair of ships of war is annually from one-fourteenth to one-tenth of their first cost. The annual expense of repairs of a ship that cost 300,000 dollars, will be above 21,000 dollars; the greatest part of this expense is in her sails and rigging, which gun-boats are free from.

The difference also in point of duration is great.

Gun-boats, when not in use, can be put under shelter, and preserved from the weather, but ships cannot; or boats can be sunk in the water or mud. This is the way the nuts of cider mills for grinding apples are preserved. Were they to be exposed to the dry and hot air, after coming wet from the mill, they would crack and split, and be good for nothing. But timber under water will continue sound several hundred years, provided there be no worms.

Another advantage in favour of gun-boats, is the expedition with which a great number of them can be built at once. A hundred may be built as soon as one, if there be hands enough to set about them separately. They do not require preparations for building them that ships require, nor deep water to launch them in. They can be built on the shore of shallow waters; or they might be framed in the woods or forests, and the parts brought separately down and put together on the shore. But ships take up a long time in building.

The ship *United States* took up two whole years, 1796 and 1797, and part of the years 1795 and 1798, and all this for the purpose of getting the use of 44 guns, and those not heavy metal.

This foolish affair was not in the days of the present administration.

Ships and gun-boats are for different services. Ships are for distant expeditions; gun-boats for home defence. The one for the ocean, the other for the shore."

Trial of Chesapeake Deserters
'Naval Courts Martial.' *XVIII 335-343*

Minutes of the Proceedings of a Court Martial, assembled and held on board his Majesty's ship *Belleisle*, in Halifax harbour, Nova Scotia, on Wednesday, August 26, 1807, to try Jenkin Ratford, of his Majesty's ship *Halifax*, for mutiny, desertion, and contempt, as set forth in a letter from her commander, the Right Honourable Lord James Townshend...

His Majesty's sloop Halifax, Halifax Harbour, August 13th, 1807
Sir, I beg leave to represent to you, that the five men, named in the margin,[3] belonging to his Majesty's sloop *Halifax*, under my command, when sent with a petty officer in the jolly-boat, in Hampton Roads, on the 7th of March last, to weigh a kedge anchor, which had been previously dropped for the purpose of swinging the ship by, taking the advantage of the dark of the evening, mutinied upon the petty officer, some of them threatening to murder him; but the rest interfering, they desisted. However, taking the boat under their own command, they succeeded in deserting, by landing at Sewel's Point.

The whole of the above-mentioned deserters, I have since been informed, entered on board the United States frigate *Chesapeake*, and were seen by me, and several of my officers, parading the streets of Norfolk in triumph, under the American flag. A few days after the desertion, I accosted one of these men, Henry Saunders, asking the reason of his deserting, and received for answer, that he did not intend any thing of the kind, but was compelled by the rest to assist, and would embrace the first opportunity of returning. At that moment Jenkin Ratford, one of the said deserters, coming up, took the arm of the said Henry Saunders, declaring with an oath, that neither he, nor any of the rest of the deserters, should return to this ship; and with a contemptuous gesture told me he was in the land of liberty, and instantly dragged the said Henry Saunders away.

Finding that my expostulating any longer would not only be useless in obtaining the deserters, but in all probability have collected a mob of Americans, who, no doubt, would have proceeded to steps of violence, I instantly repaired to the house of Colonel Hamilton, the British consul there, and related every circumstance which occurred, and applied to him, as also to Lieutenant Sinclair, of the rendezvous for the United States service, to recover the said deserters, but without effect.

Being since informed that Jenkin Ratford has been recovered, in action, on board the United States frigate *Chesapeake*, with his Britannic Majesty's ship *Leopard*, and now a prisoner on board his Majesty's ship *Bellona*, I have to request you will be pleased to direct a court martial may be assembled for the purpose of trying the said Jenkin Ratford, for the within-mentioned charges of mutiny, desertion, and contempt....

---

3 Richard Hubert, Henry Saunders, Jenkin Ratford, George North, William Hill.

A view of the harbour of St. John's in Newfoundland.

The harbour of St. John's is very commodious, and ships lie in it in perfect security, being sheltered on every side by high rocks, and the anchorage being extremely good. The approach to the harbour, although apparently hazardous, from the number of small rocky islands which are contiguous to its entrance, is in reality perfectly easy and safe. Plate 91

[After the evidence for the prosecution was heard] The prisoner was now called upon for his defence, having been told, at the examination of each witness, that he might ask any question he pleased. After retiring for a short time with the judge advocate, he returned into court, and stated, that the evidence brought against him was so strong, there was but little left for him to say in his defence; but that the reason of his hiding in the coal-hole was for fear of the Americans making him fight against his country, which he declared he would not do on any account; that he, with all the men who deserted from the *Halifax*, were persuaded by the boatswain to enter for the *Chesapeake*, to protect themselves, which they did: Lieutenant Sinclair asking them if they had not a second name. About thirty men went in the first draft with him to the *Chesapeake*, when Captain Gordon mustered them; and they were mustered again in Hampton Roads by the commodore. He requested leave to call one evidence in again, to ask his officers for a character; and then he threw himself on the mercy of the court.

Lord James Townshend, and the other officers, stated, that prior to the charges, he had always behaved himself as a quiet steady man.

The court were of opinion that the charges were proved, and adjudged the prisoner to suffer death.

The sentence of the court martial was carried into effect, at the fore yard-arm of his Majesty's sloop of war *Halifax*, on the Monday following, August 31st.

Three deserters from the *Melampus*, who were taken out of the *Chesapeake* were also tried, found guilty, and sentenced to receive 500 lashes each, but were afterwards pardoned.

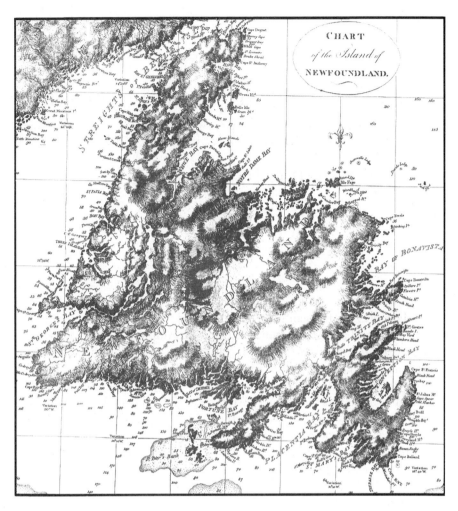

Chart of Newfoundland.

We are indebted for the annexed chart to that meritorious officer Colonel Desbarres, who was many years employed by government in surveying Nova Scotia, &c. and who published a most useful work, which we strongly recommend to our readers, entitled the *Atlantic Neptune*.

Account of Newfoundland

Newfoundland, in North America, has ever been esteemed one of the most valuable possessions of the British empire, whether considered as a nursery for seamen, or as a great source of national wealth, arising from the exchange of fish for the various productions and luxuries that spring up in the Mediterranean, &c. . . . It abounds with a vast number of harbours, some of which are very capacious, extending a great distance into the country, and interspersed with villages. The internal parts have never been perfectly explored, from the inhumanity and wanton cruelty which have been exercised towards the natives. . . . [Plate 87]

1807 – Russian Action against the Turks, and Collingwood's Return to the Levant

FOLLOWING THE WITHDRAWAL OF Vice-Admiral Duckworth from the Sea of Marmora, the Russian Navy had deployed a squadron to the Aegean, four ships and a frigate commanded by Vice-Admiral Seniavin who had been educated in the British navy. He took possession of the islands of Lemnos and Tenedos, garrisoned the latter, and then proceeded to blockade the Dardanelles. The Turkish Captain Bey hastily equipped his fleet and fought two engagements, on 19 May and 1 July, during his attempt to recover Tenedos. The Russians prevailed, with the Turks losing three ships and two frigates, but one British observer, Captain John Stewart, felt the Russians might have done more. In its biographical memoir *The Naval Chronicle* published a long letter recounting Stewart's work patrolling the islands, but it has only been possible to reprint a brief selection here.

Russian Official Account of the Late Naval Engagements Between the Turks and Russians off the Dardanelles
From 'Naval Anecdotes.' XVIII 370-374

The following is Admiral Siniavin's [Seniavin] report, relative to the actions of the 11th of May and the 19th of June, between the Russian and Turkish squadrons, together with an account of the attempt of the Turks to dislodge a detachment of Russian troops from the fort and the island of Tenedos:

"On the 7th of May, eight Turkish ships of the line, six frigates and smaller vessels, with about 50 gun-boats, passed the straits of the Dardanelles, and steered towards Tenedos. Admiral Siniavin, for several reasons, got under sail with his squadron, consisting of 10 ships of the line, and steered his course towards the island of Ymbro. The Turks, wishing to avail themselves of his absence for landing their troops upon the island of Tenedos, made two attempts for this purpose on the 8th, when they were repulsed with great loss by a division of our troops from the fortress, under the command of Major Gedeonow; of course they did not attempt to land a third time, but steered over to the coast of Natolia, and concealed themselves in the creeks.

On account of contrary winds, and a strong current, we could not make any attack on the Turkish fleet on the 8th or 9th; but on the 10th, at two in the afternoon, the wind being favourable, an attack was determined upon. However, our ships were scarcely got under weigh, when the Turks also weighed anchor, and attempted to gain the Dardanelles under full sail. Our ships pursued them to the mouth of the Straits, and cannonaded them two hours during their passage. The enemy's ships were so precipitate in their flight, that three of them were stranded between the batteries and the promontory of Asia; most of them were considerably damaged in their hulls, and had a number of killed.

The Turks, having received a reinforcement of ships of war and frigates from Constantinople, made their appearance again on the other side of the Dardanelles, on the 10th of June. They had now 10 ships of the line, six frigates, and five smaller vessels: among the former were three flag-ships, one of them a three-decker, carrying the Captain Pacha's colours, and two others with an admiral's flag. Near the island of Ymbro, they cast anchor, and formed the line of battle. In consequence of contrary winds and currents, our squadron could not approach them during three days; but on the evening of the 14th, we got under weigh with a favourable breeze.

On the 15th, being on the other side of the island of Ymbro, and unperceived by the enemy, we learnt they had weighed anchor, and steered for Tenedos. At the same time a number of boats, with Turkish troops on board, made their appearance from the coast of Asia, upon which the Russian garrison of Tenedos immediately got under arms, and occupied the most important posts and shores of the island. When the enemy's ships came within half cannon-shot of the fort, they were fired upon not only by the fort, but by the sloops lying in the harbour, upon which they made their boats approach the northern side of the island, and there attempt a landing, but they were repulsed.

Next morning, at day-break, the Turkish frigates and gunboats opened their fire upon our works, and at the same time they caused a great number of vessels, with troops on board, to approach the island from the coast of Anatolia. To oppose this landing, the Russian commandant detached 300 men; but before they could arrive at the place of destination, the Turks had succeeded in landing 1000 men, under cover of their frigates and ships of the line. The continual fire of grape and cartridge from these vessels left the small Russian detachment no choice as to the propriety of retiring.

The enemy, well knowing the weakness of the fort, flattered themselves with the hope of making themselves masters of it with little or no difficulty: accordingly, on the 17th, they again approached it with their whole squadron, and one ship of the line and a frigate kept up a cannonade against it during three hours; but when the enemy observed that our squadron approached Tenedos, they got a part of their troops on board, with the utmost precipitation, and stood out to sea.

The wind having changed in the night of the 13th, our squadron was detained till the 17th, in its passage between the island of Ymbro and the European coast; but on the 17th, with the north wind in their favour, they bore up for Tenedos, and observing that the enemy's small craft, with troops, were still upon the coast, the Russian row-galleys were ordered to attack them. A part of them were sunk by the galleys, and the rest dispersed.

As soon as the fort had been supplied with necessaries, and dispositions made for preventing the approach of the enemy's vessels, the frigate *Venus*, and the *Spitzbergen* sloop, were left to protect the coast. On the 18th, the Russian fleet were again under sail, steering their course for Lemnos, where they hoped to find the Turks. On the 19th, at day-break, they descried, as they expected, ten ships of the line, five frigates, and an equal number of small vessels. The Turks formed their line without delay. Our side followed their example, with the intention of attacking the enemy's flag-ship. Our ship *Raphail* was the headmost in our line, and when bearing down upon the enemy, it was observed that the Turks opened their fire at a very great distance. Our ship *Raphail*, on the contrary, being ordered to attack the enemy's flag-ship, retained her fire till she was within a very small distance from her opponent; but on account of receiving so much damage in her sails, as not to be able to bear up against the wind, she was driven into the enemy's line. At the same time Vice-Admiral Greig was ordered by Admiral Siniavin to attack the enemy's van, consisting of one ship of the line, and two large frigates. These frigates being soon disabled, and obliged to retire, the *Raphail* broke through the enemy's line, when she was fired upon by several of their ships of war; and Vice-Admiral Siniavin, who bore down to support the *Raphail*, was in a short time rendered unable to continue the conflict.

A calm succeeding immediately after, as it was impossible for the ships to manoeuvre, they became so far separated from the enemy's squadron, as to give them an opportunity of repairing their damages. As soon as the wind began to blow a little fresh, Admiral Siniavin made the signal for pursuing some of the enemy's ships of the line, and two frigates that were a considerable way behind the rest of the squadron.

In the following night, the ship of the Captain Bey, which was damaged more than the rest, was taken, with Becker Bey, and 774 men on board. This vessel carries 80 pieces of brass cannon, and is in every respect a very fine ship.

On the following day, Vice-Admiral Greig, with three ships, was ordered in pursuit of an enemy's ship of the line, and two frigates, that were discovered between Famo and the promontory of Asia. When the Turks found it was impossible to escape, they ran their ships aground, and, after getting the people on shore, set fire to the vessels.

Our three ships having returned to the squadron, Admiral Siniavin lost no time in proceeding to the island of Tenedos, with the view of affording the garrison the necessary assistance.

During the passage to Tenedos, on the 22d, a smoke was observed near the island of Tasso, where the Turkish fleet had been defeated, and some firing heard; and upon our arrival at Tenedos, we learned, that it arose from the burning of one of the enemy's ships and a frigate, which had been considerably damaged during the action.

The result of this last action has been the loss of three Turkish ships of the line and three frigates.

On the 26th, after Admiral Siniavin had taken proper measures for investing the island on all sides, and for cutting off all communication between the enemy and the continent, wishing to spare the effusion of blood, he sent a proposal to the commandant of the Turkish troops upon the island to evacuate it, and offering them a free passage to the coast of Asia. In consequence of this offer, on the 27th the Turkish commandant sent an officer to announce his acceptance of this proposal; and in order to relieve the garrison as soon as possible from the blockade it was under, the Turkish army, consisting of 4,600 men, was transported over to the Asiatic coast on the 28th.

Admiral Siniavin bestows very high encomiums upon the valour of Admiral Greig; the captains of the rank of post, Malagew, Schaltedg, and Krowwe; the captain of the second rank, Rtiechtochew; and Colonel Padeiski, the commandant of the garrison of Tenedos.

In these engagements we have lost 132 private, three superior officers, the captains Ignetgew, Lukin, &c. Among the wounded, 17 officers of the staff, and 392 privates. On the part of the enemy, in the ships that were taken, there were 230 killed, and 160 wounded; from which we may infer, that their whole loss must have been considerable. Of the Turkish troops that landed at Tenedos, in the various attempts upon that island, and during the blockade, which lasted ten days, the loss sustained was about 1,000 men.

Account of the Russian Admiral, Seniavin
From 'Naval Anecdotes.' *XIX 32-33*

The officer is of one of the first families in Russia. About the year 1783, being then a youth, he was sent to England by the Russian court, who obtained permission from the British government for his being admitted a volunteer in our navy. He was accordingly, by order of the Lords of the Admiralty, received on board the *Leander*, of 50 guns, then destined for the Halifax station, in America, where he served about three years. He was afterwards employed for nearly the same time in the Mediterranean, as a volunteer midshipman, on board the *Pearl* frigate, then commanded by the late Honourable Seymour Finch, brother to the Earl of Aylesford, which ship he quitted at Smyrna, in 1789, in order to render to his own country the benefit of that knowledge and experience he had acquired from us, Russia being then engaged in a war with the Turks, against whom he seemed, by nature, to be a zealous adversary. During the last war he served, and held the rank of a post captain in the Russian navy, and was one of their fleet that wintered in the Medway; but on that fleet being ordered home, and the Emperor Paul entering into the views of Buonaparte, he retired, and continued in retirement until Russia again made common cause with this country.

British Return to the Levant
From the 'Naval Biography of the Late Captain John Stewart, R.N.'
XXVIII 19-21

On her [i.e., the *Seahorse*'s] arrival at Malta, Captain Stewart was selected by Lord Collingwood, to serve in the Archipelago; his Lordship, with the British squadron, and that of Russia, were lying off the Island of Imbros, outside of the Dardanelles: Sir Arthur Paget being on board with Lord Collingwood, endeavouring to negotiate with the Turks. On the conclusion of peace between France and Russia, the Russian squadron came down the Mediterranean, and soon afterwards Lord Collingwood set sail; leaving Captain Stewart to maintain our footing in the Archipelago, and to preserve the Greek Islands, whence we had drawn our supplies and from which a great deal of trade was carrying on to Malta, from the ravages of their Turkish Agas, who had left them on our approach. . . .

The principal detail of Captain Stewart's services in the Archipelago, is given by himself, in a long letter to Mr. Loch, dated *Seahorse*, off Candia, November 7, 1807: and is particularly interesting, as containing a faithful portraiture of Stewart's sanguine and chivalric disposition, ever ready to succour the oppressed, and to chastise the oppressor. It is worthy of forming an episode, even in the beautiful *Romaunt of Childe Harolde*.

"I left Gibraltar July 14th, after putting my prizes in a fair train, and arrived at Malta after a fine weather passage of fourteen days. There I found orders to proceed to Messina for news, and then join Lord Collingwood at Tenedos, whom I found under the rocky Imbros of Homer. A position which he had taken, as from it he could fetch the Turkish fleet with the N.E. winds, which at that season are periodical. This he could not have done from Tenedos, which is to leeward, and towards which a continued strong current sets from the Dardanelles: this intention of his Lordship was in consequence of the Turkish fleet being outside of the Dardanelles, when he first arrived at Tenedos; but the moment they heard of our fleet's arrival, they moved above the first Castles; and, by the time he had worked to windward, were quite secure. They remained outside, not caring much for the Russians; who have had two actions with them, and only took one line-of-battle ship, besides driving two, I believe frigates, ashore. I leave you to judge of Siniavin's manoeuvres and conduct, when you are informed, that the Russians were some days between the Turks and the Dardanelles, that the Turks never put into any other port, and did actually land a body of men on Tenedos, who retook and held it for some time: what would we give such an opportunity! The consequence of these Russian manoeuvres is, that as they have a particular talent for burning and destroying, the town and island of Tenedos, which was one of the most productive of the small islands, are now, except the vines and fig-trees, a total desert. I went all over it - there was an abundance of game, but not a human being to be seen. I found a profusion of the finest grapes and figs, and plenty of corn for our stock. All of which every ship in the fleet used to gather in any quantity they pleased. - The town had been burnt to the ground, and was still a mass of smoking ruins. Its small harbour was totally ruined, and nearly filled up, and there was not a house but what had been perfectly gutted. All this I beheld on my return to Lord Collingwood, after visiting the Cyclades, where I had already seen most of the unfortunate inhabitants of Tenedos begging their bread. . . ."

1807 - Evacuation of
South America

IN JUNE AN EXPEDITION COMMANDED by General Craufurd and Rear-Admiral George Murray, and intended against Chile, arrived in the Plata and was diverted to reinforcement of the British forces there. General Whitelocke was put in command and on the 28th a landing was made at Ensenada, about 30 miles from Buenos Aires. The town was entered, and some of the operational objectives were reached, but the army became bogged down in intense street fighting, and eventually had to surrender. Against the heavily armed and inveterate citizen-army the small professional British force was entirely inadequate. A convention was agreed that all prisoners of war would be released, and in return the British would withdraw from all their positions on the River Plate within two months. On his return home, General Whitelocke was subjected to a court martial which lasted 32 days and in the end declared him unfit and unworthy to serve His Majesty in any military capacity.

This judgement may have been justified, but the reality was that the people of Buenos Aires had fought for their independence, and were never to accept any form of colonial government in the future.

From the 'Biographical Memoir of George Murray, Esq.' XVIII 191

On account of his father-in-law's affairs, Rear-Admiral Murray was for some time under the necessity of declining an appointment; but, when the expedition under General Craufurd had been determined on, he was selected for that service by the Admiralty, and accordingly received the command.

To what place that expedition was destined, remains, we believe, to the present time, a profound secret; but, in all probability, it was intended for some other part of South America than Buenos Ayres; as Rear-Admiral Murray had reached the Cape of Good Hope, and was afterwards directed, by the present administration, to take the command of the fleet at Monte Video.

When we sat down to compile the present memoir, we indulged the expectation, that, before it should be put to press, the public would be congratulated on the recapture of Buenos Ayres; and that, consequently, our footing would have been completely established in South America. We deeply regret, that our expectation has been wholly, and definitively frustrated; as, on the 12th of the month (September) official despatches were received by government, from Rear-Admiral Murray and Lieutenant-General Whitelocke, announcing the failure of our attempt upon Buenos Ayres, and the consequent agreement, on the part of the British commanders, to evacuate Monte Video, and the whole of Spanish South America, in two months, from the 7th of July.

The despatches were brought to England by the *Saracen*, Captain Prevost.

Admiral Murray's Dispatches

From the 'Naval History of the Present Year,' 1807
August-September

Letters on Service, September 12 1807. [XVIII 243-246]

Despatches, of which the following are copies and extracts, have this day been received at this Office from Rear-Admiral Murray, addressed to William Marsden, Esq.

Neriede, off Barragon, June 30th, 1807
Sir, I did myself the honour of informing you, by the last opportunity which sailed from Monte Video, of my proceeding from St. Helena until my arrival off Monte Video with the squadron and transports under my orders, a duplicate of which letter I now transmit.

Rear-Admiral Stirling had made every necessary arrangement for the intended expedition before my arrival; it being necessary on account of the shoals in the river, that the line of battle ships should remain at anchor off Monte Video, as well as for the protection of that place, I directed Admiral Stirling to remain with them. On the 17th instant, the second division of troops, consisting of all those who had come out with General Craufurd, being ready to proceed to Colonia, where General Whitelocke wished the whole to be assembled, Captain Prevost, in his Majesty's ship *Saracen*, taking with him the *Encounter* gun-brig and *Paz* schooner, sailed with the transports.

On the 18th, two hundred and thirteen marines of the squadron were landed at Monte Video, by request of the general, to strengthen the garrison; I likewise ordered four hundred and forty seamen to be ready to land, under the command of Captains Rowley, Prevost, and Joyce, with a proportion of officers, to assist in working the artillery, to go up in the frigates, and Captain Bayntun to proceed up the North channel to Colonia, in the *Haughty* gun-brig, with six gun-boats (Spanish prizes captured at Monte Video;) the *Medusa*, *Nereide*, and *Thisbe*, to receive the seamen intended to land, and three boats from each of the line of battle ships.

On the 21st the wind moderating, I shifted my flag to the *Nereide*, and General Whitelocke did me the honour of accompanying me; and having directed Captain Bouverie, in the *Medusa*, and Captain Shepherd, in the *Thisbe*, to proceed with the *Rolla* and *Olympia*, the last division of the troops, at noon, weighed, and stood to the southward, where we anchored in three fathoms water.

On the 24th we anchored between Ensinada de Barragon and the northern shore, the winds and weather having prevented our getting to the westward of the Oitez Bank, before. The general and myself finding time would be lost by going with this division to Colonia, sent for the troops to join at this anchorage; General Gower went for them, with orders from General Whitelocke to evacuate Colonia, if he thought it necessary; Colonia was accordingly evacuated.

On the 27th the troops from Colonia joined, with the *Fly, Pheasant, Haughty,* and the gun-boats. I ordered the *Paz* up the river, with directions to the *Staunch* and *Protector* gun-brigs to join me.

The transports having the troops and artillery on board, being in three divisions, I directed Captain Thompson, in the *Fly,* who had made himself acquainted with the river, and particularly the place intended for landing, which was near Barragon, to lead the first division, having with him the *Dolores* schooner and four gun-boats; Captain Palmer in the *Pheasant,* to lead the second division, with the *Haughty* and two gun-boats; Captain Prevost, in the *Saracen,* to bring up the rear of the third division; and Captains Bayntun and Corbet to superintend the landing of the troops.

At daylight on the 28th, the wind being favourable, I made the signal to the *Fly* to weigh with the first division, and immediately after a general signal to weigh, having ordered the *Rolla* to be placed on the west end of the bank, as a guide to the ships to join. I shifted my flag to the *Flying Fish,* and General Whitelocke went in with me. As soon as the first division of transports anchored, I made the signal to get into the boats, and immediately afterwards to put off.

Soon after nine, A.M. the first boats, with Brigadier-General Craufurd's division, landed about a mile to westward of the fort, from which the enemy had some time before withdrawn their guns. A creek being found soon after the first boats landed, the whole were got on shore without opposition, or any accident; except that several of the transports were aground, but got off without damage. . . .

Extract of a Letter from Rear-Admiral Murray, dated Nereide, off Buenos Ayres, July 8

Sir, By my letter of the 30th ult. their lordships will be informed, that the army under the command of Lieutenant-General Whitelocke was landed without opposition or accident on the 28th near Barragon, about 20 miles to the eastward of Buenos Ayres.

On the 30th, the *Nereide,* small craft, and transports, weighed, and anchored again to the westward of Quelmes; the next morning I went in shore in the *Flying Fish,* to endeavour to communicate with the army, having directed some transports with provisions to go close in, in case the army should want supplies.

Captain Corbet, in his boat, discovered some of our troops, and sent Lieutenant Blight, of the *Nereide,* on shore; he with difficulty got to them, being obliged to pass through a deep bog. On the 2d Lieutenant Blight returned and informed me he had seen General Whitelocke the evening before; that the army had suffered most severely on their march, having very deep marshes to pass, and having been obliged to leave their provisions behind them; were much in want of bread and spirits, which were immediately landed from the *Encounter* and transports. As I understood that General Gower had advanced towards Buenos Ayres, I directed Captain Thompson, in the *Fly,* with the gun-brigs, to get as near in as he could. The same day I received a letter from Colonel Bourke, Quarter Master General, to say he was directed by General Whitelocke to inform me that he had marched on, and meant to go to the westward of Buenos Ayres, requesting I would send the ships having heavy artillery there, and likewise provisions. I immediately sent the gun-boats to join the *Fly* and gun-brigs, and directed Captain Thompson to get as close in to the westward as he could. The transports with the guns, and those with provisions, as well as an hospital ship, I likewise sent there, and am happy to say they were all in shore on the 4th, ready to meet the army.

On the 5th, a firing was observed in the town; I desired Captain Thompson to make use of the gun-brigs and boats, when he could, without annoying our own people, who appeared to be both to the eastward and westward of the town. A communication was opened with the army in the morning; they had stormed and taken possession of four guns, near the citadel. Bread, spirits, and ammunition, were supplied from the ships.

On the 6th, I directed the *Encounter* to endeavour to communicate with the army on the east side of the town, and supply them with what they might require. An hospital ship was likewise sent that way.

The *Nereide* was moored up as high as she could go, being in less than three fathoms, but still nine miles from the town. At one P.M. I received a letter from Captain Thompson, saying our affairs at the west end of the town were in a most distressing state, Brigadier-General Craufurd and the whole of his brigade taken prisoners, and that a truce had been demanded and granted; at the same time requesting more transports might be moved up, in case it should be necessary to re-embark the troops.

I immediately went up to the *Staunch* gun-brig, which was about a mile from the shore, and abreast of the post occupied by Sir S. Achmuty, and ordered the *Medusa*, *Thisbe*, and *Saracen*, which were left off Barragon, to come up as high as they could with safety.

Captain Thompson, who was with the general, came off to me immediately, but was obliged to have a guard to protect him to the beach, although close to the gun-brig; but it was dark. At eight P.M. I received a note from General Whitelocke informing me he had arrived there to see what more could be done by the gallantry and exertion of the army under his command, whose sufferings in every way had seldom, under any circumstances, been exceeded. Of one thing he was certain, that South America could never be English.

The inveteracy of every class of inhabitants was beyond belief. He wished to see me, as he had sent General Gower to General Liniers, in consequence of a letter he had received from the latter.

I cannot help taking this opportunity of saying how very active Captain Thompson of the *Fly* has been, who placed the gun-boats, which were commanded by Lieutenant Frazer of the *Medusa*, and Lieutenant Heron of the *Saracen*.

Early in the morning of the 7th, the *Staunch* telegraphed to say I was wanted on shore immediately; a flag of truce was still flying at our head quarters. On my going on shore, the general shewed me the proposals made by the Spanish general, Liniers, (a copy of which I enclose,) and observed, that he was of opinion, as well as were the other generals, that it could answer no good purpose to persist, and that one great object was attained, that of getting all the prisoners back that had been taken in South America this war; that the destroying the town could not benefit us; and that he saw no prospect whatever of establishing ourselves in this country, as there was not a friend to the English in it; that the number of our prisoners the enemy had were in the power of an enraged mob; and that persisting on our part would make their situation truly distressing; the number of our killed and wounded, although not exactly ascertained, was said to be very great. Under these circumstances, and being persuaded that the people of this country did not wish to be under the British government, I signed the preliminaries, trusting that what I have done will meet their lordship's approbation. . . .

'London Gazette Extraordinary,' September 13, 1807. $^{XVIII\ 236\text{-}242}$

Copy of a Despatch received by Lord Castlereagh, from Lieutenant-General Whitelocke

Buenos Ayres, July 10, 1807

Sir, I have the honour to acquaint you, for the information of his Majesty, that upon being joined at Monte Video on the 15th of June, by the corps under Brigadier-General Craufurd, not one moment was lost by Rear-Admiral Murray and myself in making every necessary arrangement for the attack of Buenos Ayres. After many delays occasioned by foul winds, a landing was effected, without opposition, on the 20th of the same month, at the Ensinada de Barragon, a small bay about thirty miles to the eastward of the town. The corps employed on this expedition were three brigades of light artillery, under Captain Frazer; the 5th, 38th, and 87th regiments of foot, under Brigadier-General Sir Samuel Achmuty; the 17th light dragoons, 36th and 88th regiments, under Brigadier-General the Honourable William Lumley; eight companies of the 95th regiment, and nine light infantry companies, under Brigadier-General Craufurd; four troops of the 6th dragoon guards, the 9th light dragoons, 40th and 45th regiments of foot, under Colonel the Honourable T. Mahon; all the dragoons being dismounted, except four troops of the 17th, under Lieutenant-Colonel Lloyd.

After some fatiguing marches through a country much intersected by swamps and deep muddy rivulets, the army reached Reduction, a village about nine miles distant from the bridge over the Rio Chuelo; on the opposite bank of which the enemy had constructed batteries, and established a formidable line of defence. I resolved, therefore to turn this position, by marching in two columns from my left, and crossing the river higher up, where it was represented fordable, to unite my force in the suburbs of Buenos Ayres. I sent directions at the same time to Colonel Mahon, who was bringing up the greater part of the artillery under the protection of the 17th light dragoons and 40th regiment, to wait for further orders at Reduction.

Major-General Leveson Gower having the command of the right column, crossed the river at a pass called the Paso Chieo, and falling in with a corps of the enemy, gallantly attacked and defeated it, for the particulars of which action, I beg to refer you to the annexed report. Owing to the ignorance of my guide, it was not until the next day that I joined with the main body of the army, when I formed my line by placing Brigadier-General Sir Samuel Achmuty's brigade upon the left, extending it towards the Convent of the Recoleta, from which it was distant two miles. The 36th and 88th regiments being on its right; Brigadier-General Craufurd's brigade occupying the central and principal avenues of the town, being distant about three miles from the Great Square and fort; and the 6th dragoon guards, 9th light dragoons, and 45th regiment, being upon his right, and extending towards the Residencia. The town was thus nearly invested, and this disposition of the army, and the circumstances of the town and suburbs being divided into squares of 140 yards each side, together with the knowledge that the enemy meant to occupy the flat roofs of the houses, gave rise to the following plan of attack.

Brigadier-General Sir Samuel Achmuty was directed to detach the 38th regiment to possess itself of the Plaza de Toros, and the adjacent strong ground, and there take post: the 87th, 5th, 36th, and 88th regiments were each divided into wings; and each wing ordered to penetrate into the street directly in its front. The light battalion divided into wings, and each followed by a wing of the 95th regiment, and a three-pounder, was ordered to proceed down the two streets on the right of the central one, and the 45th regiment down the two adjoining; and after clearing the street of the enemy, this latter regiment was to take post at the Residencia. Two six-pounders were ordered along the central street, covered by the carabiniers, and three troops of the 9th light dragoons, the remainder of which was posted as a reserve in the centre. Each division was ordered to proceed along the street directly in its front, till it arrived at the last square of houses next the River Plata, of which it was to possess itself, forming on the flat roofs, and there wait for further orders. The 95th regiment was to occupy two of the most commanding situations, from which it could annoy the enemy. Two corporals with tools were ordered to march at the head of each column, for the purpose of breaking open the doors; the whole were unloaded, and no firing was to be permitted until the column had reached their final points and formed; a cannonade in the central streets was the signal for the whole to come forward.

In conformity to this arrangement, at half past six o'clock of the morning of the 5th instant, the 38th regiment moving towards its left, and the 87th straight to its front, approached the strong post of Retiro and Plaza de Toros, and after a most vigorous and spirited attack, in which these regiments suffered much from grape shot and musketry, their gallant commander, Brigadier-General Sir Samuel Achmuty, possessed himself of the post, taking thirty-two pieces of cannon, an immense quantity of ammunition, and six hundred prisoners. The 5th regiment meeting with but little opposition, proceeded to the river, and took possession of the Church and Convent of St. Catalina. The 36th and 88th regiments, under Brigadier-General Lumley, moving in the appointed order, were soon opposed by a heavy and continued fire of musketry from the tops and windows of the houses; the doors of which were barricaded in so strong a manner, as to render them almost impossible to force. The streets were intersected by deep ditches, in the inside of which were planted cannon, pouring showers of grape on the advancing columns. In defiance, however, of this opposition, the 36th regiment, headed by the gallant general, reached its final destination; but the 88th being nearer to the fort and principal defences of the enemy, was so weakened by his fire as to be overpowered and taken. The flank of the 36th being thus exposed, this regiment, together with the 5th, retired upon Sir Samuel Achmuty's post at the Plaza de Toros; not, however, before Lieutenant Colonel Burne, and the grenadier company of the 36th regiment, had an opportunity of distinguishing themselves, by charging about eight hundred of the enemy, and taking and spiking two guns. The two six-pounders moving up the central streets meeting with a very superior fire, the four troops of the carabiniers, led on by Lieutenant-Colonel Kingstone, advanced to take possession of the battery opposed to them, but this gallant officer being unfortunately wounded, as well as Captain Burrel, next in command, and the fire both from the battery and houses proving very destructive, they retreated to a short distance, but continued to occupy a position in front of the enemy's principal defences, and considerably in advance of that which they had taken in the morning.

The left division of Brigadier-General Craufurd's brigade, under Lieutenant-Colonel Pack, passed on nearly to the river, and turning to the left, approached the Great Square with the intention of possessing itself of the Jesuits' College, a situation which commanded the enemy's principal line of defence. But from the very destructive nature of this fire, this was found impracticable, and after sustaining a heavy loss, one part of the division throwing itself into a house which was afterwards not found tenable, was shortly obliged to surrender, whilst the remaining part, after enduring a dreadful fire with the greatest intrepidity, Lieutenant-Colonel Pack, its commander, being wounded, retired upon the right division, commanded by Brigadier-General Craufurd himself. This division having passed quite through to the River Plata, turned also to the left to approach the Great Square and fort from the north-east bastion, of which it was distant about four hundred yards, when Brigadier-General Craufurd, leaving [learning?] the fate of his left division, thought it most advisable to take possession of the Convent of St. Domingo, near which he then was intending to proceed onwards to the Franciscan Church, which lay still nearer the fort, if the attack or success of any other of our columns should free him in some measure from the host of enemies which surrounded him. The 45th regiment being further from the enemy's centre, had gained the Residencia without much opposition, and Lieutenant Colonel Guard having it in possession of his battalion companies, moved down with the grenadier company towards the centre of the town, and joined Brigadier-General Craufurd.

The enemy, who now surrounded the Convent on all sides, attempted to take a three-pounder which lay in the street, the lieutenant-colonel with his company, and a few light infantry under Major Trotter, charged them with great spirit. In an instant the greater part of his company and Major Trotter (an officer of great merit) were killed, but the gun was saved. The brigadier-general was now obliged to confine himself to the defence of the Convent, from which the riflemen kept up a well directed fire upon such of the enemy as approached the post; but the quantity of round shot, grape, and musketry, to which they were exposed, at last obliged them to quit the top of the building, and the enemy, to the number of six thousand, bringing up cannon to force the wooden gates which fronted the fort, the brigadier-general having no communication with any other columns, and judging from the cessation of firing that those next him had not been successful, surrendered at four o'clock in the afternoon.

The result of this day's action had left me in possession of the Plaza de Toros, a strong post on the enemy's right, and the Residencia, another strong post on his left, whilst I occupied an advanced position opposite his centre; but these advantages had cost about two thousand five hundred men in killed, wounded, and prisoners. The nature of the fire to which the troops were exposed, was violent in the extreme. Grape shot at the corners of all the streets, musketry, hand-grenades, bricks and stones, from the tops of all the houses, every householder with his negroes defended his dwelling, each of which was in itself a fortress, and it is not, perhaps, too much to say, that the whole male population of Buenos Ayres was employed in its defence.

This was the situation of the army on the morning of the 6th instant, when General Liniers addressed a letter to me, offering to give up all his prisoners taken in the late affair, together with the 71st regiment, and others, taken with Brigadier-General Beresford, if I desisted from any further attack on the town, and withdrew his Majesty's forces from the River Plata; intimating at the same time, from the exasperated state of the populace, he could not answer for the safety of the prisoners, if I persisted in offensive measures. Influenced by this consideration, (which I knew from better authority to be founded in fact), and reflecting of how little advantage would be the possession of a country, the inhabitants of which were so absolutely hostile, I resolved to forego the advantages which the bravery of the troops had obtained, and acceded to the annexed treaty, which I trust will meet the approbation of his Majesty.

I have nothing further to add, except to mention, in terms of the highest praise, the conduct of Rear-Admiral Murray, whose cordial co-operation has never been wanting whenever the army could be benefited by his exertions. Captain Rowley, of the royal navy, commanding the seamen on shore, Captain Bayntun, of his Majesty's ship *Africa*, who superintended the disembarkation, and Captain Thompson, of the *Fly*, who had the direction of the gun-boats, and had previously rendered me much service by reconnoitring the river, are all entitled to my best thanks. . . .

J. WHITELOCKE, Lieutenant General

The Right Honourable William Windham

A Definitive Treaty between the General in Chief of his Britannic Majesty and of his Catholic Majesty, as per the following articles:

I. There shall be from this time a cessation of hostilities on both sides of the river Plata.

II. The troops of his Britannic Majesty shall retain for the period of two months, the fortress and place of Monte Video, and as a neutral country there shall be considered a line drawn from San Carlos on the west, to Pando on the east, and there shall not be on any part of that line hostilities committed on any side, the neutrality being understood only that the individuals of both nations may live freely under their respective laws, the Spanish subjects being judged by theirs, as the English by those of their nation.

III. There shall be on both sides a mutual restitution of prisoners, including not only those which have been taken since the arrival of the troops under Lieutenant-General Whitelocke, but also all those his Britannic Majesty's subjects captured in South America since the commencement of the war.

IV. That for the promptest despatch of the vessels and troops of his Britannic Majesty, there shall be no impediment thrown in the way of the supplies of provisions which may be requested for Monte Video.

V. A period of ten days from this time is given for the re-embarkation of his Britannic Majesty's troops to pass to the north side of the river La Plata, with the arms which may actually be in their power, stores and equipment, at the most convenient points which may be selected, and during this time provisions may be sold to them.

VI. That at the time of the delivery of the place and fortress of Monte Video, which shall take place at the end of the two months fixed in the second article, the delivery will be made in the terms it was found, and with the artillery it had when it was taken.

VII. Three officers of rank shall be delivered for and until the fulfilment of the above articles by both parties, being well understood that his Britannic Majesty's officers who have been on their parole, cannot serve against South America until their arrival in Europe.

[See also Dr Harness's letter to Lord Melville on the use of citric acid, Volume II, Appendix 5.]

1807 – Combined Forces Action at Copenhagen, and the Capture of Heligoland

THE OPERATION BY 20,000 SOLDIERS, guarded by a fleet of twenty-seven ships of the line, which seized the Danish fleet and the contents of its arsenal, was one of the darkest moments in British history. It could only be justified by the argument of necessity, that the prospect of the French obtaining the use of the Danish fleet was real and immediate, and that, if possessed, it would provide such an increase in French naval power that Britain would be unable to sustain the war. This was indeed the argument made in the Duke of Portland administration's subsequent declaration, and *The Naval Chronicle* accepted it without dispute, but the nation was less convinced. Portland appeared to have adopted as despicable an approach to international affairs as that of Napoleon Buonaparte. The Treaty of Tilsit by which Russia and Prussia left the war had dangerously isolated Britain, but the raid on Copenhagen transformed a difficult neutral, Denmark, and a defeated friend, Russia, into enemies. It may be questioned whether the capture of sixteen ships of the line, fifteen frigates, six brigs and twenty-five gunboats outweighed the losses.

Naval command of this expedition had been offered to Admiral Young, and then to Sir Charles Cotton, who both declined it, but the assignment was accepted by Admiral Lord Gambier who handled the major undertaking with great efficiency. Despite his recent censure, Commodore Home Popham was appointed Captain of the Fleet over the heads of his superiors, Commodores Hood and Keats, and Captain Robert Stopford, who formally protested. Gambier valued Popham's assistance because of his experience in the area in the 1800 Copenhagen operation under Dickson, and there were rumours that Stopford was anything but efficient.

A Foreign Office official, Francis James Jackson, had been sent to request the Danes to intern their fleet in a British port out of reach of the French, and when Admiral Gambier arrived off the Danish coast Jackson repeated his request, with the same negative result. It was hardly conceivable the Danes would strip themselves of their naval defence at the very time they were most threatened by the French. The result, however, was that Lord Cathcart landed his army at Wybeck and moved into position to bombard Copenhagen. Transfer of the British garrison at Stralsund to Kioge Bay increased his force to 28,000. Gambier blockaded Zealand to isolate the battlefield, and British gunboats engaged the Danish Tricroner fort and floating batteries, where they were worsted. In return, the Danish gunboats were beaten off by British batteries mounted on the coast to protect the army's flank.

Initial Danish resistance had been feeble, because of the surprise, but the nation rallied and a volunteer army under General Castenschield poured into southern Sjaelland. On 26 August this was attacked by Sir Arthur Wellesley, and defeated. He then occupied the centre of the island to pacify it.

By the 31st the batteries were in place to bombard Copenhagen, and Congreve's new rocket system was ready for action (see Appendix 8 in this volume, pp377-387), but a renewed demand for the surrender of the fleet was rejected. For three days the city endured attack, until it was in flames and faced total destruction, when a truce was asked for. On the 7th, articles of capitulation were signed, by which the original demand for the Danish fleet to be surrendered until after the end of the war was accorded. The British were given six weeks to prepare the fleet for departure, which it ensured by assigning to the responsibility of the several ship's companies of the investing fleet the fitting out of individual Danish ships. All the stores of the arsenal were freighted onboard the warships and another ninety-two transports.

A Declaration was published explaining the necessity for the British action, but the Speech from the Throne met unprecedented protest in the House of Lords, and when on 28 January 1808 the thanks of both Houses of Parliament were voted to the naval and military commanders, officers, seamen, etc employed in the late expedition to the Baltic, the motion was opposed in both houses, on the ground that the enterprise was not of such a nature as to merit the proposed honours for the officers by whom it was accomplished. The policy of the measure, however, was not taken into discussion, and the motion was carried without a division in the Lords; in the Commons it was carried by 100 against 19 (Vol. XIX, p71). For further papers on the government's intentions, see A N Ryan, editor, 'Documents relating to the Copenhagen Operation 1807', *Naval Miscellany Volume 5*, Navy Records Society, Vol. 125 (London, 1984).

In comparison to the Copenhagen operation, that sent to capture the North Sea island of Heligoland was very small in scale, and in its diplomatic significance. However, possession of the island was important in keeping open trade to the Elbe and Weiser.

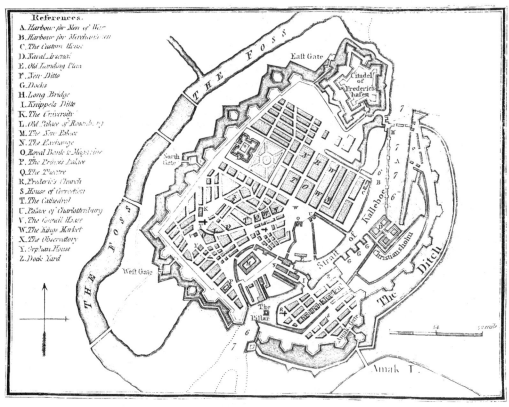

References.
A. *Harbour for Men of War*
B. *Harbour for Merchant men*
C. *The Custom House*
D. *Naval Arsenal*
E. *Old Landing Place*
F. *New Ditto*
G. *Docks*
H. *Long Bridge*
I. *Knippels Ditto*
K. *The University*
L. *Old Palace of Rosenburg*
M. *The New Palace*
N. *The Exchange*
O. *Royal Bank & Magazine*
P. *The Princes Palace*
Q. *The Theatre*
R. *Frederic's Church*
S. *House of Correction*
T. *The Cathedral*
U. *Palace of Charlottenburg*
V. *The Council House*
W. *The Kings Market*
X. *The Observatory*
Y. *Orphan House*
Z. *Dock Yard*

Plan of Copenhagen. Plate 465

From the 'Naval History of the Present Year,' 1807
August–September. XVIII 229-265

Journal of Army Operations 14 to 21 August 1807

Letters On Service, Downing Street, September 4 1807

Extract of Letter from Lieutenant-General Lord Cathcart to Lord Castlereagh, dated Head Quarters at Hellerup, before Copenhagen, August 22, 1807
I have enclosed a journal of the operations of the army from the 14th, in the morning, together with a return of the casualties which have occurred, except those of the cavalry, which are not considerable, but have not been transmitted.

Head-Quarters, Hellerup, before Copenhagen, 22d August, 1807
Journal of the Army under the command of Lieutenant-General Lord Cathcart, from the morning of the 14th August, 1807
August 14th - The fleet between Elsineur [Elsinore] and Heisingberg - calms and contrary winds - transports assembled by brigades, each under the charge of one of his Majesty's ships.

15th - The fleet worked up to Vedbeck, the reserve anchored nearest the shore, covered by the *Surveillante*, and by several gun-brigs and bombs. Major-General Spencer's brigade under convoy of Admiral Essington, with a division of the fleet, anchored higher up the Sound to make a diversion.

Coast reconnoitred, and disposition made for landing.

16th - The reserve landed at five in the morning, with the ordnance of a light brigade, and occupied the heights. The remainder of the infantry followed, with the ordnance of another light brigade. A squadron of the 1st light dragoons, horses for the two brigades of artillery, and for the staff, were also disembarked. A flag of truce was received from Major-General Peyman, commander in chief in Copenhagen, requesting passports for their Highnesses the two Princesses of Denmark, nieces to his Danish Majesty, to go from Copenhagen to Colding, which were granted.

In the evening, the army marched by their left in three columns by Neruth to Lyngbyl; the centre by Hermitage and Fortuna to Jagersborg, the left by the coast to Charlottenberg, and lay upon their arms.

17th - At day-break the army marched by their right in three columns to invest the town. The left column established a post at Bagerne's Mill, and extended from Freborg to Emdrup. That from Jagersborg by Gladsacks and Vanloes to Fredericksberg, extending to the sea on the right, and towards Falconergard on their left. The reserve from Lyngbyl marched by Bangede and Emdrup, and occupied the space between the two other divisions. Two brigades of the King's German Legion remaining at Charlottenfurd [sic] to cover the disembarkation of the cavalry and park of artillery.

Major-General Spencer's brigade landed at Skoresbard, and marched into their post on the left of the line; all the divisions giving piquets to the rear to prevent surprise from the country. Head quarters established at Hellerup. Transports assembled at Skoreshard, where the cavalry commenced disembarking. The Princesses of Denmark came out of the city on their route to Colding, and were received with the honours due to their rank by the brigade of guards, near the palace of Fredericksberg.

The piquets of the left towards the town were attacked about noon: - at the same time the enemy's gun-boats rowed out of the harbour, and cannonaded the left of the line with grape and round shot. The piquets drove in and pursued the enemy, and resumed their posts, part of the line having advanced to sustain them. His Majesty's gun-brigs and bombs having been towed as near the harbour as they could, opened a fire at a considerable distance upon the enemy's gun boats, which, after a long cannonade, retired into the harbour.

18th - At day-break the gun-boats renewed the attack upon the gun-brigs, trusting to the superior weight of their guns. The latter having, during the night, exchanged their carronades for eighteen-pounders, the gun-boats retired, but advanced again with increased numbers. A brigade of nine-pounders, from the park, having been brought to the Mill, took them in flank, upon which they turned their fire to the lines, and after cannonading for some time, were driven in, together with their field-pieces, which advanced upon the road.

Engineer tools, &c. &c. having been disembarked, a work was begun at the Mill, and considerable progress was made. The same day the cavalry moved to their quarters at Charlottenberg, Jagersborg, and Vanloes, with piquets in the country, and a chain of posts, supported by the 1st battalion of the King's German Legion from Lorgenfree and Kollekolle, under the direction of Brigadier-General V.D. Decken.

19th - The works carried on by parties of six hundred men, relieved every four hours. The gun-boats attacked at day-break, but were driven off by the field-pieces which were now protected. Some of the pipes were discovered which convey fresh water to the town from Emdrup. The frigates and gun-brigs having a favourable breeze, took their station near the entrance of the harbour, within reach of throwing shells into the town.

Four twenty-four pounders were brought into the battery at the Mill. Great progress was made in the works at that place, and in a howitzer battery in the rear of it, with traverses and cover for the men.

Brigadier-General Decken surprized and took the post of Fredericksworks, commanded by a major, aide-de-camp to the Crown Prince, who capitulated with eight hundred and fifty men and officers, with a foundry and depot of cannon and powder.

The King's household, with part of his Danish majesty's wardrobe, plate, wine, and books, were suffered to come out of the town to follow his majesty, (who has withdrawn to Colding), passports having been requested.

Some gentlemen residing in the district of Copenhagen, and in the bailiwicks towards Elsineur, having offered their services to accept the office of magistrates and superintendents of police in their respective districts, under the commander of the forces, an order was made for that purpose, and sent to be printed and published, and a commission was given, in reference to a proclamation printed and published in German and Danish on the day of disembarkation.

20th - Farther progress made in the works. More ordnance landed and mounted. A patrol on the left having reported that a body of cavalry, with a corps of infantry in their rear, had been seen in front of Roeskilde, Colonel Roeden sent a squadron to reconnoitre them, which found them assembled near that place, and immediately charged and put them to flight, leaving sixteen or eighteen men killed, and taking three prisoners and twenty-nine horses.

The dragoons pursued the enemy to the gates of Roeskilde, where they were received by a heavy fire of infantry, and returned to their quarters.

The admiral came to head quarters in the morning and returned to his ship.

21st - Lord Rosslyn's corps disembarked in the north part of Kioge bay, with two batteries of artillery, sending round the remaining transports to Skoreshard. A strong patrol of cavalry and infantry was sent to cover his landing.

Progress made in cutting off the water. Further arrangements made with gentlemen of the country. Passport granted to Prince Frederick Ferdinand of Denmark and his preceptor.

Notice given that no more passports can be granted: - at the same time a recommendation urged to the commanding general, to consider the dreadful consequences of making a capital city of such extent stand a siege and bombardment like an ordinary fortress. Great advance made in perfecting the works already in progress which covered our left.

A trench pushed forwards, and a new battery erected three hundred yards in advance. Brigadier-General Macfarlane's brigade landed at Skoreshard. - Great progress made in landing the battering-train and stores for the siege - Fascines made for a new battery on the right. These works being completed will take the enemy's line of advanced posts in reverse, and will cover and secure the advance of the army to a new position.

(Signed) CATHCART

Blockade Proclaimed

By James Gambier, Esq., Admiral of the Blue, and Commander in Chief of a fleet of his Majesty's ships and vessels employed on a particular service

Whereas I have judged it expedient, in conducting the operations of his Majesty's fleet under my command against Copenhagen, to surround the island of Zealand, and the other islands contiguous thereto, with his Majesty's ships, in order to prevent reinforcements or supplies of any kind whatsoever from being thrown into the said islands, I do hereby declare them, as well as the passage of the Great Belt, (extending from a bank or shoal named Hasteen's Ground, to the south-east end of the island of Femeren) to be in a state of close blockade, and do also hereby direct the flag officers, captains, and commanders of the said ships, to give notice thereof to any neutral vessels they may find going into any of the ports of the said islands, or into the passage aforsaid . . .

     Given under my hand on board the *Prince of Wales*, off Copenhagen, August 21, 1807,

J. GAMBIER

Journal of Navy Operations 23 to 25 August 1807
Admiralty Office, September 11

Extract from the Journal of Admiral Gambier, Commander in Chief of His Majesty's ships and vessels in the Baltic, received at the Admiralty this morning
August 23 - The battery on the left wing of the army (which is calculated to defend its advance from the annoyance of gun-boats) being completed and mounted with thirteen twenty-four pounders, the construction of mortar batteries, under cover of the above, are in progress. The enemy observing these movements, appeared yesterday to be collecting their praams and gun-boats near the harbour's mouth, in preparation for a powerful attack on our works. Our advanced squadron continuing in their position for defending the operations on shore, were, about ten A.M. attacked by three praams (carrying each twenty guns) and a considerable number of gun-boats (said to be more than thirty), in addition to the fire from the Crown battery, floating batteries, and block ships, which was continued for more than four hours. The fire was returned with great spirit from the squadron, and some attempts were made to throw Mr. Congreve's rockets, but the distance was too great to produce much effect from them. About two P.M. the gun-brigs which were farthest advanced, not being able to make any impression against so vast a force, were ordered to retire, and the firing ceased. I am happy to find the squadron received no material injury . . .

Names of the Vessels forming the Advanced Squadron, . . .

Thunder	Bomb	*Indignant*	ditto
Zebra	ditto	*Urgent*	ditto
Fury	ditto	*Pincher*	ditto
Aetna	ditto	*Tigress*	ditto
Vesuvius	ditto	*Desperate*	ditto
Cruiser	Sloop	*Safeguard*	ditto
Kite	ditto	with three armed transports,	
Mutine	ditto	and ten launches fitted	
Hebe	Armed Ship	as mortar boats . . .	
Fearless	Gun-brig		

August 24 - Having occasion to confer with Lieutenant General Lord Cathcart, commanding the army, respecting the co-operation of the fleet, I went on shore to head-quarters for that purpose. I learnt that the right wing of the army is advancing

near to the town on the south west, and are preparing mortar batteries to commence the bombardment of it. The enemy being obliged to withdraw their out-posts in that quarter, have set fire to the suburbs to prevent them from affording cover to our troops. The vessels which were in action yesterday are getting their damages repaired. No attack has been made this day by the enemy's flotilla against our advanced squadron. . . .

Supplement to the 'London Gazette Extraordinary,'
of Wednesday, the 16th of September

Blockade of Stralsund

Prince of Wales, Copenhagen-Roads, September 1, 1807
My Lord, Conceiving it to be of great importance to the success of his Majesty's arms against Zealand that every exertion should be used to deprive the enemy of the means which the merchant vessels at Stralsund may afford for transporting troops from thence to this island, I have judged it my duty to issue orders (of which the enclosed is a copy) for the blockade of Stralsund; and I hope that this measure will meet with your lordship's approbation.
    I have the honour to be, &c.

J. Gambier

The Right Hon. Viscount Castlereagh

By James Gambier, Esq. Admiral of the Blue, and Commander in Chief of a fleet of
His Majesty's ships and vessels employed on a particular service
Whereas I have received information that the French army is in possession of Stralsund, and it being essential to the service in which his Majesty's fleet under my command is employed; that no reinforcements should be sent from thence to the island of Zealand, you are hereby required and directed to station such part of the force under your orders off Stralsund, as you may judge sufficient for the above purpose, as well as to maintain a close blockade thereof; and to this end you are to direct . . .
    Given on board the *Prince of Wales*,
    off Copenhagen, August 23 1807

(signed) J. Gambier

To Commodore R.G. Keates [sic], ec. *Superb*

By command of the admiral,
(signed) Jos. Trounsell

Journal of Army Operations 22 August to 1 September 1807

Journal of the Army under the Command of Lieutenant General Lord Cathcart, from
the morning of the 22d of August to the Evening of the 1st September, 1807 . . .
Head-Quarters, Copenhagen, Sept. 1, 1807
August 22 - Brigadier-General M'Farlane's division having landed the preceding evening, joined the army, and encamped in the rear of head-quarters, Lieutenant-General the Earl of Rosslyn's division marched from the place of debarkation to Damhuis and adjacents. Arrangement and distribution settled for forming the park, and progress of providing for mortar batteries.
23d. Lieutenant-General and Earl of Rosslyn's corps joined the army, and took its position in the second line covering the centre.

The advanced squadron of his Majesty's gun-brigs and bomb vessels having taken a position near the entrance of the harbour, within the Crown battery, were attacked at ten in the morning, by all the enemy's block-ships, and some of the works; having maintained this position for several hours, they at length retired, some of them having been more than once on fire by red hot shot. The batteries near the Mill having acted with effect upon the gun-boats, the latter turned their fire upon them, but were obliged to retire with considerable loss.

24th At three in the morning the army was under arms; the centre advanced its position to the height near the road which runs in a direction parallel to the defences of Copenhagen, to Fredericksberg, occupying that road and some posts beyond it. The guards at the same time occupied the suburbs between Fredericksberg and Copenhagen, flanked by a detachment of the 79th. They dislodged a piquet of the enemy, who in their retreat concealed thirteen three-pounders, which have since been found.

All the piquets of the enemy fell back to the lakes or inundations in front of the place; our piquets occupying their ground. In the afternoon, the garrison shewed itself on all the avenues leading from the town, apparently with a design either to recover their ground, or to burn the suburbs. The several generals immediately drove them in, each in his own front, and at the same time seized all the suburbs on the north bank of the lakes, some of which posts are within four hundred yards of the ramparts.

Sir David Baird's division turned and carried a redoubt which the enemy had been some days constructing, and which was that night converted into a work against him.

The enemy set fire to the end of the suburb nearest to the place the upper part of which was occupied by the guards, and was now defended by them. In consequence of this general success, the works which had been intended and begun by us, were abandoned, and a new line was taken, within about eight hundred yards of the place, and nearer to it on the flanks.

25th. The mortar-batteries in the advanced line made considerable progress. A heavy fire was kept up by the garrison on the suburbs and buildings near the lake, which were strengthened as much as circumstances would allow. The navy and artillery were employed in landing ordnance and stores, and forwarding them to different parts of the line.

Lieutenant-General the Earl of Rosslyn's corps, which had a considerable share in occupying the suburbs, relieved the reserve, which moved into second line.

The enemy's gun-boats made their appearance in the channel between Omache and Zealand, and cannonaded the guards in the suburb. Progress was made in preparing a battery to protect the right from the gun-boats. There were frequent skirmishes with sharp-shooters on the right and centre, and several shells thrown from the lines.

26th. Sir Arthur Wellesley with the reserve, eight squadrons of cavalry, and the horse artillery, under Major-General Lisengen, the 6th battalion of the line, King's German legion, and the light brigade of artillery belonging to the reserve, marched to Roskeld Kroe. The gun-boats made an attack on the left of our position, and were twice driven in by the windmill batteries, one boat having blown up, and several others having suffered considerably. The guards were severely cannonaded by the gun-boats; the enemy likewise attempted a sortie, but was quickly driven back.

27th. At day-break the battery of four twenty-four pounders opened on the right, and drove in the gun-boats, one of which was damaged. Sir Arthur Wellesley marched in two divisions to attack the enemy in front and rear at Koenerup, but he had moved up towards Kioge, upon which Sir Arthur took a position to cover the besieging army.

General Peyman applied for an armistice of thirty-six hours to remove the patients from St. John's hospital. Four hours was proposed to him, which offer he did not accept, and several shots were fired through the said hospital.

28th. Progress was made in landing and bringing forward ordnance and stores, as well as in making batteries and communications.

29th. Sir Arthur Wellesley marched to Kioge, where he completely defeated and dispersed the enemy, taking upwards of sixty officers and one thousand five hundred men, fourteen pieces of cannon, and a quantity of powder, and other stores. The patients of St. John's hospital were removed to the chapel at Fredericksberg, and adjacent houses; the Danish general thankfully acceding to this removal, and declaring that it was not fired upon by the order or with his knowledge.

30th. Batteries nearly finished, platforms laid, and two-thirds of the ordnance mounted. New battery planned and begun, near the Chalk Mill Wharf.

31st. The enemy attempted a sortie on the right, before sunrise, and were stopped by a piquet of the 50th regiment, commanded by Lieutenant Light.

They persevered for some time, and were repulsed by the piquets with loss. Sir David Baird twice slightly wounded; but did not quit the field.

The Danish General Oxholm arrived with his officers at head-quarters, when they were put on parole, and sent to their respective homes.

In the evening one thousand five hundred prisoners were distributed in the fleet.

The batteries are in progress; all armed and completed, except the Chalk-Kiln-battery, which is close to the enemy.

The gun-boats attacked the in-shore squadron of light vessels; blew up one of them, and obliged them to retire; the gun-boats as well as the block-ship, having apparently suffered considerable damage from the batteries at the Windmill.

September 1. The mortar batteries being nearly ready for action, the place was summoned. The answer arriving late, accompanied by a desire, on his part, to take the pleasure of his Danish Majesty, the reply could not be sent till the following day: during all these days the enemy has fired from the walls and out-works with cannon and musketry upon the advanced posts, and has thrown many shells on all parts of the line, but has had no success, except in setting fire to some houses, and cutting some trees on his own side of the lakes.

(signed) CATHCART

Summons to Governor of Copenhagen

British Head-Quarters, before Copenhagen, September 1, 1807

Sir, We, the Commanders in Chief of his Majesty's sea and land forces now before Copenhagen, judge it expedient at this time to summon you to surrender the place, for the purpose of avoiding the further effusion of blood, by giving up a defence, which it is evident cannot long be continued.

The King our gracious master used every endeavour to settle the matter now in dispute, in the most conciliating manner, through his diplomatic servants.

To convince his Danish Majesty, and all the world, of the reluctance with which his Majesty finds himself compelled to have recourse to arms, we the undersigned, at this moment, when our troops are before your gates, and our batteries ready to open, do renew to you the offer of the same advantageous and conciliatory terms which were proposed through his Majesty's ministers to your court.

If you will consent to deliver up the Danish fleet, and to our carrying it away, it shall be held in deposit for his Danish Majesty, and shall be restored, with all its equipments, in as good state as it is received, as soon as the provisions of a general peace shall remove the necessity which has occasioned this demand. . . .

J. Gambier
Commander in Chief of his Majesty's Ships and vessels in the Baltic
Cathcart

His Excellency General Peyman, Governor of Copenhagen, &c.

Copenhagen September 1 1807
My Lords, Our fleet, our own indisputable property, we are convinced is as safe in his Danish Majesty's hands as ever it can be in those of the King of England, as our master never intended any hostilities against yours.

If you are cruel enough to endeavour to destroy a city that has not given any the least cause to such a treatment at your hands, it must submit to its fate; but honour . . . [etc.]

(signed) Peyman
Commander in Chief of his Danish Majesty's Land Forces
His Excellency Admiral Gambier, and Lord Cathcart, etc.

Wellesley's and Lisengen's Operations in the South

Head-Quarters, before Copenhagen, September 2, 1807
My Lord, Having stated to your lordship in my despatch of the 22d the preparation of force which was assembling under Lieutenant-General Castenschiold, and my intention of detaching a force to disperse them before they should be in a state to undertake any enterprize; I have now the greatest pleasure in transmitting the report I have received from Sir Arthur Wellesley, to whom, with the assistance of Major-General De Lisengen, and Brigadier General Stewart, that service was entrusted.

The major-general marched on the 26th of last month to Roeskild Kroe, and proceeded on the following day to attack the position at Borneruk, which was occupied according to the last reports by the Danes; Major General Lisengen having made a long detour towards the sea, for the purpose of cutting off their retreat, and attacking the rear.

But finding that the enemy had moved off by the right to Kioge, Sir Arthur Wellesley fell back to Roeskild Kroe, extending to his left to cover the besieging army until the cavalry and infantry, who had made a forced march, had time to refresh. He then proceeded to attack and defeat the enemy in a general action. The deroute appears to have been complete.

Major-General Oxholm was within a mile of this action, on his way to join General Castenschiold, with a corps collected in the southern islands, which he got over. He endeavoured to stop the fugitives, but could make no effectual resistance; this corps would have endeavoured to connect itself with some sortie from the place, and would have soon been troublesome.

Sir Arthur Wellesley has moved into the centre of the island, to disarm and quiet the country.

The only corps which appears to have kept together is the cavalry; but by the last accounts these have been found by the patrols, and will be followed up.

The general and his officers, who are mostly of their militia, have been released on a very strict parole; the general being responsible for them; but their men, one thousand five hundred, to which near one hundred have since been added, are distributed in his Majesty's line of battle ships; the dread of which will, perhaps, induce the remaining militia of this description to be averse to quitting their homes.

I trust, that it will appear that the affair of the 29th, at Kioge, is as useful as it is brilliant.

I have the honour to be, &c

(Signed) CATHCART

The Viscount Castlereagh, &c.

[Unfortunately it has been impossible to reproduce Majors-General Wellesley and Lisengen's own accounts of the action.]

'London Gazette Extraordinary,' Downing-Street, September 16, 1807

Despatches, of which the following are copies, have been received by Viscount Castlereagh, one of his Majesty's principal secretaries of state, from Admiral Gambier and Lieutenant-General the Right Honourable Lord Cathcart, K.T., the commanders of his Majesty's naval and military forces in the Baltic Sea:

Prince of Wales, Copenhagen Road, September 7, 1807

My Lord, My letter of the 5th instant will inform your lordship of the progress of the operations of his Majesty's forces against Copenhagen to that period. I have now the honour and satisfaction to add, that previous to the hour intended for opening our batteries on that night, an officer with a flag of truce came out from the town, with proposals for an armistice to settle terms of capitulation. This was accordingly done, after a correspondence between the Danish general and Lord Cathcart and myself, of which I transmit a copy; and your lordship will be informed of the stipulations agreed upon by the enclosed copy of the articles.

Our army has accordingly been put in possession of the citadel and the arsenal, and the most vigorous exertions are commenced for equipping and sending to England the Danish navy.

I have the honour to be, &c.

J. GAMBIER

[From Lord Cathcart.]
Citadel of Copenhagen, September 8, 1807

My Lord, It has fallen to my lot to have the great satisfaction of forwarding to your lordship the ratified capitulation of the town and citadel of Copenhagen, including the surrender of the Danish fleet and arsenal in this port, which are placed at his Majesty's disposal.

The object of securing this fleet having been attained, every other provision of a tendency to wound the feelings or irritate the nation has been avoided; and although the bombardment and cannonade have made considerable havoc and destruction in the town, not one shot was fired into it till after it was summoned, with the offer of the most advantageous terms, nor a single shot after the first indication of a disposition to capitulate; on the contrary, the firing which lasted three nights from his Majesty's batteries was considerably abated on the 2d, and was only renewed on the 3d to its full vigour, on supposing from the quantity of shells thrown from the place that there was a determination to hold out.

On the evening of the 5th September, a letter was sent by the Danish general, to propose an armistice of twenty-four hours, for preparing an agreement on which articles of capitulation might be founded. The armistice was declined, as tending to unnecessary delay, and the works were continued; but the firing was countermanded, and Lieutenant-Colonel Murray was sent to explain that no proposals of capitulation could be listened to, unless accompanied by the surrender of the fleet.

This basis having been admitted by a subsequent letter, on the 6th, Major-General Sir A. Wellesley, whom I had sent for, for this purpose, from his command in the country, where he had distinguished himself in a manner so honourable to himself and so advantageous to the public, was appointed, with Sir Home Popham and Lieutenant Colonel Murray to prepare and sign articles of capitulation; and those officers having insisted on proceeding immediately to business, the capitulation was drawn up in the night between the 6th and 7th.

The ratification was exchanged in the course of the morning, and at four in the afternoon of the same day, Lieutenant-General Burrard proceeded to take possession. . . .

By the naval blockade the force opposed to us has been limited to the resources of this and of the adjacent islands, separated only by narrow ferries; and almost every wish of assistance has been anticipated, and every requisition of boats, guns and stores has been most amply and effectually provided for with the greatest despatch and the most perfect cordiality and every possible attention has been paid, and every accommodation given, by every officer in that service, from Admiral Gambier downwards.

A battalion of seamen and marines, with three divisions of carpenters, were landed on the 5th, under Captain Watson, of his Majesty's ship *Inflexible*; and had the effort been made, which would have been resorted to in a few days, if the place had not capitulated, their services in the passage of the ditch would have been distinguished. . . .

I have the honour to be, &c.

CATHCART

ARTICLES OF CAPITULATION, Article II. The ships and vessels of war of every description, with all the naval stores belonging to his Danish Majesty, shall be delivered into the charge of such persons as shall be appointed by the commanders in chief of his Britannic Majesty's forces; and they are to be put in immediate possession of the dock-yards, and all the buildings and storehouses belonging thereto.

Admiralty Office, September 16, 1807

Captain Collier, of his Majesty's ship the *Surveillante*, arrived at this office this morning with a despatch from Admiral Gambier, commander in chief of his Majesty's ships and vessels in the Baltic, addressed to the Honourable William Wellesley Pole, Secretary of the Admiralty, dated *Prince of Wales*, in Copenhagen Road, 7th September, 1807, of which the following is a copy:

"Sir, The communications which I have already had the honour to transmit to you, will have made the Lords Commissioners of the Admiralty acquainted with the proceedings of the fleet under my command down to the 2d instant; [I] have now to add, that the mortar batteries which have been erected by the army in the several positions they had taken round Copenhagen, together with the bomb-vessels, which were placed in convenient situations, began the bombardment in the morning of that day, with such power and effect, that in a short time, the town was set on fire, and by the repeated discharges of our artillery, was kept in flames in different places till the evening of the 5th, when a considerable part of it being consumed, and the conflagration having arrived at a great height, threatening the speedy destruction of the whole city, the general commanding the garrison sent out a flag of truce, desiring an armistice, to afford time to treat for a capitulation. After some correspondence had passed between the Danish general and Lord Cathcart and myself, certain articles were agreed upon, of which I have the honour to transmit a copy. From these their lordships will perceive, that all the Danish ships and vessels of war, (of which I enclose a list), with the stores in the arsenal, were to be delivered up to such persons as should be appointed to receive them on the part of his Majesty. I accordingly appointed Sir Home Popham for this purpose, and having made the necessary arrangements for equipping them with the utmost despatch, I have committed the execution of this service to Vice-Admiral Stanhope, in whose ability and exertions I can place the fullest confidence.

I am happy on this occasion to express the warm sense I entertain of the cordial co-operation of the army, by whose exertions, with the favourable concurrence of circumstances, under Divine Providence, ever since we left England, for our ultimate success has been more immediately obtained. . . .

I have the honour to be, &c.

J. Gambier"

A List of the Danish Ships and Vessels delivered up by the Capitulation of Copenhagen to his Majesty's Forces, September 7, 1807

Ships	Guns	When Built	Ships	Guns	When Built
Christian the			Rota	44	1801
Seventh	96	1803	Venus	44	1805
Neptune	84	1789	Nyade	36	1796
Waldemaar	84	1798	Triton	28	1790
Princess Sophia			Frederigstein	28	1800
Frederica	74	1775	Little Belt	24	1801
Justice	74	1777	Fylla	24	1802
Heir Apparent			St. Thomas	22	1779
Frederick	74	1782	Elbe	20	1800
Crown Prince			Eyderen	20	1802
Frederick	74	1784	Gluckstad	20	1804
Fuen	74	1787	Brigs:		
Oden	74	1788	Sarpe	18	1791
Three Crowns	74	1789	Glommen	18	1791
Skiold	74	1792	Ned Elven	18	1791
Crown Princess Maria	74	1791	Mercure	18	1806
Danemark	74	1794	Courier	14	1801
Norway	74	1800	Flying Fish		1789
Princess Caroline	74	1805	Gun Boats:		
Detmarsken	64	1780	Eleven with two guns in the bow		
Conqueror	64	1795			
Mars	64	1784	Fourteen with one in the bow and one in the stern		

Frigates:
Pearl	44	1804
Housewife	44	1789
Liberty	44	1793
Iris	44	1795

The Naval Bombardment

From the 'Naval Biography of Captain Richard Dacres, R.N.' XXVI 446-450

Notwithstanding the copious details already referred to, we shall take this opportunity of relating some additional particulars of the proceedings at Copenhagen, taken, in substance, from the private papers of an officer belonging to the *Pompée*.

The first of these papers, bearing the date of September 5, describes the effect produced by the opening of the mortar batteries, by our army, on the evening of the 2d, as a most awful and terrific sight. The devastation was evident on the ensuing morning; the N.W. part of the town was soon in a blaze; it burnt with incredible fury; and was then (Sept. 7) nearly destroyed. On the evening of the 4th, our breaching batteries opened: the firing was excellent; and they had continued, without intermission. There was a battery on shore, in front of the brigade of Guards, constructed expressly for the Congreve rockets, which are known to have contributed much to the destruction of the town.[1]

A few days previously to the date of the paper (Sept. 5) an attack was made, by the Danish gun-boats, on our flotilla; and they so far succeeded, as to oblige our gun-vessels to slip, with considerable loss, and to sink an armed ship. Subsequently, however, our batteries blew up two of the enemy's gun-boats, sunk three, and compelled the remainder to retire under cover of the Crowns battery. The army complained much of these vessels, which unremittingly annoyed and flanked them in their approaches to the town. We had no proper craft to keep them in check: our gun-vessels drew too much water, and were too unwieldy; and our launches were not sufficiently powerful to cope with them. Each of them carried two long twenty-four pounders: they were managed very well; but it was remarked, that they were "much attached to long bowls."

On the 4th, our army were making their last parallel; the pontoons were all ready to lay over the ditch which surrounded the town; a breach was expected soon to be made; and the troops were all in excellent spirits, fully confident of ultimate success. It was not then known, whether the fleet was intended to have any share in the storming of the town; but nothing was seen to prevent it. The Crowns battery was formidably strong; but the *Pompée*, which drew more water than any ship there, could approach it within musket-shot; and the smaller ships of the line, frigates, &c, might approach within pistol-shot. The guns on the Crowns battery were *en barbette*, and were deemed incapable of withstanding the powerful fleet then lying in the roads. - On the evening of the 4th, the signal was made for 50 seamen, and 15 marines, to hold themselves in readiness to land, at eight on the following morning. Captain Owen, who had succeeded Captain Horlock, in the *Pompée*, was ordered to command the whole of the marines; and Captain Watson, of the *Inflexible*, the seamen. All the maindeck guns of the *Pompée* were on shore, in different batteries. - About this time, Commodore Keats was keeping

---

1 *Vide* N.C. XXI 408; XXII 27, 31, 100, 196, 201, 285, 363, 364, 367, 374, 461 [partly reproduced below in Appendix 8].

a look-out in the Great Belt; Sir Samuel Hood was at anchor, with his squadron to the southward of the island of Amag, for the purpose of preventing any supplies from reaching Copenhagen by that Channel; and Captain Stopford was cruising in the Cattegat, where he had intercepted some troops from Norway, intended for Copenhagen.

At 10 P.M. on the 5th of September (as is stated in a paper of the 7th), a Danish general came out to negotiate; on the morning of the 6th, three other officers came out for the same purpose; and, in the afternoon, Sir Home Popham and Colonel Hope went to Copenhagen. The armistice ceased at noon, on the 7th; and at one P.M. the signal was made for all lieutenants. It was then understood, that the Danes had surrendered their fleet and naval stores unconditionally; and, at four, our forces took possession.

We have heard it insinuated, but we presume not to say with what degree of justice, that Vice-Admiral S[topford] though second in command upon this occasion, appeared to know but very little of the intended operations; that, at one period, a general want of energy and spirit characterised the whole of our proceedings; and that, with many, the hope of success rested more on the innate valour of our men, than on either the talents or animation displayed by our naval leaders. Fortunately for the country, the armament, by some means or other, produced its desired result.

Protest at Popham's Command

From the 'Naval History of the Year,' 1807-1808
December-January. [XIX 68-71]

A pamphlet has just been published, entitled a "*Discourse on our late Proceedings in the Baltic,*" which contains much curious matter, relating to the Danish expedition, and to the appointment of Sir Home Popham. We submit the following passages, without introduction or comment:

Narrative of Measures pursued by the Officers who remonstrated against ceding their Rank to Sir Home Popham
The officers who felt themselves so much hurt at the appointment of Sir Home Popham to be captain of the fleet, as to represent their feeling on that occasion to the commander in chief, waiting upon him, as in conformity with the law and usage of the service,[2] and temperately, quietly, and respectfully made known their grievance to him. After some conversation, Admiral Gambier, though not perhaps approving the act, was so far from condemning the mode of application, that he said to those officers, that he felt *himself obliged* by the delicate manner in which they proceeded; and recommended to them to address an official letter to him on the subject. . . .

The fall of the Danish fleet produced a promotion of admirals, which secured two of the officers from the grievances they complained of. The third, on his return from the Baltic, was placed under orders that relieved him also from the painful situation.

The grievance was removed, and in a manner flattering to the two officers who bore the rank of established commodores. They might justly have been accused of indulging a disposition rather tending to embarrass than relieve themselves from an injury, had they on their return continued to urge their original remonstrance. It appeared essential to Sir Samuel Hood and Rear-Admiral Keats, both of whom have been in

2 The articles of war provide for the quiet and temperate representation of grievances to the admiral or commander in chief.

London since their return, to justify themselves from the imputation that appeared to be cast upon them in the private letter of Lord Mulgrave's, before noticed. That has been done, I have no doubt, in a manner perfectly satisfactory to Lord Mulgrave, and equally so to themselves. . . .

Note - Although it is ordered by the naval instructions, that a captain of the fleet shall be either a flag officer or one of the senior captains of the navy, the remonstrating officers were not ignorant that *one* precedent could have been adduced of an appointment of captain of the fleet as junior as Sir Home Popham.[3] But where, as in this case, the time of *actual* employment has been very limited: where the officer had never served in a fleet; and other objections occurred; they considered, and consider, they formed a fair and legitimate subject of remonstrance; especially as two of them, very much his seniors, were (by the new naval restrictions), though established commodores, called upon to cede their rank to him at councils and courts-martial. . . .

Comparative Services of the Remonstrating Captains, and Sir Home Popham's
. . . The remonstrating officers acknowledged no inferiority of naval information or ability to Sir Home Popham. Their actions have corresponded with their professions: and they have not been accustomed to view with respect those whose conduct has been marked by *speculative notions*. It has been said, the *local* knowledge of Sir Home Popham, made his appointment, as captain of the fleet, *requisite*. Men of versatile talents have local knowledge in all parts of the world. The remonstrating captains did not discover *any extraordinary advantage* which the public service derived from his appointment at Copenhagen; and on Admiral Gambier's advancing it as an argument at Yarmouth, he was reminded by the captains, that he might as easily derive all the advantages he promised himself from it, by taking him in a situation that would not be offensive to them, as in that in which he had been appointed to.

Note - One of the remonstrating captains, who commanded a frigate in 1790, was actually employed to cruise for *El Trusco* [*l'Etrusco?*], the foreign merchant ship, commanded by Sir Home Popham, then on her outward-bound voyage to the East Indies. She was stopped the *Brilliant* frigate, Captain Mark Robinson, on her homeward-bound voyage in 1793 or 1794.

[Lord Mulgrave did not approve of the remonstrance, but Hood and Keats were promoted to Rear-Admiral.]

State Paper; or
Declaration of His Britannic Majesty [XVIII 301-304]

His Majesty owes to himself and to Europe a frank exposition of the motives which have dictated his late measures in the Baltic. . . .

His Majesty could not but recollect that when, at the close of the former war, the court of Denmark engaged in a hostile confederacy against Great Britain, the apology offered by that court for so unjustifiable an abandonment of a neutrality which his Majesty had never ceased to respect, was founded on its avowed inability to resist the operation of external influence, and the threats of a formidable neighbouring power.

---

3 Captain Bowen. - If Sir Home Popham's services had been as regular as those of Captain Bowen, and he had not met the public disapprobation of the Admiralty, and the severe censure of a court-martial, and had not pursued rather a *speculative* than a regular line of conduct, no object would ever have been made to him.

His Majesty could not but compare the degree of influence which at that time determined the decision of the court of Denmark, in violation of positive engagements, solemnly contracted but six months before, with the increased operation which France had now the means of giving to the same principle of intimidation, with kingdoms prostrate at her feet, and with the population of nations under her banners.

Nor was the danger less imminent than certain. Already the army destined for the invasion of Holstein was assembling on the violated territory of neutral Hamburg. And Holstein once occupied, the island of Zealand was at the mercy of France, and the navy of Denmark at her disposal.

It is true, a British force might have found its way into the Baltic, and checked for a time the movements of the Danish marine. But the season was approaching when that precaution would no longer have availed; and when his Majesty's fleet must have retired from that sea, and permitted France, in undisturbed security, to accumulate the means of offence against his Majesty's dominions.

Yet, even under these circumstances, in calling upon Denmark for the satisfaction and security which his Majesty was compelled to require, and in demanding the only pledge by which that security could be rendered effectual - the temporary possession of that fleet, which was the chief inducement to France for forcing Denmark into hostilities with Great Britain; his Majesty accompanied this demand with the offer of every condition which could tend to reconcile it to the interests and to the feelings of the court of Denmark.

It was for Denmark herself to state the terms and stipulations which she might require.

If Denmark was apprehensive that the surrender of her fleet would be resented by France as an act of connivance, his Majesty had prepared a force of such formidable magnitude, as must have made concession justifiable even in the estimation of France, by rendering resistance altogether unavailing.

If Denmark was really prepared to resist the demands of France, and to maintain her independence, his Majesty proffered his cooperation for her defence - naval, military, and pecuniary aid; the guarantee of her European territories, and the security and extension of her colonial possessions. . . .

It was time that the effects of that dread which France has inspired into the nations of the world, should be counteracted by an exertion of the power of Great Britain, called for by the exigency of the crisis, and proportioned to the magnitude of the danger.

Notwithstanding the declaration of war on the part of the Danish government, it still remains for Denmark to determine whether war shall continue between the two nations. His Majesty still proffers an amicable arrangement. . . .

Westminster, September 25, 1807

The Cost of the Operation to British Subjects
From 'Correspondence,' 1813. *XXIX 16-17*

"F. Y." to the Editor

Mr. Editor, For the information of your correspondent, D.F., I take the liberty to send you the following answers to some of his questions [*vide NC*, Vol. XXVIII, p464]:

1st. The amount of the losses sustained by British subjects, by confiscation, in Denmark, in consequence of the expedition to Copenhagen, and of the seizure of Danish ships and cargoes in the ports of this kingdom, previously to a declaration of war against Denmark, was calculated, (according to the returns made in 1808, by the committees in different parts of the kingdom, appointed for the purpose of making applications to ministers for indemnification for those losses), at £500,000. It has since been ascertained, that a great many of the Danish debtors had not conformed to the decree of their government for the confiscation of British property, and the real amount of the losses is now estimated at about £280,000; but this point will soon be known more exactly, as the committees are again employed in collecting these particulars.

2d. The value of the Danish ships and cargoes, seized in our ports previously to a declaration of war against Denmark, was estimated at about £1,600,000. The number of these ships and cargoes was reckoned at 320, which at £5,000 for each ship and cargo (which was the average net proceeds of the first twenty-five which had been sold, when the calculation was made), produce the above sum of £1,600,000.

3d. The British subjects, whose property the Danes confiscated, have not received any indemnification, nor any promise of indemnification, out of the fund of the Danish droits. Applications for that purpose were made to ministers, soon after the appearance of the Danish decree of confiscation, and repeatedly since, but uniformly without success. Mr. Perceval[4] had lately shewn some disposition to relax in his opposition to the sufferers, and had desired that they would again lay before him the particulars of their case; which they did about three weeks before his assassination, but did not receive his determination. Since then, they have renewed their memorials to the present ministers, but to no purpose.

4th. I am not aware that any appropriations have been made out of the fund of Danish droits, except some presents to captors.

5th. I should suppose, that the sufferings of the British merchants, whose property was confiscated by the Danes, and who sought indemnification out of the Danish property seized by our government, have never come to the knowledge of his Majesty, the lords of the Treasury having uniformly refused to recommend their case to his consideration. It is as little probable, I think, that the case of the British sufferers ever reached the ears of the Prince Regent, as I remember seeing it mentioned in some of the papers, that his Royal Highness had, on the occasion of a grant out of the droits to the Princess of Wales, congratulated himself on an opportunity of discharging her debts, without being under the necessity of making any addition to the burthens of his Majesty's subjects.

Capture of Heligoland

Letters On Service, September 12 1807. XVIII 235-236

Extract of a Letter from Vice-Admiral Russel to the Secretary of the Admiralty, dated Majestic, off Heligoland, the 6th September 1807
I beg you will be pleased to acquaint my Lords Commissioners of the Admiralty, that I arrived at this island, and anchored close to the town, on the 4th instant, at half past two P.M. but did not, as I expected, find the *Explosion*, the *Wanderer*, or the *Exertion*, with which their lordships had intended to reinforce me.

Having found that Lord Falkland had, with his usual zeal and promptness, summoned the garrison on the 30th ultimo, and that his proposals were rejected by the

4 [Spencer Perceval, Prime Minister December 1809 until his assassination in May 1812.]

View of Heligoland. Engraved by Hall, from a drawing by W.S.H.

Mr. Editor, Enclosed I send you a sketch of Heligoland, which, in point of situation, is so singular, and at present so extremely important, that it may not be altogether an uninteresting subject for you: while making a trip to the Elbe, in the summer of 1802, accident brought us so near the island, as to enable me to take the view enclosed, which is an exact representation of that side of it which is opposed to the ocean; the island, at the time I was passing, bearing due east, and about half a mile distant. The cliffs are awfully perpendicular, from one end to the other, and appeared to be composed of a red-coloured chalk-stone, intersected with narrow horizontal seams, of a yellowish white, and so compact, that I could not but fancy it an immense fortification of brick work.

The building to the right of the church spire is the Light-house, which stands upon the highest point of the island; its southern extremity in this point of view appears shattered and broken, leaving one part a perfect pillar, nearly the whole height of the cliff: the northern extremity terminates with a sandy shoal, running some little distance into the sea, on which, by way of relieving the subject, I have wrecked a vessel, and the packet in the foreground is bearing down to her assistance.

I am, yours, &c. W.S.H.

January 18, 1808

Should this specimen of my performances please, I may perhaps travel on to Cuxhaven for you. Indeed I could send you another sketch of this island, from the south, if you should not think it "ne quid nimis."[5] Plate 266

governor, I was making my arrangements to storm him with the marines, and seamen of the squadron if he did not instantly surrender, for at this time the value of the island to us is immense.

At six P.M. however, he sent out a flag of truce, desiring that an officer might be sent in the morning to treat on articles of capitulation; and I accordingly at daylight

5 A very interesting historical and descriptive account of Heligoland, or Heilig Island, is given in the IVth volume of the *Naval Chronicle* page 377.

yesterday morning, despatched Lord Viscount Falkland and Lieutenant D'Auvergne, (first of this ship,) on that service.

At two P.M. the deputation returned with the articles of capitulation, which I immediately ratified.

With a small expense this island may be made a little Gibraltar, and a safe haven for small craft even in the winter; it is a key to the Rivers Ems, Jade, Elbe, and Eyder, the *only* asylum at present for our cruisers in these seas.

I have appointed Lieutenant D'Aubergne [sic] as acting governor until their lordships' pleasure is known; and I beg leave to add, that, from his perfect knowledge of both services, his zeal and loyalty, and a high sense of honour, I know no seaman more competent to the trust.

(Signed) T. MacNamara Russel

Extract of another Letter from the Vice-Admiral, dated on the same day
This morning the *Explosion*, *Wanderer*, and *Exertion* hove in sight round the north end of the island.

1807 – Naval News, Autumn

THE AUTUMN OF 1807 saw a succession of crises, resulting in part from the diplomatic reverberations following the seizure of the Danish fleet. *The Naval Chronicle* gave a running report on the British withdrawal from Denmark, the declaration of war by Russia, and the increasing hostility of Austria and Sweden. It also closely followed the dispute with the United States and was not at all convinced of the propriety of the British government giving up the right to search neutral warships for deserters. The crisis in Portugal, however, rapidly came to dominate. The Portuguese Prince Regent first bowed to the menaces of France and imposed a ban on British trade, and then, when a French army under Marshal Junot crossed the Portuguese border, reversed himself and agreed to accept a British escort, provided by Sir Sidney Smith, to Brazil. The evacuation of the Portuguese fleet was of paramount importance. Before the arrival of Junot in Lisbon, the commander of the Russian squadron in the Aegean, Admiral Seniavin, who had been trying to get back to the Baltic before the outbreak of war, took refuge in the Tagus. There he was blockaded by Vice-Admiral Sir Charles Cotton.

On 4 November the government proclaimed a series of Orders in Council which set the framework for Britain's resistance to the French Continental System of trade warfare. The French reply on 17 December was to be the Milan Decree, strengthening and extending the restrictions previously announced in the Berlin Decree.

From the 'Naval History of the Present Year,' 1807
September–October. XVIII 329-335

Portuguese Crisis

For some weeks the attention of the public has been irresistibly drawn to the state of affairs in Portugal. At this moment, there is every reason to believe, that a French army is in possession of that country; as, according to the latest accounts, a force of 60,000 men was rapidly approaching its frontiers.

From her geographical situation, paucity of population, &c. it has long been obvious,

95

that Portugal could oppose no effectual resistance to an attack from France, provided the efforts of that power were not counteracted by Spain; an event justly considered as hopeless. Portugal, however, possesses an advantage, which no other European state enjoys; as, under the protection of a British naval force, the government might emigrate, *en masse*, to the Brazils; and it is generally believed, that the visit of Earl St. Vincent to Lisbon, in 1806, had that object in contemplation.

Agreeable to the latest advices, the Prince Regent of Portugal remained firm in his determination to resist the unprincipled demands of Buonaparte; in consequence of which, the French and Spanish ambassadors had left the capital; all the English merchants, with their families, were making the greatest exertions to quit the country; and, under an apprehension of the immediate approach of the French army, the Portuguese royal navy, with the royal family on board, had actually dropped down below the bar, to be ready for sailing, as it was supposed, to the Brazils. Some persons, however, were of opinion, that, when all the English should have left Portugal, Buonaparte would be appeased, and the government would not feel itself under the necessity of executing its hazardous resolution.[1] Should the Portuguese have submitted to be lulled into a security of this kind, we fear that their independence, ere this, is totally gone.

Admiral Purvis's squadron, which had been employed, during the absence of Lord Collingwood, in the blockade of Cadiz, is understood to have quitted that station, according to orders, and to have proceeded to Lisbon; either to facilitate the departure of the Portuguese government, or to prevent their navy from falling into the hands of the French. That the latter object is an important one, is obvious, from the following *List of Ships of War*, which were lying in the Tagus, when Lord St. Vincent was there, in September, 1806:

Names	Guns	Their State
Princepe Real	84	Lower masts rigged, and the
Princepe de Brazil	84	lower yards are across.
Rainha de Portugal	74	"
Alfonzo de Albuquerque	74	Lower masts rigged, top-masts
Princese de Abeire	64	up, and down the lower masts,
Infante de Pedro	74	jib-booms on the bowsprit,
Meduse	74	cables bent to the spare
Belem	64	anchors: appear to have their
Maria Princeipa	74	ballast on board.
St. Sebastine [2]	74	"
Name Unknown	74	"
Name Unknown	74	"
Santa Antonia	70	In dock 7 years and 3 months.
Prince Regent	74	Building
Theriza	50	Lower masts rigged, and jib-
Gulfinia	44	boom on the bowsprit; just
Amasonia	50	caulked.

1 Several English families have reached this country, with such of their effects as they could bring away. It is said, that the demand for shipping was so great at Lisbon, that a British merchant had paid upwards of £1000 for the freight of a single vessel, to carry himself, family, and only a part of his property. - The ports of Portugal were expected to be shut against the British on the 15th of October.

2 Just undergone a good repair, and afloat.

Perolo	50	Lower masts rigged, and the
Active	36	topmasts up, and down the
Princesa de Abiena	36	masts; anchors on board, and
Andoninha	32	one cable bent.
Venus	36	Repairing, and preparing to
Ulluses	36	heave down.
Real Fonsor	28	Just repaired, and fitting.
Bon Ventura	16	Caulking.
Serpenta	22	Lower masts rigged; anchors
Delegente	22	and cables on board.
Gaivota	22	"
Real Fonza	16	"
Fereta (schooner)	8	Fitting for sea (new)
Benjamina	22	Corvette (French)
Triton	44	Lower masts rigged, topmasts and spars on board; just caulked.

N.B. One 74 gun-ship sailed the latter end of August, and the *Rainha de Portugal* arrived.

These ships, in general, were said to be in good repair; and as to construction, equal, if not superior to the British. . . .

Danish Crown Prince Rejects Capitulation, Concludes Treaty With France

The Crown Prince [of Denmark] has peremptorily refused to sanction the capitulation, signed by General Peyman, for the surrender of the fleet and arsenals to the English; Denmark has entered into a treaty of alliance, *offensive and defensive,* with France; French troops are to occupy Holstein and Sleswick; and most rigorous measures have been adopted throughout the Danish dominions, against the property and subjects of this country. Amongst other things, a proclamation has been issued, by which the principle is asserted, "that free bottoms make free goods – and the Danish ships of war are therefore strictly ordered and enjoined not to capture, bring in, or detain any ship, either of friendly or neutral nations, let the cargoes appertain to whom they may, if the ship's papers are found to be regular, and she is not loaded with contraband of war, destined for an English fleet." On the other hand – "Enemy's ships are to make enemy's goods, unless it can be satisfactorily shewn that the cargo is neutral property, and was put on board before the commencement of hostilities."

So cordial was the friendship of the Prince towards Buonaparte, and so anxiously did he anticipate his wishes, that he actually issued orders for the destruction of the Danish fleet, rather than that it should fall into the hands of the English. Fortunately, however, those orders were intercepted. Several of our transports, laden with Danish naval stores, have safely reached this country; and all the captured ships of war were expected to be ready to sail for England about the 15th of October. Nothing can more strikingly evince the chagrin and disappointment which Buonaparte has sustained by this measure, than the strictures of the *Moniteur*, and of other continental papers under the influence of France.

Notwithstanding the refusal of the Crown Prince to sanction the capitulation, it is believed, that our troops will evacuate Zealand, by the period which was originally specified; but it is conjectured, that the Crown battery and some forts upon the shore, will be previously destroyed. . . .

Sweden

The foreign journals appear to be at considerable pains to induce a belief, that Sweden is no longer friendly to this country. They also assert, that an application has been made by the British government, to that of Sweden, for a temporary surrender or deposit of the Swedish navy. Such a circumstance is not improbable; and, unless swayed by Russia, through the predominance of French influence, it is not likely that the request would be refused. . . .

No Settlement of Dispute with the United States but London makes Concessions; Incident involving HMS Jason

The negotiations between this country and America have not yet been terminated; and, in consequence of some difficulties which have arisen, or of some new points which have presented themselves, Mr. Rose, junior, has been appointed on a special mission to the government of the United States. In the mean time, the American rabble continues its inflammatory exertions, and adopts every mode, within its reach, of sowing dissention, and of instigating mutiny amongst the seamen of the British ships. A mutiny, which had broken out on board of the *Jason*, is thus mentioned, in a letter from Halifax, of the 16th of September: "His Majesty's ship *Jason* has arrived from New York under very unpleasant circumstances. While lying there, when the captain went on shore (it was obliged to be done in disguise, and by night) having occasion to send a lieutenant on shore, the moment the boat landed, the American rabble invited the crew to desert, by saying, 'Do you want your liberty? Now is your time: you are in the land of liberty!' in consequence of which the crew immediately left the boat. The officer attempted to intimidate them by drawing a pistol upon them, but was immediately surrounded by the mob, and had it not been for the interference of a captain in the American navy, he would have been tarred and feathered. He, however, escaped unhurt. After this, a still more unpleasant affair occurred: a mutiny broke out among the crew of the *Jason*. They put on the gratings, placed shot boxes upon them to prevent the officers from coming up, and rushed aft to lower the boats down, in order to desert. Fortunately the officers forced their way to the deck in spite of the precautions taken to prevent them, and upon the first lieutenant making some thrusts at them with a boarding pike, and the other officers getting possession of the small arms, they were obliged to retreat below, and surrender. Forty-five were put in irons, and they are now here for trial." From what has transpired, desertion seems to have been the main object of the mutineers. When the last accounts came away, a court martial had been sitting two days upon the offenders, but was not closed. . . .

Admiral Berkeley has been recalled from the command, on the American station, and Sir J.B. Warren goes out to succeed him.

The royal proclamation, for recalling and prohibiting seamen from serving foreign princes and states, considered as an act of his Majesty's ministers, has occasioned no slight dissatisfaction; particularly as every other act of those ministers appears to have had the welfare and honour of the country in view. The objectionable passage of this proclamation, is that which relates to the order, for his Majesty's captains, masters, &c. to claim such natural born subjects of Great Britain, as may be serving on board foreign ships of war, in a state of amity with us; and, in case of refusal, to transmit a statement of the same to the British ministers residing at the seat of government of the state so refusing, or to the Admiralty at home. It is contended, that the order for this circumlocutory mode of proceeding, is an absolute abandonment of the *right of search*, and a complete disavowal of the propriety and justice of the proceeding under Admiral Berkeley. Without dwelling upon the *particularity* of the case of the *Leopard* and *Chesapeake*, or on its total want of *precedent*, we must insist, that the conduct of Admiral Berkeley was in the strictest conformity not only to the maritime laws of England, but to the laws of every maritime power in the world. Admiral Berkeley did not claim the *right of search*, as an *exclusive* right; but in his official orders, expressly observed, that "if a similar demand should be made by the American, *he is to be permitted to search* for any deserters from their service, *according to the custom* and *usage of civilized nations on terms of peace and amity with each other.*" This, as we have just observed, was in the strictest conformity to maritime law. Amongst various claims of power, jurisdiction, and of the authority of the Lord High Admiral, we find the following statement of demand and admission: "The Lord High Admiral, by virtue of the authority he derives from the crown, MAY and DOTH require the commanders of our ships of war, to demand seafaring men, who are natural born subjects, from foreign ships, and *upon refusal* (which is a palpable injury to the prince whose subjects they are) *to take them by force*. This is an *undoubted right* of ALL maritime princes whatsoever, and hath been an ancient custom." - The justice and *legality* of Admiral Berkeley's conduct is, therefore, clearly established; and any cession of the "undoubted" right here described, is a deterioration of the rights and respectability of the country. . . .

Paget Mission to Turkey Fails

Sir Arthur Paget's mission is understood to have failed; the Porte refusing to listen to any propositions, unless our fleet should leave the Archipelago, and our troops evacuate Egypt. Such not being the intention of his Majesty's government, a continuation of hostility may, of course, be considered as determined on.

The latest intelligence from Alexandria states, that the Mamelukes and Arabs were decidedly in our favour; and, as considerable reinforcements have sailed thither from Malta and Sicily, the probability is, that we shall be enabled to retain possession of Egypt.

Lieutenant Berry Hanged for Unclean Sexual Practices
From 'Naval Courts Martial.' XVIII 342-343

On the 2d of October, a court martial was held on board the *Salvador del Mundo*, in Hamoaze, Plymouth, on charges exhibited by Captain Dilkes, of his Majesty's ship *Hazard*, against William Berry, first lieutenant of the said ship, for a breach of the 2d and 29th articles; the former respecting uncleanness, and the latter the horrid and abominable crime which delicacy forbids us to name.

Thomas Gibbs, a boy belonging to the ship, proved the offence, as charged to have been committed on the 23d of August, 1807.

Several other witnesses were called in corroboration; among whom was Elizabeth Bowden, a female who has been on board the *Hazard* these eight months. Curiosity had prompted her to look through the key-hole of the cabin-door, and it was thus she became possessed of the evidence which she gave. She appeared in court dressed in a long jacket and blue trousers.

The evidence being heard in support of the charges, but the prisoner not being prepared to enter upon his defence, he begged time, which the court readily granted, until ten o'clock the next day, at which hour the court assembled again, and having heard what the prisoner had to offer in his defence, and having maturely and deliberately weighed and considered the same, the court were of opinion, that the charges had been fully proved; and did adjudge the said William Berry to be hanged at the yard-arm of such one of his Majesty's ships, and at such time, as the Right Honourable the Commissioners of the Admiralty shall direct. Sir J.T. Duckworth was the president.

The unfortunate prisoner was a native of Lancaster, and only in his 23d year, above six feet high, remarkably well made, and as fine and handsome a man as in the British navy. He was to have been married on his return to port.

The awful sentence of the court martial was carried into execution on Monday the 19th of October, on board the *Hazard*, in Plymouth Sound, the prisoner having been removed from the *Salvador del Mundo* into that ship which lay alongside a hulk in Hamoaze. At nine o'clock he appeared, and mounted the scaffold with the greatest fortitude. He then requested to speak with the Rev. Mr. Bardwood on the scaffold; he said a few words to him, but in so low a tone of voice they could not be distinctly heard. The blue cap being put over his face, the fatal bow gun was fired, and he was run up to the starboard fore-yard-arm, with a thirty-two pound shot tied to his feet. Unfortunately the knot had got round under his chin, which caused great convulsions for a quarter of an hour. After being suspended the usual time, he was lowered into his coffin, which was ready to receive him in a boat immediately under, and conveyed to the Royal Hospital, where his friends meant to apply for his body for interment. He was dressed in a blue coat, white waistcoat, blue pantaloons, and boots. For the last week he seemed penitent, firmly collected, and prepared to meet his fate.

A curious circumstance occurred while the prisoner was in the cabin with the clergyman, receiving the sacrament: A woman came alongside the *Hazard*, and handed up a letter, signed Elizabeth Roberts, to the commanding officer, which stated, that Lieutenant Berry could yet be saved, and the person who could do it was alongside: - it was by marriage. The woman was ordered on board, and put under the care of a sentinel. When the execution was over, Captain Dilkes, with the clergyman and others questioned the woman. She said, she dreamed a dream the preceding night, that if she went on board the *Hazard* that day, and Lieutenant Berry would marry her, he would not suffer death. She was asked who advised her? She replied, that she had told her dream to some women, where she lived in dock, who recommended her to go, in consequence of her dream. She was admonished, and sent on shore.

Orders in Council Forcing British Trade on the Enemy
Important State Papers, Copied from the 'London Gazette.' XVIII 417-424

Trade of Denmark and Italian States Ordered Captured
*At the Court at the Queen's Palace, the 4th of November, 1807,
Present, The King's Most Excellent Majesty in Council*

Whereas the King of Denmark has issued a declaration of war against his Majesty, his subjects and people; and his Majesty's anxious and repeated endeavours to obtain the revocation of such declaration, and to procure the restoration of peace, have proved ineffectual; his Majesty therefore is pleased, by and with the advice of his privy council, to order, and it is hereby ordered, that general reprisals be granted against the ships, goods, and subjects of the King of Denmark . . .

Whereas France has taken forcible possession of certain territories and ports in Italy, and in the Mediterranean and Adriatic seas, and has subverted their ancient governments, and erected, in the room thereof, new governments, which, under her influence, are aiding in the execution of her hostile designs against the property, commerce, and navigation of his Majesty's subjects; and whereas diverse acts, injurious to the just rights of his Majesty, and to the interests of his kingdom, have in consequence been committed, his Majesty is pleased, by and with the advice of his privy council, to order, and it is hereby ordered, that general reprisals be granted against the ships, goods, and inhabitants of the territories and ports of Tuscany, the kingdom of Naples, the port and territory of Ragusa, and those of the islands lately composing the Republic of the Seven Islands, and all other ports and places in the Mediterranean and Adriatic seas, which are occupied by the arms of France or her allies . . .

All Neutral Trade to Any French Port to be Captured - As Reprisal for French Decree

At the Court at the Queen's Palace, the 11th of November, 1807

Whereas certain orders, establishing an unprecedented system of warfare against this kingdom, and aimed especially at the destruction of its commerce and resources, were, some time since, issued by the government of France, by which "the British islands were declared to be in a state of blockade," thereby subjecting to capture and condemnation all vessels, with their cargoes, which should continue to trade with his Majesty's dominions:

And whereas by the same orders, "all trade in English merchandize is prohibited, and every article of merchandize belonging to England, or coming from her colonies, or of her manufacture, is declared lawful prize:

And whereas the nations in alliance with France, and under her control were required to give, and have given, and do give effect to such orders:

And whereas his Majesty's order of the 7th of January last has not answered the desired purpose, either of compelling the enemy to recall those orders, or of inducing neutral nations to interpose, with effect, to obtain their revocation, but, on the contrary, the same have been recently enforced with increased rigour:

And whereas his Majesty, under these circumstances, finds himself compelled to take further measures for asserting and vindicating his just rights, and for supporting that maritime power which the exertions and valour of his people have, under the blessing of Providence, enabled him to establish and maintain; and the maintenance of which is not more essential to the safety and prosperity of his Majesty's dominions, than it is to the protection of such states as still retain their independence, and to the general intercourse and happiness of mankind:

His Majesty is therefore pleased, by and with the advice of his privy council, to order, and it is hereby ordered, that all ports and places of France and her allies, or of any other country at war with his Majesty, and all other ports of places in Europe, from which, although not at war with his Majesty, the British flag is excluded, and all ports of places in the colonies belonging to his Majesty's enemies, shall, from henceforth, be subject to the same restrictions in point of trade and navigation, with the exceptions herein after mentioned, as if the same were actually blockaded by his Majesty's naval forces, in the most strict and rigorous manner: - And it is hereby further ordered and declared, that all trade in articles which are of the produce or manufacture of the said countries or colonies, shall be deemed and considered to be unlawful; and that every vessel trading from or to the said countries or colonies, together with all goods and merchandize on board, and all articles of the produce or manufacture of the said countries or colonies, shall be captured, and condemned as prize to the captors.

But although his Majesty would be fully justified, by the circumstances and considerations above recited, in establishing such system of restrictions with respect to all the countries and colonies of his enemies, without exception, or qualification; yet his Majesty, being nevertheless desirous not to subject neutrals to any greater inconvenience than is absolutely inseparable from the carrying into effect his Majesty's just determination to counteract the designs of his enemies, and to retort upon his enemies themselves the consequences of their own violence and injustice; and being yet willing to hope that it may be possible (consistently with that object) still to allow to neutrals the opportunity to furnish themselves with colonial produce for their own consumption and supply; and even to leave open, for the present, such trade with the ports of his Majesty's dominions, or of his allies, in the manner hereinafter mentioned:

His Majesty is therefore pleased further to order, and it is hereby ordered, that nothing herein contained shall extend to subject [sic] to capture or condemnation any vessel, or the cargo of any vessel, belonging to any country not declared by this order to be subjected to the restrictions incident to a state of blockade, which shall have cleared out with such cargo from some port or place of the country to which she belongs, either in Europe or America, or from some free port in his Majesty's colonies, under circumstances in which such trade from such free port in his Majesty's colonies, direct to some port or place in the colonies of his Majesty's enemies, or from those colonies direct to the country to which such vessel belongs, or to some free port in his Majesty's colonies, in such cases, and with such articles, as it may be lawful to import into such free port; nor to any vessel, or the cargo of any vessel, belonging to any country not at war with his Majesty, which shall have cleared out from some port or place in this kingdom, or from Gibraltar or Malta, under such regulations as his Majesty may think fit to prescribe, or from any port belonging to his Majesty's allies, and shall be proceeding direct to the port specified in her clearance; nor to any vessel, or the cargo of any vessel, belonging to any country not at war with his Majesty, and which shall be coming from any port or place in Europe which is declared by this order to be subject to the restrictions incident to a state of blockade, destined to some port or place in Europe belonging to his Majesty, and which shall be on her voyage direct thereto; but these exceptions are not to be understood as exempting from capture or confiscation any vessel or goods which shall be liable thereto in respect of having entered or departed from any port or place actually blockaded by his Majesty's squadrons or ships of war, or for being enemies' property, or for any other cause than the contravention of this present order.

And the commanders of his Majesty's ships of war and privateers, and other vessels acting under his Majesty's commission, shall be, and are hereby instructed to warn every vessel which shall have commenced her voyages prior to any notice of this order, and shall be destined to any port of France, or of her allies, or of any other country at war with his Majesty, or to any port or place from which the British flag as aforesaid is excluded, or to any colony belonging to his Majesty's enemies, and which shall not have cleared out as is hereinbefore allowed, to discontinue her voyage, and to proceed to some port or place in this kingdom, or to Gibraltar or Malta; and any vessel which, after having been so warned, or after a reasonable time shall have been afforded for the arrival of information of this his Majesty's order at any port or place from which she sailed, or which, after having notice of this order, shall be found in the prosecution of any voyage contrary to the restrictions contained in this order, shall be captured, and, together with her cargo, condemned as lawful prize to the captors:

And whereas countries, not engaged in the war, have acquiesced in the orders of France, prohibiting all trade in any articles the produce or manufacture of his Majesty's dominions; and the merchants of those countries have given countenance and effect to those prohibitions, by accepting from persons styling themselves commercial agents of the enemy, resident at neutral ports, certain documents, termed "certificates of origin," being certificates obtained at the ports of shipment, declaring that the articles of the cargo are not of the produce or manufacture of his Majesty's dominions, or to that effect:

And whereas this expedient has been directed by France, and submitted to by such merchants, as part of the new system of warfare directed against the trade of this kingdom, and as the most effectual instrument of accomplishing the same, and it is therefore essentially necessary to resist it;

His Majesty is therefore pleased, by and with the advice of his privy council, to order, and it is hereby ordered, that if any vessel, after reasonable time shall have been afforded for receiving notice of this his Majesty's order at the port or place from which such vessel shall have cleared out, shall be found carrying any such certificate or document as aforesaid, or any document referring to, or authenticating the same, such vessel shall be adjudged lawful prize to the captor, together with the goods laden therein, belonging to the person or persons by whom, or on whose behalf, any such document was put on board.

And the Right Honourable the Lords Commissioners of his Majesty's Treasury, his Majesty's Principal Secretaries of State, the Lords Commissioners of the Admiralty, and the Judges of the High Court of Admiralty and Courts of Vice-Admiralty, are to take the necessary measures herein as to them shall respectively appertain.

Neutral States Free to Carry Enemy Goods to British Ports

Whereas articles of the growth and manufacture of foreign countries cannot by law be imported into this country, except in British ships, or in ships belonging to the countries of which such articles are the growth and manufacture, without an order in council specially authorizing the same:

His Majesty, taking into consideration the order of this day's date, respecting the trade to be carried on to and from the ports of the enemy, and deeming it expedient that any vessel belonging to any country in alliance, or at amity with his Majesty, may be permitted to import into this country articles of the produce or manufacture of countries at war with his Majesty:

His Majesty, by and with the advice of his privy council, is therefore pleased to order . . .

Reflagged Enemy Ships to be Captured

Whereas the sale of ships by a belligerent to a neutral is considered by France to be illegal:

And whereas a great part of the shipping of France and her allies has been protected from capture during the present hostilities by transfers, or pretended transfers, to neutrals:

And whereas it is fully justifiable to adopt the same rule, in this respect, towards the enemy, which is applied by the enemy to this country:

His Majesty is pleased, by and with the advice of his privy council, to order, and it is hereby ordered, that in future the sale to a neutral of any vessel belonging to his Majesty's enemies, shall not be deemed to be legal . . .

From the 'Naval History of the Present Year,' 1807
October-November. XVIII 425-440

Portuguese Ships to be Seized

We have heard that Sir Sidney Smith is, in the first place, to secure the Portuguese ships, and then to proceed to Madeira: the Russians are entrusted to the care and judgment of Rear-Admiral Keats.

Austria Declares War

Austria, yielding to the dictates of the usurper, is asserted, in the *Moniteur*, to have declared war against this country; and strong suspicions are entertained respecting the intentions of Russia.

Buonaparte Puts Pressure on the United States

According to the statements in the American papers, Buonaparte is also determined to compel the United States to take a decisive part in the contest with England.

Levant News; Evacuation of Alexandria

Lord Collingwood, we find, has left the Dardanelles; but Sir Arthur Paget remains there, in a frigate, to act as opportunity may require. The French ambassador has left the Turkish capital; from which it may be inferred, that the Porte is more favourable towards this country than we some time since had reason to believe.

The British troops have evacuated Egypt; the prisoners which had been taken by the Turks having been restored.

Portugal Bows to French Threat

The communication remains open with Lisbon; though, according to numerous accounts, the French troops are, or rather were, in full march for Portugal. The Prince Regent, instead of embarking for the Brazils, has issued a decree, totally excluding the British from his dominions; notwithstanding which, the official journal of the French government, has declared that *the House of Braganza shall cease to reign*, because the Prince Regent *would not seize the English merchandise which was at Lisbon*! - Every thing relating to Portugal is at present enveloped in mystery.

Plot Against King of Spain?

In Spain, a conspiracy has been discovered against the life of the king, in which his son, the Prince of Asturias, is said to be implicated. In all probability, the whole is a contrivance of that despicable character, that infamous minion of Buonaparte, the Prince of Peace.

Three Naval Expeditions Ready

We have at present three distinct naval expeditions fully equipped; but the destination of neither of them is known.

Just Out - Russian Fleet Enters Tagus

Just as this sheet was going to press, intelligence was received, of a Russian fleet having entered the Tagus.

'Supplement to the London Gazette,' of Saturday, October 31, 1807

Withdrawal From Denmark

Extract of a Despatch from Lieutenant-General the Right Honourable Lord Cathcart, K.T. addressed to the Lord Viscount Castlereagh, one of his Majesty's Principal Secretaries of State, dated on board his Majesty's ship Africaine, the 21st October, 1807

As no sort of infraction of the capitulation had been made by the Danes, who, on the contrary, acted most honourably in the strict and literal fulfilment of their engagement; with a view to the fulfilment of the articles of the capitulation on our part, it was decided to commence the embarkation of the army on Tuesday the 13th instant.

Accordingly, on that day, the eight battalions of the line of the King's German Legion, were embarked in the Arsenal; and, on the 14th, the two light battalions of the King's German Legion, together with Brigadier-General Macfarlane's brigade, viz. the 7th and 8th regiments of British, which embarked in the same ships which brought them from Hull. These corps, with the depôt and garrison company of the legion, and the sick and wounded of the army, completely occupied all the troop ships, whether for home or foreign service, which had not been appropriated to the conveyance of naval stores.

These ships having been removed to the road, were replaced by the horse ships.

On the same day the advanced posts were withdrawn from Kolhaven, Werdenberg, Corsoer, Kallenberg, Fredericksberg, Hersholm, and adjacents, and, proceeding through a chain of cavalry posts, reached the environs of Copenhagen in three marches.

The embarkation of the royal artillery, with the field and battering ordnance, having been gradually carried on from the Kalk Brauderie, that of the cavalry and foreign artillery in the Dock-yard, and that of the British regiments from the citadel, to the men of war, there remained on shore, on Sunday afternoon the 18th instant, only the brigade of guards, who moved on that day from the Palace of Fredericksberg, to the strand near Hellerup, with one brigade of British light artillery, the flank companies of the 32d and 50th regiments, with the 32 regiment, under Major General Spencer, in the arsenal; and the 4th regiment, with a detachment of royal artillery, in the citadel, under

Lieutenant-Colonel Wynch, who acted as lieutenant-governor, the 4th, or King's own regiment, having been in garrison there the whole time.

Lieutenant-General Sir George Ludlow was appointed to command the rear-guard of the army.

In the evening of the 18th instant, a gale of wind came on, which lasted twenty-four hours, and rendered further embarkation impossible, and any communication from the shore with the ships very difficult.

As soon as it became evident that the evacuation of the island, on the 19th, was impracticable, a correspondence took place between the British and Danish head-quarters, the result of which left no reason to apprehend that hostilities would recommence on either side at the expiration of the term, although the Danish general protested, in strong terms, against our retaining the citadel, which, on the other hand, it was not judged expedient to evacuate.

On the 20th the morning was calm, and as soon as it was light, the drums of all his Majesty's regiments on shore beat *the general*; and the dock-yard and harbour being entirely cleared of transports and British vessels, the corps commanded by Major-General Spencer towed out of the arsenal, under the guns of the citadel, and proceeded along the shore to Hellerup, to be in readiness to reinforce the guards. His Majesty's sloop *Rosamond* having been also towed out of the harbour, and the King's ships within reach of the three crown battery, having got under weigh, the 4th regiment marched out of the citadel, and proceeded to join the guards, covered by its own flank companies, and by a piquet of the guards.

As soon as they had marched, the bridge was drawn up, and the British fort-adjutant was sent to the Danish head-quarters to acquaint the general that he was at liberty to send a guard to take charge of the citadel; accordingly, a small detachment of the royal artillery, and of the 4th regiment, were relieved by a guard of Danish troops, the ordnance inventories and keys having been given over to the officers appointed to receive them by Major Dodecker, the fort-major, and Captain Patterson of the royal artillery. The British detachment embarked with those officers at the citadel, and proceeded to Hellerup.

As soon as the 4th regiment had joined the guards, Lieutenant-General Sir George Ludlow began the embarkation, which was completed with great expedition and regularity.

No troops of the enemy appeared, and there was no concourse of inhabitants. People of all ranks in the city, in the villages, and on the public road, were extremely civil. Had any disturbance been intended, or had any been accidentally excited, the embarkation would have been equally secure from insult, the place selected being open and level, and out of range of fire from the crown battery or citadel, but commanded by his Majesty's light ships of war.

The brow, or stage itself, from which the troops embarked, was judiciously and ingeniously contrived by Sir Home Popham, to answer equally the purposes of embarkation and defence.

A small vessel, a praam, and a floating-battery were fastened successively to each other on the beach; the two first being planked over, and the last beyond them having several guns of large calibre prepared for action in an oblique direction, and manned by seamen.

The flat-boats drew up on the two sides of the praam, and the gunboats, which also received troops, were placed beyond the floating-battery, so that, as soon as the brigade of artillery was embarked, the troops marched to their boats, and the whole put off to their respective ships; after which the floating battery and praam were destroyed.

Admiralty Office, October 31

Copy of a Letter from Admiral Gambier to the Honourable William Wellesley Pole, dated on board his Majesty's Ship the Prince of Wales, off Copenhagen, the 20th October, 1807

Sir, I have the honour to acquaint you, for the information of the Lords Commissioners of the Admiralty, that the whole of the Danish fleet being equipped, (except two unserviceable ships of the line and two frigates, which have been destroyed), and the arsenal cleared of the stores, the army has been re-embarked; and that I shall proceed with the first favourable wind to carry into execution the instructions I have received from the Lord Viscount Castlereagh.

Having so far accomplished the service on which I have been employed, I feel it my duty to state the great activity, energy, and zeal which have been shewn by Vice-Admiral Stanhope and Rear Admiral Sir Samuel Hood, in superintending the equipment of the Danish ships and the embarkation of the stores from the arsenal; nor has the same spirit been less manifest in the captains, officers, seamen, and marines, who have all executed their respective parts in the general exertion with a promptitude and alacrity, which has not only entitled them to my warmest thanks and praise, but will, I doubt not, when the aggregate result of their labour is considered, obtain for them the approbation of their sovereign, and the applause of the nation.

In the space of six weeks, sixteen sail of the line, nine frigates, fourteen sloops of war and smaller vessels, besides gun-boats, have been fitted for sea, and all the large ships laden with masts, spars, timber, and other stores, from the arsenal; from whence also ninety-two cargoes have been shipped on board transports, and other vessels chartered for the purpose, the sum of whose burthen exceeds twenty-thousand tons. A considerable number of masts and spars have been put on board the *Leyden* and *Inflexible*, which were well adapted for this purpose, and some valuable stores on board his Majesty's ships; nor can I forbear to remark, that such was the emulation among the several ships of the fleet to which the Danish ships were respectively attached for equipment, that, within nine days fourteen sail of the line were brought out of the harbour, although several of them underwent, in our hands, considerable repairs. Of the three ships on the stocks two have been taken to pieces, and the useful part of their timbers brought away; and the third, being in a considerable state of forwardness, was sawed in various parts and suffered to fall over.

On a review of the whole, I think it may be asserted, without derogating from the merit of any former service, that characteristic activity of British officers, seamen, and marines, was never more zealously exerted than on this occasion; but I must not omit, at the same time, to inform their lordships, that a very considerable proportion of the labour of the arsenal has been performed, with equal zeal and energy, by large working parties from the army, whose exertions entitle them to the same praise. . . .

I beg leave to express the great satisfaction . . . &c.

(signed) J. GAMBIER

Tzar's Protest at British Attack on Denmark

Important State Papers, Copied from the 'London Gazette.' XVIII 487-495

Declaration of the Emperor of Russia

The greater value the Emperor attached to the friendship of his Britannic Majesty, the greater was his regret at perceiving that that monarch altogether separated himself from him. Twice has the Emperor taken up arms, in which his cause was most directly that of England; and he solicited in vain from England a co-operation which her interest *required.* He did not demand that her troops should be united with his; he desired only that they should effect a diversion. He was astonished that in her cause she did not act in union with him; but coolly contemplating a bloody spectacle, in a war which had been kindled at her will, she sent troops to attack Buenos Ayres. One part of her armies, which appeared destined to make a diversion in Italy, quitted at length Sicily, where it was assembled. There was reason to believe that this was done to make an attack upon the coasts of Naples, when it was understood that it was occupied in attempting to seize and appropriate to itself Egypt. - But what sensibly touched the heart of his Imperial Majesty was, to perceive that England, contrary to her good faith and the express and precise terms of treaties, troubled at sea the commerce of his subjects. At what an epoch! When the blood of Russians was shedding in the most glorious warfares; which drew down, and fixed against the armies of his Imperial Majesty all the military force of his Majesty the Emperor of the French, with whom England was, and is now at war. When the two Emperors made peace, his Majesty, in spite of his just resentments against England, did not refrain from rendering her service. His Majesty stipulated, even in the very treaty, that he would become mediator between her and France; and finally he offered his mediation to the King of Great Britain. . . . Then it was that England suddenly quitted that apparent lethargy to which she had abandoned herself; but it was to cast upon the north of Europe new firebrands, which were to enkindle and nourish the flames of war, which she did not wish to see extinguished. Her fleets and her troops appeared upon the coasts of Denmark, to execute there an act of violence, of which history, so fertile in examples, does not furnish a single parallel. . . . His Imperial Majesty, therefore, breaks off all communication with England; he recalls the whole of the mission which he has sent thither; and no longer chooses to keep with him that of his Britannic Majesty. . . .

Declaration of His Britannic Majesty

. . . If, however, the peace of Tilsit is indeed to be considered as the consequence and the punishment of the imputed inactivity of Great Britain, his Majesty cannot but regret that the Emperor of Russia should have resorted to so precipitate and fatal a measure, at the moment when he had received distinct assurances that his Majesty was making the most strenuous exertions to fulfil the wishes and expectations of his ally (assurances which his Imperial Majesty received and acknowledged with apparent confidence and satisfaction); and when his Majesty was, in fact, prepared to employ for the advancement of the common object of the war, those forces, which, after the peace of Tilsit, he was under the necessity of employing to disconcert a combination directed against his own immediate interests and security.

The vexation of Russian commerce by Great Britain is, in truth, little more than an imaginary grievance. Upon a diligent examination, made by his Majesty's command, of the records of the British Court of Admiralty, there has been discovered only a solitary instance in the course of the present war, of the condemnation of a vessel really Russian: a vessel which had carried naval stores to a port of the common enemy. There are but few instances of Russian vessels detained: and none in which justice has been refused to a party regularly complaining of such detention. . . .

The complete abandonment of the interests of the King of Prussia (who had twice rejected proposals of separate peace, from a strict adherence to his engagements with his Imperial ally), and the character of those provisions which the Emperor of Russia was contented to make for his own interests in the negotiations of Tilsit, presented no encouraging prospect of the result of any exertions which his Imperial Majesty might be disposed to employ in favour of Great Britain.

It is not, while a French army still occupies and lays waste the remaining dominions of the King of Prussia, in spite of the stipulations of the Prussian treaty of Tilsit; while contributions are arbitrarily exacted by France from that remnant of the Prussian monarchy, such as, in its entire and most flourishing state, the Prussian monarchy would have been unable to discharge; while the surrender is demanded, in time of peace, of Prussian fortresses, which had not been reduced during the war; and while the power of France is exercised over Prussia with such shameless tyranny, as to designate and demand for instant death, individuals, subjects of his Prussian Majesty, and resident in his dominions, upon a charge of disrespect towards the French government; – it is not while all these things are done and suffered, under the eyes of the Emperor of Russia, and without his interference on behalf of his ally, that his Majesty can feel himself called upon to account to Europe, for having hesitated to repose an unconditional confidence in the efficacy of his Imperial Majesty's mediation.

Nor, even if that mediation had taken full effect, if a peace had been concluded under it, and that peace guaranteed by his Imperial Majesty, could his Majesty have placed implicit reliance on the stability of any such arrangement, after having seen the Emperor of Russia openly transfer to France the sovereignty of the Ionian republic, the independence of which his Imperial Majesty had recently and solemnly guaranteed.

But while the alleged rejection of the Emperor of Russia's mediation, between Great Britain and France, is stated as a just ground of his Imperial Majesty's resentment; his Majesty's request of that mediation, for the reestablishment of peace between Great Britain and Denmark, is represented as an insult which it was beyond the bounds of his Imperial Majesty's moderation to endure.

His Majesty feels himself under no obligation to offer any atonement or apology to the Emperor of Russia for the expedition against Copenhagen. It is not for those who were parties to the secret arrangements of Tilsit, to demand satisfaction for a measure to which those arrangements gave rise, and by which one of the objects of them has been happily defeated. . . .

His Majesty proclaims anew those principles of maritime law, against which the armed neutrality, under the auspices of the Empress Catharine, was originally directed, and against which the present hostilities of Russia are denounced. Those principles have been recognized and acted upon in the best periods of the history of Europe: and acted upon by no power with more strictness and severity than by Russia herself in the reign of the Empress Catharine.

Those principles it is the right and duty of his Majesty to maintain: and against every confederacy his Majesty is determined, under the blessing of divine Providence, to maintain them. They have at all times contributed essentially to the support of the maritime power of Great Britain; but they are become incalculably more valuable and important at a period when the maritime power of Great Britain constitutes the sole remaining bulwark against the overwhelming usurpations of France; the only refuge to which other nations may yet resort, in happier times, for assistance and protection.

When the opportunity for peace between Great Britain and Russia shall arrive, his Majesty will embrace it with eagerness. The arrangements of such a negotiation will not be difficult or complicated. His Majesty, as he has nothing to concede, so he has nothing to require: satisfied, if Russia shall manifest a disposition to return to her ancient feelings of friendship towards Great Britain; to a just consideration of her own true interests; and to a sense of her own dignity as an independent nation.
Westminster, December 18, 1807

At a Court at Windsor, the 18th of December, 1807
His Majesty having taken into consideration the injurious and hostile proceedings of the Emperor of all the Russias . . . is pleased . . . to order . . . that general reprisals be granted against the ships, goods, and subjects of the Emperor of the Russias . . .

From the 'Naval History of the Present Year,' 1807
November-December. XVIII 497-498

Britain at War With Russia

It may now be considered, that Great Britain and Russia are at war. Lord Gower, the British ambassador at St. Petersburg, has quitted that capital; an embargo has been laid upon all British shipping, merchandise, and property of every description, in the Russian ports; and, evidently under the influence of Buonaparte, the Emperor Alexander has weakly submitted to fulminate a haughty, yet feeble and sophistical, declaration against this country. . . .

Portuguese Royal Family Flee; Sir Charles Cotton Sails for Lisbon

The particulars of the embarkation of the royal family of Portugal, for the Brazils, are so amply, and so interestingly given, in the despatches of Sir Sidney Smith and Lord Strangford, that it is unnecessary to enlarge upon them. . . .

Admiral Sir Charles Cotton's expedition, with General Spencer on board, sailed from Spithead on the 20th of December, and is understood to have proceeded direct for Lisbon. It is generally believed, that, on his arrival there, he will take the command of the blockading squadron; and that Sir Sidney Smith, accompanied by General Spencer, will proceed on another expedition, the object of which is supposed to be Madeira. It has even been said, that the Prince Regent of Portugal signed an order, as far back as August last, directing the governor of that island to deliver it into the hands of the English. . . .

Jefferson Accuses Britain

Mr. Jefferson, the American president, in his message, on the opening of Congress, has indulged himself in expatiating, at great length, on the alleged injuries sustained by

America, from this country; whilst those received from France are passed over in silence. Some debates have taken place on the subject; but it is understood, that at least two thirds of the Senate, and of the House of Representatives, are in favour of peace with England.

Levant

Sir Arthur Paget has returned, without success, from his mission to the Porte. . . .

1807 – Evacuation of the House of Braganza from Lisbon

THE CRISIS IN PORTUGAL dominated attention in the autumn of 1807. Lord Strangford, the British *chargé* in Lisbon, had asked for his passport when the Portuguese Prince Regent bowed to the menaces of France and imposed a ban on British trade. He withdrew to the protection of the squadron commanded by Rear-Admiral Sir Sidney Smith, but Smith reopened communications, and when a French army under Marshal Junot crossed the Portuguese border, the Regent reversed himself and agreed to accept a British escort to the Portuguese colony of Brazil.

The Russian squadron which had been engaged against the Turks in the Aegean under the command of Admiral Seniavin, who had been trying to get back to the Baltic before a state of open hostilities developed between Britain and Russia, took refuge in the Tagus shortly before the arrival of Junot in Lisbon. To deal with the possibility that the Russians might seek to obstruct the Portuguese evacuation, a British expeditionary force under General Spencer was diverted from its intended destination of Sicily, and forces under General Moore already on Sicily were ordered to join. Vice-Admiral Sir Charles Cotton, who commanded Spencer's escort, assumed charge of the coastal blockade, while Smith conveyed the Portuguese court and the evacuated Portuguese fleet to Rio de Janeiro. Smith's services earned him rich rewards from the Portuguese Royal house, and the Portuguese fleet was to co-operate with the British in South American waters.

Relations remained good between the Russians and the Portuguese until their withdrawal, and surplus Portuguese victuals were dispensed to the Russians in preference to their falling to the French. This enabled Admiral Seniavin to face a British blockade with some confidence.

From the 'Naval History of the Present Year,' 1807
November–December. XVIII 505-510

Letters On Service, Foreign Office, December 19, 1807

A despatch, of which the following is a copy, has been this day received from Lord Viscount Strangford, his Majesty's minister plenipotentiary at the court of Lisbon, by

Plate with some account of Lisbon Harbour. This design gives a correct view of the noble harbour of Lisbon, with the castle of Belem . . .

The view is taken by Mr. Pocock, as looking to the eastward, or up the Tagus. In front is one of the vessels called Bean Cods; no less remarkable for swift sailing, than for their singular construction. In distance, the Spanish men of war are introduced, that were taken by Sir J. Jervis in the battle of the 14th of February, off Cape St. Vincent.

The harbour of Lisbon, esteemed one of the finest in the world, has sufficient depth of water for the largest ships, and can receive 10,000 sail without being crowded. For its security there is a fort at the north of the river Tagus, on each side, and a bar that runs across it, which is very dangerous to pass without pilots. Higher up, at a place where the river is considerably contracted, stands the fort, called *Torre de Belem*, under whose guns all ships must pass in their way to the city; and on the other side are several more forts. [Plate 17]

the Right Honourable George Canning, his Majesty's principal secretary of state for foreign affairs:

His Majesty's ship Hibernia, off the Tagus, November 29, 1807
Sir, I have the honour of announcing to you, that the Prince Regent of Portugal has effected the wise and magnanimous purpose of retiring from a kingdom which he could no longer retain, except as the vassal of France; and that his Royal Highness and family, accompanied by most of his ships of war and by a multitude of his faithful subjects and adherents have this day departed from Lisbon, and are now on their way to the Brazils, under the escort of a British fleet.

This grand and memorable event is not to be attributed only to the sudden alarm excited by the appearance of a French army within the frontiers of Portugal. It has been the genuine result of the system of persevering confidence and moderation adopted by his Majesty towards that country; for the ultimate success of which I had in a manner rendered myself responsible; and which, in obedience to your instructions, I had uniformly continued to support, even under appearances of the most discouraging nature.

I had frequently and distinctly stated to the cabinet of Lisbon, that in agreeing not to resent the exclusion of British commerce from the ports of Portugal, his Majesty had exhausted the means of forbearance; that in making that concession to the peculiar circumstances of the Prince Regent's situation, his Majesty had done all that friendship and the remembrance of ancient alliance could justly require; but that a single step beyond the line of modified hostility, thus most reluctantly consented to, must necessarily lead to the extremity of actual war.

The Prince Regent, however, suffered himself for a moment to forget that, in the present state of Europe, no country could be permitted to be an enemy to England with impunity, and that however much his Majesty might be disposed to make allowance for the deficiency of the means possessed by Portugal of resistance to the power of France, neither his own dignity, nor the interests of his people, would permit his Majesty to accept that excuse for a compliance with the full extent of her unprincipled demands. On the 8th instant, his Royal Highness was induced to sign an order for the detention of a few British subjects, and of the inconsiderable portion of British property which yet remained at Lisbon. On the publication of this order I caused the arms of England to be removed from the gates of my residence, demanded my passports, presented a final remonstrance against the recent conduct of the court of Lisbon, and proceeded to the squadron commanded by Sir Sidney Smith, which arrived off the coast of Portugal some days after I had received my passports, and which I joined on the 17th instant.

I immediately suggested to Sir Sidney Smith the expediency of establishing the most rigorous blockade at the mouth of the Tagus; and I had the high satisfaction of afterwards finding that I had thus anticipated the intentions of his Majesty; your despatches (which I received by the messenger Sylvester on the 23d) directing me to authorize that measure, in case the Portuguese government should pass the bounds which his Majesty had thought fit to set to his forbearance, and attempt to take any farther step injurious to the honour or interests of Great Britain.

Those despatches were drawn up under the idea that I was still resident at Lisbon, and though I did not receive them until I had actually taken my departure from that court, still, upon a careful consideration of the tenor of your instructions, I thought that it would be right to act as if that case had not occurred. I resolved, therefore, to proceed forthwith to ascertain the effect produced by the blockade of Lisbon, and to propose to the Portuguese government, as the only condition upon which that blockade could cease, the alternative (stated by you) either of surrendering the fleet to his Majesty, or of immediately employing it to remove the Prince Regent and his family to the Brazils. I took upon myself this responsibility in renewing negotiations after my public functions had actually ceased, convinced that, although it was the fixed determination of his Majesty not to suffer the fleet of Portugal to fall into the possession of his enemies, still his Majesty's first object continued to be the application of that fleet to the original purpose, of saving the royal family of Braganza from the tyranny of France.

I accordingly requested an audience of the Prince Regent, together with due assurances of protection and security; and upon receiving his Royal Highness's answer, I proceeded to Lisbon on the 27th, in his Majesty's ship *Confiance*, bearing a flag of truce. I had immediately most interesting communications with the court of Lisbon, the particulars of which shall be fully detailed in a future despatch. It suffices to mention in this place, that the Prince Regent wisely directed all his apprehensions to a French army, and all his hopes to an English fleet; that he received the most explicit assurances from me that his Majesty would generously overlook those acts of unwilling and momentary hostility to which his Royal Highness's consent had been extorted; and that I promised to his Royal Highness, on the faith of my sovereign, that the British squadron before the Tagus should be employed to protect his retreat from Lisbon, and his voyage to the Brazils.

A decree was published yesterday, in which the Prince Regent announced his intention of retiring to the city of Rio de Janeiro until the conclusion of a general peace, and of appointing a regency to transact the administration of government at Lisbon during his Royal Highness's absence from Europe.

This morning the Portuguese fleet left the Tagus. I had the honour to accompany the Prince in his passage over the bar. The fleet consisted of eight sail of the line, four large frigates, several armed brigs, sloops, and corvettes, and a number of Brazil ships, amounting, I believe, to about thirty-six sail in all. They passed through the British squadron, and his Majesty's ships fired a salute of twenty-one guns, which was returned with an equal number. A more interesting spectacle than that afforded by the junction of the two fleets has been rarely beheld.

On quitting the Prince Regent's ship, I repaired on board the *Hibernia*, but returned immediately, accompanied by Sir Sidney Smith, whom I presented to the Prince, and who was received by his Royal Highness with the most marked and gracious condescension. . .

I have the honour to be, &c.

STRANGFORD

Admiralty Office, December 21, 1807

Despatches, of which the following are extracts and copies, were received at this office on Saturday last, by Captain Yeo, of his Majesty's sloop *Confiance*, from Rear-Admiral Sir Sidney Smith, addressed to the Honourable William Wellesley Pole. . . .

Hibernia, at sea, lat. 37 deg. 47 min, long, 14 deg. 17 min. December 6, 1807
Sir, I have the satisfaction to acquaint you, for the information of my Lords Commissioners of the Admiralty, that I succeeded in collecting the whole of the Portuguese fleet, except a brig, after the gale, and that the weather was such as to allow the necessary repairs and such distribution of supernumeraries and resources to be made, as to enable Vice-Admiral Don M. d'Acunha Sottomayor to report to me yesterday all the ships capable of performing the voyage to Rio de Janeiro, except one line of battle ship, which he requested might be conducted to an English port. I meant to escort her part of the way, but she did not quit the fleet with me last night as settled. I hope, however, she may arrive safe, as she is not in a bad state, being substituted for the *Martino de Freitas*, which was at first destined to go to England, in consequence of a fresh arrangement made yesterday on the latter being found in the best state for the voyage of the two. I have detached Captain Moore in the *Marlborough*, with the *London*, *Monarch*, and *Bedford*, to attend the Portuguese fleet to the Brazils. I have thought it my duty, in addition to the usual order to take the above ships under his orders, to give Captain Moore one to hoist a broad pendant after passing Madeira, in order to give him greater weight and consequence in the performance of the important and unusually delicate duties I have confided to him. I feel the most perfect reliance in that officer's judgment, ability, and zeal. . . .

I have the honour to be, &c.

W. SIDNEY SMITH

Naval Transactions on the Coast of Portugal

From 'Correspondence.' XXI 377-394

"Sic vos, non vobis." Virg. Vit.

. . . it may be questioned whether events of equal moment ever succeeded each other with such rapidity in that space of time. One of the most ancient monarchies of the old world translated to the new. The House of Braganza (comprehending two members of the Bourbon family)[1] snatched from the longing but disappointed eyes of the French legions, under the auspices of that warrior who had already saved an empire from the grasp of their tyrant; here foiled by the only officer who had ever defeated him. We sailors remember with just pride that the sole conqueror of Buonaparte was our leader, and an Englishman; however it may suit the policy or the temper of this or that administration to forget that the MAN is Sir Sidney Smith.[2] *Sic vos, non vobis!*

As soon as the weather permitted, the utmost attention was paid to the present comfort and future safety of the illustrious voyagers and their loyal followers. Every comparative luxury that the flag-ship afforded was devoted to the royal family. Every necessary that could be spared from the others was liberally shared with the Portuguese fleet. Their own provisions were most equally distributed, and the crowd of emigrants were mustered and classed by ranks and families under the management of our officers. The painstaking required to go through such details at sea can hardly be imagined by landmen. When all was accomplished, during a run of 100 leagues to the westward, the admiral took his leave, to rejoin that division of his squadron left to observe the Tagus, making the charge of the Brazil convoy over to the able and judicious captain of the *Marlborough* (G. Moore). On the 7th of December, the *Confiance* parted company for England, with despatches. Lord S[trangford], still the admiral's guest, went home in her; and the *Hibernia* (now the flag-ship) returned to the station on the 24th. The revolutionary flag was flying on the forts and batteries along the coast of Portugal . . .

The proceedings of the squadron now became diversified only by the routine of events incidental to that line of service; among which, providing the means of subsistence, became an object of daily and increasing anxiety. The squadron was victualled from England, and watered by sending the ships in rotation to Gibraltar, to the Berlingas Islands, to the Bayonna Isles at the entrance of Vigo (an enemy's port, where a very little exertion on the part of the Spaniards might have prevented it), and even as far as the Azores and Madeira. On the 9th of January, the first convoy of victuallers arrived: but had the member for Rochester [The Honourable John Caleraft] pointed his parliamentary telescope our way, he would have perceived that famine was as much the order of the day at the Tagus, as off Rochefort.[3] On the 15th a ship hove in sight, which we hoped was the *Hindostan* storeship, with fresh supplies for our wants; but to the

---

1 Donna Carlota Juaquina de Bourbon, Princess of Portugal and Brazil, sister and presumptive heiress to Ferdinand VII, accompanied by her cousin, Don Pedro Carlos de Bourbon-y-Braganza, Infanta of Spain.

2 It is remarkable that on this occasion the admiral was acting in concert with a minister who had been his fellow prisoner in France, (M. Aranjo having been confined as a state prisoner at Paris by the Directory, in 1796) and was opposed to a general who was the first with whom he had exchanged shot in Syria. Junot commanded the vanguard of the French army marching along the coast to attack Acre in 1799, when he was surprised in the night by Sir S.S.'s guard-boats at the mouth of the brook Kishon, near Mount Carmel. He was, moreover, not long afterwards taken on his passage to France with despatches, by Sir Sidney's cruisers, and remained some weeks his prisoner, or rather his guest, for "our Christian knight" retaliated the persecution of the Temple Tower, by the hospitality of *Le Tigre's* cabin.

3 [See below, p139.]

disappointment of the hungry sailors, and to the surprise of every body, it proved to be the *Minotaur*, with the flag of a vice-admiral (Sir C. Cotton), appointed commander-in-chief on our station, not to *relieve* but to *supersede* Sir S. Smith. The vice-admiral shifted his flag to the *Hibernia* next day, exchanging his predecessor into the vacant two-decker. This arrangement was but just completed, when a gale of wind came from the eastward, which lasted with increased violence till the 23d, blowing the squadron, in a great measure, off the station, and producing the unpleasant discovery, that the *Minotaur*, fresh from home after a nominal thorough repair, and fitted for six months' foreign service, had suffered so much during the gale, and was in a state so far from efficient, that the rear-admiral reported to the commander-in-chief his opinion, that the service, as well as the honour of his flag, would be compromised by keeping it in a non-effective ship; and with the vice-admiral's assent shifted to the *Foudroyant*. The *Minotaur*, leaking and pumping, was patched up as well as could be done at sea, in order to save appearances of force for the present, with a Russian fleet of superior numbers lying at single anchor in the Tagus, and the knowledge of a French squadron of equal force being out. One really cannot help thinking that the catastrophe of the *Blenheim* ought to have served as a warning at home not to make ships undergo the ceremony of docking without doing justice to them; and then hurry them out when hardly a safe conveyance for the very stores and provisions loaded upon them, abstracted from the superior consideration of the valuable lives thus risked by the apathy of office.[4]

We considered ourselves rather fortunate in a gale having blown off shore, and consequently with, comparatively speaking, smooth water; otherwise the *Minotaur* might have been lost; and also that the Rochefort squadron had neither fallen in with any of the disabled ships when dispersed, nor attempted joining the Russians, which very feasible manoeuvre would have established a temporary superiority more than a match for us.

The first occurrence of any interest after the gale, was the return of the *Confiance* from England; which fell in with the squadron on the 24th of January. We found her gallant commander promoted by government to post rank, as a compliment for his having carried home the news of the 29th November. By him the Rear-admiral had the satisfaction of receiving despatches from the Admiralty, conveying (in terms of courtesy and encouragement, that it is to be wished naval officers were more accustomed to receive from "My Lords Commissioners") high approbation of the rear-admiral's whole conduct in the management of the service committed to his charge, and in the execution of the various orders he had received from time to time.

If the Admiralty did not go beyond praise in marking satisfaction at the conduct of their officer for what he did do, the same reproach does not lie at the door of the F.O. in rewarding its agent for what he did not do. To be sure we were not a little astonished in the squadron when we came to read in our newspapers the new Lusiad by a diplomatic pen; and the romance of the *Penates* of Braganza, so eloquently narrated to the *country gentlemen* by a ministerial orator. Our astonishment was not lessened at afterwards finding a passenger in our squadron nominated privy counsellor, promoted to the rank of minister, and dubbed knight of a "military" order, all in the twinkling of an eye, for his presumed or assumed influence over the cabinet of Portugal, in its choice between safety and destruction; while we, on board ship, had all along ignorantly ascribed the scene in which we were the actors, first to Buonaparte, and next to Sir Sidney Smith. . . .

4 [*Blenheim* foundered in a storm in the Indian Ocean off Rodriguez in February 1807.]

While these things were passing on shore, the state of the squadron was growing critical as to provisions, and more particularly as to water. The arrival of the long looked for *Hindostan* on the 2d of February, brought but a partial relief; for that ship was so full of naval stores that she could only stow provisions for the squadron equal to about one week's allowance. The *Defence* and *Elizabeth* had been sent off to Madeira for refreshments; *Plantagenet* and *Conqueror* to the Bayonnas for water; but these could not be well expected back in less than a fortnight; and we had but for three weeks left; consequently, notwithstanding the expense was curtailed to the very utmost, we found ourselves by the 7th of February getting so near our last drop, that it became a matter of serious calculation whether we should not be off, which must have been the case had not the *Elizabeth* joined on the 11th. Let party prejudice or official pride seek to disguise the truth and shift responsibility as they may, blame certainly does attach to some of our public offices, for letting two of our squadrons before the enemy at once be so hard run for the necessaries of life as Sir C. Cotton's and Sir R. Strachan's. The latter, being under the necessity of clearing the *Mediator* storeship in a gale of wind at east, was blown out to sea, so as to allow the enemy shipping out without his perceiving them; and they stole quite away owing to the *Phoenix* not coming immediately to him. . . .

Rear-Admiral Otway having joined the squadron in the *Lively* frigate on the 15th, Admiralty orders were received to put any two of the line-of-battle ships (*except the Foudroyant*) and the *Confiance*, under Sir Sidney Smith's command, in order to augment the squadron which had been detached to accompany the Prince Regent of Portugal, and of which the rear-admiral was to take upon himself the chief command, under the authority of his original commission of 27th October, 1807, now revived. The vice-admiral appropriated the *Hercule*, 74, and *Agamemnon*, 64, to this service, pointing out the former as flag-ship. But Sir S.S. representing to him that the *Hercule* was an old French prize, fitted out merely for the Copenhagen expedition, and observing that the poop, cabin, &c having been taken away to ease the ship, making it particularly awkward for a flag-officer, requested she might be surveyed, when she was reported not sea-worthy; in proof of which, part of her timbers (in the form of *snuff*) was produced. A fresh choice now became necessary; that is to say, the rear-admiral pleading for good ships upon a distant service, and the vice-admiral preferring to keep the best upon his own station. The *Conqueror* rejoined during the discussion of this matter, and was applied for; but being a favourite ship, commanded by the captain of the fleet's brother-in-law (there being, as Scrub says in the plan, "secrets in all families") it was at length decided, not to turn the rear-admiral out of the *Foudroyant*. Sir S.S. accordingly proceeded in that ship on 20th February, as commander-in-chief in the Southern Seas, from the river of Amazons to that of La Plata, good humouredly thanking his stars for a double escape from drowning in the rickety *Minotaur* or the rotten *Hercule*, and Sir C. Cotton remained in the command off the Tagus, to become known to the public and to posterity as a party to the convention of Cintra.[5]

---

5 At this period the royal navy, according to Steel's list, consisted of one thousand ships of war, and yet this country could not contrive to find three-deckers for our flag-officers, according to the approved example of the French. - N.B. It is to be observed in conclusion, that notwithstanding the junction of the *Conqueror*, which it will be recollected was a foraging ship, the very low state of the water and provisions in the squadron obliged the commander-in-chief to take as much out of the two detached ships as could possibly be spared, occasioning their deviation to Gibraltar to complete before they could undertake the voyage to Brazil.

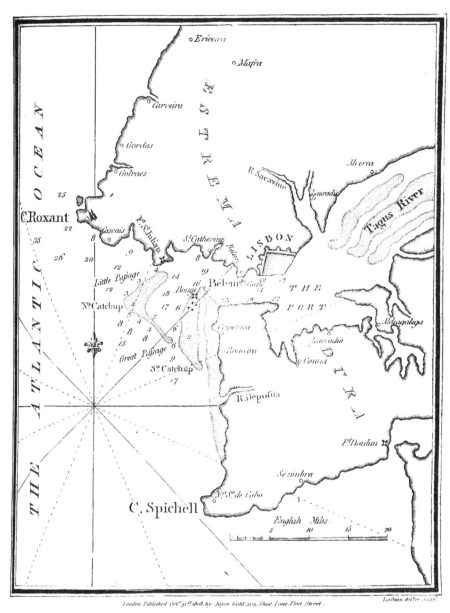

Chart of the Port of Lisbon. From the events which have recently taken place at
Lisbon, every thing relating to that port acquires fresh interest. The annexed map,
by Luffman, is therefore presented. Plate 268

Cotton Assumes Command

From the 'Naval Biography of the Late Sir Charles Cotton, Bart.' XXVII 362-382

Some time afterwards, the command of the Halifax station becoming vacant, Sir Charles
Cotton was proposed by Lord Mulgrave, as a person singularly well calculated to

conciliate the differences then subsisting between this country and America; but, not feeling himself disposed to engage in such diplomacy, the Vice-admiral waved the honour of the appointment. Lord Mulgrave, however, as if determined that his old friend should remain no longer in retirement, offered him the command off Lisbon, which he accepted, and repaired thither, in the *Minotaur*, in the month of December, 1807.

[The affair of Sir Sidney Smith's flag ship is recorded in exhaustive detail in this biographical memoir.]

Cotton's Orders

Papers Presented to the House of Commons, Relative to the Russian Fleet in the Tagus, and to the Convention Concluded with the Russian Admiral. - Ordered to be printed on the 9th of February, 1809. [XXI 234-242]

No. 1 is the following extract of an order, from the Admiralty to Sir Charles Cotton, dated on the 9th of December, 1807:

"Whereas since the orders given to Rear-admiral Sir Sydney Smith, information has been received of the entrance of a Russian squadron, consisting of seven sail of the line and two frigates, into the river Tagus, and orders have been issued for seizing and sending into port all Russian ships of war and merchant ships; and whereas it has in consequence become necessary, that the officer commanding his Majesty's ships off the Tagus should be furnished with further instructions: We do hereby require and direct you, if the Portuguese government should recur to its original intention of proceeding to the Brazils, but should represent to you that the Russian squadron interposes an obstacle to their departure, to demand possession of the principal forts upon the Tagus, as you may deem necessary for the safe passage of the squadron under your orders; and having obtained it, to proceed up the river for the purpose of attacking the Russian squadron, and conveying the Portuguese fleet out of the Tagus.

And whereas, in consequence of the recent conduct of the court of Russia, in renouncing all intercourse with his Majesty, the capture of the Russian squadron in the Tagus has become an object of the greatest importance, and Major-general Spencer, with a corps of seven thousand men, who is destined for Sicily, is directed to proceed with you off Lisbon in his way thither, to co-operate with you for the attainment of that object, and to put himself under the command of Lieutenant-general Sir John Moore, who may be expected on that station with a similar force from Sicily, and with whom Rear-admiral Sir William Sidney Smith was by our secretary's letter of the 7th ultimo, directed to co-operate; we herewith transmit to you a copy of the instructions which have been given to the Lieutenant-general by Lord Hawkesbury, one of his Majesty's principal secretaries of state, and do hereby require and direct you to co-operate with the Lieutenant-general, or in his absence, with Major-general Spencer, for the purpose of effecting the capture of the Russian squadron above-mentioned.

In the event of its not being judged prudent or practicable to make an attack on the ships in the Tagus, or in the event of the failure of such attack, you are to continue with the fleet off that river, for the purpose of maintaining and enforcing a strict blockade thereof, so as to prevent the entrance of any supplies whatever, even of provisions.

Should the Portuguese government, in consequence of the strictness of the blockade,

6 Mr. John Bell. Names, dates, and facts, are the marrow of history.

View of Chacra-Braganza, a Royal Domain, on the Rio de Janeiro, in Brazil.
Engraved by Baily, from a Drawing by R.S.

In addition to the picturesque merits of this View (the performance of an amateur,
a civilian attached to, in a high situation, the English squadron on the South-
American station), it is presumed that it will be regarded by naval men with a more
particular interest, as representing a memorial of the gratitude of the reigning house
of Braganza towards a distinguished member of their profession. Chacra-Braganza
was spontaneously bestowed on Admiral Sir Sidney Smith by the Prince of Brasil,
in commemoration of the 29th of November 1807, and to demonstrate to the world
the light in which his royal-highness regards services, which in this country do not
appear to receive any remuneration or acknowledgment beyond a letter from the
Secretary of the Admiralty conveying the approbation of the Lords-Commissioners.
This was done most certainly in the most forcible language of office: but on this
occasion it ought not to pass unobserved, that, while the naval chief who snatched
the House of Braganza from perdition, and thereby laid the foundation for the
salvation of the peninsula, was rewarded with mere words, the confidential servants
of the crown advised his Majesty to heap accumulated and unprecedented marks of
favour on a subaltern diplomatist, who, in palpable disagreement with his published
despatches, had quitted his post in despair, and left the politics of his mission to be
retrieved by the sailor. The plain unvarnished truth is, and it is high time, as well as
a duty to the profession, to place it distinctly on historical record, that Lord
Viscount Strangford, then secretary of legation, acting as *chargé d'affaires* in the
absence of Lord Robert Fitzgerald, H.M.'s envoy, quitted Lisbon the 18th
November 1807, with Admiral Sir S. Smith's secretary, in a fishing-boat, to take
refuge on board the flag-ship; his lordship considering the French influence in the
Prince Regent's cabinet to have finally prevailed, so that all idea of migrating to
Brazil was given up; in fact, previous to his departure he had nominated an agent for
prisoners of war;[6] by which act he virtually extinguished his own diplomatic

existence. The decision that was afterwards taken to withdraw, arose from a letter of
Sir Sidney's to the Portuguese minister of state (Mr. Aranjo), who, in his answer of
the 25th, notified that preparations were, at last, making, and that the Queen of
Portugal, together with all the royal family, would embark the next day. Sir Sidney
had naturally admitted the *çi-devant chargé-d'affaires* to a share in this
correspondence, in consequence of which Aranjo tacked to his despatch an
acquiescence to a contingent proposition for Lord Strangford to *re-land*; which his
lordship consequently did in a *flag of truce* sent in by the admiral: but he did not get
on board the Portuguese flag-ship till day-light on the 29th, after the convoy was
actually under weigh, and coming out of the Tagus to join Sir Sidney Smith in
Cascnës bay. The historical reader will not find his time mis-spent in comparing
this matter-of-fact statement with the contemporaneous publication of that day;
particularly the letter of Mr. Secretary Canning to the Lord Mayor of London,
dated "Foreign-office, Saturday, 19 December 1807, 1/2 past 2 P.M." which was
followed by a second Gazette Extraordinary on the same day, containing a brief
summary of the transactions in question, and concluding with a notice as follows: -
"The particulars of the above intelligence will be published in an Extraordinary
Gazette on Monday." But this engagement was not fulfilled till the following
morning of Tuesday, 22d December; when, by some unaccountable management,
instead of the admiral's despatches, reporting a naval operation of great moment,
taking the lead in their proper place, precedence was given to a flourishing letter of
Lord Strangford's [who, by-the-bye, had arrived in London during this interval of
delay in publication), purporting to have been written on board Sir Sidney Smith's
ship, the 29th November, the very day of the Lusitanian emigration: whereas it is a
notorious fact, that the first despatches from the flag-ship could not be prepared,
and were not sent off, till the 1st December, owing to impediments of various kinds
arising from unsettled weather and multiplicity of occupation.[7] Plate 395

surrender to the fleet under your command the Portuguese and Russian squadrons, you
are in that case (but in no other) to relax the blockade of the Tagus, so far as relates to
the supply of provisions to the inhabitants, and in that case only." ...

No. 4, a letter from Sir C. Cotton to Mr. Pole, dated *Hibernia*, off the Tagus,
February 8, 1808, mentions the arrival of two Russian, and one French officers, in a flag
of truce. From one of the former having found means to separate them, he understood
the Russians to be extremely dissatisfied with their situation, subject as they were to the
immediate control of the French, who had possession of all the old batteries on the
banks of the Tagus, and were daily erecting new ones. "The Russian ships," says Sir
Charles, "are said to be full of provisions of every description, completed to ten months;
all the Irish provisions, &c. that were in store previous to the entry of a French army,
having, in preference to its falling a prey to them, been sent to the Russian squadron. -
The port of St. Ubes and coast to the southward, is, I understand, to be immediately
occupied by French troops, in order to prevent a possibility of any supplies being sent
to, or communication whatever held with, the squadron under my command."

[See the Proclamation of the Prince Regent of Portugal, Vol. XVIII, pp496-497.
Readers would also be interested in the 'Manifesto, or detailed *Exposé*, in justification of
the conduct pursued by the court of Portugal towards France, since the commencement of
the revolution until the invasion of Portugal (in 1807) . .' which was published in Vol. XXI,
pp463-472, but it has not been possible to publish more than the few excerpts given above.]

7 The reader who is desirous of more ample details had better consult the 13th volume of *Cobbett's
Political Register*; *The Pilot*, evening newspaper, from No. 302 to 331 inclusive; and also the *Naval Chronicle*
for the year 1808.

1808 – The Spanish Revolt, and Other Naval News

1808 WAS A VERY ACTIVE PERIOD of the war, but there was no naval event of the first importance. Moved by this apparent weakness, *The Naval Chronicle* began to lay aside political reserve, for the first time since publication commenced in 1798. In the prefaces to the nineteenth and twentieth volumes it expressed a wish that the country and navy would unite to face the crises throughout Europe, and went so far as to wish that Lord Barham were back at the Admiralty. Lord Mulgrave had been weighed in the balance, and was increasingly to be found wanting. Further, it strongly expressed a wish for the return of Earl St Vincent to active service. Political disunity was expressed in Parliament by protests at the seizure of the Danish fleet, and protest that the proceeds from condemnation of Danish merchant ships were being used to support the comfort of the Duke of York. The debate was extended into the whole issue of the administration of Admiralty courts, and to the grant which was made to Sir Home Popham to compensate him for the loss when his trading venture to Ostend was seized. The Commons also debated the effectiveness of the arrangements to supply the blockading squadrons, and Duckworth's actions in the Dardanelles.

Early in the year, the Rochefort squadron escaped its blockade and was chased to the West Indies by squadrons commanded by Sir John Duckworth, and Rear-Admiral Sir Richard Strachan. However, it eventually made its way into Toulon. Other naval news was the capture of the Danish West Indian islands for a second time, following their return at the Peace of Amiens.

The most important event of the year was the Spanish revolt. Buonaparte had prepared the ground for direct government of Spain by an agreement with Charles IV to permit a French army to cross Spanish territory to occupy Portugal. Several Spanish fortresses were garrisoned by the French to ensure the safety of their communications. However, on 19 March Charles abdicated in favour of his son, Ferdinand VII, at the request of the hereditary nobility. In response, Napoleon, having by trickery made both Charles and Ferdinand his prisoners, installed his brother Joseph as a puppet monarch. This led to insurrection throughout the country. General Murat suppressed a rising in Madrid with reckless violence, but in the provinces the Spaniards, developing guerrilla tactics suitable to partisan warfare, prevailed. Joseph had to flee Madrid immediately after his coronation, and the French withdrew to the frontier. However, the war in Spain and Portugal was to continue for the next five years, and was to become the principal scene of British military operations. By the end of the year, Madrid and three-quarters of Spain were again in the hands of Napoleon.

On 10 June the Spanish forts at Cadiz had opened fire on the French squadron commanded by Admiral Rosilly in the harbour. Rear-Admiral Purvis blockaded the exit to prevent their escape, and four days later Rosilly surrendered. The British government ordered the Bank of England to ship $300,000 to Spain to support the Spanish government, and in July proclaimed a state of peace with Spain. The Spanish revolt led to revolt in Portugal, and an expeditionary force of 9000 men commanded by Sir Arthur Wellesley changed its intended Spanish destination to Oporto, and eventually disembarked at Mondego Bay on the road to Lisbon. There the force commanded by General Spencer joined him, and an advance was made on Junot's headquarters in Lisbon. The first engagement with a French detachment was followed by a pursuit into the mountains. When Junot learnt that British reinforcements, commanded by Generals Anstruther and Ackland, were expected – they actually arrived on the 20th – and that more were expected commanded by Sir John Moore, he resolved to strike immediately with all his forces. On the 21st he met Wellesley's force at Vimeiro on the coast road to Lisbon, attacked, and suffered a loss of 20 per cent of his army.

A few days later Wellesley was superseded by the Lieutenant-Governor of Gibraltar, General Sir Hew Dalrymple. Dalrymple agreed to Junot's request for a convention by which the French army would evacuate Portugal, but would not be considered prisoners of war, would be free to carry home their booty, and would be provided transportation by the Royal Navy. The Convention of Cintra, as it was called, roused the British public to fury. It was a victory thrown away, as the French soldiers were immediately returned by the Emperor across the Spanish border.

The least objectionable part of the convention was that which allowed for the internment at Spithead of Admiral Siniavin's squadron then sheltering in the Tagus. Admiral Sir Charles Cotton had been enforcing a rigorous blockade, which caused severe privation in Lisbon, but did not force the Russians to sea because of the sea stores they had taken over from the Portuguese. He had orders to ease the surrender of the Russian squadron, and certainly in the longer term the conciliatory attitude proved of infinite value. Although the cost was unnecessarily high, the convention did put an end to the French occupation of Lisbon and made the port available to the Royal Navy.

Despite the reluctance to go to extremes with the Russians, the Royal Navy was involved in active belligerency against the Russians in the Baltic, where the Swedish court found it better to resist the French, and overlook the action at Copenhagen, in order to have assistance with respect to Russia. In May Vice-Admiral Lord de Saumarez took command of a squadron intended to co-operate with Sweden and operate in the Danish islands, where several Spanish regiments which had been incorporated into the French army were extricated and repatriated to Spain. On 25 August Rear-Admiral Sir Samuel Hood, with two British ships of the line and a Swedish squadron, attacked a Russian fleet and destroyed one of its number.

The consternation with which the Convention of Cintra was greeted in Britain had the result of arresting British military operations in Portugal for two months, while Dalrymple, Wellesley, and Sir Harry Burrard were recalled to England. Transports needed to move the army from Lisbon into Spain were not available, because they were carrying Junot's army to Rochefort. In October, however, a British army of 13,000 under the command of Sir David Baird was landed at Corunna, and on the last day of the year news was received that it had formed a junction at Benevento with the British main force, which had been left under the command of Sir John Moore.

Napoleon continued to tighten the Continental System during 1808. The American response to the Milan Decree was to embargo all United States merchant ships in their own ports. At the beginning of January were received copies of the French Decree stripping protection from neutral vessels which submitted to inspection by British warships under the Order in Council of 11 November. On 15 February the King of Prussia stopped all commercial and political intercourse with Britain, and on 1 April the Tzar prohibited the import of foreign manufactured goods, which predominantly came from Britain. In May Napoleon annexed all the Italian Mediterranean port towns so as better to control smuggling, and in September he prohibited the importation of any colonial produce, most of which came from areas under British control.

Fundamental to all this naval activity, however, was the danger of the sea. This chapter opens with an account of the wreck of HMS *Anson* on the Lizard in the last days of 1807, and, ironically, with an idylic print of Mounts Bay on a summer afternoon.

Wreck of the Anson on The Lizard

From the 'Biographical Memoir of the Late Captain Lydiard.' XIX 452-454

For the following account of the loss of the *Anson*, we have taken the best information of the particular circumstances, that we could collect from the survivors, and more especially from Captain Sullivan, who was a volunteer on board the *Anson*.' We have also been made acquainted with several articles respecting the melancholy catastrophe,

This view of Penzance, and Mounts-Bay, from the eastward side, was drawn by Mr. Pocock, from a sketch made on the spot by Captain Walter Tremenheere of the marines, nephew to the learned Dr. Borlase, and now serving on board his Majesty's ship *Sans Pareille*: we trust a public avowal of our obligation to this gentleman will not offend him. A brigantine is introduced turning into the Bay, with a sloop on the starboard tack coming into Mouse-Hole. A fishing boat is also seen going large out of the bay. Plate 11

by Captain Lydiard's steward, who was more immediately about his person, to the last moment of his existence.

"On the 27th of December, 1807, cruising off the Black Rocks, and perceiving the approach of a gale, kept a look out for the commodore in the *Dragon*. The next morning (Monday), the gale increasing from the S.W. and not perceiving the *Dragon* in any direction, at 9 o'clock shaped our course for the Lizard, with a view of getting into Falmouth. At 12 o'clock all hands upon deck, the sea running very high, two bow ports on the starboard side, washed away by the violence of the sea, also a port abreast the main-mast, by which means she shipped a great deal of water. The captain sent for the master at this time to determine the situation of the ship, and at half past 12 o'clock or thereabout, land was seen about two miles distant, but, from the extreme thickness of the weather, we could not ascertain what part. Captain Lydiard ordered the ship to be wore to the S.E. not thinking it safe to stand in any nearer under such circumstances of weather. Soon after one o'clock the master wished him to run in again and make the land, which was supposed to be the Lizard, and that if we could make it out, we should get into Falmouth. Captain L. asked if it could be done without risk; he (the master) said he thought it could. The ship was then wore, but the weather still continuing thick, we had a cast of the lead, and having twenty-seven fathoms, we were convinced we must be to the westward of the Lizard, and immediately wore ship again, and made all sail. Soon after three o'clock, as the captain was going to dinner, he looked out of the

1 This gentleman was the particular friend of Captain Lydiard, whose first lieutenant he had been in the different services performed in the West Indies, and was promoted on the taking of Curaçoa.

quarter gallery, from whence he saw the breakers close to us, and the land a long distance a-head. The ship wore instantly, and Captain Lydiard's mind made up to come to an anchor; for had we kept under weigh, the ship must have struck upon the rocks in a few hours. The top-gallant-masts were got upon deck, and she rode very well until four o'clock on Tuesday morning, when the cable parted. The other anchor immediately let go, and the lower yards and topmasts struck. At daylight the other cable parted, and we were then so close to the land, that we had no alternative but to go on shore, when Captain L. desired the master to run the ship in the best situation for saving the lives of the people, and fortunately a fine beach presented, upon which the ship was run. Shortly after she struck, the main-mast went, but hurt no one. Captains Lydiard and Sullivan, with the first lieutenant, were resolved to remain by the ship as long as possible: many people were killed on board; the first lieutenant and a number of others washed overboard. It was the captain's great wish to save the lives of the ship's company, and he was employed in directing them the whole of the time. He had placed himself by the wheel, holding by the spokes, where he was exposed to the violence of the sea, which broke tremendously over him, and from continuing in this situation too long, waiting to see the people out of the ship, he became so weak, that, upon attempting to leave the ship himself, and being impeded by a boy who was in his way, and whom he endeavoured to assist, he was washed away, and drowned." Thus perished this gallant officer, to the sincere regret of all who had the happiness of knowing him.

From the 'Correct Relation of Shipwrecks No. XXII.' [XIX 55-57]

The following account of the loss of his Majesty's frigate *Anson*, Captain Lydiard, is extracted from a letter, written by her second lieutenant (Gill), and dated Truro, January 9: . . .

"Now commenced a most heart-rending scene to some hundreds of spectators, who had been in anxious suspense, and who exerted themselves to the utmost, at the imminent risk of their lives, to save those of their drowning fellow men; many of those who were most forward in quitting the ship lost their lives, being swept away by the tremendous sea, which entirely went over the wreck. The main mast formed a floating raft from the ship to the shore; and the greater part of those who escaped, passed by this medium. One of the men saved, reports, that Captain Lydiard was near him on the main mast; but he seemed to have lost the use of his facilities with the horror of the scene, and soon disappeared. At a time when no one appeared on the ship's side, and it was supposed the work of death had ceased, a methodist preacher, venturing his life through the surf, got on board over the wreck of the main mast, to see if any more remained; some honest hearts followed him. They found several persons still below, who could not get up; among whom were two women and two children. The worthy preacher and his party saved the two women, and some of the men, but the children were lost. About two P.M. the ship went to pieces; when a few more men emerged from the wreck. One of these was saved. By three o'clock no appearance of the vessel remained. The men who survived were conveyed to Helston, about two miles distant, where they were taken care of by the magistrates, and afterwards sent to Falmouth, in charge of the regulating captain at that port. Of the missing, we understand many are deserters, who scampered off as soon as they reached the shore. Among the officers saved, are Captain Sullivan, a passenger; Messrs. Hill and Brailey, midshipmen; Mr. Ross, assistant surgeon; and some others."

A Call for Greater Political Unity and Strategic Direction
From the Preface to Volume 19. ^{XIX v}

At the present awful crisis of civilized Europe, amidst the general wreck and degradation of the continent, whilst the storm is still raging, and the gloom of military tyranny is deepening on all sides, it is devoutly to be wished, that our endless factions and parties would think only of employing men of the most high and established professional merit. There is a dreadful stagnation in the service, a dead calm, hitherto unprecedented in the long and desperate contest in which we have been engaged. The country, and its natural bulwark, the BRITISH NAVY, wants men who will dare to act and think, without that eternal wavering, and looking to others for an opinion, which paralyses all national exertions. A greater portion of talent ought to be afloat; and we know that we deliver the general sentiments of our countrymen when we express a wish, that the venerable Lord Barham were again stationed at the helm, and the experience and determined spirit of Earl St. Vincent again seen and felt on his old station off Cadiz.
[See 'Correspondence' below, pp162-164.]

From the Preface to Volume 20. ^{XX vi-viii}

Our Correspondent, E.G.F. has been pleased to repeat the common abuse of Earl St. Vincent; which, to evince our impartiality, we have inserted. We therefore trust, he will now allow us to add, that nothing but a very superior and great character could bear up, as his lordship's has so long done, against the torrent of abuse which has so very indiscriminately been showered upon him. To whom are we indebted for the present discipline of the Navy? Where shall we meet with an admiral who at such a distance from home, and finding such a difficulty, as he did, in procuring Supplies, will continue such a blockade as his lordship's, off Cadiz harbour? Or where shall we find such officers, as those who have been brought up in the school of St. Vincent? ...

Would it were possible, in concluding our Preface, effectually to *pipe all hands* on board our good old Ship; which has so many enemies to oppose, such innumerable shoals and rocks to avoid, and such an infinite variety of expenses to support. In the midst of which they talk of another change of masters; that the board is to have a new helmsman, and, as is the fashion, that helmsman to be a landsman. We hope, in that case, he will soon find his *sea legs*; and as he is likely to chew a bitter quid or two, if he remains long at his post, we trust that he will look the tempest well in the face, and ever remember the last words of the late Admiral Villeneuve, before he left England to have his throat cut by Napoleon: *"Whatever object Buonaparte may appear to be engaged in, however distant it may seem from this Country; remember, Englishmen, it is alone directed against you. Whether at peace, or at war, Buonaparte will never rest, until he has either subdued you, or himself."*

From the 'Naval History of the Present Year,' 1807-1808
December-January. ^{XIX 66-88}

Protest in Lords at Seizure of Danish Fleet

His Majesty's speech, delivered by commission, at the opening of the present session of parliament, will be read with considerable interest and satisfaction; as it states the finances of the country to be in the most flourishing condition, and throws much light upon the present critical aspect of affairs. On the motion for the address, no division took place in either house; but, in the Lords, the following protest was entered against the passage respecting the seizure of the Danish fleet:

"*Dissentient*,

Because no proof of hostile intention on the part of Denmark has been adduced, nor any case of necessity made out to justify the attack upon Copenhagen, without which the measure is, in our conception, discreditable to the character and injurious to the interests of this country."

W. Frederick, Rawdon, Lauderdale, Grey
Vassal Holland, Norfolk, Sidmouth

For the above, and various other reasons, Lord Erskine also entered a distinct protest.

Madeira Declares for Prince Regent

By Sir Samuel Hood's despatches of the 29th of December, it will be seen that the island of Madeira surrendered to his Majesty's arms, on the 26th of that month; to be holden for the Prince Regent of Portugal, or his heirs and successors, till the free ingress and egress to the ports of Portugal and its colonies shall be re-established; or till the sovereignty of Portugal shall be emancipated from the control or influence of France.

French Order Seizure of All Neutral Ships

Buonaparte has returned to Paris, and is reported to have issued a decree, by which every neutral ship that may in future enter the ports of France shall be detained till the period of a general peace.
[See dispatches from Major-General Beresford to Viscount Castlereagh, and from Rear-Admiral Sir Samuel Hood to the Honourable W W Pole, 29 December 1807, Vol. XIX, pp80-82.]

United States Embargoes Own Shipping

Our relations with America are still in a state of great uncertainty; but the proceedings of the Senate, and of the House of Representatives, as far as they are known, are rather pacific than hostile. An embargo, however, has been laid upon American shipping in the ports of the United States. It is conjectured to be the intention of the American government to confine their ships to their ports until the belligerent powers abandon the restrictions which have been imposed on neutral commerce. Foreign vessels are not to be permitted to trade with the United States, because, it is alleged the naval superiority of this country would, in that case, place the American market entirely in the hands of England, to the exclusion of the other belligerents. The Americans are therefore to abandon all external trade, in order, it is pretended, that no preference may be given either to this country or to France, and it seems to be expected that the embarrassment which will be experienced by the states of Europe, when deprived of neutral ships as a medium of commercial intercourse, will be so great as to produce the removal of the existing restrictions.

Gale Delays Expedition

Sir Charles Cotton's expedition, having been dispersed in a gale, has been obliged to return to port.

Rochefort Squadron Sails

Intelligence has been received, that the Rochefort squadron, consisting of six sail of the line, a frigate, and a brig, sailed on the 17th of January. The same day the *Eurydice* frigate was chased by them, and near being taken, but fortunately made her escape, and the day following she joined Sir J.T. Duckworth, and gave him the information. He immediately made sail in quest of them in the *Royal George*, 100 guns, and the *Temeraire* and *Neptune*, 98 guns each; *Tonnant*, 80 guns, *Dragon*, 74 guns, and two frigates; leaving the *Dreadnought* off Brest, and despatching a brig for Sir Sidney Smith, and the *Ann* armed brig for Ireland. The flag ship of the enemy mounts 120 guns. The squadron was supposed to be about fourteen leagues from Admiral Duckworth, in the south-west quarter.

Sir Richard Strachan's squadron was also in pursuit.

Debate on the Speech from the Throne

Imperial Parliament

House of Lords, Thursday, January 21 1808

The Lords Commissioners, consisting of the Archbishop of Canterbury, the Lord Chancellor, Earls Camden, Aylesford, and Dartmouth, having taken their places; and the Commons being in attendance, the Lord Chancellor read his Majesty's most gracious Speech, which was as follows:

My Lords and Gentlemen,
We have received his Majesty's commands to assure you, that in calling you together at this important conjuncture of affairs, he entertains the most perfect conviction that he shall find in you the same determination with which his Majesty himself is animated, to uphold the honour of his crown, and the just rights and interests of his people.

We are commanded by his Majesty to inform you, that no sooner had the result of the negotiations at Tilsit confirmed the influence and control of France over the powers of the continent, than his Majesty was apprised of the intention of the enemy to combine those powers in one general confederacy, to be directed either to the entire subjugation of this kingdom, or to the imposing upon his Majesty an insecure and ignominious peace.

That for this purpose, it was determined to force into hostility against his Majesty, states which had hitherto been allowed by France to maintain or to purchase their neutrality: and to bring to bear against different points of his Majesty's dominions the whole of the naval force of Europe, and specifically the fleets of Portugal and Denmark.

To place those fleets out of the power of such a confederacy, became therefore the indispensable duty of his Majesty. . . . [Here were reviewed the proceedings at Copenhagen and Lisbon.]

It is with concern that his Majesty commands us to inform you, that notwithstanding his earnest wishes to terminate the war in which he is engaged with the Ottoman Porte, his Majesty's endeavours, unhappily for the Turkish empire, have been defeated by the machinations of France, not less the enemy of the Porte than of Great Britain.

But while the influence of France has been thus unfortunately successful in preventing the termination of existing hostilities, and in exciting new wars against this country, his Majesty commands us to inform you, that the King of Sweden has resisted

View of Puerto-Santo, near Madeira. Engraved by Baily, from a Drawing by Pocock. [Plate 368]

every attempt to induce him to abandon his alliance with Great Britain, and that his Majesty entertains no doubt that you will feel with him the sacredness of the duty which the firmness and fidelity of the King of Sweden impose upon his Majesty, and that you will concur in enabling his Majesty to discharge it in a manner worthy of this country.

It remains for us, according to his Majesty's commands, to state to you that the treaty of amity, commerce, and navigation between his Majesty and the United States of America, which was concluded and signed by commissioners duly authorised for that purpose, on the 31st of December, 1806, has not taken effect, in consequence of the refusal of the President of the United States to ratify that instrument.

For an unauthorised act of force committed against an American ship of war, his Majesty did not hesitate to offer immediate and spontaneous reparation; but an attempt has been made by the American government to connect with the question which has arisen out of this act, pretensions inconsistent with the maritime rights of Great Britain; such pretensions his Majesty is determined never to admit. His Majesty, nevertheless, hopes that the American government will be actuated by the same desire to preserve the relations of peace and friendship between the two countries, which has ever influenced his Majesty's conduct, and that any difficulties in the discussion now depending may be effectually removed.

His Majesty has commanded us to state to you, that in consequence of the decree by which France declared the whole of his Majesty's dominions in a state of blockade, and subject to seizure and confiscation the produce and manufactures of this kingdom, his Majesty resorted, in the first instance, to a measure of mitigated retaliation; and that this measure having proved ineffectual for its object, his Majesty has since found it necessary to adopt others of greater rigour, which, he commands us to state to you, will require the aid of Parliament to give them complete and effectual operation. . . .

The Speaker and the House of Commons having withdrawn,

The Earl of *Galloway* moved an address of thanks to his Majesty, in which he was seconded by Lord Kenyon.

The Duke of *Norfolk* objected to that part of the speech which related to the attack upon Copenhagen. No documents proving the necessity of that measure were before their lordships, and he therefore moved as an amendment, that the paragraph approving of that expedition should be omitted entirely.

Lord *Sidmouth* contended that Denmark had not manifested a hostile disposition towards this country. Her army was in Holstein, and her navy in ordinary: she was not at the mercy of France.

Lord *Aberdeen* defended the Danish expedition, on the ground of necessity.

Lord *Grenville* vehemently opposed it, directed the attention of ministers to Ireland, and urged the necessity of catholic emancipation.

Lord *Hawkesbury* defended the attack upon Copenhagen on the ground that government was possessed of information that there were secret engagements at the treaty of Tilsit; that the view of the parties was to confederate all the powers of Europe, and particularly to engage or seize on the fleets of Denmark and Portugal to annoy this country. They heard this from their public ministers then abroad. They heard it from their faithful ally, Portugal. They also received information of the hostile intentions of Denmark from a quarter to which they had often been indebted for the first knowledge of the designs of Buonaparte; from, or rather through the disaffected in Ireland. Ireland was to be attacked from two points - Lisbon and Copenhagen; and they never found the information of these persons, however they came by it, false. And, finally, they had a confidential communication, that in the council of the highest authorities in Copenhagen the matter was discussed, whether, on an option that they should join either England or France, an option which they understood was to be put to them, they resolved to join France. Having learnt this, ministers would have been traitors if they had not secured the fleet.

Lord *Lauderdale*, and Lord *Buckinghamshire* supported the Duke of Norfolk's amendment; which was opposed by Lord Mulgrave, and negatived without a division. . . .

House of Commons, Thursday, January 21 1808

After the reading of the speech, Lord *Hamilton* moved an address of thanks to his Majesty, which was seconded by Mr. Ellis.

In the course of the debate, Mr. *Whitbread* deprecated the Copenhagen expedition; denied all credit to ministers for the escape of the Royal Family of Portugal; contended that there was now as good an opportunity of making peace with France as ever; and particularly called upon ministers to attend to Ireland.

Mr. *Canning* defended the conduct of ministers in every point alluded to in the royal speech. No angry discussion, he said, had taken place with the court of Vienna. Strictly speaking, there was no negotiation through the medium of Austria, nor any distinct offer from Tallyrand. No remonstrances had been received from Prussia. Every hostile appearance on her part was extorted by France. In justice to the late ministers, he stated, that the expedition to the Dardanelles had been undertaken at the request of Russia. As that had not succeeded, the cause of war with the Porte had ceased. A negotiation with the Porte was entered upon, and the only difficulty was the admission of Russia into the treaty. In the middle of this, the Russian minister left Constantinople, and then a treaty was concluded by the Porte with France. As to Sweden, subsidiary negotiations were carrying on with that power, which would be laid before the house when finished. With regard to America, as no right had been claimed by Great Britain of searching ships of war, satisfaction was offered for the affair of the *Chesapeake*. But ministers had kept that affair distinct from other matters of dispute, while the Americans endeavoured to blend them. He at the same time acquitted of any serious blame the gallant officer who had the command on the American station, as his provocation was extreme. As to the policy of the orders in council, all agreed that there must be something of that sort, and the difference was only as to the degree, which was a question of inferior importance. It was proper to shew other powers that Great Britain might be as formidable as Buonaparte in some instances, though he admitted that our having a giant's strength was not a reason why we should use it like a giant.

From the 'Naval History of the Present Year,' 1808
January-February. XIX 144-176

Danish Indies Captured

The capture of the Danish West Indian islands, and the particulars of that service, are given in the official letters. This acquisition, as it tends to weaken the resources of our enemies, and to put the islands out of the grasp of the French tyrant, is certainly of considerable importance to the country.

Captain W.S. Parkinson, the bearer of the intelligence from Sir A. Cochrane, was one of the earliest followers of Lord Nelson, recommended to his notice by Admiral Sir C. Pole, Bart. and was with Captain Nelson as midshipman in the *Boreas*, when he so much distinguished himself in the West Indies during the years 1784, 5, 6, and 7. He was third lieutenant of the *Vanguard* at the battle of Aboukir [ie the Nile], and afterwards first, and returned to England strongly recommended for promotion by his Sicilian majesty, when he was made commander. This excellent officer is now raised to post rank. . . .

No Relaxation in Dutch Restrictions on Trade

There is no truth whatever in the report of a relaxation having taken place in the commercial restrictions in Holland: on the contrary, Louis Buonaparté declares, that he thinks it his duty to surpass in severity the prohibitory decrees of his brother Napoleon. He has accordingly resorted to measures far more rigid than any hitherto adopted. The ports of Holland are shut against all ships whatever, whether belonging to neutrals or allies, with the following exceptions only, viz. Armed ships of war may enter the ports of Holland with their prizes, and the merchant vessels belonging to neutral or allied powers may take refuge in the ports of Holland from the dangers of the sea; but they are to be placed under the most strict and severe quarantine, and must put to sea as soon as the weather permits. Even fishing boats are forbid to go to sea without a soldier on board each of them, who, upon his return, is bound to make a report of what passed during the fishing. This decree is accompanied by a declamatory address to the Dutch.

It invites them to fit out privateers, reminds them of the actions of De Ruyter and Van Tromp, and asks them whether the Danes are to be the only people that dare to attack the English by sea?

Prussia Withdraws Ambassador

The King of Prussia has also been compelled to withdraw his ambassador from this country, and strictly to prohibit all intercourse between his subjects and those of Great-Britain. . . .

Turkish Fleet Withdraws to Constantinople

Intelligence from Constantinople, of the 19th of December, states as follows: "The Captain Pasha, with his whole fleet, is in the harbour of Constantinople. The losses he suffered in the late battle with the Russians off Tenedos, are not yet entirely repaired. At the same time the naval preparations are continued with the utmost ardour and activity, and the Porte will soon have a very respectable fleet."

Differences with United States Reported Settled

Letters have been received from Boston, in America, to the 14th of January; which mention the arrival of Mr. Rose, the English minister, at Washington, and state, that all differences were expected to be amicably adjusted between Great Britain and the United States. This intelligence is accompanied by an improbable report, that General Moreau, some time ago stated to have left New York, had gone to the Floridas, for the purpose of taking possession of these territories in the name of the French Emperor: It is added, that the Rochefort squadron was understood to be destined to that part of America, having been fitted out to support General Moreau in the execution of this design.

Debate on Royal Expropriation of Droits
Imperial Parliament
House of Commons, February 9 1808

Sir *F. Burdett* inquired of the Chancellor of the Exchequer, whether a report which he had heard were true, that his Majesty had lately granted the sum of £20,000 to the Duke of York, from the Droits of Admiralty.

The *Chancellor of the Exchequer* admitted its truth; but observed, that the property belonged solely to his Majesty, and that such grants were not unusual.

Thursday, February 11
Sir *Francis Burdett* moved for an account of all captures made at sea by his Majesty's naval forces, since the year 1792; with the produce of each specific capture, and its application distinctly set forth: also the amount of captures now remaining in the hands of the crown.

Sir *Charles Pole* wished that the Honourable Baronet, on a matter of so much national importance, had gone more into detail. Every day convinced him of the necessity of putting the Admiralty Court into a very different situation; and he had himself prepared a motion with reference to it.

The *Advocate General* did not know distinctly what the Honourable Baronet who spoke last alluded to, nor what application such a matter could bear to the present question. The subject before the house ought to be correctly understood. The property referred to was of two kinds: one part of it was held *jure corona*, the other in the office of Lord High Admiral. The captures, before the issuing of general reprisals, belonged to the former, the captures afterwards to the latter, and these were therefore called Droits of Admiralty. The one was usually acquired prior, the other subsequently obtained under very different circumstances. In the year 1795, when the French invaded Holland, nine months elapsed before the King declared war against Holland, and encouragement was given to the Dutch to settle in neutral countries, or to emigrate to England. On their compliance, their property seized in our ports was to be restored to them, otherwise notice was given that it would be condemned. They did not accede to the proposal, and on the 15th of September, in the same year, it was condemned. The honourable member proceeded to shew other instances of the same kind with respect to Spanish, Prussian, and Danish property, in 1796, 1800, and 1807, and this was that distinction, he said, to which the King was entitled, *jure corona*. It might, he said, be satisfactory that the mode should be explained to the house in which it had been applied. The honourable Baronet who spoke last, he knew, had the interest of the navy much at heart, and he would learn with pleasure, that two-thirds of the amount had been devoted for essential services rendered to the country by that important branch of the public force. One million had been paid a considerable time since, and another within the two last years. From the same source compensation had been made to persons who had been scattered during the former war. His Majesty, he added, had also granted several sums out of it for the use and benefit of the younger branches of the royal family; and he thought his Majesty had most undoubted right to do this, unless it should be expected that he should be the only father of a family in this country who was not at liberty to shew pecuniary favours to his offspring.

Mr. *Lushington*, in opposing the motion, begged leave to mention one instance of misapplication, of a most extraordinary kind. An honourable member of that house, (Sir Home Popham) obtained leave to quit the British service; and having so done, he purchased a ship, settled at Ostend, and exchanged the vessel so procured for another named the *El Trusco*. Thus provided, the honourable gentleman sailed for India, where he loaded his ship, proceeded from thence to Dungeness, and there ran in, or, to speak more intelligibly, smuggled in part of the cargo. After some transactions, in which Lieutenant Bowen, of the *Brilliant*, was concerned, the ship came within the jurisdiction of the court of Admiralty. Proceedings were thereupon instituted, and claims were put in by the honourable baronet, to the amount of £100,000; and he demanded the restoration of the vessel, as being his own property. In that court he avoided process, and absconded. Captain Robinson, who was the captor, received nothing; but in September, 1805, his Majesty, in compliance with the recommendation of Mr. Pitt, Mr. Long, and another lord of the treasury, made the honourable Baronet a present of the sum of £25,000. He presumed that this would not be reckoned among the rewards assigned for meritorious services: it was, in truth, a reward to an officer of the navy, for having violated the laws of his country.

Sir *Home* rose and said, it was impossible that he could avoid complaining of the manner in which he was thus made the subject of such an attack, which was greatly aggravated, because, being done at a sudden, he was quite unprepared to defend himself. He trusted, however, that the house would believe, that, whether in India or at home, the good of his country was an object nearest his heart. If he had adopted the mode

alluded to by the honourable gentleman, he could tell him there was nothing derogatory
in it; it was the best that a man of his then rank in the service could attempt, to enable
him to improve in his profession. He defied the honourable gentleman, or any other
person, to prove a single act that constituted him a smuggler; and he should be happy to
see all the papers relating to him and his conduct, from the India House, produced and
laid before the public.

[Papers relating to this subject were ordered printed by the House on 22, 24
February, 2, 3 and 4 March 1808, and were reprinted in *The Naval Chronicle*, Vol. XIX,
pp312-321 and 406-408.]

The *Advocate General* stated, that Sir Home Popham, when in India, was known to
persons in the highest offices there, to be a British subject; that he was very much
countenanced by them; and in consequence of the services he had rendered the East
India Company, by taking the soundings of Prince of Wales' island, and other parts in
those seas, he had received such recommendations to the Court of Directors, as had
procured him some very valuable presents from them. From India he had, however,
sailed to China, and at Canton had taken in a cargo of tea, without any license from the
India company, which rendered the transaction a breach of the law, and as such the
cargo was liable to forfeiture. But it was not a droit of the admiralty; it was not what had
fallen to the King as a capture in time of war, but was merely what became vested in his
Majesty as a forfeiture, in consequence of the cargo being illegal, for want of a license
from the India company. With this cargo of tea, the honourable baronet was proceeding
to Ostend, in the ship *El Trusco* [*l'Etrusco?*], when she was met with and seized by his
Majesty's ship the *Brilliant*; and the ship and part of the cargo were condemned, for the
benefit of the captors; but this part of the cargo, which was the property of the honourable
baronet, became vested in the King as a forfeit; and under all the circumstances of the
case, it became a question whether it was a fit forfeiture for the crown to take advantage
of. On a mature and deliberate consideration of the case, he was of opinion that it was
not; and therefore he advised the remission of it, which accordingly took place.

After some further discussion, the Chancellor of the Exchequer submitted an
amended motion, adopting the whole of that submitted by Sir Francis, excepting that
part which called for the statement of the application of these funds since 1792.

On a division, there appeared, for the amendment 82/ Against it 57 - Majority 25.

Report of Operations against Danish West Indies
From the 'London Gazette Extraordinary,'
February 9, 1808

Downing-Street, February 8, 1808
Captain Berkeley, first aide-de-camp to General Bowyer, arrived yesterday morning at
the office of Viscount Castlereagh, one of his Majesty's principal secretaries of state,
with a despatch from the general, of which the following is a copy:

Santa Cruz, December 27, 1807
My Lord, Being in a state of preparation and readiness to move a sufficient force
against the Danish islands in these seas, in consequence of your lordship's despatch of
the 5th of September, no time was lost (after the arrival of his Majesty's final commands,
signified to me by Lord Hawkesbury's letter of November the 3d, in your lordship's
absence, by the *Fawn* sloop of war, which arrived early on Tuesday morning the 15th

View of Brimstone Hill, Island of St. Christopher. Engraved by Baily, from a Drawing by G.T. Plate 369

instant at Barbadoes) in embarking the troops at Barbadoes on board the men of war appointed to receive them by Rear-Admiral Sir Alexander Cochrane, who immediately despatched others to the islands to leeward to take on board such as were under orders in each of them, with directions to proceed to the general rendezvous, the whole of which, except one hundred rank and file of the 90th regiment from St. Vincent's, joined the admiral before or soon after our arrival off the island of St. Thomas, on the 21st instant. It was then thought proper to send a summons to Governor Von Scholten, in charge of Brigadier General Shipley and Captain [William Charles] Fahie commanding his Majesty's ship *Ethalion*, to surrender the islands of St. Thomas, St. John, and their dependencies, to his Britannic Majesty, which he did the next day on terms agreed upon between him and Major-General Maitland and Captain [Francis] Pickmore, of his Majesty's ship *Ramillies*, which were afterwards approved of and ratified by Rear-Admiral the Honourable Sir Alexander Cochrane and myself, a copy of which I have the honour to enclose, and hope they will meet with his Majesty's approbation.

On the 23d, in the evening, after leaving a garrison of three hundred men of the 70th regiment, with an officer and detachment of the royal artillery, at St. Thomas's, under the command of Brigadier-General Maclean, whom I have also directed to assume the civil government of the same, until his Majesty's pleasure is signified thereon, we proceeded to Santa Cruz, the Admiral having previously sent his Majesty's ship *Ethalion*, with Brigadier-General Shipley and Captain Fahie to summon that island; who returned the next morning, the 24th, with a letter from the governor, offering to surrender it to his Majesty, provided we would allow three Danish officers to view on board the ships the number of troops brought against it, which we permitted, that his excellency's military honour might thereby not be reflected on. These officers having made their report to their governor, returned early the next morning, the 25th, to the flag-ship with a message, that the governor was willing to treat for the surrender of the island, when Major-General Maitland and Captain Pickmore were again sent on shore to settle the terms of capitulation, a copy of which I also transmit; which being approved of by the admiral and myself, troops were landed, and the forts and batteries taken possession of in the name of his Majesty the King of the United Kingdoms of Great Britain and Ireland, a royal salute being fired on the British colours being hoisted. . . .

I have the honour to be, &c.

HENRY BOWYER
General and Commander of the Forces

[Correspondence and Articles of Capitulation are printed in Vol. XIX, pp158-166.]

Admiralty Office, February 9, 1808

Copy of a letter from Rear-Admiral the Honourable Sir Alexander Cochrane, K.B. &c. to the Honourable W.W. Pole, dated on board his Majesty's ship Belleisle, St. Croix, December 27, 1807

Sir, Be pleased to inform the Lords Commissioners of the Admiralty, that in obedience to their lordships' orders, received by his Majesty's sloop *Fawn*, no time was lost in embarking the troops previously destined for the expedition against the Danish islands of St. Thomas and St. Croix. As the artillery, ordnance, and commissary stores had been for some time on board of vessels hired for the purpose, we were enabled to leave Carlisle bay on the 16th instant, General Bowyer doing me the honour of accompanying me in the *Belleisle*.

On the 19th we reached Sandy Point, St. Christopher's, and received some troops from that garrison; and on the 21st, anchored off St. Thomas, where we were joined by reinforcements from Antigua and Grenada, and the troops held in readiness to land at a moment's notice.

Brigadier-General Shipley and Captain Fahie had been previously sent forward in the *Ethalion*, charged with a summons to the Governor, to surrender the island, a copy of which, and his answer are enclosed. Soon after they returned, accompanied by three Danish officers, Major General Maitland, and Captain Pickmore of the *Ramillies*, were sent on shore with powers to negotiate with the governor for capitulating, which was agreed to on the enclosed terms, and signed in the evening.

Having on the morning of the 22d taken possession of the island and its dependencies, the first division of the troops intended for the attack of St. Croix was embarked in the frigates and sloops of war; and the same officers again sent forward, charged with a similar summons to the governor. On the morning of the 24th, they rejoined with an answer, and about noon the squadron anchored off the town of Frederickstadt, when three Danish officers (as at St. Thomas) came on board, and it was arranged that the governor should, on the following morning, the 25th, meet Major-General Maitland and Captain Pickmore, to settle the terms of capitulation, which was accordingly done, and the fort taken possession of by the troops in the evening; and last night the garrison and town of Christianstadt, on the other side of the island, were also given up. . . .

I have the honour to be, &c.

ALEXANDER COCHRANE

[Attached were lists of vessels found in the harbours of the captured islands, Vol. xix, pp168-169.]

Debates on the Blockade, and on Naval Supply Organisation

From the 'Naval History of the Present Year,' 1808
February-March. XIX 243-264

Imperial Parliament

House of Commons, Wednesday, February 24, 1808

In a committee on the American Treaty Bill, Mr. *Whitbread* made a severe attack upon ministers for their intention to prevent the exportation of jesuit's bark to France; he considered this as making war upon the sick. If, he observed, it once became the policy of this country to starve the continent, the evil might be visited on ourselves. The ports of the Baltic were shut; and we were provoking a war with America, while we might be in want of corn. If we pressed this, they might say that we might starve, and reap in that fatal vengeance the fruits of our own detestable policy.

The *Chancellor of the Exchequer* said, that the present bill only imposed a duty on bark. The prohibition was to be the subject of a separate bill. But as Mr. W. had said, that no inconvenience would be felt from this on the continent, there appeared in his own view no good reason for his motion.

After much conversation, the house divided upon the amendment proposed by Mr. Whitbread, that the words "Jesuit's Bark" should be omitted. - For the original motion, 167; against it, 76. . . .

March 3 1808

Mr. *Calcraft*, pursuant to notice, rose to make a motion on the situation of the squadron under the command of Rear-Admiral Sir Richard Strachan, when the enemy escaped from Rochefort. It was reported, he said, that the gallant officer, Rear-Admiral Sir R. Strachan, had been obliged to leave his important station in Basque Roads, where he blockaded the enemy's squadron in Rochefort, for want of stores. If it should appear that no stores were sent to the squadron, the House would see that the public service had been retarded by neglect. When the gallant admiral was obliged to leave his station, and cruise in the offing, he met the *Superb, Collossus* [sic], *Mediator*, and another ship of war. After taking stores from these ships, he was obliged to proceed to the Ferrol squadron, and obtain a further supply of provisions before he could follow the enemy. What excuse ministers would make to the House and the public for this palpable breach of duty, he did not know. The papers he intended to ask for, were, accounts of all stores and provisions furnished Sir R. Strachan's squadron, while on the Rochefort station; also, for copies of letters which passed between the Admiralty, Lord Gardner, and Admiral Young respecting this squadron. He was induced to require the production of those documents, having been informed that the squadron had been reduced to two-thirds of their daily allowance, with only five days' beef and fifteen days' bread, without wine and spirits on board, before they were relieved by the *Collossus*, &c . . .

The Honourable *W. Wellesley Pole* said . . . He was enabled to describe the state of the squadron after the enemy escaped from Rochefort. From the despatches received bearing date the 18th of January, the day subsequent to the escape, it appeared, that on that day the squadron under Sir R. Strachan divided the provisions sent from England.

La Parquette-Rock, near Brest, at Half-tide. Engraved by Baily, from a drawing by
G.T. 1813.
   The subject of the annexed plate is one of a number of rocks which lie off
Camaret, a sea-port town (according to Malham) on the west coast of France, to the
south of the channel or entrance into Brest. The road is good, excepting that it is
open to the North, which is well defended by forts on the land. By its being so
much within St. Mathew's Point to the N.W. with the point of the bay, the sands and
rocks, which run far out to the W. and W.S.W. the force of the swelling seas from the
bay of Biscay, must, however, be much checked, so as to render it a tolerable
anchoring place. It has 10 fathoms at a distance of little more than half a mile from
the East coast of the bay. To sail for it, make the length nearly of the East point of
Bertheaume Road on the North coast, and then steer S.S.E. a little easterly, for the
road of Camert, which lies in a bight of the land. [Plate 468]

They had then ten weeks' bread, six weeks' water, and other provisions; about that time
they were employed in clearing the *Mediator*. She was filled with provisions, and had
been sent by the orders of the Admiralty. She sailed on the 21st of December, and
arrived on the 18th of January. She had vegetables on board for the squadron, forty live
bullocks, and other stock for the refreshment of the men. The honourable gentleman
had complained that a sufficient force was not sent out. On the 15th, the squadron was
joined by the *Spencer*, but, in consequence of tempestuous weather, she could not be
cleared of her provisions until the 18th. The *Bellerophon* joined on the 22d, which
supplied six weeks' bread and five days' water. They also received from the *Cumberland*
live stock. On the 23d, a transport arrived with provisions; and Sir R. Strachan, so far
from wanting provisions, sent her back, without touching her cargo. He denied that Sir
R. Strachan had been compelled to go to Ferrol for provisions. He had left his anchorage
at Basque Roads to cruise in the offing, rather than remain in danger of a lee-shore. By
[but for?] tempestuous weather, he might have seen the Ferrol squadron. On the 23d,
he received the first information of the escape of the enemy; but it was not until the
29th that he received certain information that they had escaped. He afterwards attempted

to make Ferrol; but could not get there in consequence of the wind. He was inclined to think the gallant officer did not go to the Ferrol squadron, because, in his despatches, he did not state one tittle to induce a belief to that effect. The honourable gentleman did not know the state of the country. It was known to be difficult to keep up the blockading squadrons. In November, twelve sail of the line were stationed at St. Helen's, to watch the Russian squadron; eleven sail of the line were sent, under Sir Sidney Smith, to the Tagus, in December to protect the royal family of Portugal; and Sir Samuel Hood was despatched with a squadron of three sail to the Madeiras. There never was more exertion shewn, than in relieving the blockading squadron at Rochefort. As the honourable gentleman had attacked the Admiralty upon the subject of the Rochefort squadron, it might be satisfactory to state, that Sir Samuel Hood was despatched up the Mediterranean in pursuit of that squadron. Brest was also blockaded, and a respectable force stationed on the coast of America, to look after that country, if required.

[An *Account of Provisions, and Pursers' Necessaries, remaining on board each Ship of the Rochefort Squadron, on the 23d of December, 1807* and another for 18 January 1808, together with some correspondence concerning supply, was published in Vol. XIX, pp326–327. Sir Charles Pole's reply to Wellesley Pole, rejecting the official efforts at justification, was published in the Memoir of his Public Services, in Vol. XXI, pp280-282. The majority against the resolution was 77. On 21 March 1809 Admiral Pole opened an extensive debate on the weaknesses in the Victualling department, which the administration claimed to be addressing, Vol. XXI, pp289-292, 440-441. See also Appendix 1, Volume I, pp317-319.]

Escape of French Prisoners from a Prison Ship

From 'Naval Anecdotes.' XIX 285-286

Early on Thursday morning, the 7th April, eleven French prisoners made their escape out of the *Vigilant* prison-ship, at Portsmouth, by cutting a hole through one of the ports of the ship, and swimming to the *Amphitrite*, a ship in ordinary which is fitted up for the abode of one of the superintendent-masters. There they clothed themselves with the great coats of his boat's crew, lowered down the boat, and went and took possession of one of the finest unarmed vessels in the harbour, called the master-attendant's buoy-boat. - They immediately got her under weigh, and sailed out of the harbour at about five o'clock that morning, and, it is supposed, reached either Cherburgh [sic] or Havre in the evening. Several persons saw the vessel go out of the harbour, but no one suspected in whose possession she was. There were three men on board her, whom they have taken to France. The vessel is valued at upwards of £1,000 being in every respect well found. The commissioners' yacht was sent after her, but their escape was not known in time to make the pursuit successful: she returned in a few hours.

Fruitless Pursuit of Rochefort Squadron; America Unfriendly

From the 'Naval History of the Present Year,' 1808
March-April. XIX 332-352

We fear that our gallant admirals have made an unfortunate chase of it after the wily enemy; for some of Lord Nelson's old *Agamemnons* turn their quids, and look very sour upon it. The ill success both of Sir Richard Strachan, and Admiral Duckworth, is certainly peculiarly hard just at this time. It was of the utmost importance for Europe, that either the certainty of the escape of the French squadron, or its destination, should before this time have been ascertained.

Sir John Duckworth, after an unsuccessful cruise, comprising an extent of upwards of 13,000 miles, anchored in Cawsand Bay on the evening of the 18th of April, with the following ships:

Ships	Guns	Commanders
Royal George	110	Vice-Admiral Sir J.T. Duckworth
Neptune	98	Captain Williams
Temeraire	98	Captain Hamilton
Tonnant	80	Rear-Admiral De Courcy
Dragon	74	Captain Scott

It appears that Sir John directed his course for Madeira, where he made a short stay; and from thence he proceeded to the West Indies. On the 15th of February, as they were off Martinique, they fell in with Admiral Cochrane's squadron, which was blockading that harbour closely with six sail of the line, and several frigates. Gaining no information of the enemy there, the squadron repaired to St. Kitt's and Nevis, where they watered on the 18th and 19th of the same month. Then they ran down the islands as far as St. Domingo, but still neither heard nor saw any thing of the enemy. To the coast of America they next bent their course; and, on the 11th of March, they arrived off the Chesapeake, and continued to cruise on that station until the 21st of that month. The Americans by no means evinced a friendly disposition towards our squadron; they would not furnish a drop of water, the smallest quantity of fresh provisions, or even common vegetables, although the ships were on short allowance. Such being the unfriendly disposition manifested towards our countrymen, the squadron steered, on the 21st of March, for England. In their way they called at Newfoundland, and at the Western Islands, where they were furnished with a supply of fresh provisions, water, &c. thence they made the coast of Ireland; but they heard nothing concerning the Rochefort fleet.

Sir J.T. Duckworth's squadron is going to refit and victual directly for Channel service.

Various are the conjectures respecting the Rochefort fleet. . .

Chesapeake Incident Satisfactorily Adjusted

Mr. Rose, having satisfactorily adjusted the affair respecting the *Leopard* and *Chesapeake*, with the American government, reached England, in the *Statira* frigate, on 22d of April.

Marigalante Captured

By a Barbadoes paper, of the 8th of March, we are informed of the capture of the island of Marigalante, on the 3d of that month, by the *Cerberus*, *Circe*, and *Camilla* frigates, and *Express* brig, under the command of Captain Selby. The island was taken by surprise, and no serious resistance was attempted. Two hundred and fifty stand of arms, and about one hundred and fifty barrels of gunpowder, fell into the hands of the captors. . . . .

Blockade Puts Pressure on Russian Squadron

At the date of the latest accounts from our squadron off Lisbon, it was hourly expected that the Russian fleet would attempt to put to sea, in consequence of the great scarcity of provisions. Bread was 16d per lb. and meat 8d. Buonaparte was endeavouring to raise £10,000,000 in Portugal. The enemy's force in the Tagus consisted of nine sail of the line, two frigates, and three brigs. The British squadron was amply supplied with water and provisions.

Revolution in Spain

A complete revolution has been effected in Spain; the King having abdicated his throne, in favour of his son, the Prince of Asturias. Whether this event has been produced by the populace, or by the agency of Buonaparte, is yet unknown. The latter is the more probable.

Batavian Expedition

Sir Edward Pellew has proceeded on an expedition against Batavia. . . .

Blockade of the Russian Squadron in the Tagus
From 'Naval State Papers.' *XXI 235-239*

Papers Presented to the House of Commons, Relative to the Russian Fleet in the Tagus, and to the Convention Concluded with the Russian Admiral. - Ordered to be printed on the 9th of February, 1809 . . .
No. 5 is a letter from Sir C. Cotton to Mr. Pole, dated March 29, 1808, stating that Mr. Setarro, (formerly contractor, or agent for supplying the British army and navy with provisions, but now commissary to the French army) had come on board the *Hibernia*, to request permission for the importation of flour, for the relief of the suffering inhabitants of Lisbon. To this request Sir Charles gave a decided negative. Mr. Setarro also requested permission for about fifteen merchant vessels, which were lying in the Tagus, to proceed to the Brazils. Sir Charles replied, that all persons of respectability attached to their Prince would meet with no obstacle to their intention of proceeding, but that they must first pass under an examination. . . .

Nos. 7 and 8, relate to the following order from the Admiralty to Sir Charles Cotton for the provisional relaxation of the blockade of the Tagus [16 April, 1808]:

". . . the proposals which you are herein directed to make should if possible be transmitted at the same time to the Portuguese commander, (Don Gomes Frero) to the civil government of Lisbon, and to Vice-admiral Seniavin [commander of the Russian squadron in the Tagus]; and lastly (should Mr. Setarro have come to you on the part of General Junot) to the French commander also.

In the communications above mentioned, you are expressly to declare, that the blockade of the ports of Portugal has not been established with any view of inflicting the calamity of famine on the natives of Portugal, but on the contrary, that you deeply lament their sufferings, as the inevitable consequence of a necessary operation of war; that Lisbon, having become in the hands of the enemy a port of equipment for the invasion of his Majesty's dominions, the rigid enforcement of a strict blockade has followed as an indispensable measure of self defence, a measure which can neither be withdrawn or relaxed whilst the port of Lisbon shall retain that character; that the relief of the suffering inhabitants of Portugal rests, therefore, entirely with those who

View of Lisbon Rock. Drawn and engraved by Bennet. ^{Plate 251}

exercise the powers of government at Lisbon; that the interest and compassion with which his Majesty considers these sufferings, have induced him to authorize you to offer the most liberal terms of maritime capitulation, by which the pressure of blockade may be removed, and the people be entirely relieved from distress; but, that in the event of the rejection of the terms proposed, you are at the same time commanded to render the blockade still more rigorous. . . .

1st. The ships of war of the Emperor of Russia, now in the Tagus, shall be delivered immediately to you, to be held as a deposit by his Majesty, and to be restored to his Imperial Majesty within six months after the conclusion of a peace between his Majesty and the King of Sweden, together with any other powers, being the allies of his Majesty at the time, and the Emperor of Russia.

2dly. Vice-Admiral Seniavin, with the officers, sailors, and marines under his command, to return to Russia without any condition or stipulation respecting their future services.

3dly. The Portuguese ships of war and merchant vessels to be delivered over to you . . .[etc.]"

No. 10 encloses to Mr. Pole, the copy of a proclamation which Sir C. Cotton had issued to the Portuguese, on the 28th of April, pointing out the means by which they might obtain a relief from blockade.

No. 11 is a letter from Sir C. Cotton to Mr. Pole, dated May 18, stating the events which had been occasioned by the above mentioned proclamation. The following is an extract:

". . . With respect to Vice-Admiral Seniavin, and the Russian squadron, Mr. Setarro said the following questions had been agitated: - 'What would be the conduct of the

Russian Admiral if the French met with a disaster in Spain, and were opposed in Portugal?' - To which the generally ascribed reply is, 'That Russia, not being at war with Spain or Portugal, the fleet could not act in any manner hostile to either of those countries.'

'What would be the conduct of the Russian Admiral should the British fleet enter the Tagus?' - To which the reply ascribed in like manner is, 'Unless a very commanding and superior force rendered such a measure improper - Fight them.'"

No. 12 is a letter from Sir C. Cotton to Mr. Pole, dated June 12, recommending that 5 or 6,000 British troops should be landed, to occupy the forts on the Tagus (as, from intelligence received, the French had not above 4,000 men at Lisbon), to enable the fleet to enter and take possession of the maritime means in the Tagus.

No. 13 Sir C. Cotton states his having requested 5 or 6,000 men from Sir Hew Dalrymple [Deputy Governor of Gibraltar], for the purpose above mentioned.

From 'Naval Anecdotes.' XIX 380-382

Sir Thomas Louis's Sword

At a Court of Common council, held at Guildhall on the 6th of May, the Chamberlain of the city stated to the court, that the sword which had been voted to Admiral Sir Thomas Louis had not been presented to the admiral, his country having lost the services of that gallant officer by his death, previously to the sword having been made. It was thereupon unanimously resolved to present the sword to Sir John Louis, a post captain in his Majesty's service, and son of the deceased.

Admiral Rainier's Will

The late Admiral Rainier has left property to the amount of nearly £250,000 and after providing amply for his near relations, has made the following bequest:

"I bequeath one-tenth part of my personal property to the Chancellor of the Exchequer for the time being, towards the reduction of the national debt, in acknowledgment of the generous bounty of the national establishment of the royal navy, in which I have acquired the principal part of the fortune I now have, which has exceeded my merit and pretensions."

From 'Correspondence.' XIX 385

Mr. Editor, You must be a devilish lucky fellow, or else a precious conjurer, if you ever get my old friend Tom Hardy to send you a memoir of his life: for I see you have hung him up, with a variety of other intended officers, on the wrapper of your last Chronicle. However, as no officer better deserves to have his name recorded in your work, I send you his for a fac-simile.

[Signature, dated *Triumph* Downs, 1800.]

Rochefort Squadron at Toulon

From the 'Naval History of the Present Year,' 1808
April-May. XIX 419-440

No satisfactory intelligence has yet reached us from the Mediterranean. Despatches,

View of the east end of the island of Madeira. Engraved by Cook, from a painting by Northcote, R.A. ^{Plate 270}

however, have been received from Lord Collingwood, of the date of April 26; at which time, the Rochefort and Toulon squadrons were in Toulon, and the Carthagena squadron was at Port Mahon.

Expedition in Support of Sweden Sails

On the 10th of May, the expedition under the command of Sir J. Saumarez and Rear-Admiral Keats, sailed from Yarmouth Roads. The naval force consisted of nine sail of the line, five frigates, six sloops, and 13 gun-brigs, with upwards of 200 sail of transports, with troops; 80 of which had horses on board. Several gun-boats accompanied the expedition, made upon a new construction, drawing only two feet of water, and carrying a long 18-pounder and a carronade. The *Margate* sloop of war, in working out, got athwart the hawse of the *Stately*, and received some damage in her rigging, which prevented her from proceeding with the expedition. This force is understood to have proceeded to Norway, in aid of the King of Sweden, who still offers the most determined resistance to his enemies.

The Swedish fortress of Sweaborg has been surrendered; one of the articles for its surrender stipulating, that "*the flotilla shall be restored to Sweden, according to the particular return made thereof,* after the conclusion of peace, IN CASE THAT ENGLAND SHOULD ALSO RESTORE TO DENMARK THE FLEET WHICH SHE TOOK LAST YEAR."

The governor and officers, commanding at Sweaborg, have been cashiered.

According to the latest accounts from Sweden, the island of Gothland was surrounded by Swedish ships; and it was expected, that the whole Russian armament would be captured.

Naval Force Arrives at Copenhagen

A British naval force has arrived off Copenhagen. A letter from that place, dated May 3, says: "The long expected English expedition arrived here yesterday, under convoy of an English ship of war; about 40 transports passed through the Sound in two divisions. At noon, 15, under the convoy of two brigs, arrived opposite Chronenburgh [sic], and our gun-boats and cruisers were making bold attacks, with the view of cutting some of them off."

A very spirited action has recently been fought off Bergen, between his Majesty's frigate *Tartar*, commanded by Captain Bettesworth, and six Danish gun-boats and a schooner. We lament to say, that the service has experienced a severe loss, in the death of Captain Bettesworth, who fell in the conflict. . . .

Portuguese and British Properties to be Restored

The British government has announced its intention of restoring all such property as belongs to Portuguese subjects now within this realm, or who are with their lawful sovereign in the Brazils. With respect to the property of those who are unhappily under the government and authority of France, an especial reference is to be made to the Prince Regent; and, until his pleasure shall be known, no distribution of it is to take place.

The island of Madeira has been restored to the dominion of Her Most Faithful Majesty.

The Portuguese minister in this country is said to have communicated to Mr. Canning the agreeable information, that his government holds itself responsible to the subjects of his Britannic Majesty, for all the losses which they sustained by the acts of the Portuguese government prior to the Prince Regent's leaving Lisbon but particularly for those which were occasioned by the decree of the 8th of November last. . . .

Despatches for America

Mr. Pinckney, the son of the American minister, in London, and a Mr. Lewis, who recently arrived in this country, from America, set out, on their return thither, on the 18th of May. They are understood to be the bearers of very favourable despatches, towards America, from the British government.

French Decree against American Shipping

On the 17th of April, Buonaparte issued a decree, at Bayonne, which, in consideration that the American government has laid an embargo on the ports of the United States, declares, that, in future, every American ship shall be considered as coming from England, and shall therefore be put under sequestration. A report has been directed to be made to him, of all the American ships that have arrived in French ports, since the 1st of January last. . . .

[This was intended against those British shippers who evaded the Continental System by disguising themselves as Americans.]

Spain

A counter-revolution has been effected in Spain; the *new* king having already restored the crown to his father. . . .

From the dreadfully convulsed state of Spain, the people entertaining the bitterest animosity against the French, strong expectations are entertained, that the French ships in the harbour of Cadiz will be seized and delivered over to the English, as prize; and that the Spanish ships will also be delivered over, in trust.

Fleet to be Increased, Deserters Pardoned

A proclamation was issued, on the 4th of May, for pardoning all such deserters, seamen and marines, as may have deserted since the 10th of October, 1805, provided they return to the service by the 31st of December, 1808. . . .

An order has been issued to increase the number of the Royal Marines serving in the navy, as follows: 25 to a ship of the first rate, 20 to a second rate, 15 to a third rate, 10 to a fourth rate and large frigates, and in proportion to smaller ships. . . .

Imperial Parliament
Debate on the Seizure of Danish Merchant Ships

House of Lords, Tuesday, May 17 1808

Lord *Sidmouth* [Addington, the former prime minister] rose to make his promised motion, respecting the Danish ships. It had been laid down, he said, by the most learned civilians, that it was contrary to the municipal laws to detain foreign vessels previously to a declaration of hostilities, unless our own vessels had been first detained. It appeared, however, that Danish ships and property had been made subject to seizure, while the merchants entered our ports as friends, before any declaration of war had taken place. In June last, when the expedition at Yarmouth excited alarm among the subjects of Denmark, they became lulled into a false security, and, by August following, 320 vessels were seized, and declared lawful captures. The proceeds of those ships and cargoes he calculated at two million sterling. - The noble viscount moved three resolutions: - first, that it appeared that friendly traders had been seized in our ports, and at sea, by our cruisers, contrary to the laws of nations. Secondly, that it would be expedient, for the honour of the British nation, to advise his Majesty to suspend, during pleasure, the proceeds of ships and cargoes adjudged prizes under the circumstances before described by the Admiralty courts. Thirdly, that such ships should be restored to their owners, and the seamen cease to be prisoners of war.

The *Lord Chancellor* [John Scott, Lord Eldon] contended that the ships and subjects of Denmark had not been detained contrary to the laws of nations. He therefore moved the previous question to the first resolution; and on a division, the numbers were - For the resolution, 16 - Against it, 36. - Majority, 20.

A second division occurred on the resolution for restoring the condemned ships, which was also negatived. The numbers were - For the resolution, 16 - Against it, 37. - Majority, 21. . . .

Debate on the Expedition to Constantinople

House of Commons, Friday, May 20 1808

Mr. *Taylor* rose, to make his long-promised motion, relating to the expedition against Constantinople. In a long speech, he recapitulated the various treaties that had been

The annexed plate, presenting a view of the Government House, in Funchal, the town residence of the Governor of Madeira, is from a drawing of Mr. Westall's.

The rooms of the house are large, but they are not well furnished; and every thing that they contain, intended as ornamental, is extremely clumsy. . . . The harbour towards the sea is well defended by a castle and several batteries; but on the land side it is much exposed; a great oversight in the engineer, as there are several bays, at a very short distance, where an enemy might safely disembark, and march thence to the very walls without opposition. [Plate 293]

concluded between Turkey, Russia, and this country, for a series of years back. From the perusal of all the treaties, it seemed to him evident, that the fleet sent by the then government of this country, with a view to commit hostilities against Constantinople, was impolitic in the extreme, in so far as regarded the interests of this country, and in direct violation of our treaty with the Sublime Porte. It might be urged that Turkey went to war with our then intimate ally, the Emperor of Russia, and that we were bound to assist him. This assertion, however, he would not permit to be made, as it was evident, from the official documents then before the house, that the aggressions had proceeded entirely on the part of Russia. The good disposition of the Turks towards the people of England, might be authenticated by the first military and naval characters in the country: he therefore conceived it incumbent on the members of the late administration to defend their conduct to the country at the failure of the expedition sent to the Dardanelles, though not so disastrous, was certainly as disgraceful to the national character as the loss of Monte Video of Buenos Ayres [sic]. The Honourable member then moved, as a preliminary resolution, "That his Majesty's fleet appeared before Constantinople, remained ten days, and retired, without effecting any object."

Mr. *Thomas Grenville* contended that the Turkish fleet was easily assailable, at the time the expedition arrived at Constantinople, and that the force sent thither was quite sufficient for the purpose for which they were sent to Constantinople. From this conclusion the inference was also to be drawn, that the late ministers were fully vindicated

in the steps they had taken respecting that expedition, and that they were justified in
the expectation which they entertained of the co-operation of the Russian government;
by their sending to the assistance of Lord Collingwood eight sail of the line. He
complained of being deprived of the report made by Sir Thomas Louis to Lord
Collingwood, of the state of the forts of the Dardanelles, and of the Turkish fleet at the
same period, which would have elucidated this matter, and corroborated the conclusion
and inferences which he had drawn. He imputed the failure of the expedition to adverse
winds, which, for the space of six weeks, prevented the timely approach of our ships,
added to the activity of General Sebastiani, who disciplined the Ottoman troops, and
provided for them French officers and engineers, who, with an army of 200,000 men,
must have baffled any effort which we could make, either by land or sea. The honourable
gentleman adverted to the expedition of Alexandria, and laboured to shew, that
notwithstanding the result, it was planned on the wisest principles, and for the most
prudential purposes. He blamed the present administration for giving it up; the station
being, both in a naval and military point of view, one of the first importance on the coast
of Egypt.

Mr. *Canning* admitted the propriety of preserving amity with Russia, but he did
not consider that by breaking with the Ottomans, we could preserve the relations of
amity with the Court of St. Petersburg; for the attack on Constantinople only shewed a
narrow and grasping selfish policy, directed all to our own interest, and wholly neglected
the interest of Russia as our ally.

But the great imputation to be cast on the expedition to the capital of the Turkish
empire was, that with an affectation of proceeding upon an amicable negotiation, an
attack was made on the out-works of that capital by attacking and passing the Dardanelles.

The right honourable gentleman imputed misconduct to the late administration in
fitting out the expedition, and read a letter sent from Admiral Louis to Sir John
Duckworth, stating, that more troops were necessary to effect the enterprize. It was
necessary to attack the castles of Cestos and Abydos, in order to force the passage of the
Dardanelles. From the account transmitted by Admiral Duckworth, these castles were
formidable, and had the Turks been allowed to raise fortifications another week, it would
have been impossible to force the passage. It had also been said, that 5,000 men were in
Constantinople, and what could 2,000 British troops do against such an army? The
truth was, that the troops were not employed in the expedition, but were sent to
Alexandria, when they might have taken possession of the castle on the Asiatic side of
the Strait, without annoyance from the forces at Constantinople. As he conceived the
subject had already occupied a considerable time, he would not prevent other members
from expressing their opinions, but concluded by moving, that the other orders of the
day be read.

Mr. *Windham* observed, it was not known that more troops were requisite for the
expedition, until Admiral Louis wrote to Admiral Duckworth, on the 22d of January,
for an additional force. Eight days previous the admiral had said, "I can go up with
three ships," and it was evident that a sufficient force at one time was not sufficient at
another.

After some further discussion, the question was negatived without a division.

May-June. ^XIX 501-504^

Buonaparte Deposes Spanish Royal Family - Revolt Follows

The latest intelligence from Spain is of the most interesting description. Buonaparte having removed the whole Spanish Royal family, has caused his brother Joseph to be nominated as the successor to the vacant crown.

The Spaniards, however, determined to resist the invader, have risen *en masse* in several provinces. Ferrol is reported to be in possession of the patriotic party; and proclamations against the French have been issued at Arragon, Leon, the two Castiles, Valencia, and Murcia. The Spanish troops in Oporto are said to have risen upon the French detachment at that place, to have overpowered it, and, after imprisoning the general and his officers, to have marched into Spain, and joined their countrymen in arms.

French Squadron at Cadiz to be Surrendered?

According to the latest official advices, received by our government, the proposal of Admiral Purvis to the governor of Cadiz, to resign the French fleet as prize, and the Spanish in trust, had been rejected; owing, as it was supposed, to the influence of the French commander. Later accounts, however, state, that the French fleet has been given up to Admiral Purvis.

Spanish Patriots Supplied

Several noblemen, as deputies from the Spanish patriots, have arrived in London, and have experienced the most favourable reception from our ministers. Great quantities of ammunition have been sent off to Spain; and Sir Arthur Wellesley's expedition, which was understood to be destined against the Spanish possessions in South America, is believed to have sailed from Cork, to assist the Spanish patriots of the mother country.

English Prisoners Released

The two last deputies who arrived from Spain reached the Admiralty on the 26th of June. They came from Corunna, where Captain Tremlett, of the *Alcmene*, landed, and was at the sittings of the committee. Every English prisoner, to the amount of 120, was released, and sent to our squadron: the greatest enthusiasm prevailed; all the troops, to the amount of 20,000 regulars, and 300,000 patriotic citizens, were in full march for Madrid, to avenge their brethren who had fallen in the massacre of the 2d of May. Captain Tremlett, it is said, had released twelve Spanish vessels, which he had captured off their own coast.

Rumours of a Victory

Accounts of a still more recent date - on which, however, though derived from a respectable source, we cannot wholly depend - represent Murat to have been actually defeated, in the neighbourhood of Madrid ...

Baltic Squadron Inactive

Our Baltic expedition, according to the last advices, was lying inactive off the Swedish coast; some changes, it is supposed, having taken place in the military councils of Sweden. ...

As the large cutter belonging to *le Tigre*, was coming on shore with Captain Hollowell, the Rev. Mr. Pennington, and several other gentlemen, it being nearly low water, she struck on the stock of an anchor, which stove her bottom, went through her, and being fast, she sunk. On this being perceived by the Deal boatmen, they immediately launched to their assistance, and fortunately succeeded in getting the gentlemen and boat's crew out, and saved most of her materials. The boat, upon the flowing of the tide, floated off, and was towed on shore at Sheerness.

[In a letter to the Editor, 'Mercator' had pointed out earlier in the year that the boatmen in the Downs were uniquely discouraged from dragging for lost anchors because these were seized by the Lord Warden, and the salvage did not cover their expenses. 'These anchors are very injurious to the shipping, if they are permitted to remain under water. When a ship brings up among them, her cable frequently gets foul of the sunk anchors, and is in a short time, by the friction which takes place, completely cut through. Thus not only a great expense is incurred by the destruction of the cables, but the vessels are exposed to the imminent danger of shipwreck.' (Vol. XIX, pp202-204).]

French Shoot Briton as Spy

The *Plymouth Telegraph* gives the following information. "Mr Hammond, formerly pilot of the *Saturn* (a person well known in this neighbourhood), has been arrested, in France, as a spy, and shot, by order of the French government. Other accounts state, that he was beheaded, and his body dragged round the town, the name of which is not mentioned. He had been sent from the *Saturn* on board *l'Aigle*, Captain Wolfe, to reconnoitre the French coast, and landed at a port near l'Orient; he had been on shore twelve days, and was preparing to come off in a boat, when he was arrested by two custom-house officers. He received a pension of £50 per annum from our government, for the information he obtained some time since, by landing on the enemy's coast. He was a Frenchman by birth, but had been many years in our service, in the course of which he had more than once risked his life, by making incursions into France, and returning, in an open boat, to our ships off the coast."

Editorial: Have Confidence in the Spaniards
From the Preface to the Twentieth Volume. *XXv*

It is painful to observe, even in this early state of the struggle, which the Spaniards are making with the long experienced and veteran soldiers of the French tyrant, a disposition in our Country immediately to despond, whenever even reports prevail respecting a retreat, or a temporary check of the Spanish patriots. On the contrary, it is astonishing, that the raw, and, one would have thought, undisciplined troops of Spain, should have already made the resistance they have done; and, when the Corsican [ie Napoleon] has hurried, in a great alarm, to command his soldiers in person: when such an overwhelming multitude has been marched, and still continues marching to the Spanish frontier. It is not ten defeats that will overcome the Spaniards: and it should be remembered, that what may be lost by them in the field, may be recovered by them in their mountains. ...

Lines on the Death of Captain Jervis. [XX 14]

Sunk in the silent lethargy of woe,
Her tear-swoll'n eyes fix'd mournful on the ground,
Britannia comes, with solemn steps and slow,
Wide streams her sea-green hair with cypress crown'd.
          [etc.]

New Evidence on Alleged Yachting Outrage at Sea

From 'Naval Anecdotes.' [XX 15-16. See also XIX 377]

A letter from Penzance, bearing date the 13th of May, and published in different London prints, having stated that a gentleman's pleasure boat was sunk on the 9th of that month between Portland and St. Alban's, by a Belfast trader, and that the act was accompanied by circumstances of wanton barbarity, a strict investigation of the transaction was instituted by the owners of the said trader; the master and mate of her being examined on oath, depose as follows:

"Samuel Montgomery, master of the brig *Venus*, of Belfast, maketh oath, that, on Monday, the 9th of May, on his voyage from London to Belfast, off Portland, about 8 o'clock, P.M. deponent discovered a small vessel, ketch-rigged, about two miles to windward, bearing down upon him. He being then close hauled, beating to the westward, wind W.S.W., called the watch that all hands might be on deck, supposing her to be an enemy; he then altered his course in order to avoid her, but perceiving that she still followed him, he hoisted colours, opened his ports, and fired a shot a-head of her. After this some time elapsed, the strange sail still following him, without attending to his signal, or shewing colours, when a shot was fired at her; she then hoisted English colours, and without altering her course, continued to bear down upon deponent's vessel; when within call, deponent hailed the strange vessel, desiring her to keep off, which not being attended to, a second shot was fired at her: this shot, deponent believed, carried away her mizen. After this a few more shots were fired at her, deponent repeatedly hailing in the intervals, without receiving any reply. The vessel having at length neared, a person from the strange vessel called out that she was a pleasure-boat belonging to Mount's Bay, bound from thence to London. All firing then ceased, with the exception of one gun from the gangway, which was discharged without deponent's orders, and said shot did not strike her. Two men then came off from the strange vessel, one of whom said, that the cause of their following the trader proceeded from their supposing her to be a gun-brig, and that they wished to inform the lieutenant, that the Channel fleet were in Torbay. When demanded why he did not obey the signals, or answer when hailed, he replied, that he was inexperienced in steering, or making signals; that they heard themselves hailed, but were afraid to venture upon deck: that his brother was in bed, and the master below. By this time it appeared that the small vessel was so much injured, it was impossible to prevent her sinking, which she did shortly after. Her crew, three in number, were taken on board the trader, all apparently intoxicated, when every attention and accommodation were afforded them by deponent, who caused them to be landed in safety in Torbay the day following. Previous to their going ashore, they expressed their gratitude for the civility and attention shewn them, and begged deponent's acceptance of a valuable compass, acknowledging that the unpleasant accident was to be ascribed to their own inexperience.

George Joy, Magistrate for the county of Antrim,

> Sworn before me at Belfast, 31st May, 1808,
>
> SAMUEL MONGOMERY

From the 'Naval History of the Present Year,' 1808
June–July. XX 54-80

French Cadiz Squadron Surrenders

The French squadron in Cadiz harbour, the capture of which we anticipated at page 502 in our 19th volume, surrendered to the Spaniards on the 14th of June.

In addition to the official advices from Lord Collingwood, announcing this event, which will be found in their proper place (*Letters on Service*), we subjoin the following particulars, extracted from the *Seville Gazette*:

Royal Isle of Leon, June 10
At a quarter past three in the evening of the 9th instant, the batteries on the channel del Trocadero opened upon the French squadron, consisting of five ships of the line and one frigate. Those of the arsenal, of the Caracca, of the store-houses and magazines situated at the point of the Cantero, followed immediately; and were supported by the flotilla stationed in the said arsenal, and by that on the Cadiz station, which anchored opposite Fortuis, while the French ships themselves lay in the canal of the arsenal, in such a position, that they were out of reach of the cannon of the castles, as well as of our own squadron. The French ship of the line *Algeziras*, finding herself greatly annoyed by the mortar-battery of the Cantero, directed the whole of her fire against it, and succeeded in dismounting its ordnance, but without killing any of the men. The gun-boat No. 17, commanded by Ensign (of frigate) Valdes, and Escalera's mistico were sunk, but no lives lost, as, during the whole of the engagement, we had but three of four killed, and as many wounded. With respect to the enemy, we are unacquainted with the extent of their loss. Their ships have suffered in their hulls, but not in their masts, the *Algeziras* alone having lost her fore-top-mast and cross-jack-yard. A few shot from the enemy's frigate fell into the arsenal, one of which killed one of the slaves. Three reached the stores, but did no harm; 136, the magazines which were empty; and others, various other places. One of the enemy's gun-boats blew up, and three boats were lowered from the stern of one of their line of battle ships, but whether with people in them is not known. The firing on both sides ceased at eight o'clock; and, during the remainder of the night, our batteries continued to throw a few shells, and the French did the same, so that it did not appear to be an action, but rather minute-guns fired upon the death of a general officer, until nine this morning, when the engagement was renewed with greater activity on both sides, to three o'clock in the afternoon, at which time the *Hero*, Rossilly's flag-ship, hoisted a Spanish flag on the fore. Upon this, the *Prince*, one of our ships of the line, hoisted a flag of truce, fired one gun, and sent off her barge. She was an hour and a quarter upon this mission; and, on her return to the *Prince*, she was observed going to Cadiz. Our general was afterwards summoned to that city, and is not yet come back (half past nine), so that the result is not known. The firing, of course, had discontinued ever since the said hour of three. This evening they are erecting a battery of eight 24-pounders, close to the bridge of the new town, which, in case matters should not be adjusted, will be ready tomorrow morning, and, from its advantageous situation, may annoy the enemy very much. The *Argonauta* (a ship of the line, formerly belonging

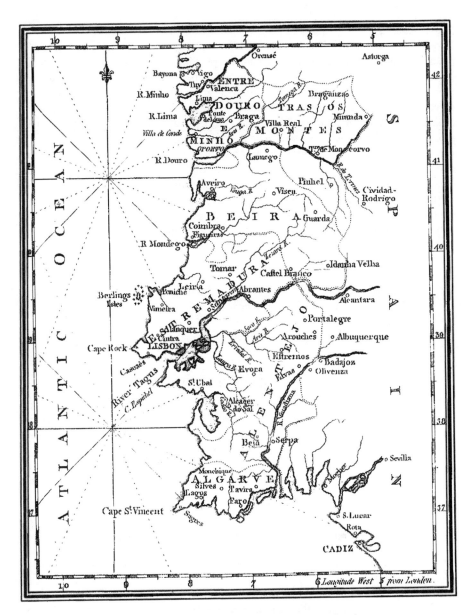

Chart of Portugal. Engraved by Luffman. ^{Plate 326}

to the French, who exchanged her for one of ours) also went out of the Caracca this evening, for the purpose of taking up a favourable position to fire upon them, together with a large merchantman, within half cannon shot. The latter is a little below Puntales, and provided with artillery; and it is said that there are, in both, furnaces for heating red-hot balls. The French kept up a very heavy fire during the afternoon, particularly the head ship and the frigates.

Cadiz, June 14

Last night it was notified to the French squadron, that a new battery of thirty 36-pounders and eight 24-pounders, was ready to open upon it, within half cannon shot, in case it should not surrender. This morning, at seven, no answer having been returned, the signal for general action was made on board the *Prince*; upon which the French surrendered at eight. The officers wanted to fight to the last, but the crews revolted against them, and compelled them to strike. The general of our squadron immediately repaired, in his barge, on board the French admiral's ship, and returned to his own with the French general. The many vessels which were in readiness, either to give assistance in case of shipwreck, or to remove the crews, in case they surrendered, went alongside the ships of the line, and, in the course of the day, the latter were manned by our sailors, all the French having been previously removed. The seamen have been conducted to the four towers in the Caracca, the marines to Puntales, and the officers on board a ship in the bay, which has been fitted out for that purpose, and is called Ponton. . . .

French Ships Taken at Cadiz

Ships	Guns	Ships	Guns
Neptune	84	*Argonaut*	74
Pluton	74	*Algesiras*	74
Hero	74	And a frigate	

Gibraltar Supplies Spanish Patriots

We are informed that Sir Hew Dalrymple, the Deputy Governor of Gibraltar, when the first application was made to him by the patriots of Spain, instantly supplied them with 10,000 muskets, 2000 barrels of gunpowder, a variety of entrenching tools, and 100,000 dollars in money, without waiting for the *orders* of government.

Every Englishman must experience the sincerest pleasure, on ascertaining the formidable check which the career of Buonaparte has sustained, by the patriotic exertions of the Spaniards . . .

All Warlike Operations against Spain Suspended

At a Court at the Queen's Palace, the 4th of July, present, the King's most excellent Majesty in Council

His Majesty having taken into his consideration the glorious exertions of the Spanish nation, for the deliverance of their country from the tyranny and usurpation of France, and the assurances which his Majesty has received from several of the provinces of Spain, of their friendly disposition towards this kingdom; his Majesty is pleased, by and with the advice of his Privy Council, to order, and it is hereby ordered:

First, That all hostilities against Spain on the part of his Majesty, shall immediately cease.

Secondly, That the blockade of all the ports of Spain, except such as may be still in the possession, or under control of France, shall be forthwith raised.

Thirdly, That all ships and vessels belonging to Spain shall have free admission into the parts of his Majesty's dominions, as before the present hostilities. . . .

Other Spanish News, Wellesley Sails

Several thousands of Spanish prisoners have been liberated by the British government, furnished with money and clothes, and sent off to join their fellow-countrymen, in opposition to the invading armies of Buonaparte.

Sir Arthur Wellesley sailed from Cork, with an expedition, the express object of which, is to assist the Portuguese.

Another very powerful expedition, intended to act in conjunction with that of Sir Arthur, is also on the eve of sailing.

Great quantities of arms, ammunition, and money, have likewise been sent to Spain from this country.

Whole armies have been swept away by the invincible valour of the Spaniards, whose patriotic spirit has extended to their neighbours, the Portuguese. Oporto has been *twice* taken from the French; and, when the last accounts came away, the Portuguese flag was flying in every town and fortress throughout the kingdom, with the exception of Lisbon. General Junot had posted himself in the citadel; but, as all his supplies were cut off, it was expected that he must soon surrender. The surrender of the Russian fleet, in the Tagus, to the British flag, was also daily expected.

Buonaparte, according to the latest continental intelligence, continued at Bayonne. Joseph Buonaparte, the *French*, alias the *Corsican* king of Spain, had entered his *new* territories; but, from the cool reception which he every where experienced, it was thought that he would not proceed far into the interior.

Baltic Squadron Returns

The English expedition to the Baltic has returned, without having either accomplished or attempted any thing. Various reasons have been assigned for this inactivity; but the real cause, we believe, remains a secret to the public. - The troops, transports, &c. are to form part of the grand equipment in aid of Spain.

Peace between Russia and Sweden?

A belief is very prevalent, that peace is on the eve of taking place between Russia and Sweden.

Dispatches Reporting the Surrender of the French Squadron in Cadiz

Letters on Service, Downing-Street, July 9, 1808

A despatch, of which the following is a copy, together with enclosures, have been received from Major-general Spencer, by Viscount Castlereagh, one of his majesty's principal secretaries of state, dated off Cadiz, June 12, 1808.

His Majesty's Ship Atlas, off Cadiz, June 12, 1808
My Lord, The French squadron, consisting of five sail of the line and a frigate, having placed themselves in a defensive position, in the channel leading to the Caraccas, and out of the reach of the works of Cadiz, and having refused to listen to any terms, I have great satisfaction in reporting that the Spanish gun and mortar-boats, and the batteries erected for this purpose on the isle of Leon, and near Fort Louis, commenced hostilities

against the French ships at three o'clock in the afternoon of the 9th, and the firing continued without interruption on both sides till night. It was renewed on the part of the Spaniards on the morning of the 10th, and partially continued till two, when a flag of truce was hoisted by the French, but the terms proposed being inadmissible, the Spaniards intend to recommence hostilities with an additional battery, to the eastward of Fort Louis, consisting of thirty twenty-four pounders.

Admiral Purvis and myself wished to have co-operated in this attack, but the Spaniards feeling themselves confident in their own force, have declined our offers of assistance.

The Supreme Council of Seville have nominated commissioners, and applied last night for passports, and a frigate to convey them to England, and they are also equally anxious to send feluccas with despatches to South America.

Information having been received that a small French corps was assembling at Tavira, with a view of entering Spain by the river Guadiana, we have been requested to proceed against this corps, and either to attack them on the coast, or endeavour to prevent the further prosecution of their plans against Spain. I accordingly propose to sail immediately for this object, Lord Collingwood approving of it.

Admiral Purvis had already detached three ships of war off the mouth of the Guadiana, and has offered every other necessary assistance, which Lord Collingwood has since confirmed.

[Copies of correspondence with General Morla, Captain-General of Andalusia and Governor of Cadiz, and between him and Admiral Rosilly commanding French naval forces in the Bay of Cadiz, were attached.]

July 12

Extract of a Despatch from Major-General Spencer to Viscount Castlereagh, dated on board his Majesty's Ship Windsor Castle, off Ayamonte, June 17, 1808

My Lord, I avail myself of the opportunity afforded by the passing of the *Nautilus* from Lord Collingwood to Sir Charles Cotton, to congratulate your lordship on the surrender of the French squadron of five line of battle ships and one frigate, in the harbour of Cadiz, to the Spanish arms on the 14th instant; on which day the Spanish colours were flying in all the French ships. The particulars of this important and interesting event will, no doubt, be fully communicated to your lordship by Lord Collingwood.

It is also very satisfactory for me to inform your lordship, that the movement I have made to this quarter, at the request of General Morla, has been attended with the happiest effects. The French troops are retiring in every direction towards Lisbon, except some very insignificant parties left to occupy the different small forts and posts on this side of Portugal. The Portuguese people are rising in all parts, encouraged greatly by our presence here; and the Spanish frontier on the Guadiana is thus effectually secured from any attack of the French.

[It has not been possible to reprint here Vice-Admiral Lord Collingwood's dispatch of 14 June 1808 reporting on the Spanish action against the French squadron.]

Extract of a Despatch from Major-General Spencer to Viscount Castlereagh, dated on board his Majesty's Brig Scout, off Lagos, June 21, 1808

My Lord, The French fleet having surrendered on the 14th, and the Spanish commissioners having since embarked for England, I beg leave shortly to recapitulate the different events which have led to these desirable objects, and to state to your lordships the present situation of Spain and Portugal, as far as I have obtained correct information.

The general feeling of the Spaniards had been for some time excited to the utmost degree of indignation at the conduct of the French. The information of the forced renunciation of the crown of Spain by Charles IV, Ferdinand, and all the royal family, in favour of Buonaparte, appeared to be the signal for a universal opposition to the views of France.

The Council of Seville, one of the principal provincial jurisdictions in Spain, have laid hold of some statutes in their constitution, which authorized their rejecting the orders of the Supreme Council of Madrid when that capital shall be in the power of foreign troops. They have therefore assumed an independent authority in the name of Ferdinand VII, whom they have proclaimed king; and, after some previous steps, they have formally declared war against France, and have appealed to the Spanish nation to support them; and their supremacy has been acknowledged by the councils of several other provinces.

In Andalusia they collected from fifteen to twenty thousand regular troops, and have put arms in the hands of upwards of sixty thousand peasants. General Castaneos is appointed commander in chief; and I understand they propose, out of the first levies, to augment the establishment of the old regiments, to double their present numbers.

Provincial assemblies are also forming in most of the large towns, and different depôts fixed upon for raising volunteers.

They have a proportion of near four thousand cavalry, and a large quantity of artillery, as Seville is a foundry, and one of the largest depôts in Spain.

All accounts agree, that in every part of Spain the insurrections have commenced almost at the same period; many small detachments of the enemy, and many officers, have been cut off.

General Dupont was on his march to Seville, and had already passed the Morena mountains when the insurrection took place. He was pushed on to Cordova, and, by the interception of despatches, we learn he is strengthening himself there, and purposes to wait for reinforcements. In the mean time the Morena passes in his rear have been occupied by five thousand Spaniards, the road has been broken up; and, I trust, all communication has been cut off.

General D'Alril had received orders to join him at Seville with four thousand men, who were to assemble at Alcorentin, but our arrival off Ayamonte, and the arming of all Spain, and the alarms in Portugal, having prevented this movement, I trust that General Junot will not now be able to detach any troops from Portugal, though we understand a French corps has been collected at Elvas, but I do not think it can exceed four thousand men, though the reports of its strength are very various.

At Faro the Portuguese have already risen, have taken or destroyed a detachment of about two thousand men, have seized the arms and ammunition of the province, which the French had collected in a depôt, and also about forty thousand dollars in gold, which the French general had amassed.

[It has not been possible to include the dispatch from Captain G A Creyke, of HM sloop *Eclipse*, dated 20 June 1808, detailing the revolutions at Oporto.]

Extract of a Letter from Captain Digby, of his Majesty's Ship the Cossack, addressed to the Right Honourable Lord Gambier, Admiral of the Blue, &c., and transmitted by his Lordship to the Honourable W.W. Pole
His Majesty's Ship Cossack, off Saint Andero, June 25, 1808

My Lord, The last opportunity I had of writing to your lordship, I acquainted you of my intention to go to St. Andero immediately, and afford every assistance in my power to the loyal inhabitants, and bring off any British subjects that might wish to come away, in the present uncertain state of the country; and I had intelligence that the French frigate in passage, accompanied by several gun-boats, was expected to make a descent on that part of the coast. Owing to the strong easterly winds, and long calms, I did not get there till the 21st. The signal-post displayed a flag of truce, which was answered by both ships. The captain of the port, Don Vincento Camino, came on board: he told us the French army was soon expected to make an attack on the pass in the mountains that guarded the approach to the town; he invited us to anchor in Sardenero Bay, which we did at five P.M.; until he had made his report to the bishop, who was the present governor, he wished us not to land. No boat returning by one o'clock the next day, I concluded that some sudden attack or unexpected event must have taken place. In the afternoon a brig came out of the harbour full of people of all descriptions, who had left the town on the report that the French were advancing. I immediately got under weigh, and sent Captain Daly, of the *Comet*, up the harbour, to gain some confirmed intelligence, and should the report prove true, to reconnoitre the fort, and find out where the principal magazine was, and, if it was possible, to destroy it. Between eight and nine P.M. Captain Daly returned with certain information, that the French army had gained the pass, and had halted only a few miles from the town, and were expected to enter that night or next day.

Captain Daly also had made every possible observation, and had himself spiked the guns in two forts near the town, and he requested to go and destroy the magazine, and the guns in the forts that guard the entrance of the harbour. I should certainly have sent the boats that night, but the great chance of their being taken by surprise, should the enemy advance, and the night being very dark and squally, with every appearance of bad weather, made me defer it till the next morning; at day-light we stood into the bay, and manned and armed two boats from each ship, under the orders of Captain Daly; he was accompanied by Lieutenant H.M. Herbert, of the *Cossack*, and Lieutenant Read, of the Royal Marines, and several of the younger officers, who all volunteered their services; they left this ship soon after six o'clock, and landed about eight, spiked all the guns in fort St. Salvador de Ano, and fort Sedra, and wedged shot in the chambers of them, which renders them quite useless; the magazine was at some little distance, and had five hundred whole barrels of powder in it, besides quantities of other stores; all of which was completely destroyed, in great part by throwing it over the cliffs into the sea, leaving sufficient to blow up the magazine: the train was laid for a considerable distance, and it was let off about ten o'clock, which instantly levelled the whole building to the ground. Finding some more powder in fort Sedra, a train was laid to it, which took effect, and blew part of the house and storehouse in it up; the two other forts on the west side of the bay they could not attempt, as the surf was so high it was impossible to land, and to walk round was too far from the boats, as they had not a moment to spare, having heard, before they set fire to the first train, that the French had entered the town, and they expected a strong guard at the forts; the boats left the shore by eleven o'clock, and had just got round the point of De Ano, when a considerable body of

French dragoons appeared on the hill, and took post near the smoking ruins of the magazine. I am sorry to say, Captain Daly, and Lieutenant Read, are much scorched, particularly Lieutenant Read, in setting fire to the last train, but am happy to find that his eyes are safe, and that he is doing well. Captain Daly speaks in high commendation of the zeal and exertion of every officer and man employed with him.

Launch of the Caledonia

The *Caledonia* man of war was launched at Plymouth, on the 25th of June, between five and six o'clock in the evening. She is the largest, and is generally considered to be the finest ship ever built. Her plan was designed by Sir William Rule, one of the surveyors of the navy; and she was laid down in the year 1796. Her dimensions are as follows:

Length on the gun deck	205ft	0in
Extreme breadth	53	6
Depth in the hold	23	2
Burthen (more than)	2605 tons	

On the lower, or gun deck, she has 17 ports on each side, middle deck 18, upper deck 17, quarter deck 8, and forecastle 2. She will mount the guns, from 18 to 32 pounders, besides carronades. Her stern is elegantly neat and light, without that profusion of carved work which formerly decorated ships of her class, having only the unicorn supporting the arms of Scotland. - Her head is a bust of a female figure, emblematic of her name, with the plaid bonnet, and thistle "*of the Saxon-green*," and bag-pipes, the favourite musical instrument of Caledonia, on each side, carved by Mr. Dickerson [sic], in a manner that does great credit to his taste and judgment. - Her mainmast is 119 feet in length, and 39 inches in diameter; the weight of her anchors is ninety-three hundred and two quarters.

Imperial Parliament
Debate on Sir Home Popham's Commercial Activity
House of Commons, Tuesday, May 31 1808

Mr. *Lushington* brought forward his long-promised motion respecting Sir Home Popham, and the ship *l'Etrusco* [earlier named *El Trusco*]. He observed, that the legislature had years ago, prohibited any trade between Ostend and the East Indies. Sir Home Popham had, however, gone to Ostend, in the year 1787, having previously applied to the East India Company for leave to go to India for two years. That was refused, but at length he prevailed, on an assurance that he would reside during that time at a Danish settlement, called Fredericksnagore, relinquishing his half-pay as a lieutenant in the navy. He got to India in a foreign vessel, and it appeared, that in the year 1789, he was trading illegally, and that by that traffic he had realized a considerable sum. He was connected with a house at Ostend, of the most notorious description for illegal trade, and he soon after returned to Europe. The captain meditated a second voyage, but it did not appear he got fresh leave from the Admiralty. In his second expedition, therefore, he made the voyage under Tuscan colours, for which a sum of £62 10s had been paid. He made the voyage out and home, and was not aware that in so doing he was violating the laws of his country. After this, in the *Etrusco*, he came to the Cove of Cork, where he pretended he was taken under convoy by the *Diadem*; but that was not the case. A lieutenant on board that ship was ready to prove that there was a prize-master on board the *Etrusco* at the time, and he could prove that fact at the bar, if necessary. He then proceeded to accuse Sir Home with having, on a variety of occasions, resorted to false papers for purposes of deception; and concluded, by moving a resolution, - "That Sir Home Popham, in these illegal transactions, had acted contrary to his duty, as a British subject, and to his honour, as a man, and as an officer; that the grant which he had received was a misapplication of the public money, and would operate as a discouragement, in future, to the British navy.". . .

After a long debate [which produced no new material], the motion was negatived, by 126 against 57.

Foreign Minister's Statement on Spain
Monday July 4, 1808

This being the last day of the session, Mr. *Whitbread* put some questions to ministers, as to the intentions of his majesty's government, relating to Spain; in answer to which, Lord *Castlereagh* observed, that the grateful task at length presented itself, of announcing to the House, that it had been determined to give that struggling nation every aid that we could afford. As to his majesty's ministers not having laid before Parliament any proposal concerning Spain, he did not think it, in the present state of affairs, necessary. In due time that would be done, and although a vote of credit was not asked for, yet, whatsoever dispositions might be arranged and agreed on for the desirable object, he had the satisfaction of saying, that by the liberality of the House, means were in hand to enable them to give the assistance which might be immediately required; and should more be requisite, the law furnished his majesty with the power of calling together Parliament, at a very short notice, by which any further or greater supplies, as they might be wanting, might be furnished.

Reports of Naval Revision to be Tabled

On the motion of Mr. *Wilberforce*, an address was voted to his Majesty, that he would be graciously pleased to direct, that there be laid before the House, copies of the 4th, 5th, 6th, 7th, 8th, 9th and 10th Reports of Naval Revision.

New Naval Hospital
From 'Naval Anecdotes.' XX 113

The Lords of the Admiralty have ordered a royal naval hospital to be erected upon the Denes, Yarmouth, capable of containing 300 patients; from plans by Edward Holl, architect, under the inspector-general of his Majesty's naval works.

Critique of Barham's and St Vincent's Leadership
From 'Correspondence.' XX 125-129

Remarks on the Parliamentary Duties of Naval Officers (Letter IV)
Sir, In the preface to the volume of the *Naval Chronicle* just completed, you venture to

say, "we know we deliver the general sentiments of our countrymen, when we express a wish that the venerable Lord Barham was again stationed at the helm, and the experience and determined spirit of Earl St. Vincent again seen and left on his old station off Cadiz."[2]

Our walks through life, Sir, must lead us among men of very distinct opinions, for I hardly meet a man who does not most earnestly deprecate such appointments. I am a great admirer of Lord Barham, and think most highly of his respectability and worth; but the character of the Board of Admiralty, when he presided there, was of a dry, unconciliating, cold, depressing nature; and I never saw less animation in the service than in those days. Why do not your friends pant for the return of Lord Spencer, where the enlightened statesman, the steady man of business, the accomplished gentleman, and a very considerable knowledge of the navy and its officers, made all things easy, the service beloved, and animation pervaded all ranks. There was certainly an error of considerable magnitude respecting the mutiny at Spithead, otherwise I have always heard the conduct of his lordship at the head of the Board highly approved of. I shall perhaps, at a future time, offer you some remarks on that unhappy period, as they may apply to the management of men in more fortunate situations. But to return to Lord Barham. It is so long since his lordship was at sea, that he can hardly be said to possess any experience of the naval service of the present day, so much has it changed, and I will with pleasure add improved. I repeat, sir, that I very much esteem Lord Barham, with whom I have been formerly acquainted, and have been obliged by; but in speaking of a man in his public character, the consideration of the private must cease, and I could not let the paragraph in your preface pass without one negative to your assertion, even when so very respectable a name was brought forward.

The other character, whose return to the command of a fleet you seem to think would be *unanimously* welcomed, has been so much and so very freely canvassed by the public, that his lordship need not be surprised if your panegyric should have called forth some animadversions. I am as ready as any man to extol his blockade of Cadiz, his rigid and excellent economy of stores (at that time), his judicious and spirited conduct during the dreadful days of mutiny; and I am not one of those who would shade his laurels of the 14th of February beneath those of Lord Nelson. His attack of the Spanish fleet on that day must be for ever eminent in our naval annals; nor can the greater victories of succeeding days ever prevent the name of Earl St. Vincent from standing high, very high in our list of naval *victors*; I was about to write *heroes*, but I cannot find any good definition of the latter word, that applied direct to the character of his lordship. The glories of the 14th of February may perhaps have dazzled him beyond the powers of his mind to bear - for there are not many minds strong enough to surmount success and its consequent applause, particularly whilst possessed of very high power. But from the days of the *Foudroyant* upwards, the ruling passion and the predominant character have been the same. His lordship's wound, and the capture of the *Pegase*, merited not a reward; and I know hundreds of officers who would have been ashamed to receive it, for an action under such circumstances.[3]

As a conqueror of Martinique, the earl and his comrade are stated to have exacted as severe pecuniary claims as ever a subdued country was subjected to;[4] and I question whether any people ever suffered more totally unnecessary hardships and deprivations,

2 Having expressed this sentiment, which some may consider to be a partial one, we feel ourselves called upon to give place to the present animadversions of our Correspondent, E.G.F. observing, however, that we most pointedly deprecate every species of personal attack. - Ed.

or that the feelings of officers were so insulted and wounded, as when his lordship
commanded the Channel fleet. Do you want his lordship in power because he is a
reformer of abuses? What were his own emoluments when living ashore at Torbay,
Cawsand Bay, or even in London, or perhaps Essex; whilst all under his command were
suffering the confinement and attendant deprivations of the inhabitants of a town in a
close siege? These are not the characteristics of a man I wish to see possessing any sway
in Great Britain. I must add, that the manner in which the few reforms that were made
under his lordship's auspices were so conducted as to lose all their good effect, by making
reform appear hateful. Is it possible that the circumstances which took place between
his lordship and the Navy Board, and the published correspondence between him and
Sir John Orde, can have been taken into consideration, and after that a wish expressed
to see power vested in such hands? Were his lordship's talents tenfold superior to what
they are or have been, yet his mode of rule appears to me so truly *anti-British*, that I
cannot wish to see him in power in any extremity. The system by which the ships in
commission during the late short peace were managed, reminded me of the days of
terror and *espionage* which marked the career of Robespierre; and when was the navy of
Britain so long fitting for sea as at the breaking out of the present war? I have heard it
said, that his lordship simplified the service by reducing the number of ranks, he himself
constituting the *first*, and all the admirals, captains, officers, and men under his command,
the *second*. . . .

I remain, sir, &c

E.G.F.

From the 'Naval History of the Present Year,' 1808
July–August. [XX 142-143]

Spanish Victory

We are much gratified, in being able to state, that the intelligence from Spain continues
to be of the most favourable description.

By one splendid victory, the entire province of Andalusia has been freed from the
presence of the French, with a loss, to the vanquished, of from 14,000 to 20,000 men.
The French general, Gobert, was killed in the action; and the other two generals, Dupont
and Wedel, were taken prisoners of war.

The contemptible usurper, Joseph Buonaparte, had ventured to Madrid; but, in
consequence of the reverses of the French, he left that capital abruptly, after a stay of

---

3 This remark appears to be deficient in candour. Public honours and rewards, unless notoriously
misbestowed, ought never to be called in question; as, in addition to the satisfaction which they impart to
the individual immediately concerned, who feels his services warmly appreciated by his country, they
operate as powerful stimulants to future and general exertion. The case of Earl St. Vincent, however,
requires no apology. The capture of the *Pegase* was generally acknowledged to be a gallant exploit; and, on
that subject, Admiral Barrington, in his official letter to the Admiralty, says: "My pen is not equal to the
praise that is due to the good conduct, bravery, and discipline of Captain Jervis, his officers and seamen."
Vide. Naval Chronicle, Vol IV page 9. - The *Foudroyant* and the *Pegase* were closely engaged for three
quarters of an hour; and, respecting the wound which Captain Jervis received, it so severely affected him
as to endanger his sight; nor, we believe, have the consequences ever been completely removed. - Ed
4 On this point, before he forms his opinion, the reader will do well to consult the vindicatory letter of Sir
John Jervis and Sir Charles Grey, addressed to the Duke of Portland, in the IVth volume of the Naval
Chronicle, page 14, *et seq.* - Ed. [Unfortunately, it has not been possible to reproduce this extremely long
letter in the Consolidated Edition.]

only a few days, taking with him the regalia, and most of the valuable movables, in plate, &c. from the palace. . . .

Austria to Fight France?

Extensive military preparations are going forward in Germany; and the general opinion is, that Austria meditates an immediate attack upon France. - Any circumstance of this nature must be favourable, as tending to divert the attention of Buonaparte from his main object - the subjugation of Spain.

British Forces Free Spanish Soldiers in Denmark

The emancipation of upwards of 10,000 Spanish troops from the yoke of France and Denmark, under the auspices of the British navy, as will be seen by the official despatches of Admiral Keats, given in the *Extraordinary Gazette* of August 24, is another joyful event, which reflects much credit on all the parties concerned.

Anecdote of Sir Roger Curtis
From 'Naval Anecdotes.' XX 199-200

Having received orders while in London to take command of a squadron at Portsmouth, the admiral travelled, for despatch, without servants, plainly dressed, in the mail coach. As it frequently happens in this sort of conveyance, the passengers were unknown to each other, and Sir Roger found himself in company with a young man, who proved, by his uniform, to be a mate of one of the East Indiamen then lying at the Motherbank. When they had proceeded within a few miles of Petersfield, the young officer pulled out some bread and cheese from a bundle, and invited his fellow-travellers to eat. During their repast he entertained them with sea phrases, which induced the admiral jocosely to ask him many simple questions relating to nautical tactics; among others, he demanded how sailors could see at night, and whether they were not compelled to tie the ship to a post, or tree, until morning? The mate was not backward in bestowing a few hearty d—ns upon the ignorance and lubberly lingo of the admiral, who laughed heartily at the joke; and he not only bore the rough observations of the sailor with good humour, but the contemptuous grins of his fellow-passengers. On their arrival at Portsmouth, the admiral shook hands with the mate, and went on board his ship. The same day Sir Roger came on shore in his broad gold-laced hat and uniform: he was attended by several of his bargemen, and while walking up Point-street, he met his later fellow-passenger, the mate of the Indiaman. Before the latter could recover from his surprize, Sir Roger accosted him with, "What cheer, messmate; you see I am not the lubber you took me for; but come, as I breakfasted out of your locker this morning, you shall *splice the main-brace* with me this evening; then you may square your yards, and run before the wind to the Motherbank." The mate, with astonishment, apologized, as well as he was able, for the liberty he had taken with the admiral, who soon released him from his embarrassment, and advised him, over a bottle, never to be decoyed in future by false colours, but to look sharply at the mould and trim of every vessel he met, before he suffered her to surprize him.

From the 'Naval History of the Present Year,' 1808
August–September. XX 229-233

Angry Reaction to Convention of Cintra

The account of the victories in Portugal, obtained by Sir Arthur Wellesley on the 17th and 21st of August, were received by people of all ranks with the most generous enthusiasm; but the dissatisfaction which afterwards pervaded the public mind, on the appearance of the *Extraordinary Gazette*, relating to the evacuation of Portugal and the surrender of the Russian fleet is indescribable. A defeat, unless it had been marked by cowardice, could not have produced so vexatious, so mortifying a sensation. It is said that, at the time of signing the disgraceful convention, by which we have given away advantages with the pen, more than tantamount to those which we had gained by the sword, the British army consisted of 32,000 men, while that of the French, beaten, and in an enemy's country, amounted to only 15,000!

That the evacuation of Portugal is an object of importance, must not be denied; but that a proudly victorious army should suffer a routed enemy to depart, with their arms in their hands, with 800 horses, with all their artillery, with 60 rounds of ammunition, with all their baggage, with all their *private property,* of which they had plundered the wretched people whose country they had been ravaging; and that they should even furnish the means of conveying these marauders to their own country - to the very spot which of all others they would wish to reach - in order that they might again be immediately employed against ourselves or our allies, is indeed passing strange. It appears as though we had been granting a boon to Buonaparte, of the most invaluable description.

Nor does the acceptance of the Russian fleet, as a mere temporary deposit, to be restored *unconditionally*, at the period of peace, seem less astonishing. That all its officers and seamen should be conveyed to their own shores, giving them an immediate opportunity of acting against our own gallant ally, the King of Sweden, is an act unprecedented in history.

This is, at present, a delicate subject to speak upon; but it must be admitted, that an official letter to government, more palpably deficient in information than that of Sir Hew Dalrymple, the British commander-in-chief, never appeared. . . .

The terms of the armistice, or *provisional* convention, on which the *definitive* one was founded, and which, by some, is charged entirely upon Sir Arthur Wellesley, appear even more infamous and more disgraceful than those which were ultimately agreed upon. According to those, the Russian fleet would have totally escaped; as, had it not been for the objection of Sir Charles Cotton, who seems entitled to some credit for his conduct, the following article, which a plea of idiocy could scarcely excuse, would have been carried into effect:

"The neutrality of the port of Lisbon shall be recognized for the Russian fleet – that is to say, that when the English army or fleet shall be in possession of the city and port, the said Russian *fleet shall not be disturbed during its stay, nor stopped when it wishes to sail, nor pursued when it shall sail, until after the time fixed by the maritime law.*" . . .

We much doubt whether our military commanders will be able to justify their conduct to the satisfaction of government, or of the public. Orders are believed to have been sent out for the recall of Sir Hew Dalrymple, and the country is loud in its demands for a full and impartial investigation of the subject.

Amongst the Portuguese, the convention is understood to have excited even a more abhorrent dissatisfaction than it has in this country. Two gentlemen, from the provisional government of Portugal, reached London on the 24th of September, having left Oporto on the 11th. Together with other despatches, they were charged with a solemn protest against the leading terms of the convention. They are also said to have laid some very serious complaints before our government, through the medium of the Portuguese ambassador, respecting the conduct of the British military commanders, as well previously as subsequently to the battle of Vimeiro. These we at present refrain from stating. . . .

Hood Attacks Russian Fleet in the Baltic

Sir Samuel Hood, as will be seen by our "*Letters on Service*," has acquired fresh laurels by an attack upon the Russian fleet in the Baltic. The enemy, after losing one of their line-of-battle ships, took shelter in Port Baltic; where, when the last accounts came away, they were closely blockaded. They had fortified both sides of the harbour, but appeared in great confusion, having struck their yards and top-masts, and moored so close to the shore, that it was thought a strong north-west wind would strand them. According to report, the Russian admiral had proposed to dismantle his fleet, till a peace should take place; an offer which was rejected by the British commander.

Collingwood Understood to Return off Toulon

It is Lord Collingwood's intention, when he leaves Cadiz, to resume the command of the squadron off Toulon, and to take all the line-of-battle ships with him into the Mediterranean: three frigates only to be left off the former port. The despatches sent to his lordship in the *Pickle* were not lost, though they went down in her: the admiral found out a Maltese diver, who after three days' exertion found them. The *Caesar*, 80, Rear-Admiral Sir R. Strachan; *Eagle*, 74 Captain Rowley; *Formidable*, 98, Captain Fayerman; *Standard*, 64 Captain T. Harvey; (besides the *Repulse, Queen*, and *Windsor Castle*), and the *Lavinia* frigate, are coming home.

French Commerce Restrictions Relaxed

Buonaparte's anti-commercial decrees have undergone some relaxation; and the following goods are now permitted to be exported from Holland: - butter, geese, Geneva, earthenware, rushes, flower roots, files and pans, hoops, dried hides, cambrics, leather, plants, paper, pipes, Sach. Saturni, ground bark, bricks, starch, tobacco, tarras, flax, fruits; clover, garden and flower seeds, madders, &c.

Ships of the Line to be Layed Up

We understand that government purpose to pay off immediately nineteen or twenty sail of the line, and to transfer the crews to smaller vessels of war, which are to be sent to the Baltic and other quarters, where they are most wanted. It is no longer deemed necessary to keep up large fleets, since the enemy is no where in sufficient force to meet them. . .

Another Female Sailor
From 'Naval Anecdotes.' [XX 293]

A young woman, who called herself Rebecca Ann Johnson, was lately brought before

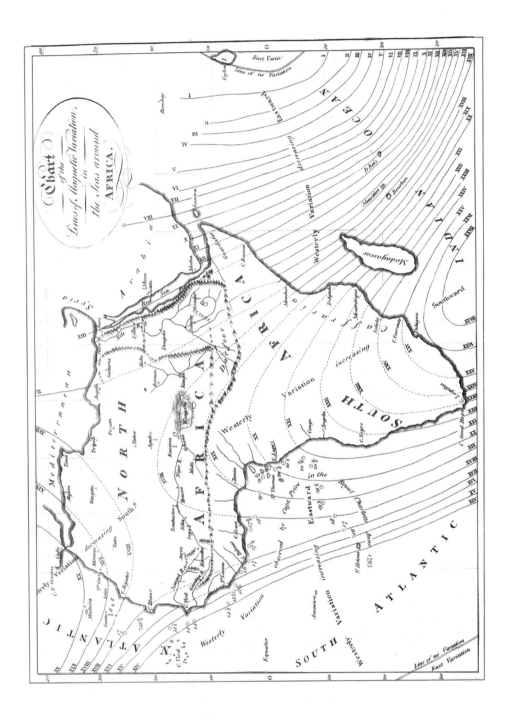

the lord mayor, dressed in sailor's clothes, she having been found in the streets the night before in a distressed and weak condition. She admitted that she was a female, and had been apprenticed by her father-in-law, at Whitby, to a ship in the coal trade, called the *May Flower*, John Read, master; that she had served four years out of the seven without her sex having been discovered; that she was bound when she was thirteen; that her father-in-law had likewise bound her mother to the sea, who was killed at the late bombardment of Copenhagen. A Mrs. Lesley, who keeps the Bull public house, in Half Moon Alley, Bishopsgate-street, stated, that she was found near her house in a very exhausted state: she confessed that she had run away from the ship she was apprenticed to, and had not eaten or drunk any thing the whole day; that some humane men took compassion upon her, thinking she was a poor sailor boy, and brought her to their house, where they gave her some nourishment. From her weak state, they suspected her sex, which she acknowledged, and said that her ship was at Woolwich, and that the mate of the ship had chastised her for not getting up. The lord mayor ordered her to be provided with female attire, and to be taken care of, till she could be sent to her parish.

From the 'Naval History of the Present Year,' 1808
September-October. XX 323-326

Knighthood for Keats

We sincerely congratulate both the naval profession, and the country at large, on the merited honour which Admiral, now Sir Richard Goodwin Keates [Keats], has received from his sovereign, in being created one of the knights companions of the most honourable Order of the Bath. Should the war continue, we hope one day to see this great officer with his flag hoisted in the Mediterranean - a station that more particularly than any other requires great professional and political talents.

Hallowell Sails to Mediterranean

Captain B. Hallowell, one of the select band who followed Nelson to the Nile, and who particularly distinguished himself in that overthrow of republican pride and ambition, has sailed for the Mediterranean in the *Tigre*. . . .

Messengers from France and Russia

The arrival of French and Russian messengers just as this part of the Chronicle was going to press, occasioned various conjectures. A cabinet council was held, October 25, which was attended by all the ministers in town. . . .

Hemp

The Transport Board continues to engage large coppered ships for long voyages. Many

Chart of the Lines of Magnetic Variation in the Seas Around Africa. (Copied by permission from Major Rennell's Appendix to Mr. Park's *Travels*.)
   A great part of Mr. Park's geographical memorandums are totally lost; but fortunately his bearing by compass during a great part of the way, are preserved. In other parts he has preserved only the calculation of latitude and longitude, arising from them; which, however, of course furnish the means of obtaining the bearings, if necessary. Plate 18

of those vessels are to proceed to India for the purpose of bringing home hemp, the directors of the East India Company having engaged to furnish government with *twenty thousand tons of hemp* annually for the next three years, the whole of which is to be brought home in ships especially fitted and prepared for the purpose, so as to prevent the articles from imbibing an improper heat on their voyage to England.

The culture of hemp is rapidly extending in Canada; and there is much reason to hope, that in a few years we shall, through this medium, be rendered independent of the foreign markets.

Sir Sidney Smith's Honours
From 'Naval Anecdotes.' XX 438-439

At Brazil, on the 14th of June, 1808, Sir Sidney Smith gave an entertainment to the whole Portuguese royal family and court, on board his majesty's ship *London*. On quitting the ship, the Prince Regent presented to the rear-admiral, with his own hands, the standard of Portugal, to be borne as an augmentation to his coat of arms, and declared the revival of the Order of the Sword, instituted by Don Alfonso V. surnamed the African, in 1459, of which order Sir Sidney Smith is to be created grand cross. All the English captains before the Tagus, under his command on the 29th of November, [were] to be commanders, and the first lieutenant of each ship, knights of the same; also Mr. F. Hill, his majesty's secretary of legation to that court. His royal highness conferred medals on the four captains composing the squadron detached by Sir Sidney Smith to accompany the Portuguese fleet to Brazil.

Sanguinary Engagement of Amethyst with La Thetis
From the 'Memoir of the Public Services of Captain Michael Seymour.'
XXI 94-95; see also XX 418

The *Amethyst* had been cruising off l'Orient fourteen weeks: during this time violent gales of wind had prevailed, and consequently added to the perils of a coast at all times, we believe, sufficiently dangerous.

On the night of the 10th of November, 1808, we find the *Amethyst*, however, in the watchful perseverance of her duty, standing so close in to the north-west point of Groa, that it became impossible for an enemy to escape; the proof of which has been fully exemplified, by the ineffectual endeavours of the French frigate. The night was unusually dark, not a star to be seen, and every thing indeed favoured the attempt. About seven the flash and report of cannon were distinctly seen and heard from a battery on the French coast, in a direction contiguous to the alarm and signal post. The conjecture of the moment supposed it in consequence of the near approach of the *Amethyst*; but it was in reality directed against their own frigate, of the sailing of which they were ignorant. About half-past seven a sail was descried just ahead: it was supposed a small armed vessel, or something still more contemptible, and the deception of night favoured the supposition. A musket was ordered to be fired: no notice was taken: she grew larger. The *Amethyst* still continued under an easy press of sail. A gun was now fired, and the crackling noise of this shot was heard as it passed through the cabin windows. This by the enemy was instantly returned, and the veil of darkness which had hitherto obscured her was now removed, by the lights flying in every part of her; every inch of canvas was

View of the Harbour of Rio de Janeiro. Engraved by Bennet, from a drawing by Pocock.

The entrance to this harbour, which is a very good one, is not wide; but the sea breeze, which blows every day from ten or twelve o'clock till sun-set, makes it easy for any ship to go in before the wind; and it becomes wider on approaching the town, abreast of which there is room for the largest fleet, in five or six fathoms water, with an oozy bottom. At the narrow part, the entrance is defended by two forts. [Plate 259]

set; her boat cut from her stern, and a ship of war appeared anxious for escape though capable of resistance. The *Amethyst* immediately spread more canvas, but allowed her to gain a little, lest her apprehensions might induce her to run on that shore which was then so near them. About nine, however, those apprehensions were at an end, and the *Amethyst* closed fast. Her adversary, now finding all hopes of escape at an end, made her best dispositions to receive the *Amethyst*, and before ten o'clock the action commenced, which continued, with very little intermission, until about twenty minutes after twelve. The French ship fell on board the *Amethyst* a little after ten. She extricated herself from that situation; but, at a quarter past eleven, she intentionally laid the *Amethyst* on board; and from that time, until the moment of her surrender, which was about an hour, the contending ships were locked together, the fluke of the *Amethyst*'s best bower anchor having entered the foremost main-deck port of *la Thetis*. After great slaughter, *la Thetis* was boarded and taken possession of, and some prisoners were received from her, before the ships were disengaged. The *Triumph*, commanded by Sir Thomas Hardy, shortly afterwards came up; and, subsequently, the *Shannon*, which took *la Thetis* in tow.

In this long and sharply contested action, the rigging of the *Amethyst* was much cut; and 19 of her crew were killed, and 51 wounded. The loss of the *Thetis*, however,

The annexed plate, engraved by Bailey, from a drawing by Mr. Pocock, represents
H.M.S. *Thunderer*, of 74 guns, Captain Badford, in a Storm, off Crookhaven, in the
night of December 10, 1808.[5] After being nearly wrecked, off the Mizen Head, she,
by the superior skill and pilotage of the master (Mr. A. Barclay), ran through a
narrow pass, and anchored safe in Bantry Bay. Plate 360

was still more shocking to humanity; as, exclusive of her captain, she had 172 men
killed, and 102 wounded; amongst whom were all her officers, excepting three.

When the great disparity of force between the *Amethyst* and *Thetis* is considered,
the conquest achieved is marked by particular brilliancy. The *Amethyst* mounted only
36 guns, the *Thetis* 44; consequently, from her larger size, her metal was of superior
weight; her crew, consisting of 360 men, besides 106 soldiers, had served for years
together; added to this, Mons. Pinsun, entrusted with the command of *la Thetis*, was a
man of approved courage, much beloved by his men, and deserving in every respect the
commendation of an excellent officer . . .

[At a meeting of the common council of the city of Limerick, held on 13 February
1809, the following resolution was unanimously agreed to:

'That the freedom of the city be presented to Captain Michael Seymour, of his
majesty's ship *Amethyst*, in a heart of oak box, ornamented with gold, accompanied
with the following address . . .' (Vol. XXI, p157). The official French account was
published in Vol. XXII, pp93-94.]

5 N.C. XXIII 398.

1808 – Convention of Cintra

THE CONVENTION OF CINTRA, negotiated by the newly-arrived British commander-in-chief, General Sir Hew Dalrymple, a few days after Wellesley's victory at Vimeiro, was a national disgrace. Portugal was liberated without further loss of blood, and the blockade of Lisbon could be brought to an end, with the Russian squadron being interned at Spithead, but the provision that the French would be transported to France in British ships, with all their booty, and then be free to re-cross the Spanish frontier and enter a war in which the odds were in any case on the side of the French, was unacceptable. The French in Portugal were in such desperate straits that, had the convention not been signed, they would inevitably have been forced to surrender without any concession of substance. Admiral Sir Charles Cotton refused to co-sign the convention until it was made clear that any French contributions demanded of the Portuguese should be cancelled, and that all French ships of war became prizes. *The Naval Chronicle* was indignant that the Russians should be accorded the status of internees, considering the Russian declaration of war, but the government was happy with an arrangement which might facilitate a rapid termination of the state of hostilities.

Admiral Cotton's Demands
From the 'Naval Biography of the Late Sir Charles Cotton, Bart.'
XXVII 382-386

[In 1812 *The Naval Chronicle* wrote:] The arrival of the army, the battles which were fought, the change of commanders, and the convention of Cintra that followed, are circumstances which have been too often before the public. It should be known, however, that, bad as that convention was; mortifying and degrading as it was to the feelings of Britons; it received considerable and important amendments from Sir Charles Cotton, who thrice returned it to its projectors unexecuted, and whose opinion thereof is forcibly expressed, in the following correspondence with Sir Hew Dalrymple upon the occasion:

Hibernia, off Cascaes, August 25, 1808
Sir, The French having evacuated St. Ubes, of which I am informed this morning, and

173

of the Portuguese army expected there every hour, amounting certainly to 4,000 or 5,000 men, makes me suggest the propriety of detaching one half or more of the troops now at Maceira, under the command of Lieutenant-General Sir John Moore, to be landed at St. Ubes, or near it, that, with the assistance of the loyal Portuguese, possession might certainly be taken of the left bank of the Tagus, and effectually prevent the retreat of the French army to Elvas. I suggest this on the presumption that the preliminary articles I read yesterday can never be acceded to, so as to form a definitive treaty so much in favour of the French army, twice beaten, and 30,000 British troops in Portugal. Without great alteration of those articles, I can never accede to such a treaty.

I have the honour to be, &c.

C. COTTON

Lieutenant-General Sir Hew Dalrymple, &c.

Hibernia, off the Tagus, August 27, 1808
Sir, I enclose for your inspection and approbation, articles that I should conceive might be consented to on the part of the enemy, and would modify them, that I could in some measure be justified in acceding to. I am told, from correspondents in Lisbon, that the French expected nothing less than unconditional surrender, and to return as prisoners of war to France. The Portuguese and some Spaniards are in possession of St. Ubes, where I should have sent the 32d regiment yesterday, had not the wind come round to the southward, and the knowledge I received that the cessation of hostilities was extended to four days from the 26th. The enemy had taken almost all the troops from the different forts along the bay, and sent them over to Palmella, a height between Lisbon and St. Ubes, apprehensive of an attack from the army now at St. Ubes; the weather, looking threatening, has forced me to weigh with the fleet: but I shall again return to my anchorage the moment I can with safety, and endeavour at all events to preserve communication with the shore.

I am, &c.

C. COTTON

Lieutenant-General Sir Hew Dalrymple, &c.

Enclosure
Article 12th. The forts of St. Julien and the Bugio, as well as those to the right of St. Julien, are to be given up and garrisoned by British troops at the ratification of the present treaty.

To be added to Article 16th. "All arrears of contributions, requisitions, or of any claims whatever made by the French government upon the kingdom of Portugal, or any individual residing therein, which remain unpaid at the signing of the treaty, are considered as cancelled."

Article 17th. Insert after "property movable and immovable," "shipping excepted;" again, after "in either case their property," insert "with the above exception."

In addition to the 17th Article, besides the foregoing, the following is to be added:

"No property belonging to any Portuguese, or the subjects of any power in alliance with Portugal, at the time of the entry of the French army into that kingdom, that has been confiscated on account of political opinions, or under any other pretext, shall be removed, but restored to the proper owners. It is also to be clearly understood, that the stipulations in favour of persons carrying away their private property, is not to be made the ground work of any commercial speculations."

In addition to the 19th Article, "The arms, artillery, baggage, and all other property whatsoever belonging to the Spanish troops in Portugal, to be delivered up to them."

Article 5th of additional Articles, to be struck out altogether.

Additional article. - "The French ships of war, and all other vessels, to be delivered over with all their stores, sails, and equipments, subject only to such arrangements, respecting such ships of war and merchant vessels as shall be subsequently agreed upon and concluded on the part of his Britannic Majesty, and that of his Royal Highness the Prince Regent of Portugal."

C. COTTON

Lieutenant-General Sir Hew Dalrymple, &c.

Extract of a Letter from Admiral Sir Charles Cotton to Sir Hew Dalrymple
Hibernia, off the Tagus, 28th August, 1808
My letter to you of the 27th, will have informed you of my knowledge of the further suspension of hostilities, and of my sentiments respecting the treaty about to be entered into with the French Commander-in-chief, for the evacuation of Portugal. Brigadier-General Beresford, also, if enabled to land, will have explained to you my reasons for not acceding to the treaty as it now stands. I have no instructions from government on the subject, but if there has been any confidential communication to yourself, or any of the general officers lately arrived from England of the wishes of his Majesty's Government to dislodge the enemy from Portugal, by treaty, or any concessions in their favour it may be thought proper to make, I cannot but conform and sacrifice my opinion to those instructions. Fully expecting a conference at Cascaes, as proposed, I did not enter with Lieutenant-Colonel Murray so fully into the objections as they occurred to me on the articles of the basis on which the treaty was to be made. The conveyance of the plunder to France, which may be greatly covered by the unqualified allowance to respect all nominal private property, both French and of those natives who choose to leave their country with them, may have the worst consequences both to us and those loyal Portuguese whom we are come to assist; to us, as the means of adding some millions perhaps to Buonaparte's treasury, at a time when all his former resources from Spain are cut off; and a perpetual source of discord with the Portuguese, for suffering their property to be carried away.

The responsibility thus incurred, of refusing to ratify what had already received the signature of the commanding, and other generals, whose local and particular knowledge of the situation of the opposing armies, and of the state of the country, must be presumed to have been much more accurate than that of the naval Commander-in-chief, was very great. We have been informed, however, upon unquestionable authority, that, when the intelligence of Sir Charles Cotton's refusal to ratify the convention, as first proposed, reached the vicinity of Vimeiro, it excited the admiration of the whole army; and it was the known advice, and opinion of the hero, who had then recently commanded that army, that the pending negotiation for a convention, should, in consequence of the Admiral's refusal, be broken off, and hostilities recommenced. What national disappointment, and subsequent discontent, would not such a measure have prevented! The bare act of refusal, however, ought to exonerate the lamented subject of this memoir from all participation of the odium which attached to that instrument, "of some of the articles of which, his Majesty felt himself obliged formally to declare his disapprobation." [*Vide* His Majesty's Speech, at the Opening of Parliament, on 19 January 1809; below p179-181.]

In former times, and under more fortunate circumstances, the responsibility which the Admiral took upon himself, would have met with unqualified applause. The British army had not attained, at the period immediately referred to, the distinguished glory, and splendid pitch of prowess, which, under its matchless leader, it has since enjoyed. The chief projector and bearer of the convention to the British Admiral, thought, perhaps, that, to inform his countrymen of a bloody battle, was sufficient; and that its particulars and consequences, were points on which no enquiry would be hazarded. Happily, however, this is no longer the case; for Britons can now look forward with as much hope, confidence, and pleasure, to the details of siege, or to the meeting of hostile armies in the field, as they have long been accustomed to do, to the attack of a maritime fort, or to the conflict of opposing fleets upon the ocean. Under the blessing of heaven, the army, as well as the navy, has, upon every recent occasion, contributed to gratify the most prodigal desires for national fame; and the glorious achievements of both, individually or collectively, separately or conjunctively, will remain imperishable memorials thereof, as long as deeds of heroic valour can charm, and acts of dauntless intrepidity animate, the grateful hearts of Britons!

Of the convention for the surrender of the Russian ships, much has been said, and much might be added, respecting the relative situation of Great Britain and Russia, at the time of its negotiation. In this place, however, we shall content ourselves with observing, that the conduct of Sir Charles Cotton, upon that subject, was swayed by political circumstances, of which the public were altogether ignorant.

The object of the British naval expedition having been closed, Sir Charles left the Tagus on the 20th of December 1808, and returned to England in the *Hibernia*.

Dalrymple's Dispatches
From the 'Naval History of the Present Year,' 1808, August-September.
XX 239-256

Letters on Service, Downing Street, September 16, 1808

A despatch, of which the following is a copy, was received yesterday evening from Lieutenant-general Sir Hew Dalrymple, commanding his majesty's troops in Portugal, addressed to Lord Viscount Castlereagh, one of his majesty's principal secretaries of state, and brought by Captain Dalrymple, military secretary to Sir Hew Dalrymple.

Head-quarters, Cintra, September 3, 1808
My Lord, I have the honour to inform your lordship that I landed in Portugal, and took the command of the army on Monday the 22d of August, the next day after the battle of Vimeiro, and where the enemy sustained a signal defeat, where the valour and discipline of British troops, and the talents of British officers were eminently displayed.

A few hours after my arrival, General Kellermann came in with a flag of truce from the French general-in-chief, in order to propose an agreement for a cessation of hostilities, for the purpose of concluding a convention for the evacuation of Portugal by the French troops. The enclosed contains the several articles at first agreed upon and signed by Sir Arthur Wellesley and General Kellermann; but as this was done with a reference to the British admiral, who, when the agreement was communicated to him, objected to the 7th article, which had for its object the disposal of the Russian fleet in the Tagus, it was finally concluded that Lieutenant-colonel Murray, quarter-master-general to the British army, and General Kellermann should proceed to the discussion of the remaining articles, and finally to conclude a convention for the evacuation of Portugal, subject to the ratification of the French general-in-chief, and the British commanders by sea and land.

After considerable discussion and repeated reference to me, which rendered it necessary for me to avail myself of the limited period latterly prescribed for the suspension of hostilities, in order to move the army forwards, and to place the several columns upon the routes by which they were to advance, the convention was signed, and the ratification exchanged the 30th of last month.

That no time might be lost in obtaining anchorage for the transports and other shipping, which had for some days been exposed to great peril on this dangerous coast, and to ensure the communication between the army and the victuallers, which was cut off by the badness of the weather, and the surf upon the shore, I sent orders to the Buffs and 42d regiments, which were on board transports with Sir Charles Cotton's fleet, to land and take possession of the forts on the Tagus, whenever the admiral thought it proper to do so. This was accordingly carried into execution yesterday morning, when the forts of Cascais, St. Julien, and Bugio were evacuated by the French troops, and taken possession of by ours.

As I landed in Portugal entirely unacquainted with the actual state of the French army, and many circumstances of a local and incidental nature, which, doubtless, had great weight in deciding the question; my own opinion in favour of the expediency of expelling the French army from Portugal, by means of the convention the late defeat had induced the French general-in-chief to solicit, instead of doing so by a continuation of hostilities, was principally founded on the great importance of time, which the season of the year rendered peculiarly valuable, and which the enemy could easily have consumed in the protracted defence of the strong places they occupied, had terms of convention been refused them.

When the suspension of arms was agreed upon, the army under the command of Sir John Moore had not arrived, and doubts were even entertained whether so large a body of men could be landed on an open and a dangerous beach, and that being effected, whether the supply of so large an army with provisions from the ships could be provided for, under all the disadvantages to which the shipping were exposed. During the negotiation, the former difficulty was overcome by the activity, zeal, and intelligence of Captain Malcolm of the *Donegal*, and the officers and men under his orders, but the possibility of the latter seems to have been at an end, nearly at the moment when it was no longer necessary.

Captain Dalrymple of the 18th dragoons, my military secretary, will have the honour of delivering to your lordship this despatch. He is fully informed of whatever has been done under my orders, relative to the service on which I have been employed, and can give any explanation thereupon that may be required.

Admiralty-Office, September 16, 1808

Captain Halstead, first captain to the squadron under the command of Admiral Sir Charles Cotton, Bart. commander-in-chief of his majesty's ships and vessels on the coast of Portugal, arrived yesterday at this office, with despatches from the admiral to the Honourable William Wellesley Pole, of which the following are copies:

Hibernia, off the Tagus, September 3, 1808
Sir, Enclosed herewith, for the information of the Lords Commissioners of the
Admiralty, is a copy of a convention, entered into by Lieutenant-colonel Murray and
General Kellermann, for the evacuation of Portugal by the French army; such a
convention having been ratified by Lieutenant-general Sir Hew Dalrymple, myself,
and the French commander-in-chief. British troops, consisting of the 3d and 42d
regiments, were, on the 2d instant, landed to occupy the forts of Cascais, Saint Antonio,
Saint Julien, and the Bugio, and no time shall be lost to embark the French troops,
agreeably to the said convention. . . .
     I have the honour to be, &c.

C. COTTON

Hon. W.W. Pole, &c.

Hibernia, off the Tagus, 4th September 1808
Sir, Herewith I have the honour to enclose to you, for the information of the Lords
Commissioners of the Admiralty, a copy of a convention¹ entered into by me with Vice-
admiral Seniavin, commanding the Russian fleet in the Tagus, by which it will appear
to their lordships that such fleet has been surrendered to me, to be held by his majesty
as a deposit, until six months after the conclusion of a peace between Russian and
England.
     I have charged Captain Halstead, first captain of the *Hibernia*, and captain of the
fleet, with the delivery of this despatch to their lordships; he was sent by me to negotiate
the convention with Vice-admiral Seniavin, and will be able to explain every particular.
     To Captain Halstead I feel greatly indebted for his able advice and assistance upon
all points of service; his zeal and diligence have been exemplary, and entitle him to my
highest commendation.
     Rear-admiral Tyler has been directed to superintend the first division of the Russian
fleet, which I purpose sending under his protection immediately to Spithead; to him
(since with me) I have been indebted for every assistance, and to the captains, officers
and crews of those ships that have been employed throughout a tediously protracted
blockade (by whom every exertion has been made with a degree of cheerfulness doing
them infinite honour). I feel extremely grateful, and deem it my duty to offer every
possible testimony of my approbation in their favour.
     I have the honour to be, &c.

C. COTTON

Hon. W.W. Pole, &c.

List of the Ships referred to in the foregoing Convention

Twerday, Vice-admiral Seniavin,
               Captain du 1er rang Malayoff, of 74 guns, and 736 men.
Skoroy, Captain du 1er rang Schelling, of 60 guns, and 524 men.
Ste. Helene, Captain du 2nd rang Bitchenskoy, of 74 guns, and 598 men.
S.Cafael, Captain du 2nd rang Rushnoff, of 74 guns, and 610 men.
Ratvizau, Captain du 2nd rang Rtishchoff, of 66 guns, and 549 men.
Silnoy, Captain-lieutenant Malygruin, of 74 guns, and 604 men.

---

1 A copy of the convention enclosed in the letter from Sir Hew Dalrymple.

Motchnoy, Captain-lieutenant Rasvosoff, of 74 guns, and 629 men.
Rafael, Captain-lieutenant Dournoff, of 26 guns, and 222 men.
Fregatte *Kildnyn*, Captain-lieutenant Dournoff, of 26 guns, and 222 men.
Yarrowslavl, Captain du 2nd rang Milkoff, of 74 guns, and 567 men.
   Total- 5635 men.

(Signed) MALIVJEFF, le Capitaine de Pavilion

Why Admiral Cotton Agreed to Intern the Russians
State Papers, 'Papers Relative to the Russian Fleet.' XXI 239-240

No. 15 is the following letter from Sir C. Cotton to Mr. Pole, with additional proposals made by the Russian admiral:

Hibernia, in the Tagus, 7th September, 1808
... I beg leave further to observe to their Lordships, in addition to my before-mentioned letter, that upon the whole, the Russian squadron having entered the Tagus previous to the departure of the Prince Regent of Portugal; having committed no act of hostility against Portugal, or joined the French in opposing us, as they were repeatedly requested to do; and having their Lordships' instructions for my conduct towards them upon a former occasion (the supposed famine in Portugal) I feel satisfied their Lordships will approve of the favourable terms that have been granted.

City Petitions for an Inquiry into the Convention
From the 'Naval History of the Present Year,' 1808, September-October.
XX 323-324

The convention of Cintra has astonished, and still continues to perplex every one, as much as the appointment of Sir Hew Dalrymple to the chief command astonished himself, when he first received it at the Government House, Gibraltar. The City has exercised its high privilege of petitioning the king to direct an inquiry to be made into an event which appears to throw such disgrace on our arms and character. The papers in the interest of government have deprecated this conduct in the metropolis; and, in the mean time, the arrival of Sir Arthur Wellesley and of Sir Hew keeps the public mind on the tip-toe of expectation. ...

The Speech from the Throne, and Earl St Vincent's Protest at the Convention of Cintra

Imperial Parliament XXI 66-71

House of Lords, Thursday 19 January 1809

The session of Parliament was opened this day by commission: the Commissioners were, the Archbishop of Canterbury, the Lord Chancellor, the Earl of Camden (president of the council), and the Duke of Montrose (master of the horse).
   The ususal forms having been gone through, the Lord Chancellor read the following speech:

My Lords and Gentlemen

We have it in command, from his majesty to state to you, that his majesty has called you together, in perfect confidence that you are prepared cordially to support his majesty in the prosecution of a war which there is no hope of terminating safely and honourably, except through vigorous and persevering exertion.

We are to acquaint you, that his majesty has directed to be laid before you copies of the proposals for opening a negotiation, which were transmitted to his majesty from Erfurth, and of the correspondence which took place with the governments of Russia and of France; together with the declaration issued by his majesty's command on the termination of that correspondence.

His majesty is persuaded, that you will participate in the feelings which were expressed by his majesty, when it was required that his majesty should consent to commence the negotiation by abandoning the cause of Spain, which he had so recently and solemnly espoused.

We are commanded to inform you, that his majesty continues to receive from the Spanish government the strongest assurances of their determined perseverance in the cause of the legitimate monarchy, and of the national independence of Spain: and to assure you, that so long as the people of Spain shall remain true to themselves, his majesty will continue to them his most strenuous assistance and support.

His majesty has renewed to the Spanish nation, in the moment of its difficulties and reverses, the engagements which he voluntarily contracted at the outset of its struggle against the usurpation and tyranny of France; and we are commanded to acquaint you, that these engagements have been reduced into the form of a treaty of alliance; which treaty, so soon as the ratification shall have been exchanged, his majesty will cause to be laid before you.

His majesty commands us to state to you, that while his majesty contemplated with the liveliest satisfaction, the achievements of his forces in the commencement of the campaign in Portugal, and the deliverance of the kingdom of his ally from the presence and oppressions of the French army, his majesty most deeply regretted the termination of that campaign by an armistice and convention, of some of the articles of which his majesty has felt himself obliged formally to declare his disapprobation.

We are to express to you his majesty's reliance on your disposition to enable his majesty to continue the aid afforded by his majesty to the King of Sweden. That monarch derives a peculiar claim to his majesty's support, in the present exigency of his affairs, from having concurred with his majesty in the propriety of rejecting any proposal for negotiation to which the government of Spain was not to be admitted as a party. . . . [etc.]

The Earl of *Bridgewater* moved an address of thanks to his majesty; which was seconded by Lord *Sheffield*; after which Earl *St. Vincent* observed, that he could not suffer the question to be put on the address, without claiming their lordships' attention for a few moments. Though he could not concur in every part of it, yet it was not his intention to propose any amendment. His principal motive for rising was, to express his unqualified disapprobation of the whole of the conduct of ministers; of every thing they had done with respect to Spain, of every thing they had done with respect to Portugal, of almost every thing they had done since they came into power, and particularly for the last six months. The noble lord who seconded the address had talked of the vigour and efficacy of their measures. Vigour and efficacy indeed! when their whole conduct was marked by vacillation and incompetence. If such men, so notoriously incapable, were not immediately removed, the country was undone.

There was one part, however, of the address and of the speech in which he cordially agreed - that which condemned the armistice and convention [of Cintra]. It was the greatest disgrace that had befallen the British arms, the greatest stain that had been affixed to the honour of the country since the Revolution. He was not at present disposed to enter into an examination of the manner in which the naval part of that expedition had been conducted: opportunity would arise for discussing the extraordinary arrangement that had been made respecting the fleet in the Tagus. He would not withhold from ministers whatever praise might be due to them. He would give them credit for providing plenty of transports; but what was the merit of these exertions? Any one who offered a little more than the common market price might hire as many as he pleased; but ministers not only offered that market price, but a great deal more than they should have done. And how were these employed? Why, in conveying Junot and his runaway ruffians, with their plunder and exactions, all the plate and precious stones, and rare exhibitions of art, the fruits of their robberies of churches, palaces, and private houses, to France. . . . [etc. etc.]

If the House would do their duty, they would go in that dignified manner that became them to the foot of the throne, and implore his majesty to remove from his councils those men whose measures would bring inevitable ruin on the country. . . .

On the Responsibility for Cintra
From 'Correspondence.' XXI 209-211

Letter to the Editor from "E.G.F.", March 3, 1809
Mr. Editor, having in a former letter stated to you the opinions I had seen and heard respecting the conduct of our late naval commander-in-chief in Portugal, I should be wanting in justice if I did not acknowledge, that in the course of the late debate in Parliament, there appeared some exculpations which were not before in the possession of the public. It appears that he was not the original inventor of the abominable naval convention, but only retains the demerit of having applied it to practice, when the victory of *Vimeiro*, and other circumstances, had totally changed the relative situations of the parties. This appears to me a very great and important *error in judgment.* Now it is not long since, Mr. Editor, that Sir Robert Calder beat an enemy superior in force to the fleet under his command, and captured two sail of the line. The hopes and expectations of the nation, however, raised as they had been to a high pitch from the recollection of former splendid naval victories, were disappointed; a LEGAL trial quickly ensued, and the victorious admiral was *severely reprimanded for an error in judgment,* in not having made a proper use of his victory: and although I am of opinion that a different conduct was due to an old, faithful, and meritorious officer, he has not since had an opportunity afforded him of correcting the error that he was censured for committing. Now the admiral in his defence gave some very cogent reasons, which might well have influenced him in the conduct he pursued;[2] but what could have

---

2 The more frequently I peruse the trial of this meritorious officer, the less am I enabled to discover how the sentence given could have been produced from the evidence which appears in the minutes. Surely Sir R. C. has had hard measures dealt to him. - *Vide* Nav. Chron. Vol. XVII p. 99, et seq. [Reprinted in Volume III.]

influenced Sir H. Burrard to refuse to follow up the victory gained by Sir A. Wellesley, even when urged to do so by the victorious general, whose valour and abilities he had witnessed? In a late debate in the lower house of Parliament, it was said (according to the newspapers) by one of his majesty's present ministers, that there was no specific charge against either of the generals, and that the *opinion* that had been asked of certain officers ought to satisfy the nation. These said ministers may have some reasons not to bring forward a charge, but after a diligent perusal of the proceedings of the board of inquiry, I feel, and the country sorely feels, that there lies a very heavy and serious charge against Sir Harry, in not following up the victory, and in consequence being the great, if not sole cause, of the subsequent conventions, of our ships bearing their disgraceful burdens to the ports of France, and of Junot being so soon at the head of a division of the French troops in Spain. Where does a shadow of blame attach to Sir R. Calder, without the heaviest clouds of error hanging over Sir H. Burrard? . . .

1808 – Co-operation with the Swedish Navy

IN MAY 1808 VICE-ADMIRAL DE SAUMAREZ escorted to Gothenburg the British Army under Sir John Moore, which had been brought back from Sicily at the end of 1807 to meet the crisis in Portugal, and then redeployed. In June it was re-embarked for more urgent duty in Spain, but at the end of July and early August the remaining British forces in the Baltic, concentrated in the southern Danish islands, were active in extricating and repatriating part of the Spanish Army under the Marquis de la Romana, which had been serving with the French. On 25 August Rear-Admiral Sir Samuel Hood, with two British ships of the line and a Swedish squadron, attacked a Russian fleet and destroyed one of its number.

Evacuation of the Spanish Troops in Denmark

From 'Letters on Service,' Admiralty Office,
August 16 1808. ^{XX 154}

Copy of a Letter from Vice-Admiral Lord Collingwood, Commander-in-Chief of his Majesty's Ships and Vessels in the Mediterranean, to the Honourable W.W. Pole, dated on board the Ocean, off Cadiz, July 25, 1808
Sir, I have the pleasure to acquaint you, for the information of the Lords Commissioners of the Admiralty, that the French troops under General Dupont, consisting of about eight thousand men, surrendered themselves prisoners of war, on the 20th instant, having lost about three thousand killed in some partial actions which took place on that and the three preceding days.

General Wedel, with about six thousand, who had arrived to reinforce Dupont, has capitulated, on conditions of his corps being embarked and sent to Rochefort. . . .

London 'Gazette Extraordinary,' Admiralty-Office,
August 23, 1808. ^{XX 159-164}

Despatches, of which the following are copies, have been this day received at this Office from Rear-Admiral Keats. . .

To the Officers of his most Catholic Majesty's Troops
Superb, off Langeland, August 5, 1808

Sirs, I have the honour to inform you, that I have received from my government the most positive instructions to endeavour to communicate with the Spanish officers commanding the troops of that nation in the vicinity of my command, and to concert with them measures to secure their retreat, from any place of embarkation which they may possess, and for placing them in a state of security, until transports for their reception can be provided to convey them to Spain, for which, as well as the necessary provisions, measures have already been taken, and indeed of the arrival of them I am in hourly expectation. Until that period shall arrive, they are welcome to share in the accommodation and provisions of the ships under my command; but as that might not afford ample means at present, although I am in expectation of the commander-in-chief, I would suggest, under the pressure of circumstances, the removal of the troops to some of the islands in the Belt, for their perfect security. But as a measure of this magnitude to the interests of the Spanish nation would necessarily require a concerted plan, lest by attention to partial interests the general one might suffer, I request an unreserved and confidential communication, either to the ships off Nyborg, that stationed off Langeland, or any of his Britannic majesty's ships in the Belt; and through the bearer of this, or by any other means, I propose sending on Sunday, unless I should earlier receive some person on board, a flag of truce under some pretext to the Spanish post at Spoysberg, and if this should be safely received, I wish, in token of it, a small guard might parade in some conspicuous situation at noon to-morrow, near the English ship at anchor, or under sail near Spoysberg.

In my present situation it is impossible, ardently as I enter into the views of my government and the Spanish nation, to attempt to lay down any fixed plan. My services, and that of every Englishman under my command are devoted to the cause; but before measures can be adopted, we must communicate, agree on, and combine as far as it may be possible, the interests of the Spanish troops in Jutland and Zealand, with those in Funen and Langeland. I shall keep a ship for some days off Spoysberg; and every ship under my command will be on the look-out to receive any boats that may approach them.

I have the honour to be, &c.

R.G. KEATS

To his Excellency the Marquis de la Romana, Commander-in-Chief of the Spanish Troops in Denmark
Superb, off Langeland, August 7, 1808

Understanding from the Spanish officer that the accompanying paper (thought unnecessary now to send) is the true state and situation of the Spanish troops in Denmark, and its dependencies, the following, according to the various circumstances that present themselves to my view, appears to form a plan that promises the fairest prospect of success to ensure their security and ultimate embarkation.

Those in Zealand I would propose to force their way to the peninsula, of which Halskon, near Corsoir, forms the projecting point towards Sproe. That isthmus appears capable of being defended, or at least seems to afford the means of defence for a few days, till I could remove them to the island of Sproe.

Those at Frederisca, by seizing on vessels, might possibly force an embarkation, and unite with those on Funen, which might perhaps be favoured by some movements of troops at Odense.

Separate, or united with those in Jutland, I apprehend those in Funen could secure themselves in the Presqu'Isle (peninsula), which terminates near the island of Romsoe, of which the pass near Kurteminde appears to form the gorge, and I could, if necessary, remove them to Romsoe; it would greatly facilitate the necessary naval operations, and might enable me to send a ship of the line towards Frederisca, to favour the troops in Jutland, if those in Langeland should be thought in security on that island: if they should, the other troops might be landed at leisure on that island, and the whole embarked from thence; but if the troops at present there are incapable of maintaining themselves at that place, in that case I must leave a ship of the line and a sloop, which could at almost any time receive them on board, and convey them to any other place that might be approved of, till transports could be procured for their reception. My means (three ships of the line and half a dozen small vessels at most), are not perhaps sufficient to embrace all these objects at once; but the zeal and exertion of the officers and ships' companies would greatly diminish the difficulties, and I should be much aided in lending assistance to the troops at Frederisca, if, as I have before said, those in Langeland should be considered capable of maintaining that post without any immediate support. I am aware some sacrifices of horses, and perhaps cannon, might be necessary, and we must be prepared to encounter even unforeseen difficulties; naval arrangements and movements are ever dependent, in some degree, on weather; but I should hope to surmount them all. It would of course be right to drive in cattle, and take whatever provisions might be practicable with the troops as it would not only save our present supply, which, the victuallers not having at this moment arrived, is rather scanty for the Spanish army, but would put me at ease on that score, provided any unavoidable delay should intervene, and prevent my sending supplies to them on shore.

In my present uninformed state, I am not in a situation to judge how far it might be in the power of, or deemed preferable by the Spanish commander, to seize Nyborg. It would secure the inactivity of the gunboats in that port. But such measure might possibly involve the safety of the troops in Zealand and Jutland, by inducing the Danes to act hostilely, when otherwise they might be disposed to wink at, or make no serious efforts to impede the quiet removal of the Spanish troops.

But if the principle of the plan should be approved of, and deemed feasible by those in command, I would recommend the movement to be general. That it be agreed to act upon it in all its parts the same day, except a discovery should take place, in which case each part should act immediately without hesitation.

I acknowledge I should have little expectation of the success of any negotiation for the peaceable removal of the troops; but a declaration, immediately after the movement shall have commenced, of the peaceable and unoffending object in view, accompanied with a threat of retaliation in the event of any hostile opposition on the part of the Danes or French, might perhaps be found advantageous.

In stating the naval force at present under my command, it is right to observe, I am in expectation of more ships, and have been informed, that a sufficient supply of provisions for all the Spanish troops is now on its passage to me.

I have the honour to be, &c

R.G. KEATS

N.B. I have just heard that the expected supply of provisions is in part arrived, which obviates difficulties on my part.

Rear-Admiral R.G. Keats to Vice-Admiral Sir James Saumarez
Superb, off Sproe in the Great Belt, August 11, 1808

I have the honour and satisfaction to inform you, that by an immediate and zealous pursuit of the measures recommended in the duplicate of instructions received by the *Mosquito*, on the 5th inst. his Excellency the Marquis de la Romana, and nearly six thousand of the Spanish troops under his command, were embarked this morning at Nyborg, which place he took possession of on the 9th.

By a combination of the same plan, more than one thousand have joined us this morning, by sea, from Jutland, and another thousand are thrown into Langeland, to strengthen the post held by the Spanish forces in that island, where it is proposed to land the remainder the moment the circumstances of weather will permit of our moving. The arrival of the Spanish officer in the *Edgar*, on the 5th, of whose spirited escape to the squadron you were informed by Captain Graves, greatly facilitated our means of communication.

No doubt could be entertained of the honour and patriotism of soldiers, who, indignant at the proposal of deserting their allegiance, though surrounded by hostile battalions, planted their colours in the centre of a circle they formed, and swore on their knees to be faithful to their country. All were equally anxious of returning to it. But one regiment in Jutland was too distant and too critically situated to effect its escape; and two in Zealand, after having fired on the French general, Frison, who commanded them, and killed one of his aides-de-camp, have been disarmed.

Some untoward circumstances having occasioned suspicion, and made a premature execution of the plan necessary, the wind and current being adverse, I left the *Superb* on the 8th, and went in my barge to the *Brunswick*, off *Nyborg*, and two hours after my flag was hoisted. On the 9th the general took possession of the town.

Although the Danish garrison yielded to circumstances, an armed brig of 18 guns, the *Fama*, and a cutter, the *Salorman*, of 12, moored across the harbour near the town, rejected all remonstrance on the part of the Danes, and every offer of security made by the general and myself. The reduction of these vessels being absolutely necessary, and the Spanish general unwilling to act hostilely against Denmark, such small vessels and boats as could be collected, were put under the command of Captain M'Namara, of the *Edgar*, who attacked and took them. On this occasion, I have to lament the loss of Lieutenant Harvey, an officer of much merit, of the *Superb*, and two seamen wounded; the enemy had seven killed and thirteen wounded.

I should have noticed, that the Spaniards, irritated at the opposition their friends who came to their support met with, departed in some measure from the general's intention, and fired some shot at them before they struck.

Expedition being deemed of the greatest importance, I shifted my flag to the *Hound*, in the harbour; and as neither of the three ships of the line, from circumstances of the weather, could be brought near in, fifty-seven sloops or doggers, found in the port, were fitted by the seamen, into which great part of the artillery, baggage, and stores, were embarked that night and the following day, and removed to the point of Slypsharn, four miles from Nyborg, where the army was embarked safely, and without opposition, this morning, notwithstanding the very unfavourable state of the weather, and they are now under the protection of his majesty's ships at the anchorage, off the island of Sproe.

Some sacrifices of horses and stores were conceived necessary by the general; and as I considered it right, under the peculiar circumstances, to enter into the views and wishes of the Marquis de la Romana, every unavoidable act of hostility was rigidly abstained from, for I did not consider it any to bring away the brig and cutter that rejected our offer of security, and forcibly opposed our entrance into the port; and I even undertook to liberate the vessels employed as transports, provided no interruption was made by any to the peaceable embarkation of our friends. . . .

Such guns as could be brought against us were spiked, and the embarkation was covered and most effectually protected by the *Minx* gun-brig, and the two prizes, and by the very judicious disposition of the gun-boats, under the command of Captain May, of the royal artillery, who volunteered, and whose services on this and other occasions were highly useful.

It is not easy to express the joy and satisfaction felt by every class of the army at this event; and no circumstance, I believe, could have afforded more real pleasure to us all. One, the regiment of Zamora, made a march of eighteen Danish miles in twenty-one hours.

I transmit herewith for your further information, copies of such letters as I deemed it requisite to address to his Excellency the Marquis de la Romana and the governor of Nyborg on this occasion. The replies to the former were verbal, through a confidential officer, and the latter were made personally.

I have the honour to be, &c.

R.G KEATS

Note. Since this letter was concluded, we entertain some hopes that part of the regiment of Jutland, we thought lost, has escaped to the post at Langeland by the western channel.

Anglo-Swedish Action against the Russians

'Letters on Service,' September 20 1808. [XX 247-248]

Copy of a letter from Vice-Admiral Sir James Saumarez, K.B. Commander-in-chief of his Majesty's Ships and Vessels in the Baltic, to the Honourable W.W. Pole, dated on board the Victory, off Rogerswick, the 30th of August, 1808

Sir, You will please to inform the Lords Commissioners of the Admiralty, of my arriving off Oro yesterday evening, pursuant to my intentions, to effect a junction with the Swedish fleet, which I had received an account from Rear-admiral Nauckhoff was blockaded by the Russian fleet, consisting of thirteen sail of the line-of-battle ships, besides frigates. It was not before this morning that I was informed by the commander of the Swedish frigate *Champan*, that the Rear-admiral Nauckhoff, after being joined by Sir Samuel Hood in the *Centaur*, and *Implacable*, had sailed from Oro road on the 25th, in pursuit of the Russian fleet; and on the day following, had succeeded in capturing and destroying the Russian line-of-battle ship *Sewolod*, off Rogerswick, and in which port the remainder of the enemy's ships had been compelled to shelter themselves. I immediately made sail for Rogerswick, where I arrived this afternoon, and had the satisfaction to find the Swedish fleet, with the *Centaur* and *Implacable*, at anchor, watching the Russian force in the harbour.

I enclose to you, for their lordship's information, the duplicate of a letter which I have had the pleasure to receive from Rear-admiral Sir Samuel Hood, detailing the account of his proceedings with his majesty's ships under his orders, and the squadron of his Swedish majesty, under Rear-admiral Nauckhoff, and of the meritorious conduct of Captain Martin, of the *Implacable*, in bringing the enemy's sternmost ship to action, and which struck her colours to the *Implacable*, but was afterwards rescued by the approach of the enemy's whole force, which had obliged Sir Samuel Hood to recall her. I also enclose the copy of a letter from Captain Martin to the rear-admiral, in which he gives due credit to Lieutenant Baldwin, and Mr. Moore, the master, and the other officers and men of the *Implacable*.

The Russian admiral having sent a frigate to take the disabled ship in tow, she was again attacked by the *Implacable*, and the *Centaur* laying her on board in the most gallant manner, and by the exertions of Captain Webley and Lieutenant Lawless, and Mr. Stode, master of the *Centaur*, her bowsprit was lashed to that ship, and there was every prospect of her being got off; but she having unfortunately grounded, rendered it impossible, and she was set on fire, after the prisoners and wounded men were taken from her.

Too much praise cannot be bestowed on Rear-admiral Sir Samuel Hood, for the gallantry he displayed with the two ships under his orders, in his pursuit of the enemy's fleet, when the bad sailing of the squadron of his majesty's ally prevented their coming up with them, and bringing on a general action. The brave and highly-meritorious exertions of Captain Martin and Captain Webley, with the officers and men under their orders, entitle them to the highest commendation in my power to bestow, and excited the amazement and admiration of the gallant Swedes who witnessed their heroic bravery and perseverance.

The present position of the Russian fleet within the batteries at the entrance of the harbour, leave but slender hopes of their being attacked with any probability of success. Admiral Nauckhoff has requested a body of land forces be sent from Finland, with a view of taking possession of the island of East Raga, which would effectually command the harbour; but as the enemy have been occupied in placing it in the best state of defence, it is very doubtful if a descent upon the island could be effected. I beg to assure their lordships, that every endeavour will be practised with the force under my orders jointly with the Swedish squadron, that can tend to the further defeat of the enemy.

I propose to detach a small squadron, under the orders of Captain Martin, towards Cronstadt; and I shall order the *Africa* to repair to her station off the Malmo channel, calling off Carlscrona for the convoy appointed to sail from that port for England.

[It is impossible to reproduce here Rear-Admiral Sir Samuel Hood's letter of 27 August giving further particulars of the action. Readers are referred to the Navy Record Society Vol. 110, *The Saumarez Papers, The Baltic 1808-1812*, A N Ryan (ed.), London, 1968. See also the reprint of the 'Russian Official Account of the Late Naval Action in the Baltic', Vol. XXI, pp99-101.]

1809 - Naval News,
Winter and Spring

DURING 1809 THE DOMINANT CONSIDERATIONS for Britain continued to be the progress of the war on the continent, especially in the Iberian Peninsula where the British army and navy were co-operating with the regular and irregular units of the Spanish Juntas, and the need to address Napoleon Buonaparte's efforts to rebuild the naval forces of France and the French vassal states. The year opened and closed with disasters. At the beginning of the year, the British army under Sir John Moore found itself facing impossible odds in northern Spain and had to be evacuated through Corunna at the end of January, after a well-fought rear-guard action in which Moore lost his life. Wellington's campaign in the south was more successful, and the Navy provided useful support for Spanish forces which drove the French out of Vigo, Santander, Corunna and Ferrol. In the Mediterranean, the British navy under Collingwood's command-in-chief supported the vicious and undecided action between the French and Spaniards. At the end of the year Rear-Admiral Martin destroyed a relief convoy out of Toulon.

Of considerable interest is the report published in *The Naval Chronicle* of the forceful way in which Captain Stewart defended British interests in the Aegean, by protecting the Greek vassals of the Ottoman against a return of their masters, and how this led to negotiations at the Porte for a joint Anglo-Turkish naval operation against the Russians in the Black Sea.

Of major concern was the possible loss of the Spanish fleet to the French, and a squadron of the Mediterranean fleet was moored in Cadiz Roads. Its task was to co-operate with the Spanish navy, with which good relations prevailed, but also to ensure that it should on no account be surrendered to the French. The squadron at Ferrol was an object of concern. Until the French were driven out of Ferrol in June, there was a risk that the Spanish squadron would be seized, or persuaded to co-operate with their old allies. The arrival of a French naval force at Ferrol could

189

have been decisive, and that prospect added to the alarm when in April the Brest fleet escaped its blockade, and got into Basque Roads in the mouth of the Charante. Admiral Gambier was sent Lord Cochrane, a young fire-eater, to lead a fireship attack. The operational results were moderately successful, and certainly dramatic, but the service repercussions of Lord Mulgrave's insensitive intervention from the Admiralty were entirely unfortunate.

The Franco-Dutch fleet building in the Scheldt was considered so threatening that the largest British amphibious operation of the war was mounted to destroy it. The raid, which sailed from the Downs at the end of July, was also intended to provide relief for the hard-pressed Austrians. The Earl of Chatham who commanded the army, however, was temperamentally quite unsuited to the job. Having failed to maintain the momentum of operations, so that the French were able to concentrate for the defence of Antwerp, he decided to withdraw, leaving a garrison in Flushing. Disease swept through the garrison and forced the withdrawal of the survivors at the end of the year.

On the Italian coast British naval operations continued to achieve satisfactory results and, in the Caribbean, Cayenne, Martinique, St Lucia, the Saints and finally St Domingo fell to British arms. More ominous for the future was the continued inability to resolve American complaints about the exercise of naval control over maritime trade.

From the 'Naval History of the Present Year,' 1808-09 December-January. XXI 60-61

Fighting Withdrawal at Corunna

From the great interest and importance of the subject to the country at large, we have been induced to give the military as well as the naval details of the *Gazette*, relating to the disastrous, though glorious, battle of Corunna, on the 16th of January.

It will be seen, that Sir John Moore, the gallant commander-in-chief of the British army, with several other distinguished officers, fell in the sanguinary conflict; and, according to report, we had previously lost not fewer than 7,000 men, in the course of our retreat to Lugo, and thence to Corunna.

Much as we deplore the loss, the great and heavy loss, we have sustained, we have the satisfaction of knowing, that not the slightest blame attaches to any of the officers or men concerned. The retreat of Sir John Moore is justly considered as one of the most masterly upon record.

War Should Take Amphibious Form - Editorial

The peninsular form of Spain presents an excellent opportunity for carrying on the war, agreeably to a plan which the late Lord Nelson so often and anxiously pressed on the attention of government: which was, to embark the army when hard pressed by a superior enemy, and land them on some other part of the coast, where it could act with a greater prospect of success; and to continue repeating this plan of attack, as a sure means of harassing and separating the great armies which the French can bring into the field.

A plan of this nature it was, in all probability, Sir John Moore's intention to pursue; but, in consequence of the great loss and fatigues of the army, it has been found expedient for it to return to England. Whether, when recruited, it will be again sent out, is doubtful.

In the royal speech, at the opening of Parliament, it was intimated, that the most vigorous assistance would continue to be afforded to Spain, as long as that country should continue true to itself; and, as recently as the 26th of January, since the distressing news of the battle of Corunna arrived, Lord Mulgrave has, in the most decisive manner, repeated that declaration.

If it be true, however, that the British officers have brought back the army upon their own responsibility, and contrary to the expectation of ministers, it seems to intimate that the affairs of Spain are in a very hopeless state; and we trust that, before another man shall be sent from our shores, the most satisfactory information will be received of the *will*, as well as of the *power*, of the Spaniards to co-operate, with the utmost cordiality, in resisting, and endeavouring to exterminate, the usurpers.

The last accounts from the Spanish coast were brought by a ship which was off Corunna on the 18th of January; at which time, it is said, the whole town was in flames. It is conjectured, that the Spaniards had resisted the entrance of the French; and that, from motives of revenge, the sanguinary invaders had set fire to the place.

A French officer of high rank, supposed to be either Soult or Junot, is said to have fallen in the battle of Corunna.

We lament to state, that we have sustained considerable injury from the elements as well as from the sword; some of our transports, returning from Spain with troops, having been entirely lost, and others greatly damaged.

January-February 1809. ^{XXI 156-157}

Escape of the Brest Fleet

From Mottley's 'Telegraph,' Portsmouth, Saturday, February 25, 1809

This morning arrived the *Racoon* sloop of war, Captain Welsh, with intelligence of the *Escape of the French Fleet at Brest* - The *Racoon* was on her passage to Cadiz, when, on Thursday noon last, off Ushant, she fell in with the *Lyra* sloop of war, Captain Bevians, which ship had been just despatched to Plymouth, by the reconnoitring frigate stationed off Brest, with intelligence, that all the ships of war that were ready for sea in Brest had escaped out, either on Monday night last, or early on Tuesday morning. They had not been seen by any of the ships on that station - the course they steered is not known, nor is their destination - the wind was northerly. Captain Welsh, conceiving it to be of essential importance that early information should be communicated to the Admiralty of the circumstances, made every possible haste to this port: on his arrival here, it was immediately communicated to London by telegraph.

It is supposed that, as Lord Gambier, who sailed from Torbay on Tuesday afternoon, was not in his station on Thursday, his lordship had received the information, and had gone in pursuit. The opinion as to their destination is divided between Cadiz and Martinique. It is apprehended that they will be joined by the six sail of the line, (two of which are three deckers) which the French took possession of at Ferrol. The following ships sailed from Torbay with Lord Gambier, *viz.* - *Caledonia*, 110, Admiral Lord

Gambier, Captain Sir H. Burrard Neale (captain of the fleet), Captain Bedford; *Royal George*, 100, Vice-Admiral Sir John Thomas Duckworth, Captain Dunn; *St. George*, 98, Rear-admiral Eliab Harvey, Captain Hillyar; *Dreadnaught* [sic], 98, Rear-admiral Southeby, Captain Salt; *Temeraire*, 98, Sir C. Hamilton; *Achille*, 74, Sir Richard King; *Impetueux*, 74, Captain Lawford; *Christian VIIth*, Captain J. Hancock, acting; *Warspite*, 74; Honourable Captain Blackwood. - The *Hero*, 74, Captain Newman, looked into Torbay on Wednesday, and then proceeded for the station off Ushant, to join his lordship. - The Brest fleet is believed to consist of ten sail of the line and several frigates.

The *Barfleur*, 98, Captain Linzee; *Zealous*, 74, Captain Boys; and the *Elizabeth*, 74, Honourable Captain Curzon, sailed from Plymouth on Monday, to cruise off Ferrol.

Sailors March to Collect Their Pay
From 'Correspondence.' XXI 115-116

Chatham, January 26, 1809
Mr. Editor, Several false reports being in circulation respecting a late visit of the crew of the *Standard* to London, and their application to the Lords of the Admiralty, I send you the following account, the correctness of which you may depend on:

The *Standard* and *Thunderer* arrived here together from the Mediterranean; the *Thunderer*'s crew were paid off, and had liberty for fourteen days; the *Standard*'s crew, conceiving they had a right to the same indulgence, both ships having been on the same station, petitioned the Lords of the Admiralty to that effect, and their application was granted. Thinking their commander was tardy in complying with the order of the Lords of the Admiralty, when called upon, on Wednesday se'nnight, to wash decks and scrub the ship, they refused, and went aft in a body to the quarter-deck; they requested to know why their leave was kept back, and entreated it should be immediately granted. The first lieutenant told them it was the captain's wish (who was absent on leave) that only a watch should have liberty at once, and on their return, the other watch should have the same indulgence. They replied in one voice, "No, all or none." On Thursday, the whole of the crew were granted fourteen days' liberty, but were not paid off. On their getting on shore they formed into a body, and marched for London, with a drum and fife, and union jack flying - many of the poor fellows without a farthing in their pockets. On their arrival at the Admiralty, they sent their petty officers forward, with a petition, stating the hardship of being allowed liberty without receiving a part of their pay. They were told it was unusual to grant liberty, except when the ship was paid off, but from the good character their captain had given them, it was granted to them, and they must return immediately to Chatham; that orders should be sent that night for payment to be made to them next morning, and entreated they would conduct themselves peaceably and quietly; that they would be accommodated for that day on board the receiving ship off the Tower, and be supplied with provisions; and that also the Gravesend boats should be engaged to take them down by that night's tide. They complied in the most orderly manner, and arrived at Chatham on Saturday morning; but the ship's books not being made up, they were informed they could not be paid until Monday last. They appeared satisfied, and said they wished for no more indulgence than the *Thunderer*'s crew had received. Their conduct has been perfectly peaceable throughout. [Anon.]

[This little drama led to C M Pole asking a question in the Commons on 27 February

1809. The Admiralty First Secretary, William Wellesley-Pole, firmly defended the administration. Vol. XXI, p254.]

From the 'Naval History of the Present Year,' 1809
February–March. XXI 249-252

Brest Squadron Appears at Rochefort

Early on the morning of the 24th of February, the enemy's squadron, which had escaped from Brest, consisting of eight sail of the line, appeared off Rochefort, in a widely extended semi-circle. Their first object, there is no doubt, was to capture the squadron of three sail of the line under Captain Beresford, which had been at anchor in Basque Roads. But Captain Beresford had fortunately learnt the preceding day, that the French admiral had struck his flag, and gone to L'Orient to bring out the squadron lying there, in order to join in the attack upon the British squadron off Rochefort. In consequence of this information, Captain Beresford got under weigh, and stood off, and very soon after he observed the entrance into the bay of the French squadron. Here the enemy was joined by three sail of the line lying in Rochefort, which, exclusive of smaller vessels, make his force consist of eleven sail of the line. . . . When joined by the whole of the squadron there, it would consist of 14 sail of the line (two of which are three-deckers) two 50-gun ships, 10 frigates, and several small vessels. . . .

Lord Gambier, in the *Caledonia*, took the command of the blockading squadron off Rochefort, on 8th of March. Should the squadron from L'Orient have proceeded to the West Indies, they will probably fall in with Sir John Duckworth's squadron, which there is no doubt has proceeded in that direction in search of the Brest fleet.

Oporto Fleet Sails

The escape of the [merchant] fleet which had been so long weather-bound at Oporto, and which crossed the Bar on the 23d ult. is a matter of consolation, considering the menaced condition of that country. The property on board is estimated at the value of £400,000 and insurances have been done at Lloyd's to that amount. There are from eight to ten thousand pipes of wine in the fleet. . . .

Proserpine Captured

The Dutch papers, as well as the private letters from Holland, state the capture of his Majesty's frigate *Proserpine*, in the Mediterranean, by two French frigates, *la Penelope* and *la Pauline*: she was carried into Toulon. From the French official accounts, it appears that the *Proserpine* had been very audacious, frequently standing so close to the shore as to look into the port of Toulon. This provoked the French admiral, who sent out against her the two abovementioned frigates. Once she escaped by flight, but on a second occasion her pursuers came up with her about half past four o'clock in the morning. An engagement ensued, which was fought close alongside for three quarters of an hour; at length the *Proserpine* struck to her two opponents. The enemy states the *Proserpine* to have had 11 men killed, and 15 wounded, and that both the French frigates came out of the action without the loss of a man killed or wounded.

Danish Naval Crews Refuse Duty

Private accounts from Holland state, that the crews of two Danish ships of the line lying at Flushing had refused to obey the orders of the French government. They were ordered to sail for Brest, but the captain declined compliance till they received instructions from their government; upon which they were arrested. The crews having likewise declared their resolution to refuse obedience, a representation of the affair was at length sent to the Danish government.

Change at Admiralty

The Honourable John Hope has resigned his appointment as one of the Lords of the Admiralty, and has set off for Scotland. Captain Moorsom has succeeded him. . . .

Saumarez to Command in Baltic

Sir James Saumarez is to have the chief command of a large fleet, which is to be sent to the Baltic, and Sir Samuel Hood is to accompany him. They will hoist their flags on board the *Victory* and *Centaur*. The following line of battle ships are to compose part of the fleet:

Vanguard	74 guns	Captain Glynn
Minotaur	74	Thompson
Standard	64	Harvey
Ardent	64	Vashon
Dictator	64	Pierson
Ruby	64	Hall
Africa	64	Barrett

Besides several frigates and bomb-vessels.

CAPTURE OF THE *PROSERPINE*. Engraved by Baily, from an original drawing.
    The subject of the annexed plate will be best explained by the subjoined narrative from an officer of the *Proserpine*. Of the plate itself it will be sufficient to say that -
No. 1. Is a view of the *Proserpine*, as seen by the enemy's frigates.
No. 2. Represents her at the time when the enemy was first seen from the *Proserpine*'s Larboard Gangway.
Narrative of the Capture of the Proserpine, Captain Charles Otter
On the evening of the 27th February, 1809, the *Proserpine* was at her station off Cape Sicie, and had in the day reconnoitred the French fleet in the roads and inner harbour; two frigates had been making a short excursion, and went in again towards dusk and anchored. Several sail of small coasting vessels were out, and running down along shore towards Marseilles, which induced Captain Otter to run in and endeavour to cut some of them off: failing, however, in that attempt, and having little wind, we stood off again for the night, and strict orders were given to keep a very sharp look out during the night, and to stand in again in time to catch some of them in the morning. Having the middle watch to keep, I went early to bed; the ship was nearly becalmed; at about five or six miles from the Cape, and on my relieving the deck, I found her, as near as I could guess, in the very same place, and not a breath of wind; it was as fine a moonlight morning as I ever saw; but the moon being to seaward, prevented us from seeing vessels that then might be running along

N.º 1

N.º 2

Pub.d 30 Nov.r 1816 by Joyce Gold, Naval Chronicle Office, 103 Shoe Lane, London.

shore, and our ship being between them and the moon, gave them decidedly the advantage. Mr. Brown, the master of the ship (and who died afterwards in France), was the officer of the watch, and kept a constant good lookout all the watch. Mr. Carslake, first lieutenant of the ship, had left orders for the men to scrub their hammocks on the main deck, and that the mate of the watch should occasionally

attend to the same; this caused me sometimes to quit the deck for a few minutes.¹ At
4 o'clock, I asked Mr. Brown how I should mark the log; he answered, "head round
the compass" [ie ship's head constantly swinging]. I then called Mr. Rigby, second
lieutenant, to relieve Mr. B. and on coming on deck, I heard a man at the look-out
on the larboard gangway, sing out, "I think I see a vessel, Sir." Mr. Brown took a
glass, and on looking, told me he thought she looked like a man of war: he ran down
to the captain, and I went and called all the officers; when I had gone on deck again,
I looked through my glass, and plainly discovered two ships, with all sail set, and
very close to us, yet I could scarcely make them out with the naked eye. All hands
were immediately called, and we in vain (it being calm) attempted to escape the
enemy, who was coming up fast, with a fine land breeze; we made the private night
signals, but no answer.

At length we got a little breeze, and as Captain Otter knew the ship sailed faster by
the stern [ie trimmed deep aft], he ordered the two bow guns into the cabin, to
answer the double purpose, I suppose, of stern-chasers and ballast. At about twenty
minutes past four, one of the ships² ranged up on the larboard side, looking very
large - her ports all up; lights on the maindeck fore and aft: she had shortened sail,
and was perfectly ready for commencing the action; the other ship was coming up on
our starboard side, when the wind entirely died away, leaving the poor little
Proserpine in a very hopeless situation; as by this time we discovered two seventy-
fours coming down to assist in this unequal combat. Captain Otter took the hint,
and beat to quarters; when they heard our drum, they gave us a whole broadside,
which salute we returned in as politie a manner as we could: the ship yawed a little,
and left the other ship in a safe position astern, where she continued raking us all the
action, without our being able to fire a gun at him, as the two bow guns had been left
by those who were getting them aft, when we beat to quarters, and were no small
nuisance, as on our larboard side two guns were disabled for twenty minutes by
them, till they were got to their places; very fortunately they fired high in the ship
astern, to prevent our escape by flight, as they had before witnessed that we could
sail very fast: at a little after five the ship alongside piped *à la bordage*! and the cry of
Vive l'Empereur! à la bordage! rent the air; a little breeze which sprung up would
have favoured them in this design, had not the captain called all the officers, and
consulted with them; the result of which was, that as the *Proserpine* was almost a
wreck, her rigging, masts, and sails cut to peices, 41 hands short of complement,
with no chance of being able to save the ship, and the two seventy-fours coming up

1 When below superintending scrubbing hammocks, one of the men was scolding an old man who had
two twin sons on board, for breaking his rest to wash for them, as he said they were big enough to do it
themselves; he said, "Oh! they will grow up men soon, and then will not forget my doing this for them; and
provided that a shot does not take my head off, they will treat me to many a glass for washing for them now."
Less than two hours after he said the words, a shot actually took his head clean off, and the heart-rending
scene I was a witness to, on the boys finding out that it was their father, would beggar description; he was
the only man killed outright.

2 *Penelope.*

3 The marine who was mortally wounded, knew his end was very fast approaching, and begged to die on
board the *Proserpine*; but he was sent on shore to the hospital at Toulon, and although he could scarcely
speak from his wounds, when he passed under the stern of *Le Majestueux*, Admiral Gantheaume's flag-
ship, seeing numbers on her poop looking at the boat, which was the *Proserpine*'s cutter, he made an effort
to raise himself up in his cot, and sung out loud,

"You Frenchmen, don't talk of your fighting,
Nor boast of this deed you have done;
Don't think that Old England you'll frighten,
So easy as Holland and Spain."

He then attempted to sing God save the King, but could not, from loss of blood and exertions, being too
faint; this poor fellow was firm and collected to his last moments, and is a proof of that sterling and truly
British heroism for which our brave seamen and marines have ever been noted.

fast, it was necessary to surrender, to save the lives of the crew: the colours were then ordered to be struck; after which they fired two broadsides at us, took possession of us, and carried us into Toulon: the two ships that took us were the *Penelope* and *Pauline*, 44-gun frigates, 360 men each; the *Proserpine* had one seaman killed outright, one marine mortally wounded (died three days afterwards),[3] and eleven seamen, marines, &c slightly wounded. The French officers said they had no killed or wounded, but several of the crew secretly told us that they had several killed, and that there were many wounded men sent at night to the hospital. Thus the *Proserpine* was taken by a superiority of force, which is evident: she mounted in all 40 guns, and had, including sick, boys, women, and children, 214 persons on board; they mounted, in the whole, 102 guns, and had when they attacked us 720 men in good health. The action commenced at 25 minutes past 4, and ended at 10 minutes past 5 A.M. when, to our mortification, we saw an English frigate, which came on purpose to relieve us. This proved to be H.M.S. *Cambrian*. [Plate 473]

Peace Negotiations With the Porte

From the 'Naval Biography of the Late Captain John Stewart, R.N.'
XXVIII 41-44

[Part of a letter to the author of the 'Memoir' from Robert Adair, in 1808-9, Minister Plenipotentiary to the Porte, dated:]

Queen Street, May Fair, April 3d, 1812 . . .
Returning from my mission at Vienna, in the spring of 1808, I landed at Malta; where, soon afterwards, Captain Stewart arrived in the *Seahorse*, with some important information respecting the state of affairs in Turkey. This intelligence was immediately forwarded to Lord Collingwood, and likewise to Mr. Canning, then secretary of state for foreign affairs; who lost no time in making out a commission for me to renew the negociations. After transacting some business in England, I returned to the Mediterranean, and reached Palermo on the third of August. During this important interval, the conduct of Captain Stewart had been most judicious. Steadily adhering to the conciliatory system with which he had set out, his disinterestedness was never shaken, even by the temptation of advantages fairly within his reach, but he regarded his instructions to capture and distress the Ottoman trade, rather as the means of bringing a mistaken enemy to his senses, than as a source of emolument to himself. On the other hand, and in conformity with the same spirit, which is ever best allied to firmness, while he suffered the inhabitants of the Archipelago to carry on their traffic from island to island unmolested, he strictly enforced two conditions on the Turks, as the price of his forbearance; the one, that they should collect no revenue in the Greek Islands, the other, that no Turkish ship of war should appear in those seas. It is not, therefore, to be wondered at, that the Greeks regarded him rather as their protector than their enemy, and that, as such, they should venerate him to this hour. With every disposition, however, to give a marked character of mildness to the hostility which two nations, so long friendly, were now compelled to exercise against each other, he found it impossible, on one occasion, to avoid inflicting upon the Turkish marine, one of those severe lessons, which every naval state, in hostility with us, has been doomed to experience in its turn. It happened, that under a pretence of destroying pirates, the Captain Pacha thought fit, this year, to send a squadron of frigates into the Aegean Sea; in contravention of the understood compact already mentioned. Information of this having reached Captain

Stewart, he proceeded immediately in search of them, and coming up with two of the
frigates and a galley off the island of Scopolo, he remonstrated with the Turkish
commodore upon his proceedings. On being made acquainted, by that officer, with the
purpose for which he had been sent out, Captain Stewart readily offered to take that
service upon himself, provided he would return to port; but he told him, at the same
time, that if he remained there, he must attack him. The Turk, scarcely thinking his
adversary in earnest, and relying upon his immense superiority; his own ship mounting
52 guns, and his consort 34, while the *Seahorse* had but 38 in all; preferred the risk of an
engagement: and after seeing his comrade driven out of the action, so completely beaten
and crippled as to render it doubtful whether she could gain a port, he was himself
compelled to surrender, at the end of a conflict of four hours, in which (to use Captain
Steward's words in his official letter) "*he was rendered a motionless wreck*," with the loss
of 350 men.

This event, the glorious details of which are in every one's knowledge, happened a
very few days before my arrival at Palermo. When I learned it, I confess that, on a first
view, I could not but consider it as extremely embarrassing. It was impossible to judge,
either what change so desperate an encounter might not produce on the pacific
dispositions of the Turks: or whether the encounter itself, might not rather have been
occasioned by a previous alteration in those views; and this embarrassment, coming in
addition to what I had also just learned of a fresh revolution at Constantinople, in which
the Sultan, to whom I was accredited, had been deposed, and most of the ministers
supposed to be friendly to us, had been put to death, caused me to hesitate for a moment
as to the course most proper to be pursued.

From any apprehensions, however, as to the bad effects likely to result, from Captain
Stewart's vigorous proceeding with the Turkish frigates, I was relieved, on my first
interview with him. Indeed I soon found that, in one sense, it was likely to assist rather
than impede my negotiation. As, besides the benefit of the example, it enabled me to
ascertain the true character of the revolution which had just happened, and which at
first sight appeared fatal to my mission.

Having embarked on board the *Seahorse* on the 3d of December, we proceeded to
the Dardanelles, and anchored off Tenedos on the 26th. We remained there until the
arrival of a Turkish plenipotentiary to open the conferences with me; and then removed
to Barbieri bay, an anchorage between the first and second line of castles which defended
the Straits. During our stay at Tenedos I thought it advisable, although the negotiation
had not yet commenced, that the Turkish trade, which at this time was carrying on with
considerable activity, should be suffered to pass unmolested to the capital. Captain
Stewart acceded without hesitation to my wishes, and by this additional act of
disinterestedness, helped to keep alive, and to confirm the prevailing good humour of
the Divan; a service the most essential, as it afterwards turned out, for on the very day
preceding my first conference with the Turkish plenipotentiary, another insurrection
broke out at Constantinople, and was followed by the death of the deposed Sultan, the
slaughter of ten or fifteen thousand Turks, and the burning of a third part of the city.

In this, as in the whole of his preceding conduct, I conceived myself greatly indebted
to Captain Stewart, for the success of the negociation entrusted to me. There are other
points of his public services at this period, on which I might descant, were I not restrained
by obvious considerations. Between the commencement of the negotiation and its close,
which was not until the 5th of January, 1809, and during the time which we afterwards
passed together at Constantinople, where he remained until the end of March, nothing

occurred to assist me further in tracing out the distinct lines of his character, except in its amiable and social parts . . .

I am, Sir, Your very obedient humble servant,

ROBERT ADAIR

(1809.) Before Captain Stewart left Constantinople, he sent the following account of the Turkish navy to Lord Collingwood, dated March 24th:

"My Lord, I am at last able to leave this place, where I have been detained much longer than I wished; but at the express desire of Mr. Adair, who required my assistance in two or three things which he had to settle with the Turkish Government: particularly to assist at a conference that was held relative to a proposed co-operation in case of their being at war with Russia.

On the 23d instant, I attended Mr. Adair to the Porte, where we met the Reis Effendi, a person of the Ulema, called the Plenipotentiary of the conference, and Wakid Effendi: The principal subject was the co-operation of a British squadron in the Black Sea, to attack, or at least threaten, Sebastopolis [sic] and the Crimea; and thus draw a large detachment of the Russian troops from the Danube. The Turks held themselves equal to meet the Russian fleet in the Black Sea; but said, that a British force would both give confidence to their fleet, and inspire fear in the enemy. They asked for four sail of the line, two frigates, and four bombs, the latter in case Sebastopolis should be attacked from the sea. I learnt from Mr. Adair, that he had had communication with your Lordship on the subject of the Black Sea, where the impossibility of protecting the retreat of a British squadron had been discussed: I, therefore, asked the Turkish ministers, if the British government sent the ships they required, would they take the necessary steps for destroying the cannon on the north side of the Bosphorus, in case of the rapid advance of the Russians? Their answer was, "that though they had no idea of such an advance, still there could be no doubt they would do so;" and they added, "*but if the Russians were to get there, our Empire in Europe is gone*; and surely England, on whose account we are now going to war, would not grudge the injury which a few of our ships might sustain." Mr. Adair told them of the crippled state of your Lordship's fleet, and the probability that you could not spare any ships: they said, the assurance of his application to the government for them, was sufficient, as they counted every thing on our friendship. I added, that unless the squadron sent into the Black Sea, before the N.E. winds set in, it could not get up there this year. They seemed to think, that the very idea of being attacked in the Black Sea by our squadron, would make a strong impression on the Russians. I afterwards told them all I knew about the Archipelago; recommended their attention to the fortresses of *Suda*, *Napoli*, and *Romania*, &c. &c. and, above all, pressed their immediately securing, or turning away from the Islands, all the Russians, and French partizans. They begged me to give them all the information I could in writing; which I did the next day. They asked a good deal about Buonaparte's Berlin Decree, and our Orders in Council; a copy of all which I left with Mr. Adair for them. By all I can learn, my Lord, the Russians have eight sail of the line, four frigates, and a number of small vessels fit for sea, two or three of which are three-deckers; they are at Sebastopolis; which port I have not been able to get a good account of, as no merchant ships go there: I enclose an account extracted from a book, containing descriptions of the different places in the Black Sea: An Austrian captain told me, it is strongly fortified on both sides of the entrance. The Turks have fifteen sail of the line, ten of which (*viz.* three 3-deckers, and seven 2-deckers) are nearly ready for sea. One 74 is just launched, and the other four refitting; they have five frigates nearly ready for sea, and two refitting: they have besides in Constantinople, seven corvettes, two bombs, and two brigs; three sail of the line are building at Militine, Bondroum, and Rhodes. I went up the Bosphorus in a boat as far as the Buyulidari: till you come to that place there are no batteries to signify, but from thence to the Black Sea, are a great many, and seemingly in better order than the batteries in the Dardanelles passage.

The Caimacan Ali Pacha has been made Captain Pacha, and will take upon himself the office the moment the Grand Vizier arrives: he is a man of great bravery, but no sailor. Said Ali was made Pacha by the Janizary party after the late revolution, and the Sultan always determined to remove him, as soon as his own authority should be consolidated. Said Ali is banished to Broresa: he persuaded Sir A. Paget, that he was a great friend to the English; on the contrary, he seems to have been totally inimical to them, and to be connected with the French: he undoubtedly protracted the negotiation, by suggesting and urging the claim for restitution of ships. A claim Mr. Adair always suspected came from French advice, and which I have no doubt did."

Parliamentary Discussion of American Attitudes to the Exercise of Sea Power

Imperial Parliament XXI 255

House of Commons, Monday March 6

Mr. *Whitbread* made the following motion relating to America: - "that an humble address be presented to his Majesty, representing to his Majesty, that in consequence of the decree of Berlin of the enemy, the orders in Council had been issued by his Majesty's government, both equally contrary to the usages of nations; that, however, it had been at the same time vested in his Majesty to rescind these orders as circumstances might require; that America, feeling the danger likely to accrue from those measures to the neutral trade, had laid an embargo on her ports, prohibiting all commercial intercourse with foreign states; that America, willing to put an end to these inconveniences, and finding the enemy to persist in his Berlin decree, had made an offer to this country to remove the embargo with respect to us, should we, on the other hand, consent to rescind the orders in Council; that this offer, on the part of America, was just in its principle, and advantageous to Great Britain, as it would infallibly secure to us the trade of America: though this offer had not at first been accepted, that we still believe it is in the power of his majesty's government to restore a good understanding between the two countries; and that therefore we heartily pray his Majesty may be pleased to adopt such measures as are calculated to restore a good understanding, and to re-establish the commercial intercourse between this country and America."

This motion was negatived by 145 against 83.

Additional Honours Conferred on Sir Sidney Smith by the Court of Portugal

From 'Naval Anecdotes.' XXI 298

The public papers have lately contained many contradictory accounts of the state of affairs at the court of Brazil, but we are as yet very scantily supplied with genuine intelligence; we therefore conceive the following document will be read with interest, as authentic testimony of the sentiments of that court relative to the person and services of the British admiral commanding in those seas. It is somewhat singular that Sir Sidney Smith's conduct should be viewed in so different a light at the Admiralty from what it is by our ally, that he has just been unexpectedly superseded in a manner, which we fear will be considered by the worthy admiral as the most abrupt.

To Don Domingos Antonio de Souza Continho. London
Palace of Rio de Janeiro, 6th August, 1808
His Royal Highness the Prince Regent, our Sovereign Lord, being desirous to shew the estimation in which he holds the high merit, abilities, and valour of Sir Sidney Smith, rear-admiral and commander-in-chief of his Britannic majesty's naval forces in the Southern Seas; his royal highness has been pleased to grant him the honour of enabling him to bear the arms of Portugal, quartered with his own, and to bear them as the French express it, *on shield and banner,* that he, and his descendants, may use them, and in default of issue, his representatives in both the male and female lines: but as the said Sir Sidney Smith cannot do this without his Britannic majesty's licence, his royal highness orders that your excellency will request this faculty through Mr. Canning, his minister of state for foreign affairs, signifying the great pleasure and satisfaction his royal highness will receive by his Britannic majesty's being pleased to accede to this his particular desire. Your excellency will make known this minister's answer as soon as possible. His royal highness flattering himself that this just request will not meet any difficulty. God preserve your excellency.

D. RODRIGO DE SOUZA CONTINHO

Debate on Securing the Spanish Squadrons
Imperial Parliament
House of Lords, Friday, March 24 1809. XXI 438-439

Lord *Aukland* expressed a wish to receive some explanation from ministers relative to the great omission of not adopting measures to secure the numerous and powerful Spanish squadron, comprising three three-deckers, and several large ships of the line, which were stationed at Ferrol, from falling into the hands of the enemy. This he thought was a circumstance easy to have been effected, when he considered the state of circumstances for a long interval of that part of the Peninsula, and the long presence of a powerful British force. He did not mean, however, that this most important object was to be effected by force, but it might have been done by means of arrangement, in a way in which the interests of the Allied Nations might both have been consulted. He therefore moved, "That there be laid before the House copies, or extracts, of instructions sent out to the officers commanding the British naval and military forces, relative to the securing the Spanish squadron at Ferrol from falling into the hands of the enemy."

Lord *Mulgrave* said, the topic to which the motion referred was one of equal delicacy and importance. He would not say that farther information officially may not be laid before the House on this subject, but he begged leave now to state, that his Majesty's government were by no means unmindful of that important object; that the British admiral in command in that quarter had offered to take those ships under his protection; but it was represented to him by the Spanish commanders, that Ferrol was sufficiently strong to be able to resist the attacks of the enemy, and that the ships in question would be of essential service in enabling them to repeal such attacks. He must add, that under the present relative circumstances of the two countries, such a discussion as the Noble Lord's motion must produce, would be injurious to the public service.

The Duke of *Norfolk* said, he felt rather alarmed than satisfied at the statement just made by the Noble Lord. Such arguments might as well be used by the Spaniards in the case of Cadiz, should we propose any steps for the security of the squadrons in that port.

Earl *Grey* was of opinion, that measures should be adopted to prevent the squadrons now in Spanish ports from falling into the hands of the enemy. It was not at Cadiz alone, but at Carthagena there was a powerful squadron ready equipped and manned, which was very dangerously situated. With reference to the negotiations which may be going on, it would be as well not to press the discussion at present; but a most severe responsibility rested upon ministers with respect to their conduct relative to Spain.

Lord *Aukland* at length consented to withdraw his motion.

Monday, March 27 1809

The Earl of *Liverpool* laid before the House a copy of a treaty, offensive and defensive, entered into by his Majesty with the government acting for, and in the name of his Catholic Majesty the King of Spain and the Indies, dated 14th January last.

Lord *Selkirk* was desirous of ascertaining, whether the recent negotiation with the American States applied only to making satisfaction for the abrupt conduct of our commander on that station, or whether it went generally to other topics as well as to that.

The Earl of *Liverpool* answered, that any question on the subject of that negotiation was at present ill-timed, and very ill suited to present circumstances.

From the 'Naval History of the Present Year,' 1809 March-April. XXI 315-316; 348-349

Fire Ship Attack on Basque Roads

It will be seen, in our succeeding "*Letters on Service*," that four sail of the Brest fleet were totally destroyed, in Basque Roads, on the 12th of April (the anniversary of Rodney's brilliant victory in the West Indies) by the frigates, fire-ships, and bomb vessels of Admiral Gambier's fleet, under the immediate command of Captain Lord Cochrane. Sir Harry Neale, the captain of the fleet, reached town with this interesting and important intelligence on the 21st; and, for two succeeding evenings, the Admiralty, Horse Guards, Treasury, Somerset House, &c were brilliantly illuminated.

Martinique Surrenders

Official advices had previously been received of the complete surrender of the Island of Martinique to his Majesty's arms. . . .

United States Passes 'Non-Intercourse' Act

The United States of America, in a spirit of inveterate hostility towards this country, have passed the Non-Intercourse Act, as a substitute for the Embargo, which has been removed. All commercial intercourse with England and France, on the part of America, is thus precluded; but, as the United States have thought proper to consider Holland as a *neutral* and *independent* State, it is evident that they expect, through that really vassal country, to give France every commercial advantage which she might be able to derive from a direct trade. Now is the time to prove the value and efficacy of the British Orders in Council!

Harvey to Stand Trial

The 1st of May has been appointed for the trial of Rear-admiral Harvey, by court martial, on a charge of breach of discipline. It is said that upon Lord Cochrane's joining the fleet, Admiral Gambier gave orders, that a boat, boat's crew, and an officer, should instantly be provided by every ship under his command; the whole of the men being required to volunteer. Upon receiving these orders, Admiral Harvey addressed his ship's company, and, after stating the nature of them, declared, that he himself in his own person volunteered, and invited as many as chose to follow his example; in consequence of which the greater part of his officers and men enrolled themselves along with him. A list of these being conveyed to the *Caledonia*, Lord Gambier's flag ship, his Lordship is reported to have stated, that these were not generally the kind of volunteers he wanted; as Lord Cochrane was to command the expedition, of which appointment he (Lord Gambier) had himself some reason to complain, inasmuch as it seemed to indicate that there was no officer in his fleet fit to take charge of the service; but that Admiralty Orders to this effect had been received, which of course he must obey. Hereupon Admiral Harvey is stated to have expressed the greatest dissatisfaction, and to have bestowed upon Lord Gambier himself, epithets descriptive of other qualities than those which he has evinced in his profession, such as *Jesuit*, *Methodist*, and *Psalm-singer*; and all this in the presence of Captain Bedford, of the *Caledonia*, who desired to know if it were meant, that this reply should be conveyed to the commander-in-chief: to which the other answering, in the heat of passion, in the affirmative, the communication accordingly took place, and the letter for a court martial was the result.

Russia

An expedition is reported to have been sent to Archangel, to destroy several men of war which are building in the dock-yard at that place.

Laurel Captured

His Majesty's ship *Laurel* is taken by the French frigate *Canonnier*, and carried into the Isle of France [Mauritius]. It is stated that the killed and wounded on board the *Canonnier* amounted to 180; the *Laurel* 5 killed and 14 wounded. The *Canonnier* had 44 twenty-four pounders, the *Laurel* 22 nine-pounders, and was totally dismasted before she struck.

Dutch Deserters Reach Britain

An open boat, with eleven deserters from Flushing, was picked up at sea, by the *Fly* sloop of war, and carried into the Downs. They consist of four seamen, two Danish and two Dutch, belonging to the Dutch admiral's flag-ship; the remainder was a corporal's guard, consisting of the corporal and six privates. It appears that the sailors had formed a plan with the soldiers, while on guard, to attempt their escape: in which they succeeded, without having experienced even a pursuit. These men state, that the fleet in Flushing ready for sea consists of ten sail of the line, all seventy-fours; but that they are very badly manned, as their crews comprise many raw conscripts, and the Danes who had been sent on board were dissatisfied, and persist in their refusal to serve on board French or Dutch ships. The discontent was further increased by a great scarcity of provisions in the fleet. They add, that a great number of seamen and soldiers would gladly follow their example, had they an opportunity. They had been three days and nights at sea, with scarcely any sustenance.

April–May. *XXI 428-429*

Buonaparte Triumphantly Enters Vienna

At page 316, we announced, that hostilities had been commenced by Austria against France. A series of battles has since taken place, in most of which the French were decidedly victorious; and, to crown the success of the campaign, Buonaparte, after a short and ineffectual resistance, entered Vienna, the capital of the Austrian empire, on the 12th of May. The Emperor Francis is reported to have made overtures for peace, which were rejected; but this report is not generally believed. The Austrians are yet in considerable strength, and a formidable opposition, by the Archduke Charles, is still confidently expected.

Austrian Army Makes Gains in Italy

In Italy, particularly in the department of the Tyrol, and in Poland, the Austrians have obtained some important advantages.

Insurrection in Westphalia

A formidable insurrection has broken out in Westphalia which threatens the existence of King Jerome's sovereignty; and Colonel Schill, a Prussian officer, of considerable talent and enterprise, has seized upon Bremen, and is spreading his forces throughout Brunswick and Hanover. These are all serious and useful diversions in favour of Spain and Portugal.

Wellesley Victorious at Oporto

In the latter country Sir Arthur Wellesley has retaken Oporto, and defeated Marshal Soult, in three successive actions. At the date of the last accounts, it was expected that he would cut off his retreat into Galicia, where Marshal Ney was stationed.

Russia

Russia is said to have declared war against Austria.

Sweden

The gallant, but unfortunate King of Sweden, was *compelled* to sign what is imprudently termed a *voluntary* Act of Abdication, on the 29th of March.

America

Respecting our relations with America, a very serious sensation has recently been excited in the mercantile world. About the 22d of May, government received despatches from Mr. Erskine, the British Envoy at Washington, announcing the adjustment of the differences between this country and the United States; and that, in consequence of the alleged revocation of our Orders in Council, with respect to America, the head of that government had issued a proclamation, authorising the renewal of the trade with Great Britain, after the 10th of June. It appears, however, from the statements of the Earl of Liverpool and Mr. Canning, in Parliament, that government will not ratify the arrangements of Mr. Erskine, who, they assert, has acted diametrically opposite to both the spirit and letter of his instructions. But, to prevent as much as possible the loss and inconvenience which might accrue to the American merchants, from acting on the faith of the agreement between Mr. Erskine and the government of the Untied States, an Order in Council has been issued, suspending the blockade of the ports of Holland, from the 9th of June to the 20th of July; thereby allowing, for that period, a free trade from America direct to Holland. Licenses are also to be granted to the British merchants, to trade to Holland, during a certain period.

Mutineers of the Bounty

From 'Naval Anecdotes.' XXI 454-455

Accounts have been received from the squadron in the Southern Seas, under Rear-admiral Sir Sidney Smith. They sailed from Rio Janeiro [sic] on the 7th of March: it being the anniversary of the Prince of Brazil's arrival in that country, they fired a royal salute in sailing out of the harbour. On the 13th of March they were in latitude 26 deg. 33 min. S. and longitude 30 deg. 51 min. W. The last advices left them at sea, all well, on the 16th of March, off the island of Trinidada [sic]. The only intelligence of any moment is comprised in the following extract from the log-book of the American ship *Topaz*, of Boston, Folgar, master, *viz.*

Extract from the log-book of Captain Folgar, of the American Ship Topaz, of Boston
Captain Folgar relates, upon landing upon Pitcairn's Island (or Incarnation, off Quiros), in lat. 25 deg. 2 min. S. long. 130 deg. W. by lunar observation, he found an Englishman of the name of Alexander Smith, the only person remaining of nine that escaped in his Majesty's late ship *Bounty*, Captain W. Bligh.
   Smith relates, that after putting Captain Bligh in the boat, Christian, the leader of the mutiny, took the command of the ship, and went to Otaheite, where a great part of the crew left the ship, except himself, Smith, and seven others, who each took wives, and six Otaheitean men as servants, and shortly after arrived at this island, where they ran the ship on shore, and broke her up. This event took place in the year 1799. About four years after their arrival, a great jealousy existing, the Otaheiteans secretly revolted, and killed every Englishman except himself, whom they severely wounded in the neck

with a pistol ball. The same night, the widows of the deceased Englishmen rose and put to death the whole of the Otaheiteans, leaving Smith the only man alive upon the island, with eight or nine women, and several small children. He, when he recovered, applied himself to tilling the ground, so that it now produces plenty of yams, cocoa nuts, bananas, and plantains, hogs and poultry in abundance.

There are now some grown up men and women, children of the mutineers, on the island, the whole population amounting to about 35, who acknowledge Smith as father and commander of them all. They all speak English, and have been educated by him, Captain Folgar represents, in a religious and moral way.

The second mate of the *Topaz* asserts, that Christian, the ring-leader, became insane shortly after their arrival on the island, and threw himself off the rocks into the sea; another died of a fever, before the massacre of the whole took place.

The island is badly supplied with water, sufficient only for its present inhabitants, and no anchorage. Smith gave to Captain Folgar a chronometer made by Kendall, which was taken from him by the Governor of Juan Fernandez.

1809 – Operations on the Coast of Spain: Corunna, Rosas and Vigo

THE CONVENTION OF CINTRA had enabled the French to concentrate their force to oppose the army under Sir John Moore which had marched to cross the Spanish frontier from Lisbon on 27 October 1808 and had been reinforced from England with troops landed at Corunna on 13 October under Sir David Baird. Moore had received much less support from the Junta of Galicia than expected, and had begun to withdraw from an exposed position, but was persuaded by the government in Madrid and the British minister, Mr Frere, to march for the capital. When the true position became clear, that Napoleon Buonaparte was himself in the field against the British army with no less than 70,000 men, a retreat by forced marches became essential. Because the transports were not immediately available at Corunna, a stand had to be made against Marshal Soult's advanced corps, which proved to be one of the more remarkable triumphs of British arms. Moore was himself killed, but the bulk of the army was able to embark.

The defence assistance provided by the navy in the defence of Rosas and Vigo was on a smaller scale but nonetheless important.

Letters on Service, London 'Gazette Extraordinary'
Downing Street, January 24, 1809. XXI 79-84

The Honourable Captain Hope arrived late last night with a despatch from Lieutenant-general Sir David Baird to Lord Viscount Castlereagh, one of his majesty's principal secretaries of state, of which the following is a copy:
[In the body of the letter Captain Gordon is mentioned as the bearer of the despatches.]

His Majesty's Ship Ville de Paris, at Sea, January 18 1809
My Lord, By the much lamented death of Lieutenant-general Sir John Moore, who fell in action with the enemy on the 16th instant, it has become my duty to acquaint your lordship, that the French army attacked the British troops in the position they occupied in front of Corunna, at about two o'clock in the afternoon of that day. A severe wound which compelled me to quit the field a short time previous to the fall of

Sir John Moore, obliges me to refer your lordship for the particulars of the action, which was long and obstinately contested, to the enclosed report of Lieutenant-general Hope, who succeeded to the command of the army, and to whose ability and exertions, in direction of the ardent zeal and unconquerable valour of his majesty's troops, is to be attributed, under Providence, the success of the day, which terminated in the complete and entire repulse and defeat of the enemy at every point of attack. The Honourable Captain Gordon, my aide-de-camp, will have the honour of delivering this despatch, and will be able to give your lordship any further information which may be required.

I have the honour to be, &c.

D. BAIRD, Lieutenant General

Right Hon. Lord Viscount Castlereagh

His Majesty's Ship Audacious, off Corunna, January 18 1809

Sir, In compliance with the desire contained in your communication of yesterday, I avail myself of the first moment I have been able to command, to detail to you the occurrences of the action which took place in front of Corunna on the 16th instant. It will be in your recollection, that about one in the afternoon of that day, the enemy, who had in the morning received reinforcements, and who had placed some guns in front of the right and left of his line, was observed to be moving troops towards his left flank, and forming various columns of attack at that extremity of the strong and commanding position which on the morning of the 13th he had taken in our immediate front. This indication of his intention was immediately succeeded by the rapid and determined attack which he made upon your division which occupied the right of our position. The events which occurred during that period of the action you are fully acquainted with. The first effort of the enemy was met by the commander of the forces, and by yourself, at the head of the 42d regiment, and the brigade under Major-general Lord William Bentinck. The village on your right became an object of obstinate contest. I lament to say, that soon after the severe wound which deprived the army of your services, Lieutenant-general Sir John Moore, who had just directed the most able disposition, fell by a cannon-shot. The troops, though not unacquainted with the irreparable loss they had sustained, were not dismayed, but by the most determined bravery not only repelled every attempt of the enemy to gain ground, but actually forced him to retire, although he had brought up fresh troops in support of those originally engaged.

The enemy finding himself foiled in every attempt to force the right of the position, endeavoured by numbers to turn it. A judicious and well-timed movement which was made by Major-general Paget with the reserve, which corps had moved out of its cantonments to support the right of the army, by a vigorous attack, defeated this intention. The major-general having pushed forward the 95th (rifle corps) and 1st battalion 52d regiments, drove the enemy before him, and in his rapid and judicious advance, threatened the left of the enemy's position. This circumstance, with the position of Lieutenant-general Fraser's division (calculated to give still further security to the right of the line) induced the enemy to relax his efforts in that quarter. They were however more forcibly directed towards the centre, where they were again successfully resisted by the brigade under Major-general Manningham, forming the left of your division, and a part of that under Major-general Leigh, forming the right of the division under my orders. Upon the left, the enemy at first contented himself with an attack upon our piquets, which, however, in general maintained their ground. Finding, however, his efforts unavailing on the right and centre, he seemed determined to render the attack upon the left more serious, and had succeeded in obtaining possession of the village through which the great road to Madrid passes, and which was situated in front of that part of the line. From this post, however, he was soon expelled, with considerable loss, by a gallant attack of some companies of the 2d battalion 14th regiment, under Lieutenant-colonel Nicholls; before five in the evening, we had not only successfully repelled every attack made upon the position, but had gained ground in almost all points, and occupied a more forward line than at the commencement of the action, whilst the enemy confined his operations to a cannonade, and the fire of his light troops, with a view to draw off his other corps. At six the firing entirely ceased. The different brigades were re-assembled on the ground they occupied in the morning, and the piquets and advanced posts resumed their original stations. Notwithstanding the decided and marked superiority which at this moment the gallantry of the troops had given them over an enemy, who, from his numbers, and the commanding advantages of his position, no doubt expected an easy victory, I did not, on reviewing all circumstances, conceive that I should be warranted in departing from what I knew was the fixed and previous determination of the late commander of the forces to withdraw the army on the evening of the 16th, for the purpose of embarkation, the previous arrangements for which had already been made by his order, and were in fact far advanced at the commencement of the action. The troops quitted their position about ten at night, with a degree of order that did them credit. The whole of the artillery that remained unembarked having been withdrawn, the troops followed in the order prescribed, and marched to their respective points of embarkation in the town and neighbourhood of Corunna. The piquets remained at their posts until five on the morning of the 17th, when they were also withdrawn with similar orders, and without the enemy having discovered the movement.

By the unremitted exertions of Captains the Honourable H. Curzon, Gosselin, Boys, Rainier, Serret, Hawkins, Digby, Carden, and Mackenzie, of the royal navy, who in pursuance of the orders of Rear-admiral de Courcy, were entrusted with the service of embarking the army; and in consequence of the arrangements made by Commissioner Bowen, Captains Bowen and Shepherd, and the other agents for transports, the whole of the army was embarked with an expedition that has seldom been equalled. With the exception of the brigades under Major-generals Hill and Beresford, which were destined to remain on shore, until the movements of the enemy should become manifest, the whole was afloat before day-light. The brigade of Major-general Beresford, which was alternately to form our rear-guard, occupied the land front of the town of Corunna; and that under Major-general Hill was stationed in reserve on the promontory in rear of the town. The enemy pushed his light troops toward the town soon after eight o'clock in the morning of the 17th, and shortly after occupied the heights of St. Lucia, which command the harbour. But notwithstanding this circumstance, and the manifold defects of the place, there being no apprehension that the rear-guard could be forced; and the disposition of the Spaniards appearing to be good, the embarkation of Major-general Hill's brigade was commenced and completed by three in the afternoon. Major-general Beresford, with that zeal and ability which is so well known to yourself and the whole army, having fully explained, to the satisfaction of the Spanish governor, the nature of our movement, and having made every previous arrangement, withdrew his corps from the land front of the town, soon after dark, and was, with all the wounded that had not been previously moved, embarked before one this morning. Circumstances forbid us to indulge the hope, that the victory with which it has pleased Providence to crown the efforts of the army, can be attended with any very brilliant consequences to Great Britain. It is clouded by the loss of one of her best soldiers. It has been achieved at the termination of a long and harassing service. The superior numbers and advantageous position of the enemy, not less than the actual situation of this army, did not admit of any advantages being reaped from success. It must be, however, to you, to the army, and to our country, the sweetest reflection that the lustre of the British arms has been maintained, amidst many disadvantageous circumstances. The army which had entered Spain, amidst the fairest prospects, had no sooner completed its junction, than, owing to the multiplied disasters that dispersed the native armies round us, it was left to its own resources. The advance of the British corps from the Duoro afforded the best hope that the south of Spain might be relieved, but this generous effort to save the unfortunate people, also afforded the enemy the opportunity of directing every effort of his numerous troops, and concentrating all his principal resources for the destruction of the only regular force in the north of Spain. You are well aware with what diligence this system has been pursued. These circumstances produced the necessity of rapid and harassing marches, which had diminished the numbers, exhausted the strength, and impaired the equipment of the army. Notwithstanding all these disadvantages, and those more immediately attached to a definitive position, which the imperious necessity of covering the harbour of Corunna, for a time, had rendered indispensable to assume, the native and undaunted valour of British troops were never more conspicuous, and must have exceeded even what your own experience of that invaluable quality, so inherent in them, may have taught you to expect. When every one that had an opportunity, seemed to vie in improving it, it is difficult for me, in making this report, to select particular instances for your approbation. . . .

To you, who are well acquainted with the excellent qualities of Lieutenant-general Sir John Moore, I need not expatiate on the loss the army and his country have sustained by his death. His fall has deprived me of a valuable friend, to whom long experience of his worth had sincerely attached me. But it is chiefly on public grounds that I lament the blow. It will be the conversation of every one who loved or respected his manly character, that, after conducting the army through an arduous retreat with consummate firmness, he has terminated a career of distinguished honour by a death that has given the enemy additional reason to respect the name of a British soldier. Like the immortal Wolfe, he is snatched from his country at an early period of a life spent in her service; like Wolfe, his last moments were guided by the prospect of success, and cheered by the acclamation of victory; like Wolfe also, his memory will for ever remain sacred in that country which he sincerely loved, and which he had so faithfully served. It remains for me only to express my hope, that you will speedily be restored to the service of your country, and to lament the unfortunate circumstance that removed you from your station in the field, and threw the momentary command into far less able hands.

I have the honour to be, &c.

JOHN HOPE, Lieutenant-General

Lieutenant-General Sir D. Baird

Supplement to the London 'Gazette Extraordinary'
Admiralty-Office, January 24, 1809. *XXI 83-84*

Copy of a Letter from the Honourable Michael de Courcy, Rear-Admiral of the White, to the Honourable W.W. Pole, dated on board his Majesty's Ship the Tonnant, at Corunna, the 17th and 18th instant

January 17, 1809

Sir, Having it in design to detach the *Cossack* to England as soon as her boats shall cease to be essential to the embarkation of the troops, I seize a moment to acquaint you, for the information of the Lords Commissioners of the Admiralty, that the ships of war, as per margin,[1] and transports, under the orders of Rear-Admiral Sir Samuel Hood and Commissioner Bowen, arrived at this anchorage from Vigo on the 44th and 15th instant. The *Alfred* and *Hindostan*, with some transports, were left at Vigo to receive a brigade of 3,500 men, that had taken that route under the Generals Alten and Crawford [Craufurd?].

In the vicinity of Corunna the enemy have pressed upon the British in great force. The embarkation of the sick, the cavalry, and the stores went on. The night of the 16th was appointed for the general embarkation of the infantry; and, mean time, the enemy prepared for attack. At three, P.M. an action commenced; the enemy, which had been posted on a lofty hill, endeavouring to force the British on another hill of inferior height, and nearer the town. The enemy were driven back with great slaughter; but very sorry am I to add, that the British, though triumphant, have suffered severe losses. I am unable to communicate further particulars, than that Sir John Moore received a mortal wound of which he died at night; that Sir David Baird lost an arm; that several officers and many men have been killed and wounded; and that the ships of war have received all such of the latter as they could accommodate, the remainder being sent to transports.

The weather is now tempestuous, and the difficulties of embarkation are great. All except the rear guard are embarked, consisting perhaps at the present moment of 2,600 men. The enemy having brought cannon to a hill overhanging the beach, have forced a majority of the transports to cut or slip. Embarkation being no longer practicable at the town, the boats have been ordered to a sandy beach near the light-house, and it is hoped that the greater part, if not all, will still be embarked, the ships of war having dropped out to facilitate embarkation.

January 18

The embarkation of the troops having occupied the greater part of last night, it has not been in my power to detach the *Cossack* before this day: and it is with satisfaction I am able to add, that, in consequence of the good order maintained by the troops, and the unwearied exertions of Commissioner Bowen, the captains, and other officers of the navy, the agents, as well as the boats' crews, many of whom were for two days without food, and without repose, the army have been embarked to the last man, and the ships are now in the offing, preparatory to steering for England. The great body of the transports having lost their anchors, ran to sea without the troops they were ordered to receive, in consequence of which there are some thousands on board the ships of war. Several transports, through mismanagement, ran on shore. The seamen appeared to have abandoned them, two being brought out by the boats' crews of the men of war, two

[1] *Ville de Paris, Victory, Barfleur, Zealous, Implacable, Elizabeth, Norge, Plantagenet, Resolution, Audacious, Endymion, Mediator.*

were burnt, and five were bilged. I cannot conclude this hasty statement without expressing my great obligations to Rear-Admiral Sir Samuel Hood, whose eye was every where, and whose exertions were unremitted.

[P.S.] Hazy weather rendering the *Cossack* obscure, I detached the *Gleaner* with this despatch.

Cochrane's Coastal Operations

From the 'Memoir of the Public Services of the Right Honourable Lord Cochrane, K.B.' XXII 13-15

No sooner had they attempted to shake off the galling yoke of their oppressors, than the English, ever sympathising with those feelings which result from a sense of the inestimable blessings of liberty, proffered the most generous assistance; and, independently of his duty, as a British officer, we have reason to believe, that Lord Cochrane found himself impressed with the warmest interest, in favour of the patriots of Spain. Certain it is, that he made every exertion in their behalf, that could be made with a single ship; and that he both deserved and acquired the approbation of Lord Collingwood, the commander-in-chief. - In the month of July, 1808, while cruising off Catalonia, he formed the resolution of rescuing the castle of Mongal, which commands an important post between Barcelona and Gerona, from the hands of the French, by whom it had been seized. Accordingly, on the 31st of July, he attacked and carried that fortress; which, as soon as the military stores it contained had been delivered over to the patriots, he destroyed.[2]

Lord Cochrane next appears off the coast of Languedoc, where, in September, 1808, he blew up, and totally destroyed the newly-constructed "semaphoric" telegraphs at Bourdique, la Pinede, St. Maguire, Frontignan, Canet, and Foy; together with the houses attached, fourteen barracks of the gens-d'armes, a battery, and the strong tower upon the lake of Frontignan. The telegraphs here mentioned were considered as of the utmost importance to the safety of the convoys accustomed to pass along the coast of France; as, by their signals, they constantly apprised them of the approach of any English cruiser that might appear. Alluding to this service, the commander-in-chief, in his official letter, says: "Nothing can exceed the activity and zeal with which his lordship pursues the enemy. The success which attends his enterprises clearly indicates with what skill and ability they are conducted; besides keeping the coast in constant alarm, causing a total suspension of trade, and harassing a body of troops employed in opposing him, he has, probably, prevented those troops which were intended for Figueras, from advancing into Spain, by giving them employment in the defence of their own coasts." It appears, indeed, from Lord Cochrane's statement, that the comparatively insignificant force which he landed upon this occasion, drew about 2,000 troops from the fortress of Figueras, to the defence of the French coast.

Towards the close of the year (1808) the *Imperieuse*, with other ships, was employed in the Bay of Rosas, to assist the Spaniards in defending the fortress of that place; and Lord Cochrane, with his accustomed alacrity and spirit, landed, and took upon himself the defence of Trinity Castle, an outwork of the garrison, on which its preservation depended. At the time (November 22) the garrison, which consisted of only about eighty Spaniards, was on the point of surrendering. With this handful of men, joined

2 [See Vol. XX, p327.]

by a similar number of seamen and marines, from the *Imperieuse*, Lord Cochrane made the most astonishing exertions; and, on the 30th of the month, when a general assault was made upon the castle, by 1,000 picked men, he drove the assailants back, with the loss of their commanding officer, storming equipage, and all who had attempted to mount the breach. At length, finding it impossible to resist the overwhelming numbers of the French, the citadel of Rosas capitulated, on the 5th of December; and, as farther resistance, in Trinity Castle, would have been "useless and impracticable," Lord Cochrane blew up the magazines, and returned to his ship.

The Defence of Rosas

Letters on Service, Admiralty Office, January 31, 1809. XXI 165-167

Extract of a Letter from Vice-Admiral Lord Collingwood, Commander-in-Chief of his Majesty's Ships and Vessels in the Mediterranean, to the Honourable W.W. Pole, dated on board the Ocean, off Toulon, the 1st of December, 1808
The *Excellent*, having been relieved on the service at Rosas by the *Fame*, joined me on the 24th, and Captain West gave me a relation of events that have lately occurred there, in his letter dated the 21st ultimo, which I enclose, together with a list of killed and wounded seamen and marines of that ship and the *Meteor* bomb, employed on the same service.

But for the presence of his Majesty's ships in that bay, and the powerful assistance which Captain West, with the companies of those ships, afforded the Spaniards, both on shore and by the fire from them, there is every reason to believe the citadel of Rosas and castle of the Trinity would both have fallen; they were ill provided with every thing necessary to a siege; the works of the citadel in bad repair, and the garrison not sufficiently numerous for the duties of its defence.

Captain West's ability, and the valour and perseverance of his officers and men, removed as many of those defects as it was possible, and gave such severe checks to the enemy as made it necessary they should proceed by rules of art against a place that with their great force they intended to take by a *coup-de-main*, which has given ample time for the Spanish government to reinforce the garrison, and replenish the stores, &c. of this important post.

The French have on this occasion practised those arts which Frenchmen are very expert in. A person was employed, it seems, to intercept the letters written by Colonel O'Daly, the commandant of the garrison of Rosas, to the Supreme Junta of Gerona; and they were two or three weeks without having any knowledge of what was passing: - at the same time their emissaries gave out that the English had taken possession of the fortress, and suspended the Spanish officer from the duties of his office. The Junta wrote to Captain West, informing him of part of those reports, and begging he would inform them of the circumstances which had caused this change. It was afterwards discovered to be an artifice of the enemy to prevent reinforcements coming.

In another instance the French have shewn much art, by abandoning their usual system of terror, desolation, and plunder; and in the neighbourhood of Figueras and Rosas have lately treated the Spanish inhabitants with more kindness to their persons, and forbearance of their property, endeavouring to attach them by a feigned moderation.

The Spaniards are very sensible and very grateful for the support given to them by the English; the animating example of Captain West, his skill, and the gallantry of his

View of La Guayra, on the Spanish Main. Engraved by Rickards, from a drawing by G.T.
   La Guayra is in the province of Caracas, on the Spanish main, in the longitude of 10° 37' north, latitude 66°1/4 west. It is very strongly fortified. [Plate 249]

officers and men, is deserving of every praise; in the sortie he made at the head of his seamen and marines, when they attacked the enemy's advanced post, and rescued the miquelets [partizan irregulars], their conduct and their courage were admirable; several men were wounded, and Captain West's horse was shot under him, before they were obliged to retire, to prevent being cut off by the cavalry, which was advancing for that purpose. Captain Collins, of the *Meteor*, conducted the bombardment with great ability, and was indefatigable in the annoyance he gave the enemy by it. Lieutenant Howe, of the royal marines, belonging to the *Excellent*, commanded a detachment of that corps, which was thrown into the castle of Trinity for its defence; and in two assaults made by the enemy with large bodies of troops, this officer, and the marines under his command, were highly distinguished for the gallantry which they displayed, and the resources they found, where almost every thing was wanting.

   The enemy suffered a very considerable loss of men in these assaults; but unless measures have been taken to raise the siege, I am apprehensive this very important post will be reduced.

[Captain John West to the Right Honourable, Vice-Admiral Lord Collingwood, dated:]

His Majesty's Ship, Excellent, Rosas Bay, November 21, 1808
My Lord, I have anxiously waited an opportunity to inform your lordship of the investment of this port by the enemy, with a force computed at five or six thousand men.

On the evening of the 6th instant, the enemy was first observed in motion between Figueras and Catillern, and, on the following morning, was in complete possession of the heights that encompass this bay. On the same day at noon, a small body of the enemy entered the town of Rosas, which, in an instant, was cleared of its inhabitants, who either fled to their boats or the citadel for protection; but a well directed fire from the *Excellent* and *Meteor* bomb, both within point-blank shot of the town, obliged the enemy precipitately to retire. On the first appearance of the enemy, Colonel O'Daly, governor of this fortress, made application to me for assistance, when I immediately reinforced his garrison with the marines of the *Excellent* (with the exception of an officer and twenty-five men, who had been previously detached to Fort Trinité), and an officer and fifty seamen. On the 7th, the enemy took possession of several houses and ruins in the rear of the town as an advanced post, from which he has been repeatedly dislodged by the citadel and the guns and shells of his majesty's ships in the bay. On the 8th at noon, observing a body of miquelets hard pressed by the enemy from their advanced post, I was induced to make a sortie from the citadel with the seamen and marines, and the officers commanding them, but the very superior force of the enemy, who endeavoured to surround us, obliged us to retire, but not till my officers and men had displayed a spirit and courage which gave me the most lively satisfaction. I am sorry I am obliged by this little affair to send your lordship a return of wounded men.

Late on the evening of the 9th I received from the governor the unpleasant advice, that a large breach was made in the rampart of the citadel by a part of the bulwark falling down, sufficiently capacious to admit twenty-five men abreast. I proffered to the governor every assistance that the urgency of the moment required, and directed Captain Collins to immediately weigh and place the *Meteor* as near the shoal as possible, to flank the breach in the event of an attack. I sent at the same time two boats to enfilade the beach [breach?] with the cannonades; fortunately the lateness of the hour precluded the enemy gaining information of the event. The following morning I sent an officer and a part of seamen to assist in repairing the breach, directing the seamen and marines in the citadel to be employed on the same service. By every exertion the rampart was placed in a state of security for the night, the defence of which was entrusted to an officer and forty seamen, whom I sent on shore for that purpose. On the 3d day I was happy to see the repair completed, and the work as defensible as it was previous to the disaster.

On the morning of the 15th instant, at eight o'clock, the enemy was bravely repulsed; but in a moment again advanced in greater force, when two of the outer gates were broken open; but by a most galling and steady fire of musketry and hand-grenades from the fort, the enemy was a second time obliged to retire with great loss, leaving their leader, a chief of brigade, and many others, dead under its walls, and the second in command carried off desperately wounded. Expecting a third assault would be made, I threw in a reinforcement of thirty marines, with a captain and subaltern, by means of a rope ladder, which was effected without loss, and with one man but slightly wounded, during an incessant fire of musketry.

I cannot speak in terms of sufficient praise of the officers and men in their glorious defence of Fort Trinité, on which occasion five marines were wounded, and one Spaniard; but I have the satisfaction to enclose to your lordship a letter I have received from the Spanish officer commanding its garrison, which does him great honour.

No further attempt was made on this fort till the 20th instant, when the enemy opened a battery of three heavy guns from a height commanding it; but as yet has made no impression on its walls. The *Lucifer* bomb had been throwing her shells the two preceding days to prevent the enemy making a lodgment on this height; but was compelled to retire, after being struck three times by the battery. During the previous night the enemy threw up an extensive entrenchment three hundred yards from the citadel, and at daybreak opened a fire upon the ships in the bay from three large mortars, which obliged us to retire out of their reach: the bomb vessels, from having a longer range of shells than the enemy, were enabled to throw them with effect.

Fort Trinité, from its insulated situation and strength, I am of opinion, may stand a long siege. But I am not so sanguine with respect to the citadel, whose garrison is very inadequate to its defence, and having, as I conceive, a vulnerable point. I waited on the governor on Sunday last, to take my leave, when he informed me, that he was in expectation of a reinforcement; but I am apprehensive the blockade of the enemy in Barcelona will prove an obstacle to his expected success. . . .

I have, &c.

JOHN WEST

Right Hon. Vice-Admiral Lord Collingwood, &c

Admiralty Officer, March 11 1809. XXI 259-260

[Lord Cochrane to Vice-Admiral Lord Collingwood, and by him forwarded to the Honourable W W Pole, Admiralty First Secretary.]

Imperieuse, Bay of Rosas, December 5, 1808

My Lord, The fortress of Rosas being attacked by an army of Italians in the service of France, in pursuance of discretionary orders that your lordship had given me, to assist the Spaniards wherever it could be done with the most effect, I hastened here. The citadel, on the 22d ultimo, was already half invested, and the enemy making his approaches towards the south-west bastion, which your lordship knows was blown down in the last war by the explosion of a magazine, and tumbled into the ditch; a few thin planks and dry stones had been put up by the Spanish engineers, perhaps to hide the defect; all things were in the most deplorable state, both without and within; even measures for their powder, and saws for their fusees were not to be had - hats and axes supplied their place. The castle of Trinidad, situated on an eminence, but commanded by heights, was also invested; three twenty-four pounders battered in breach, to which a fourth was afterwards added, and a passage through the wall to the lower bomb proof being nearly effected, on the 23d the marines of the *Fame* were withdrawn. I went to examine the state of the castle, and, as the senior officer in the bay had not officially altered the orders I received from your Lordship, to give every possible assistance to the Spaniards, I thought this a good opportunity, by occupying a post on which the acknowledged safety of the citadel depended to render them an effectual service. The garrison then consisted of about eighty Spaniards, and were on the point of surrendering; accordingly I threw myself into it, with fifty seamen and thirty marines of the *Imperieuse*. The arrangement made I need not detail to your Lordship; suffice it to say, that about one thousand bags, besides barrels and palisadoes, supplied the place of walls and ditches; and that the enemy, who assaulted the castle on the 30th, with a thousand picked men, were repulsed with the loss of their commanding officer . . .

I have, &c.

COCHRANE

Operations in Galicia

Letters on Service, Admiralty Office, April 12, 1809. ^{XXI 333-336}

Copy of a Letter from Captain George-M'Kinley, of his Majesty's Ship Lively, to the Honourable W.W. Pole, dated on board that Ship, Vigo, the 29th of March 1809

Sir, As I have thought it of importance that my Lords Commissioners of the Admiralty should have the earliest intelligence of the surrender of Vigo, I have despatched Mr. T. Furber, senior lieutenant of this ship, (in a vessel hired for the purpose,) with a copy of my letter on that subject to the Honourable Vice-Admiral Berkeley.

I have the honour to be, &c.

GEORGE MCKINLEY

Lively, Vigo, March 29, 1809

Sir, In consequence of a letter I received at Villagarcia from Captain Crawford, of the *Venus*, off Vigo, informing me that the loyal peasantry were in considerable force around the castle and town of Vigo, and that the presence of another frigate would very much contribute to the surrender of that fortress, I joined him on the evening of the 23d instant.

The next morning I went to the head quarters of Don Joao de Almanda de Sanzo e Silva, who commanded the patriots. At the instant, a summons was sent to the Governor of Vigo to surrender at discretion, which led to a negotiation between him and the French, which continued till the 26th, when Don Pablo Murillo, commanding a regular force of 1,500 men, composed of retired soldiers in this province, arrived, and sent in a summons to surrender. In consequence of which, on the following day, the proposals (No. I [enclosure]) were brought on board by Don Pablo Murillo, accompanied by three French officers. The answers to them (No. II.) were delivered at five P.M. by Captain Crawford, who concluded the capitulation which I have the honour to enclose; and the whole of the garrison, consisting of a colonel, forty-five officers, and about thirteen or fourteen hundred men, were embarked the next morning.

I should be wanting in every feeling of an officer, were I not to acknowledge the liberal attention and zealous services of Captain Crawford.

It also becomes most gratifying that I am enabled to inform you of the spirit and determination of the Spaniards, to expel from their country, the invaders of all that is dear to a brave and loyal people. No doubt of success could have arisen, had the enemy persisted in holding out, from the able and prompt conduct of Don Pablo Murillo, and the good order of his troops, the strongest proof of his zeal in the just cause of his king and country, and the ardour of the peasantry is beyond all description.

I have the honour to be, &c.

GEORGE MCKINLEY

[Enclosures included the articles of capitulation and a return of the French forces.]

Admiralty Office, June 21, 1809. ^{XXII 78-79}

Copy of a Letter from the Honourable Captain Irby, of his Majesty's ship Amelia, addressed to Admiral Lord Gambier, and transmitted by his Lordship to the Honourable W.W. Pole

10th June, 1809

My Lord, Acting in obedience to your lordship's order of the 15th ult. I received information of an attack being about to be made by the Spanish Patriots, on the French troops in possession of the town of St. Andero [Santander]; and having established signals between his Majesty's ship under my command and the fortress of Golezand, I proceeded off this place in company with his Majesty's ship *Statira*, she having joined me on the 8th inst. but a strong wind and current prevent our getting up till this day, when, on our approach, firing was observed in every direction on the shore, and several vessels trying to effect their escape out of the harbour, which were captured as per margin,[3] one boat only getting away; more must have escaped but were prevented through the activity of Captain Boys, in his Majesty's ship *Statira*. They appear fine vessels, and have several of the French army on board, with chief part of the hospital Staff. The corvette is the same lately so gallantly engaged by Captain Skinner, in his Majesty's sloop *Goldfinch*, and since by the *Black Joke* Lugger, and has proved a great annoyance to our trade. I learn by a Spanish officer, who came to me from the shore, (aide-de-camp to General Ballestero,) and by our own boats which I sent on shore, that the French Troops have all surrendered, and that the town is in possession of the Spanish patriots under the command of General Ballestero. . . .

I have the honour to be, &c.

FREDERICK PAUL IRBY

Admiralty Office, July 4, 1809. [XXII 79-80]

Copies of two Letters from Captain M'Kinley, of His Majesty's Ship the Lively, to the Honourable William Wellesley Pole

Lively, Vigo, June 7, 1809

Be pleased to inform my Lords Commissioners of the Admiralty, that, yesterday evening, an express arrived from a Spanish Officer at San Payo to Commodore Juan Don Carransas, that the Conde de Morona was retiring with his Division of the Galician army from Pontevedra to that place, and desiring boats might be there to convey the troops across the river, (the bridge having been broken down on the 7th of May,) Commodore Don J. Carransas requesting assistance, Captain Winter with the *Cadmus* (who had been obliged to put back from stress of weather) immediately sailed up the river with the Portuguese schooner *Curiosa*, under my orders from the Honourable Vice-admiral Berkeley, the *Tigre* Spanish schooner of war and as many boats and vessels as could possibly be collected.

This retrograde movement caused me much anxiety, and I very early this morning went up in the barge to San Payo, where I found Brigadier-General Carrera strongly posted on the south side of the bridge (the Conde de Morona being at Redondela), and in my interview with him, I learnt that the enemy, after the Brigadier-General had taken Santiago, united his forces from Lugo to those of Corunna, amounting to eight thousand men, two thousand five hundred cavalry, with several field-pieces and some twelve pounders.

This force being very much superior to the Brigadier's, he retreated to Caldas and Pontevedra, where the Conde de Morona joined. From the excessive and continued heavy rains we have had of late, much of the ammunition was unavoidably damaged, and Pontevedra being too distant to receive any more when attacked, the falling back on such a strong position was well conceived and most ably executed. On a height, above

---

3 Listed were a corvette, *La Mouche*, a brig, a schooner and two luggers.

the bridge they had a battery of two eighteen-pounders, and this army was increased to between six and seven thousand men armed, and three thousand fine young men without arms, one hundred and twenty horse, nine field pieces, acting under the immediate direction of the Brigadier-General.

At nine the enemy appeared on the other side, in great force, and although the Galician troops had undergone much fatigue, and suffered greatly from the inclemency of the weather, to which they had been constantly exposed, yet, on the approach of the enemy nothing could exceed the animation and spirit of the soldiers, all was alacrity and confidence, and I left the Brigadier-General, and was saluted by the enemy from their field-pieces, but without hurting us, although nearly within musket-shot; at half-past nine they opened their fire on the Spaniards, which was most spiritedly returned and their field artillery was moved with great alacrity and well served.

On my return on board I landed my marines and twenty-five seamen at the Castle (having taken them on board some days past); and Lieutenant Colonel Carroll, in the most zealous and handsome manner, offered his services to assist Captain Crawford in defence of the Castle, sixty soldiers, whom he brought from Gijon with him, (part of our army,) at his earnest request were landed, and I supplied them with arms; and every thing was put in the best possible order of defence by Commodore Don Juan Carransas, Don Bernardo Gonçalez the Governor, and Captain Crawford, of his Majesty's ship *Venus*.

I have the honour to be, &c.

GEORGE McKINLEY

[On 7 June the French army, commanded by Marshal Ney, attacked the Spanish position and was repeatedly repulsed. In consequence the French had to evacuate Corunna and Ferrol.]

1809 – Capture of Cayenne, Martinique, and the Saintes

IN THE WEST INDIES the tide was flowing with the British. On 12 January the French colony of Cayenne, bordering on Brazil, capitulated to British and Portuguese forces, and the French frigate *Topaze*, of 48 guns, laden with troops and provisions for its relief, was captured eleven days later by cruisers. At the end of January, Martinique and St Lucia fell to forces under the command of Rear-Admiral Sir Alexander Cochrane and Lieutenant-General Beckwith, following which British forces were landed on the Saintes. On 14 February the *Hautpoult* was captured when the small squadron sheltering in the group of islands was forced to try to escape, and on the 17th the islands capitulated to Major-General Maitland. The successes were partly attributable to the care which was being taken of the health of men ashore, and especially to the employment of black soldiers who were acclimatised. This experiment, in imitation of the French, had been agreed to reluctantly by the island governments, and was an important development, both in the context of the war and in that of world social history.

Capture of Cayenne

Letters on Service, Admiralty Office,
April 15, 1809. *XXI 337-340*

Captain James Lucas Yeo, of his Majesty's ship the *Confiance*, has, with his letter dated at Cayenne, the 9th February last, transmitted to the Honourable William Wellesley Pole, copies of his letters to Rear-Admiral Sir William Sidney Smith, detailing his proceedings in the expedition against the above settlement.

Having, in conjunction with the Portuguese land forces, under the command of Lieutenant-colonel Manuel Marques, taken possession, on the 8th December last, of the district of Oyapok, and on the 15th of the same month, with the *Confiance* and a Portuguese sloop and cutter, reduced that of Approaque; Captain Yeo, together with the lieutenant-colonel, proceeded to the attack of the island of Cayenne with the

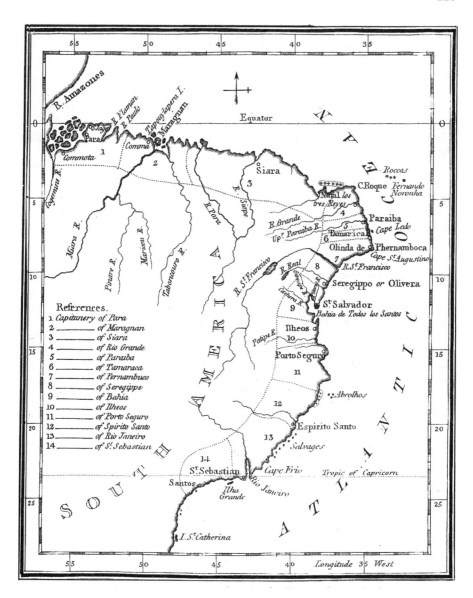

Chart of Brazil. Plate 417

Confiance, two Portuguese sloops, and some smaller vessels, having on board five hundred and fifty Portuguese troops. The following is a copy of Captain Yeo's letter on this subject.

His Majesty's Ship Confiance, Cayenne Harbour, 15th January, 1809
Sir, My last letters to you of the 26th ult. informed you of the arrival of the Portuguese troops at Approaque. On the 4th inst. it was determined by Lieutenant-colonel Manoel [sic] Marques and myself, to make a descent on the east side of the island of Cayenne. Accordingly all the troops were embarked on board the small vessels, amounting to 550,

and 80 seamen and marines from the *Confiance*, and a party of marines from the *Voador* and *Infante* brigs. On the morning of the 6th all dropped into the mouth of the river. In the evening I proceeded with ten canoes and about 250 men, to endeavour to gain possession of two batteries: the one Fort Diamant, which commands the entrance of the river Mahuree, the other Grand Cane, commanding the great road to the town of Cayenne. The vessels, with the remainder of the troops, I entrusted to Captain Salgado, of the *Voador*, with orders to follow me after dusk, to anchor in the mouth of the river Mahuree, and wait until I gained the before-mentioned batteries; when, on my making the signal agreed on, he was to enter the river and disembark with all possible despatch. I reached Point Mahuree at three o'clock next morning, with five canoes; the others being heavy could not keep up. We then landed in a bay half way between the two batteries. The surge was so great, that our boats soon went to pieces. I ordered Major Joaquin Manoel Pinto, with a detachment of Portuguese troops, to proceed to the left, and take Grand Cane; while myself, accompanied by Lieutenants Mulcaster, Blyth, and Read (of the royal marines); Messrs. Savory, William Taylor, Forder, and Irwin, proceeded to the right with a party of the *Confiance*, to take Fort Diamant, which was soon in our possession, mounting two twenty-four and one brass nine-pounder, and fifty men. I am sorry to add, that Lieutenant John Read, of the Royal Marines, a meritorious young officer, was mortally wounded, as also one seaman and five marines badly. The French captain and commandant, with three soldiers, were killed, and four wounded. The major had the same success: the fort mounting two brass nine-pounders and forty men; two of the enemy were killed. The entrance of the river being in our possession, the signal agreed on was made, and by noon all were disembarked. At the same time I received information of General Victor Hughes having quitted Cayenne, at the head of a thousand troops, to dispossess us of our posts. Our force being too small to be divided, and the distance between the two posts being great, and only twelve miles from Cayenne, it was determined to dismantle Fort Diamant, and collect all our forces at Grand Cane. I therefore left my first lieutenant, Mr. Mulcaster, with a party of the *Confiance*, to perform that service, and then join me. On arriving at Grand Cane, I perceived two other batteries about a mile up the river, on opposite sides, and within half gun-shot of each other: the one on the right bank called Treo, on an eminence commanding the creek leading to Cayenne; on the other, at the opposite side, at the entrance of the creek leading to the house and plantation of General Victor Hughes, and evidently erected for no other purpose than its defence. At three o'clock I anchored the *Lion* and *Vingaza* cutters abreast of them, when a smart action commenced on both sides for an hour; when finding the enemy's metal and position so superior to ours, the cutters having only four-pounders, and many of our men falling from the incessant shower of grape-shot, I determined to storm them, and therefore directed Mr. Savory (the purser,) to accompany a party of Portuguese to land at General Hughes' battery; at the same time proceeding myself, accompanied by Lieutenant Blyth, my gig's crew, and a party of Portuguese troops, to that of Treo; and though both parties had to land at the very muzzles of the guns keeping up a continual fire of grape and musketry, the cool bravery of the men soon carried them, and put the enemy to flight: each fort mounted two brass nine-pounders and fifty men. This service was scarcely accomplished, before the French troops from Cayenne attacked the colonel at Grand Cane. Our force then much dispersed, I therefore, without waiting an instant, ordered every body to the boats, and proceeded to the aid of the colonel, who, with his small force, had withstood the enemy; and after a smart action of three hours, they retreated to Cayenne. At the same time, 250 of the enemy appeared before Fort Diamant; but perceiving Lieutenant Mulcaster prepared to receive them, and imagining his force much greater than it was, they, on hearing the defeat of their general, followed his example.

There was yet the strongest post of the enemy to be taken, which was the private house of General Victor Hughes: he had, besides the fort above-mentioned, planted before his house a field-piece and a swivel, with an hundred of his best troops. It is situated on the main, between and three miles in the interior, at the end of an avenue the same length from the river; on the right of which is a thick wood, and on the left the creek Fouille. I have also to remark, that there is nothing near appertaining to government, or for the defence of the colony. On the morning of the 8th I proceeded, accompanied by Lieutenant Mulcaster, Messrs. Savory and Forder, with some seamen and marines of the *Confiance*, and a party of Portuguese troops, with a field-piece, to take the said post; but as my only object was to take the post, for which I had force sufficient; and though I might lose some men in taking it, there could be no doubt as to the result: I therefore requested, for the sake of humanity, he would not attempt to defend a place not tenable; but that I was determined, if he made a useless resistance in defending a private habitation, against which I gave him my honour no harm was intended, I would consider it as a fortress, and would level it to the ground. The enemy's advanced guard allowed the flag of truce to approach them within a boat's length; then fired two volleys at them, and retreated. I then landed; but reflecting it was possible this outrage was committed from the ignorance of an inferior officer, I sent Lieutenant Mulcaster a second time, when on his approaching the house, they fired the field-piece at him. Finding all communication that way ineffectual, yet wishing to preserve the private property of a general officer, who was perhaps ignorant and innocent of his officer's conduct, I sent one of the general's slaves to the officer with the same message, who returned with an answer that any thing I had to communicate must be in writing; at the same instant he fired his field-piece as a signal to his troops, who were in ambush on our right in the wood, to fire, keeping up a steady and well-directed fire from his field-piece at the house. It was my intention to have advance with my field-piece; but finding he had made several fosses in the road, and the wood being lined with musketry, not a man of whom we could see, and the field-piece in front, I ordered ours to be thrown into a foss, when our men, with cheers, advanced with pike and bayonet, took the enemy's gun; they retreated in the house, and kept up a smart fire from the windows; but on our entering they flew through the back premises into the wood, firing as they retreated. Every thing was levelled with the ground, except the habitations of the slaves.

As we received information that about 400 of the enemy were about to take possession of Beauregard Plain, on an eminence which commands the several roads to and from Cayenne, it was determined between the lieutenant-colonel and myself to be before hand with the enemy, and march our whole force there direct. We gained the situation on the enemy on the 9th, and on the 10th Lieutenant Mulcaster and a Portuguese officer, (Lieutenant Bernardo Mikillis,) were sent into the town with a summons (No. I [enclosure]) to the general. In the evening these officers returned, accompanied by Victor Hughes's aide-de-camp, requesting an armistice for twenty-four hours, to arrange the articles of capitulation. This being granted, and hostages exchanged, on the 11th the lieutenant-colonel and myself met the general, and partly arranged the articles. A second meeting on the morning of the 12th finally fixed them, (No. II) and on the morning of the 14th, the Portuguese troops and British seamen and marines marched into Cayenne, and took possession of the town. The enemy, amounting to 400, laid

View of St. Eustatius, from the Eastward. Engraved by Bennet, from a drawing by Pocock.

It may be more properly termed a huge pyramidical rock rising out of the waves, than an island; yet, for its size, it is incomparably the most valuable of all the Caribbees. Tobacco is its chief product; and that plant is cultivated, on its sides, to the very top of the pyramid, which terminates in a plain, surrounded by woods, but having a hollow in the middle, which serves as a large den for wild beasts. Plate 316

down their arms on the parade, and were immediately embarked on board the several vessels belonging to the expedition; at the same time the militia, amounting to 600, together with 200 blacks, who had been incorporated with the regular troops, delivered in their arms. . . .

I am, &c.

JAMES LUCAS Yeo

Capture of Martinique and the Saintes

Admiralty-Office, March 28, 1809. XXI 317-318

Copy of a Letter from the Honourable Rear-Admiral Sir Alexander Cochrane, K.B., Commander-in-Chief of his Majesty's Ships and Vessels at the Leeward Islands, to the Honourable W.W. Pole, dated on board the Neptune, off Martinique, the 4th of February, 1809

Sir, Having on the 20th January received a letter from Lieutenant-general Beckwith, informing me that in consequence of some alteration of circumstances he was induced to proceed on the attack of Martinique, and expressing a wish to see me at Barbadoes, in order to make the final arrangements, I lost no time in meeting him there for that purpose; and having embarked all the troops, I committed the principal landing of the army intended to be put on shore at Bay Robert, to Captain Beaver, of his Majesty's ship *Acasta*, who had Lieutenant-general Beckwith, the commander of the forces, with him; Major-general Sir George Prevost, commanding the division, being embarked on board the *Penelope*. By the enclosed letter from Captain Beaver, their Lordships will see that he completed this service, with his usual ability, on the 30th of January, and morning of the 31st, whilst the other division, under Major-general Maitland, was landed on the 30th at Saint Luce, under the superintendence of Captain Fahie, of the *Belleisle*, who had formed the most judicious arrangements for the purpose.

About six hundred men were detached on board his Majesty's ship *York*, under the command of Major Henderson, of the Royal York Rangers, to take possession of the battery at Point Solomon, in order to secure a safe anchorage for the men of war and transports: after effecting this the Rangers pushed on, and invested the fort of Pigeon Island, on which a mortar was brought to bear so early as the 1st instant, but not finding the fire of that sufficient, nine others, including howitzers, were landed, five of which were got up to the top of a commanding height, by the very great exertions of Captain Cockburn, of the *Pompée*, and the seamen under his orders, who ably gave support to Brigadier-generals Sir Charles Shipley and Sichelin, in completing the batteries, which opened last night, at six o'clock, with such effect, as to oblige the enemy to capitulate this morning; and one hundred and thirty-six persons that were in the fort, surrendered themselves prisoners of war. Our loss consisted of two seamen killed, and one soldier of the Royal York Rangers wounded; the enemy's of five killed and several wounded.

In order to cut off the retreat of the enemy, I previously sent the *Aeolus* and *Cleopatra* frigates, and the *Recruit* sloop of war, to the upper part of Fort Royal Bay; when this was perceived, the enemy set fire to, and destroyed the *Amphitrite* frigate, of forty-four guns, and all the shipping in the harbour; having, on our first landing, burnt the *Carnation* at Marin, also a corvette at St. Pierres on the following night.

The army under Lieutenant-general Beckwith having advanced towards the heights of Surirey, fell in with the enemy on the 1st instant, who was defeated with considerable loss; since then two actions have taken place, which has given to his Majesty's forces possession of the before-mentioned heights, commanding Fort Bourbon. The enemy upon this abandoned the lower fort, or Fort de France, having destroyed the guns, and from the different explosions I suppose they have blown up the magazines.

Major-general Maitland reached Samantin on the 2d without opposition, and has since formed a junction with the Lieutenant-general. I am now moving the squadron to the Fort Royal side of the Bay, so as to embrace the double view of an early communication with the head quarters of the army, and affording the supplies necessary for the siege of Fort Bourbon on both sides.

From the zeal which has manifested itself in each service, I make no doubt but the batteries will soon be in a fit state to open upon the enemy, and I hope before long, that I shall have the satisfaction to communicate to their Lordships that the fort has surrendered.

The militia who were forced to serve, have returned to their homes.

I have the honour to be, &c.

ALEXANDER COCHRANE

The London 'Gazette Extraordinary'
Admiralty-Office, April 12, 1809. ^{XXI} _323-333_

Captain Joseph Spear, of his Majesty's sloop the *Wolverine*, arrived at the office this morning with despatches from Rear-admiral the Honourable Sir Alexander Cochrane, K.B. commander-in-chief of his Majesty's ships and vessels at the Leeward Islands, addressed to the Honourable William Wellesley Pole, of which the following are copies:

Neptune, Fort-Royal Bay, Martinique, February 25, 1809
Sir, By my letter of the 18th, a duplicate of which accompanies this, together with one of the 4th, the Lords Commissioners of the Admiralty will have been informed, that it was intended to open a fire on the enemy from four batteries on the succeeding day in addition to his own guns turned upon him from Fort Edward, which was accordingly done at half-past four in the afternoon, the time appointed.

The enemy at first returned the fire with spirit, but it gradually slackened until the following morning, and then entirely ceased, except at long intervals, which made it evident he was beaten from his guns.

While the batteries were kept constant firing on the enemy from the western side, Captains Barton and Nesham, of the *York* and *Intrepid*, with about four hundred seamen and marines, continued to be employed in getting the heavy cannon, mortars, and howitzers up to Mount Surirey from the eastern side of the fort, which was a service of the utmost labour and difficulty, owing to the rains and deepness of the roads; but notwithstanding which, a battery of four twenty-four pounders and four mortars was finished by the 22d, and the guns mounted ready for service.

On the following day several more guns were got up, and ready to be placed in an advanced battery, intended to consist of eight twenty-four-pounders; a similar battery was preparing to the westward, and the whole would have been in a state to open on the enemy by the 26th, had not a flag of truce been sent from the Fort on the 23d, with proposals for a surrender, on the principle of being sent to France on parole; but Lieutenant-general Beckwith, the commander of the forces, and myself, not judging it proper to accede to such terms, the batteries, which had before opened their fire, recommenced the attack at half-past eight o'clock in the evening, and continued it without intermission during the night.

The next morning, a little past six o'clock, one of the magazines in the fort blew up with a great explosion, and soon afterwards three flags of truce were hoisted by the enemy, and hostilities ceased on our part.

A letter was then received from the Captain-general Villaret Joyeuse, requesting that commissioners might be appointed on both sides to settle the terms of capitulation, which was agreed to, and Lieutenant-general Sir George Prevost and Major-general Maitland were named by the commander of the forces, and Commodore Cockburn by me. These officers were met by the general of artillery, Villaret (the Captain-general's brother), and Colonels Montfort and Boyer, in a tent erected for the purpose between the advanced piquets on each side, when the terms were settled and ratified before midnight; a copy of which I have the honour to enclose.

This morning a detachment of troops took possession of the Bouillé Redoubt and the ravelins and gateway of Fort Bourbon on the land side; and the garrison (a return of which, as well as the rest of the prisoners taken since the commencement of the siege, is enclosed) will be embarked in the course of eight days in transports, and his Majesty's ships *Belleisle* and *Ulysses* will proceed with them as a guard to Europe. . . .

I have the honour to be, &c.

ALEXANDER COCHRANE

[Enclosures included the terms of capitulation, returns of the French garrison, of the batteries erected, killed and wounded in the squadron, of the squadron, and the General Memorandum issued to the squadron.]

Admiralty Office, May 23, 1809. XXI 435-436

Copy of a Letter from Rear-Admiral the Honourable Sir Alexander Cochrane, K.B. Commander-in-Chief of His Majesty's Ships and Vessels at the Leeward Islands, to the Honourable W.W. Pole, dated on board the Neptune, off the Mona Passage, the 17th of April, 1809

Sir, Having in my letter, (No. 637,) dated the 7th instant, informed the Lords Commissioners of the Admiralty of the arrangements that had been made between Lieutenant-general Beckwith and me for the Reduction of the Saintes, and, if possible, to secure the French squadron of three ships of the line and two frigates, then at anchor there, which it is ascertained were sent to this country expressly for the relief of Martinique; I have now the honour to acquaint you, for their Lordships' information, with our subsequent proceedings, which have been attended with the capture of *Le D'Hautpoult*, a fine new ship, of seventy-four guns, of the largest class.

The troops, under the command of Major-General Maitland, arrived at the Saintes on the 13th instant, and were landed the following day with little loss; the direction of all naval operations connected with the army having been left entirely with Captain Beaver, of the *Acasto*, who conducted that service with all the correctness and celerity which I expected of him.

On the afternoon of the same day two howitzers and mortars began to play upon the enemy's ships; and I received information that one of the line had weighed one of her anchors, but that the others did not appear to be preparing for sea.

I must here call their Lordships' attention to the situation of the Saintes, which have three passages the enemy could escape through, and these being situated in different directions made it particularly difficulty to guard by five ships of the line, so as to bring an equal force to meet the enemy at either point.

At half-past nine in the evening, the concerted signal was made for the enemy's ships having put to sea; but the signals were for their having gone both to Windward and to Leeward of the islands, which was literally the case, as I am informed the two frigates proceeded one way, and the three line-of-battle ships the other.

The *Neptune* being at the time off the south-west passage, made sail to join the *Pompée* stationed under the west end, which ship I found had closed with, and was in chase of three ships, apparently standing to the W.S.W. but from their appearance in the dark, I did not suppose them to be of the line.

At this time I was particularly at a loss how to act, for if those ships should be the enemy's small men of war, and the line-of-battle ships reported to be preparing for sea, should remain behind, the withdrawing of the squadron from the Saintes would have been fatal to the troops landed the preceding day. The night was very dark, and it was not possible to determine whether the whole of the ships making off were of the line or not, although we crossed so near the sternmost, that her shot struck the *Neptune*, and killed one man and wounded four. When day-light approached they were clearly discovered, and every endeavour used to come up with them, the *Pompée* being the only line-of-battle ship in company, and the frigates not joining until the following day. Some ships were seen from the mast-head, to whom I sent to signify, by a sloop of war, the course we were steering.

The superiority of the enemy's sailing, left little chance for the *Neptune* getting up, unless some of the ships were disabled, and if any accident had happened to the *Pompée*'s Masts, they must inevitably have all escaped; I therefore directed Captain Fahie to endeavour to cripple the sternmost ship, without bringing on the collected fire of the three, then in line abreast. In this attempt he was most gallantly supported by Captain Napier, of his Majesty's sloop *Recruit*, who kept close up, although fired at from all their stern-chase guns, and did every thing that was possible to be done to cut away the enemy's masts and rigging, and continued on this service during the whole chace, which lasted until this morning at half-past three, when *Le D'Hautpoult* was brought to action by the *Pompée* and *Castor*, as will more fully appear by Captain Fahie's letter, here inclosed.

I should not render justice to that excellent officer was I to withhold the praise due to him for his unremitted attention during so long and arduous a pursuit, and his taking such advantages of the enemy's situation as they occasionally occurred.

I have much to regret in the loss of those that have fallen and suffered on the occasion, a list of whom is enclosed.

As the other two ships of the enemy separated on the morning of the 17th, at two o'clock, their route cannot be well ascertained, I suppose they made sail to the southward, and will pass through the Sambrero passage. They had outsailed this ship so much as to be at too great a distance to be observed when they parted, we of course followed the *Pompée*'s lights.

I am now waiting until the *Pompée* and the prize are refitted, to proceed to the windward; and I have detached the *York* and *Captain*, with two frigates and a sloop of war, to the northward to try to intercept the enemy's two ships that have escaped.

Until their Lordship's pleasure is known, I have commissioned the prize, and appointed Captain Napier to the command of her, as a reward for his spirited conduct during the chase.

I have the honour to be, &c.

ALEXANDER COCHRANE

Admiralty Office, June 2, 1809. ^{XXI 500-505}

Major-General F. Maitland to His Excellency Lieutenant-General Beckwith, Commander of Forces, and by him forwarded to the Right Honourable Lord Viscount Castlereagh

Camp, at the Saintes, April 18, 1809
Sir, I have the honour to transmit you a report of the proceedings of his Majesty's troops detached for the reduction of the Saintes.

We sailed from Fort Royal Bay on the 12th; Captain Beaver, of his Majesty's ship *Acasta*, who was commodore of the division, left the squadron under charge of Captain Carthew, of his Majesty's ship *Gloire*, and went forward to meet Rear-admiral Sir Alexander Cochrane. The 13th was passed in examining the enemy's positions and in making arrangements.

The disembarkation was fixed to be at six o'clock in the morning of the 14th, but a bad night separated our ships. By ten they were collected. Soon after, the *Acasta* led in, through a very narrow channel which was buoyed on each side. The *Gloire, Narcissus,* and *Circe* followed; the *Intrepid* about an hour after, but the *Dolphin* not until next day. His Majesty's ships anchored opposite to the little bay, Bois Joly. The landing was meant to have been at the next to eastward, called Ance Vanovre. As much time, it was then seen, would be lost by persevering to go to Ance Vanovre, because the boats would have had a long row against wind and current, we landed at Ance Bois Joly; a secure landing, though a stony beach, protected by the fire of the frigates. We experienced no opposition except a cannonade from the Isle of Cabrit, the guns of which fired over the ridge among the shipping.

When advanced to the first ridge, we found the enemy occupied the great mountain which is above eight hundred feet high, called Mount Russel. This was immediately on our right, nor could we advance. The rifle companies of the 3d and of the 4th battalions 60th regiment, were ordered to dislodge the enemy. The exertion of these companies, under Captains Dolling and Lupton, was great; the ascent no less steep than an angle of fifty degrees, covered with bush and prickly pears, they most gallantly effected the service, and drove back the enemy, who suffered considerably. The rifle companies were supported to their right by the flank companies of the 3d West India regiment, and one company of the Royal York Rangers, led by Lieutenant-colonel Campbell, deputy adjutant-general, whom I detached for this service. We had now a strong position. Before us were the enemy's three forts, showing stout garrisons, and three line-of-battle ships, and two frigates in the harbour. The large ships were full of men. We found, however, we could not advance without being flanked on our left by the fort on Isle de Cabrit. Two eight-inch howitzers were immediately landed, a battery quickly constructed by Lieutenant Hobbs, of the Royal Engineers. Brigadier-general Stehelin, of the royal artillery, and all his officers and men, were most strenuous, and before six that evening our battery opened on the enemy's squadron at a very fair distance. About an hour after, there were indications that the French squadron was about to push out, and by eight it was not doubtful. Not a moment was lost; Captain de Courcy, of the quarter-master-general's department, was sent by me to Captain Beaver, of the *Acasta,* and we fired six rockets from a headland, at five minutes interval, being the signal fixed on by the admiral. About ten at night, the three French line-of-battle ships were seen to go through the windward passage. Next morning, the 15th instant, the *Intrepid* was the only line-of-battle ship in sight.

The difficulty of advancing on the west side of the island, forced us to reembark the greater part of our troops, to land at Ance Vanovre, but as the enemy occupied a strong and commanding position on the east side of this bay, Lieutenant-Colonel Prescot, with the flank companies of the 3d West India regiment, and the two rifle companies of the 60th and Major Henderson, with the reserve, were ordered to descend from Mount Russel to protect the landing, and to dislodge the enemy. This was well executed, and we gained a favourable position, whence our mortars could reach Fort Napoleon at a proper distance, as well as the fort on the islet. A mortar battery of two thirteen-inch, and four ten-inch was immediately begun, and carried on with unremitted exertions; all our men volunteering every labour. Between the enemy's forts Napoleon and Morelle, and us, was a middle ridge, which was on the back of the town, and held by the enemy. On the night of the 15th, a strong piquet of the enemy was surprised by two companies of the Royal York Rangers, commanded by Captain Starke and Lieutenant White. The

View of the islands of Redonda and Nevis, in the West Indies. Engraved by Hall, from a drawing by G.T. Plate 255

French had one officer and seventeen men bayonetted, and twelve prisoners were brought away. This affair was highly creditable to the officers named. The night following we determined to occupy the middle ridge, and confine the enemy within his works. Major Alen was ordered with the two flank companies of the 3d West India, and a flank company of the 8th West India for this service; he was supported by part of the Royal York Rangers, under Major Henderson. The position advanced from Forts Napoleon and Morelle to recover this ground. A sharp action took place, the whole of the York Rangers, and the rifle companies of the 60th, supporting our black troops. The ground lay open in great part to the grape shot from Forts Napoleon and Morelle, and to round shot from Islet de Cabrit; but all our troops were undaunted; - none were more brave or active than the flank companies of the 3d West India regiment, and a flank company of the 8th West India, under Major Alen. The enemy was driven back with loss, and our possession of the ground completely secured. On this occasion our loss was about thirty men, killed and wounded.

I omitted to say that the two French frigates, both loaded with flour, took their chance of escaping on the forenoon of the 15th. They went through the windward passage, keeping a little from the wind to gain the shore of Guadaloupe. The leading frigate was engaged by his Majesty's ship *Intrepid*. This frigate however doubled the point of Vieux Fort, was followed by the other, and both escaped into Basse Terre.

About the middle of the day, yesterday the 17th, the French commandant, Colonel Madier, sent a flag of truce to enter into terms. They expected what we would not concede, and they submitted to what we were willing to grant. They are prisoners of war.

I understand their number to be from seven to eight hundred; of this number, six hundred were landed by the French squadron.

We are to take possession of the forts this evening at four o'clock.

I have the honour to be, &c.

F. MAITLAND, Major-General

His Excellency Lieutenant-general Beckwith,
Commander of the Forces

Imperial Parliament

House of Commons, Friday April 14, 1809. *XXI 509-510*

Lord *Castlereagh* called the attention of the House to the services of the navy and army in the West Indies, in the conquest of Martinique. That capture had never been effected under circumstances more glorious than in the recent instance. It was a proud circumstance for the country, that whilst we had an army of 50,000 men on the Continent of Europe, government had been able to collect a force of 10,000 men for offensive operations against Martinique, without detaching any troops from Europe. Though the gallantry of the troops had been most distinguished, there was one circumstance which peculiarly characterized this conquest, namely, that from the effectual measures taken by the Officers of Health, the object of the expedition had been accomplished with less loss by disease than at any former time. Every favour, too, consistent with the interests of the public, had been shewn to the inhabitants of Martinique, who had behaved with the greatest good-will towards their captors.

[At the beginning of July 1809 the last French garrison in the Spanish half of Hispaniola surrendered, and one of the French frigates, *la Furieuse*, which had escaped from the Saintes, was captured by the sloop *Bonne Citoyenne* in August. At the end of the action both ships were in a near sinking condition and it was only with great difficulty that they were brought into Halifax. Vol. XXII, pp346-348.]

1809 – Action at Basque Roads

ADMIRAL LORD GAMBIER'S BLOCKADE of the Brest fleet into Basque Roads in the mouth of the Charente put the British squadron in a dangerously exposed position. The Admiralty sent him four 'explosion ships' and instructions to give Captain Lord Cochrane command of a force of fire-ships to attack the enemy at their moorings, where they were protected by sand bars, strong tides and batteries. Rear-Admiral Eliab Harvey's violent reaction to Gambier's employment of Lord Cochrane led to his being sent home and court-martialled. The operation, undertaken on the night of 11 April, was a partial success. The explosion ships were fired prematurely, but the fire-ships got through the boom and, when the tide allowed, the fleet entered the roads and destroyed those ships which did not manage to escape up the Charente by throwing overboard their guns and stores so that they could pass the bar. One ship of 120 guns, five 74s and two frigates were driven on shore and either totally destroyed or rendered useless, while one 80, two 74s, a 50 and three frigates were burnt. To Cochrane's overwrought mind, however, Lord Gambier's support had been too slow. On his declaration to the Admiralty that he would use his vote in the House of Commons, of which he was a member, to oppose a vote of thanks to Lord Gambier, the latter requested a court-martial, which fully exonerated him and discredited Cochrane.

Destruction of the French Fleet in Basque Roads, With a Plan of the Harbour, &c. By an Officer of His Majesty's Ship Valiant (With an Engraving) XXI 403-407

Mr. Editor, As a public despatch is not calculated to include many of the minute particulars relating to a naval operation, but merely to pencil out a broad outline, and sum up the final result, I beg leave to fill a few of the chasms with such particulars as fell under my immediate observation, during the late attack on (and I may say destruction of) the French fleet in Basque Roads. On the 11th of April, 1809, the French fleet were

[The engraving of Basque Roads.] Plate 13

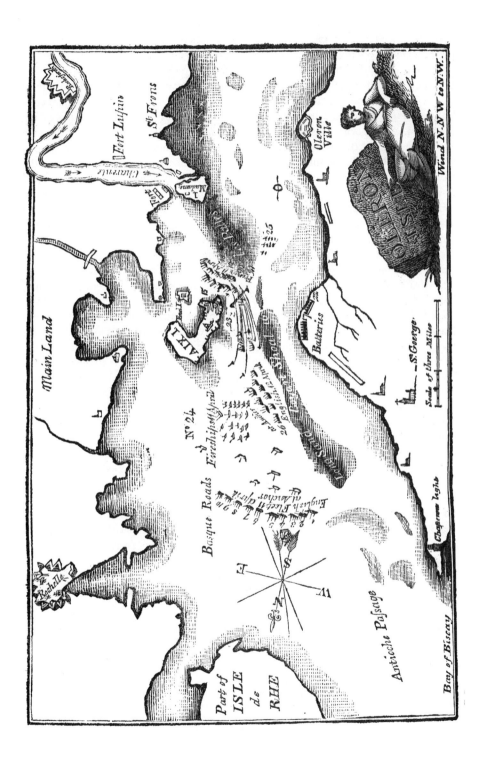

anchored in two lines, between Isle D'Aix, and a shoal to the southward of that island (Les Pattes). The channel was narrow, and between them and the outer roads was placed a kind of boom (No. 14), composed of cables, secured by anchors, and floated by buoys, &c. which they believed capable of resisting fire-ships; while the batteries of Isle D'Aix on one side, and Oléron on the other, secured them from open attack by ships of war. I learned, however, afterwards from a French officer, that they had a number of boats out every night, ready to tow off any fire-vessels, in case we succeeded in breaking the boom. As the wind was strong from the northward all the afternoon of the 11th April, they judged the precaution of boats unnecessary; not expecting that we should attempt any thing that night. Our officers, however, having assembled on board the *Caledonia* for orders, repaired to their respective fire-ships, and in the evening dropped down to the place marked No. 24 in the plan, where they lay at anchor till about 9 o'clock; they then got under weigh, and in an hour afterwards there were 18 or 20 vessels in a blaze. From the ships in Basque Roads, they appeared to form a chain of ignited pyramids, stretching from the Isle D'Aix to the Boyart shoal; while Congreve's rockets flying through the air in various directions, and liké comets, dragging a fiery train behind, formed a scene at once the most grand and terrific that can well be imagined. The *Mediator* was the first to strike the boom, and providentially, from the strength of the wind and tide, she broke the gallic barrier, and thus destroyed the palladium of their hopes! A brisk cannonade now commenced from the batteries on the Isle D'Aix, and likewise from several of the French ships, whose vivid flashes glancing like electric fires through the volumes of smoke and flame, emitted by the fire-ships, heightened the sublimity of the scene . . . At this moment the channel being opened by the successful impulse of the *Mediator*, a train of at least a dozen fire-ships drifted directly towards the French fleet, which in the utmost consternation, cut their cables, and ran aground on the shoal marked (Les Palles) in the chart; two fire-ships actually fell foul of two French men of war, but by great exertions they (the French) disengaged themselves, and suffered the rest to drive peaceably up towards the Charente. . . .[1]

A telegraphic communication having taken place between Lord Gambier and Lord Cochrane, the English fleet got under weigh (12th April) and dropped down nearer to the enemy, where they are represented in the plan (26); it having been intended that the *Caledonia* and *Caesar* should engage the batteries, but too little water having been found for this operation, the *Valiant* and *Revenge*, ships of the line, were ordered to anchor off the Boyart shoal (No. 12 and 13) within range of shell, in company with the *Aetna* bomb and several frigates. At this time the enemy were making every exertion to heave their ships off the shoal, which many of them effected, and stood up towards the entrance of the Charente; four, however, of their ships, namely the *Varsovie, Aquilon, Tonnérre,* and *Calcutta* seemed completely fixed; at one o'clock, therefore, Lord Cochrane in the

---

1 A thousand rockets were discharged at the enemy during this attack, fifty having been placed in the tops of each fire-ship, which, as the fire ascended into the rigging twenty minutes or more after the ship was abandoned, were flying about in all directions amongst the French ships, thus giving our fire-vessels a power of distant conflagration, as well as that by absolute contact. The enemy ceased firing, and shut down their ports, as the prisoners informed us, on seeing this unexpected discharge; nor can it be doubted that many took effect; and although by their exertions the enemy prevented the immediate burning of any of their ships, still this shower of fire must have added infinitely to their terror and confusion, and have greatly contributed to drive them from their anchorage, which was the foundation of all our future successes. In like manner one of the fire vessels carried in by the first Lieutenant of the *Hero*, armed with a volley of 50 rockets on one side, was laid ashore on the Isle of Aix, and the whole going into the batteries in one flight, silenced a very heavy fire of cannon and musketry.

Imperieuse weighed anchor, and stood in between the Boyart and Isle D'Aix, close to the former, and followed by the *Aetna* bomb.

The batteries from Oléron now opened; and the shells pitched in every direction around the *Imperieuse* and *Aetna*; while the 42-pounders from Isle D'Aix went over them in the contrary direction; regardless of these, they steadily pursued an equidistant course between the two islands, and in twenty minutes they passed the Scylla and Charybdis without any loss: they now steered for the western edge of the shoal, and having proceeded to that part marked (21) in the plan, they opened their fire on the French ships which were aground at (18 and 19); the batteries on the fortified point of Isle D'Aix (23 and 15) at the same time opening a tremendous cannonade on them in return. The *Valiant* and *Revenge*, accompanied by the *Indefatigable*, *Pallas*, *Emerald*, *Unicorn*, and *Aigle* frigates, at half-past two o'clock, weighed anchor, and took the same route which the *Imperieuse* and *Aetna* had done before, the shot and shells passing over them without producing any effect; these ships having come to an anchor off the edge of the shoal, opened a well-directed fire on the French ships, (under a heavy discharge from Isle D'Aix) particularly on the *Ville de Varsovie* and *Aquilon*, while the *Calcutta*, in all probability, struck to the *Imperieuse*, whose judicious position, and inimitable fire, exceeded all praise. The French ships, after firing for some time from their sterns, &c. struck their colours, many of the crew betaking themselves to their boats; while the *Tonnérre*, either by accident or design, caught fire, and in half an hour blew up, with a most awful and magnificent explosion; previously to this, however, the *Calcutta* was in flames, but did not explode till past seven o'clock, when she blew up, and exhibited the most terrific and sublime spectacle the human mind could contemplate, or the eye survey, without emotions of terror! . . . Almost all of those ships which escaped destruction by fire, were aground in various directions, between Isle D'Aix and Isle Madame: two or three days after the action, a frigate was burnt near Fuel Isle, and the others must have experienced, many of them, irreparable, and all, considerable damage, as we could see them heaving overboard their ammunition and stores, in order to prevent their going to pieces on the shoals. No farther operations, however, were deemed practicable, on account of the intricacy of the Channel, and the numerous protecting batteries which now surrounded the French ships in every direction.

The *Valiant* was aground five hours, and the *Caesar*, which came down late in the afternoon, was likewise on shore; but fortunately they all got off early on the morning of the 13th of April, without any material injury, leaving a squadron of frigates out of gun-shot to the westward of the shoal, at (No. 25) in the plan, where they lay in despite of the enemy; though in passing to and from our fleet they were exposed to a cannonade from both sides. . . .

[Admiral Lord Gambier's service letters provide detailed accounts of the action in Basque Roads. Most of these were published as part of the documentation presented at his court-martial. The first letter to be published in *The Naval Chronicle* was Lord Gambier's victory despatch of 21 April, but the following, which was published as part of the proceedings of Lord Gambier's court-martial, ought to be placed first.]

Gambier's Despatches

From the Trial of Admiral Lord Gambier. [XXII 109]

Copy of a Letter from the Right Honourable Lord Gambier, dated 26th March, 1809,
to the Honourable William Wellesley Pole, Admiralty First Secretary

Caledonia, in Basque Roads, March 26th, 1809
It is proper I should state, for their lordship's information, the position in which the
French fleet is at present anchored, near to the Isle D'Aix, that their lordships' may be
able to form a judgment of the success that may be expected to attend an attack upon
the enemy's fleet, in either of the modes directed by their lordships, in your letter above
mentioned.

The enemy's ships are anchored in two lines, very near to each other, in a direction
due south from the fort, on the Isle D'Aix, and the ships in each line not further apart
than their own length; by which it appears, as I imagined, that the space for their
anchorage is so confined by the shoalness of the water, as not to admit of ships to run in
and anchor clear of each other. The most distant ships of their two lines are within
point-blank shot of the works upon the Isle D'Aix: such ships, therefore, as might
attack the enemy, would be exposed to be raked by the hot shot, &c. from the island, and
should the ships be disabled in their masts, they must remain within the range of the
enemy's fire until destroyed, there not being sufficient depth of water to allow them to
move to the southward out of distance.

The enemy have taken their position apparently with the view, not only to be
protected by the strong works upon the Isle of Aix, but also to have the entrance to the
Charente open to them, that, in case of being attacked by fire-ships, and other engines
of the kind, they can run up the river, beyond the reach of them.

With respect to the attempt that may be made to destroy the enemy's ships with
shells, &c. I am not competent to give an opinion, until it is ascertained whether the
bombs can be placed within range of their mortars to the enemy's ships, without being
exposed to the fire from the Isle of Aix.

I beg leave to add, that, if their lordships are of opinion that an attack on the
enemy's ships, by those of the fleet under my command, is practicable, I am ready to
obey any orders they may be pleased to honour me with, however great the risk may be
of the loss of men and ships.

I have the honour to be, &c.

GAMBIER

Letters on Service, Admiralty Office, April 21 1809. [XXI 344-346]

Sir Harry Neale, Bart. First Captain to Admiral Lord Gambier, commander-in-chief
of his Majesty's ships and vessels employed in the Channel Soundings, &c. arrived here
this morning with a despatch from his lordship to the Honourable William Wellesley
Pole, of which the following is a copy:

Caledonia, at Anchor, in Basque Roads, April 14, 1809
Sir, The Almighty's favour to his Majesty and the nation, has been strongly marked in
the success he has been pleased to give to the operations of his Majesty's fleet under my
command; and I have the satisfaction to acquaint you, for the information of the Lords

2 *Ville de Varsovie,* of 80 guns; *Tonnérre,* of 74 guns; *Aquilon,* of 74 guns; and *Calcutta,* of 56 guns.

Commissioners of the Admiralty, that the four ships of the enemy named in the margin[2] have been destroyed at their anchorage, and several others, from getting on shore, if not rendered altogether unserviceable, are at least disabled for a considerable time.

The arrangement of the fire vessels placed under the direction of Captain the Right Honourable Lord Cochrane was made as fully as the state of the weather would admit, according to his lordship's plan, on the evening of the 11th inst.; and at eight o'clock on the same night they proceeded to the attack under a favourable strong wind from the northward, and flood-tide, (preceded by some vessels filled with powder and shells, as proposed by his lordship, with a view to explosion), and led on in the most undaunted and determined manner by Captain [James] Wooldridge, in the *Mediator* fire ship, the others following in succession, but owing to the darkness of the night several mistook their course and failed.

On their approach to the enemy's ships, it was discovered that a boom was placed in front of their line for a defence. This however the weight of the *Mediator* soon broke, and the usual intrepidity and bravery of British seamen overcame all difficulties. Advancing under a heavy fire from the forts in the Isle of Aix, as well as from the enemy's ships, most of which cut or slipped their cables, and from the confined anchorage, got on shore, and thus avoided taking fire.

At daylight the following morning, Lord Cochrane communicated to me by Telegraph, that seven of the enemy's ships were on shore, and might be destroyed. I immediately made the signal for the fleet to unmoor and weigh, intending to proceed with it to effect their destruction. The wind however being fresh from the northward, and the flood-tide running, rendered it too hazardous to run into Aix Roads, (from its shallow water), I therefore anchored again at the distance of about three miles from the forts on the island.

As the tide suited, the enemy evinced great activity in endeavouring to warp their ships (which had grounded) into deep water, and succeeded in getting all but five of the line towards the entrance of the Charente, before it became practicable to attack them.

I gave orders to Captain Bligh, of the *Valiant*, to proceed with that ship, the *Revenge*, frigates, bombs, and small vessels, named in the margin,[3] to anchor near the Boyart Shoal, in readiness for the attack. At twenty minutes past two P.M. Lord Cochrane advanced in the *Imperieuse* with his accustomed gallantry and spirit, and opened a well-directed fire upon the *Calcutta*, which struck her colours to the *Imperieuse*; the ships and vessels above-mentioned soon after joined in the attack upon the *Ville de Varsovie* and *Aquilon*, and obliged them, before five o'clock, after sustaining a heavy cannonade, to strike their colours, when they were taken possession of by the boats of the advanced squadron. As soon as the prisoners were removed, they were set on fire, as was also the *Tonnérre*, a short time after by the enemy.

I afterwards detached Rear-admiral the Honourable Robert Stopford in the *Caesar* with the *Theseus*, three additional fire ships (which were hastily prepared in the course of the day), and all the boats of the fleet, with Mr. Congreve's rockets, to conduct the further operations of the night against any of the ships which lay exposed to an attack. On the morning of the 13th, the rear-admiral reported to me, that as the *Caesar* and other line-of-battle ships had grounded and were in a dangerous situation, he thought it advisable to order them all out, particularly as the remaining part of the service could

3 *Indefatigable, Aigle, Emerald, Pallas, Beagle, Aetna* bomb, *Insolent* gun-brig, *Conflict, Encounter, Fervent,* and *Growler.*

be performed by frigates and small vessels only; and, I was happy to find that they were extricated from their perilous situation.

Captain Bligh has since informed me, that it was found impracticable to destroy the three-decked ship, and the others which were lying near the entrance of the Charente, as the former, being the outer one, was protected by three lines of boats placed in advance from her.

This ship and all the others, except four of the line and a frigate, have now moved up the river Charente. If any further attempt to destroy them is practicable, I should not fail to use every means in my power to accomplish it.

I have great satisfaction in stating to their Lordships how much I feel obliged to the zealous co-operation of Rear-admiral Stopford, under whose arrangement the boats of the fleet were placed; and I must also express to their lordships the high sense I have of the assistance I received from the abilities and unremitted attention of Sir Harry Neale, Bart. the captain of the fleet, as well as of the animated exertions of the captains, officers, seamen, and marines under my command, and their forwardness to volunteer upon any service that might be allotted to them; particularly the zeal and activity shewn by the captains of line-of-battle ships in preparing the fire vessels.

I cannot speak in sufficient terms of admiration and applause, of the vigorous and gallant attack made by Lord Cochrane upon the French line-of-battle ships which were on shore, as well as of his judicious manner of approaching them, and placing his ship in the position most advantageous to annoy the enemy, and preserve his own ship; which could not be exceeded by any feat of valour hitherto achieved by the British navy.

It is due to Rear-admiral Stopford, and Sir Harry Neale, that I should here take the opportunity of acquainting their lordships of the handsome and earnest manner in which both these meritorious officers had volunteered their services before the arrival of Lord Cochrane to undertake an attack upon the enemy with fire ships; and that had not their lordships fixed upon him to conduct the enterprise, I have full confidence that the result of their efforts would have been highly creditable to them.

I should feel that I did not do justice to the services of Captain [William] Godfrey of the *Aetna*, in bombarding the enemy's ships on the 12th, and nearly all the day of the 13th, if I did not recommend him to their lordships' notice; and I cannot omit bearing due testimony to the anxious desire expressed by Mr. Congreve to be employed where ever I might conceive his services in the management of his rockets would be useful; some of them were placed in the fire ships with effect, and I have every reason to be satisfied with the artillerymen and others who had the management of them, under Mr. Congreve's direction.

I send here with a return of the killed, wounded, and missing of the fleet, which, I am happy to observe, is comparatively small. I have not yet received the returns of the number of prisoners taken, but conceive they amount to between four and five hundred.

I have charged Sir Harry Neale with this despatch, (by the *Imperieuse*) and I beg leave to refer their lordships to him, as also to Lord Cochrane, for any further particulars of which they may wish to be informed.

I have the honour to be, &c.

GAMBIER, 15th April

P.S. This morning three of the enemy's line-of-battle ships are observed to be still on shore under Fouras, and one of them is in a dangerous situation. One of their frigates (*L'Indienne*), also on shore, has fallen over, and they are now dismantling her. As the tides will take off in a day or two, there is every probability that she will be destroyed.

Since writing the foregoing, I have learnt that the Honourable Lieutenant-colonel Cochrane (Lord Cochrane's brother), and Lieutenant [William] Bissell of the navy, were volunteers in the *Imperieuse*, and rendered themselves extremely useful, the former by commanding some of her guns on the main-deck, and the latter in conducting one of the explosion vessels.

Names of the Ships in Aix Roads, previous to the Attack on the 11th April, 1809

L'Ocean, 120 guns, Vice-admiral Allemand, Captain Roland - Repaired in 1806; on shore under Fouras.
Foudroyant, 80 guns, Rear-admiral Gourdon, Captain Henri. - Five years old; on shore under Fouras.
Cassard, 74 guns, Captain Faure, Commodore. - Three years old; on shore under Fouras.
Tourville, 74, Captain La Caille. - Old; on shore in the river.
Regulus, 74 guns, Captain Lucas. - Five years old; on shore under Madame.
Patriote, 74 guns, Captain Mahèe. - Repaired in 1803.
Jamappe, 74 guns, Captain Fauvau. - On shore under Madame.
Tonnérre, 74 guns, Captain Clement de la Rouciere. - Nine months old, never at sea.
[Burnt]
Aquilon, 74 guns, Captain Maingon. - Old. [Burnt]
Ville de Varsovie, 80 guns, Captain Cuvillier. - New, never at sea. [Burnt]
Calcutta, 56 guns, Captain La Tonie. - Loaded with flour and military stores. [Burnt]
Frigates
Indienne, Captain Porteau. - On shore near Isle Enel, on her beam ends.
Elbe, Captain Perengier.
Pallas, Captain Le Bigot.
Hortense, Captain Allgand.
N.B. One of the three last frigates on shore under Isle Madame.

[Appended was a list of casualties totalling 2 officers, 8 men killed; 9 officers, 26 men wounded; 1 man missing.]

[A series of letters to the editor written by 'Brontes' describing Congreve's rocket system have been published as an appendix to this volume. The following reprint from *The Morning Post* was published almost immediately after the first report of the action, and expressed the public feelings which led to the over-hasty enrolment of Lord Cochrane as a Knight of the Bath.]

Gallantry of Lord Cochrane
From 'Naval Anecdotes.' XXI 368-375

. . . We therefore think it unjust to withhold from the public, that although Captain Wooldridge most truly did "lead on the *Mediator fire-ship* in the most undaunted and determined manner," and of whom Lord Cochrane has been publicly heard to speak in terms of unbounded praise, as well as of sincere regret for his severe sufferings; yet it is equally true that Lord Cochrane personally conducted the *explosion* ship, which had been charged by himself in a manner than which nothing was ever contrived to be more dreadful.

His lordship caused about 1,500 barrels of gunpowder to be started into puncheons, which were placed end-upwards: upon the tops of these were placed between 300 and 400 shells, charged with fusees, and again, among and upon these were between 2 and 3,000 hand grenades. The puncheons were fastened to each other by cables wound round them, and jammed together with wedges; and moistened sand was rammed down between these casks, so as to render the whole, from stem to stern, as solid as possible, that the resistance might render the explosion the more violent.

In this immense instrument of destruction, Lord Cochrane committed himself, with only one lieutenant and four seamen; and after the boom was broken, his lordship proceeded with this explosion ship towards the enemy's line.

Let it be recollected, that at this moment the batteries on shore were provided with furnaces to fire red hot shot, and then his lordship's danger in this enterprise may be properly conceived.

The wind blew a gale, and the tide ran three knots an hour. When the blue lights of the fire-ships were discovered, one of the enemy's signal ships made the signal for fire-ships; which being also a blue light, the enemy fell into great confusion, firing upon her with very injurious effect, and directly cut their cables.

When Lord Cochrane had conducted his explosion ship as near as was possible, the enemy having taken the alarm, he ordered his brave little crew into the boat, and followed them, after putting fire to the fusee, which was calculated to give them 15 minutes to get out the reach of the explosion. However, in consequence of the wind getting very high, the fusee burnt too quickly; so that, with the most violent exertion against wind and tide, this intrepid little party were six minutes nearer than they calculated to be, at the time when the most tremendous explosion that human art ever contrived took place, followed by the bursting at once in the air, of near 400 shells, and 3,000 hand-grenades, pouring down a shower of cast metal in every direction! But fortunately our second Nelson was spared; the boat having reached, by unparalleled exertion, only just beyond the extent of destruction. Unhappily this effort to escape cost the life of the brave lieutenant, whom this noble captain saw die in the boat, partly under fatigue, and partly drowned with waves, that continually broke over them. Two of the four sailors were also so nearly exhausted that their recovery has been despaired of. Such were the perils our hero encountered, and which have hitherto been buried in silence. When they reached their ship, the *Imperieuse*, it is known that Lord Cochrane was the first to go down to the attack, and was for more than an hour the only English man of war in the harbour. His attack and capture of the *Calcutta*, which had one-third more guns than the *Imperieuse*, has been properly spoken of.

The repetition of his explosions was so dreaded by the enemy, that they apprehended an equal explosion in every fire-ship; and immediately crowding all sail, ran before wind and tide so fast, that the fire-ships, though at first very near, could not overtake them, before they were high and dry on shore, except three 74s, besides the *Calcutta*, which were afterwards engaged, taken, and burnt. ...

A total silence as to the objects this squadron had in view, and which have been prevented by Lord Cochrane's destruction of it, has hitherto deprived the nation of the fair means of justly appreciating the extraordinary advantages which have accrued along with his addition to our naval glory; for it has now been learnt, that this squadron was to have gone to Ferrol, where it would have gained a great additional naval strength: from thence proceeding to Toulon, it was to receive on board 40,000 troops, intended to take possession of Cadiz and the fleet; and after that they were to proceed to the West Indies, to succour Guadaloupe and Martinique; for which service, one of the seventy-fours that was burnt was laden with six hundred thousand pounds worth of stores and ammunition. . . .

From the 'Memoir of the Public Services of the Right Honourable Lord Cochrane, K.B.' *XXII 15-18*

[*The Naval Chronicle*'s 'Memoir' was published within a few months of the action, and just as the controversy over Cochrane's criticism of Gambier was at its height.]

Howsoever reprehensible Lord Gambier might have been, in not himself attacking the enemy; or howsoever injudicious or improper it might be, in the Admiralty Board, to select a junior officer - one who even had not previously been attached to the Channel fleet - for so important an attempt, passing over many veterans in the service, no censure can possibly alight upon Lord Cochrane. To him all praise is due. If we are to accredit his own statement, as given in evidence by Sir H.B. Neale, on the trial of Admiral Harvey, it is not even to be imputed to him that he solicited the appointment. In a conversation which took place between Admiral Harvey and Lord Cochrane, on the arrival of the latter in the Channel fleet, respecting the intended attack, Sir H.B. Neale represents his lordship to have expressed himself to the following effect: "I assure you I did not seek it; I went to town; and in a conversation, either with Lord Mulgrave or the Board of Admiralty, it was mentioned to me that the expedition was composed of bombs and fire-ships, for the purpose of destroying the French fleet in the Isle of Aix. I answered, that it was a service very easy to be executed. I was asked, if I would undertake it. I answered, 'Yes'."

The plan of the expedition, we believe, was entirely entrusted to his lordship; agreeably, as we have heard, to a proposal which he, some years ago, submitted to the Admiralty Board, for destroying an enemy's fleet at anchor. . . .

How far the reasons, here adduced for the delay [in the fleet moving into Basque Roads], may be deemed satisfactory, by a Court of Naval Inquiry, we know not; but, from the suspension of the vote of thanks to the commander-in-chief, &c. intended to be proposed in Parliament, and from Lord Gambier having solicited that an inquiry into his conduct may take place, it is evident that some doubt as to their validity exists. It is said, that, when one of his Majesty's ministers communicated to Lord Cochrane their intention of moving for the thanks of Parliament to the commander-in-chief, his Lordship answered, if no other person should oppose the motion, he would rise in his place for that purpose. On being asked, on what ground, his reply was, "The log-book of the *Caledonia*;" alluding, as it may be supposed, to the proofs which must there appear, of the delay which had taken place, in the operations of the fleet, subsequently to the display of his signal, already mentioned.

For the welfare and credit of the service, we sincerely hope, that every doubt may be cleared up, to the general satisfaction of the parties more immediately concerned, and of the country at large.

As a special mark of royal favour, in consideration of Lord Cochrane's signal services, in Basque Roads, on the 12th of April, his Majesty was graciously pleased, on the 25th of the same month, to invest his lordship with the honourable Order of the Bath.

Portrait of the Right Honourable
Lord Cochrane, K.B. Engraved
by Nesbit, from a drawing by
Pocock. Plate 288

[The reports heard by *The Naval Chronicle* proved to be essentially correct when, later, Cochrane's correspondence with the Honourable William Wellesley Pole, Admiralty First Secretary, was published as part of the records of Admiral Gambier's court-martial. Vol. XXII, p113.]

Lord Gambier's Further Despatches

From the Trial of Admiral Lord Gambier. XXII 109-113

The Right Honourable Lord Gambier, 10 May, 1809, to the Honourable W.W. Pole. London, 10 May, 1809

Sir . . . From communications I have since had with their lordships, I am led to understand, that a more full and detailed account than I have transmitted, of the proceedings of the fleet under my command, during the whole of its operations in Basque Roads, would be desirable; I shall, therefore, in making such a statement, endeavour to omit no incident that may be in any degree connected with those operations, or serve to elucidate the various movements and proceedings of the fleet; persuaded that doing so cannot fail to promote the satisfaction which, in common with the officers and men under my command, I feel upon that occasion, and on the success which has resulted from it. . . .

The *Unicorn*, *Aigle*, and *Pallas*, I directed to take a station near the Boyart Shoal, for the purpose of receiving the crews of the fire-ships on their return from the enterprise, to support the boats of the fleet which were to accompany the fire-ships, and to give assistance to the *Impérieuse*, which ship was still further advanced. The *Whiting* schooner, *King George*, and *Nimrod* cutters, were fitted for throwing rockets, and directed to take a station near the same shoal for that purpose.

The *Indefatigable*, *Foxhound*, and *Aetna* bomb, were to take a station as near the fort on the Isle of Aix as possible; the two former to protect the bomb-vessel, whilst she threw shells into the fort.

The *Emerald, Dotterel,* and *Beagle* sloops, and *Growler, Conflict,* and *Insolent* gun-brigs, were stationed to make a diversion at the east end of the Isle of Aix.

The *Redpole* and *Lyra* I directed to be anchored by the master of the fleet (one near the Isle of Aix, and the other near the boyart), with lights hoisted, to guide the fire-ships in their course to the attack; and the boats of the fleet were ordered to assemble alongside the *Caesar,* to proceed to assist the fire-ships, under the superintendence of Rear-Admiral Stopford.

With these pre-concerted movements the fleet was at this time unmoored, in readiness to render any service that might be practicable; but being anchored in a strong tide-way, with the wind fresh from the N.W. upon the weather tide making, it was again moored, to prevent the ships falling on board each other.

At about half-past eight P.M. the explosion vessels and fire-ships proceeded to the attack; at half-past nine, the first explosion vessel blew up; and at ten, most of the fire-ships were observed to be on fire; the enemy's forts and ships firing upon them. Many of the fire-ships were seen to drive through their fleet, and beyond the Isle of Aix.

Shortly after day-light, Lord Cochrane, who, in the *Imperieuse,* lay about three miles from the enemy, made the signal to me, by telegraph, that seven of the enemy's ships were on shore, and that half the fleet could destroy them. It was visible from the *Caledonia* what ships were aground, and that two or three had made their escape up the Charente. I immediately ordered the fleet to be unmoored, and at half-past nine weighed and ran up nearer to the Isle of Aix, with a view, when the time of the tide should render it advisable, that some of the line-of-battle ships might proceed to attack the enemy's ships on shore; but the wind blowing fresh from the N.N.W. with a flood tide, I judged it was unadvisable to risk any of them at that time in so perilous a situation. The fleet was therefore anchored. I made the signal for each ship to prepare, with spare or sheet cables out of the stern ports, and springs on them, to be in readiness for any of them to go in, that I might judge necessary; in the meanwhile, I ordered three additional fire-ships to be prepared.

Observing the *Imperieuse* to advance, and the time of flood nearly done running, the *Indefatigable, Aigle, Emerald, Pallas, Beagle, Aetna,* and gun-brigs, were ordered in to the attack; at 2:20 P.M. the former opened her fire upon the enemy's ships a-ground, and the others as soon after as they arrived up. I then ordered in the *Valiant* and *Revenge* to support them, and they soon joined in the action.

The enemy's ship *Calcutta* struck her colours at 4:10 P.M. and the *Ville de Varsovie* and *Aquilon,* in about an hour afterwards; all three were taken possession of by the boats of the advanced squadron, and set on fire as soon as the prisoners were removed; a short time after, *le Tonnérre* was set on fire by the enemy.

Perceiving, towards the close of the day, that there were some of the enemy's grounded ships lying further up towards the Charente, which appeared to be exposed to further attacks, I sent in the three additional fire-ships, and all the boats of the fleet, with Mr. Congreve's rockets, accompanied by the *Caesar* and *Theseus,* under the direction of Rear-admiral Stopford, with discretional orders, for his acting as he should think fit, and according as circumstances should render it expedient.

On the following day (the 13th) the rear-admiral, perceiving that nothing further could be effected by the line-of-battle ships, which had grounded, as had also some of the frigates, and how imminent the danger was in which they lay, and being satisfied that the remaining part of the service could be performed only by frigates and smaller vessels, he most wisely took advantage of a providential shift of wind, and returned, with the line-of-battle ships, to Basque Roads. Captain Bligh, on his return, reported to me, that it was found impracticable to destroy the enemy's three-decked ship, and others, which were lying at the entrance of the Charente, as the former (which was the outer one) was protected by three lines of boats, placed in advance from her.

During the remainder of the 13th, the *Aetna* was employed in throwing shells, the *Whiting* schooner in firing rockets, and the other small vessels in firing upon the enemy's ships which were assailable. At 2:50 the *Aetna* bomb, and small vessels in-shore, began their fire upon the enemy's ships at the entrance of the Charente, and continued to do so during the remainder of the day.

On the 15th, in the morning, (the day on which I dispatched Sir H. Neale to their lordships, in the *Imperieuse*), three of the enemy's line-of-battle ships were observed to be still a-ground, under Touras, and one of them in a dangerous situation; one of their frigates (*l'Indienne*) also on shore, had fallen over, and the enemy were dismantling her.

It blew very strong from the westward the whole of the 15th and 16th, so that no attempt could be made to annoy and harass the enemy; on the latter day their frigate, which was on shore, was discovered to be on fire, and blew up soon after.

All the remainder of the enemy's ships got up the river by the 17th, except one, (a two-decker) which remained a-ground under the town of Touras; in the afternoon of this day it was observed, that another of the enemy's frigates had got on shore up the river and was wrecked, which was afterwards confirmed by the master of a neutral vessel from Rochelle.

On the 19th it blew too violent for any of the small vessels to act against the enemy; but, on the 20th, the *Thunder* bomb having arrived, and the weather having become more moderate, I sent her to assist the *Aetna* in bombarding the enemy's ship, on shore near Touras. The *Aetna* had split her 13-inch mortar on the 15th, consequently had only her 10-inch effective; and the *Thunderer*'s 15-inch was also rendered unserviceable, this day, from the same cause.

The following day I went in by boat into the Roads, on board the *Aigle* and *Pallas*, to reconnoitre the enemy's ship above mentioned, and ascertain what further operations could be carried on for her destruction. That evening, and the succeeding days, the wind was too violent and unfavourable.

On the 23d I gave directions to Captain Wolfe to put two of the *Aigle*'s 18-pound long guns into each of the four gun-brigs, and use every means in his power to drive the enemy out of the ship near Touras, and attempt to set her on fire: the whole of the 24th was employed in this attempt: the 10-inch mortars throwing their shells occasionally, but without success; and, as Captain Wolfe reported to me, that this attack made very little impression upon the enemy, and that the ships and vessels which were advanced above the Boyart Shoal, in order to carry these operations, were in a situation much exposed to attack from the enemy's gun-boats, &c. I considered any further attempt would be fruitless, and therefore withdrew them from their advanced position.

The enemy's ships continued a-ground near Touras until the night of the 28th, when, having lightened her considerably, and applied great exertion to get her afloat, the spring tides having set in, they succeeded in their attempt, and got her up the river.

Their lordships will perceive, from the foregoing statement, as well as from their own knowledge of the local situation of the scene of action, that I was obliged to have a second object in view, for besides the destruction of the enemy's ships, the greatest care was required that his Majesty's fleet should not be sacrificed; the state of the tides and wind was most materially to be attended to, and, without reference to the chart of the anchorage, nothing can better exemplify the limited space and danger of the navigation, than the circumstance of one of the enemy's line-of-battle ships having, on their fleet entering the Roads in February last, run on shore on the shoal of the Pallas, and being there totally wrecked. . . .

When it is considered with how little, or comparatively no loss, this most important service has been performed, their lordships, I am persuaded, will agree with me, that there is great cause for rejoicing at the result of the undertaking.

Various and Changing Views on Lord Cochrane

From 'Correspondence.' *XXI 395-412; XXV 211-213*

Extract of a Letter from an Officer of his Majesty's Ship Revenge, of 74 guns, dated off Rochefort, 13th April, 1809

. . . for two hours and a half we encountered yesterday a dreadful fire from the batteries and some of the enemy's ships; we were *the first ship of the line in,* and, thank God, considering our situation, we were very fortunate, only three killed and fifteen wounded; our men behaved nobly, and knocked an 84-gun ship almost to atoms; we understand she had 60 killed, and as she was lying aground she was burnt: last night the sight was glorious, four line-of-battle ships in flames, and their blowing up was awfully tremendous. We had just water enough for the *Revenge* to get without the range of the shot, where we lay at anchor all night; and this morning we were *the last line of battle ship that came out.* . . .

Letter from a midshipman apparently serving in Insolent, to his mother

Our captain observing one of the enemy's ships in a proper situation for attack, immediately bore down, and we hove to under her stern, and engaged *L'Aquilon,* of 84 guns, for thirty minutes; at the end of which time, we found ourselves drifted opposite the broadside of our adversary. We were now in the most imminent danger of being sunk; and had we not given her a good drubbing before, this would certainly have been our lot. We tacked immediately, and resumed our station across her stern; and after several severer broadsides, she struck to us. *I believe that we are the first brig of 18 guns that ever took a line-of-battle ship:* About six o'clock our second lieutenant set fire to the *Calcutta,* (one of our prizes), it proving impossible to get her off. About two hours afterwards she blew up with a terrible report: we now compelled the enemy to set fire to the *Tonnérre,* of 74 guns; she blew up a short time after the *Calcutta.* Thus, my dear Mother, ended this *glorious day*!

Extract from a letter to the Editor from "An Eye-Witness" May 4, 1809

The destruction . . . of the ships in Basque Roads, in one of the enemy's *strongest and best ports,* is a victory of a new class: it proves that he is no where safe, and points out a mode of warfare which defies the utmost caution he can adopt. But there is another point not to be forgotten in this estimation - that Buonaparte cannot conceal the extent of this misfortune, and the bravery of the British navy, from his subjects. It was done in the presence of a large army, prepared to embark in the devoted squadron, and before thousands of the French people, who there beheld an English frigate leading in to the attack of their line-of-battle ships, and fearless of their batteries. Surely, Sir, when these points are fairly considered, it gives a claim of the utmost importance to this service, even where the *Gazette*-account leaves it. But there is no doubt, from subsequent information, that the discomfiture, if I may not use the term *destruction*, is nearly total: there are not above one or two of these ships that can ever probably go to sea again - and those not without a thorough repair. Yet were they not in this ruined condition, they have been driven into a corner, where they may be blocked up for ever; nor do I therefore hesitate to say, that not *one* ship of this fleet *will ever go to sea again*; and I know not how a victory can be well more important or complete.

To the Editor from "An Eye-Witness"
[This second letter was published considerably later, after the author's arrival in Madras, when he had had time to cool his support for Lord Cochrane.]

Madras, May 10th, 1812
Mr. Editor, . . .No man, believe me, is more ready than myself to bestow every praise and credit on Lord Cochrane; but let the others who were concerned in this glorious enterprise, share that meed of approbation and credit which is their due. It is well known to the whole fleet, and which this writer does not contradict, that Captain Wooldridge did lead in the *Mediator* fire-ship, in the most undaunted and determined manner; and that Lord Cochrane has always been ready to bear testimony to the bravery, as well as to the sufferings of that gallant but much neglected officer; the latter of which were greater than it can be almost supposed human nature to exist under. For the shocking manner in which the officer was scorched, I appeal to Lord Cochrane himself, as well as all those who had an opportunity of witnessing the dreadful state he was in on board the *Imperieuse*, after the destruction of the *Mediator*. That his Lordship prepared the explosion vessel, and committed himself in her with a lieutenant and four men, is well known: but at the same time it is as well known, and acknowledged, both by his Lordship, and by those employed with him, that the vessel exploded before the boom was broken; nor was she ever within that boom. He is also correct, when he says, that the fuse did not burn as long as was expected, though it burnt sufficient time to allow his Lordship and boat to be perfectly clear before the explosion took place; neither was the lieutenant (whose name was Bissell) or any other person hurt in the boat, but all arrived safe on board the *Imperieuse*, not more exhausted and fatigued than it was natural to expect those must be who had laboured at the oar against strong wind and tide. He goes on to tell us, that the repetition of the explosions was so much dreaded by the enemy, that they immediately crowded all sail before the wind, and that the fire-ships could not overtake them. . . . Suffice it to say, that the fortunate circumstance of the *Mediator*, a ship of that bulk and weight, being fitted as a fire-ship, was the means of the success with which his Majesty's arms were so gloriously crowned, as all the other fire-ships were so small and light, being mostly transport brigs, that none of them could possibly have forced the boom, but would all have burnt on the outside of it, as was expected by the enemy. And it is well known, particularly to Mr. Fairfax, the master of the fleet, who was an idle spectator in the *Lyra*, light vessel, and had the most correct means of judging, that none of the enemy's ships, except the frigates, did cut their cables, until they were well assured that the passage had been forced, which they scarcely thought possible; but, on the contrary, considered their own fire, which they opened, and that of the Isle d'Aix, a certain destruction to those who should have the temerity of attempting it. I have also heard him and several officers who were in the fire-ships, declare, that the *Mediator* was not fired till long after the boom had been broken, many minutes after the explosion vessel exploded, or until she was within the buoys of the French admiral in the three-decker. The *Mediator*, I have been assured by an officer

then on board her, was fortunately so very near the explosion vessel, that the greatest part of the shells, &c. passed over her, although her decks were almost covered afterwards by the falling pieces. The situation of this ship was observed by Lord Cochrane, by the light of the explosion, and who feared very much she had occasioned the destruction of that ship, till he saw her on fire afterwards, for she was very distinguishable by her immense size; and when it was reported to Lord Cochrane, that Captain W. and his officers were alongside the *Imperieuse*, wounded, he expressed his regret, fearful it might have happened from the explosion.

Captain W. was immediately promoted by the Admiralty, and was presented with a gold chain and medal by order of his Majesty; thereby reviving an ancient custom, which had almost become obsolete, of rewarding services performed in fire-ships. He was also presented with a sword, value £100 from the Patriotic Fund, as were both his lieutenants, N.B. Clements, and James Pearl, of the value of £50 and the former promoted to the rank of commander: the latter, unfortunately for him, not having served two years, according to the late regulations, was not eligible for promotion.

Trial of Admiral Harvey

From the 'Naval History of the Present Year,' 1809
April–May. [XXI 428-429]

The first object of naval importance, and on which we touched in our preceding Retrospect, has been the trial and sentence of Admiral Harvey. We could not but take a lively interest in the trial, which we have detailed at full length; and must own we felt sincerely at seeing this brave man, after receiving sentence, walking up alone from the Sally Port to his house. He left Portsmouth immediately. This trial will afford a memorable example of the impartial discipline of the British navy; and prove to every common seaman in the service, that no one can transgress its rules with impunity.

[It has not been possible here to reproduce the trial report. Harvey was sentenced to be dismissed from His Majesty's service (see Vol. XXI, pp420-428). Less than a year following the dismissal, he was reinstated in rank, and he continued to advance through the ranks until he was made Admiral of the Blue in 1819.]

The Trial of Admiral Lord Gambier [XXII 107-130; 215-242]

[The report of the trial running to sixty pages, it has only been possible to reproduce here enough of the highly technical and interesting evidence to support the complete exoneration the court gave Admiral Gambier.]

On Wednesday, the 26th of July, a court martial was assembled on board his Majesty's ship *Gladiator*, at Portsmouth, for the trial of Admiral Lord Gambier, respecting his conduct as commander-in-chief of the Channel fleet, between the 17th of March and 29th of April, agreeably to the following Order:

"*By the Commissioners for executing the officer of Lord High Admiral of the United Kingdom of Great Britain and Ireland, &c.*"

Whereas Admiral the Right Honourable Lord Gambier has, by his letter to our secretary of the 30th of May, 1809, requested that his conduct as commander-in-chief of the Channel fleet, employed in Basque Roads, between the 17th day of March and the 29th of April, 1809, may be inquired into by a court martial:

And whereas by the log books and minutes of signals of the *Caledonia, Imperieuse,* and other ships employed on that service, it appears to us that the said Admiral Lord Gambier on the 12th day of the said month of April, the enemy's ships being then on shore, and the signal having been made that they could be destroyed, did for a considerable time neglect or delay taking effectual measures for destroying them [etc.] . . .

Captain Lord Cochrane sworn and examined. . . .

Q. It appearing by the signal log of the *Caledonia* that you made several signals for the ships of the fleet to come up, and of the situation of the enemy, was it your opinion that it would have been expedient for the commander-in-chief to have sent in half the fleet, or any part of it, to destroy the enemy's ships, considering tide, &c. and was it your opinion such ships could have again got out in safety? A. I did make the signal; the *Imperieuse* being the nearest ship placed by his lordship in the guidance of the fire-ships; and having had the charge of these vessels, I thought it proper to communicate to his lordship the state in which they appeared to me to be, which I did by the signals mentioned - (produces some papers). These are copies of the minutes which I made at the time; the time may not be precisely accurate, but the circumstances are perfectly correct, and well known by all the officers in the fleet.

[Some discussion took place upon Lord Cochrane's referring to his minutes, after which the examination proceeded.]

It is my opinion that a much smaller force than half the fleet would have been sufficient; the signal was directed by the *Caledonia* to be repeated. I ordered the signal to be made that two sail of the line was enough, which I have since understood was not made, but that the officer repeated the previous signal. The fact was, he thought it would be an insult to make that signal, and therefore he repeated the former signal, leaving it to the discretion of the commander of the fleet to send what portion of the fleet he might think proper. From the time that the first signal was made in the morning, until about eight o'clock, it was ebb tide; the tide was going to windward. At eight o'clock it was low water. There is anchorage out of range of shot or shell for at least six sail of the line. The *Imperieuse* passed in going in close to the Boyart, it was then nearly high water; about half past one or two o'clock in the day of the 12th, when going in. Coming out it was also high water. In both of which courses there was sufficient depth for vessels of any size; the impression of my mind is, for vessels of any size, at any time. . . .

Q. When you went in on the 12th did you so go in, pursuant to signals of the commander, or did you do so without orders, by signal or otherwise? A. I did so in compliance with what I considered the spirit of the orders I had received. The doing of it was my own act. The entry in the log-book of the *Imperieuse*, that I weighed at half-past eleven, is not correct, as will appear by the log-books of the fleet. I weighed at one o'clock; the *Aetna* rather preceded me.

Q. It appears by the log that you made signal of distress; what was the nature of distress of your ship, and did any one mind what came to your assistance, and was there any unnecessary delay in that respect? A. I inquired by hailing [a passing brig], what attack was intended to be made on the enemy. The commander replied, he was ordered to bombard; I directed the commander of the brig to go close, and that I should protect them. It was then one o'clock. The French three-decker swung to her hawsers, and the last of their ships began to move. I had had the charge of the fire-ships; they had failed of every expected purpose. I knew what the tongue of slander was capable of, and although I admit that the feelings of my Lord Gambier for the honour and the interest of his country, were, and are, as strong as my own, yet personal considerations were not enough; the expectations of my country, the hopes of the Admiralty, and my own prospects, were about to vanish. I weighed anchor, and ran in, and went beyond the possibility of return; I ordered sail to be made after the sternmost ships of the enemy, and in standing in, I made the signal that the chase was superior to the chasing ship, because the *Ville de Varsovie* and *Calcutta* were both afloat, and immediately afterwards, that we wanted assistance, which signal is absurdly coupled with the words "being in distress." When we got up to the Boyart, we opened our fire upon the *Calcutta* and *Ville de Varsovie*. The *Calcutta* was broadside on, the *Varsovie* lay with the stern towards us, she being under sail, and the *Aquilon* was in the same position, the latter did not fire for a long time, they were employed clearing away their stern to get guns out. When we anchored it was about two o'clock. Some brigs had anchored as marked in chart No. 2 [which was not printed], for the protection of the bomb, and were firing, but too far off to be of any use. I made the signal for them to close, but as there is no flag to express brigs only, without frigates or large vessels, most of which were commanded by my seniors, I explained as far as lay within my means, that this signal was intended for them by firing from the main-deck, the quarter-deck shot did not reach them. This signal, I was afterwards told, gave considerable offence, and so soon as I learnt that from Sir Harry Neale, I declared to Lord Gambier, that it was not my intention, in the slightest degree, to hurt his lordship's feelings. I had then no time to express, by a tedious telegraphic communication, what I meant to convey. We were all busily employed, when it was reported to me that several sail of the line and frigates were coming to our assistance. About three the *Revenge* and several frigates came within hailing. I hauled them to anchor, or they would ground, we having taken our berth on the very edge of the shoal - it was the falling tide. Several that had anchored opened their fire on all the ships that were within reach, the *Varsovie, Aquilon*, and *Calcutta*. I made signal that the *Calcutta* had struck, and sent a boat to inform those who were firing at her, that our boat was then on board of her; on which the *Indefatigable* and others turned their fire to the *Varsovie* and *Aquilon*: I ordered our people to cease firing; there were then ships enough to destroy the enemy without the *Impérieuse*; our people were much fatigued, they therefore rested themselves, with the exception of those ordered to repair their rigging; the other ships continued to fire on the *Varsovie* and *Aquilon* until they struck, which was about six o'clock. The *Calcutta* was set on fire; the enemy in a consternation kindled it still more: our boats were employed shifting the prisoners; the French were deserting several of their ships with every boat that belonged to them, and pulling and sailing for the Rochefort river; an attempt was intended to have been made to burn the enemy's ship *Ocean*. Captain Bligh volunteered this service. Captain Maitland regretted that on account of Captain Bligh's previously having undertaken it, that he was deprived of that opportunity of distinguishing himself. I was too much fatigued to undertake it myself, I could scarcely stand through excessive fatigue; the reason it was not done I only learnt since seeing the public despatches in the papers. As the French had taken to their boats to land the people, they were all ashore that night, and the next morning there were two or three chasse marées in their stead, lightening the enemy's ships, by taking articles from them. There was no delay whatever to the best of my belief after the signal for assistance was made, on the part of Lord Gambier, in ordering the vessels to our assistance; but had the attack been made in the morning when the tide was falling, until past eight o'clock, and when the enemy's ships were all, with the exception of two, fast aground, a three-decker and two others, as shewn in chart No. 2, lying close together to windward, with their masts and yards apparently locked, in which position they continued until one o'clock, it is my opinion that seven sail of the enemy, including the three-decker, might have been destroyed with facility, by two sail of the line, assisted by the frigates and smaller vessels; and it is my opinion, that after the hour of half-past eleven, when the enemy's two ships that remained at anchor until the British fleet weighed, the frigates alone, assisted by the smaller vessels, might have destroyed the whole of the above-mentioned ships, the rear of which afterwards were attacked. . . .

Q. Your lordship having stated that if two or three sail of the line, in coming in, had borne close on the Boyart, had laid their main and foretopsails aback, and taken the tide under their lee, so as to enable them to bear round, and go up to the enemy's two line-of-battle ships, then afloat, was there space enough for either one, two, or three sail of the line to have taken up an anchorage, with even part of her broadsides to bear on those two ships, without taking the ground? - A. I did not consider the tide under the lee as a point essential to the bearing up. There was sufficient room. I can speak with positive certainty, for we in the *Imperieuse*, when working out from the position which we occupied, as shewn by Chart No. 3, tacked repeatedly, and traversed all the space between the shoal of the Boyart and the buoys of the enemy's ships, where they had been anchored in line, and from which they had cut. I should not have stood so far towards these buoys had it not been that the enemy seemed little inclined to disturb us, which I not only attributed to the ruinous state of the works [on Isle d'Aix], but concluded that they were in want of powder or other military stores. I should not have chosen, however, any distant station, but should probably have brought up alongside of them, and on that side directly opposite to Aix. The three-decker, and other ships on shore, two for which after appeared to have their masts locked together, could have given no material disturbance to such a position, and these three might have been destroyed by one seventy-four, had she been sent to attack them, or even by a frigate or two, while the two French line-of-battle ships were occupied at their anchors, as is above supposed; when I arrived at the outer anchorage, I mentioned to Lord Gambier that as there could be no jealousy with respect to Admiral Stopford, that it would be a matter essential to the service to send the admiral in with the frigates and other vessels, whichever his lordship thought best, as his zeal for the service would accomplish what I consider yet more creditable than any thing that had been done; I apologised for the freedom which I had used with his lordship, and stated that I took that liberty as a friend, for it would be impossible, things remaining as they were, to prevent a noise being made about it in England. I said, "My Lord, you desired me to speak candidly to you, and I have used that freedom; I have no wish or desire but for the service of our country," to which his lordship replied, that if I threw blame, it would appear, as arrogantly claiming all the merit to myself. I assured his lordship I had no such intention, and mentioned at the same time that it was not my desire to carry despatches, or to go to London with Sir Harry Neale, upon the occasion. His lordship immediately after delivered to me an order directing the above. When I weighed I had the satisfaction of hearing that the signal had been made for Admiral Stopford, but whether to execute the above purpose by the frigates, or other means, I do not know.

Lord Gambier declined asking Lord Cochrane any questions at present.

Admiral Stopford was next sworn and examined. . . .

Q. When the *Imperieuse* made the signal that the enemy's ships were on shore, and the fleet might destroy them, would you, with the experience you have as flag officer, have thought it prudent or proper to send or lead in the fleet to destroy them? - A. In my opinion the dislodgment from the anchorage of the enemy's ships by fire-ships, removed but a small part of the obstacles. With the wind as it then was, and the broadside of the enemy's ships still commanding the passage, we should have been so crippled in going in and in working out a passage a little more than a mile, I think I should not have risked the ships had they been under my command. . . .

The evidence for the prosecution closed here, and the Court adjourned to Saturday, July 29; when Lord Gambier stated, that he should be ready to proceed on his defence on Monday. The Court having assembled on Monday, on the President's desiring the witnesses to withdraw, as usual, Lord Cochrane submitted to the Court, that it was not the custom of courts martial to exclude the witnesses from the Court during the defence.

The President - Lord Cochrane; it is the wish of the Court, in the present instance, that the witnesses should be excluded.

Lord Cochrane - The trial of Admiral Harvey is a case in point, where the witnesses were allowed to remain in Court during the reading of the defence.

The President - My Lord, the Court has discussed the measure in the present instance, and it is its wish that you should withdraw.

Lord Cochrane bowed and withdrew.

Lord Gambier was then called upon for his defence, which the Judge Advocate was permitted to read for him, as follows. . . .

Upon the 10th of April, at half-past four P.M. the *Beagle* arrived, with the twelve fire-ships from England. When I issued orders to the commanders of sloops and first lieutenants of line-of-battle ships [placed in command of the fire-ships] which I had prepared, it was found altogether impracticable to proceed to the attack on the night of the 10th, though much pressed by Lord Cochrane, and it may be considered a most fortunate circumstance that the attempt was deferred; for it appears by a general order found on board one of the enemy's ships, and now delivered into court, that the French, to protect their fleet from attack, had equipped 73 launches, and other boats, in five divisions, to guard it from surprise during the night, and to tow off our fire-ships on their approach; and the tranquillity of the 10th would have afforded the enemy full opportunity of availing themselves of this protection; but of this they were deprived, by the very blowing weather on the subsequent night, when the fire-ships were sent in. I have here to notice, that some days previous to the attack, I had, to deceive the enemy, adopted the precaution of ordering out of the Roads vessels of every description, that were not to be engaged in the intended operations. . . .

At about half-past eight P.M. [on the 11th] the explosion-vessel and fire-ships proceeded to the attack; at half-past nine two of the explosion-vessels blew up; and at ten most of the fire-ships were observed to be on fire, the enemy's forts and ships firing on them. Many of the fire-ships were seen to drive through their fleet, and beyond the Isle d'Aix. The night was extremely dark; it blew a strong gale with a high sea, and the service thereby became of such increased hazard as scarcely to admit of a hope of the officers and men ever returning.

It is right I should here observe, that, although from these and other untoward circumstances, several of the fire-ships failed in their object, I could not discover (after the fullest investigation) that blame was imputable to any of the officers who commanded them.

The explosion-vessel, conducted by Lord Cochrane in person, also failed in their object, as will be seen by a reference to the small chart I now deliver into court, which points out where two of them blew up: the third broke adrift, and did not explode.

The situation in which, and the time when these vessels blew up, proved prejudicial to the enterprise in several respects. Their premature explosion, contrary to the expressed intention of Lord Cochrane, that they should blow up in the midst of the enemy's boats, to deter them from towing off our fire-ships in their approach, served as a warning to the enemy, whose ships were observed instantly to shew lights; and several of the officers who commanded the fire-ships not doubting but that the explosion had taken place near to the enemy's fleet, steered their ships and set them on fire accordingly, by which means several were in flames at a greater distance from the enemy than was intended, and so as to endanger our advanced frigates. In fact, had not Captain Wooldridge, and some of the other officers, wholly disregarding the explosion, taken their fire-ships in a proper direction for the enemy, it is more than probable that none of them would have produced any effect whatever on the enemy's fleet.

But although not one of the enemy's ships was actually destroyed by means of fire-ships, yet the terror excited by their approach induced the enemy to cut their cables, and exposed them, by their running aground, to the attack which ensued.

I now come to the proceedings of the 12th of April, which commence with the signal that the enemy could be destroyed, and which destruction it is imputed to me I delayed or neglected. . . .

These movements of the enemy's ships were not, as I submit to the Court, to be prevented by any means that I could adopt with the smallest chance of success, and without his Majesty's ships being put to the most unwarrantable peril, and when, as Rear-admiral Stopford has, in his evidence, on the part of the prosecution, most emphatically described, "Ours would have been all the loss, and the enemy's all the advantage."

The wind blew directly in, so that in the event of our ships being crippled, while the flood-tide was running, which appeared inevitable, it would have been impossible for them to have worked out, or to have retreated to an anchorage out of the reach of the enemy's shot and shells; the consequence of which could scarcely have been less than their utter destruction.

These serious impediments induced me to delay the attack until the latter part of the flood, in order to give any ships, which might be disabled on their approach, a chance of returning, by means of the receding tide.

Had the wind been favourable for sailing both in and out, or even the latter only, there could have been no doubt that the sooner the enemy's ships were attacked the better. . . .

Lord Cochrane has expressed an opinion, that two or three sail of the line sent in on the morning of the 12th, might, by running up, on the verge of the Boyart shoal, have passed to leeward of the two French ships remaining at anchor. This, I declare to have been absolutely impracticable; as well from the raking fire of the two ships afloat and of the upright ones on shore on our approach, and the fire of the batteries, as from the shoal water close under their lee. The testimony of Captain Rodd, the only witness examined on this point, on the part of the prosecution, corroborates my opinion, which I have no doubt will be further supported by the evidence of other competent witnesses I propose calling.

With respect to the force of the Aix batteries, I apprehend that what appeared to Lord Cochrane, and to the master of his ship, as ruins of the fort, were in fact materials for improving or increasing the works. Indeed, can it be natural to suppose, that the enemy, who are so active in forming batteries wherever they can be useful, and whose engineers are considered to be equal to any, would of all moments choose that for dismantling, or blowing up works, when they expected those works would be most required; for it is very certain, the enemy was as fully apprized of our intentions of attacking their fleet as myself. And it will, perhaps, be considered less likely that the enemy should weaken their defences on the Isle d'Aix, raised evidently for the protection of their fleet, when at the same time they were endeavouring to form others on the Boyart shoal as further protection for it. . . .

Previous to my leaving Basque Roads, one of the enemy's frigates was set on fire by themselves at the entrance of the Charente, another was observed to be wrecked up that river. The number of ships that escaped without injury, did not, from the best information, exceed one or two line of battle ships, and two frigates; what may have been the fate of the remainder, I leave to be considered by the Members of this Honourable Court, who are well qualified to judge of the condition of ships which had been so long and so repeatedly aground.

By the foregoing narrative, as well as by the log and signal log of the *Caledonia* (to which, as also to every correct log of the fleet, I am as desirous to refer as Lord Cochrane may be) it will, I conceive, be seen, that I fully meet the charge which has been preferred against me; and if the impression arising out of this inquiry should prove less favourable to Lord Cochrane, than that which may have been produced by my letter to the Lords Commissioners of the Admiralty of the 14th of April, his Lordship must be sensible, that as the instigator of this Court Martial, he will himself have been the cause of this change of sentiment. . . . Had I pursued any of the measures deemed practicable and proper in the judgment of Lord Cochrane, I am firmly persuaded the success attending this achievement would have proved more dearly bought than any yet recorded in our naval annals, and, far from accomplishing the hopes of my country or the expectations of the Admiralty, must have disappointed both. If such, too, were the foundation of his Lordship's prospects, it is just they should vanish before the superior considerations attending a service involving the naval character and most important interests of the nation.

[Lord Gambier was most honourably acquitted. On Thursday, 25 January 1810, Lord Grenville moved in the House of Lords for a vote of thanks of Lord Gambier, and on Monday, 29 January Lord Cochrane tried to interest the Commons in his version of events in Basque Roads, but received little support. The Lords and Gentlemen strongly approved the vote in both houses. Vol. XXIII, pp149, 155-157.]

The Fault Lay with the Admiralty
From 'Correspondence.' XXII *104-106*

A.F.Y. to the Editor
"Present Management and Discipline of the Navy, Letter XIII"
Sir, In my first letter to you, I ventured to make some observations on the constitution and conduct of the Board of Admiralty, as relative to the discipline and management of the navy, and I am induced at present to offer some few farther remarks, which arise from parts of the court martial just finished.

If I could flatter myself that the exposition of the causes and consequences of the late events in Basque Roads would meet the eye of their immediate author, I should also flatter myself that the recurrence of such deplorable mistakes would be in future avoided.

Let it be remembered that it was the palpable mismanagement in the designation of Lord C., gallant and able as he may be, which has occasioned courts martial on *two* British admirals, has occupied the time of many officers for several weeks, and caused a degree of heart burning which will not soon be allayed. As the power of the Board was certainly adequate to the appointment, I must probably confine my charge to mismanagement, and not to an absolute infringement of discipline, although that has been materially injured by the consequences. It appeared so evident, that the step to be taken, was the sending a simple order to Lord G. to appoint a flag officer, and such captains as he should judge proper from those under his command, to make an attempt on the French fleet as soon as the additional means of destruction arrived, that I can only in one way account for the omission. I conclude that it must have been wholly owing to the inexperience of ____ [presumably the First Lord, Lord Mulgrave] in naval affairs, and to his not consulting the experienced naval officers associated with him. I am borne out in my suspicions by documents before the public. Lord G.'s letter of March 11, 1809, is not addressed to the *Board* of Admiralty, but to the *Military* 1st Lord, though wholly on naval matters. These *demi*-official correspondences are always bad: they appeared so on the trial of the gallant Cornwallis, and appear no less insulting to the naval service in general, and the naval Lords of the Admiralty in particular, on the present occasion. Lord C. has, I believe, publicly allowed that his appointment originated in a private conversation; and in Lord M.'s letter to Lord G. of May 29, the first lord seems all in all, and we hear of more private conversations. I am of opinion that the experienced judgments of the naval lords might have prevented the late court martial, but there is somehow or other a natural difference in the idea of discipline in the two services. From a bare surmise of a very young officer, it appears, as far as I can observe, that Lord M. deemed a court martial on Lord G. as quite proper, while very lately a court of inquiry was held to be quite sufficient on the Cintra generals, one of whom refused to follow up a victory and attack a beaten foe, and the whole nation was indignantly demanding a trial.

In all the affair now under discussion, there have appeared to me the same want of attention to the feelings of naval officers, and disregard of the interests and discipline of the service, which I fear are become part of a system, a systematic neglect of "Briton's best bulwarks!" There never was an instance of an *interloper*, however excellent he may have been, that has done good. Had the burning of the French fleet and arsenal at Toulon[4] been entrusted to officers of the fleet who had seen the whole service there, it would have been more effectually done than it was. What indignation was caused by the appointment of the late Sir Hyde Parker, in July 1792, to superintend the manoeuvres of Lord Hood's fleet; and the instance before us, is apparent to all men. Look at the list of the evidences on Lord G.'s trial; would not the gallant captains of the *Theseus* and

---

4 With respect to this allusion, made by our ingenious correspondent, to the burning of the Toulon fleet, we cannot agree with him in considering Sir S. Smith's volunteering that service, being on the spot, and at the "*eleventh hour*," quite a parallel case to the specific appointment from home of Lord C. to the Basque Road enterprise; but we shall make it our business to consult a naval friend on this point, whom we know to be able, and hope to find him willing, to give the public full and particular information of what passed at the conflagration of Toulon, in the utmost detail. We have always understood that, in the hurry and bustle attendant upon a scene of evacuation, no preparations were even thought of for disposing of the French fleet, till Sir S.S. suggested it that very morning. - Editor.

Bellona, (and many others) have equally dared the cannon's mouth with the noble lord who was sent to snatch the laurel from their brows, and will any man underprice their judgments when put in comparison with his? I admire the gallantry and skill of the noble lord as much as any man can do, and I could expatiate with pleasure on his many eminent actions, but I must ever regret his appointment to the execution of the late enterprise.

It is a very serious thing, Mr. Editor, and a heavy stroke on the discipline of the navy, when a commander-in-chief, high in rank and character, is reduced to the necessity of standing as a prisoner at the bar of a court; the most honourable acquittal to himself, does not efface the evil done to the service, and it is peculiarly baneful when, as in the present case, it originates with a very junior officer. But this evil, when traced to its source, will, I am convinced, be found to arise from the lamentable inexperience in naval matters in the man where the contrary talent is so much wanted; in his assuming more than usual individual power to himself, and neglecting to avail himself of the experienced judgments of the naval officers who are his associates in the commission, however low he may hold them in the exercise of its powers. . . .
[Other letters by A.F.V. on Naval Discipline are located in Appendix 6, Volume III.]

Report of the French Court Martial XXII 453-455

We mentioned that several of the French captains, engaged in the affair of Basque Roads, in April last, had been brought to trial. We are now enabled to give the following additional particulars.

The account of the loss of the *Calcutta* was given by her captain, Lafon, and his officers, jointly. It states, that whilst preparing to engage a British frigate, they were surprised by the explosion of a catamaran, and soon after, being nearly surrounded by fire-ships, one of which their cannon sunk, they cut their cables to avoid the others, and about midnight grounded; but after lightening the vessel, succeeded the next morning in getting off with the tide. They were then attacked by two of our frigates and two bomb-vessels. Notwithstanding their disadvantageous position, and the paucity of their numbers, the whole crew, consisting of only 230 men, they returned our fire, when, about three o'clock, two other British ships joined in the attack. At four, convinced of the impossibility of saving the ship, they forsook it, having only twelve men wounded, and none killed, and set it on fire, when they repaired on board the admiral, who sent them to Rochefort.

The loss of the frigate *l'Indienne* is thus accounted for in the journal of her captain, signed by all her officers. Having placed his vessel at a short distance from the boom, which protected the French line, she was suddenly covered with fire by two explosions which took place at the boom within the lapse of forty minutes, and discovered to his view the approach of several brigs and fire-ships, which burst through the boom, and advanced kindling against the fleet. In order to avoid them, he passed through the French line, and after several astonishing escapes, grounded, and waited for the return of the tide. The next day he was astonished at finding that not a single French vessel had suffered by the effects of the explosions and fire-ships. That day was spent chiefly in vain efforts to get afloat, and in witnessing the destruction of the *Ville de Varsovie*, the *Calcutta*, *Aquilon*, and *Tonnérre*. On the 15th he was attacked, as well as the *Ocean* and *Regulus*, by six British gun-boats, a small frigate, and two cutters; but after an action of several hours, that flotilla was obliged to retire. Having thrown the greatest number of his guns, almost all his powder, ammunition, and provisions into the sea, without being able to get completely afloat, he was obliged to send to the admiral for ammunition and assistance, both of which were not afforded him in an effectual manner. On the 14th he formed a battery on land, which was served by part of his crew. At four o'clock five British brigs and a bomb-vessel attacked the *Regulus* and *Foudroyant*, and continued bombarding them until seven in the evening, without compelling them to alter their position. On the 15th he succeeded in getting the frigate perfectly afloat, and threw almost the whole of his remaining cannon into the sea. In the evening he descried the approaching catamarans, and took precautions in consequence. On the 16th the frigate was driven aground by the wind a second time. Her masts were on the point of falling overboard; she was filling fast with water, and her sides began to gape, when her captain called a council of war, which determined that every hope of saving her being lost, it was necessary to abandon her; she was set on fire, and the crews landed near Fouras, from whence they repaired to Rochefort.

The captains of *la Ville de Varsovie* and *Aquilon* having been taken prisoners, their statement of the loss of their ships could not be transmitted to the court martial.

Captain La Caille, of the *Tourville*, one of the ships that escaped, having been accused of leaving his ship for several hours, whilst she was in presence of the enemy, and the accusation being corroborated by the minutes of his journal, was also compelled to give an account of his conduct before the officers composing the court martial. It appears, that when the first catamarans exploded, the French frigate, *la Pallas*, whilst endeavouring to avoid a fire-ship, ran on board the *Tourville*, which then cut a cable, and was soon after threatened by the *Regulus*, to which a fire-vessel had fixed itself. The *Tourville* then manoeuvred to avoid the surrounding perils, but got aground, and the captain ordered the gunpowder barrels to be opened, in order, should the ship catch fire, that they might be immediately drowned by means of water pipes; but his apprehension proved unfounded. On the arrival of a pilot, he attempted to gain the mouth of the river but with little hopes of success.

On the 12th, whilst several British frigates engaged the *Ville de Varsovie*, the *Calcutta*, and *Aquilon*, the *Tourville* threw away her heavy guns and cannon balls, and sent all her inexperienced and weak sailors and boys on shore, keeping only the stoutest men and marines on board. The pilot, convinced of the impossibility of saving the ship, took French leave, and the captain was informed that several fire-ships were coming against the *Tourville*, and conscious in his grounded position of inability, to avoid or remove them, ordered the whole crew to land, and was the last who quitted the ship. The wind having undergone a favourable change, and no fire-ships having reached their destination, the captain and crew returned on board with the same pilot, whom they had found on shore, and who now expressed his belief that the ship could be got afloat, on account of the alteration in the wind. Several British bomb-vessels and other ships approached at that critical moment to engage the *Ocean* and *Tourville*, both of which answered their fire effectually. The next night they succeeded in getting afloat, and sailed for the mouth of the river, but through the want of experience in the pilot, were grounded on

Chart of the position of the French Fleet in Aix Roads, on the 11th and 12th of April, 1809, when attacked by the English Fleet, under the command of Admiral Lord Gambier, Engraved by Simpkin, from a drawing by Mr. Fairfax, master of the Fleet. Plate 289

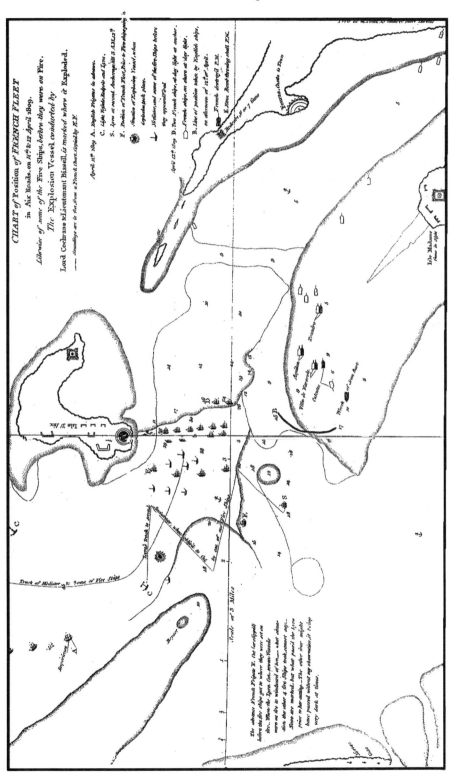

the other side near Fouras. On the 15th they were set afloat by the morning tide, and on the 16th, anchored at the mouth of the river, off the point of Vergeron.

The examination of the officers of the fleet, which follows, in length far exceeds that which took place on the investigation of Lord Gambier's conduct, on the same occasion. In general, as far as it goes, it appears to be in favour of the captains whose ships were lost.

We have been favoured with the accompanying chart and communication (the accuracy of which may be relied on) by Mr. Fairfax, first master of his Majesty's ship *Caledonia*, who, on the evening of the 11th of April, 1809, was appointed by the Right Honourable Lord Gambier to place vessels, with lights, for the purpose of pointing out the passage to the French fleet in Aix Roads. Mr. Fairfax performed that service with great credit and ability in his Majesty's brig *Lyra*.

Correspondence about Pyrotechnics XXI 408-412

Extract from a letter to the Editor from F.F.F., dated London, May

. . . If conjectures may be attended to, a great revolution is about to take place in maritime skill and machinery. Battles in future may be fought under water: our invincible ships of the line may give place to horrible and unknown structures, our frigates to catamarans, our pilots to divers, our hardy, dauntless tars, to submarine *assassins*, coffers, rockets, catamarans, infernals, water worms, and fire devils. How honourable! how fascinating is such an enumeration! how glorious, how fortunate for Britain are discoveries like these! How worthy of being adopted by a people, made wanton by naval victories, by a nation whose empire are the seas.

[It was this letter which stimulated 'Brontes' to write the five letters describing the development and capabilities of the Congreve war rocket, which have been located together in Appendix 8 on Gunnery, below p377-387.]

1809 – Naval News, Summer

IN THE EARLY SUMMER OF 1809 the news from the Austrian front was not good, and a major expeditionary force was prepared for operations with a wider strategic purpose of diverting French forces from Bavaria. *The Naval Chronicle* learnt that Britain was not to attack French positions in the Scheldt, but this rumour was certainly a measure of disinformation, as was soon after reported in the 'Naval History'.

The Naval Chronicle was disturbed that the King's Speech on the Opening of Parliament did not even mention the need to address American concerns about British exercise of maritime rights.

From the 'Naval History of the Present Year,' 1809
May-June. XXI *497-498*

A great and noble mind now actuates the armies of Austria and the Confederates. It will, however, be still a hard and severe labour to oppose the wide influence of French corruption, aided by the wretched politics of Russia. Spain still keeps her head above water; Sir Arthur Wellesley continues successful, and Buonaparte has certainly sustained a severe defeat and is retreating. But why is Lord Wellesley at an enormous expense to be sent out to Spain for only a few months, and then to return: and why are the troops kept on board the numerous transports at Spithead, and in Portsmouth harbour, losing the golden opportunity and their own health? These and various other questions are constantly asked, but are never answered.

No Change at Admiralty

The reports of a change at the Admiralty have proved fallacious, and the resignation of Lord Mulgrave and the raising of the *Royal George* are given up for the present. The trial of Lord Gambier has been put off for some weeks to collect the witnesses, and begins to take a more decided character than was at first expected. It is at all events a great misfortune to the service to meet with such impediments and clogs, whatever may be the result.

No Mention of America in King's Speech

It is remarkable, that, in his Majesty's Speech, at the prorogation of Parliament, no mention whatsoever is made respecting America. The Speech of Mr. Madison, the American President, at the opening of the extra Session of Congress, on the contrary, dwells on scarcely any other topic than the renewal of amity with England, and the necessary alterations which that renewal will cause, in the respective departments of government. The event, which the Americans erroneously believe to have been accomplished, appears to give great and almost general satisfaction throughout the territories of the United States; and despatches have been forwarded to the American minister at Paris, instructing him to urge the revocation of the Berlin decrees.

Major Expeditionary Force Assembling

A new and formidable expedition, intended to create a diversion in favour of Austria, is in great forwardness. An embarkation of 12,000 troops is taking place at Portsmouth; and the entire number of soldiers, it is said, will amount to nearly 40,000. The naval part of the expedition is to be entrusted to Rear-admiral Sir Richard Strachan, with Sir Home Popham under him. The military commander-in-chief has not been mentioned; nor is it yet known against what point the attack will be directed.

An attempt to destroy the enemy's fleet, in the Scheldt, is said to have been in contemplation by government, but to have been abandoned, in consequence of the escape of a person, considered as a spy, who had obtained a knowledge of the intention.

June-July. XXII 75-77: 173

Austrian Forces Suffer Major Defeats

Every flattering hope, respecting the emancipation of the Continent, has again vanished. After several weeks of inaction, between the main French and Austrian armies, on the banks of the Danube, two sanguinary battles were fought, on the 5th and 6th of June, which terminated in the retreat of the Archduke Charles to the Bohemian frontier. It was at first believed, that his retreat had been effected in good order; that the French had suffered at least equally; and that, from the loss which the enemy had sustained, they were unable to pursue. On the 10th of the month, however, the Rear of the Austrian army was overtaken; and, in the midst of an engagement which ensued, on the 11th, Prince John of Lichtenstein arrived at the out-posts of the French army, with proposals for an armistice. Buonaparte immediately ordered the firing to cease; fifteen days' notice of the intended recommencement of hostilities, was agreed to. The terms of the armistice are wholly in favour of the French, who, it is feared, will extort a peace from the Emperor Francis, of the most humiliating description. Buonaparte is said to have returned to Paris.

Expedition Sails for the Scheldt

We are happy to find, that the British expedition, announced at page 498 of the preceding volume, has not been countermanded, nor even suspended, in consequence of the disastrous intelligence from Germany. It sailed from the Downs in four divisions, on the 27th of July; and, from the subsequent favourable state of the wind, there is every reason to suppose, that it reached the first place of its destination, at a very early period. Sir Richard Keates [Keats] is the senior naval officer, and the Earl of Chatham is the military commander-in-chief. The Portsmouth division alone consists of 13 sail of the line, besides other ships and transports, with 15,000 troops on board; and the total number of men employed, including seamen and marines, is estimated at nearly 80,000; a force so truly formidable, that we cannot be surprised at the alarm which it is understood to have excited on the enemy's coast.

Official Statement

The following statement, of the primary object of this expedition, is given by a paper apparently in the confidence of government:

"The operations will commence by landing the numerous gun-boats on board the fleet either in the West Put, at the entrance of the Scheldt, or Sluys Roads, comprehending the coast of Cadsand (according as the weather may prove,) where the men-of-war are to anchor. The immediate intention is to embark on board the boats the troops destined for the main attack of the island of Walcheren, in the West Put, and the most judicious precautions have been projected to prevent the enemy's gun-boats from annoying them. The first attack, however, will be made upon Cadsand, and south Beveland will immediately after be assailed. The possession of the former being necessary to the future operations, it is to be attacked by the whole of a strong brigade, led on by the gallant Marquis of Huntly; and this brigade, if necessary, is to be joined by another, as nearly the whole of the brigades of the right wing will at this juncture be in the Wieling Channel. Schowen, Dayveland, and North Beveland will at the same time be attacked, and in this enterprize the brigade of guards will be employed. In the van squadron will be embarked the brigade of General Hope, which is destined either for Domburgh or the Veer Gat, as circumstances may deem expedient; and this brigade will also have a view to the service of Tenegoes [sic], on South Beveland. One of the brigades is to be held in readiness to land below the Nolle Battery, in the event of the enemy sending any great force to Zoutland to repel our force; by which means his retreat to Flushing may be cut off. The principal attack upon the island of Walcheren is to be made by the Portsmouth division, commanded by General Coote, and a brigade is to be allotted for a service of demonstration. The rowing boats to a great amount are to precede the flat boats, and when they are within reach of grape from the shore, they are to open upon the enemy, drawing off in equal divisions to the right and left, making room for the flat boats to push in, and covering them till the field artillery is ready to move forward. The bombs to take certain stations, and to be ready to commence a bombardment when directed."

The possession of the Islands of Walcheren and Cadsand will give us the entire command of the Scheldt, the ports of which, since Buonaparte has annexed Walcheren to France, have been made the chief nursery of the French navy. They at present contain a considerable number of ships of war ready for sea, and many on the stocks in a state of great forwardness; all of which, we trust, will be either taken or destroyed, and Buonaparte be thus deprived of his last means of fitting out a naval force for our annoyance. It is thought, that our occupation of Walcheren will not be of a temporary nature; for it is understood to be tenable by us in all seasons of the year; and, besides its advantages, as a naval station, it will have the important effect of neutralising a considerable portion of the enemy's territory.

The destruction of the French flotilla, at Boulogne, is conjectured to be a secondary object of the expedition; and it is not unlikely, that several other parts of the enemy's coast may feel the effects of British prowess before it returns.

Lord Gambier's Trial

In consequence of the sailing of the expedition having been protracted beyond the expected period, the trial of Admiral Lord Gambier did not commence till Wednesday the 26th of July. [Highlights of the most interesting technical evidence have been published above at pp247-253.] . . .

Elbe

On the 5th of June, a small English squadron, consisting of four gun-brigs and two sloops, from Heligoland, arrived at Cuxhaven, and drove the enemy out of that place, demolished the batteries, and obliged the Municipality to lay down the buoys in the Elbe, which had been taken up by the French. The military force of this little expedition was only 120 men. The Dutch troops who were left in possession of the place fled, and the inhabitants testified the greatest joy at seeing the English flag once more flying in their port.[1]

Spain

According to the latest intelligence from Portugal, Sir Arthur Wellesley, having formed a junction with General Cuesta, was marching towards Madrid. Joseph Buonaparte is again reported to have abandoned that capital.

The British arms have again been triumphant in Spain. Sir Arthur Wellesley achieved a brilliant victory at Talavera, on the 27th and 28th of July; for which he has been elevated to the peerage, by the title of Baron Douro and Viscount Wellington.

---

1 The official letter from Captain Goate was published in Vol. 22 p. 85.

1809 – Scheldt Expedition

THE SCHELDT EXPEDITION was the largest British amphibious operation in the war, and the greatest disaster suffered by British arms during it. The objectives were to destroy the naval force that Emperor Napoleon was developing in the Scheldt, protected by the difficulties of navigation but close to the heart of England, and to provide a diversion which might provide assistance for the hard-pressed Austrians. Parliament published many of the service letters relating to the expedition. The most important of those which deal with the planning and launching of the expedition are reproduced here. A more personal view of the naval part of the operation was provided by a journal kept by a medical man, Doctor William Cullen–Brown, who served in a bomb vessel, HMS *Aetna*.

The army Commander-in-Chief was Sir John Pitt, the second Earl of Chatham. He had been First Lord of the Admiralty between 1788 and 1794, when his indolence earned him the soubriquet of 'the late Earl of Chatham'. He was Master-General of the Ordnance from 1801 to 1806, and was consoled for his disappointment when General Wellesley was appointed to command in the Peninsula by this appointment to command on the Scheldt. Edward Baines, in his 1817 *History of the Wars of the French Revolution*, wrote, "unfortunately, the formidable strength, and the complete equipment of the troops, were rendered useless; and when it was known that the command was to be conferred on the Earl of Chatham, a man proverbial for indolence and inactivity, the nation no longer looked forward to the result with confidence." Naval command was entrusted to Rear-Admiral Sir Richard Strachan. Chatham's attempt to cast the blame for failure on to Strachan ensured his own political ruin.

The expedition sailed from the Downs on 28 and 29 July, and on 1 August Flushing was invested. It was bombarded with Congreve's rockets and, on the 14th, from the sea by ships' guns. On the 2nd the garrison capitulated. Chatham failed to exploit this victory by a rapid move up the Scheldt.

263

THE SOUTHERN PART OF THE UNITED PROVINCES.

Naval State Papers

Relating to the Expedition to the Scheldt, presented by his Majesty's Command to both Houses of Parliament. XXIII 113-134; 200-241

This extensive collection of papers is arranged under four heads: *Intelligence*; *Preparation of the Naval Force*; *Departure of the Armament, and Subsequent Operations*; and, *Evacuation*.

Intelligence:

No. 12, dated off West Capel, March 3, 1809, contains the following information from Captain [Commander James?] Boxer:

"The enemy's fleet in Flushing consists of the following force: ten ships of the line (including a 50-gun ship), two frigates, and a few smaller vessels; the line-of-battle ships are fitting *slowly*; during the last week they were employed getting iron ballast, water casks, and gun carriages on board; the frigates are rigged and nearly ready for sea, and it is supposed the fleet will be ready to haul out of the harbour about the latter end of the present month. The line-of-battle ship on the stocks at Flushing is not in a forward state, but the greater part of those at Antwerp, it is believed, will be ready to come down about July or August next. The Danish officers in the fleet are very discontented; several of whom have deserted. No reinforcements of troops have arrived on the island, their numbers at present are supposed to be about 4,000, besides the burgers."

No. 13, dated two days later, mentions, that the enemy's fleet in Flushing, except two, have their topmasts on end.

No. 14, from [Vice-] Admiral [Sir George] Campbell to Lord Mulgrave, dated March 6, announces the arrival of a great number of troops in the neighbourhood of Flushing; that the ships of war, in the dock, were expected to be completed in about three weeks; and that four brigs, laden with provisions for the West Indies, were ready to sail the first opportunity. . . .

No. 19, dated March 24, mentions, that all the ship-builders and carpenters had been ordered away from Flushing to the interior, for the purpose of constructing rafts to transport troops across the Rhine, in consequence of the war with Austria. . . .

In No. 22, dated *Venerable*, in the Downs, April 5, Sir R.J. Strachan, addressing Lord Mulgrave, says: "Captain Boxer has sent me a sketch of Flushing, and although it is roughly done, I forward it to your lordship, as it will give you an idea of the basin where the ships of war lay. I am told the guns on the works at the town are mounted on old works faced with stone or brick. Captain Boxer has not sent me any account of the batteries on the Cadsand side, but I understand there is one on the point of Breskin, opposite Flushing, and also at the point below Borcelen, on the South Beveland side. It seems to be a general opinion that much resistance is not to be expected at Flushing, and the reports of the deserters, lately come over, favour the opinion; but when I consider the defence of Flushing, I am decidedly of opinion that a squadron, let it be ever so well attended by gun-vessels, could do little against the ships of the enemy in the basin, and would be exposed to be set on fire by the batteries of the enemy; therefore, it is advisable not to make any attempts on the town without the co-operation of an army. If a squadron should be anchored clear of existing batteries above the town, it would be an object to

Chart of the Southern Part of the United Provinces. Drawn and engraved by Luffman. Plate 291 take up such an anchorage, to prevent the enemy from escaping up the river when the town is attacked. By the accounts of to-day it seems probable, that all the ships of the enemy, by this time, are at anchor in the Scheldt, and in a situation to run up the river, if attacked; six were at anchor, and the others were preparing to go out of the basin; Lieutenant [James] Duncan says, he thinks one of the ships of the line, as well as the frigates, had Dutch colours up."

No. 32, contains some loose intelligence from a deserter; and also (addressed to the Secretary of the Admiralty) the following *Memorandum of observations made by — at the ports of Boulogne, Calais, Dunkirk, Ostend, Antwerp, and the Island of Flushing.*

At Boulogne there are about 600 craft of different descriptions, that compose the flotilla, but they are in such a state of wreck, as well in their rigging as in their bottoms, which are worm-eaten, that they will require to be nearly rebuilt to be of service.

At Calais there are about 70 craft of the flotilla in the same state.

At Dunkirk there are two old frigates, and about ninety vessels of the flotilla in the inner Basin; and there are in the outer basin, above fifty fine merchant vessels, fit for transports, many of which are prizes taken from the English.

At Ostend there are about forty small vessels of the flotilla, and a few merchant vessels which are in a very bad state.

In consequence of repeated disputes, which have taken place between the Dutch and French officers employed on this flotilla service, a considerable division of the Dutch flotilla have returned to Holland through the canals.

At Antwerp, there are about fifteen vessels of the flotilla, but they are unserviceable; and at Flushing there are only seven of about thirty tons with one gun in the bow.

Ships of war on the Stocks at Antwerp, and observations on the Arsenal

At Antwerp there are on the stocks ten eighty gun ships, and three of them are nearly finished, though it is probable they will not be launched this winter. The situation chosen by Buonaparte for the building of ships of war was occupied by 1,500 houses in the beginning of 1804, and was the most ancient part of the city of Antwerp; but it is at present reduced to ways and slips, for ships, and is capable of being extended to the placing of 20 ships of the line on the stocks at the same time, and their resources for building, from the Black Forest through the Rhine, are inexhaustible. The mechanics employed on the building these ships are all young men, and are chosen from among the conscriptions levied. They are formed into military order, as well as into labouring order. There are a company to each ship building, under the superintendence of a captain; and to every two ships there is a superintending builder; and every Sunday they are exercised to military discipline. The work is carried on with amazing rapidity, but perfectly performed. At Flushing, in the basin, are the following 74 gun ships; *Charlemagne, Commerce de Lyon, Anversois, Caesur, Duquesclin, Dantzick,* and *La Ville de Berlin,* with a new Dutch frigate: and on the stocks are two 74 gun ships, a frigate and a brig: in the roads are the *Princess Caroline* frigate and a brig belonging to the French.

At Ramskeys are seven gun-boats, with one gun on the prow, as has been observed of the flotilla at Flushing. Distributed among all those vessels at Flushing, (French and Dutch,) there are not 800 men of all descriptions.

There are at Campvere[1] about 40 sail of smugglers, and belonging to them, from 300 to 500 prime English seamen, who, as well as the Dutch, would rejoice to see the

French removed from their favourite smuggling port, which they have converted into a naval arsenal, and which arbitrary conversion has created great disgust. . . .

No. 41, contains the following information, in a letter from Captain Bolton of the *Fisgard*, to Sir R. Strachan, dated East Capel Roads, July 7:

"Examination of the Weiling channel proves it to be safe, and sufficiently capacious for any enterprise. The fortifications on the island of Cadsand consist as far as I have been able to discover, of two small batteries, one apparently of five, the other of thirteen guns; the landing is good on any part of the shore. The coast between east and west Capel is precisely as I left it. On west Capel point is a Fleur d'Eau battery of seven or eight guns, and to the north of the church is another, about a cable's length from the beach, of seven guns en barbet, and I do not think there is any gun mounted between this battery and east Capel; preceding to Camvere a little above house point is a small battery of three or five guns, and at Camvere there is another of about seven, neither do I see any difficulty of landing or navigation on any part of the coast. . . .

Agreeably to your desire, I shall give my opinion on the proper points of landing and attacking Flushing; this will depend on the wind.

If the attack is made with wind southerly (as far as S.S.W.) the Weiling channel will be most advisable for the large ships to pass up, as after passing the Elboog those intended to batter Flushing can bear up to their stations, as well as the ships that cover the troops landing about Zoutland, of which there can be no difficulty if the weather is moderate; at the same time the divisions assigned for landing and attacking Camvere and west Capel, will have a smooth beach between west and east Capel. If the attack is made with the wind northerly, the Duerloo will be the best channel for the ships to advance up. But, if it blows fresh, the whole of the debarkment must be made between west Capel and Flushing, and nothing can be done on the east Capel side, unless a division sail up at once to Camvere, through the Vere Gat; - provided the attack is made with the wind this way (northerly), a strong portion of heavy armed light draught of water vessels should be appropriated for the attack of west Capel: they can lie close to the shore, and this point secured, the troops and stores might be landed at the jetties in smooth water; there is a passage of four fathoms through the east Gat, and when inside the Calloo, eight or ten fathoms all the way along shore to Flushing; all the smugglers are well acquainted with this passage, and I shall endeavour to find it out. Vessels of light draught can pass at high water over the banks. There will be one advantage in attacking with the wind northerly, the ships damaged in battering Flushing may bear away to refit, and be succeeded without difficulty by the reserve, which may be kept anchored out of gun shot in the Duerloo.

You will perceive by the sketch [which unfortunately was not published], I had not only placed a vessel on Thornton's ridge, but also one on the Hinder; this is to enable the large ships to pass in safety between those shoals should they have to cross over to Blackenbury, to proceed through the Weiling.

If the attack from the northward is decided upon, the best place of rendezvous would be the 17 fathom, or Brei Bank. They might there pass between the stone banks, through the stone deep round the Rassen and up the Duerloo; and the battering vessels through the east Gat to the west Capel, the division to Camvere round the Baujart to the Veer Gat.

---

1 ['Campvere' and 'Vere' are spelt variously throughout the original text.]

From all the information I have been able to collect, the troops on the island do not amount to 3,000 men."

In No. 42, an enclosure from Captain Bolton states, that, in the Roompot, there is plenty of room for vessels to lie perfectly out of gun-shot of Walcheren or Schoen; and that the fortifications of the latter place are insignificant. . . .

The next series, under the head "*Preparation of the Naval Force*," comprises thirty-two papers.

No. 1, is a Memorandum of the Board of Admiralty, dated June 9, 1809, as follows:

"It is the opinion of the sea Lords of the Admiralty, that in the first instance the island of Walcheren should be taken: they do not take upon them to say where the landing should be made, or how the military force should be distributed; this should be arranged between the General and Sir Richard Strachan. The fleet may be broken into divisions, calculated to convey and protect any given number of troops to any given point; and it is presumed that we shall be able to master any floating force the enemy can produce, and to assist the army in the attack of any batteries that may have been erected on the banks of the river.

In going up the river it may be expedient to take possession of Terneuse on the left bank, but the right bank of the river must be secured as the armament proceeds; and having attained it as far as Bathz, the naval force would be capable of protecting and conveying the whole army in a very short space of time to Sandfleet, or any other point below the narrow part of the Scheldt, at which the general may think it proper to land. An arrangement may be made for putting on shore about fourteen thousand men at the first trip, by flat boats, launches, &c. and the remainder of the army could follow from ships to be anchored close to the shore. The fleet can also undertake to bring the army off from the neighbourhood of Sandfleet, but the fleet cannot go into the narrow part of the Scheldt, unless the army are in possession of both banks of the river. Fire vessels, however, will be prepared, and every means held in readiness for taking any advantage that may offer of acting against the enemy in the narrow part of the river for the destruction of their ships.

[Rear-Admiral] Sir Richard Strachan is ordered into port, and all the details of the expedition should be settled between that officer and the general who is to command. The naval force destined for the service, is in such a state of forwardness, that if an embarkation return were furnished, the ships could, in a very few days, be at their stations.

100 flat boats will carry	5,000 men
70 gun-boats	700
26 long boats and ship's launches	520
40 barges	400
26 small vessels, and 20 vessels from dock-yard, &c	5,000
30 gun-brigs to be advanced with 100 men each	3,000
	14,620

72 gun-boats, carrying 24-pounders, to attend the fleet; also twenty-six cutters and small vessels. These boats should be furnished with Shrapnell's shells; and a detachment of artillery ought to be appropriated to them.

In further aid of the transport service it would be proper to collect as many revenue vessels as possible; and when the expedition is about to sail we should lay hold of all Folkstone and Deal cutters, all Berwick smacks that may be in the river, and such Harwich packets and vessels of that description as can be procured." . . .

No. 21, from Vice-admiral Campbell to Mr. Pole, dated *Agincourt*, Downs, July 15, contains, as an enclosure, the following:

Arrangement for the Embarkation of troops in the Downs

Agincourt	900	4th Foot	I Battalion,	1,008
Monmouth	900		2 "	930
Powerful	600			1,938
York	600	6th Foot	I "	971
Serapis	300	50th Foot	I "	853
Venerable	300	91st Foot	I "	520
Lavinia	300			2,344
Salsette	300	9th Foot	I "	932
Statira	300	38th Foot	I "	750
Bucephalus	300	42d Foot		799
Heroine	300			2,481
St. Fiorenzo	300			6,763
Thalia	300	To be embarked in the Downs on
Circe	300	board of men of war.
Terpsichore	390			
Amethyst	200			
Camilla	100			

No. 26, is as follows:

Orders from the Lords Commissioners of the Admiralty to Sir R. Strachan, dated 17th July 1809. . . .

3d – In the arrangement for the conveyance of the troops on board his Majesty's ships, it is proposed that fifteen thousand troops should be embarked at Spithead, on board the ships of the line, frigates, and sloops at that anchorage. This force is intended for the reduction of the island of Walcheren, and it has thus been distributed on board the larger ships of war, in order that this division of the army may be readily landed, and that the ships of that description may be exposed as little as possible to the intricate navigation of the Scheldt. You will avail yourself of every opportunity of collecting the vessels of the country for the further conveyance of the troops employed in the first instance in the island of Walcheren; and you are, as far as possible, to make your arrangements in such a manner as may enable you at the same time that you afford the most effectual assistance to the army in the reduction of the island of Walcheren, to take care that the line-of-battle ships employed in the conveyance of troops for that enterprise, may not be pushed higher up the river than may be absolutely necessary for that object; and you are to bear in mind, that although in carrying on the subsequent operations in the Scheldt, the services of the officers and men belonging to those ships may be wanted for gun-boats, launches, or flat boats, to assist the army on shore, or for other services, the ships themselves are not to be risked amidst the shoals and narrows of the river, unless you shall deem it to be absolutely necessary for giving effectual aid to the army, or for destroying the enemy's fleet; objects which would, however, justify such risk.

4th – You are to keep a sufficient number of ships at the Nore, to receive the proportion of the army consisting of three thousand men, intended to be embarked in his Majesty's ships at that anchorage, with directions to join you in the Downs the moment the troops shall be embarked; but, as it is of importance that the line-of-battle ships attached to your squadron, now in the Downs, should be kept in all respects fit for the most effectual service, as they may be required for attacking batteries, for covering the landing of the troops in Walcheren, and to attend the army in its progress up the river, for the purpose of keeping in check the enemy's line-of-battle ships, or of attacking them if practicable; You are not to embark more than two hundred soldiers in any of the said ships of the line, the remainder of the seven thousand troops, destined to be conveyed by ships of war from the Downs, must be distributed in such manner as you may judge best for his Majesty's service, among the frigates and other ships and vessels of war. . . .

[In Lord Porchester's resolution in the House of Commons, 26 March 1810, censoring the administration for the Scheldt expedition, it was stated that the armament consisted of '39,000 land forces, 37 sail of the line, 2 ships of 50, 8 of 44 guns, 24 frigates, 31 sloops, 5 bomb-vessels, and 23 gun-brigs'. Vol. XXIII, p423.]

Departure of the Armament, and Subsequent Operations:

No. 2, from Sir R. Strachan to Mr. Pole, dated *Amethyst*, Downs, July 24, contains copies of all the Admiral's instructions to the different flag and divisional officers in the expedition; accompanied by the following remarks:

"You will observe, Sir, that the first object is the possession of Cadsand, which service I have confided to Captain Owen, and he is to co-operate with the Marquis of Huntley, whose division is embarked in the ships under his orders.

The main object, as their Lordships have been already apprized, is Walcheren, which is to be possessed by the troops embarked in the squadron at Portsmouth, under the direction of Sir Eyre Coote and Rear-admiral Otway.

The other object is, to possess the south side of Schowen, for the advantage of commanding the Roompot Channel, with a view of giving every facility and acceleration to the transport of the troops to South Beveland; and this service being confided to Lieutenant-general Sir John Hope, and branching out into more consequence and arrangement than I had at first an idea of, I considered it right to appoint Rear-admiral Sir Richard Keats to take charge of the squadron, and to co-operate with the lieutenant-general accordingly. Captain Plampin will be the next senior officer, and will, I am satisfied, render any information to the rear-admiral that he may be in possession of from his former intercourse with that country.

The last division is for the Vere Channel, which I have entrusted to Sir Michael Seymour, and I think, from some arrangements which I have in contemplation, that much benefit will be derived from [to] the general service, from an early possession of this channel, and pushing it forward under prudence to Tergoes, to shorten the route of Sir John Hope.

Having now laid before their Lordships my general outline of operations, I have only to assure them that I shall endeavour to give a superintending eye to the whole, and if the event should fortunately be such as to enable us to effect the landing at Domberg, I shall be very well able to do so.

After the Earl of Chatham is satisfied that his footing at Walcheren is of so commanding a nature as to preclude the necessity of re-embarking his troops, I shall then order the Portsmouth division of ships to the Downs, with all others which I can spare, for the double purpose of relieving their Lordship's minds from the anxiety which they have expressed about these particular ships, in the fourth paragraph of their instructions, and to enable them to apply their services in any other way.

I shall lose no time in pushing up the river according to their Lordships' instructions, taking every possible precaution to avoid the numerous shoals; preliminary steps to which have been taken, and a card of explanation printed for the information of every ship.

I am very glad to find that their Lordships have so fully estimated the difficulty and intricacy of the navigation of the Scheldt, because they will be less surprised if I should not be able to carry up the line-of-battle ships; but, in such an event, I beg you to assure them, that I shall make every disposition to attack the enemy's fleet with the frigates and flotilla under my command."

No. 5, encloses a letter from Captain [William] Bolton, to Sir R. Strachan, dated *Fisgard*, East Capel Roads, July 23; announcing that the enemy's fleet, amounting to eleven sail of the line, had just dropped down the Scheldt, and anchored close off the town of Flushing. . . .

No. 7, from Sir R. Strachan to Mr. Pole [the Honourable William Wellesley Pole], dated *Amethyst*, Downs, July 25, contains the following statement:

"Having received information that the enemy's fleet has moved down the river, and anchored close in to Flushing, I think it right to proceed to sea without a moment's loss of time, and I shall sail immediately.

All the arrangements have been made some time, and we have waited only for a fair wind, and the arrival of [Rear] Admiral [Sir Robert Waller] Otway, to proceed to sea with the whole armament; but as Admiral Otway may arrive on the first movement of a change, I have, with a view of gaining as much time as possible, made dispositions for his fleet. Boats are to be sent to him the moment he reaches the anchorage; and by way of hastening the arrangements for the rowing gun-boats, I have despatched Captain Janverin to Dungeness to wait his being off that place, with a plan for their covering the landing of the troops, even under the strongest opposition, in any place we may be able to land at.

I have left Rear-admiral Sir R. Keats to attend to the duty in the Downs, and to issue the necessary orders which I have given him for the following order of sailing.

Captain [Edward William Campbell Rich] Owen, with Lord Huntley's division, to sail first.

After he is under weigh, Sir R. Keats to sail for Schowen, anchoring in the first instance under the Bangart. Sir John Hope's division of the army is embarked in this squadron.

After Sir R. Keats has made sail, then Admiral Otway is to sail with the grand division for Walcheren.

I have also given Captain Sir Home Popham an order to receive the Earl of Chatham on board, to proceed to sea with him whenever his lordship pleases. . . ."

Rear-Admiral Strachan's Despatches

From 'Letters on Service,' Admiralty Office,
August 7, 1809. XXII 140-142

Lieutenant James Duncan, commanding his Majesty's hired cutter the *Idas*, arrived yesterday evening at this office with despatches from Sir Richard John Strachan, Bart. and K.B. Rear-admiral of the white, &c. addressed to the Honourable William Wellesley Pole, of which the following are copies:

Venerable, off the Veer Gat, August 4, 1809
Sir, You have been already acquainted that I had hoisted my flag in the *Amethyst*, and that it was my intention to have preceded the expedition, in company with the *Venerable*, on board which ship Lord Chatham had embarked; but finding the public service might suffer from the commanders-in-chief being separated, I therefore shifted to the *Venerable*, and sailed from the Downs at day-light on the 28th ultimo.

I have now to acquaint you, for their lordship's information, of my arrival on the evening of that day in the Stone Deeps, with the *Amethyst* and several smaller vessels, where I was joined by the *Fisgard*, Captain Bolton, who had with great judgment placed vessels on the various shoals off this coast. After dark, Lieutenant [James] Groves, of this ship, with some skilful pilots in Deal boats, were despatched to sound the Roompot Channel, and to station vessels at its entrance.

Early next morning, the 29th, the division of Lieutenant-general Sir John Hope, conducted by Captain [Walter] Bathurst, in the *Salsette*, joined me, as did also Rear-admiral Sir Richard Keats, in the *Superb*. This zealous officer had the command of the blockading squadron off the entrance of the Scheldt, but observing the armament pass, he, with his usual promptitude, left that squadron under the orders of [Rear-Admiral Alan Hyde] Lord Gardner, and resumed the charge of Sir John Hope's division; I therefore directed the rear-admiral to shift his flag to the *Salsette*, and to proceed to the Roompot.

The entrance to that Channel is very narrow, and as I was aware of [Captain] Sir Home Popham's local knowledge of the insular navigation before me, I entrusted to that officer the service of leading Sir Richard Keats' division in, and which he did with great skill in the *Sabrina*, Captain Kittoe; the whole was anchored in safety opposite Zeerickzee, situation between the islands of Schowen and North Beveland.

That afternoon Rear-admiral Otway, with the left wing of the army, under [Major-General] Sir Eyre Coote, joined me in the Stone Deeps, but it blew too fresh to have any communication.

On the morning of the 30th, Sir Home Popham returned with a letter from Sir Richard Keats, acquainting me that the division under his charge were all safely anchored; and I was likewise informed that there was sufficient space in the Roompot to contain all the ships, to which anchorage Sir Home Popham undertook to conduct them; and as it blew fresh, with all the appearance of an approaching gale, the squadron was instantly got under sail, and led in by the *Venerable*, when they all came to in safety off the Veere Gat.

As soon as the ships were secured, measures were instantly taken to prepare to land the army on the Island of Walcheren. I did not wait for the gun-boats coming up, but ordered those who happened to be near the *Venerable*, together with the mortar brigs, to push in shore to cover the landing, and to force the Derhank battery.

Having thus accomplished this first object, I lost no time in directing the bombs and gun-vessels to proceed up the Veere Gat, off Cambere; and having given Sir Home Popham (who, at the request of Lord Chatham, had remained on shore with his Lordship,) permission to employ them as the service might require, he the next morning began to cannonade Cambere, which had been summoned, but held out. The fire of the gun-boats was exceedingly well directed, and did much damage to the town.

The officers and crews engaged in that service, had a great claim to my admiration for their conduct. Three of our gun-boats were sunk. In the afternoon it blew fresh, and as the strength of the tide prevented the bombs from acting, I directed the flotilla to fall back, preserving a menacing position.

At night, Captain Richardson, of the *Caesar*, who was in the dyke on shore, threw some rockets at the nearest battery of Camvere, and soon after the commanding officer of the town sent out an offer to surrender. A copy of the terms acceded to by Lieutenant-General Frazer, and Captain Richardson, the senior naval officer on the spot, accompanies this letter.

The army under Sir John Hope landed at South Beveland, on the 1st of this month; and, by a letter from Sir Richard Keats, of yesterday's date, I find the whole of the island is in our possession, the enemy's ships are all above Lillo, and those most advanced as high up as Antwerp.

We are getting our flotilla through the Slough into the Western Scheldt, to prevent succours being thrown into Flushing by the canal of Ghent.

When the Rammekens battery is taken, we hope to pass the lighter vessels to the Western Scheldt, for the purpose of following up the other objects of the Expedition.

I cannot conclude this letter without acknowledging the assistance I have received from Rear-Admiral Otway, and how much I approve of the arrangements he made for landing the division under Sir Eyre Coote; which was carried into effect by Lord Amelius Beauclerc, and Captain Cockburn, with much skill and activity. . . .

I have, &c.

R.J. STRACHAN

A Medical Officer's Point of View

A Letter to a Friend, From Dr. William Cullen-Brown

In 'Correspondence.' XXII 206-213; 287-290

His Majesty's Ship Aetna, July 30, 1809, off Ter Veer, in the Isle of Walcheren, Province of Zealand

That I may not be worse than my promise to you, at my departure, I sit down to transmit some account of the operations of the Expedition hitherto, by extracting from a journal I keep, the chief particulars, which, however, are hitherto, till to-day, but uninteresting.

"July 28th, Downs. This morning, at six o'clock, the whole of the Grand Expedition got under way, with a fair wind for Flushing. We are now going along at the rate of eight knots and a half an hour before the wind; and it is not improbable that we may commence operations in the course of to-morrow. To-day is doubly memorable to me, as being the commencement of this other Grand Armada, and the anniversary of my birth day. At twenty years of age, when I was puffed up with college pride, and looked forward to the accomplishment of mighty schemes, I should have been sadly mortified, had any one predicted, that at thirty three years of age I should have advanced no farther in establishing myself in the world than I have done. But I fear I have neglected catching Shakespear's "tide in the affairs of men" at the proper time: yet, how many are there, men of education too, that would gladly embrace my present situation!

10 o'clock P.M. We are now at anchor on what they call Thornton's Ridge, about 18 miles from the Isle of Walcheren. We shall hardly be prepared to attack Flushing to-

morrow; and the bombarding in all likelihood is reserved for the day after (Sunday), when a desperate conflict will be the result.

July 29th. This morning, at 9 o'clock, following the motions of the fleet, we got under way with a fine breeze in our favour. - Half-past 11 o'clock. We have again anchored about three leagues from the Isle of Walcheren. The transports have not yet come up with us, and the gun-boats have still their guns to get out of the line-of-battle ships; a heavy sea at the same time is running. All these things contribute to retard our progress.

July 30th. We weighed anchor at 7 o'clock this morning; and are now approaching fast to the coast. All is anxious expectation. I have supplied most of the officers and men with cotton to stuff their ears with; so much even do they dread the concussion of the mortars who have been accustomed to them. I have arranged every thing on my part to meet the worst. - Half-past 5 o'clock P.M. Most of the flat-bottomed boats full of troops are rowing for the shore: the frigates are ranged along the shore to cover their landing.

Eight o'clock. A great number of the troops are now landed, and have formed themselves in line on the beach. A heavy fire has been kept up for some time between a battery on shore and our ships; in the mean time our troops are pouring in with all despatch, and will continue to do so during the course of the night. Repeated volleys of musketry have been fired, and are still firing: the great guns are now hushed: we have just dropt our anchor: a height, where a signal post is erected, has been taken possession of by some sailors, who have hoisted the British colours there.

July 31st. This morning, at 6, again got under way. We understand from a captain in the navy, having the command of some gun-boats, with which he was landing the soldiers last night, that only two men were wounded at their disembarkation. . . .

Eleven o'clock. The ice is now broken! We have fired off our ten and thirteen-inch mortars, from the explosion of which I had been taught to apprehend so much. By stuffing my ears with cotton, and pressing them with my fingers on the word for making ready being given, I find no manner of inconvenience from the concussion. I have had the hardihood, standing close by the great brass mortar, to try the effect of its sound on my ears open, and never experienced a more disagreeable sensation. My ears have continued ever since ringing. At the very first firing of the mortar, the lock of my cabin door has been forced off, and the boards of the bulkhead have drawn their nails. This, however, is but the prelude to what is to follow. A tremendous fire has been kept up, and is still going on, between the town and our ships, which last, however, are too far distant from it. The tide is now turning; and such a force of bomb-vessels, gun-brigs, gun-boats, and flat-bottomed boats, will shortly assail the place, almost in close contact with it, as there will be no resisting. The multiplicity of ships to be seen almost as far as the eye can carry, forms a beautiful sight, and highly gratifying to the feelings of an Englishman. A post captain has just been aboard of us, with the intelligence, that the inhabitants of Ter Veer require from us the same terms of capitulation that the French did at Cintra! The firing, after a cessation of half an hour on both sides, has recommenced.

Noon. We are again weighing anchor to get nearer to the town. The intelligence just now received is, that thirty of our troops are killed and wounded together. We are now fast approaching the town. Things become more and more interesting and critical every moment.

Quarter before one. After dropping up about three quarters of a mile, we have again let go our anchor, and taken a proper position for carrying on our bombarding effect. Six o'clock P.M. Our collected force here has been playing away on the town with little intermission till now. What damage the place has sustained, we cannot ascertain; but many of our shells must have told well. My former commander, Mr. Leach, of the *Cracker* gun-brig, who has just been on board of us, has been so much exposed to the enemy's fire, his ships having got aground, that he has been under the necessity of deserting her, at least for the present. We are still ignorant of the operations of our troops ashore.

Twelve o'clock at night. An officer in a boat has been round the different ships from the commander-in-chief ashore, desiring us to desist from hostilities till farther intimation. We have fired off forty-two shells in the course of this day.

August 1st. We have remained at anchor and actionless the whole of the day. In the course of the day, the Dutch troops, amounting to 400, were permitted to march out of the town with the honours of war, when ours entered into it.

August 2d. At 6 o'clock A.M. got under way to proceed towards Rammekens, with a pilot of the country. At 11 o'clock again dropped anchor five or six miles below the fort. At half-past eleven, in consequence of being sent for, I went on board the *Harpy* brig. A poor man, belonging to one of the gun-boats, manned from the *Bellona*, had been shot through both arms from Rammekens, and was brought, in consequence, for assistance to the *Harpy*. Before my arrival, Mr. Parsons, surgeon of the *Harpy*, with Mr. Mortimer, assistant-surgeon of the *Charger* gun-brig, had amputated the right arm; and the tourniquet was already fixed on the other. Both arms had been shockingly fractured and lacerated. The man expired in five or six minutes after my arrival. He had been shot an hour and a half before getting on board of the *Harpy*: his death, as it appeared to myself, Mr. Mortimer, Mr. Parsons, and the assistant-surgeon of the *Safeguard*, was imputable to the loss of blood he had sustained, and the shock the nervous system had received. I dressed another man, who had been shot in the integruments of the head by a grape-shot, or musket-ball, and one who had received a severe bruise on the nose, without any of the bone being shattered, in the same gun-boat. The battery fired first at the boat, and appears to have employed grape-shot.

Between 1 and 2 o'clock. We have again weighed anchor, and are fast drifting up to the battery. At three dropped our anchor.

August 3d. To-day at 10 A.M. weighed anchor, and between 11 and 12 got aground on the sand-bank called Calot. - 4 o'clock. We are again afloat, and about to weigh anchor. We are now about two miles from the fort we are going to attack, as appears from three shells we have thrown having fallen in the Rammekens.

Eleven o'clock P.M. We remain still in the same situation. A party of the gun-room officers went ashore this afternoon on the Isle of South Beveland, where a torrent of rain forced us to scamper in different directions. Mr. Steele, the marine artillery officer, and myself, took refuge in a barn, where we entered into conversation with two very agreeable men in uniform, who had betaken themselves to the same retreat. They afterwards proved to be Lord Yarmouth and Major Dormer, who are here at present, in a small vessel they have hired from Dover, for the purpose of observing the operations of the Expedition. A fire has been seen blazing for upwards of an hour past, which is supposed to be part of Flushing in flames. Our troops, it is said, have made several breaches in it.

August 4th. This day has been a continued gale of wind, accompanied with heavy rains, and as much cold as we might expect to find in the month of December. The

British flag was seen flying in the Rammekens about 10 o'clock this forenoon; and in consequence no hostilities have taken place since. A gun-boat, No. 47, has been upset by a squall just under the fort, and three poor fellows unfortunately drowned: two of them were below at the time coiling away the cable. The life of one of them, who was swept away by the current, might easily have been saved, had they had a row-boat of any description, which, however, none of these gun-boats are allowed; the bad consequence of which has already been repeatedly experienced by them. The lives of the rest of the crew, amounting to twenty-eight, including the lieutenant, were saved by that very useful set of men, the Deal boatmen, employed on this occasion by government, who have conveyed them on board our ship. These gun-boats appear to be little attended to: the service in them is peculiarly severe: officers and men are almost equally destitute of comfort and accommodation; their victualling is neglected, and the risk they run extreme. It was but the other night that a man was wounded in one of them, and died without being seen by a medical man. Another man, who was suddenly taken ill, probably with a spasm in his stomach in consequence of exposure to all manner of hardships, died before there was an opportunity of applying to another ship for assistance. The immediate employment of one or two doses of a powerfully diffusible stimulus, in all likelihood would have saved the man's life. This, then, is the third fatal accident in these boats that has come under my own observation. It is an apparent mismanagement, which, however, I fancy is inseparable from the nature of this service."

[The journal of the action against the Scheldt batteries continued until 31 August, by which time Dr Cullen-Brown was clearly able to observe Antwerp using a telescope.]

1809 – Naval News, Autumn

THE NEWS IN THE LATTER HALF OF 1809 was dominated by the disastrous outcome of the Scheldt Expedition. The news from Spain was only better because the British army managed to escape into Portugal, and the warning that the United States was on the point of concluding an alliance with France was definitely ominous. Better news came from the Mediterranean, where the navy was successfully interrupting the communications of the French army, both by sea and along the coast. Of interest to naturalists, amongst the 'Naval Anecdotes' *The Naval Chronicle* published a reported sighting of a mermaid; the accusation from a correspondent that the money committed to the Sea Fencibles was a profligate example of political jobbing is also of interest. Napoleon's divorce from his Empress, so that he could marry a woman more likely to give him children who could continue his dynasty, did not impress the editor of *The Naval Chronicle*.

From the 'Naval History of the Present Year,' 1809
August-September. XXII 243-245

Disastrous Sick List Threatens Scheldt Expedition

At page 133 [not reproduced], we had the pleasure of announcing the successful progress of the Scheldt Expedition; but it is now our irksome duty, to state, as will be seen at length, by the succeeding *"Letters on Service,"* that all attempts to destroy the hostile fleet at Antwerp have been abandoned. As it is understood, that a Court of Inquiry is to be holden on the conduct of the military commander-in-chief, we shall not venture to prejudge the question; but, in the mean time, we beg leave most particularly to direct the attention of our readers to the gallant Sir R. Strachan's letter, of the date of August 27. It will, we conceive, be found very fully to exhibit *his* opinion on the subject.

It is not at present known, whether Government intends to retain, or to endeavour to retain, possession of the Island of Walcheren; but, from the dreadful mortality which prevails amongst our troops there, it seems to be the general wish of the country, that it should be abandoned. The returns of sick, on the 20th of September, were stated at upwards of 9,000! *Nine* thousand out of *fifteen*! We much doubt, whether any advantage can possibly result from the retention of Walcheren, to compensate for so horrible a sacrifice of life and health.

Cabinet Changes

It seems not unlikely, that the sudden dissolution of the British Ministry may have prevented a determination on this important point. The Duke of Portland, Lord Castlereagh, Mr. Canning, and several other Cabinet Ministers, have given in their resignations; but, amongst the *efficient* members who remain, are *Lord Mulgrave* and the *Earl of Chatham*! The Lords Grenville and Grey have been sent to, for the purpose of assisting in the formation of a new Ministry; but nothing farther is known, than that great difficulties are likely to be encountered, in the accomplishment of this object.

No News of Austria

England is at present quite in the dark, respecting the proceedings between France and Austria. It is not even known, whether peace has been actually signed between those powers.

Peace in the North

Peace has been signed between Russia and Sweden.

Wellington Quits Spain

Lord Wellington has been obliged to abandon Spain, and to fall back upon Portugal; but we have had the satisfaction of learning, that the whole of the Spanish fleet in Ferrol have been completely fitted out for sea, by a squadron sent for that purpose from the Tagus, and that the last ship sailed for Cadiz on the 16th of September.

America, Alliance With France in the Wind

The American Government has enforced its Non-intercourse act against this country; the *Wasp* American sloop of war, was to sail for France on the 16th of August, with a messenger, bearing proposals to the Cabinet of the Thuilleries [Tuileries], as the basis of a treaty; and it is expected, that the negotiations will terminate in an offensive and defensive alliance between France and the United States. Mr. Jackson, the English envoy to America, was within four days' sail of New York, on the 22d of August; but very little hope is entertained of his being able to effect a settlement of the differences between this country and America.

Senegal Surrenders

Admiralty Office, August 26, 1809

A letter has been received at this office, from Captain Columbine, late commander of his Majesty's ship the *Solebay*, addressed to the Honourable William Wellesley Pole, and dated on board the *Derwent* sloop, off Senegal, the 20th of July, 1809, giving an account of the surrender of that settlement to his Majesty's arms. Some depredations having been committed on the trade in the neighbourhood of Senegal, by small privateers fitted out there, Captain Columbine, and Major Maxwell, commanding the garrison at Gorée, determined to make an attack upon the place, and proceeded against it on the 4th of July, with the *Solebay, Derwent* sloop, and *Tigress* gun-vessel, and some merchant and smaller vessels, having on board a detachment of one hundred and sixty men from

Gorée. The enemy at first appeared disposed to offer some resistance, but the detachment being landed, together with one hundred and twenty seamen and fifty marines, the enemy's force, consisting of one hundred and sixty regulars, and two hundred and forty militia, retreated, and on the 13th a capitulation was signed, by which the Island of St. Louis, and its dependencies, were surrendered to the British forces, the garrison being conveyed to France as prisoners of war, not to serve against his Majesty or his allies, until regularly exchanged.

The only loss sustained by the English on this service, has been that of Captain Frederick Parker, of the *Derwent*, Mr. Francis Atterbury Sealy, midshipman of that sloop, and six seamen, drowned in attempting to cross the Bar of Senegal. Captain Columbine speaks in high terms of the conduct of the officers and men employed on the occasion. On the 11th of July, the *Solebay*, in moving up the river, got on shore and was wrecked; all her men and part of the stores were saved.

From 'Naval Anecdotes.' XXII *190–191; 276–284*

Spanish Entertainment, in Compliment to Admiral Purvis

On the 2d of July an elegant entertainment was given by Lieutenant-general De Narva, admiral in the Spanish navy, to Admiral Purvis, and the officers of the British squadron at Cadiz, attended by a numerous assemblage of the first rank there. At the upper end of the dining hall were displayed the flags of England and Spain crossed, and their fly tied together. On each person's plate a printed paper was found, containing some lines in Spanish, in allusion to the union of the national colours, which were read by one of the party, amidst the loudest acclamations of *vivas*. The following was the substance:

> Spain and Britain, fam'd in story!
> Now unite to crush the foe!
> Dauntless Nations, crown'd with glory!
> Lay the haughty Tyrant low. [etc.]

Tendency of Currents

The following letter furnishes an excellent illustration of a well-known fact, that the general tendency of currents in the ocean is from the East towards the West:

Neptune, St. John's Road, Antigua, June 29, 1809
Sir, As the enclosed letters,[1] picked up in a bottle, on the windward part of the island of Martinique, on the 18th of April last, tend to elucidate the state of the current in the Atlantic Ocean, I enclose them to you, with a request that you will be pleased to make the circumstance known to the Lords Commissioners of the Admiralty.

The bottle appears to have been thrown overboard by the *Princess Elizabeth* packet, going to the Brazils, on the 6th of September, 1808, in lat. 14 deg. 45 min. and long. 25 deg. and it must have been carried about 2020 miles in 224 days, which gives nine miles per day on a west course.

I am, &c.

ALEXANDER COCHRANE

Honourable W.W. Pole

1 Several letters were found in the bottle, addressed to individuals.

Mermaid

Letter from Mr. William Munro, Schoolmaster, of Thurso, to Dr. Thorrence,
regarding a Mermaid seen by him some years ago
Thurso, June 9, 1809

Dear Sir, Your queries respecting the Mermaid are before me. From the general scepticism which prevails among the learned and intelligent about the existence of such a phenomenon, had not your character and real desire for investigation been too well known to me, for supposing that you wished to have a fertile imagination indulged by a subject of merriment, I would have been disposed to have concluded, that in this instance you aimed at being ranked among the laughing philosophers, at my expense. Sensible, however, that this is not the case, and taking it for granted that you are sincere, I shall endeavour to answer your queries, though there is little probability that any testimony which I can give respecting the Mermaid, will operate towards convincing those who have not hitherto been convinced by the repeated testimonies adduced in support of the existence of such an appearance. About twelve years ago, when I was parochial schoolmaster at Reay, in the course of my walking on shore of Sandside Bay, being a fine warm day in summer, I was induced to extend my walk towards Sandside Head, when my attention was arrested by the appearance of a figure, resembling an unclothed human female, sitting upon a rock, extending into the sea, and apparently in the action of combing its hair, which flowed around its shoulders, and of a light brown colour. The resemblance which the figure bore to its prototype, in all its visible parts, was so striking, that had not the rock on which it was sitting been dangerous for bathing, I would have been constrained to have regarded it as really an human form, and to any eye unaccustomed to the situation, it must have undoubtedly appeared as such. The head was covered with hair of the colour above mentioned, and shaded on the crown; the forehead round, the face plump, the cheeks ruddy, the eyes blue, the mouth and lips of a natural form, resembling those of a man; the teeth I could not discover, as the mouth was shut; the breasts and abdomen, the arms and fingers of the size of a full grown body of the human species; the fingers, from the action in which the hands were employed, did not appear to be webbed, but as to this I am not positive. It remained on the rock three or four minutes after I observed it, and was exercised during that period in combing its hair, which was long and thick, and of which it appeared proud, and then dropping into the sea, which was level with the abdomen, from whence it did not reappear to me. I had a distinct view of its features, being at no great distance on an eminence above the rock on which it was sitting, and the sun brightly shining. Immediately before its getting into its natural element, it seemed to have observed me, as the eyes were directed towards the eminence on which I stood. It may be necessary to remark, that previous to the period I beheld this object, I had heard it frequently reported by several persons, and some of them persons whose veracity I never heard disputed, that they had seen such a phenomenon as I have described, though then, like many others, I was not disposed to credit their testimony on this subject. I can say of a truth, that it was only by seeing the phenomenon I was perfectly convinced of its existence.

If the above narrative can in any degree be subservient towards establishing the existence of a phenomenon, hitherto almost incredible to naturalists, or to remove the scepticism of others who are ready to dispute every thing which they cannot fully comprehend, you are welcome to it, from, dear Sir, your most obliged, and most humble servant.

List of Nautical Fellows of the Royal Society of London, 1809

William Bentince, Esq. Rear-admiral of the White.
William Bligh, Esq. Captain R.N.
Philip d'Auvergne (titular Duke of Bouillon) Rear-admiral of the White.
John Elliott, Esq. Admiral of the Red.
Sir Andrew Snape Hamond, Bart. Captain, Ret.
Sir John Henslow, Knt. Surveyor of the Navy.
William Johnstone Hope, Esq. Captain R.N.
Joseph Huddart, Esq.
George Lord Keith, K.B. Admiral of the White.
Sir Charles Maurice Pole, Bart. Admiral of the Blue.
Sir Home Popham, Captain R.N.
Matthew Smith, Esq. Captain R.N. Superann.
Sir Philip Stephens, Bart. late Secretary to the Admiralty.
Charles Stirling, Esq. Rear-admiral of the White.
Sir George Young, Knt. Admiral of the White.

Correspondence on the Sea Fencibles. ^{XXII 373-374}

AGRICOLA to the Right Honourable Lord Mulgrave, First Lord of the Admiralty, &c. &c.

My Lord, As the head of the Admiralty, I wish to draw your lordship's attention to the establishment of the Sea Fencibles, which, though a force in name only, cannot cost the nation much less than £200,000 per annum. The public benefit derived from these corps I have never been able to learn, as they are enrolled to serve *only* in case of invasion. Their officers have no command over them; and the amount of their present service is merely to muster once a week, and for which each man receives a shilling. But it is not so much the establishment in general, as the enormous pay given to the *officers*, that I wish to hold up to public notice. The senior captain on each station received £1 10s a day, or £547 10s a year. According to Steel's Navy List, there are round the coasts of England, Wales, and Ireland, (Scotland is not mentioned, though that land of cakes is not, I dare say, without these good things) 143 of these captains so paid. The number of inferior officers is not stated; but these captains are receiving from the public, on the average, more than double their regular pay when on their proper element, and exposed to all kinds of dangers and hardships. I need not inform your lordship as a soldier, that no lieutenant-colonel commanding a battalion in the line, receives more than half the pay allowed to the captains of the Sea Fencibles for *doing nothing*. In a first rate man of war, the captain's pay is no more than £1 5s per diem, and decreases gradually according to the rate, to 12s. In all our domestic military branches, the pay is inferior, and properly so, to that of the regulars. The Militia officers have less pay; the Local Militia still less, and that for the period of being embodied only. Most corps of volunteers have no pay at all; and yet the officers of these Sea Fencibles, which at the best can be considered but as a species of volunteers – these officers, I say, are allowed more than double their regular pay when fighting the battles of their country. This, surely, my lord, is a most monstrous waste of the public money, and which must be put an end to. These are not times for such profuse liberality to one branch of the public force, when all others are cut to the quick, and the whole nation is groaning under the weight of its enormous burdens. Should government think it desirable to keep the seafaring men on the coast, in a kind of nominal service, they may be placed under the inspection of the officers on the *Impress Service*; who, from the very nature of their duty, would keep them in much greater control; and by so doing, £100,000 per annum would be saved to the public. To your lordship's candour and patriotism, I submit the consideration of this subject; and, I trust, with the kingdom in general, that this statement will not be made in vain.

[This view of the Fencibles was by no means universally approved. See Vol. XXIII, pp37-40.]

From the 'Naval History of the Present Year,' 1809
October–November. ^XXII 433-435^

Reports of a Victory Over the Toulon Fleet

Reports have prevailed, ever since the middle of November, of a victory having been gained over the Toulon fleet, by Lord Collingwood, in the Mediterranean. From the numerous concurrent statements which have arrived, *via* France, Holland, and Spain, scarcely a doubt can be entertained of a battle having been fought, about the 26th of October; but whether the whole of the Toulon fleet, or only a division of it, were engaged, is uncertain. . . .

Walcheren to be Evaluated

After much hesitation and indecision, numerous orders and counter orders, and an enormous sacrifice of men, it now appears that the pestilential island of Walcheren is to be evacuated. Sixty transports arrived at Flushing on the 22d of November; the troops on board of which were to be employed in embarking the cannon, and military and naval stores at that port, and in removing every thing from the arsenal which might be useful to the enemy. The fortifications are to be levelled.

America

Government have received despatches from Mr. Jackson, our ambassador in America, by Mr. Erskine, our late Minister there. These communications are reported to be of a pacific character, and refer to the intercourse which had taken place between Mr. Jackson and the American Executive; but they are not decisive as to any of the points in dispute, Congress not having assembled at their date. Mr. Erskine left the Chesapeake on the 28th October, and he is said to have expressed an opinion, that both the government and the people of America are adverse to a rupture with this country.

Wellesley to be Foreign Secretary

The Marquis of Wellesley has arrived from Spain, having consented to accept the office of Secretary of State for the Foreign Department.

Spain

The interior of Spain and Portugal remains nearly in *statu quo*. In the latter country, the English troops have suffered much from illness. . . .

View of the Peak of Fogo, Cape de Verde Islands, from the S.S.E. Engraved by
Baily, from a drawing by G.T. Plate 418

Baltic News

An armistice has been agreed upon between Sweden and Denmark.

November-December. XXII 498-499; 517

Peace Negotiations

A negotiation between this country and France is expected. It is at least certain, that,
through the medium of the Austrian ambassador, an overture has been made by
Buonaparte; determined on, as it is said, ever since the 21st of November. ...

A cartel, for the general exchange of prisoners, is understood to have been established
between this country and France.

Despatches, supposed to be of a pacific nature, were some time ago received from
America; but we have since learned, that the intercourse between Mr. Jackson (our
envoy) and the American government, has experienced an abrupt suspension, if not an
absolute termination. ... Mr. Jackson is said to have arrived at Baltimore, on the 8th
of November, intending to embark for England; but that, in consequence of despatches
which were sent after him by the American government, he meant to return to
Washington. ...

Buonaparte has given peace to Sweden, on terms nearly the same as those which
that power had previously obtained from Russia.

Spain

Some changes, of a popular nature, have taken place in the Spanish government, and greater exertions than ever are making against the French. The Spaniards have sustained a serious defeat in the vicinity of Madrid from an over-anxiety to obtain possession of that capital; but they are reassembling their forces with great alacrity.

Wellesley at Foreign Office

The Marquis Wellesley has accepted the office of Foreign Secretary; and a report is current, that, prior to the meeting of parliament, Lord Melville will be placed at the head of the Admiralty. . . .

Buonaparte Divorces

Just as this sheet was going to press, we received the intelligence, through the medium of the *Moniteur*, that, on the 16th of December, a decree was passed for dissolving the marriage of Buonaparte and his wife Josephine. These high and illustrious personages "sacrifice their conjugal happiness to the welfare and interest of their country." Buonaparte conceives, that, though he has reached the age of 40, he may live long enough to educate *in his views and sentiments, the children which it may please Providence to give him*! Josephine is to preserve the title and rank of Empress Queen, with an annual income of 2,000,000 francs. - We have not yet heard who is destined to be the *envied* and *happy* bride.

Through the same channel with the above, we learn that the Duke del Parque was defeated on the 28th of November, with a loss in killed, wounded, and prisoners, of upwards of 5,000 men.

Cruiser Success in the Baltic

His Majesty's squadron in the Baltic, under the command of Vice-Admiral Sir James Saumarez, and the cruisers under his orders on the different stations incident to that extensive command, have captured and destroyed 430 vessels of various descriptions within the present year; the aggregate burden of which exceeds 25,000 tons, navigated by 2,300 men, with 130 guns of different calibres. Of this grand total 340 vessels, with 1900 men and 100 guns, including 14 stout cutter privateers, and upwards of 20 armed schooners, are Danes, that Government having fitted out a great number of vessels of the latter class for supplying Norway with grain during the unexampled scarcity occasioned by the present war, which they are compelled at all risks to attempt. The remaining 90 vessels, with 430 men and 30 guns, belonged to Russia, and were captured in the Gulf of Finland during the short summer season, in which are included an Imperial schooner, ten gun-boats, and as many armed transports, for carrying supplies to the Russian army in Finland and Bothnia, besides the loss sustained in the very severe attacks on the Russian flotillas at Percola and Aspo on the 7th and 25th of July, amounting in killed and drowned to 200 men.

Mediterranean

Vice-admiral Thornborough has arrived from the Mediterranean, in the *Apollo*, 38, Captain Taylor.

Gales

The late gales have been exceedingly destructive upon our coast. That of the 11th of December was felt by our fleet in the Scheldt with equal severity. Upwards of twenty transports and a brig with wine, were stranded, and the greater part lost.

1809 – Withdrawal from the Upper Scheldt

THE EARL OF CHATHAM'S FAILURE to take the initiative following the capitulation of Flushing gave the French and Dutch the time to concentrate their forces for the defence of Antwerp. On 27 August, despite Sir Richard Strachan's offer to support a move into the upper Scheldt, Chatham made the decision to withdraw, leaving a garrison on Walcheren to support the blockade of the estuary, and to facilitate British trade to the continent. Taking advantage of his ministerial position he submitted an apologia directly to the King, describing the events leading to the decision in terms critical of Sir Richard Strachan, who defended his own conduct in a letter to the Secretary of the Admiralty. Parliament later condemned Chatham's outdated conception of the constitution.

Naval State Papers

Relating to the Expedition to the Scheldt, presented by his Majesty's Command to both Houses of Parliament. *XXIII 218-219*

No. 29, dated *St. Domingo*, off Batz, the 27th August [1809], is the much-talked-of letter of Sir Richard Strachan [to the Honourable Wellesley Pole], of which only a wretchedly-mutilated extract was given in the *Gazette* of September 2. We here insert it, with its enclosures, all of which are very important documents.[1]

"Sir, I conclude you have received my letters of the 22d instant. I have now to acquaint you, for their Lordship's information, that the flat boats and every description of vessels being assembled, and every necessary arrangement made on the part of the navy, for landing the army near Santoliet on the beach, which had been previously reconnoitred, and not hearing from the Earl of Chatham respecting his intentions, I communicated with his lordship on the 24th instant, and on the following day I found his lordship had not come to a determination, on account of the increased force of the enemy, and the army getting sickly; and that he had sent for the generals to consult. I

---

1 [Vol. XXII, pp342-343. Unfortunately, it has not been possible to reproduce all of the enclosures here.]

therefore, on the morning of the 26th (to bring matters to a conclusion) wrote to his lordship, a copy of my letter accompanying this.

I soon after went on shore to the meeting of the lieutenant-generals of the army, taking with me Rear-admiral Sir Richard Keats; I found them decidedly of opinion that no operations could be undertaken against Antwerp with any prospect of success at this advanced season of the year, and the enemy increasing in strength, and our own forces diminished by sickness; and that, as the taking of Lillo and Liefkenshoeik would not ensure our obtaining the ultimate object of the expedition without Antwerp being reduced, and the country near these fortresses being inundated, it was also their decided opinion, that the army ought not to make any attempt on them. I had already, in the most unqualified manner, offered every naval assistance to reduce these fortresses, and also in aid of every other operation of the army; conceiving the subject of the deliberations of the generals perfectly military, I withdrew with Sir Richard Keats.

The ships of the enemy which were above the town of Antwerp about five miles, have come down, and are now extended along the river face of it, except two of the line lower down in the reach above Liefkenshoeik; and four frigates next to Lillo; an immense number of small gun-boats are on the boom; behind them a crescent of sixty gun and mortar brigs. The battery between Lillo and Fredrick Hendrick is finished; it has ten guns. The enemy has been driven from that which he was constructing on the Doel side with loss, by the fire of our bombs and gun-vessels. Our stock of water is reducing fast, the wells on the island are nearly exhausted by the army on shore, the people in our boats begin to get sickly, and the army on South Beveland exceedingly so. We are dropping the transports down towards Waerden, by way of clearing this place, where we lay so thick, that we are exposed to fire-vessels, if the enemy had any enterprise. He is secure behind the boom, which is seen just at the water's edge, from any such attempt on our part. I think no time should be lost in communicating the foregoing circumstances. . . .

I have the honour to be, &c.

R.J. STRACHAN"

[Lord Chatham's account of 29 August to Lord Viscount Castlereagh gave further detail of the massive force the enemy had brought against the British expedition (Vol. XXII, pp343-344).]

In Lord Porchester's resolution in the House of Commons, 26 March 1810, censoring the administration for the Scheldt expedition, it was stated that 'on the 19th of August, a malignant disorder shewed itself amongst his majesty's troops; and that, on the 8th of September, the number of sick amounted to upwards of 10,948 men'. . . .

VI. That it appears by the report of the physician appointed to investigate the nature and causes of the malady to which his Majesty's troops were thus exposed, that the disease is one which prevails periodically in the islands of Zealand, and is of peculiar malignity there, and which constantly follows as a law of season, appearing towards the end of summer, becoming more severe in the autumnal months, declining in October, and nearly ceasing in November: that perfect recoveries are rare, convalescence never secure, and that the recurrence of fever quickly lays the foundation of complaints, which render a large proportion of the sufferers inefficient for future military purposes.

VII. That of the army which embarked for the service in the Scheldt, 60 officers, and 3,900 men, exclusive of those killed by the enemy, had died before the 1st day of

February last; and on that day 217 officers, and 11,269 men were reported sick. [Vol. XXIII, pp423-424.]

The Earl of Chatham's Statement of his Proceedings,
dated 15th October, 1809; presented to the King,
14th February, 1810. ^{XXIII 222-229}

In submitting to your Majesty a statement of my proceedings in the execution of the service your Majesty was graciously pleased to confide to me, and of the events which occurred in the course of it, it is not my intention to trouble your Majesty with any further details of the earlier parts of our operations, which, having terminated in the speedy reduction of Walcheren by your Majesty's troops, and the occupation of the adjacent islands, and of the important fort of Batz, received at the time your Majesty's most gracious approbation; but to confine myself principally in the narrative, which I am anxious to be permitted to bring under your Majesty's view, to the consideration of the two following points, as most immediately applying to the conduct and final result of the expedition to the Scheldt: 1st. The ground upon which, after the army was at length assembled near Batz, a landing in prosecution of the ulterior objects of the expedition was not deemed advisable; 2dly. Why that army was not sooner there assembled, in readiness to commence further operations.

With respect to the former proposition, I am inclined to think that it is so clear and evident, that no further operations could at that time, and in the then sickly state of the army, have been undertaken with any prospect of success; that it would be unnecessarily trespassing on your Majesty to enter into much more detail on this point than has been already brought before your Majesty, in my despatch of the 29th of August: and the chief object of this paper will be directed to shew to your Majesty, that the second point, namely, why the army was not brought up sooner to the destination from whence its ulterior operations were to commence, is purely a naval consideration, and that the delay did in no shape rest with me, or depend upon any arrangements in which the army was concerned, every facility, on the contrary, having been afforded by their movements to the speedy progress of the armament.

In doing this, it will, I conceive, be necessary, for the sake of perspicuity, that I should take up the consideration of this business from its commencement.

Your Majesty will permit me here to recall to your recollection the change which took place in the original project formed for the attack of Antwerp, and of the French fleet in the West Scheldt, in consequence of the opinions of the general and staff officers to whom this question was referred; and a combined operation of the army and navy, the whole, with the exception of the force to be left for the reduction of Walcheren, to proceed up the West Scheldt, was accordingly determined on.

Upon the practicability of such an operation being at once carried into execution, which was, however, the ground-work of the expedition, and which alone, in the opinion of all persons consulted, seemed to afford any prospect of success, even in the most sanguine view of the subject in all other respects, I must confess, I entertained great doubts, till the communication of a distinct official opinion, given on this point by the Lords of the Admiralty, decided in the affirmative this important question.

At the same time it is to be remarked, that the occupation of Walcheren, which, by some persons, it had been thought possible to leave behind us, and the reduction of Flushing, which it had once been proposed only to mask, were deemed indispensable to the security of the fleet, in case of disaster; and accordingly a considerable separate force was allotted to this service; and, in this view, it was besides distinctly agreed upon, that a vigorous attack by the navy upon the sea front should be made at the same time that the troops, after effecting their landing, advanced to invest Flushing; it being hoped that by a powerful co-operation from the sea, at the moment the troops had presented themselves before the place, the labour and delay of a regular siege might have been avoided, and a considerable portion of the force, allotted to this service, set at liberty to follow the army up the Scheldt. How far this expectation was fulfilled, or whether the assurance given that the whole of the armament (the part to be landed at Walcheren excepted) should be at once transported up the Scheldt, in prosecution of the ultimate objects of the expedition, was carried into effect, or was wholly disappointed, the information already before your Majesty, will have, in a great measure shewn, and which it will be my duty to bring more particularly under your Majesty's view, when I detail the subsequent course of our proceedings.

From what cause this failure ensued, whether it arose from insufficient arrangements on the part of the admiral, or was the unavoidable result of difficulties inherent in the nature of the expedition itself, it is not for me, considering it entirely as a naval question, to presume to offer my opinions upon it to your Majesty.

It may, however, be here proper to remark, that, in all the projects which have at various times been brought forward on the subject of an attack upon the island of Walcheren and the Scheldt, the necessity of having a wind a good deal to the westward, with moderate weather, has always been insisted on. Without these advantages, in the one case, the passage would be difficult; in the other, the surf would prevent a landing on the points deemed most favourable in other respects. In the present instance, owing to the wind blowing strong from the westward, the surf was actually such as to prevent a landing on either of the points first fixed on for that purpose by the admiral; and the situation of the gun-boats and transports at anchor in the Stone deep becoming very critical, and the gale increasing, he found it necessary to carry such part of the fleet as was arrived for safety into the Roompot, and by which means the division of the army destined for the attack of Walcheren was enabled to effect its landing from a more sheltered anchorage on the Bree Sand, to the westward of Fort den Haak. At this time, the division under Lieutenant-general Lord Rosslyn, as well as that under Lieutenant-general Grosvenor, also the cavalry, artillery, &c. were not arrived; but they were afterwards, on their making the island, ordered by the admiral into the Veer Gat. It is, however, particularly deserving of attention, that this measure, though in itself one of great advantage, as far as it applied to the division destined for the attack of Walcheren, by placing the transports, storeships, and small craft in security, was, if carried further, certainly not a little at variance with the leading purpose of the expedition, namely, the running with the right wing, and the advance of the army at once up the West Scheldt, at the same moment that the attack upon Walcheren was proceeding: but that even this need have delayed it for more than three or four days, unless on account of naval difficulties, which it will be for the admiral, not for me to explain, I deny; for as soon as Ter Verre and the fort of Rammekins [Rammekens] fell, which happened on the 3d of August, the passage of the Sloe was open to the transports and gun-vessels; or they might have entered by the Durloo or by the Zoutland passages, the batteries of Dyskook, or Vygeeteer, and the Nolle, having been all carried by the army early on the 1st of August; and on the same day the battery of Borslen, at the south-west end of South Beveland, was abandoned on the movement of a detachment from the corps under Sir

John Hope; and I know of nothing (but this, of course, is a point for the admiral to speak to) to have prevented the line-of-battle ships and frigates from coming in and passing up above Flushing, in the first instance, according to the plan originally decided upon.

Before, however, I pursue further the details of the proceedings of the army, governed as they necessarily were (until a footing should be gained on the continent) by the movements of the navy, I must for a moment refer to two separate operations; the one under Lieutenant-general Lord Huntley and Commodore Owen, and the other under Lieutenant-general Sir John Hope and Rear-admiral Sir Richard Keats; but both directed to assist and ensure a rapid progress up the Scheldt, had the admiral found it practicable in other respects. With respect to the former, which was destined to destroy the Cadsand batteries, and particularly that of Breskens, had it been carried at once into effect, and that the admiral could have availed himself of it, to take the ships up the West Scheldt, by the Weeling[2] passage, it would have been of the utmost advantage; but it was certainly rather fortunate it did not take place at a later period, as after all the transports, store-ships, &c. were ordered into the Veere Gat, and the plan of running at once up the West Scheldt, by the Weeling Channel, seemed abandoned, the object of destroying the Cadsand batteries ceased, and a landing there would only have been an unnecessary risk, and a very inconvenient separation of our force, and of course occasioned great delay in collecting it for ulterior operations. It must not however be forgotten, that the difficulties here turned out to be much greater than had been at all foreseen before we sailed. In the first place, the beach was so exposed, that in blowing weather it was found impossible to land, and, from what cause I know not, the Marquis of Huntley's division could not be taken up, in the first instance, high enough to attack the Bresken's battery, the only one, from its situation, of much importance. In addition to this, the enemy, who had been represented by all the intelligence communicated to me to be very weak, almost actually without troops in that quarter, appeared to be well prepared, and in considerable force. Under these circumstances, according to Lord Huntley's report, Commodore Owen appears to have experienced great disappointment in not having the support of Lord Gardner's fleet and of his boats; but his lordship, as I believe, could never enter the Weeling channel at all; nor indeed was I ever acquainted with what instructions were given to him on this head.

When it was found that Lord Huntley's division could neither land nor proceed by the Weeling passage, up the Scheldt, as I had intended they should, it was determined to withdraw them; but from the boisterous state of the weather, it was some days before this could be effected. As soon as it was accomplished, they were passed over to South Beveland.

With respect to Sir John Hope's operation, it was more prosperous. The object of it was this: In the original arrangement for carrying the army at once up the West Scheldt, Sir John Hope's division was included; but just before we sailed, the admiral received intelligence that the French fleet was come down abreast of Flushing, and seemed to threaten to oppose our passage up the Scheldt.

In this view, it was conceived that, by a landing on the north side of South Beveland, the island might be possessed, and all the batteries taken in reverse, and thereby the position of the French fleet, if they ventured to remain near Flushing, would be, as it were, turned, and their retreat rendered more difficult, while the attack on them by our

---

2 [Spelt variously throughout the original text.]

ships would have been much facilitated; and for this object, the division of Sir John Hope rather preceded, in sailing from the Downs, the rest of the fleet.

The navigation of the East Scheldt was found most difficult, but by the skill and perseverance of Sir R. Keats, this purpose was happily and early accomplished, though the troops were carried a great way in schuyts and boats; and this division was landed near Ter-Goes, from whence they swept all the batteries in the island that could impede the progress of our ships up the West Scheldt, and possessed themselves on the 2d of August of the important post of Batz, to which it had been promised the army should at once have been brought up.

Sir John Hope remained in possession of this post, though not without being twice attacked by the enemy's flotilla, for nine days before any of the gun-boats under Captain Sir Home Popham were moved up the Scheldt to his support.

But it will be recollected that both these operations tended directly to forward the original purpose of a rapid progress up the Scheldt, the former by opening the Cadsand channel, could the landing of Lord Huntley's division have been effected; the second, by covering the progress of our fleet along the coast of South Beveland; while this division, under Sir John Hope, was, at the same time, so far advanced towards the destination at which the reset of the armament was to be assembled.

It will now only be necessary for me to bring before your Majesty the dates at which the several parts of the armament were enabled, according to the arrangement of Sir Richard Strachan, to pursue their progress up the Scheldt. In this place, however, it may be proper that I should previously advert to the grounds on which the 3d division under Lieutenant-general Grosvenor, as well as the two light battalions of the King's German Legion, (composing part of the force destined, in the first instance, to proceed against Antwerp) were landed at Walcheren and employed before Flushing.

Your Majesty will be pleased to recollect, that the troops which sailed from Portsmouth, under Lieutenant-general Sir Eyre Coote, were destined for the service of Walcheren, and had been considered as sufficient for that object, according to the intelligence received, and the supposed strength of the enemy; though, at the same time, certainly relying for the first efforts against Flushing on the promised co-operation of the navy, and on their establishing, as was held out, in the first instance, a naval blockade, except on the side of Veer and Rammakins. Unfortunately, however, this did not take place; and for several nights after the army was before Flushing, the enemy succeeded in throwing from the opposite coast, probably from the canal of Ghent, considerable reinforcements into the place, which enabled him constantly to annoy our out-posts and working-parties, and finally to attempt a sally in force, though, happily from the valour of your Majesty's troops, without success. This proving very harassing, particularly from the great difficulty of communication between the several parts of our line; I determined, in order to relieve the troops and press forward the siege with as much vigour as possible, to avail myself, for the time, of the services of these corps; but it is to be remembered, that this was only done because I saw no movement making to push forward a single vessel up the West Scheldt; and it therefore seemed more advisable to have their assistance before Flushing, than that they should lie inactive in the Veer Gat; and they might at any time be re-embarked from Rammakins in a few hours, whenever their transports could be brought up from Veer, and there was the least chance of our proceeding to our ulterior destination.

I have already stated that Rammakins surrendered on the evening of the 3d of August. Immediately upon this event, feeling, as I did, great uneasiness at the delay which had already taken place, and at the departure from the original plan, I wrote a letter to the Admiral, then at Ter Veer, expressing my hope that the ships would now be able to enter the West Scheldt by the Sloe Passage, and that no time should be lost in pressing forward as speedily as possible our further operations; and I requested, at the same time, that he would communicate to me the extent of naval co-operation he would afford, as well as for the future blockade of Flushing, as with a view to protecting the coasts of South Beveland, and watching the passages from the Meuse to the East Scheldt, as this consideration would govern very much the extent of force I must be [obliged?] to leave in South Beveland, when the army advanced. To this letter he did not fully reply till the 8th of August; but I had a note from him on the 5th, assuring me the transports should be brought forward without delay; and I had also a very long conversation with him on the morning of the 6th, on the arrangements to be taken for our further operations, when I urged, in the strongest manner, the necessity of not losing a moment in bringing up the cavalry and ordnance ships, transports, store-ships, victuallers, &c. &c. in order that the armament might proceed without delay to its destination; and I added my hopes, that they would receive the protection of the ships of war, none of which had yet entered the West Scheldt.

To all of this, and to the several arrangements explained to him in detail, he fully assented.

In his reply to my letter of the 4th, on the 8th of August, he acquaints me that several of the smaller vessels, of different descriptions, had passed through the intricate passage of the Sloe, and that he had ordered the frigates to pass up the West Scheldt, to be followed by the line-of-battle ships; and he gave hopes that he should be able to go up the river with the flotilla on the 10th of August at furthest, and that the frigates and line-of-battle ships should follow, as they came in, in succession.

The frigates, however, did not pass Flushing till the evening of the 11th, and the line-of-battle ships only passed to the anchorage, above Flushing, on the 14th, the second day of the bombardment.

These ships began to proceed up the river on the 18th, and arrived on the 19th; one division as high as the bay below Waerden, the other off the Hanswent, where they remained; the *Courageux* passed above Batz; the cavalry ships only got through the Sloe Passage into the West Scheldt, from the 20th to the 23d, and arrived off Batz on the 22d and 24th; the ordnance-ships and store-ships passed through from the 22d to the 23d, and arrived at their destination off Batz on the 24th and 25th; the transports for Lieutenant-general Grosvenor's division only came up to receive them on the 19th, on which day they embarked, and those for Major-general Graham's division on the 20th and 21st; and they arrived off Batz on the 24th. The corps of Brigadier-general Rottenburgh, and the light divisions of the German Legion, proceeded to join the Earl of Rosslyn's division in South Beveland.

From this statement, your Majesty will see, that, notwithstanding every effort on my part with the Admiral, the armament was not assembled at the point of its destination till the 25th, and of course that the means of commencing operations sooner against Antwerp were never in my power.

It now became at this advanced period of my duty to consider very seriously the expediency of landing the army on the continent. On comparing all the intelligence obtained as to the strength of the enemy, it appeared to be such as to leave (as stated in my despatch of the 29th of August) no reasonable prospect of the force under my command, after accomplishing the preliminary operations of reducing Fort Lillo as well as Liefkenshoeik on the opposite side of Antwerp, without the possession of which the destruction of the ships and arsenals of the enemy could not be effected; and in addition to this, the sickness which had begun to attack the army about the 20th, and which was hourly increasing to an alarming extent, created the most serious apprehensions in the minds of the medical men, as to its further progress at that unhealthy season, and which fatal experience has since shewn to have been but too well founded.

Your majesty will not be surprised, if, under these circumstances, I paused in requiring the admiral to put the army on shore. That a landing might have been made, and that any force that had been opposed to using the field would have yielded to the superior valour of British troops, I have no doubt; but then, any such success could have been of no avail towards the attainment of the ultimate object, and there was still less chance that the enemy would have given us the opportunity. Secure in his fortresses, he had a surer game to play; for if ever the army, divided as it must necessarily have been in order to occupy both banks of the river, exposed to the effects of inundation on every side, and with all its communications liable to be cut off, while the force of the enemy was daily and hourly increasing, had once sat down before Antwerp, it is unnecessary for me to point out to your Majesty, how critical must, in a short time, have been their situation. But when, added to this sickness to an alarming extent had begun to spread itself among the troops, and the certain and fatal progress of which at that season, was but too well ascertained, it appeared to me, that all further advance could only tend to commit irretrievably the safety of the army which your Majesty had confided to me, and which every principle of military duty as well as the direct tenor of my instructions alike forbade.

In this state of things, I considered that there was left me no alternative, but to pursue the course I have already stated, for your Majesty's information, in my despatch of the 29th of August; and that conduct I now most humbly, but at the same time with perfect confidence, submit to your Majesty's judgment.

I shall here close this report; which has, I fear, already detained your Majesty but too long; by observing that wherever it has been necessary for me to advert to the disappointments experienced, through the arrangements of the admiral, in the naval co-operation I have been taught to expect, I have confined myself to stating the facts; abstaining, as it became me, from all comment, and leaving it to the admiral, in such report as he may make of his proceedings, to bring under your Majesty's view the circumstances which may have occasioned them; and, above all, to account for the difficulties which prevented the investment of Flushing (a point never even doubted of before) as well as to shew the obstacles which presented themselves to the early progress of the armament up the West Scheldt, which operation I had always looked upon as the primary object of his instructions, and on the accomplishment of which our best hopes of success in any of the ulterior objects of the expedition principally, if not wholly depended.

From a letter from Rear-Admiral Sir R.J. Strachan, to J.W. Croker, Esq. respecting the statement of the Earl of Chatham
London, March 5, 1810

... Feeling perfectly conscious that every exertion had been made by me in forwarding the objects of the expedition, and that no blame could be justly imputed to myself or the navy, I could not possibly suspect that Lord Chatham, to the irregularity of presenting immediately to his Majesty such a paper as that which I have received, had added the impropriety (to use no stronger term) of endeavouring to exculpate himself by private insinuations against the conduct of others. . . .

Observations on the Earl of Chatham's Statement of his Proceedings, . . . R.J. Strachan, Rear-Admiral, London, March 5, 1810

. . . I have in vain endeavoured to ascertain the foundation upon which the assertion rests, that it "was distinctly agreed upon that a vigorous attack by the navy upon the sea front should be made at the same time that the troops after effecting their landing advanced to invest Flushing, it being hoped that by a powerful co-operation from the sea at the moment the troops presented themselves before the place, the labour and delay of a regular siege might have been avoided." I cannot find any instructions, orders, letters, or communications, either previous to our departure from the Downs, or subsequent, alluding to any such agreement, and can have no difficulty, not merely in asserting that no such agreement was made, but that from the nature of the thing itself, it is quite impossible that any such agreement could have been made.

It certainly was in contemplation, if the enemy's fleet had remained in the lower part of the river, more particularly in the vicinity of Flushing, to have pushed a fleet of line-of-battle ships into the Scheldt to attack them, and a squadron for that purpose, among other objects, was ready, under the orders of Lord Gardner. With that squadron I intended to have proceeded to the attack of the enemy's fleet, if it had not retreated up the river before the armament arrived on the coast of Zealand.

It was also in my contemplation, by means of that squadron, to cooperate with the army in any attack upon Flushing, wherein the assistance of the navy should be thought desirable. This is proved by my orders to Lord Gardner of the 16th and 20th of July; but it is so far from being true that this view of mine was the result of any agreement preconcerted with Lord Chatham, as the Statement seems to imply, that the first spontaneous offer of such co-operation on my part was passed by without any immediate notice by his lordship. This offer was contained in my letter of the 8th of August, to which I shall shortly have occasion to allude. . . .

It had been at one time proposed before we quitted London, to land the whole army in Tholen and South Beveland, as presenting fewer difficulties than the navigation of the Scheldt, which under the most favourable circumstances must always be liable to various contingencies. This proposal was, I understand, a good deal discussed, and on this point it is only necessary to refer to my instructions to Sir R. Keats, when he was directed to give every assistance in the transporting the troops in South Beveland and Tholen.

Another plan had been proposed, of disembarking in the Slough, marching across South Beveland, embarking again at Bathz [Batz], and landing at Santfliet.

This plan appeared to be approved by many good judges of military operations, for one proof of which I may refer to the Minutes of Evidences, page 197.

The third plan which was suggested as preferable to either of the former, provided we met with no obstacles, was to proceed directly up the West Scheldt, and this was ultimately adopted, because, by keeping the troops in the transports, it promised to preserve them in an efficient state until their immediate service should be called for. To this arrangement the command of the Weiling passage was thought to be necessary, for which reason a respectable force was destined to occupy Cadsand. . . .

I selected Commodore Owen, an officer of great intelligence and professional talent, for the purpose of co-operating with the Marquis of Huntley; I gave him every latitude of discretion; the quarter-master-general sent Lord Huntley a copy of the commodore's instructions, and I apprehend there is no position or part of the beach between Sluys and the Ghent canal, on which he would not have attempted to effect a landing, if any proposition or request had been made by Lord Huntley to that effect.

I only require on this point that a dispassionate attention should be paid to my orders, that my letter of the 2d July to Lord Gardner, coupled with that of the 16th, should be read with attention, and that a reference should be made to the evidence of Commodore Owen and the Marquis of Huntley, which I think unequivocally prove, that no application was ever made to me for a proportion of boats beyond what was carried by Commodore Owen's squadron.

Our original determination of landing in Zoutland Bay was laid aside, in consequence of intelligence received at Deal of the preparation of the enemy on that part of the coast, and a memoir was drawn up on this subject, which was submitted to Lord Chatham and Lord Castlereagh, and approved of by both; and it was consequently intended to land on Domburgh Beach; but on our arrival at Walcheren, the surf was found to be so heavy on Domburgh Beach, in consequence of a strong westerly wind, the landing there was impossible; it became therefore absolutely necessary to take shelter in the Roompot and Veergat, and the constant succession of gales for many days after our arrival, made it impossible, independently of other obstacles, to recur to the original intention of entering the western mouth of the Scheldt.

Upon the change in our measures, which was thus forced upon us by the untoward state of the weather, I must here beg leave to offer a very few remarks. It is admitted by Lord Chatham to have been in some respects advantageous, by placing the transports and small craft in a place of security, and by facilitating the disembarkation of the troops on the Bree Sand.

His lordship further states, that by this change of the destination of the fleet the occupation of Cadsand became unnecessary, and that if it could have been accomplished it would have occasioned a very inconvenient separation of our force. On the other hand, this change of destination necessarily tended to produce some delay in the naval operations, by forcing us to proceed by a circuitous instead of a direct navigation; but the main question is, how far it necessarily tended to retard the attainment of the ulterior objects of the expedition.

I have already stated, that for the purpose of obtaining those objects, three paces had been proposed, the last of which, as I conceived, had been selected as the most advantageous, only upon the supposition of our encountering no obstacles to the navigation of the whole fleet up the West Scheldt. ...

With respect to the immediate difficulties which may have operated as an objection to the disembarkation of the troops on South Beveland, and to their subsequent march across that island, he need only refer to the opinions of the naval officers who were employed in the Slough, by which I think it will appear that 20,000 men, and 4,000 horses, might have been landed from the Slough in 48 hours, [and] that cavalry and ordnance horses might easily perform this march from the Slough to Bathz in thirty-six hours, the distance being from thirty to thirty-five miles. With regard to artillery, it was stated by Sir John Hope, in answer to a question as to the number of guns found in Bathz and Waerden, which might have been used for ulterior objects, that there were twelve 24-pounders in the battery at Waerden, and fourteen or fifteen at Bathz, all of which, as the general believed, were on travelling carriages. I might add, that the quantity of ordnance and ordnance stores taken on the island, as appears by the return in Journal

Proceedings, page 15, was such as I should suppose to be sufficient for all the possible wants of the army.

When, therefore, Lord Chatham contends in his statement that the second point, namely "why the army was not brought up sooner to the destination from whence all its operations were to commence, is purely a naval consideration," his position is certainly true in words, but is certainly incorrect in its implied meaning. It is obvious that the army might have marched to Bathz in the course of a few days, but it is also obvious that it could not be conveyed on board a fleet of 400 transports, besides frigates, sloops, and flotilla, through a very intricate channel, without some delay. The difficulty of conducting such a fleet at all, through the mazes of such a navigation, can only be appreciated by professional men; it was very greatly increased by an adverse wind, blowing for some time with such violence, as to render the expedient of warping (the only means of proceeding) totally impracticable; such obstacles to our progress were only to be overcome by great exertions and perseverance, by a considerable, but not, as I trust, an unnecessary expenditure of labour and time.

I can only say, that I made every arrangement, by appointing the most active officers to every separate part of each service, and that I had every reason to be satisfied with their zeal, activity, and exertion.

Having anticipated many of these difficulties, I attempted, in a conversation with Lord Chatham on the 1st August, to impress them on his lordship's mind, and I inferred from his answers, that he intended to modify his plans in consequence, and to proceed by South Beveland instead of the West Scheldt. - Under this persuasion I directed Admiral Otway to take command of the fleet employed before Walcheren, that I might be at liberty to employ my whole attention in forwarding the different preparations necessary to facilitate the progress of the army to the destination from whence its ulterior operations were to commence.

I immediately directed Sir Home Popham to proceed through the Slough with several sloops of war, all the bombs, gun-brigs, and gun-boats, and use every exertion in getting the flotilla into the West Scheldt, that it might in the first instance co-operate with Commodore Owen in completing the naval blockade of Flushing, and to be ready to proceed to Bathz at the shortest notice, whenever its services should be required there, for the purpose of prosecuting the ulterior objects of the expedition.

I also instructed him to hasten as much as possible the progress of the transports through the Slough.

The subsequent news of the rapid occupation of South Beveland and of the fort of Bathz, with a quantity of artillery and ammunition in the other forts adapted to our future operations, and also of the facility which might be afforded to our arrangements for crossing to Santfliet [Sandvliet], by a ford reported capable of being passed by some part of the army, further strengthened my opinion that the landing in South Beveland with all the cavalry and infantry would be the only means of rapidly approaching towards the ultimate objects of the expedition.

Accordingly, in my interview with Lord Chatham on the 6th, I stated fully the difficulties I had to encounter from the untoward state of the weather, and from the intricacy of the channel in passing the vessels through the Slough, as also from the difficulties made by the pilots, who refused to take charge of the vessels, or even to carry the line-of-battle ships into the West Scheldt.

The strong impression I felt upon this subject induced me to deviate from the line of conduct I have always adopted in relation to military matters, of not interposing any opinion; and I ventured to propose to his lordship to commence the disembarkation by landing the cavalry immediately on South Beveland, and marching them to Bathz, which might be followed by all the infantry not occupied in the siege of Flushing; stating that much delay and difficulty would arise in getting our numerous vessels and transports through the Slough; that in addition to the frigates which were already under orders to proceed into the West Scheldt, I should be able in a day or two to get a sufficient portion of sloops and flotilla, including the transports I ordered to be armed, and the launches of the fleet to be fitted with carronades, to increase the flotilla through the Slough to send up to co-operate with the army at Bathz, and such a limited number of transports as might contain articles essential to the first advance of the army. I also informed his lordship that every possible exertion was making to accomplish the passage through the Slough, on the nature of which exertions, being wholly technical, such as buoying and anchoring small transports on the side of the shoals, and making arrangements for warping (the wind being still adverse) it cannot be necessary for me to dwell.

That Lord Chatham fully understood the nature and extent of the obstacles to our getting into the West Scheldt, which I described, is obvious from his letter of the 7th of August written after the interview, in which I had explained them, and ventured to propose the remedy of landing the cavalry, &c. on South Beveland. . . .

Lord Chatham seemed to think it necessary that all the men of war and transports should assemble at the Upper Scheldt, at Bathz.

My opinion on this subject I have already stated. It is to be remembered that the French fleet had retreated above Lillo, so that the presence of our line-of-battle ships on the West Scheldt could not be necessary until the army should have been assembled at Bathz, and even then, unless it should have been deemed inexpedient for the army to have advanced upon Antwerp, until we should have broken the boom of Lillo, I still think that not more than four ships could have been required for that purpose. In the mean time our flotilla would have been amply sufficient to have protected the passage of the army from Bathz to Santvliet, as I should not have agreed to any proposition for crossing the army unless I had been quite certain that I had the most ample means of giving it the fullest protection. Being, however, particularly anxious to pursue the line of conduct most congenial to his lordship's wishes, and consequently best adapted to promote a cordial co-operation, I promised every exertion in carrying his intentions into execution.

Accordingly, on my return from Lord Chatham, I continued my arrangements for accelerating the various complicated objects which were to be attended to.

The first part of the flotilla which got through the Slough, were applied to the cutting off the communication between Cadsand and Flushing; because his lordship had regretted (though without urging it as a subject of complaint), that supplies had been so often thrown into Flushing. In fact, until after the 7th of August, the weather continued so bad, with the wind at S.W. and S.S.W. that we were unable to interrupt the communication of the enemy, as the only vessels by which we could effect it were constantly driven in by the gales, and could not keep the sea. The wind which was most adverse to us, was most favourable to the enemy, who could from Cadsand run before it into Flushing without the possibility of interruption.

On the 7th we were able, by the weather moderating, to establish the sea blockade of Flushing; and on the 9th a considerable body of the flotilla, under the command of Sir Home Popham, was carried through the Swatchway of the Caloot Sand at the entrance of the Slough Passage, and proceeded to Bathz, where they arrived on the

11th. At the same time a squadron of frigates passed Flushing to join the flotilla, and proceeded on the following day up the Scheldt.

With respect to the line-of-battle ships, great difficulty had occurred from the objections of pilots, but I regretted this less because I had considered these ships, if in consequence of my offer they should be called for by Lord Chatham, as applicable to the co-operation in the attack upon the town; and having placed the different divisions of the fleet employed in the various services in the East Scheldt, at Bathz, in the Slough, and in the West Scheldt, under the command of officers of responsibility, with directions to press the passage of the transports through the Slough, I remained in the vicinity of Walcheren for the purpose of communicating with Lord Chatham, as I conceive it my duty to do, until he should think it right to proceed to South Beveland. The ships of the line, therefore, whose immediate presence at Bathz did not, for the reasons which I have just mentioned, appear to me at all necessary, did not pass Flushing until the attacks on the 14th. The *Courageux*, which ship was intended to go up the river when the frigates did, proceeded early in the morning of the 15th. I detained the others, as the anchorage at Bathz was very confined, and, at that time, extremely crowded, but they were only a few miles lower down, and within reach of going up in one tide whenever it should be required of them to proceed up the river.

The transports proceeded up the river in different divisions as fast as the difficulties I have stated could be overcome, and in consequence of the arrangements made, and the exertions of the officers employed, with fewer accidents than I believe have ever occurred to so large a fleet in such a navigation. . . .

I trust that it was owing to no defect of zeal on my part, and I am sure it was owing to no want of exertion on the part of the many excellent naval officers whom I have the honour to command, that the progress of a fleet which it was necessary to warp, or in less technical language, to haul by human labour, through the windings of a most intricate channel, and often directly in the teeth of the wind, appeared so tardy that Lord Chatham "saw no movement making to push forward a single vessel to the West Scheldt." The exertions of the naval officers and men were not rendered less irksome by the persuasion that the labour which, though incessant, often proved unavailing, might have been spared to them at the expense of a short march across the island of South Beveland. To impute to me or to the navy, under the name of delay, the loss of time which was passed by me in constant solicitude, and by the men in unremitting toil, is not what I should have expected from Lord Chatham.

1809 – The Destruction of Baudin's Squadron and Convoy from Toulon

TOWARDS THE END OF OCTOBER, twenty large transports escorted by a small squadron of three sail of the line and four frigates was sailed from Toulon under Rear-Admiral Baudin to relieve the besieged garrison of Barcelona. Collingwood detached Rear-Admiral George Martin to chase them, and the line-of-battle ships and one of the frigates were run ashore between Cette and Frontignan, where they were set on fire by their crews to prevent them falling into British hands. The transports took refuge in Rosas Bay, but the boats were dispatched under Captain Hallowell to burn or cut them out, which was done with complete success in the sight of thousands of spectators.

Details Respecting the Destruction of Baudin's Squadron and Convoy from Toulon
From 'Naval Anecdotes.' XXII 457-460

In addition to the official accounts of the late victory in the Mediterranean, which are given in a subsequent sheet, the following private letter, written by an officer on board his Majesty's ship *Sultan*, and dated off Cape St. Sebastian, November 1, 1809, will be found to contain much interesting information:

"A few circumstances which have taken place lately may be worth your reading. We left the Island of Minorca on the 13th of October, with about fifteen sail of the line, two frigates, and four sloops of war, having information that it was the enemy's intention to relieve the garrison of Barcelona, with fifteen sail of the line and nine frigates, besides a number of transports with provisions and troops on board. On the 15th, we reached the coast of Catalonia, between Cape St. Sebastian and Barcelona, where we found it was the admiral's intention to cruise for the enemy, which I think was most judiciously planned by his lordship [Vice-Admiral Lord Collingwood] to fall in with them, was it

299

their intention to do so. From the 15th to the 22d, nothing particular occurred; our fleet keeping within a few leagues of Cape St. Sebastian, the admiral having frequent communication with the shore, *via* Gerona, which the French were besieging, and, it was thought, would not gain possession of.

On the 22d, about nine P.M. we observed a sail in the E.S.E. coming down on us under a crowd of sail, making signals for the enemy's being near, which were repeated with guns and false fires, until the admiral answered it, and made the signal to us that the enemy's ships were supposed to be near. Our whole fleet were instantly under a crowd of sail, anxious to meet the common foe. You may easily imagine how much our anxiety must have been for the sight of day-light. On the morning of the 23d, we understood, the happy tidings of the enemy's ships being near, reached the admiral through the vigilance of Captain Barrie, of his Majesty's ship *Pomone*, who was left watching them off Toulon. At 9 A.M. the *Pomone*, being the weathermost ship of our fleet, made the signal for the enemy's ships being in sight, 37 in number, seven of which were of the line, one frigate, and the rest transports.

The signal was immediately made for Rear-admiral Martin, in the *Canopus*, to chase with seven other ships, the *Sultan* included as one; two of them, by a shift of wind, lost sight of the flying squadron during the night. About three P.M. the enemy's transports separated from the ships of war, the former steering to the N.N.W. the latter to the E.S.E. with the wind at N.E. seemingly in great confusion. At dark we lost sight of the enemy. At eight P.M. the wind about east, tacked to the northward (considering that they would push for their own coast), and continued under a great press of sail all night and next day, with the ships as per margin.[1]

The 24th, squally weather, with drizzling rain and thick weather. At five P.M. the *Tigre* being the headmost ship, made the signal for four sail in the N.N.E. which we soon discovered to be part of the enemy's squadron: a crowd of sail was instantly spread on every ship of our little fleet, in hopes of bringing them to action before night: at dark we again lost sight of them, and were approaching the shore fast, our headmost ship being in 17 fathoms water; hauled our wind for the night, and made short tacks, in order to keep the enemy within us. The vigilance and sound judgment of Rear-admiral Martin cannot be too much praised in keeping the track of the enemy; and I must confess, that the captains of the ships under his command deserve the greatest credit, for being able to keep company with him under all circumstances, the weather thick, unsettled, and the *Canopus* being a very fast sailing ship.

On the morning of the 25th, about seven A.M. we discovered the enemy's ships in the north, three of the line, and one frigate. Our whole squadron, following the example of our admiral, were soon under a press of sail, wind S.E. blowing fresh, and every prospect of bringing them to action. Now, my dear Sir, you may easily imagine how much we were all disappointed to find we had such a small proportion of the enemy's ships to deal with; as honour is the general order of the day, we shall get but little credit for what we have done. Two of the finest ships of the French navy, having 16 ports on their lower gun-decks, burned to the water's edge; one of the line, and one frigate, driven on shore in the small harbour of Cette, in the gulf of Lyons. It is generally believed by those who pretend to know the place, that the line-of-battle ship which

1 *Canopus*, Rear-admiral Martin, Captain Ingles; *Renown*, Captain Durham; *Tigre*, Captain Hallowell; *Sultan*, Captain Griffith; *Leviathan*, Captain Harvey; *Cumberland*, Captain Wodehouse.

went into Cette, must have been considerably injured in her bottom, and that she never again can appear at sea without being metamorphosed.

Again for the narrative of our proceedings - About 11:30 A.M. we were approaching the enemy very fast, and had every thing prepared for anchoring with springs on the cables: we were nearing the shore very fast, which made this precaution necessary. At 11:40 A.M. the enemy shewed a disposition to run their ships on shore. At 11:52 A.M. two of the line-of-battle ships of the largest class, of two decks, one of them having a rear-admiral's flag flying put their helms up, and run both on shore within pistol shot of each other, about six miles N.E. of Cette harbour; some of our ships were then in seven fathoms, others in five. Our ships immediately hauled their wind to avoid the same danger; the enemy having themselves done all that we could wish for the destruction of two of their own ships, without our firing a single gun at them: therefore we have sustained no loss. The *Tigre* and *Leviathan* chased the other line-of-battle ship and frigate, but could not come up with them: they therefore reached the small harbour of Cette. The ship of the line must be inevitably considered as destroyed; and we doubt whether the frigate will ever again leave that harbour. The harbour of Cette is well known by our Mediterranean traders; and I believe a vessel drawing above 16 feet water, was never before known to enter it; the swell is high, and they were observed to beat over the shoal water outside of the Mole Head.

The squadron now experienced the want of a frigate, and which had unavoidably lost sight of us from the thickness of the weather, and, no doubt, anxiety of their captains to keep sight of the enemy. The wind being now dead on the shore, with a good deal of sea, it would have been highly imprudent, in my humble opinion, to have anchored one of our ships of the line, which a small ship might have done, to prevent the enemy from landing any thing out of their ships.

At one P.M. a number of boats assembled round them, and they were seen to be busily employed in landing their crews, as well as cutting every thing away, and dismantling their ships. A little after four P.M. both ships' mizzen masts went by the board: at dark we stood to the southward with our small squadron, and tacked in the night, with an intention to be close in with the wrecks by day-light; the wind failing us, we did not close with them until towards evening on the 26th; found one with her foremast only standing; the other her fore and mainmast, apparently quite destroyed by the swell of the sea. At 7:30 P.M. they landed all their people, and set fire to the two ships, and by eight they were completely on fire, fore and aft. At 10:30 P.M. they exploded: it was one of the most grand sights ever seen; we were within six or seven miles of them at the time; it being then calm, serene, and a clear moon-light night, made the prospect more beautiful.

27th, light airs and foggy weather, making the best of our way to join the fleet. We are full of anxiety to know what has become of the remainder of the enemy's ships, as we left ten sail of the line, three frigates, and one sloop in chase of them. I hope they will be able to give as good an account of them as we have done with the four in question. You will see that I leave ten sail of the line, we only sailed with fifteen from Mahon. Know then, that the *Conqueror* joined us on the coast of Catalonia; she has, for these some months past, with two frigates and one sloop, been blockading the port of Barcelona.

This fate, I hope, will be a death blow to the enemy in that quarter, and relieve the Spaniards of their unwelcome visitors at that place. I think it must now fall.

The 30th, joined the fleet off Cape St. Sebastian; found five or six of the convoy taken and destroyed, the rest of the convoy effected their escape during the night, and got into the Bay of Rosas. Two line-of-battle ships, three frigates, and three sloops, have just made sail to endeavour to destroy the convoy at Rosas. I hope they will succeed. Captain Hallowell, in the *Tigre*, has the direction of the squadron.

Since joining the fleet, I understand the ships of war, that I have given you an account of, were all that sailed from Toulon with the convoy in question; we therefore must have mistaken the *Pomone*'s signal on the 23d; she was at a great distance, and seven may very easily be mistaken for three, as it proved to be three of the line and one frigate.

November 1. The *Tigre* and her little squadron are joining, after having destroyed, as I am given to understand, ten sail by fire; and four sail have actually joined us, three of them brigs, and one settee; the settee is armed with fourteen guns, and one of the brigs with ten guns. I am sorry to say, this has not been done without some loss on our side; we have lost in killed, one lieutenant and one mate; also about 30 seamen in killed and wounded, including officers."

Despatches Reporting the Action
Letters on Service, The 'London Gazette Extraordinary'
20 November 1809. XXII 500-505

The Honourable Lieutenant William Waldegrave, of the *Ville de Paris*, arrived here this morning with despatches from Vice-admiral Lord Collingwood, commander-in-chief of his Majesty's ships and vessels in the Mediterranean, addressed to the Honourable William Wellesley Pole, of which the following are copies: . . .

Rear-Admiral George Martin to Vice-admiral Lord Collingwood
Canopus, at Sea, October 27, 1809
My Lord, In obedience to the signal for the *Canopus* to chase E.N.E. I stood that way the whole of the night of the 23d, and the following day, in company with the *Renown*, *Tigre*, *Sultan*, *Leviathan*, and *Cumberland*. In the evening four sail were seen, to which we immediately gave chase, and pursued them till after dark; when, from shoal water, and the wind being direct on the shore, near the entrance of the Rhone, it became necessary to keep to the wind during the night. The following morning (the 25th) the same ships were again seen and chased between Cette and Frontignan, where they ran on shore - two of them (an 80-gun ship, bearing a rear-admiral's flag, and a 74) at the latter place, and one ship of the line and a frigate at the former. From the shoal water and intricacy of the navigation, it was impossible to get close enough to the enemy's two line-of-battle ships near Frontignan, to attack them when on shore; for in attempting to do so, one of his Majesty's ships was under five fathoms water, and another in less than six. On the 26th, I sent the boats to sound; meaning, if possible, to buoy the channel (if any had been found) by which the enemy's ships could be attacked; but at night we had the satisfaction to see them set on fire.

From the circumstances under which the ship and frigate ran on shore at the entrance of the port of Cette, I have little doubt the former will be lost; and the frigate must certainly have received considerable damage; but they cannot be got at on account of the batteries.

Your Lordship must be well aware, that nothing but the great press of sail carried by his Majesty's ships, and the good look-out kept, could have enabled them to close

View of the Rock and Tower of Scylia, Mount Aetna in the distance. Engraved by Hall, from a drawing by Pocock. ^{Plate 359}

with those of the enemy from the distance they were at the time they commenced the chase.

I have the honour to be

G. MARTIN

Vice-Admiral Lord Collingwood, Commander in Chief &c.

Lord Collingwood to the Honourable William Wollesley Pole
Ville de Paris, off Rosas, November 1, 1809

Sir, When the enemy's convoy was chased on the 23d ultimo, their transports separated from the ships of war, and, under the protection of an armed store ship, two bombards, and a xebec, made for the Bay of Rosas. When the ships of war were disposed of, as related in my letter of yesterday, the convoy became the object of my attention; and on the 29th the *Apollo* was sent off Rosas to examine what vessels were there, and how far they were in a situation assailable.

The next day I appointed the ships, as per margin, for this service, under the orders of Captain Hallowell, to bring them out if the wind was favourable, or otherwise to destroy them.[2] The state of the wind and sea would not permit this operation until last night; when, after dark, the ships bore up for the Bay, and anchored about five miles from the castle of Rosas, under the protection of which castle, of Trinity Fort, and of several other newly erected batteries, the convoy, consisting of 11 vessels, five of them armed, as per accompanying list, were moored.

2 *Tigre, Cumberland, Volontaire, Apollo, Topaze, Philomel Scout,* and *Tuscan.*

The boats being arranged in separate divisions, the whole were put under the orders of Lieutenant Tailor, first lieutenant of the *Tigre*, and proceeded to the attack of the enemy; who, although he could have had no previous intimation of such an enterprise against him, was found vigilant and completely on his guard. The ship, which was a smaller sort of frigate, was enclosed in boarding nettings, and a gun-boat advanced ahead of her for the look-out. On being hailed, and the alarm gun fired, our boats stretched out, the crews at the highest pitch of animation filling the air with their cheers; each division took the part previously allotted to it; the armed ship was boarded at all points, and carried in a few minutes, notwithstanding the spirited and sturdy resistance which the enemy made; all their armed vessels were well defended, but the British seamen and marines, determined to subdue them, were not to be repelled, even by a force found to be double that which was expected; and, besides the opposition made by the vessels, the guns from the castle, the forts in the bay, the gun-boats and musketry from the beach kept a constant fire on them. On the opening of day, every ship or vessel was either burnt, or brought off, aided by the light winds which then came from the land, and the whole of the convoy that came from Toulon for the supply of the French army in Spain has been destroyed, with the exception of the frigate, which escaped to Marseilles, and one store-ship not since heard of. . . .

I have the honour to be,

COLLINGWOOD

1809 – Evacuation From Walcheren

THE CONTINUED OCCUPATION of Walcheren Island after the withdrawal from the Upper Scheldt proved disastrous, because the army proved to be unable to control the Walcheren Fever. The enemy had no need to risk engagement when it became apparent that Flushing was no more than a hospital and a morgue. Finally there was no choice but to abandon the fortifications and dock facilities, which had been repaired at great expense and which were now demolished by the army engineers supported by the navy.

The evacuation was detailed in the Naval State Papers published by order of Parliament. Captain Tomlinson's legal troubles, apparently occasioned by his complaint to the Navy Board about the equipment of the fire-ships, ends the Walcheren papers.

Naval State Papers

Relating to the Expedition to the Scheldt, present by his Majesty's Command to both Houses of Parliament. XXIII *301-308*

The fourth head - *Evacuation* - comprises twenty-seven papers.

No. 1, is a letter from Sir R. Strachan to Lord Mulgrave, dated *St. Domingo*, off Borslen, September 18; in which the writer says:

"I am very anxious, I do assure your lordship, to see you, for the purpose of communicating matters connected with this island; which, in my opinion, ought not to be given up. It is a post of great importance as a naval station; and also with a view to future operations on the Continent; particularly as it is not certain Austria has made peace with France. This island, under popular government, (by popular I mean pleasing to the inhabitants, by placing the superior ones in authority, and governing by their own laws) may be productive of great advantages to England, in regard to trade with the Continent, similar to that established at Heligoland. I do not apprehend it is more unhealthy than any of the low parts of Kent; but the troops being at present generally infected, owing to the nature of the service to which they have been exposed, it may be proper they should be withdrawn, and replaced with other regiments."

Enquiry into the Disaster at Walcheren
Imperial Parliament

House of Commons, Monday, March 26 1810. ^{XXIII 423-425}

Lord Porchester, pursuant to notice, moved the following resolutions, respecting the Scheldt expedition; previous to which, in a speech of great length, he entered into an extensive review of the origin, progress, and failure, of that disastrous undertaking.

[Of most interest are the 'second set of resolutions relating to the retention of the island of Walcheren'.]

I. That lieutenant-general Sir Eyre Coote, having on the 9th of September, been left in command of Walcheren, with an army of about 15,000 men, did, on that day, make an official report on the state of the island, the extent of force required effectually to guard it; the nature and condition of its defences, and the number of men then sick and unfit for duty; representing, that after such his exposition, his Majesty's ministers would be the best judges of the propriety or possibility of keeping the island; and adding, that the advantages must be great indeed which could compensate the loss of lives and treasure, which the retention must necessarily occasion.

II. That on the 23d of September, Sir Eyre Coote stated to his Majesty's ministers, that the alarming progress of disease was such, that if it should continue in the same proportion for three weeks longer (as he added, there was every probability it would) our possession of the island must become very precarious.

III. That on the 6th of October, Sir Eyre Coote, after stating that the number of sick was increasing, and that the effective force was thereby rendered so trivial, as to make the defence of the island, if it should be attacked, extremely precarious, did express his anxiety to be informed of the intentions of his Majesty's government as to the future state of Walcheren.

IV. That notwithstanding these and many other pressing representations, on the alarming condition of the troops, and the danger to which they were exposed, his Majesty's ministers did neglect to come to any decision until the 4th of November, and that the final evacuation of Walcheren did not take place until the 23d of December.

Despatches Reporting the Withdrawal from Flushing

Letters on Service, Admiralty Office, 19 December 1809. ^{XXIII 77-84}

Rear-Admiral W.A. Otway to Rear-Admiral Sir Richard Strachan, K.B., Commander-in-Chief
Caesar, Flushing Roads, December 11, 1809

Sir, I have the honour to communicate to you such circumstances as have occurred previous to your arrival, and subsequent to my last official communication.

The transports necessary for the embarkation of the army having arrived the 25th ult. on the following day the measures that I had previously concerted with Lieutenant-general Don for the destruction of the basin, arsenal, and sea defences of Flushing, agreeable to instructions from the Earl of Liverpool, dated the 13th and received on the 17th, were begun.

On this service six hundred seamen and artificers from the fleet were employed, under the orders of Captain Moore, of his Majesty's ship *Marlborough*, assisted by Captains Tomlinson and Henderson, of the fireship service. The navy having completed the portion of work allotted to them, and Lieutenant-colonel Pilkington, commanding the royal engineers, having reported to Lieutenant-general Don that his mines for the destruction of the gates and piers at the entrance of the basin were ready, the whole of the army, with the exception of the rear-guard, was embarked on the afternoon of the 9th instant.

The mines were exploded yesterday at low water, and appear to have fully answered their object: the whole of the east side of the basin had been previously completely destroyed, but as the port of Flushing west of the basin lies considerably below the high water mark, any material injury of the west bank would have caused the immediate inundation of the whole town; therefore our work on that side has been confined to the demolition of the careening wharf and pits.

It was at first intended to defer the burning of the storehouse and other buildings in the arsenal until our final departure, but, from the probability that with a strong east wind the flames might communicate to the town, the whole was set fire to yesterday, and is totally destroyed.

Thus Flushing is rendered useless to the enemy as a naval arsenal; and the basin, which afforded very secure retreat for several ships of the line during the winter, is for the present effectually destroyed, and can only be restored by great labour, and at an immense expense.

I have the honour to be,

W.A. OTWAY, Rear-Admiral

Rear-admiral Sir Richard Strachan, K.B. Commander-in-Chief, &c.

Downing Street, December 30, 1809
Commodore G.W.C.R. Owen to Rear-Admiral Sir R.J. Strachan, Bart. and K.B.

His Majesty's Ship Clyde, off the North Foreland, December 28, 1809
Sir, In obedience to the direction of Rear-Admiral Otway, I have the honour to lay before you the following detail of my proceedings in carrying into execution the orders to evacuate that part of the island of Walcheren, with the duties of which I had the honour to be charged.

Of our previous state of preparation you have been acquainted, and that all the stores, guns, and ammunition not judged immediately necessary to our defence, had been withdrawn and put on board, and every arrangement made in the beginning of December.

I have likewise had the honour to report to you, that the enemy's anxiety to complete his works on Wolversdyke and south Beveland, for the purpose of clearing the Slou [sic], and driving our advanced divisions from the channels which lead to it, had obliged me to commence a system of offensive operations, and the result thereof has likewise been submitted to you.

I had further to inform you of the necessity I felt for shifting my pendant to the *Cretan*, that I might be better situated to direct our movements.

Our flotilla held their forward stations when, on the morning of the 23d, I received your letter, acquainting me that you intended to quit Flushing on that day, provided the wind would permit the line-of-battle ships to pass the Duerloo. I immediately made preparation likewise to withdraw. The boats assembled, and embarked the rear guard of the army, under the direction of the honourable Captain Cadogan; whilst the few remaining guns of Veer and Armuyden points were rendered useless, and every other article of stores was taken off.

In the meantime our advanced divisions fell back, and collected at their defensive stations, but it was two o'clock before those duties were completed, and there was no chance of clearing any considerable part of our force from the Veer Gat before dark, whilst the wind, which was very light, hung so far to the westward, as to leave me doubtful of your succeeding with the line-of-battle ships; I therefore ordered the *Clyde* only, whose draught of water might embarrass us, to shift out to the Roompot whilst I sent an intelligent person to Flushing for information of your movements.

Colonel Pack (with whom it has been my good fortune to co-operate) was good enough to offer the Town-major of Ter Verre for this duty. Captain Clements of the 71st regiment, who returned to me at five o'clock, with the information that every thing was clear except two frigates, and a two-decked ship, and the stay of these seemed to be the effect of chance alone, and I concluded they would follow in the morning. Captain Clements found the towns of Middleburgh and Flushing occupied by Burger guards, and at four on the following morning, the gates of Veere were likewise given to the Burgers.

At day-light of the 24th, I made the signal for our distant ships to move, but the transports at the entrance of the Gat did not succeed in getting out till dark.

Captain Davis's division of the gun-boats however reached the Roompot, and were disarmed.

It was whilst this movement was making, and which was much retarded by the baffling winds, I learnt of your arrival in the Roompot; and it was in the pause the shift of wind and tide occasioned that you did me the honour to join me in the *Cretan*, and sanction my proceedings.

On the morning of the 25th, our guard boats were recalled, the *Pallas* got out to the Roompot, and a movement of our whole flotilla made; but as it then came on to blow, you ordered it to take a position off the Fort Den Haak.

Encouraged by our retreat, the enemy's advanced division of gun-boats moved through the Wolversdyke channel to the station heretofore occupied by our advance, but on our anchoring, returned again to its former station. As however we had decidedly given up Ter Verre, three rowboats with Dutch troops, crossed over there from Campere, and in the course of the afternoon some Schuyts followed likewise with Dutch troops, and by sunset the enemy had posted sentinels at Den Haak.

On the 26th the wind got round to the N.E. and you (seeing every prospect of our getting out) had sailed for England, the wind however backed again to the westward of north, and I did not think it right to disarm any more of the gun-boats, then the division of acting Captain Rich.

All the merchant vessels had got clear of the Veere Gat, but one gun-boat was aground. I sent Captain Carteret with two divisions to cover her, and to protect the disarmed boats, which I ordered once more to anchor off Den Haak.

The enemy's gun-boats had in this while anchored in a line off Ter Veere, but again abandoned that position and returned to Wolversdyke.

The morning of the 27th was as favourable as could be desired; the several convoys sailed soon after day-light with a gentle breeze at east; the two disarmed divisions of gun-boats parted company whilst the remainder were disarming, which done, the whole squadron was a-weigh by half-past one, and fairly in the Stone Deep by sun-set. I there met Captain Mason, in the *Fisgard*, with his squadron, and learnt that all was clear from Flushing.

The wind and weather have been so favourable and fine, there is no doubt all will reach Sheerness in safety, I should hope, to-day. . . .

G.W.C.R. OWEN, Commander

Rear-Admiral Sir R.J. Strachan, Bart. and K.B.

Sir Richard Strachan's Reasons for not Sinking Vessels to Block Up the Scheldt

From 'Naval Anecdotes.' XXIV 22

The following are Admiral Strachan's reasons, given to the Admiralty, for not sinking vessels to block up the Scheldt:

"The public anxiety, though under a state of delusion, has been led to imagine, that nothing is more easy than to block up the navigation of a river where the channel is narrow; and I am ready to confess, no person's opinion was more eagerly bent than mine to this persuasion, on the first sensation which was produced from the impression of theory; but that idea was materially altered by the effect of observation and practical research. I had taken steps to prepare vessels, before I was satisfied of the inexpediency of doing so.

Captain Peake, a very active and intelligent officer, who was stationed at Batz with the marine brigade, ascertained the rise of the tides to be *from twenty to twenty-four feet*; and, on the 2d of September, which happened to be the dead of the neaps, he was directed to measure the rise of the tide; the wind was then at S.E. certainly the most checking wind in the Scheldt, and yet it rose 18 feet.

After this statement of facts, I venture to submit to their lordships' consideration, whether with such a rise of tide, and in a situation where the genius and activity of French mechanics could be employed without any interruption, there was the least prospect, by sinking vessels, to prevent or even to impede the navigation of that part of the river; for it must be evident, that any thing raised above the level of low water could easily be removed; and, without claiming the advantage of what they could work under water, I think it will not be denied, that nothing is more practicable than to get ships across such a narrow bank as any description of vessels would form that we could sink: the enemy's ships might be without difficulty lightened to eighteen feet.

It appears, on a final calculation, that it will be necessary to destroy twenty-six large ships, and twenty-one smaller ones, to accomplish this purpose."

The Navy Board's Revenge on Captain Tomlinson

From the 'Memoir of the Public Services of Captain Nicholas Tomlinson.'
XXV 112-128

[According to the author of *An Appeal to the Public, in behalf of Nicholas Tomlinson, Esq., Captain in his Majesty's Navy, &c. &c.*, from which a considerable portion of the information in the present memoir is drawn, subsequent to his volunteer service at Copenhagen in 1801 (*vide* Schomberg's *Naval Chronology*, Vol. III, p194),] "Captain Tomlinson was not only reinstated, but re-employed, being appointed soon after to the command of the Sea Fencibles, at Southend, in Essex. While stationed on that coast, his mind, ever active, and constantly panting after *real* service, on the proper element for a British sea officer, in 1809, suggested to the Admiralty the plan of an attack on the enemy's fleet, in their own ports, by means of fire-ships. Previously to this, Captain

Tomlinson not only improved the old plan, but pointed out a new, and more efficacious disposition of this description of vessels, which was approved by the Board of Admiralty; and he himself was soon after actually employed, with *confidential and secret instructions* from the Lords Commissioners, to fit out, and command all the fireships, which were *ordered to be* completed according to this method.

The Board of Ordnance displayed great activity and zeal, upon this occasion; but from the Navy Board, the stores demanded were not obtained; and the expedition actually left England *without them*; although the Secretary to the Admiralty, relying on the exertions of the Commissioners of the Navy, had informed Captain Tomlinson that "they should be supplied in due time," no less than four weeks before the armament left the Downs. Such conduct necessarily produced complaints on the part of Captain Tomlinson, who *feeling himself responsible for the event*, and knowing that this was the only species of force that could possibly come in contact with the enemy's fleet near Antwerp, not only remonstrated with the Board in question, but was at length under the absolute necessity of stating his wants, and disappointments, to a superior tribunal [i.e. the Admiralty]." . . .

To what extent these stores were actually required, or employed, in the progress of the Scheldt expedition,[1] we are not informed; but, in the destruction of the basin, arsenal, and sea defences of Flushing, Captain Tomlinson obtained the high approbation of Captain Moore, of the *Marlborough*, whom he assisted in that service.[2] The fire-ship in which he was embarked having been wrecked, he returned to England in the *Isis*. . . .

To the Right Honourable the Lords Commissioners for executing the Office of Lord High Admiral, &c. &c. the Humble Memorial of Nicholas Tomlinson, a Captain in the Royal Navy

The fire-ship in which your memorialist was embarked being wrecked, he returned to England in the *Isis*, and resumed his command of the Sea Fencibles in Essex; but he had not been many days in England, and was returning home, when he learnt with astonishment and indignation, that his house was beset, and his numerous family alarmed by Bowstreet officers, who were sent to seize on his person, at the instance of the Navy Board, (in a county where he is a magistrate, and on a spot where he long exercised an important naval command) under pretence that he had "uttered" i.e. transmitted to the Navy Office, *in the course of his duty, as commander of the Pelter*, a forged voucher in the year 1795, to the amount of £29 5s from a *Sub-Tradesman*, who swore in open court before three of your Lordships, that he had never seen your Memorialist before; therefore he could not be acquainted with his hand writing, to detect a forgery if there was one: and this must have been known to the deputy solicitors of the Navy Board, as they had this man up from Dartmouth two or three times before on this business; and as the voucher in question was given to your Memorialist, with others, he supposes he transmitted it to the Navy Board, but it was not necessary to pass your memorialist's (or even the shipwright's) accounts, and this was known at the Navy Office, for their own secretary pointed out that circumstance to the police magistrates while your memorialist was present; *therefore he could have no interest in it!*

---

1 The reader who may wish to be informed of the particulars of this expedition, may be gratified, by referring to the NAVAL CHRONICLE Vol. XXII pages 75, 133, 140, 154, 158, 164, 170, 171, 243, 312, and 434; and Vol. XXIII pages 77, 113, 200 and 301 [and see the relevant chapters above].
2 Vide NAVAL CHRONICLE Vol. XXIII page 78.

That your memorialist's accounts for the *Pelter* had been *audited and lying on the shelf at Somerset House, upwards of FOURTEEN YEARS,* when he was called upon, he believes, *contrary to all precedent,* to prove the authenticity of the voucher above-mentioned, at the peril of his life, and great injury of his character and fortune: but your memorialist respectively submits, that if (after the lapse of so many years) they had reason to suppose any thing was wrong in his accounts, an impress against his pay to the amount of £29 5s until an explanation had been obtained, would have fulfilled all the purposes of public justice, and been in conformity to the naval instructions, and the usage of the service; for this mode of procedure was strictly followed in respect to two or three gallant officers, of high rank, at the close of the American war, who were actually mulcted in large sums; but they were not attempted to be hunted down at the public expense, by police officers, and attorneys; for they were employed in important commands pending the investigations of their accounts, and subsequent to paying the money. - And although the Navy Board were in constant correspondence with your memorialist on the public service, they did not require any explanation from him, agreeably to the custom of the navy, which every officer of rank and character has a right to expect from the commissioners; but thief-takers were sent, at their instance, *to drag your memorialist from his command at Southend,* on a warrant obtained from a police magistrate at Bow-street, selected for the purpose, and upon affidavits manufactured in another place; without the knowledge or consent of Mr. Graham, the sitting magistrate of the day; and he was actually on the Bench, when the deputy solicitors to the Navy Board, their secretary, and the police magistrates alluded to, &c. retired into a private room without his knowledge or approbation; and by accident only, Mr. Graham discovered what had been going on, and he has declared he never met with more iniquity in all his practice in that office; and the warrant was thus obtained against your memorialist upon affidavits,[3] *antedated,* which he has been informed were not even read to their witnesses; who afterwards *contradicted upon oath,* before the magistrates, what they had sworn to in those affidavits! *And these were the men that were* carried before a grand jury to get a bill found, *and then to the Old Bailey, to swear away the life of your memorialist!!*

That the magistrate above alluded to, being asked how he could grant the warrant against your memorialist without interrogating the witnesses, acknowledged to Mr. Graham, the police magistrate, (while your memorialist was present) that he had been imposed upon by the representatives of the *deputy* solicitors of the Navy Board; but he promised never to take their word again, upon such occasions, or to grant any more warrants on their representations: for the correctness of the above statement your memorialist begs leave to refer your Lordships to Mr. Graham, who is *officially* acquainted with the whole of this business. - And your memorialist most respectfully submits, that if this case is allowed to grow into a precedent, no officer can sleep secure in his bed, that has ever transmitted a voucher to the Navy Office; for, according to this example, they may begin with the admiral of the fleet, and descend to the junior officer that ever sent a voucher to that office, fifteen or perhaps fifty years before; and hold up this authority *in terrorem,* to overawe and intimidate, *at the public expense,* any officer who may have just cause, as he had, to represent their neglect to your Lordships: for it has been officially reported at the Admiralty (for Mr. Yorke's information) by the magistrate who investigated this business, that any other officer, *however exalted,* might

---

3 "Affidavits dated 23d January, but sworn to on Saturday, 3d February, 1819."

have been taken to Bowstreet, with as much propriety as your memorialist was, under pretence that some voucher sent to the Navy Office many years before was forged; though it might, as in this case, have been impossible for him to detect it.

That on hearing his house was beset by police officers, your memorialist came to London for legal advice, and his solicitor applied to Mr. Knight, one of the deputy solicitors to the Navy Board, to fix a time to have their complaint investigated by the police magistrates, and your memorialist would attend; but this reasonable request was refused by Mr. Knight, who insisted on his being first in custody (*and of course manacled*) before he would appoint a meeting, and he therefore wrote the following note to your memorialist's solicitor:

"Mr. Knight's compliments to Mr. Taunton, and when he has notice that Captain Tomlinson has surrendered to the warrant, he will apply to Mr. Nares, to fix a time for the examination. *Great Marlborough-street, Friday Evening.*"

Your memorialist most respectfully submits, *that this contemptuous treatment of its superior officers, by such men, must tend to bring the navy into contempt, and depress the high and honourable spirit that now prevails among all classes of its officers*; and humbly doubts the propriety of allowing these *deputy attorneys* to trifle with their honour, *at the public expense*, as in this case.

That your memorialist's solicitor, not succeeding with Mr. Knight, made the same application to the police magistrate, who appointed a hearing on Saturday the 24th of February last, when your memorialist attended; but the solicitors to the Navy Board refused to appear, insisting (as your memorialist was informed) on a previous commitment; and they did not obey until the Tuesday following, when a third summons had been sent by Messrs. Graham and Nares, when an investigation took place before those magistrates; and after hearing counsel on behalf of the Navy Board (seeing no grounds for its having been granted) they discharged the warrant against your memorialist, after he had been put to the expense of near two hundred pounds in law charges, and bringing up witnesses from distant parts of the country.

That your memorialist can form no reason for this unexampled severity on the part of the Navy Board, against a brother officer, except that he had thrown the responsibility of the probable failure of the fire-ships, *for want of proper stores*, off his shoulders, and perhaps they found it had fallen upon their own; for however lightly it may *now* be thought of, it was *then* a matter of the first consideration; for at *that time*, the success of the armament might, and was thought to, depend in a great measure on the fire-ships under the command of your memorialist.

Had the persecution of your memorialist ended when this complaint was dismissed by the police magistrates, he would not have troubled your Lordships with this appeal to your justice; but after their complaint had been discharged, *and Mr. Knight, who appeared to conduct it, had acknowledged to Mr. Graham, before his own counsel, while your memorialist was present, that he was convinced of his innocence, and that their accusation had originated in a mistake*; yet they afterwards carried most of the same witnesses before a grand jury, *who had contradicted themselves before the police magistrate*, to get a bill found, and your memorialist was in consequence put to the charge of *more than four years' half pay*, to defend his life and honour at the bar of the Old Bailey.

Having laid these his wrongs and suffering before your Lordships, your memorialist humbly trusts, that you will grant him such redress, and relief, as may in your Lordship's wisdom and justice seem meet.

Dated: *"Witham, Essex, 5th December, 1810"*

Representation of Bull and Cow Rocks, and part of Dursey Island, on the west coast of Ireland. Engraved by Baily, from a Drawing by G.T. in 1807.
A frigate is running for Bear Haven, with a signal for a pilot. Plate 411

It appears to be the opinion of the writer of the "*Appeal*" that Captain Tomlinson, by his previous remonstrances and complaints, had drawn down the high displeasure of the Navy Board; but, by way of *excuse* for the prosecution which was afterwards commenced against this officer, he observes –

"The Navy Board had been lately accused of gross *neglect*, by those appointed to investigate its conduct; and was further charged with permitting one of its accountants to obtain improperly *upwards of £285,000 of the public money:*[4] the Commissioners doubtless imagined, that in an age famous for punishing petty crimes and pardoning great ones, a fine opportunity now presented itself, for redeeming their characters with the public at large; and, accordingly, having allowed a Leviathan of a defaulter to escape, they were determined, if possible, to entangle a shrimp!" . . .

[The Admiralty Board offered no relief.]

Thus it appears, that, notwithstanding the absolute innocence of Captain Tomlinson, as to the charges on which he had the extreme mortification of being brought to the bar of the Old Bailey; notwithstanding his general and acknowledged merit as an officer, he has incurred a positive loss of between five and six hundred pounds, independently of the severe irritation and distress of mind which the proceedings must have excited, in himself, and in his family – Under this consideration of his case, we have only to offer him the advice of the poet – to live in hope, and to reserve himself for more prosperous circumstances.[5]

[This account of Captain Tomlinson's plight led to a letter from 'An Old Seaman' suggesting that he sue for damages. Vol. XXV, pp206-207.]

4 "See Fifth Report of the Committee on the Public Expenditure, pages 1, 2, and 3."
5 "Sperate et vosmet rebus servate secundis." Virgil

1810 – The Scheldt Enquiry and Other Naval News

THE FAILURE OF THE SCHELDT EXPEDITION, its irrelevance to the campaign which defeated Austria, the reverses suffered in Spain, and the illness of the King, which could no longer be ignored, made the winter of 1809–1810 a dark time for Britain. The desultory negotiations which had been attempted with the French for a peace settlement came to nothing, and even the negotiations to exchange prisoners of war collapsed. The dispute with the United States over the exercise of British maritime power continued to fester.

The malaise was reflected in Parliament. The speech from the Throne on 23 January had to be read by commission, and in both houses there were amendments proposed. The debate focused on the war in Spain, and votes of thanks were made to Lord Wellington and his army for their skill and gallantry at the battle of Talavera. On a motion by Lord Porchester, the House agreed to an inquiry into the conduct of the Earl of Chatham, and generally into the Walcheren fiasco. To ensure full discussion, he called for a committee of the whole House. Despite ministerial protest, the House supported him.

In the debate on the Scheldt expedition Mr Whitbread especially singled out for criticism the Earl of Chatham's violation of the concept of ministerial solidarity by his directly addressing the King with his version of events, in which he attempted to lay the blame for failure on Rear-Admiral Sir Richard Strachan. Against ministerial protest, the House voted for a return of all communications between the Earl of Chatham and the King. The examination of evidence took the Walcheren committee from 2 February to 26 March, and then Lord Porchester moved resolutions to the effect that the expedition had been undertaken when there was little rational prospect of success, at a time of year when a well-known epidemic was to be expected, and that the withdrawal had been delayed unresponsibly. The severest censure was called for, but after four days' debate Porchester's resolutions were negatived in a very full House by small margins, and amendments approving the ministerial action passed.

Public interest in the debate had been muted because Charles Yorke had enforced the standing rule excluding strangers from the House. As a reward, he was appointed First Lord of the Admiralty. Having taken a position under the Crown, however, he had to stand for re-election, and the electors of Oxford made him pay for his assault on the freedom of the press. He had to find a safe seat in Cornwall. Sir Francis Burdett, member for Westminster, publicly objected to the extra-judicial action of the House in committing to Newgate prison without criminal trial the writer of a handbill objecting to the exclusion. On a vote of the House he was imprisoned in the Tower, an event which caused enormous public protest.

The affairs of Parliament, and the struggle for civil liberties, give the impression that the public had lost much hope of the war ever reaching a satisfactory conclusion. The news from the continent suggested that Napoleon believed that he had all but triumphed, and had time to consolidate. Following the defeat of the Austrian army, his separation from his childless wife, Josephine, opened the way for him to propose marriage to a young Austrian archduchess, Maria Louisa. Emperor Francis I and Archduke Charles agreed to the alliance, which took place by proxy on 11 March, and hoped for better things. From Spain there continued to arrive news of French triumphs. *The Naval Chronicle* was most interested in the ability of the defences of Cadiz, with British assistance, to withstand the assault, and so prevent the Spanish Cadiz fleet falling into French hands.

The death in harness of the Mediterranean fleet commander, Vice-Admiral Collingwood, saddened his friends, and perhaps demarked the end of the heroic era at sea.

In Sweden, on 29 May, the Crown Prince died suddenly and under pressure from Emperor Napoleon, Julian Bernadotte, one of his Marshals, was chosen by the estates of Sweden in August to be his successor. Bernadotte arrived in Sweden to take up his duties in October. Obediently, Sweden declared war on Britain, but Bernadotte proved less than a perfect instrument of Napoleon's power. The declaration specifically stated that it was made at the instigation of France, and Bernadotte made it clear in his address to the realm in November that he would seek above all to keep Sweden out of active conflict.

Napoleon's brother Louis, who was the puppet king of the Netherlands, also proved unwilling to follow French dictates to the destruction of the people he governed. Netherlands west coast harbours were vital to Napoleon's plans, now tacitly abandoned, for the invasion of England, and had been made available on demand, with the assistance of Dutch soldiers and sailors, but the same harbours were also principal points of entry for British merchandise. Enforcement of Napoleon's Continental System trade barrier caused tremendous suffering, and eventually Louis ordered the modification of the controls. This Napoleon would not tolerate. For a while Louis complied with his brother's dictates, but his humanity revolted at the suffering this caused, he abolished all controls and abdicated in July in favour of his eldest son. However, Napoleon had not approved of that measure, and decided on the direct annexation of the Netherlands to France. This was followed by the annexation of the Hanse Towns.

Britain was also to suffer for its economic strategy. In 1810 all restraint on American trade was lifted by the Madison administration, conditional upon the belligerents mending their ways. Napoleon obfuscated. London grudgingly decided to exempt American traders from the provisions of the orders-in-council regulating trade, but there continued to be incidents.

It was a relief to look to the West Indies. After the fall of Martinique, Guadaloupe was the only important possession of the enemy in America. Early in the year a force of six thousand men commanded by Sir George Beckwith succeeded in its capture. The decisive tactical move was the deployment of the reserves under Brigadier-General Wale to make a surprise advance through the mountains to attack the enemy position in the rear. After their surrender, Beckwith went on to accept the surrender of Eustatius without opposition. At sea, on the other hand, a French squadron of two 48-gun frigates and another two armed *en flûte* and carrying reinforcements for Guadaloupe caught a British frigate, *Junon*. Her people put up a stiff fight, for an hour and a quarter, before surrendering.

Good news also came from the East Indies where, in September 1809, a raid had been conducted on the French establishments on the Isle of Bourbon which served to support French cruiser warfare in the Indian Ocean, but were now destroyed. For that purpose ships operating out of Simons Bay in South Africa were employed, and soldiers from the garrison of the recently captured island of Rodriguez. Later in the year came news of the capture of the Isle de France.

The precarious balance of British politics was to be subjected to severe strain late in the year. The fragile state of King George's mind was subjected to an unbearable blow when his youngest and favourite daughter, Princess Amelia, fell ill, and eventually died. On her deathbed she slipped a ring onto his finger with a lock of her hair made into it, and the words 'remember me' engraved on it, and by the time she expired, on 2 November, sorrow had deprived him of reason. Three times during the autumn and winter of 1810 Parliament met, and adjourned because there was no commission to stand in the place of the sovereign, but eventually it became evident that the King would not soon recover. Out of necessity, but in defiance of constitutional forms, Lord Perceval obtained the agreement of both Houses of Parliament to ask the Prince of Wales to assume the powers of Regent. It was expected that the Prince would replace Perceval with Earl Grey and Lord Grenville, but the King's mental health suddenly began to improve and, for the time, the constitutional crisis passed.

From the 'Naval History of the Present Year,' 1809-1810
December-January. XXIII 67-69

Commons Vote for Inquiry into Walcheren Failure

It will be seen, by our report of the proceedings of Parliament, on the first night of the session, that ministers had a considerable majority, in each house. In the Commons, however, on the third night of debate, the opposition had a majority of nine, in favour of Lord Porchester's motion for an inquiry into the causes of the failure of the Walcheren expedition. Whether this event may lead to a dissolution of Ministry, we cannot pretend to say; but certainly it must gall them sorely. They are, however, but little entitled to pity or commiseration; for, had it not been for an over-weening confidence, the result of their first night's success, they would have suffered Lord Porchester's motion to be carried without a division; a measure by which, as inquiry had been repeatedly promised, they could have lost nothing; particularly as the opposition were not anxious to commence the inquiry, before the requisite information should be before the house.

Irenic Failure

The prospect of a negotiation for peace between France and England has nearly vanished. Buonaparte has refused to accede to our proposition of treaty in conjunction with Spain and Portugal; though, it is said, he has offered to restore the latter country to the house of Braganza, and to erect South America into a monarchy, under Ferdinand VII.

Some new arrangements are said to be in contemplation, for the exchange of prisoners between Great Britain and France, on terms more liberal than heretofore.

Dutch Narrowly Avoid Annexation

The absolute annexation of Holland to France has, for a time, been abandoned; but Buonaparte, though he has consented to a certain modification of his obnoxious Berlin and Milan decrees, has adopted new, and more severe regulations, to prevent all commercial intercourse between the English and Dutch.

New Rules for French Privateers

The French minister of marine has also promulgated a code of laws for the government of privateers and the distribution of prizes, chiefly with a view to encourage individuals to embark their property in speculations of that kind. By these, the masters of privateers are directed to ransom, burn, or destroy, all vessels to or from Great Britain or her colonies, provided the estimated value does not exceed £10,000; but all vessels exceeding in value that sum are to be sent to France. In regard to ransomed ships, the masters of privateers are directed to take the mate and two seamen as hostages, or security, for the payment of the stipulated sum; if the money is paid the men are to be liberated and sent home, but in default of payment are to be imprisoned as debtors to the nation.

American Negotiations - New Trade Restraints

Some important negotiations are understood to be going forward between France and America; but their probable result is unknown.

View of Fannet Point and Signal Station, Lough Swilly. Engraved by Baily, from a Drawing by G.T., 1815. Plate 481

It will be seen, by the Speech of his Majesty's Commissioners, at the opening of Parliament, that the American minister has expressed a wish for the continuance of amity between this country and the United States; and the last despatches which Mr. Pinkney received from France are said to be favourable to our future negotiation with America, which is expected to be chiefly carried on between the Marquis Wellesley and Mr. Pinkney; no ambassador having been sent from England, in the room of Mr. Jackson.

It appears, from the last received American papers, that the legislature of the United States has again embarked in the war of commercial restrictions. A bill, intended as a substitute for the Non-intercourse Act, had been read a second time in the House of Representatives, and was expected to pass into a law. Its principal object is, to prevent importations from Great Britain or France, or their colonies, except in vessels owned wholly by Americans. All vessels sailing under the flags of Great Britain and France are therefore prohibited, with some exceptions, from entering the ports of the United States. The President is authorized to remove, by proclamation, the prohibitions on trade with Great Britain or France, upon learning that our orders in council, or the decree of Buonaparté, have been rescinded.

Vote of Thanks for Lord Gambier

On the 29th of January, a vote of thanks to Lord Gambier was agreed to, on a division, by 161 against 39; Lord Cochrane's motion for producing the minutes of the Court Martial, having been previously rejected by 171 against 19.

Indian Mutiny Quelled

An alarming insurrection among our troops, in India, has been completely quelled.

Bourbon Defences Destroyed - East Indiamen Recaptured

By the arrival of the extra ships *Monarch, Lord Keith,* and *Earl Spencer* at Portsmouth, on the 7th of January, under convoy of the *Princess Charlotte*, we received the intelligence of the capture of the Isle of Bourbon, in the Indian Ocean.

This object was effected, on the 21st September, by the cruizing squadron from the Isle of France, under Commodore Rowley, in the *Raisonable,* 64, *Boadicea, Sirius,* and *Nereide* frigates, and *Otter* sloop of war, assisted by a party of the 56th Regiment, and some Bombay Sepoys, under Lieutenant Keating. From farther information, it appears, that about 350 soldiers, and 200 royal marines, were landed before day-break, and soon carried three of the forts. The squadron went in and fired their broadsides, and then hauled out; the *Sirius* frigate, Captain Pym, stood in again, and anxious to avail himself of the only opportunity that presented itself, he asked leave, and was permitted, by signal from the Commodore, to anchor, and accordingly, in the most gallant style, carried his little ship in and placed her within pistol-shot of the beach, and half-musket shot of the *Caroline* French frigate, and the two East Indiamen and a French brig of war, and opened so heavy a fire on them from his English bull-dogs, that in 20 minutes (the troops at the same time charging through the town) the whole struck their colours. Both army and navy joined in praise of this brilliant enterprize, declaring they had never seen or thought it possible for a ship to keep up so tremendous a fire as the *Sirius* exhibited on that occasion; and we understand it was principally owing to the very great exertions of Captain Pym, his officers and crew, that the two Indiamen were saved from being burnt; or that any of the stores and goods from the shore were taken off and put on board the *Streatham*.

Raid on the Isle de Bourbon

Letters on Service, Admiralty-Office, February 13, 1810. XXIII 251-260

Despatches, of which the following are copies, have been received at this office by John Wilson Crocker, Esq. from Vice-admiral Bertie, Commander-in-chief of his Majesty's ships and vessels at the Cape of Good Hope, addressed to the honourable William Wellesley Pole.

La Bourbonaise, Table-Bay, November 16, 1809
Sir, I have the honour to congratulate their lordships on the beneficial effects that have already manifested themselves to the interest of his Majesty's service, and particularly those of the honourable East-India company, by the measures their lordships have been pleased to adopt for the blockade of the Isles of France and Bourbon, and by the prompt reinforcement they have been pleased to place under my orders, for the furtherance of this object; the communications from Captain Rowley and Lieutenant-colonel Keating, copies of which are forwarded herewith, fully explain the nature of the services performed; the able manner in which they have been conducted, and the unanimity, zeal, and discipline, which have distinguished the whole proceeding, merit the highest approbation, and to which I feel that no comment or encomium of mine can render sufficient justice.

The objects proposed by Captain Rowley and Lieutenant-colonel Keating in undertaking this enterprise were very considerable, and have succeeded in every point; all the batteries, guns, mortars, at St. Rosa, St. Paul's, St. Gill's, and St. Luce in the Island of Bourbon, have been effectually and completely destroyed, and in their harbours the enemy can no longer find that protection for their own ships or their captures, which they were accustomed to seek, when the rigour of the blockade opposed their entrance into the Isle of France.

Their naval force is reduced on this station, by a frigate (*La Caroline*) of forty-four guns, and a corvette (the *Grappler*) of eighteen guns, besides merchant vessels; but what is still more gratifying is the recovery out of the hands of the enemy of the honourable company's ships *Europe* and *Streatham*, with a considerable part of their cargoes, being the only two ships belonging to the East-India company which have, within my knowledge, been brought within the limits of this station since my arrival on it. . . .

I have the honour to be,

A. BERTIE

Raisonable, off Port Louis [Isle de France], August 23, 1809
Sir, The harbour of St. Paul's having long been the rendezvous of those French cruizers, and such of their prizes as have escaped the vigilance of our look-out ships off the Isle of France, and *La Caroline* French frigate having succeeded in entering that port with two homeward bound indiamen richly laden, I considered it practicable, both from the reports of Captain Corbett, of the *Nereide*, who is perfectly acquainted with the coast, as well as from my own observations, and from information received from prisoners, that the place might be carried with the assistance of a detachment of the troops from Rodriguez, to assist by land in an attack on the batteries. Having communicated my opinion to Lieutenant-colonel Keating, commanding the troops there, he immediately acceded to the measure, and in the most handsome manner offered to embark with all the troops that could be spared from the defence of the place. I have therefore detached the *Nereide, Otter*, and *Sapphire*, to bring them down; and as soon as they arrive shall proceed with the whole of our force to the attack of the place. I have in the meantime sent the *Boadicea* to blockade the port, and trust that these measures will meet your approbation.

I have the honour to be, &c.

J. ROWLEY

To Vice-admiral Bertie

Raisonable, St. Paul's Road, 29th September, 1809
Sir, Having acquainted you by my letter of the 28th August with the reason which induced me to request the assistance of Lieutenant-colonel Keating, commanding the troops at Rodriguez, to co-operate with his Majesty's ships in an attack on St. Paul's, I have now further to acquaint you, that being joined by the *Nereide, Otter,* and *Wasp* schooner, having on board a detachment of the 56th Regiment, and of the 2d regiment native infantry, amounting in the whole to 368 men, under the command of Lieutenant-colonel Keating, and the *Sirius* having joined, we proceeded at dusk on the evening of the 20th for the Isle of Bourbon; the force intended to be landed were the detachment of his Majesty's and company's troops, reinforced by the marines of the squadron, and a party of about 100 seamen from this ship and the *Otter*, under the command of Captain Willoughby, whose zeal induced him to volunteer the command of so small a party. As secrecy and despatch were essential to the success of the expedition, the whole of this force, amounting to 604, were embarked with five additional boats on board the *Nereide*, Captain Corbett, who, from his perfect acquaintance with the coast, as well as his known skill and activity, was entrusted with this important service.

On our approach towards the bay of St. Paul's, to prevent suspicion, the *Nereide* preceded the other ships, and being anchored close to the beach, the whole of the detachment were landed with the greatest celerity, without any alarm being given to the enemy, and proceeded towards the batteries, which were successively stormed and carried with the greatest gallantry, and several of the guns pointed on the ships in the roads; in the mean time the squadron stood into the bay, and according to the plan agreed upon, when the movements of the troops enabled them to act, opened their fire on the shipping, which was warmly returned by *La Caroline* frigate, the indiamen her prizes, and those batteries which, from their distance from the first point of attack, were enabled to continue their fire; but these being finally carried, our ships preparing to anchor, and the *Sirius* having already taken a close raking position a-head of *La Caroline*, they found it necessary to surrender, having made an honourable resistance, and by nine o'clock the whole of the batteries, town, and shipping were in possession of his Majesty's troops and squadron.

The squadron having anchored in the roads close off the town of St. Paul's immediate exertions were made to secure *La Caroline* and the rest of the shipping, whose cables being cut had drifted on shore, and they were hove off without material injury.

The guns and mortars at the different batteries and on the beach being spiked, their carriages burnt or destroyed, and magazines blown off under the directions of Captain Willoughby, the whole of the troops, marines, and seamen, were embarked soon after dark on board of the different ships: Thus, Sir, have we completely succeeded in the objects of the expedition, by the capture of the enemy's shipping, the destruction of all the defences of the only safe anchorage in the island, and which has always been a place of shelter for their cruizers and prizes when prevented from entering the ports of the Isle of France, besides the rescue of property to an immense amount out of the hands of the enemy.

It is impossible for me to do justice to, or sufficiently express the high sense I entertain of the gallantry and skill of Lieutenant-colonel Keating, which were equally conspicuous in planning and conducting this affair; and the bravery shewn by the troops in successively carrying the batteries, was eminently distinguished. . . .

On the morning of the 22d we could have but little communication with the shore, on account of the surf on the beach, but we observed the enemy collecting on the heights, and in the afternoon they appeared in force, advancing towards the town from St. Denis, upon which it was considered advisable by Lieutenant-colonel Keating and myself, to destroy the stores containing the public property. From the state of the surf on the beach, the marines were selected for this service, with a small party of seamen, and Captain Willoughby again volunteered his services on the occasion: the Lieutenant-colonel himself accompanied the party, and a large and valuable magazine, the only one we could ascertain to be public property, was fired, and the party re-embarked without loss. On the morning of the 23d, the troops, marines, and seamen, all in boats, were in readiness to land under cover of the *Nereide*, when we were informed that the enemy, under the command of General de Bruleys, had retreated to St. Denis in the night. The Commandant St. Michiel being disposed to negotiate, the Lieutenant-colonel and myself agreed to sign the terms, of which the enclosed is a copy, since which time the troops and seamen have been actively employed in shipping the property found in the public stores, consisting of provisions and some ordnance stores, and a part of the cargoes of the captured indiamen, which had not been fired at the same time as the others, on the supposition of its being private property; the cargoes of the indiamen alone being valued by them at three millions of dollars.

As the captains of the captured indiamen were found in the place, I have replaced them in their former situations, with such of their people as we can collect, and are fitting their ships for sea. A strong party has also been employed completing the destruction of the batteries, by bursting the guns and mortars, or heaving them off into deep water, carrying off the shot and shells, &c. . . .

I have, &c.

J. ROWLEY

To Vice-admiral Bertie, &c.

[Rowley's account of this raid was supported by one sent by Henry S Keating, Lieutenant-Colonel, 56th Regiment, and Governor of Rodriguez, to Fras Warden, Esq, Chief Secretary to the Government, Bombay, 29 September 1809, which was published, with the articles of capitulation, in Vol. XXIII, pp256-258.]

From the 'Naval History of the Present Year,' 1810
January-February. XXIII 147-148

Spanish Defeat in Andalusia

The French army, under Marshal Soult, having succeeded in the important object of passing the Sierra Moreua, have penetrated into the province of Andalusia; the Spaniards have been defeated, with considerable loss; the enemy have obtained possession of Cordova, and of Seville; the Supreme Junta - several of the members of which were suspected of treason - have been dispersed; a new Junta, or rather a Council of Regency, has been assembled at Cadiz; and a formidable Spanish army, amounting, as it is said, to 23,000 men, under the Duke of Albuquerque, being in that city and its environs, the most vigorous measures have been adopted for its defence. The batteries, which commanded the harbour, have been destroyed; and, to prevent the Spanish fleet from falling into the hands of the French, should they obtain possession of Cadiz, it has been moored outside of the British squadron. - The city is crowded with fugitives, to the number, as it is reported, of 100,000; who fled from Seville, and other places, on the approach of the French. Several families are known to have left Cadiz, for England; and every facility has been given for the escape of those whom necessity or choice compelled to fly.

Assistance Sent from Gibraltar

A detachment of 1,200 English troops has been sent from Gibraltar, to assist the Spaniards in the defence of Cadiz.

Another detachment of troops, from Gibraltar, has taken possession of the Island of Ceuta.

The French, it is believed, expected to surprise Cadiz; and it is conjectured that the Toulon fleet, which is understood to have sailed from Toulon on the 22d of January, had an intention of co-operating with the army, in the attack upon that place. A report, however, was very prevalent, when this sheet was put to press, that Lord Collingwood had overtaken the enemy, on the 24th or 25th, totally defeated them, and captured or destroyed nearly every ship. The British and French fleets were estimated at sixteen sail of the line each.

Portugal

The British government, it appears, persist in its intention of defending Portugal. Lord Wellington, in addition to his *double* peerage, and the thanks of Parliament, is to have an annuity of £2,000 for himself and his two next heirs, for the *victory* of Talavera!!

Corfu

The English are understood to have taken possession of the island of St. Vito, which commands the harbour of Corfu.

Black Sea

An English squadron is understood to be blockading the Russian ports in the Black Sea.

Revolt in South America

A revolution, favourable to the cause of Ferdinand the VIIth, has taken place at La Paz, the centre of the Spanish dominions in South America. The consequences of this event are likely to be favourable to the commerce of Britain; the South American ports having been thrown open on liberal terms.

Report of the Scheldt Expedition Published

The attention of the public has been for some time much occupied by the inquiry which is going forward respecting the Scheldt Expedition. The papers which have been laid before Parliament upon the subject, have reached an extent almost unprecedentedly voluminous; notwithstanding which, we hope, in the course of the present volume, to present our readers with a full and faithful abstract of their contents, of the examinations of the witnesses, and of the consequent debates in Parliament.

Strachan to Demand Court Martial

It is reported that Sir Richard Strachan, in consequence of some oblique reflections on the naval part of the expedition, in Lord Chatham's narrative, intends to demand a court martial upon his conduct.

It is remarkable also, that Sir Richard Keats's evidence is materially at variance with the statements of his lordship.

February–March. XXIII 244-246
Guadaloupe Captured

In the midst of this political warfare, Captain Wilby, aide-de-camp to Lieutenant-general Sir George Beckwith, commanding his Majesty's forces in the Windward and Leeward Islands, arrived on the 15th of March, with an account of the capture of the valuable island of Guadaloupe. The expedition, with the squadron under the command of Vice-admiral the Honourable Sir Alexander Cochrane, sailed from Martinique on the 22d of January, and the result was in every respect most honourable to the enterprise and valour of our brave countrymen. We only trust, that we shall be able to retain the valuable acquisitions we have again wrested from the French, who have now received a death blow to their West India commerce. It will also enable us to keep the Americans in

View of Ape's Hill, on the Barbary coast. Engraved by Baily, from a drawing by
Bennet.

As a naval and military station, Ceuta is of more importance than Gibraltar, and is,
in fact, the key of the strait; inasmuch as the navigation thereof is carried on nearer
to the African than to the European shore.

For this place, by a suitable equivalent, it would, in the opinion of many, be highly
desirable to effect an exchange with Spain, when saved from French sovereignty.
Gibraltar, perhaps, important as it is, might be offered; for it is a possession of more
glory than advantage; and, in our hands, will ever, under a settled order of things, be
a bar to cordial connection between the two nations. This consideration appears to
deserve the notice of the English ministry. A project was on foot, for possessing
ourselves of Ceuta, by a *coup de main*, in 1808; but, being too long delayed - as is
frequently the case, in this country of deliberation and preparation, where the
phrase, "secret expedition," means any thing rather than secret or expeditious - it
proved abortive. [Plate 377]

check, inasmuch as all their favourite and lucrative trade with the West Indies, must
now pass through our hands.

When the *Hazard* left Guadaloupe, the French frigate *Nereide*, of the largest class,
which escaped from St. Maloes some time ago, hove in sight off Basseterre, where two
of our frigates and two sloops were lying at anchor; discovering the island to be in our
possession, she stood back, which our squadron perceiving, immediately slipped their
cables, and all four were in close pursuit when the *Hazard* came away, and there is little
doubt of her being captured.

[Vice Admiral Cochrane's service letter recounting this action was published in
Vol. XXIII, pp339-344.]

Porchester Proposes Vote of Censure on Scheldt Expedition

On Monday, the 26th of March, Lord Porchester, agreeable to notice, brought forward a string of resolutions in censure of the Scheldt expedition; exonerating both the navy and army from blame. Lord Castlereagh spoke in defence of the policy and conduct of the expedition, and was followed by Mr. Ponsonby on the other side. On the 27th the debate was resumed, and General Craufo[u]rd moved an amendment to Lord Porchester's resolution, in favour of ministers. Another adjournment took place, and the debate was again resumed on the 29th; the House having been occupied the whole of the preceding evening respecting a libelous breach of privilege committed by Sir F. Burdett, in a publication concerning the committal of J.G. Jones to Newgate, for contempt of Parliament. - Lord Chatham had some time previously resigned, in consequence of a vote of censure passed on him by the House of Commons. . . .

Baltic

The French, it is said, are about to take possession of the ports of the Baltic. For the purpose, as we presume, of counteracting this measure, an expedition is now fitting out at Yarmouth.

The Electorate of Hanover was formally annexed to the Kingdom of Westphalia, on the 1st of March. . . .

Threat to Gibraltar?

It is conjectured, that, should the French succeed in making themselves masters of Cadiz, their next attempt will be upon Gibraltar. In contemplation of this, every precaution has been used to ensure the safety of that fortress. - A very formidable expedition has for some time been fitting out, the naval command of which is to be entrusted to Sir Sidney Smith and Commodore Owen. In the opinion of some, it is destined to assist in the protection of Gibraltar; but, according to others, it has in view some important object in South America. If it be not necessary for the defence of Gibraltar, we should be better pleased if it were going to the Mauritius; the capture of which would deprive Buonaparte of the *last* of his "colonies and commerce."

American Negotiations Look Happier

The relations between Great Britain and America have assumed a favourable aspect. Lieutenant Elliott, in the *John Adams* frigate, sailed from Cowes about the 26th of March, with the *project* of a plan for the adjustment of all differences between the two countries, drawn up by the Marquis Wellesley and Mr. Pinckney. The disposition of the inhabitants of the United States also appears to be more amicable than formerly; and a circumstance which will probably operate forcibly in our favour is, that Buonaparte has sequestrated and ordered for sale all the American property in France. General Armstrong, after ineffectually remonstrating against this measure, is said to have demanded his passports.

Russian Ships at Trieste and Venice to French Marine

A letter from Trieste states, that the Russian fleet, which has been ceded by Russia to France, consists of four sail of the line, besides frigates and corvettes. These vessels are partly at Trieste, and partly at Venice. The Russian crews have already set out on their return home, and the French have taken possession of the vessels.

Treaty Between France and Holland
Naval State Papers. XXIII 471-472

Article I. Until the English government shall have solemnly revoked the restrictions contained in their Orders in Council of 1807, all kinds of trade between the ports of Holland and the ports of England are prohibited. If there should be occasion for granting licenses, those only shall be valid which are issued in the name of the Emperor.

II. A corps of troops of 18,000 men, (including 3,000 cavalry) and consisting of 6,000 French and 12,000 Dutchmen, shall be distributed at all the mouths of rivers, along with officers of the French customs, in order to take care that the stipulation in the above article be fulfilled. . . .

VIII. His Majesty the King of Holland shall, in order to co-operate with the force of the French empire, have a squadron of nine ships of the line and six frigates, armed, provisioned for six months, and ready for sea on the 1st of July next; and shall also have prepared a flotilla of 100 gun-boats, or other armed vessels. This force must be maintained during the whole period of the war, and kept constantly in a state of readiness.

Inquiry into the Scheldt Disaster
Imperial Parliament
House of Commons, Friday January 26, 1810. XXIII 152-153

Lord *Porchester* rose for the purpose of moving, that a committee be appointed to inquire into the conduct and policy of the Expedition to the Scheldt. His reason for going first into an inquiry into this precious specimen of the military plans of ministers was, that it was the most calamitous of any. A great deal of boasting had been made about the wonderful exploits achieved at Walcheren - about the destroying a Dutch dock, and the blowing up of a Dutch sluice. But it happened that the enemy spoke differently, and had had the impudence to tell ministers no injury had been done which could not be speedily repaired. It was said, that this expedition was intended principally as a diversion in favour of Austria. After the fatal battle of the 6th of July, the armistice followed on the 12th, and it was after this we chose to administer assistance to the dead. It was after this we proceeded, by an expedition to Walcheren, to relieve Austria, who was fallen never to rise again! The expedition was sent to a place where it could be of no service to Austria; where it was impossible the diversion could extend beyond the first *coup-de-main* at landing. The place was the very worst that could be chosen for such an expedition. Why was not Antwerp the first object of attack? For it was not until a month after the sailing of the expedition, that a consultation was held on the propriety of our movement against Antwerp; but our wise men thought it better to try the effect of a sudden attack, after a month's notice given to the enemy. He now came to the worst part of all. When the expedition to Antwerp was abandoned, why were the soldiers left to fall victims to pestilence? Why did ministers, instead of evacuating Walcheren, make costly preparations to maintain it? How could this serve Austria? Would Buonaparte have given less favourable terms to Austria, had our troops been withdrawn? No, certainly not. Next, as to that most important point, the selection of a commander, he would ask, without any disparagement to Lord Chatham, why did not ministers confide the army to some experienced veteran, in whom the army confided. He could not, however, but approve of the appointment of one of their own body to command the expedition, when he considered how such an ill-judged plan might ruin the fame of an able general. If ever there was a time when it became the House to call loudly for inquiry, it was the present. Therefore, for England's honour and England's security, let an inquiry be voted; and let something be done which would animate the hope of an expiring world. The Noble Lord concluded with moving, that the House would resolve itself into a Committee to inquire into the Expedition to the Scheldt.

[The House divided, with a small majority of members, 195 to 186, approving the inquiry, which opened in Committee of the Whole House on 2 February 1810. On 5 February a Secret Committee was appointed by the House to view confidential communications (Vol. XXIII, pp158-161).]

Monday, February 12. *XXIII 162*

Mr. *Hutchinson* observed, that the great object of the late expedition was to destroy the enemy's arsenals at Antwerp, together with the ships of war which were stationed there, as well as those on the stocks. Now it appeared, that on the 29th of August last, the Earl of Chatham wrote to ministers, that the possession of Antwerp could only be obtained by a regular siege, to which his army was unequal, and that without the fall of that fortress, the ulterior object of the expedition, the destruction of the French fleet, was placed beyond our reach. He could scarcely believe it possible that ministers could have determined on the expedition, without knowing the defences of Antwerp. If they were ignorant of its being a fortified place, their ignorance was grossly culpable; but if they knew it to be a fortress completely defensible, their idea of taking it by a *coup-de-main* was ridiculous, and their whole plan culpable in the extreme. He wished, therefore, that all the information of which ministers were possessed, relative to the nature and plan of the defences of Antwerp should be laid before the House; being persuaded that on this very point the whole policy of the expedition would turn. The honourable member concluded by moving - 1st, for any plan or plans in the possession of ministers of the fortifications of Antwerp; 2dly, the same with regard to Forts Lillo and Liefkenshoek; the substance of all the intelligence possessed by ministers, relative to the defences of Antwerp.

[On 23 February the Commons debated the propriety of Lord Chatham's giving the King an account of his proceedings which was not passed to him through a Secretary of State. This constitutional irregularity led to Chatham's resignation as Master-General of the Ordnance (Vol. XXIII, pp330-336).]

House of Commons, Monday, March 26, 1810. *XXIII 423-425*

Lord *Porchester*, pursuant to notice, moved the following resolutions, respecting the Scheldt expedition; previously to which, in a speech of great length, he entered into an extensive review of the origin, progress, and failure, of that disastrous undertaking. . . . [Resolution VI and VII reprinted above at p287.]

VIII. That the expedition to the Scheldt was undertaken under circumstances which afforded no rational hope of adequate success, and at the precise season of the year, when the malignant disease, which has proved so fatal to his Majesty's brave troops, was known to be most prevalent; and that the advisers of this ill-judged enterprise are, in the opinion of this House, deeply responsible for the heavy calamities with which its failure has been attended.

[A separate set of resolutions condemned the administration for delaying the withdrawal from Walcheren. The House, however, after five days of debate, preferred a motion of General *Craufurd* approving the actions of the administration and lamenting the loss of lives.]

House of Lords, Friday, June 1 1810. *XXIII 503*

Earl *Darnley*, after expatiating on the calamitous result of the Walcheren Expedition, and stating that we had lost no less than 20,000 men by it, moved for returns to be laid before the House, of all the persons that had been afflicted with the Walcheren sickness; that had been recovered and again relapsed; and the number of those now in a state of convalescence; distinguishing each class, from the 1st of January to the 1st of June 1810. - Ordered.

Portuguese Subsidy Announced
House of Lords, Friday, February 16 1810. *XXIII 247*

Marquis Wellesley brought down a message from his Majesty, informing their lordships that his Majesty had entered into an arrangement respecting Portugal, by which he had agreed to advance pecuniary succours for the support of an army of Portuguese troops, not exceeding 30,000 men.

Addenda to the Biographical Memoir of the Late Right Honourable Cuthbert Lord Collingwood, Vice-Admiral of the Red Squadron XXIII 379-382

In the biographical memoir of Lord Collingwood, which appears in the XVth Volume of our Chronicle, the professional services of his lordship, previously to, and at, the glorious battle of Trafalgar, are fully recorded. Subsequently to that period, his public career is well known; and, to repeat the substance of his Lordship's "Letters on Service," which have been already faithfully registered in various parts of our work, would be altogether superfluous. The following original letter from Lord Collingwood, comprising that epitome of his services, from which our memoir was chiefly drawn up, will, however, we doubt not, be regarded as a valuable document.

Mr. Joyce Gold, publisher of the Naval Chronicle
Queen, at Sea, 7th January, 1806
Sir, You have really made a request to me, that notwithstanding I have every desire to comply with your wish, I find great difficulty in; that is, in writing any thing relating to myself, that can be very interesting or entertaining to the public: - my life has been a continued service at sea, but unmarked by any of those extraordinary events, or brilliant scenes, which hold men up to particular attention, and distinguish them from those officers who are zealous, and anxious for the public service.

I went into the navy at a very early period of my life, in the year 1761, in the *Shannon*, under the protection and care of a kind friend and relation, the late Admiral Braithwaite, to whose regard for me, and the interest he took in whatever related to my improvement in nautical knowledge, I owe great obligations: I served with him many years, and afterwards with Admiral Roddam. - In 1774 I went to Boston with Admiral Graves, and in 1775 was made a lieutenant by him on the day the battle was fought at Bunker's Hill, where I was with a party of seamen, supplying the army with what was necessary to them. In 1776 I went to Jamaica lieutenant of the *Hornet* sloop, and soon after the *Lowestoffe* came to the same station, of which Lord Nelson was lieutenant; we had been long before in the habits of great friendship, and it happened here that Admiral Sir Peter Parker, the commander-in-chief, being the friend of both, whenever Lord Nelson got a step in rank, I succeeded him; first in the *Lowestoffe*, then in the *Badger*, into which ship I was made a commander in 1779, and afterwards the *Hinchinbroke*, a 28-gun frigate, which made us both post captains: the *Hinchinbroke* was in the spring of 1780 employed on an expedition to the Spanish main, where it was proposed, by the River San Juan, and the Lakes Nicaragua and Leon, to pass by a navigation of boats into the South Sea. The plan was formed without a sufficient knowledge of the country, which presented difficulties that were not to be surmounted by human skill or perseverance. The river was difficult to proceed on from the rapidity of the current, and the several falls over the rocks, which intercepted the navigation, and the climate was deadly; no constitution could resist its effects. At the port of San Juan I joined the *Hinchinbroke*, and succeeded Lord Nelson, who was promoted to a larger ship: but he had received the infection of the climate before he went from the port, and had a fever from which he could not recover until he quitted his ship, and went to England: my constitution resisted many attacks, and I survived most of my ship's company, having buried in four months 180 of the 200 which composed it. Mine was not a singular case, all the ships that were as long there suffered in the same degree: the transports' men all died, and some of the ships having none left to take care of them, sunk in the harbour; but transport ships were not wanted, for the troops they brought were no more; they had fallen, not by the hand of an enemy, but sunk under the contagion of the climate. From this scene I was relieved in August 1780, and in December following was appointed to the command of the *Pelican*, a small frigate of 24 guns. In August the following year, a severe hurricane blew, in which she was wrecked, being cast on the rocks of the Morant Keys, in the middle of a most tremendous night; the next day with great difficulty the ship's company got on shore on rafts, made of the small and broken yards, and on those small sandy hills, with little food and water, we remained ten days, until a boat went to Jamaica, and the *Diamond* frigate came and took us off.

The ship I next commanded was the *Sampson*, of 64 guns, which ship at the peace of 1783 being paid off, I was appointed to the *Mediator*, and went to the West Indies, where, with Lord Nelson, who then commanded the *Boreas* on the same station, I remained until the latter end of 1786. From 1786 to 1790, I was in Northumberland, making my acquaintance with my own family, to whom I had hitherto been as it were a stranger. In 1790 an armament being prepared against Spain, I was appointed to the command of the *Mermaid*, and went to the West Indies with Admiral Cornish; but affairs with Spain and Russia being accommodated, and no prospect of having employment at sea again soon, I went into the North, and was married, and thought I was settling myself in great comfort; but I was mistaken; for in eighteen months the French war broke out, and in 1793 I was appointed captain of the *Prince*, Rear-admiral Bowyer's flag-ship, and served with him until he was wounded in the action of the 1st of June, in the *Barfleur*. After that ship I commanded the *Hector* and *Excellent*, in which ship I went to the Mediterranean, blockading Toulon; and in this ship I was on the 14th of February, 1797, in the action off Cape St. Vincent; in 1799 I was appointed to the rank of rear-admiral, and soon after hoisted my flag in the *Triumph*, in which ship and the *Barfleur* I served until the end of the war.

On the re-commencement of hostilities I was again employed in the Channel fleet, in a variety of ships, by which means I was always in a complete one, without having the inconvenience of quitting my station for the purpose of replenishing.

In May, 1805, I was appointed to command a squadron on foreign service. I remained before Cadiz, maintaining the blockade of that port, until Lord Nelson superseded me in my command in September last.

In this sketch of my life you may perceive, Sir, how great a part of it has been spent at sea; since the year 1793, I have only been one year at home; to my own children I am scarce known; yet while I have health and strength to serve my country, I consider *that* health and strength due to it; and if I serve it successfully, as I have ever done faithfully, my children will not want friends.

I am, Sir, your most obedient, and very humble servant,

COLLINGWOOD

P.S. Mr. Bowyer, at the Historic Gallery, Pall Mall, has my miniature portrait.

Lord Collingwood's Coffin

From 'Naval Anecdotes.' XXIII 448

It is proper to be recorded, that the remains of Lord Collingwood are deposited in the very stone coffin which Cardinal Wolsey had prepared for himself. It had remained, as lumber, in a room adjoining St. George's Chapel, Windsor; and for its last purpose was given as a present by his Majesty.

Correspondence on the Honourific Rank of 'General of Marines' XXIII 398-400

To the Right Honourable S. Perceval
Sir, By the decease of Lord Collingwood, the sinecure appointment of Major-general of Marines has become vacant, and as on former occasions, has been filled up by an admiral.

At such a period as the present, it might have been supposed, before you resolved to gratify any sentiment of private inclination, to which this vacancy in your patronage might give rise, that as a minister you would have paused before you determined on the revival of the above useless, and it may be said, contemptible appointment; useless it cannot be denied, inasmuch as there is not the execution of even a shadow of duty to plead in its behalf; and in point of fact it has no more reference to the useful corps of which it bears the name, than it has to the Archbishop of Canterbury . . . [etc.]
May 10th A. TEMPLAR

From the 'Naval History of the Present Year,' 1810
April-May. XXIII 420-422

Cadiz Continues to Resist the French

Cadiz still holds out against the French. On the morning of the 21st of April, however, the enemy opened a most heavy and destructive fire upon the Matagorda fort, from masked batteries, mounting twenty-one 24 pounders and nine mortars. The fire was returned with the utmost vigour and effect. The defence of the fort of Matagorda was entrusted to a party of British troops and sailors: it is situated in the main land, opposite to Port Puntal, and in a great measure commands the entrance to Puntal Roads. The Spanish colours, of course, were kept flying; but the men, during the heat of the cannonade, kept up constantly calling out, "Up with the British colours." - About noon on the 21st, the flag-staff was shot away, and then there was a general cry for the hoisting of the English colours. The fire kept up by the French was so destructive, that it was necessary to evacuate the fort about noon on the 22d, after considerable loss had been sustained. . . .

Hood Escorts Fleeing Spanish Three-Deckers

Advices from Carthagena, dated the 24th of April, state, that through the exertions of Colonel Roche, two Spanish three-deckers, namely, the *San Carlos*, and *Ferdinand VII* of 130 guns each, have been saved from falling into the hands of the enemy, who, 8000 strong, entered Murcia on the 23d, and on the following day were within six leagues of Carthagena. In aid of this important service, Sir Samuel Hood sent from Minorca, at the request of Colonel Roche, the *Hibernia* and *Northumberland* ships of the line, which escorted the Spanish ships either to Minorca or Gibraltar.

St Maura Captured

An expedition consisting of upwards of 2,000 men, under the command of General Oswald, sailed from Zante against St. Maura (the ancient Leucadia) on the 29th of March. It surrendered, after ten days' bombardment, and the French commander, General Camus, and 22 officers, were conveyed by an English flag of truce to Brendisi.

[Service Letters from Admiral Sir Charles Cotton and Captain George Eyre were published in Vol. XXIV, pp165-168.]

Turkish Vessels Seized at Trieste

In pursuance of the plan for attacking Turkey, the whole of the Turkish vessels, in the port of Trieste, have lately been seized and sequestrated. The Ottoman government has, nevertheless, expressed its intention of maintaining, inviolate, its treaty with Great Britain. . . .

Maltese Government to Army

One of the last acts of Lord Mulgrave's naval administration, if we mistake not, was to take the government of Malta (on Admiral Sir R.G. Keates [Keats] declining it) from the profession to which it had been so judiciously entrusted by the late Lord Nelson, and to assign it to the army; with whom it will probably now in future remain. We have also heard, and from no common authority, that his lordship had contemplated the same alteration in what has hitherto been the naval government of Newfoundland. Such things must ensure, when a general is placed at the head of our naval department, he naturally feels a superior interest for his own profession.

Good Man Needed for Collingwood Replacement - Editorial

Much might be said, and we trust some of our Naval Correspondents will take up the subject, respecting the necessity of sending not only an experienced seaman, but also an able statesman, to take the command in the Mediterranean.

May-June. XXIII 500-502

Swedish Crown Prince Dies

The Prince of Augustenburgh, known of late as the Crown Prince, and intended heir of the Swedish usurper, was seized by an apoplexy, while reviewing some corps of cavalry, on the 29th of April; in consequence of which, he fell from his horse, in the front of the line, and instantly expired. It is conjectured, that this event will facilitate the expected revolution in favour of the family of Gustavus. The daughter of Lucien Buonaparte is said to have been destined for the wife of the Crown Prince, had he lived. The Duke of Oldenburgh, a near relation of the Emperor of Russia, it is now reported, will be declared heir to the Swedish throne. In the mean time, a coolness, if not an actual feeling of hostility, appears to have taken place between France and Sweden. In consequence of the King of Sweden having refused to exclude British ships of war from his ports, and to suffer French consuls to reside there, a considerable quantity of Swedish property has been sequestrated in France. On the other hand, Sir James Saumarez maintains the strictest blockade of all the ports in the Baltic, not suffering any ship, of any nation, to enter them without a British license.

New French Naval Operation in the Wind

Buonaparte, having terminated a tour of naval inspection along the French and Dutch coasts, returned to Paris on the 1st of June. He is supposed to have some maritime enterprise in contemplation. Great preparations are said to be making in the French and Dutch ports; the Toulon squadron has some time been reported ready for sea; considerable activity is represented as prevailing in the dock-yards at Venice; the Russian ships of war, which were ceded to France, have been repaired; and, from the continued intercourse which is maintained between the courts of France, Russia, and Denmark, it almost appears, as though a new Northern Confederacy were forming. We wish it may be so; as, in all probability, we shall then be furnished with another opportunity of punishing the temerity of the Emperor and King. Sir Richard Strachan is keeping a sharp look-out off Flushing; where the enemy's force is said to consist of four line-of-battle ships, one frigate, two praams and nineteen brigs, all apparently ready for sea.

Prisoners of War

The terms for an exchange of prisoners, between England and France, are understood to have been finally agreed upon.

Cadiz Still Resists French Siege

The last accounts from Cadiz, speak of the means which that city possesses for its defence, and of the condition of the allied army, in terms as satisfactory as could reasonably be expected. The enemy have opened their batteries on the Trocadero against Puntales, but without effect; and it appears to be the general opinion, that they cannot do much mischief to the town from Matagorda. The communication between the garrison by water, with the Caraccas, is perfectly established and secure. The fear of the want of water no longer exists. A spring has been discovered, pure in its quality, and so abundant as to be sufficient for the demand, if the inhabitants were increased to three times their present number. At the end of May, the force in Cadiz amounted exactly to 6,500 British, 1,500 Portuguese, and 11,000 Spanish troops. An addition of 4,000 Spaniards was then hourly expected from Alicant, and not only these reinforcements have since arrived, but a fresh arrival has increased the British force, and carried it to full 7,000 men, making the whole about 24,000; a large force no doubt, but not numerous enough to cope with the enemy, should they succeed in collecting the numbers which it is apprehended they intend to employ in the siege. In the mean time, most of the works are finished, and the whole were expected to be completed about the beginning of July; and then the island of Leon would be as strong as it is well possible for art to make it. Government have received despatches from Curaçoa, announcing that a revolution has been effected in South America, extending from the valuable settlement of Vera Cruz, along the adjacent isthmus, to the southern extremity of the Caraccas . . .

US Repeals Non-Intercourse Act

The American government has at length recovered its senses so far, as to repeal the Non-intercourse Act. British ships of war continue to be prohibited from entering the American ports; but our merchantmen are to be allowed a free trade, at least until the next meeting of Congress; unless, in the interim, France should revoke her Decrees, and Britain should afterwards refuse to rescind her Orders in Council. But, of this, there can be no reasonable apprehension; for, as the British Orders in Council were measures merely retaliative on those Decrees, the removal of the former would naturally follow that of the latter. The president of the United States is, however, invested with the power of renewing the Non-intercourse Act, against either of the Belligerent Powers, which might refuse to rescind its restrictive acts, after the Decrees of its opponent had been annulled. It must now, we conceive, be admitted, that the repeal of the Non-intercourse Act furnishes the most decisive proof of the wisdom and efficacy of the British Orders in Council; for, could the Americans, by any means, have evaded them, they never would have conceded a point on which they had laid so great a stress. Our ports will now shortly be crowded with American traders; a circumstance particularly favourable, as, in consequence of a deficiency of grain in France, its exportation from that country has been prohibited.

Canadian Revolt Suppressed

An insurrectionary spirit, in Canada, we are happy to find, has been quelled, without any serious mischief.

French Horror in Sumatra

The East India Company's settlement of Tappanoolly, on the coast of Sumatra, was captured by the French on the 12th of April. The circumstances attending the capture, were so unjust, cruel, and atrocious, that, should the knowledge of them reach the French government, it is to be hoped, a severe punishment will be inflicted on the perpetrators.

Promotions and Appointments [XXIII 517]

Yeo

The Gazette of June 2 contains his Majesty's permission to Sir James Lucas Yeo, Knt. commander of the royal Portuguese military order of St. Bento d'Avis, to assume certain armorial bearings, in honorary compensation for his gallant conduct at various times, but particularly in attacking the town and fort of El Muros, on the coast of Spain, on the 4th of June, 1805. He led this attack with 50 men against 250, killed the governor with his own hand, and compelled the enemy to surrender. His Majesty has since been pleased to confer upon him the order of British knighthood. . . .

Calder

Vice-admiral Sir Robert Calder, Bart. is appointed commander-in-chief at Plymouth, *vice* Admiral Young.

[Volume XXIV was dedicated to Sir Robert Calder. On 31 July 1810 Calder was promoted to Admiral of the Blue Squadron (Vol. XXIV, p169). And the opening entry in volume XXV, the Memoir of the Public Serices of Captain Henry Inman, had an extended passage criticising the condemnation of Calder. In Vol. XXVII, pp441-452 appeared an 'Additional Biographical Memoir' of Calder, giving more detail of his early career.]

From the 'Naval History of the Present Year,' 1810
June-July. XXIV 66-72

Louis Napoleon Abdicates Throne of the Netherlands

The abdication of King Louis, which took place by proclamation, on the 1st of July, is an event of some importance to the naval interest of this country. The motives assigned by Louis for this act are, that the unfortunate state of Holland arose from the displeasure which his brother Napoleon had conceived against him; that all his endeavours to remove that displeasure, or to meliorate the sufferings of his subjects, had been unavailing; that he considered himself to be the only obstacle to the termination of the differences which subsisted between France and Holland, and to the return of his brother's *good-will* to the latter country.

The abdication was in favour of Louis's eldest son, Napoleon Louis, or, in default of him, of his second son, Charles Louis Napoleon. The young Prince being a minor, the Queen was declared Regent, to be assisted by a Council of Regency.

Netherlands Annexed to France

Agreeably to an arrangement, announced at the time of King Louis's abdication, a number of French troops entered Amsterdam, without resistance, on the 4th of July; and, as was anticipated, the absolute annexation of Holland to France almost immediately followed. A *Senatus Consultum* to the following effect, received the formal sanction of Buonaparte on the 10th: the Dutch territory to form a component part of the French empire; the Duke of Placenza (Le Brun) to be president of the council for the government of Holland; one-third of the revenues of the country to be applied to the extinction of the Dutch national debt; and, ranking after Paris and Rome, Amsterdam to be the third city of the French empire.

Louis's abdication appears to have been his own voluntary act and deed, without the sanction, or even privity, of his brother. He privately disappeared from Amsterdam, on the night of July 12th. He was at first thought to have escaped to Tonnigen, where he meant to take shipping for America; but later accounts mention, that he has joined his brother Jerome, at Cassel. . . .

View of Southampton Pier. Engraved by Baily from a Drawing by Bennet. Plate 485

Commercial Treaty with Brazil

A commercial treaty has been concluded between his Britannic Majesty and the Prince of Brazils, which is highly advantageous to the commercial interests of this country. British subjects and shipping are put upon the same footing as those of Portugal. We are at liberty to trade with St. Catherine's, Goa, and, in short, with all the Portuguese possessions in every part of the world ...

Spanish America Declares Independence

The supreme government of the Caraccas, as it is now denominated, have issued a proclamation, declaring South America independent of Spain, and of every other European or foreign power. It appears, however, from a Caraccas gazette of May 11, that future obedience is promised to the parent state, should Spain be rescued from the grasp of Buonaparte, and a consultation be formed, connecting America with the European monarchy, on the basis of equal liberties and laws. The district of Maracaybo and Coro, in the province of Venezuela, continue their allegiance to Ferdinand VII.

America

The *John Adams* frigate, with despatches from Mr. Pinkney and General Armstrong (the American ministers at London and Paris) have safely reached America.

July–August. *XXIV 154-156*

French Replace Berlin System with Tarifs

Were it not that no confidence whatsoever can be placed in the conduct of so unprincipled a tyrant, we should be induced, from some recent occurrences, to augur favourably of Buonaparte's future intentions. On the 5th of August, he issued a decree, allowing the importation of colonial produce; and though the importation duties which he has imposed, are exceedingly heavy, they are not so oppressive, considering the nature of the articles, and the want of them which prevails in France, as to prevent very extensive purchases. This decree is, of itself, a virtual abrogation of the famous Berlin and Milan edicts; and, consequently, it affords a complete and decisive triumph to the operations of the British orders in council, which were simply retaliative on those edicts: coupled with this measure, however, and bearing the same date, is an official letter from the French Minister of foreign affairs to General Armstrong, the American Ambassador at Paris, expressly announcing, "That the decrees of Berlin and Milan *are* revoked; and that from the 1st of November, they will cease to be in force; it being understood, that, in consequence of this declaration, the English shall revoke their orders in council, and *renounce the new principles of blockade* which they have attempted to establish"; or, that the United States, conformably to the act of Congress of the 1st of May, "shall cause their rights to be respected by the English." . . .

British Licenses Available for Exporters

Profiting by the facilities thus offered, we understand that British licenses, allowing the exportation of sugar, coffee, &c. are ready for delivery; the imports in return to consist of wheat, meal, burr-stones, and one third of each cargo, of wine. Government is said to have refused brandies, which Buonaparte intended should form part of the return cargoes.

Prisoners of War

Another circumstance, which, if it bear not an absolutely pacific aspect, must be considered as a material relaxation of the unnecessary severities of war, is the arrangement for a general exchange of prisoners between this country and France, which is now understood to have been finally settled. . . .

Algiers at War with France

The Dey of Algiers has declared war against France.

Anholt to be Defended

The island of Anholt, in the Baltic, which has been for some time in our possession, is to be strengthened by every possible means, so as to be capable of repelling any attack that may be made on it by the Danes. Captain Maurice, of the navy, who distinguished himself in the defence of the Diamond Rock in the West Indies, is appointed to the command of this post, which is likely to become one of great importance.

Milford Haven Dockyard Abandoned?

At Milford Haven an order has been received from the navy-board to discharge the workmen on the new dock-yard walls and other buildings, which has spread a general gloom over that place, lest its rising prosperity should be checked by so unexpected a measure. Various surmises are naturally formed, some thinking it probable that the dock-yard will be removed to the opposite side of the haven; others that it will be abandoned altogether, in consequence of the new project of a naval arsenal at Northfleet.

[The plan to develop a facility at Northfleet was later abandoned, when it was decided to construct a mole at Plymouth to increase the anchorage there. See 'Naval Literature', review of 'Twelve Letters, addressed to the Right Honourable Spencer Perceval. . .' by James Manderson, Esq, Captain in the Royal Navy (Vol. XXVIII, pp143-147).]

First Lord Inspects Sheerness

On Friday, the 27th of July, the Right Honourable Mr. Yorke, First Lord of the Admiralty, accompanied by his brother Sir J.S. Yorke, one of the junior Lords, arrived at Sheerness. The next morning Admiral Stanhope hoisted the Admiralty flag, when the ships at the Great and Little Nore saluted with 19 guns. Mr. Yorke and his brother minutely examined every part of the dock-yard, for the purpose of determining if the alterations shall take place that were recommended. At three o'clock they went out of harbour in the Commissioner's yacht, and proceeded up the River Thames, when every ship at the Great and Little Nore saluted as they passed with 19 guns.

State of Forces at Cadiz

The following are the English ships now at Cadiz: *Temeraire*, of 98 guns, Rear-admiral Pickmore; *Tonnant*, of 80, Captain Stackpoole; *Blake*, 74, Captain Codrington; *Rodney*, 74, Captain Burlton; *Eagle*, 74, Captain Rowley; *Achille*, 74, Sir Richard King; *Zealous*, 74, Captain Boys; *Atlas*, 74, Captain Saunders; and *l'Impetueux*, 74, Captain Lawford.

The following is the present state of the Spanish Navy here.

AT CADIZ

Santa Anna	120	St. Pablo	74
Prin. D'Asturias	120	St. Justo	74
Neptuno*	80	L'Asia	70
Algesiras*	74	St. Julian	60
L'Heroe*	74	La Prueba	40
Pluton*	74	Atocha	40
Glorrio (very old)	74		

Conde de Ragla (unserviceable) 125

The *Venditor*, and another of two decks, prison ships, are reparable.

* Formerly French, of Rosilly's squadron.

AT SEA, FROM THIS PORT

St. Elmo	74	El Minto	50
St. Lorenzo	74	A frigate	40
St. Fulgentio	74		

At Gibraltar, two First Rates.

August–September. *XXIV 245-253*

Amboyna Captured

We have the satisfaction of announcing, that, on Monday the 24th of September, Captain Buchanan, of the Royal Navy, arrived at the Admiralty, with despatches from Rear-admiral Drury, brought in the *Sarah Christiana,* packet, containing intelligence of the surrender of the Dutch settlement of Amboyna, on the 17th of February, to a detachment of an European regiment, and of artillery from Madras, supported by 300 seamen and marines from his Majesty's ships *Dover, Cornwallis,* and *Samarang.* This valuable capture was made with the loss of five men only killed, and nine men and one officer wounded. . . .

[Service Letters describing this action were printed in Vol. xxiv, pp335-347.]

Gulf Pirates Chastised

Another very agreeable piece of intelligence is, that our expedition against the pirates in the Persian Gulf, under the orders of Captain Wainwright and Colonel Smith, has terminated with complete success. The particulars will appear in a subsequent part of the present volume.

Gallant Action off Alderney

Among our *Letters on Service,* will be found a short account of a very gallant action off Alderney, in which the *Queen Charlotte* hired armed cutter beat off a French vessel of much superior force. . . .

Almeida Surrenders to French

The fortress of Almeida surrendered to the enemy on the 27th of August; but that circumstance appears to have had very little effect on the relative positions of the hostile armies on the Portuguese frontier.

Successful Raids on Spanish Coast

In Spain, the aspect of affairs is extremely favourable to the patriots. On the 23d of August, as will be seen by our *Letters on Service*, an expedition sailed from Cadiz, under the command of Commodore Cockburn, and General Lascy, which was very successful in its result. A landing was effected near the town of Moguer, from which the French were expelled with considerable loss. Some prisoners were taken; and it is said, that an immense booty fell into the hands of the allies [Vol. xxiv, pp333-336].

'King' Murat of Naples Worsted

General Murat, Buonaparte's King of Naples, has suffered so much from the numerous conflicts of his flotilla with the British naval force off Sicily, as to be obliged to postpone, *sine die*, his long-threatened attempt to invade that island.

French General Elected King of Sweden

Contrary to expectation, the French General Bernadotte has been elected successor to the throne of Sweden! *So perfect was the harmony*, says the Gallicised Stockholm Gazette, which prevailed on this occasion, *that not more than half an hour was occupied in the deliberations!* That this election has been carried by dint of Corsican intrigue, there cannot be a shadow of doubt. . . . The reigning King of Sweden, it is said, is about to retire, in consequence of indisposition; the reins of government, it is probable, will, therefore, be immediately placed in the hands of Bernadotte.

Prussian Ports Occupied

Buonaparte has taken possession of all the Prussian ports on the shores of the Baltic, and has seized all the British and colonial produce which they contained. He is also said to have demanded permission for 25,000 French troops to pass through Holstein to Zealand, which has been peremptorily refused. The King of Denmark, however, has laid a strict embargo upon the shipping in all his ports, and has adopted a variety of measures restrictive upon commerce. It is conjectured, by some, that the progress of Buonaparte in the North will arouse the Emperor Alexander to a sense of his danger; but on this point we are not sanguine.

Activity at Boulogne

The Boulogne flotilla is again in a state of complete activity; and Buonaparte, we find, has appointed a new council of marine, for the purpose of assisting the minister at the head of that department.

More Problems with American Negotiations

There seems to be quite a spell cast on our trans-atlantic negotiations. No sooner is one stumbling block removed but another starts up. We consider the following occurrence as connected with that sort of fatality we have alluded to:

Encounter with American Brig

The American papers mention a sort of encounter between the British brig *Moselle*, Captain Boyce, and the American brig *Vixen*, Captain Trippe, which took place near the Bahamas. The only details we have of it are given by an American on board the *Vixen*. The affair took place on the 24th of June. We are told, "that the *Moselle*, a 20-gun brig, was lying at anchor under the Stirrup Roy, near the Bahama Islands. The *Vixen*, carrying 14 guns, approached her under full sail, with her pendant and ensign hoisted. The commander of the *Moselle* hoisted French colours, and sent a boat on board the *Vixen*, requesting Captain Trippe to come on board the British vessel. This was refused, and the captain of the *Moselle* fired a shot at the American; several musket-balls were, it is said, also fired from the boat into that vessel. The American prepared for action, but first thought proper to send his boat, with an officer to demand an explanation. Captain Boyce returned for answer, that he was extremely sorry for having fired, and that the only reasons for his having done so, were, that he could not distinguish the American colours; and that having been informed two French privateers were fitting out in the American States, he supposed the *Vixen* might be one of them. This explanation was deemed sufficient by the American captain, who immediately made sail in a different direction. One man, on board the American brig, was slightly wounded in the mouth by a splinter." - The writer of the letter asserts his conviction, that Captain Boyce, when he fired, knew the *Vixen* was an American vessel, and that he only wanted to provoke an action; we must suspend our opinion on the subject, however, till we hear the account given by Captain Boyce.

The conduct of the American commander has been deemed perfectly satisfactory by the government of the United States; but the republican party talk of *demanding satisfaction* from England, for this *new insult* offered to the American flag.

War Possible between US and France

General Armstrong has left Paris, for America; and, though some of Buonaparte's late commercial regulations seem to favour the Americans, it is thought by many, that a declaration of hostilities will shortly take place between France and the United States.

French Squadron at Toulon XXXVII 39

From "Thessaly" to the Editor, 18th December, 1816
Admiral Allemand had the chief command of the French marine at Toulon. This officer's professional character was very respectably mentioned, though his deportment in private was by no means engaging: he was, however, a favourite with his master. After the appointment of Admiral Allemande to this command, his efforts were unceasing, to give as much instruction to those under his authority, as the small space of water he could venture upon would admit of. He regularly exercised yards and sails; and frequently unmoored, and stood down the harbour, as far as Cape Sepet. He was occasionally more enterprising. During a short period that the British squadron was blown some distance off the coast, the French admiral ran outside Cape Sicie, the extreme headland which forms the harbour of Toulon, with nine sail of the line and four frigates. He was, however, within the observation of the in-shore squadron, and it was very apparent that, notwithstanding all the practice, the mode of managing his ships was very inexpert. Encouraged by this trip, in a few days afterwards he ventured out with 11 sail of the line, five frigates and a corvette; the British fleet lay becalmed at a considerable distance, whilst the French stood out to sea with an off-shore breeze. The in-shore squadron, however, consisting of the *Repulse*, Captain Halliday, the senior officer, the *Alceste* frigate, the *Philomel* sloop of war, was on its station, well in with the land, when the French fleet appeared, and this gallant and judicious officer formed his little force into a compact line, and, under easy sail, kept merely out of gun-shot of the enemy's van . . .

[On 31 August 1810 Rear-Admiral Boudain sailed when the Mediterranean fleet was at some distance and managed to escort home two large storeships which were being blockaded into the road of Porquerolle, at one of the Hieres islands. The *Philomel* brig was nearly captured, but Captain Halliday brought his frigates and HMS *Repulse* into action to extricate her.]

From 'Naval Anecdotes.' XXIV 286-290

Conversion of the St Raphael into a Dry Dock

The *St. Raphael,* one of the Spanish line-of-battle ships taken by the squadron under

View of St. John's Harbour, Antigua. Engraved by Medland, from an original drawing by Pocock.

We have spared no expense to give this beautiful drawing of Mr. Pocock its full force. It is taken from the westward, and discovers St. John's harbour, just open, with a headland on the right, to the southward, called *Ship's Stern*, with Rat Island, and Fort Johnstone, on the left. Some vessels are also seen in distance, within the harbour. In the fore-ground is a Bermudian sloop, and a *Pelfàugua*, a two-mast boat used by the Caribs, very few of which are now to be met with, and those only at Martinique and St. Lucia. They are excellent sea boats, and are used by them with safety in the roughest weather. Plate 153

the command of Sir R. Calder, being found in too bad a state for a sheer-hulk, has been purchased by Mr. Hawker, of Plymouth, for the purpose of being made into a dry dock: - the stern is to be cut off, and a pair of gates hung in its stead. - A ship of a similar class was used for the same purpose in the River Thames some years since, and made a profitable return to the undertaker. It is to be lamented that one of the same kind is not introduced at Plymouth. Stonehouse Pool is a favourable spot, and there is little doubt but it would turn out a good speculation. The *St. Raphael* was sold for £1,870.

Naval Happiness

Admiral Pakenham, on landing once at Portsmouth, boasted to a friend, that he had left his whole crew the happiest fellows in the world. Being asked, "Why?" he answered, "*I have flogged seventeen*, and they are happy it is over, and all the rest are happy that they have escaped."

The Hydrostat

On the 27th of August, an experiment was made on the Seine, at Paris, with a machine called a *hydrostat*, in presence of two commissioners appointed by the government, and a great concourse of spectators. The result of the experiment proves, that a diver shut up in the machine can remain under water at pleasure, and with the help of pincers, can pick up things at the bottom of the water.

[See reports of early submersibles in Appendix 2 on Ship Design in Volume I, pp334-365.]

Breaking Up of Old Ships will Save Thousands
From 'Correspondence.' *XXIV 394-395*

19th October, 1810

Mr. Editor,   With pleasure I observe the Board of Admiralty have adopted a plan for reducing in a material degree the expense of our navy, as will appear by the accompanying list of ships condemned by the Navy Board at their late visit to the Dock-yards; but, although they comprise only a part of the old lumber with which our navy is overloaded, and which thereby appears more important in respect to numbers than it really is; still, when we consider that those ships are each on an average an annual expense of at least £300 to the public, this reduction in the annual expenditure is certainly of equal, if not of greater, importance, than the recently-adopted economical plan of discontinuing the allowance of an almanack, or a half-penny biscuit, to a few of the clerks in the public offices. Those ships, as I have before observed, cost the public in their present state, £22,000 at least every year, exclusive of the expense of repairing occasional damages, &c.; this money will not only be saved to the public by the adoption of this judicious plan, but a considerable sum (not under £20,000 at least) will be added to the public purse by the sale of such as are condemned for that purpose; besides which, a farther advantage will accrue to the public by breaking up others, from which an immense quantity of very serviceable timber will be obtained for the use of the dockyards. This single example shews clearly the necessity that long existed for a change at the Admiralty; and, under a leader disposed to listen to the suggestions and opinions of professional men of ability, the public may now look to the Admiralty Board with some degree of confidence for many useful and salutary regulations.

I remain, Mr. Editor, yours &c.

NEPTUNE

Ships condemned by the Navy Board, at their late visit to the Dockyards,
to be broken up and sold

To be broken up

84	*Juste*		*Alarm*
74	*Hercule*		*Andromeda*
44	*Expedition*		*Andromache*
38	*Vertu*		*Boston*
	Immortalité		*Santa Gertruyda*
	Engageante	28	*Amphitrite*
32	*Juno*		*Brilliant*

22	*Myrmidon*	*Vesuvius*
20	*Sphinx*	*Zebra*
	Peterel sloop	*Aimwell* gun-brig
	Fairy	*Indignant*
	Don Carlos	*Arundel* hulk
	Wolf	*Yarmouth*
	Terror bomb vessel	

To be sold

38	*Fama*	*Mondovi*
20	*Fuerté*	*Rattlesnake*
	Prompte	*Railleur*
	Argus sloop	*Rambler*
	Bergere	*Sheerness*
	Camelion	*Sylph*
	Colombe	*Trompeuse*
	Eugenie	*Torche*
	Epervier	*Valorous*
	Flyvende Fisk	*Virginie*
	Hippomenes	*Incendiary* fire-ship
	Investigator	*Nile* cutter
	Lilly	*Volunteer* gun-boats
	Morgiana	*Project*

From the 'Naval History of the Present Year,' 1810
October–November. XXIV 417

Prisoners of War - No Deal!

The negotiations for an exchange of prisoners, between this country and France, has finally terminated. The details relating to this transaction, so truly disgraceful to the French government, will be found in a subsequent part of the volume.

Exiled King Lands at Yarmouth

Gustavus Adolphus, the exiled King of Sweden, having been so fortunate as to escape from the Continent, landed at Yarmouth, on the 12th of November, and has since resided, in a very private manner, in the metropolis. Apartments have been allotted him at Hampton Court.

November–December. XXIV 490-492

The King's Illness

The King's illness still continues;[1] in consequence of which certain arrangements are making, for the Prince of Wales to assume the office of Regent, with limited powers. – An outline of the proceedings will be seen in our Parliamentary report.

POW Negotiator Returns

The inferior species of diplomatic communication lately held with France, through the medium of the Transport Board, for a cartel of exchange of prisoners, has failed of success; and our negotiator, a Mr. Mackenzie, has returned from his mission to Morlaix. We have some opinions of our own on that transaction, which want of room precludes the possibility of inserting here.

Swedish Declaration of War

Since our last, the Duke of Sudermanland, now reigning in Sweden by the title of Charles XIII, has issued a declaration of war against England, dated at Stockholm, 19th November.

Americans to Tighten Economic Sanctions

But this does not appear to be the only blow which seems to await English commerce. The dispute with the United States of America relative to our restrictions on their maritime trade is of so long standing, and has been so confused by the volumes which the lawyer like statesmen on both sides have piled together, that it is difficult to render the matter intelligible to *unlearned* readers. The matter at present stands thus, that unless we rescind certain of our public acts called "Orders of Council," some of which are now become partly laws, all intercourse between this country and the American States will be interdicted after the 2d of February next, while the commercial communication between France and those states will be contingently open, that power having revoked the regulations under the name of "decrees," by which the French ruler had answered our restrictions on neutral navigation, but with still more violence: both parties having declared to America, that "as long as she submitted to the regulations of the one party, she must expect to be obliged to submit to those of the other." It is no question of mere justice demanded by special compact, and being so, no consideration of mere expediency should stand in the way of good faith. After which, we have little hesitation in saying, that we hope the obnoxious orders will be repealed: and due homage being thus paid to the immutable principles of justice in a particular case, we are thoroughly convinced we shall stand on better ground for the grand stand that sooner or later we must make for the Sovereignty of the Sea, to the plain, simple, unqualified and absolute assertion of which we must make up our minds, or else debase them to become first an inferior nation, and then a vassal to France. This is our opinion. If we were to offer advice, all we should say is, *look before you leap.*

1 The subjoined answer of Dr. Willis, to the question from the Committee of the House of Commons - "What is the distinction between mental derangement and insanity?" - presents a striking picture of the nature of the King's malady: "I consider the King's derangement more nearly allied to delirium than insanity; whenever the irritation in his Majesty arises to a certain point, he uniformly becomes delirious. In delirium, the mind is actively employed upon past impressions, upon objects and former scenes, which rapidly pass in succession before the mind, resembling, in that case, a person talking in his sleep. There is also a considerable disturbance in the general constitution; great restlessness, great want of sleep, and total unconsciousness of surrounding objects. In insanity there may be little or no disturbance, apparently, in the general consititution; the mind is occupied upon some fixed assumed idea, to the truth of which it will pertinaceously adhere, in opposition to the plainest evidence of its falsity; and the individual is acting always upon that false impression: in insanity, also, the mind is awake to objects which are present. Taking insanity, therefore, and delirium, as two points, I would place derangement of mind somewhere between them. His Majesty's illness, uniformly, partakes more of the delirium than of the insanity. . . .

From 'Naval Anecdotes.' XXIV 448-455

Admiralty Signals

Lloyd's, December 6, 1810

All masters of vessels passing up and down the Channel are recommended by the Committee of this House, on the appearance of an enemy's cruiser in the day or night, to make signals, either by firing guns, burning false lights, or setting off rockets, by which it is hoped, from the number of his Majesty's ships cruising in the Channel for the protection of the trade, many vessels will be retaken, if not preserved from capture. It is also recommended to all masters of vessels to attend particularly to the signals at the respective signal stations on the coast, as explained underneath:

For 'an enemy's frigate or frigates'	– one ball above a flag
For 'the enemy's small cruizers'	– two balls above a flag
For 'an enemy's ship or vessels close under the land'	– three balls above a flag

N.B. These signals will be hoisted at the yards, the ball perpendicular, and a pendant at the mast-head; and no signals made at the signal posts but those above-mentioned, are to be attended to by merchant vessels.

This Notice is given, in order to prevent any inconvenience to the trade until the Signals issued from the Admiralty shall be delivered from the different Custom-houses when vessels clear out.

[See also Appendix 1, Volume I.]

Death of French Admiral Bruix

Goldsmith, in his *Secret History of the Cabinet of Buonaparte*, presents a curious contrast between the conduct of Admiral Bruix, who commanded the flotilla at Boulogne, and that of the Grand Judge, who presided at the trial of General Moreau, and who afterwards suffered himself to be beaten by the newly-made Emperor. "There existed," says Goldsmith, "difference of opinion about some naval operations between the admiral and the tyrant, who was very abusive; Bruix answered him with spirit, when Buonaparte struck him in the face with his fist, upon which the admiral drew his sword, and would have run him through the body, but was prevented by the officers who were present; this quarrel took place on the beach of Boulogne, and many people saw it. Bruix pulled off his epaulets, and stamped upon them, as also upon his cross; he resigned his post as admiral and as counsellor of state: he died very soon after, and no doubt by poison. It was propagated by the agents of Buonaparte, that he died of a broken heart, from having received this insult; but this cannot be true - he had resented it as a man of spirit. I remember being one day with Rèal, who shewed me a passage in a book written in England, which stated that Buonaparte kicked his ministers; "No, no," says Rèal, "he does not kick, but gives *coups de poing* (blows with the fist.)"

"Discovery of Papers Relating to the Chevalier De La Peyrouse."

We copy the following statement from the *Times* newspaper, which professes to have received it through a channel entitling it to implicit belief.

"An officer of the name of Edwards, belonging to the 8th regiment of light dragoons, which has been long on service in India, was proceeding to New South Wales in the *Venus*, for the benefit of his health. When the vessel was off Van Diemen's Land, Lieutenant Edwards and some others landed for the purpose of amusing themselves, and seeing a little of the country. After walking about for some time, some of the company perceived an inscription cut in the bark of a tree, the characters of which were nearly obliterated or filled up. The date, however, was legible, which, by a singular coincidence, proved to have been inscribed exactly that very day seventeen years [ago]. As the whole of the inscription, from the circumstances we have stated, could not be deciphered, the company returned on board giving up all idea of further research. The extraordinary discovery having made a deeper impression on Mr. Edwards than it did on his fellow passengers, he determined to make another attempt to decipher the inscription; for which purpose he went on shore the next morning, accompanied by some persons to whom he had imparted a portion of his zeal and curiosity. Their first proceeding was to clear away the bark from the tree, by which means they found that the impression on the body of the tree was so strong as to be legible. They ascertained from it that something of consequence was buried at the root of the tree.

Mr. Edwards immediately set to work with an iron instrument they had brought on shore, and after digging for a short time, it came in contact with a glass bottle, and broke it, but fortunately the contents were not injured. Upon examination they were found to consist of four letters; two of which were addressed to persons at that time filling situations in the government of France, and the other two to ladies. A paper also accompanied the letters, which were carefully sealed, requesting whoever should find them to forward them to their respective addresses. Mr. Edwards, under these circumstances, as well as in observance of the sentiments which should animate an officer and a gentleman, did not feel himself warranted in opening the mysterious papers, but carried them in the state they were found to the Governor of New South Wales, at whose disposal he was anxious to place them. The Governor, however, considering Lieutenant Edwards as best entitled to the merit of the discovery, submitted to him the propriety of transmitting them himself to the British government. This suggestion was adopted, and Mr. Edwards forwarded the letters unopened with an account of the manner in which they were discovered, by the *Dromedary* storeship, to his father in London; who, in conformity with his son's request, has placed them in the hands of the Secretary of State for the Colonial Department.

That the letters contain some information relating to the fate of that very able and much-lamented mariner Peyrouse [La Pérouse] is most probable; for the latest intelligence obtained of him was not far removed from the date of the inscription, when he was continuing his researches in the same quarter."

It is supposed that the letters have been transmitted to France, by Government, precisely in the state that they were received. - The subjoined letter, which was addressed to the Editor of the *Times*, in consequence of the above statement, is deserving of perusal:

"Sir, In the article relative to Chevalier De La Peyrouse, in your paper of this day, you say, "the latest intelligence obtained of him was not far removed from the *date* of the inscription, when he was continuing his researches in the same quarter." In another part of the same article that date is said to be "exactly 17 *years*," from the time of the discovery of the inscription on the tree, on Van Dieman's Land, by Lieutenant Edwards. I wish the period of Mr. Edward's discovery had been stated; but as it appears from the context to be of a date not very remote, I shall consider it as having taken place within the last two years. Now, I saw *la Boussole* and *l'Astrolabe*, under the command of Monsieur De La Peyrouse, enter Botany Bay, and anchor there, on the 26th of January, 1788. On the 24th of February following, I breakfasted and dined with the Chevalier De La Peyrouse on board *la Boussole*. A few days after, three of the French officers crossed from Botany Bay to Port Jackson, where they dined, passed the day, and remained till next morning, as the guests of myself and some other British marine officers. On or about the 12th of March, 1788, La Peyrouse sailed from Botany Bay; and, as *I believe*, was never after heard of.

I shall subjoin my name and place of address, although it is not necessary that they should appear, should you consider this communication worthy of a place in *The Times*.

I have the honour to be, your very obedient servant,

W....T...., Colonel of Royal Marines

Woolwich, November 6, 1810"

"P.S. Mons. De La Peyrouse told me, that he had sailed from Brest in August, 1785. Except himself and the Chevalier Clonard, who commanded the other ship, all the French officers with whom I conversed were eager to return to Europe; but they believed in general that their voyage of discovery would not terminate in less than four years from its commencement; for which period of time, *I have reason to believe*, the equipment of the expedition was calculated."

[The letters were opened in the French Ministry of the Marine, and proved to be written by officers on board Rear-Admiral D'Entrecasteaux's squadron, and dated 24 and 25 February 1793 (Vol. XXV, p130).]

Suggestion That Passing Ships Should Identify Themselves

From 'Correspondence.' XXIV 457-458

Mr. Editor, In many instances I have witnessed the impropriety of men of war passing each other, and sometimes very close, without exchanging numbers. It would certainly be conducive to the good of the service, were every ship falling in with another to make known her name; as I have, I assure you, seen ships of war pass each other, when each had information to communicate: and once it was my fortune to belong to a vessel, in which a number of officers and men were passengers for ships (supposed) at the port we were bound to; when, owing to the above cause, we *actually* passed through a squadron, of which those very vessels constituted a part.

Under the consideration that such is *frequently* the case, I submit that it would be not only *proper*, but *necessary*, that an order should be enforced "for strange vessels, when casually meeting, *invariably* to make known their number;" as, by this means, they might *possibly* prevent officers from pursuing an useless voyage, of probably *half*, if not the *whole*, extent of the Atlantic.

I am, &c.

NIHIL

Adriatic Service

[The Adriatic littoral was dominated by the French, but the Royal Navy was able to operate freely there and ensure that the resources of Venice were not developed into a dangerous hostile naval force.]

Letters on Service
Admiralty Office, 24 November 1810. *XXIV 501-503*

Copy of a Letter from Admiral Sir Charles Cotton, Bart. Commander-in-Chief of his Majesty's Ships and Vessels in the Mediterranean, to John Wilson Croker, Esq. Dated on board the San Josef, off Toulon, September 12, 1810

Sir, I cannot desist from forwarding to the Lords Commissioners of the Admiralty, the enclosed detailed account of a gallant enterprise performed by the boats of the *Amphion*, *Active*, and *Cerberus*, which resulted in the surrender of the garrison of Grao, and the capture and destruction of a convoy of the enemy from Trieste.

I have the honour to be, &c.

C. COTTON

Amphion, Gulph of Trieste, June 29, 1810

Sir, A convoy of several vessels from Trieste were chased into the harbour of Grao by the boats of the *Amphion* yesterday morning, and the officer (Lieutenant Slaughter), on his return, reported that they were laden with naval stores for the arsenal at Venice. As the Italian government are making great exertions at the present moment to fit out their marine at that port, the capture of this convoy became an object of importance, and I was the more induced to attempt it, as its protection (it was said) consisted only in twenty-five soldiers stationed at Grao, an open town in the Friule; the sequel will shew that we were both deceived as to the number of the garrison and the strength of the place; and if I should enter too much into detail in relating to you the circumstances attending its capture, I trust, Sir, you will consider it on my part as only an anxious desire to do justice to the gallant exertions of those who were employed on the occasion.

The shoals of Grao prevented the near approach of shipping of burthen; the capture of the convoy therefore was necessarily confined to boat service, and I telegraphed to his Majesty's ships *Cerberus* and *Active* on the evening of the 28th, that their boats and marines should assemble alongside the *Amphion* by twelve o'clock that night. It fell calm in the early part of the evening, and conceiving, from our distance from Grao, that the boats of the *Active* (who was considerably in the offing) would not arrive in time, I wrote to Captain Gordon to request they might be sent immediately; I mention this, as it will account why that ship's boats and marines were not in the station assigned them in the attack, and that no possible blame can be imputed to the officers and men employed in them for their not being present, as distance alone prevented them. Captain Whitby, of the *Cerberus*, very handsomely volunteered his services on this occasion; but I considered it as a fair opportunity for my second lieutenant (Slaughter), (the first lieutenant being absent having been detached on other service in the barge the day before,) to distinguish himself, and he has fully in every way justified the confidence I had in him.

The convoy were moored in a river above the town of Grao, and it was absolutely necessary to be first in possession of it; the defences of the town were two old castles, almost in ruins, with loopholes for musketry, and a deep ditch in their front, extending from one castle to the other. The boats from the *Amphion* and *Cerberus* put off from the ship about forty minutes past eleven, and the marines of both ships under Lieutenants Moore and Brattle (of marines), and Lieutenant Dickenson, of the *Cerberus*, the whole under the command of Lieutenant Slaughter, landed without musket-shot to the right of the town before day-light, and instantly advanced to the attack, the launches with carronades under Lieutenant O'Brien (third of the *Amphion*) accompanying them along shore. It had been intended that the *Amphion*'s and *Active*'s should have landed to the right of the town, and the *Cerberus* to the left, but the former boats not arriving, Lieutenant Slaughter very properly took the *Cerberus*'s with him, and left the gig to direct the *Active*'s to the left; of course they had much further to row, and, much to the regret of all, did not get on shore till after the place was taken. A very heavy firing commenced about dawn of day, the enemy considerably stronger than was imagined, and, assisted by a numerous peasantry, kept up a very destructive fire on our men whilst advancing, who purposely retired a little to the left, taking shelter under some hillocks, and what the unevenness of the ground afforded; they were followed by the French troops, who, conceiving this to be a retreat on the boats, quitted their advantageous position and charged with the bayonet. It no longer became a contest to be decided by musketry; they were received with the steadiness and bravery inherent in Englishmen; both officers and men were personally engaged hand to hand, and out of the number killed of the enemy in this encounter, eight were bayonet wounds, which will convince you, Sir, of the nature of the attack.

A struggle of this kind could not last long, and the French troops endeavoured, in great confusion, to regain their former position; they were closely pursued, and charged in their turn, which decided the business, and the whole detachment of the enemy, consisting of a lieutenant, serjeant, and thirty-eight privates of the 81st regiment (all French men) were made prisoners, leaving our brave men in possession of the town, and twenty-five vessels laden with stores and merchandize. The *Active*'s boats landed at this moment, to the left, and her marines, under Lieutenant Foley, were of great use in completely securing the advantages gained. Every exertion was now made to get the convoy out of the river; but it being almost low water it was late in the evening before they could be got afloat, and much labour and fatigue were occasioned, being obliged to shift the cargoes into smaller vessels to get them over the Bar. About eleven o'clock in the forenoon an attack was made on the town by a party of French troops coming from Maran, a village in the interior; the force nearest them, under Lieutenants Slaughter, Moore, and Mears of the *Active*, instantly attacked, assisted by the launches in the river, and the enemy, finding all resistance ineffectual, after losing two killed, threw down their arms and surrendered. In this latter business a lieutenant and twenty-two men of the 5th regiment of light infantry (all French troops) were made prisoners. The same intrepidity which had ensured success before, was equally conspicuous on this second occasion. About seven in the evening I had the satisfaction of seeing the whole detachment coming off to the squadron, which I had anchored about four miles from the town, directly the wind allowed, and every thing was secured by eight o'clock. A service of this nature has not been performed without loss; but every thing considered, it falls short of what might have been expected from the obstinate resistance met with. . . .

W. HOSTE

Admiral Sir Charles Cotton

Message of Buonaparte to his Senate - Canal to be Built to Baltic

From the 'Naval History of the Present Year,' 1810-1811
December-January. XXV 81-82

The message of Buonaparte to his senate, on the 10th of December [1810] (of which, omitting the introductory paragraph, the following is a copy), is very interesting in a naval point of view:

"The orders published by the British council in 1806 and 1807, have rent in pieces the public law of Europe. A new order of things govern the universe. New securities becoming necessary to me, the junction of the mouths of the Scheldt, of the Meuse, the Rhine, the Ems, the Weser, and the Elbe, with the empire, the establishment of an inland navigation with the Baltic, have appeared to me to be the first and most important.

I have ordered the plan of a canal to be prepared, which will be executed in the course of the five years, and will connect the Seine with the Baltic.

Those princes will be indemnified, who may find themselves circumscribed by this great measure, which is become absolutely necessary, and which will rest the right of my frontiers upon the Baltic."

Evacuation of the Spanish Royal Dockyard at Carthagena

From the 'Naval Biography of the Late Sir Charles Cotton, Bart.' XXVII 387-389

Pursuant to his appointment [as successor to Lord Collingwood to command-in-chief in the Mediterranean], Sir Charles Cotton proceeded to the Mediterranean, in the *Lively* frigate, in the month of March, 1810. On his arrival, he hoisted his flag in the *San Josef*, and during the succeeding sixteen months, as appears from existing documents, he conducted the affairs of the fleet with universal satisfaction to the officers under his orders, and with important advantage to his country. To Sir Charles Cotton are we indebted for the salvation of the Spanish fleet, at Carthagena. The preservation of the naval stores at that arsenal, was, also wholly to be ascribed to the judgment exercised by Sir Charles, in supplying the transports requisite for their removal. The prompt and efficacious assistance, however, which he afforded, for the removal of ship timber, of all descriptions, and of considerable value, from Carthagena, which, at that time, could not be procured in Europe, will best be estimated by the following very handsome letter from Colonel (now General) Roche, an officer of distinguished talents in the Spanish service -

Carthagena, 13th February, 1811
Sir, I avail myself, with great satisfaction, of the opportunity just afforded me of the *Leviathan*'s calling off this port, to acknowledge the receipt of your very obliging letter of the 29th ultimo, by Captain Adams, of the *Invincible*, and to express my most sincere thanks, for the prompt and efficacious manner you have, not only on the present, but all former occasions, forwarded the public service, carrying on at this place. And I beg you, Sir, to permit me to take the liberty of assuring you, that I have never ceased expressing, not only to his Majesty's ministers, but to every other person with whom I have ever spoke upon the subject, that the entire salvation of all the Spanish squadron and valuable naval stores from this arsenal, is solely due to your extreme readiness in affording, upon every occasion, the necessary assistance for their removal.

Nothing could, absolutely, be more lucky or opportune, than the arrival of the

Invincible; nor could it be possible to select an officer in the service, more likely to effect all our wishes than Captain Adams. The consequence, therefore, of your good judgment will be, the immediate removal of ship-timber, of a description not to be bought, at the present day, in Europe, and the value of which, when laid in, was not less than about £90,000. The masts and oak plank, surpass every idea you can form of them; and I will take care, that an order shall be sent from the Spanish government, (through Mr. Wellesley) that the commandant at Mahon shall supply you with any quantity of these stores that you may stand in need of for our fleet.

Captain Adams will tell you, that every possible exertion is using, to load the transports we have, but I reckon that we shall want, at least, twelve more large ones. I have been obliged to employ about 400 soldiers, to drag the spars and timber out of the ponds where they soak, and to assist in loading the ships. Sebastiani's corps has again retired upon Baza, but we cannot be a moment certain, that he will not return.

Freyre's force at Murcia, is about 12,000 infantry, and 2,000 cavalry. It is said the Duke of Alburquerque is coming to command it.

Nothing can well be more discouraging, than the prospect of affairs at this part of the world - grain is extremely scarce - if they increase the army here, it cannot be fed, and if they do not increase it, there is no chance of withstanding the enemy.

I am fully sensible of the soundness of your advice, Sir, about the ultimate advantage, in case of the worst, of proceeding to Mahon with my corps; Alicant, for this reason, is extremely desirable. It would never enter my thoughts, however, to abandon Spain while a hope remained of doing any good, or of being of any use, unless you ever see the occasion of throwing a force into Mahon: if ever that moment should occur, or any other, in which you may wish for the assistance of from 3, to 5,000 men, I will, without one moment's hesitation, take the whole responsibility upon myself, and place myself, with confidence and satisfaction, at your disposal.

The *Leviathan* is about to sail. I have not time to add more, than to assure you, Sir, of the very high respect with which I remain,

Your most faithful and obliged humble servant,

K. ROCHE

Admiral Sir Charles Cotton, Bart.

1810 – The Capture of Isle de France

IN THE SUMMER OF 1810 plans were finalised for the capture of the Isle de France, to eliminate French cruisers from the Indian Ocean. In August there was a major setback when a squadron commanded by Captain Rowley seized the Isle de la Passe in the entrance to Port Southwest in order to prevent the return of French cruisers which had captured several Indiamen. They failed to stop all but one of the captives running their guns into harbour, and when Captain Pym tried to cut them out, three frigates were lost by running on the reefs. In November, however, Rear-Admiral Sir Thomas Bertie arrived with a fleet of seventy ships and transports from Bombay and South Africa, carrying an army of 10,000 commanded by Major-General John Abercromby, second son of the dead Sir Ralph. The governor of Isle de France capitulated to overwhelming odds, on the condition of repatriation to France.

French Documents Respecting the Late Naval Operations in the Indian Seas XXV 234-238

That the future historian, as well as the contemporary reader, may be in possession of all the facts and documents respecting the late naval operations in the Indian seas, it is our intention, in addition to the British *Letters on Service*, already given, to preserve the whole of the French reports, &c. upon the subject. These, with our map of the Isle of France, and the consequent illustrative particulars, relating to that island, to the Isle of Bourbon, and to Rodriguez, will exhibit a series of well digested historical, military, and commercial information, respecting our newly-acquired insular possessions, superior, we presume, to what can be met with in any other publication.

We shall commence the French Documents with the following.

Report of Captain Duperre, commanding a squadron of his Imperial Majesty's Forces

General, The events which have succeeded each other with such rapidity under your eyes, have not allowed me a moment, since my arrival, to acquaint you with the operations of the squadron under my command during my late cruise. I hasten to discharge this duty.

Having sailed on the 14th of last March, the squadron proceeded to the latitude

ISLE of FRANCE.

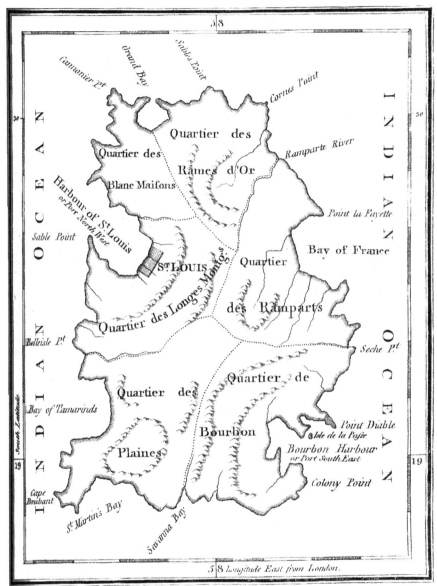

Chart of the Isle of France. Engraved by Luffman. ^{Plate 331}

you had appointed, in which it captured two vessels, one from China, and the other from Bengal. On the 1st of June, as there was no longer any chance of prizes, I quitted the cruising ground, and steered for St. Augustine's Bay, to repair damages and refresh the crew. I found there an English whaler, which was foundering, and could not be taken possession of; I ordered her to be burned. The squadron in a few days left the Bay well caulked and equipped.

A few days after, at day-break on the 3d of July, we perceived three sail, within sight of Mayotte Island, to which we gave chase.[1] I soon discovered that they were three Company's vessels. They were making off on the opposite tack, about eight miles to windward. The *Bellona* being an admirable sailer, afforded a chance that I should be able to bring them to action about the middle of the day; but the currents of wind did not favour her, although they did the *Minerva*, who got within cannon-shot of them at three o'clock. As soon as I had given the signal for attack she gallantly ranged along their line to windward, engaged them within pistol-shot, passed the headmost ship for the purpose of obliging her to fall back, and driving her to leeward, broke their line and engaged them again. The brilliant manoeuvre was on the point of being crowned with the most complete success, when the frigate in an instant lost her main-top-mast and fore-top-gallant-mast. Fortunately at this time I had got into the enemy's wake, in which I continued under a press of sail. The unexpected success he had obtained appeared to give him courage. He restored his line. I made the signal for a decisive engagement. At half-past five I passed to leeward of his line, which was formed in close order. I placed myself opposite the centre vessel, which appeared to be that of the commander, but in such a way that I could partially direct my fire against the whole three, which I engaged within less than pistol-shot at six o'clock.

The enemy at first kept up a brisk fire; their small arms were vigorously exerted. At seven o'clock the headmost ship gave herself stern-way, for the purpose of getting under shelter of the vessel next to her, which becoming exposed by such a manoeuvre to the whole of my fire, called out that she had surrendered. I wished to take possession of her, and put a boat out for that purpose, but it was unfortunately swamped. The head-most vessel having endeavoured to pass under my stern, I suffered her to do so, and found her on the other side within pistol-shot. I attacked her vigorously, and at the second broadside she struck, and extinguished all her lights. The manoeuvre she had made brought her close to leeward of the *Minerva* and *Victor*. I left her to these vessels, and proceeded to take possession of the ship that had struck, and to compel the third to surrender. I soon came up with her, and at the second broadside her lights were pulled down. I sent to take possession of these two vessels, and steered for the *Minerva*. I came up with her at ten o'clock, and was exceedingly astonished to find her alone. The captain informed me that the vessel which had struck, and which I had given up to him, taking advantage of the excessive darkness of the night, and particularly of the confidence derived from her having surrendered, had, contrary to the laws of honour and of war, escaped from under his guns. It was necessary to man the two other ships, called the *Ceylon* and the *Windham*, coming from the Cape and proceeding to Madras. They carried each 30 guns, and had 400 soldiers on board each vessel, belonging to the 24th regiment of foot; a general officer, a colonel, and the colours were on board, which accounts for their obstinate resistance. The disgraceful runaway was called the *Astle* [? — Castle?], and was the strongest ship of the three.

---

1 The Island of Mayotte, or Mayotta, is the most southerly of the Comora Islands; about 240 miles from the coast of Africa, and 150 from the island of Madagascar; in longitude 61° 10' east of Ferro [approximately 45° east of Greenwich], latitude 13° 15' south. It is rather low, but abounds with provisions and fruit, and is inhabited all along the sea-shore. According to a French writer, the natives are of such a particular humour, that they will not conclude a bargain of the value of half a rial in a day's time; nor will they buy a yard of cloth, without calling all their relations and neighbours, to fix the price they should give for it.

On the 20th of August, in the morning, I got sight of the mountains of Port Imperial, in the Isle of France. At noon, I could see the port. The National flag was flying on the Isle de la Passe, and the signal, "the enemy are cruising off La Mire." A three-masted vessel was at anchor under the fort, with French colours. I determined to touch there, or at least to take my direction from it. The sloop was a-head; the *Minerva* followed her. The *Victor*, on doubling the fort, received some shot both from it and the frigate, and both instantly hoisted the English flag. It first struck me that all this part was in possession of the enemy. I made the signal to the squadron, which was still under sail, for close order, and to keep to windward. It was too late for the *Minerva*; she and the *Ceylon* had already entered the pass. In a few minutes she went through it, engaging the fort and the frigate. There was no longer hesitation. The passage was to be forced, the squadron carried in, and a diversion effected that might be useful to the country. I made sail, throwing out a signal to follow me. The *Windham* from some indecision was unable to do so. I entered the passage under easy sail, and the fire of the fort and the frigate. I gave the latter my whole broadside as I passed under the stern within cannon-shot. As soon as I had entered I discovered the French flag flying every where. The Isle de la Passe alone appeared to me to be in possession of the enemy. I joined my squadron, and gave orders that it should take a more advanced ground of anchorage, which was instantly done. I was informed from the shore of the situation of the island. On the 21st I placed the squadron near the shore, with the rear towards the rocks which skirt the bay, and the van close to the coral reef. On the 22d the *Nereide* [British] frigate, which was at anchor under the *Isle of La Passe*, was joined by the *Sirius*. Both of them made a movement to attack me. Your Excellency being aware of the weak state of my crews, in consequence of the prizes I had taken, and the engagements I had fought, sent me a detachment of fifty men from *la Manche* and *l'Entreprenant* sloop, with the necessary proportion of officers. I immediately stationed them on board the different vessels. The plan of attack was frustrated by the *Sirius* getting on the reef in the Channel, where she remained till night. On the 23d two more frigates made their appearance, and joined the former two at their anchorage at four o'clock. From the preparations they made, I had not the smallest doubt that they would attack me.

I have the honour, &c.

G.V. DUPERRE

On board the Bellone, Port Imperial Road, 10th September, 1810

Letters on Service

Admiralty Office, December 15, 1810. ^{XXV 72-74}

Copy of a Letter from William Shield, Esq. Commissioner of his Majesty's Navy at the Cape of Good Hope, to John Wilson Croker, Esq. dated at the Cape, the 24th September, 1810

It is with the deepest regret I acquaint you, for the information of the Right Honourable the Lords Commissioners of the Admiralty, with the loss of a part of his Majesty's squadron on this station.

The account I have now the honour to present to you, came to my knowledge by his Excellency Lord Caledon having had the goodness to send, for my perusal, despatches he received last night by the late master of the *Sirius* from the governor of Bourbon. I have transcribed and enclosed such part thereof as may lead their lordship's judgment to the extent of this disastrous event.

The Isle de la Passe had fallen by assault from a party landed by two of the frigates, subsequent to which, the [French National frigates] *Bellona*, *Minerva*, and *Victor* arrived and ran into Port South East, with their prize the Honourable East India Company's ship *Ceylon*, taken in company with the *Windham*, after a gallant resistance, on their way from the Cape to Madras, with part of the 24th regiment on board.

The *Windham* was turned from Port South East, and recaptured by the *Sirius*, but the troops had been removed to the *Bellona*.

Captain Pym appears to have immediately determined on attacking these ships, and to his not being aware of the difficulties of the navigation within the port is to be attributed his failure and the loss of the King's ships. The *Sirius* and *Magicienne* were burnt by their crews, after doing every thing that was possible to extricate the ships from the situation they had fallen into. The *Nereide* after every officer and man on board were either killed or wounded, fell onshore a mere wreck, and was taken possession of by the enemy.

I am sorry to add to this list of misfortunes, that the *Ranger* transport, laden with provisions for the squadron, and having some stores on board, has also fallen into the hands of the enemy.

The transports having the troops on board, and which were to have sailed yesterday from hence without convoy, will be prevented putting to sea by the arrival of this lamented intelligence.

If it should prove that I have not been exactly correct in the information I have now given, I hope for their lordship's indulgence, and that they will impute it to my anxiety to give them the most early intimation of so important an event.

I have the honour to be, &c.

W. SHIELD

P.S. Captain Willoughby has lost an eye, and is otherwise wounded, and is in the hands of the enemy.

[A year later it was reported that 'Captain Willoughby, who lately fought his frigate, in the East Indies, till she had lost nearly every man, is unfortunately now totally deprived of sight. He lost one eye in the action at the Dardanelles, and the other is dark, owing to a wound which he received at Port-au-Prince [Port Southwest]. The country has thus lost the services of one of her most gallant and meritorious officers.' Vol. XXVI, p31.]

Copy of a Letter from Captain Pym, of his Majesty's late Ship the Sirius, addressed to Captain Rowley, of the Boadicea

L'Isle de la Passe, August 24, 1810

Sir, By my last you were informed of my intention to attack the frigates, corvette, and Indiamen in this port.

Magicienne having joined just as the recaptured ship was about to make sail, I sent Captain Lambert orders to bring her and the gun-brig with all despatch off L'Isle de la Passe; and that the enemy in Port Louis should not be alarmed, I made all sail round the south side, and although blowing very hard, reached L'Isle de la Passe next day. At noon *Nereide* made signal ready for action; I then closed, and from the situation of the enemy, decided on an immediate attack; and when her master came on board as pilot, made signal to weigh, but when within about a quarter of an hour's run of the enemy, he unfortunately run me on the edge of the inner narrow passage. We did not get off (and that with wonderful exertion) until eight o'clock next morning. At noon on the 23d the *Iphigenia* and *Magicienne* came in sight; the enemy having moved further in, and making several batteries, as also manning the East India ship, and taking many men on board the frigates, I called them to assist in the attack, having all the captains and pilot on board, and being assured we were past all danger and could run direct for the enemy's line, we got under weigh, and pushed for our stations, viz. *Sirius* alongside the *Bellona*, *Nereide* between her and the *Victor*, *Iphigenia* alongside *la Minerva*, and *Magicienne* between her and the East India ship; and just as their shot began to pass over us, sad to say, *Sirius* grounded on a small bank, not known; Captain Lambert joined his post, and had hardly given the third broadside before his opponent cut her cable. *Magicienne*, close to *Iphigenia*, ran on a bank, which prevented her bringing more than six guns to bear; poor *Nereide* nearly gained her post, and did in the most gallant manner maintain that and the one intended for *Sirius*, until *Bellona* cut. All the enemy's ships being on shore, and finding *Sirius* could not get off, the whole of them opened their fire on *Nereide*; and even in this unequal contest, and being a-ground, she did not cease firing until ten o'clock, and sorry am I to say, that the captain, every officer and man on board, are killed or wounded.

Captain Lambert would have immediately run down with the enemy, but there was a shoal a very little distance from and between him and them; he did all that could be done, by keeping open a heavy, although distant fire; nothing was wanting to make a most complete victory, but one of the other frigates to close with *la Bellona*.

I must now inform you, that the moment we took the ground, every possible exertion was made to get the ship off, by carrying out stream and kedge anchors; but both anchors came home together. I then got a whole bower cable and anchor hauled out, (not a common exertion for a frigate) as also the stream, and although having the one with the capstan, and the other with purchase on purchase, we could not move her one inch, from the nature of the ground, and the very heavy squalls at that time. We continued lightening every thing from forward, and made many severe but fruitless attempts to heave the ship off before daylight, but all to no effect. At that time the *Nereide* was a perfect wreck, *Magicienne* in as bad a situation as *Sirius*, no possibility of *Iphigenia* closing with the enemy, the whole of the enemy on shore in a heap. We then tried the last resource, by warping the *Iphigenia* to heave us off, but could not get her in a proper situation until the 25th in the forenoon.

I had a survey by the captains, masters, and carpenters, in which they agreed it was impossible to get the ship off; I had the same report yesterday from Captain Curtis, and that his men were falling very fast; I ordered her to be abandoned at dusk and burnt; and as the enemy's frigates cannot get off, I though it most prudent to preserve L'Isle de Passe, by warping *Iphigenia* for its support; and having no prospect of any other immediate support, I thought it most prudent to quit my ship, then within shot of all the enemy's posts and ships, and only being able to return their fire from two guns. After seeing every man safe from the ship, Lieutenant Watling and myself set her on fire; and, I trust, Sir, although my enterprise has been truly unfortunate, that no possible blame can be attached to any one; and never did captains, officers, and men go into action with a greater certainty of victory; and, I do aver, that if I could have got alongside the *Bellona*, all the enemy's ships would have been in our possession in less than half an hour. My ship being burnt, I have given up the command to Captain Lambert, and have recommended his supporting and protecting this island with his ship and ship's companies of *Sirius* and *Magicienne*. . . .

I have, &c.

S. PYM

[Captain Joshua Rowley's and Captain Charles Gordon's letters accounting the action in Port Southwest, and the subsequent recapture of *Africaine*, were published in Vol. xxv, pp159-164.]

Admiralty Office, February 12, 1811. ^XXV 157-164

Copy of a Letter from Vice-Admiral Bertie, Commander-in-Chief of his Majesty's Ships and Vessels at the Cape of Good Hope, to John Wilson Croker, Esq. dated on board his Majesty's Ship the Africaine, St. Paul's, Isle of Bourbon, the 13th October 1810

Sir, Following the intentions communicated by my letter addressed to you of the 26th August, I have the honour now to acquaint you, for the information of their lordships, that having made the necessary dispositions and arrangements previous to my departure from the Cape, I hoisted my flag on board the *Nisus*, and sailed on the 4th ultimo, in that ship for the Isle of France. Having made the land on the 2d instant, I proceeded to reconnoitre Port South East, and from thence to Port Louis; where, having cruised forty-eight hours, and not falling in with any ship of the blockading squadron, I proceeded to this anchorage for information of them, where I found lying his Majesty's ships *Boadicea, Otter,* and *Staunch* gun-brig, together with his Majesty's ships *Africaine* and *Ceylon*, which had been taken and recaptured from the enemy, and the imperial French frigate *La Venus*, also captured from the enemy.

The details, copies of which I have the honour to transmit herewith, will fully explain to their lordships the circumstances of the occupation of the Isle de la Passe, as well as the subsequent unfortunate result of a very gallant attack made on the enemy's ships in Port S.E. with the *Sirius*, Captain Pym, and *Magicienne*, Captain Curtis, the *Iphigenia*, Captain Lambert, and the *Nereide*, Captain Willoughby, which ended in the unavoidable destruction of the two former of his Majesty's ships, and the surrender to the enemy of the *Iphigenia* and *Nereide*, the latter after a glorious resistance almost unparalleled even in the brilliant annals of the British Navy.

A momentary superiority thus obtained by the enemy has been promptly and decisively crushed by the united zeal, judgment, perseverance, skill, and intrepidity of Captain Rowley, in his Majesty's ship *Boadicea*; the value and importance of whose services, long conspicuous and distinguished as they have been, have fully justified the selection and detention of him as the senior officer conducting the blockade of this station; and who, in the present instance, almost alone and unsupported but by the never-failing energies and resources of his active and intelligent mind, under circumstances, as may be easily imagined, of extreme anxiety, mortification, and disappointment, in a few hours not only retook his Majesty's ships *Africaine* and *Ceylon*, but captured also the largest frigate possessed by the enemy in these seas, and has thus restored the British naval pre-eminence in this quarter, which his talents have long so successfully contributed to maintain.

Nor can I omit to offer the tribute so justly due to the memory of the gallant Corbett, of his Majesty's ship *Africaine*, whose meritorious eagerness to check the triumph of an exulting enemy impelled him to an unequal contest, in which he nobly fell, defending the cause of that country, to whose service his valuable life had been most usefully, most honourably devoted.

Under the pressure of these events, the arrival of the *Nisus* was to be considered as most opportune, as every exertion had been already employed with a view to the equipment of the *Africaine* and *Ceylon*, which ships, though severely cut up in the masts and rigging (the lower masts being unfit for further service), had fortunately, at the time of their recapture, part of their crews on board. Fully concurring in the expediency and the absolute necessity of this measure, the adoption of which, and the carrying into effect with the least delay, if of the most serious importance to the ultimate success of the operation, now ripe for execution, against the Isle of France, and having found it further practicable to equip the *Venus* in furtherance of this object, I have not hesitated to commission her for the time being, under the name of the *Nereide*, in commemoration of the gallant defence of his Majesty's ship bearing that name, notwithstanding the very many local difficulties and disadvantages with which we have necessarily had to contend in the execution of these plans. The squadron, now on the eve of sailing from these roads, consisting of the ships named in the margin,[2] exhibits a striking and no less gratifying instance of what may be effected by British exertion and British perseverance.

I should at the same time, be very deficient, were I not to avail myself of the opportunity now afforded me, of expressing the obligations of the service to the lieutenant-governor and commander of the forces on this island, Lieutenant-colonel Keating, to whom it is indebted, not only for the application of every civil means at his command, but for that spirit of zealous emulation wherever the navy is concerned, which has most anxiously anticipated the appropriation of every resource to its service, and the influence of which has been extended throughout this division of the army.

Among other vessels captured by the enemy I regret to mention the *Ceylon* and *Wyndham*, Honourable East India Company's ships, and the *Ranger* transport, from the Cape, having on board provisions and stores for the squadron; I am happy to add that the *Wyndham* has since been re-taken, and is arrived here, and the *Venus* was found to have on board the greater part of the stores and provisions taken in the *Ranger*, both of which circumstances have been particularly advantageous, the lower masts of the *Wyndham* having been applied to the *Africaine*, and the victualling of the squadron being, by means of the provisions found in the *Venus*, completed to four months.

It is further of still greater moment that I should apprize you, for the information of their lordships, that Major-general Abercromby, who, with his whole staff, was embarked in the *Ceylon*, and who is entrusted with the command of the expedition against the Isle of France, was recaptured in that frigate.

As the squadron will proceed to sea in a few hours after the closing of these despatches, I trust I shall stand excused to their lordships in deferring to a future opportunity the several returns and details of the squadron, as well as a statement preparing, of work performed in each department, which, in the short space of three weeks, through the unremitting and unwearied exertions that have been displayed, has been such as to complete the equipment of the squadron, and to render the whole thoroughly effective.

I should add, that the light brigade of the troops from hence are embarked, to the number of six hundred men, on board the five frigates, and are doing duty as marines, until their services shall be required on shore.

I have, &c.

A. BERTIE

London 'Gazette Extraordinary,' February 13, 1811. [XXV 164-170]

Lieutenant Cator, acting as commander of his Majesty's sloop the *Otter*, arrived here

2 *Boadicea, Africaine, Ceylon, Nisus, Nereide.*

this morning with despatches from Vice-admiral Bertie, commander-in-chief of his Majesty's ships and vessels at the Cape of Good Hope, to John Wilson Croker, Esq. Secretary to the Admiralty, of which the following are copies:

Africaine, in Port Louis, Isle of France, December 6, 1810
Sir, I have the honour to announce to you, for the information of their lordships, the capture of the Isle of France and its dependencies, comprehending the extirpation of the naval force of the enemy in these seas, and the subjugation of the last remaining colonial territory of France.

By my communication addressed to you on the 12th of October last, and forwarded to England by the *Otter*, from Bourbon, I had the honour to acquaint you, that I was on the point of resuming the blockade of the Isle of France; accordingly arrived off this port on the 19th, and, finding the whole of the enemy's ships in the harbour, and two only apparently in a state of forward equipment, I left Captain Rowley, with the *Boadicea*, *Nisus*, and *Nereide*,[3] to watch the movements of the enemy; and having previously detached the *Ceylon* and *Staunch* to convoy the division of troops from Bourbon to Rodriguez, I proceeded with the commander of the forces, (Major-general the Honourable John Abercromby) who had embarked in the *Africaine*, towards that anchorage. On the 24th, I was joined by Rear-admiral Drury, with a division of his squadron as per margin;[4] and taking under my orders for the time being, the rear-admiral, with the ships under his command, I was enabled to strengthen the blockading squadron, by detaching the *Cornelia* and *Hesper* for that purpose; and, with the others, made all sail for Rodriguez, where the squadron arrived on the 3d of November, and found lying there the division of troops from Bombay. On the 6th arrived the division from Madras, under convoy of the *Psyche* and *Cornwallis*. On the 6th, Rear-admiral Drury sailed with the *Russel*, *Phaeton*, and *Bucephalus*, to resume his command in India. On the 12th, arrived the division from Bourbon, under convoy of the *Ceylon*.

The divisions from Bengal and the Cape not arriving by the 20th, the season being so far advanced, and the anchorage (surrounded by reefs) by no means secure, more particularly for so large a number of ships, I determined on weighing with the whole fleet on the morning of the 22d, proposing the convoy should cruise to windward, until joined by one or other of the divisions. Very fortunately, intelligence was received on the night of the 21st, that the Bengal division, under convoy of the *Illustrious*, was in the offing. General Abercromby deemed it, as well as myself, advisable they should not anchor; but that, having communicated with the convoy, and given them such supplies as they might essentially require, we should proceed to the attack of the Isle of France, without waiting the junction of the troops expected from the Cape. The whole fleet accordingly weighed for the anchorage, and on the morning of the 29th bore up for the point of debarkation it had been determined to occupy in Grande Bay, about 12 miles to windward to Port Louis, where the *Africaine* leading in, and the several ships of war following with the convoy; according to a previous arrangement, the whole fleet were at anchor by ten o'clock, A.M. consisting of nearly seventy sail; and the army, with their artillery, stores, and ammunition, the several detachments of marines serving in the squadron, with a a large body of seamen, disembarked the same day, without a single loss or accident; a division of ships still maintained a vigilant blockade of the port; another division remained for the protection of the convoy at the anchorage; and a

3 Late *la Venus*, captured by Commodore Rowley, as announced in the Gazette of yesterday.
4 *Russell, Clorinde, Doris, Phaeton, Bucephalus, Cornelin, Hesper.*

View of Bombay Castle. Engraved by Bailey, from a Drawing by W. Westall. The
Fort of Bombay is by far the strongest and most regular fortification in India. All
the arms, and naval stores, for the Malabar coast, are kept in this castle. Plate 281

third, under my more immediate command, shifted their station as circumstances
required, to keep up a more effectual communication with the army as it advanced, and
which was dependant for its supplies of provisions and stores wholly on the resources
of the navy.

On the 2d instant, the Governor-general, De Caen, proposed terms of capitulation,
and commissioners being appointed on either side, a capitulation was signed and ratified
on the morning of the 3d inst., at the British head-quarters; a copy of which I have the
honour to transmit for their lordships' information.

In a combined operation of this nature, the ultimate success of which must
essentially, in a great degree, be made to depend upon a zealous and emulative co-
operation and support through each graduation; and, in the present instance, where
these features have been so eminently conspicuous in every rank, and in every situation
and circumstance, the recommendation of particular individuals to their lordships' more
immediate notice, may be deemed superfluous.

It is, however, from a sense of justice, that I record the services of Captain Beaver,
of his Majesty's sloop *Nisus*, whom I intrusted with the superintendence of the whole
arrangements for the disposition and debarkation of the army; and whose abilities and
experience, on similar occasions, particularly qualified him to undertake this important
duty. Nor should I omit to bear testimony to the unwearied exertions of Captain
Patterson, of his Majesty's ship *Hesper*; and of Lieutenant B. Street, commanding the
government armed ship *Emma*, who were employed for many successive nights in
sounding, and (as it has been proved) gained a perfect knowledge of the anchorage on
the enemy's coast; and who were equally strenuous in their services, in various ways, on
shore. . . .

I have the honour to be, &c

A. BERTIE

Appendix 8 – Gunnery and Pyrotechnics

THE PAPERS COLLECTED in this appendix, apart from their obvious value in the study of naval weapons systems, also supplement those brought together in Appendix 1, Volume I, on Naval Strategy and Tactics. These latter, to be effective, must be derived as much from the technical limitations of weapons as they are from those of ship design and human psychology.

In 1800 was published an article discussing the gunnery advantages and disadvantages of close-range action, and three essays reprinted from the French *Moniteur*. The author of the first of these identified the gunnery practice of British fleets as the principal reason for their repeated triumphs. The second essayist from the *Moniteur*, on the other hand, ascribes British success to the quality of their gunpowder, and to the fact that the officers and ships' companies of British ships were responsible for fitting and storing their own ships. The third essay develops the theme of the limitations of French artillery. A letter to the editor published as part of the series, however, focused its attention on the morale of men on the gundeck. In 1800 was also published the first of the technical papers on guns and equipment which were to continue with increasing sophistication until after the conclusion of the war in 1815. In 1809 experiments were recorded on the power of French and English gunpowder, a flame-thrower was demonstrated at Woolwich, and 'Brontes', who may have been a paid correspondent for *The Naval Chronicle*, began a series of letters on the technical development of Congreve's rockets. In 1811 a report was printed on improvements which Thomas Bertie had made to the mounting of 42-pdr carronades, and a report on Fulton's torpedoes which, having been offered to the British government, were now being offered to that of the United States. Vice-Admiral Hunter's proposal to use counter-weights to run out guns after their recoil is a curiosity, which has only been reproduced here as a plate. Considering its obvious impracticability, it is a little surprising it was published in the first instance. Interest was growing in new forms of ordnance. Besides the Congreve rocket, papers in *The Naval Chronicle* exhibited an interest in pyrotechnics delivered by cannon shot, fire-ship or submersible. The crisis of the American war also stimulated interest in improving the capacity of the carronade to engage on equal terms the long guns of American super-frigates.

Document List

[Readers should refer to the main text of Volume III, pp61-70 to find descriptions of the coffers used for incendiary attack on Boulogne in 1804, and to pp239-240 above for the description of the explosion ships used in the attack at Basque Roads in 1809.]

1800 - The [Dis]Advantages of Close Action III 363-64

When Ships in action are opposed to each other at a small distance, the velocity of cannon balls is so great, that in penetrating a Ship's side, few or no splinters are torn off; and by these more men are commonly killed and wounded, than by the ball itself. For the same reason, a close shot does less damage also to the Ship itself, than a distant one; for a quick-flying ball makes an aperture less than its own diameter, whereas a spent one produces innumerable deadly splinters, at the same time shivering the object it strikes, and making wide and extensive rents in it. The proportion of the wounded to the killed, is also greater in distant than in close fight, on account of the great number of small splinters; and we have an experimental proof of this, in comparing the action in Fort Royal Bay in April 1781, with that near Dominica in April 1782. In the former, the enemy having kept far to windward, and engaged at a great distance, the proportion of the wounded to the killed was considerably more than four to one, whereas in the latter, where the greater part of the battle was close, the proportion of the wounded to the killed was little more than three to one. This idea, adds Dr. Blane, is well illustrated by the manner in which Captain Nott, of the *Centaur*, was killed in Fort Royal Bay. This brave man, having carried his Ship nearer the enemy than the rest of the line, but nevertheless at a great distance, had his signal made to keep the line, and having gone into his cabin, as it is said, to examine the import of the signal, a cannon ball struck him in the groin, and it was so far spent that it stuck in his body. It tore away an whole plank of the ship's side, the splinters of which killed a young gentleman, the only person near him.

1800 – Questions and Answers Relative to Naval Gunnery [IV 53-56]

Question What are the dimensions of a truly fortified iron gun?
Answer A truly fortified iron gun ought to measure eleven diameters of the bore as the circumference of the base ring, nine diameters at the trunnions, and seven at the circumference of the muzzle ring.
Question What are the dimensions of a truly fortified brass gun?
Answer It should measure two diameters less at each place of measurement than the iron gun; that is to say, nine diameters of the bore as the circumference of the base ring, seven at the trunnions, and five [at] the muzzle ring.
Question How are you to discover when a gun quadrates, or hangs well in her carriage?
Answer Every gun ought to measure in length seven times her own diameter at the vent; the trunnions ought to be placed at the distance of three diameters from the base ring; then there will remain four diameters in distance from the muzzle.
Question How can you discover whether the carriage is proper and of due length for the gun?
Answer A carriage ought to be five eighths the length of the gun, and the eye will easily discover if it is wide enough and high enough, or too high.
Question How do you dispart a gun in order to take proper aim at a given object?
['Dispart': the difference between the semi-diameter of a gun at the base ring and at the swell of the muzzle which must be allowed for in taking aim; or a sight mark on the muzzle to compensate for the difference in semi-diameters.]
Answer Insert a priming wire into the vent, and let it touch the lower part of the metal of the bore; mark the wire close to the vent, take it out, and rest it on the lower metal of the rose at the muzzle, and the distance between the muzzle ring and marked part of the wire is the height of the dispart.
Question How will you find the thickness of the metal at vent, trunnions, and muzzle?
Answer I will take the diameter of the gun at the vent, and lay it down thus [————],

which will express the diameter; then I will insert a priming wire into the vent, and let it rest on the lower metal; mark it close to the vent, and taking it out, lay the mark on the line of the diameter, thus [——/—]. I will then crook the end of the wire a little, that it may enter the vent, and inserting it a second time, turn it round till it catches the upper metal of the bore; then mark it again close to the vent, set off the distance on the same line of the diameter, and mark how far it reaches from the other end of the line, thus [a/b/a]; then will "a" and "a" represent the thickness of the metal, and "b" the bore of the gun; and if the portions "a""a" of the line are equal to each other, the thickness of the metal is equal, and of course the gun centrally bored. I will then girth the gun at the trunnions with a waxed twine, and if it measure nine diameters of the bore, the gun is so far truly fortified. Observing the same operation at the muzzle, where it is to measure seven diameters, the process is complete.

Question How are you to discover whether a gun is truly bored?

Answer Take a spare sponge-staff and fix on it a rammer-head, strike a chalk line on it from one end to the other, and put it into the gun as far as it will go, keeping the chalk line uppermost, and exactly in the centre; then prick down the vent with a priming wire; and if you find on taking out the rammer you have pricked into the chalk line, you may reasonably conclude the gun is truly bored; but if you miss the chalk line, that it is not.

Question How do you discover when a gun is honeycombed?

Answer Take a spring searcher with five prongs,[1] and a reliever, muzzle the searcher, and ram it home in the gun; take off the reliever, and keep turning the searcher backwards and forwards; you will easily discover whether it catches; when it does, mark the staff close to the muzzle, then turn the searcher again as before, and whenever it catches again, mark the staff as in the former instance; so that by laying the staff when drawn out on the outside of the gun, you may clearly judge where the honeycombs are.

Question How can you discover the depth of the honeycombs?

Answer Take a searcher with one prong, and a reliever; arm the end of the prong with wax; then ram it home in the gun; take off the reliever, and turn the searcher till it catches, then will the impression made in the wax show the shape and depth of the honeycomb.

Question How deep must a honeycomb be to render the piece unserviceable?

Answer If the honeycomb on either side, or on the lower metal between the breech and the reinforce ring, is three tenths of an inch deep, the gun is to be condemned; if on the upper metal, four-tenths; if on any part without or beyond the reinforce ring, five-tenths are sufficient.

Question How are you to discover whether a gun is sound or cracked?

Answer By striking a smart blow on the gun with a hammer. If it rings clear, it may be concluded the gun is sound; if the gun jars, or emits a hoarse sound, 'tis most probable the gun is cracked. - Or the following method may be taken: - stop the vent, and light a piece of touchwood; put it into the gun, and stop the muzzle securely; let the touchwood remain in the gun four or five minutes; if the gun is cracked, the touchwood will burn out; if the gun is sound, extinguished.

---

1 A most ingenious instrument invented by the late General Desaguliers, and since brought to the greatest perfection, has totally superseded the use of this contrivance. All guns intended for sea service are now previously examined by proper officers belonging to the Ordnance-Board, who, by means of this instrument, being able to ascertain, with the greatest precision, the internal state and defects of any gun, after a very short examination, of course reject all those which, either from natural defect, or subsequent injury, appear unfit for His Majesty's service.

Question How is a shot to be fitted to a gun?

Answer By dividing the diameter of the bore into twenty equal parts, the diameters of the shot ought to be nineteen of those parts.

Question How are you to find the proper proportion of powder?

Answer Eighteen pounders, and all inferior calibres, require half the weight of the shot; for all above, there are certain rules to find the proper proportion by.

Question How is a gun to be secured, if it breaks loose?

Answer By cutting down the hammocks, tripping the gun, and lashing it to the ring bolts of the side till fine weather.

Question How is a gun to be cleared when a bit is broke in it?

Answer By drawing the gun, and sprinkling powder with a ladle from the breech to the muzzle; this done, drive in a tight tampion with a small score in it, and blow the gun off.

Question If a shot has fetched way in the gun [ie rolled away from the charge], how is it to be secured?

Answer By damping the powder, or splitting the tampion; then insert a rope sponge of a small size, and drive the wad home.

Question Suppose in loading your gun the shot sticks by the way; if you fire the gun, it splits, and you cannot draw the gun, what must be done to free it?

Answer The powder must be damped, and while that is soaking, some powder must be mealed, and the gun primed, getting as much powder down the touch-hole as possible; then fire the gun off.

Question Suppose a ship going to sea immediately, it is required that all things should be ready for action; what must they be?

Answer The powder filled, the powder horns and partridge or grape shot between the guns, hammered shot in the buckets, crows and hand crows, levers at the guns; nets and cheeses of wads fore and aft; the match-tubs in their places, the matches ready, the lockers full of shot, the spare tackles and breechings ready, wet swabs at the door of the magazine and heads of the ladders; the boxes of hand grenades ready for the tops.

Question How thick ought the metal of a gun to be at the vent?

Answer One diameter and a quarter of the bore in thickness.

Question How many men are necessary to a gun in case of engagement?

Answer One man to every five hundred weight of metal.

1800 - French Naval Tactics ^{IV 142-148; 222-229}

A stimulation of spirit among the people in France to a new organization of their Marine, to attain which ends, the most vigorous and energetic measures are resorted to by the Consulate, appears to engage the pens of individuals. These, however, are probably in the pay of government, as they have chosen the official paper, (the *Moniteur*), in that country, for a discussion on the subject. The first Essay, the writer of which flatters himself that he has discovered - "What is the cause of the naval superiority of the English over the French," is here presented:

Essay I

Reducing the possible Causes of this Excellence to Three, he considers that in the two first of them, the superior architecture of the ships and the superior theoretic skill of the officers, the advantage is on the side of the French. In the third, the direction of the artillery on board ship, he considers the whole superiority of the British Navy to consist.

"The French," he observes, "direct their guns at the rigging, which is above all the body of the vessel. Three fourths of the space thus aimed at, form a void, so that three-fourths of the balls thus fired lose themselves in the air. From the uncertain elevation which is given to the guns when they are directed against the rigging, the balls which strike the masts, must necessarily strike them one above the other; and experience proves, that fifty strokes of this kind against a mast do not break it, for though they may make the mast useless for the future, they do not dismast the vessel during the combat. - The yards are still less exposed than the masts on account of the oblique manner in which they present themselves to the enemy. The damage done to the cordage is not difficult to be repaired, especially as the enemy must commonly be in a line from which they cannot depart, in order to profit of this momentary advantage. Notwithstanding the great number of balls which pass through the sails, they generally serve till the end of the engagement.

Thus it appears, from the effect of directing the cannon in this manner, that it cannot secure the dismasting of the vessels, and that the damage which it does to the yards, to the cordage, and the sails, is not of great consequence. And thus also it is evident, that when the guns are pointed principally against the rigging, the hulk of the ship cannot be struck, the guns cannot be dismounted, nor any considerable number of men killed or wounded: from which it follows, that the crew of the enemy being so little injured, his valour, his force, and consequently the briskness of his fire, cannot be much enfeebled.

The English direct their shot always against the hull of the vessel. It is thus that they succeed in striking between wind and water, in dismounting guns, and in killing such a number of the crew. In the first case they force their enemy to take away a number of men from the management of the guns for the service of the pumps, and nothing is so fatiguing or dispiriting as this. When a fear of sinking is induced, men are not much disposed to contend for victory. The dismounted guns cannot then be replaced. The carnage which is produced among the crew diminishes its number, and spreads terror and alarm among the survivors to such a degree, that their courage, their force, and consequently the briskness of their fire, must abate.

When the cannon are directed against the hull of the vessels, the balls which pass above must pass almost at the same height, so that those which strike the masts hit them nearly at the same point, and it is this which injures the most precisely in the manner which can bring it by the board.

It appears to follow, from the above reasonings, that the manner in which the English direct their guns must produce a much greater effect than that employed by the French, and that the superiority of the English Marine in battle consists in the better employment of its artillery, that is to say, in the better directing of it. The facts which have taken place in the principal combats of this war support these reasonings. On the 1st of June, 1794, the English had two vessels dismasted, the French had eleven. In the battle of the Nile the former had one, the latter had six. The English dismasted vessels were those which lost the greatest number of men. - Other similar facts might be added, but they are so well known that it is unnecessary to enter into so wide details.

In order to make the truth of the preceding reasonings, and the utility of their application more full, let us examine into the conduct of the English Admirals in battle, with a view of seeing whether they have sought by fineness of manoeuvring, the advantages of position, &c. or if they have depended upon the manner of directing their artillery. On the 1st of June, 1794, Admiral Howe, being to windward of the French, who expected him, made the signal to his fleet, that each ship should manoeuvre in such a manner as to attack his adversary in the enemy's line. Thinking himself secure of victory, he only added to this signal another, which instructed them to get to leeward of the French, with a view of rendering their retreat, after defeat, more difficult. Admiral Duncan, in the battle of the Texel [Camperdown], acted precisely in the same manner with Howe, believing himself, like him, sure of success, he passed to leeward of the Dutch, in order to prevent them, after the battle, from retreating into their ports, which were to leeward. When the advantage of the wind is in possession, as in the two preceding cases, and when, instead of profiting of the advantage which this position affords, it is only sought to oppose ship to ship, it is to be presumed that great confidence is placed in the manner of directing the guns.

Admiral Nelson did not attack the whole French line [at the Battle of the Nile] – but why did he not do it? It was because his enemy being at anchor, allowed him to employ all his vessels against a part of theirs, and because the French rear-guard, from its position and the state of the wind, could only be a spectator of the destruction of the advanced guard and of the centre.

The conduct of Admiral Rodney on the 12th of April, 1782, and of Howe on the 29th of May, 1794, may be opposed to the ordinary tactics of the English; but it ought to be examined why they acted in this manner. On the 12th of April, 1782, the French had the advantage of the wind, and sailing better than the English, could keep themselves at a distance, which was not consistent with the English tactics. Rodney found himself obliged to break their line, in order to fight them nearer. The conduct of the French enabled him to succeed. On the 29th of May, 1794, the French had also the advantage of the wind over the English, and as they did not shew themselves disposed to come sufficiently near, to engage in a decisive affair, Admiral Howe, in order to force them to it, endeavoured to break their line. This manoeuvre did not succeed. It is known in what confusion his fleet then was, and what the French Admiral had in his power to do. It may be supposed, from the conduct of the French in the battle, that their intention was only to get clear of the English vessels, so as to avoid a decisive affair, and they have so much this habit, that in the battle of the Nile, in which almost all the vessels were at anchor, they nearly gained it. The headmost vessel of the English line, to which a French vessel surrendered, and which, on the following morning, set sail to prevent the flight of the two French ships and of the two frigates which escaped, and whose fire she received in passing, had only one man killed and a few wounded. – The second vessel ahead of the English line had only two men killed, though a French vessel surrendered to her alone. Other similar examples might be adduced.

To convince one's self of the superior utility of killing as many as possible of the enemy, rather than of injuring their ships, it is only necessary to read the official account of the English captains who have been taken, to shew that it is always the greatest loss of men which has forced them to surrender. If the superiority of the English Marine does not depend on the manner of their directing their artillery, upon what does it depend? Why are the continual defeats which their enemies experience never interrupted by the chances of war? The French have reduced naval tactics to a system. The English never study it; they have not even a school for the Marine. The facility with which they triumph over their enemies, has made them neglect the study of a theory surely necessary for the perfect knowledge of the practice which it teaches.

It may be said, perhaps, that the English vessels are manned with better sailors, and a greater number of them, than the French – but, in a battle, there is only a certain number chosen to perform the manoeuvres, the remainder attend to the guns, and a sailor is not better for this than another man. The French have cannoneers; - the English have none. Are the English sailors more brave than the French? They should be, if bravery consists in a great measure in the confidence which one has in the means of displaying it, and in the smallness of the danger which a person believes that he runs. The habit of conquering also makes them engage in battle with an enthusiasm and courage, which men accustomed to defeats and severe losses cannot have. Do the English soldiers resemble their sailors? - No; the French troops are to them, in this respect, what the English sailors are to the French sailors, and for the same reasons.

It appears, from these new observations, that the superiority of the English Marine consists in the manner of their directing their guns, and that the excellence of its officers and sailors in the day of battle, is only the natural consequence of this.

If its own means of victory were employed against this Marine, it would not long continue to be the principal support of a government which is the greatest obstacle to the triumph of the cause of liberty."

Essay II
In answer to the Preceding, by a French Author

To the Editor of the *Moniteur*, In conformity with your invitation, I entreat you to have the goodness to insert the following reply to the memoir upon the Marine which lately appeared in your Journal.

"The English Marine was defeated by the French Marine under Louis the XIV. It has been defeated in our times by Suffrein, and De Estaing - since the Revolution, by Richery, Lejoiaille, Richer, and Sirie.

The Author of the Memoir has forgotten to mention among the qualities necessary to form a good Marine, 1st. Presence of mind, for improving every favourable circumstance, and remedying any unfavourable one, in the officer who commands. 2d. Practice in those who execute orders. 3dly, and lastly, The military spirit in both, without which all other qualities become of no use.

The French vessels are better than the English; but every Captain in England, along with his crew, sees to the fitting out, the rigging, and the stowing of his Ship. This is not the case in France.

Though the best books on tactics have been written by officers of the French Marine, it does not follow that the acting Naval officers are the best tacticians. Unfortunately those who have practice, are unacquainted with theory; and those who are acquainted with theory, have not hitherto attained practice. This remark applies to all, from commanders in chief to the lowest who aspire to this dignity, but there must be excepted from it, a small number of officers of merit, in different ranks, who could form an excellent squadron, were they to employ themselves in sea affairs.

The French sailors are composed of conscripts and requisitionaries, who are novices in the art of sailing. The largest number and the best part of the old French sailors, disgusted with the little attention paid to the Marine, and the kind of contempt in which it has been hitherto held, have passed into foreign service, and are universally much esteemed wherever they are employed. And in opposition to the opinion of the author of the Memoir, I am persuaded that the skill of private individuals has great influence on the success of a Naval engagement, though less than on that of a land action.

The success of a sea-fight depends on the talent of the commander in chief, for making arrangements; on that of the Captains for executing orders, and supplying, by their own intelligence, what is wanting in them; and on that of the crew for managing and manoeuvring the vessel, and directing the artillery.

There is no order in the Marine for directing the fire rather in one way than another. The exercise teaches to fire a-head, in stern or in broadside, to dismast, at the hull or at the rigging, and to sink. In an engagement the guns are pointed in one or other of these manners, according to circumstances.

There is no instance, as has been alleged by the author of the memoir, of a mast having received fifty shots without falling. A single shot is sufficient for the purpose.

I shall now explain why so few cannon shots have effect at sea: in the month of Frimaire, year 7th, the small division armed at Toulon to carry ammunition to Bonaparte, was lying in the Road when orders were received from the Minister to prove the powder of a magazine. The commander of that division, Citizen Hubert, having at that time observed the bad quality of the powder of his division, demanded that it should be proved. I assisted at that proof, and the most favourable trials did not carry the balls so as to have effect above seventy-five toises, whereas they ought to have been carried one hundred and fifteen toises. But a Commissary of Marine was employed to receive the powder, and a contractor had manufactured it.

The powder of our division was the same with that of the fleet of Aboukir. Thus you perceive that it is not necessary to suppose a defect in the manner of pointing the cannon at sea. The balls of the enemy strike on board; ours fall half way.

The English have no Maritime Prefects, nor Superintendents, nor even Commissiries.

They have no Marine Artillery-men, because their sailors know the management of the guns, and if they did not recruit by pressing, they would have no naval troops. The commanders take care of the arming of their fleets and ships; and except the Treasurer, they have no administration either at sea or in port. They have not attained the highest point of perfection, but at least they have not sacrificed the leading, to secondary points. They have thought, with reason, that he whose head is responsible for the success of an operation, ought alone to be trusted with the choice of the materials, and the execution of the movements which are to conduce to that success.

Though these Reflections are rather long, they are necessary to reply to the Memoir which you have inserted; and though you do not know me, I hope the subject is interesting enough to procure them a speedy insertion. - Health and respect,

RIVORE, a Sailor."

Essay III
"By an Officer of the Marine Artillery."

Sir, The author of the memoir upon the Marine, some time ago inserted in the *Moniteur*, has treated this interesting question so as in some measure to awaken the attention of every sailor, and of every Marine Artillery Man. This subject appearing to be rather out of the sphere of a private officer, I may be blamed for publishing the following observations, which I would not presume to hazard did not I believe that they may be of greater utility than those contained in the Memoir. But this is of little consequence. Should they only attract the criticism of the officers of the Marine Artillery, I shall have attained my object; for this would be one means of drawing them from the apathy in which they seem to be held.

The author has fixed upon three causes, which he thinks sufficient to give superiority in naval combats: 1st, a superior excellence of ships. 2d, a more profound knowledge in the officers of naval tactics; and 3d, the more advantageous use and direction of the artillery.

The author next having, in some way or other, demonstrated that the two first causes are in favour of the French, concludes that it is the bad use we make of our artillery that is the cause of our reverses.

It appears to me that he would have been more just had he concluded, that our defeats arise merely from the inferiority of our artillery.

The two first points not being within my sphere, and having been already resolved, I shall now, in concert with the author, examine what is the influence of the third.

It cannot be doubted that this influence is very great in naval engagements, since it is well known that artillery is employed in them as the principal agent - that if it often prepares the victory to land armies, it must by sea not only prepare but determine it. I am far from thinking that much does not depend upon the skilful manoeuvring of the ships, but can these manoeuvres be always executed under the superior fire of an enemy's artillery?

The author states, that "*The French direct their guns at the rigging, which comprehends every thing that is above the body of the vessel, that three-fourths of this space is a void, and consequently, that three-fourths of the balls so directed, must lose themselves in air.*"

The last phrase is not correct, for the balls do not lose themselves in air, but in water. "*From the vague elevation which is given to the balls when they are fired at the rigging, the balls which hit the masts must necessarily strike them one above the other; and experience proves, that fifty cannon shots received in this manner by a mast will not break it, &c.*"

When the rigging is fired at, it is only at a distance from which some kind of advantage may be expected by this direction of shot. Thus, when a vessel is precisely distant from its adversary that space which a gun will carry without giving it elevation, then it is unnecessary to allow much, and the degree necessary may be exactly determined. But when the guns are fired beyond this distance it becomes necessary to give them elevation, on account of the distance. Then it is that their muzzles conceal the hull of the enemy's vessel, and even its rigging, if the distance is considerable, from the eye of the officer who points the guns, and it is from hence, no doubt, that the author has supposed the fire was directed at the rigging of the enemy's vessel when it is only proposed to reach it. I will agree that when the Marine cannoneer fires beyond the distance of point-blank shot, he has nothing which indicates to him how much he elevates or lowers his piece; that he does not know the precise degree in which he has elevated or lowered it at the moment of the departure of the ball. Hence it follows, that besides its being possible that he may be able to bring back, for several shots, his piece to the same degree of elevation that it had before, it necessarily follows that the balls must lodge in the masts, or strike them precisely one above the other.

"*The English always direct their guns at the hulls of the vessels, &c.*"

The Author ought to have established a term of comparison from which we could set out, in order to estimate the effects of artillery. Let us suppose any fixed distance; it is evident that every shot directed at the hull of the enemy's vessel at the distance of two cables length, cannot miss it, since it is impossible that the balls can miss it by diverging laterally, and as the degree to which they fall cannot exceed seventeen or eighteen feet; but if we suppose a distance of six cables length, the guns ought no longer to be directed at the hulls of the enemy's vessels, for the balls would touch the water at about a third part of that distance, and would never reach the vessels. It would be necessary in this case to give the guns a certain elevation. Their muzzles will then conceal the object from the cannoneer, who will be obliged to take his aim by the sides of the gun - a method which cannot but produce error, and of which, the practice is only recommended for want of better means. It is not uncommon, with such uncertain methods of pointing, for the best trained cannoneer to mistake one degree or even more in the elevation of the gun, which causes him to miss every part of the enemy's vessels; since at the distance we are supposing, the fall of the balls must be from two to three hundred feet. I think it too tedious and useless to point out all the errors which might arise from lateral pointing.

When guns are fired at a greater distance than the gun carries point-blank, they are almost always aimed by chance. There can therefore be no security that they will strike any determined part of the enemy's ship; but they are fired in the hope that they will strike it some where or other. It is easy to see from this, how ridiculous it would be to aim so as to sink it in this case.

"*When the guns are directed at the body of the enemy's vessels, the balls which pass above must pass almost at the same height, so that those which strike the masts must strike them nearly in the same place.*"

What the author says here is true; when the guns are fired at a distance which they will carry point-blank, I think I have already proved, that beyond this distance there can be no security that the balls will in any degree strike.

Thus the instructions which the author has given respecting the management of artillery at sea, only relate to firing point-blank. His views are undoubtedly not confined to this point; he has given room to hope that in a second memoir he will explain them for the instruction of the officers of the Marine Artillery.

"*It may be supposed from the conduct of the French in battle, that their intention was only to get clear of the English vessels, in order to avoid a decisive action.*"

I suppose that the intention of the French sailors when they are engaged, is to do all the ill possible to the enemy, and that if the effect does not correspond with their intention, it is the fault of the arms which they use.

I shall only cite one fact to give an idea of the effect of our artillery. Upon the return of the French and Spanish fleets, commanded by Admiral Bruix, they fired 900 cannon shots at least, at an Algerine corsaire, without the smallest effect. I do not believe that in a combat of this nature, there was ever so much unavailing firing.

Though the preference ought to be given to directing the guns so as to make them strike the hull of the enemy's vessel, I do not think that this opinion of the author ought to be considered as an exclusive principle. For instance, in a particular engagement the commander of a ship, the superiority of whose artillery over that of its antagonist is discernible, ought, it appears to me, to save the enemy's vessel, and only to fire at the rigging.

The author, in examining the conduct of the English admirals in battle, asserts that they have neglected manoeuvring, with the advantages of position, and that they have reckoned solely on the superiority of their artillery. The English admirals have done what every able general will do, when having the superiority of force, he can, by combating the enemy's armament in parallel order, fight it along the whole extent of its front and destroy it completely.

The author observes, "*that the English have only produced one contemptible work upon Naval Tactics.*" But they have produced several excellent ones upon artillery, which is at least as essential. *"That they have no marine school."* We have in opposition to that, no school for artillery. *"Lastly, that they have no Naval Corps of Artillery."* It may now be asked, if we have any? If that body which we know by the name, is organized as it ought to be? If the men who compose it are chosen, and if they are commanded at sea by the officers who trained them?

The only French author who has written upon the subject of the Naval Artillery is citizen Texier Norbie. His work, though modern, appears to me incomplete, because he has not taken notice of the great changes made in the land artillery in 1765, and since that period, nor of the discoveries which have arisen from the discussions which the subject of artillery has under gone, although he could not be unacquainted with them. It is true that it does not seem to have been his object in his researches to appreciate the importance or advantage of these changes, nor to make any application of them to the naval artillery.

The land artillery having been carried to a pitch of perfection, which has attracted the attention of all military men, and even of the learned of Europe, it would have been surprising, if the naval artillery had not reaped some improvement from this perfection, were it only in those parts of its construction or management which are analogous or similar to those of the land artillery, if it had had a corps destined particularly to its service, of which the officers had been artillerers [sic]. This corps not having existed, the Naval Artillery has undergone very little change.

I have proved that our Naval Artillery does not furnish any means of taking a sure aim. It is still more defective with respect to its mounting, because this is not established on any rational principle; some of them being contrary to the simplest rules of mechanics, it would be impossible to resolve them all into one. I conclude, that in every respect it is inferior to that of the English. We have indeed the melancholy experience of this. It would not then be sufficient to secure us constant success, merely that we have perfected the construction of our vessels, that we have investigated deeply into naval tactics, and formed good naval officers; it would still remain necessary to improve our artillery, and to render it, if possible, superior to that of the enemy. I shall offer some leading ideas as to the the means which I think best adapted to make it regain this superiority.

It will be necessary to make our artillery lighter, which may be done without danger, as is proved the example of the English, and of our allies the Spaniards, whose artillery is one fourth lighter than ours; to fix the dimensions of the guns upon an accurate knowledge of the laws of cohesion, of the force of tenacity in the particles of cast iron, and of the effect of the powder which tends to break them.

It will be necessary to adapt to our guns *bousous de mire*[2] and *bausses mobiles*, similar to those with which field-pieces are provided, but of which the properties will be more extended, and the use more sure, without requiring any greater skill on the part of the cannoneer.

The next thing requisite will be, to facilitate the means of taking aim by the sides of the gun; some method of making fast the guns, so that their weight being nearer to the centre of gravity as to the vessel, the motion may be made less, which must also be provided.

The carronades ought to be cast a-new, as their construction, as well as that of their frames, is evidently bad.

2 The translator is unacquainted with the English terms for this and the following expression (*bausses mobiles*), but what is meant by *beuteus de mire* is the small mark near the muzzle of the gun, to direct more steadily the aim of the person who points it.

Schools of artillery for the naval service ought to be established, in which officers, by being taught a good theory, may be prepared for serving usefully.

A corps of Marine Artillery, of chosen men, ought to be formed; to the officers of which ought to be granted, the power of directing the artillery at sea, and that of commanding and disciplining their cannoneers. These officers not being then so completely null as they are at present on board our vessels, would have the glory of being able to contribute to our success, the only one of which they could be jealous.

The zeal which animates me for the honour of the corps to which I am proud of belonging, will plead my pardon for the faults of this essay. If I am deceived in the conclusions which I have drawn, I eagerly wish that some officers, more masters of the theory and practice of the profession, may, by making it known, propose better.

For The Naval Chronicle

Mr. Editor, The *Moniteur*, or in other words, the official gazette of France, of which you have given a translation, having thought proper to obtrude some observations upon the comparative naval tactics of France and England, and to draw from those observations a particular inference, the remarks with which I shall trouble you are intended as an answer to those observations. I shall, however, answer the *Moniteur* rather substantially than regularly, and shall reply more to the result of his arguments, than criticise his individual paragraphs. The remarks of the *Moniteur* are evidently the language of Consular command. It is an obvious finesse of government, to excite their navy to the hope of rivaling their army. The *Moniteur* insists that the superiority of a marine force, when in action, must depend on three things: 1. The better condition of the vessels - 2. The greater naval skill of the officers - 3. The better use of the artillery. I grant to the Consulate Gazette that such things are the causes, but not the only causes of superiority. There is one other cause, and that, fortunately for this country, a cause which is as much a property of our nature, as fog and beef are the characteristics of our island: that cause, Sir, is the matchless firmness of our seamen!

The *Moniteur* remarks, that the continual victories of the English at sea must arise from the imprudence of the French in firing at our rigging, rather than at our hulls; but English seamen are disposed to insist, that fire as they may, at hull or rigging, the French fleet always shall, and always must, be beaten. England, says the *Moniteur*, has had but one author who has written on naval tactics, and he was not a seaman: all their knowledge, therefore, he adds, must be drawn from French authors. The author alluded to by the Gazette of France is Clarke. Clarke has written a book, and the most excellent book it is, upon *Naval Tactics*; and by the principles of that book, in some measure, have the French, Spaniards, and Dutch, been severely chastised. But Clarke is not the only author, although the others have not published any elaborate treatises on the subject. Admiral Russell (not to go farther back) was an author on naval tactics. Boscawen, Hawke, Rodney, were authors of the same sort. Howe, Hotham, Jarvis, Duncan, and Nelson, have published upon the same topic. There is a publication called *A Quarter Board*, composed of pages of most important composition. The authors above-mentioned have been rather nervously concise than eloquently diffuse. "Point your guns well, my lads; don't throw away a single shot; see but their whiskers and you will singe them."

The letter of the *Moniteur* insinuates, that the cause of the invariable defeats of the French proceed from their firing at our masts and rigging; and that the uniform victories of the English are the natural result of firing at the French hulls. It is not here intended to reply to the individual arguments used in the *Moniteur* to substantiate his statement. It is more to the purpose to resort, in the first instance, to the truer source of British triumph, and the cureless cause of French defeat. When a very valiant captain of a French line of battle ship, whose vessel was sunk, after a most handsome resistance, was saved from the impending peril of drowning, by the commander of a British ship, in Lord Howe's memorable action, the prisoner, in the fullness of his gratitude for his life preserved, and a great part of his crew rescued from perdition, having thanked the English captain with a candour correspondent to his courage, very frankly declared, that nothing in the world could stand against the broadside of a British man of war, which he pronounced to be a perfect *hail-storm* of bullets.

When the surviving first officer of a line of battle ship, taken in an action between the French fleet in the Mediterranean, and the British fleet under Admiral Hotham, had, some days afterwards, his sword returned to him, he congratulated himself upon receiving it, and at the same time observed, that he had been obliged to thrust that sword through the bodies of several of his seamen, to make the remainder stand to their guns: he at the same time asked the First Lieutenant of the Admiral's ship, on board of which the Frenchman was a prisoner, how the English officers contrived to keep their men to their guns? "We have no necessity to keep them to their guns," replied the Lieutenant, "for the Devil himself could not drive them from them;" and, pointing to his speaking trumpet, said, "We have only to make them hear, they will be sure to obey." In short, Sir, the hail-storm, as the first-mentioned officer emphatically described it, is the true and only cause of conquest on one side, and the irresistible impulse that dismays, disconcerts, and defeats the other party; and as to John Bull, the hail-storm, with all its concomitant thunder and lightning of artillery, has no other effect upon him than to make him pelt away in return till he has silenced and subdued his antagonist.

It is not here intended to draw illiberal or national comparisons; the letter in the *Moniteur* has set no such example, and requires no such return, much less is it designed to vaunt any preternatural prowess; and, less than all is it meant to allude to the numbers sacrificed to give a temporary colouring of success to the French armies. There is no affinity between the two services. The hail-storm here alluded to, is the hail-storm of the main. It is sufficient just to observe, that pushing hundred upon hundred, and devoting to death thousand after thousand, to fatigue the enemy by continuation of slaughter, may answer the purposes of desperation on shore; but such temerity afloat, whether applied to the hull or rigging of the British ships, will only augment destruction, and ensure defeat to their assailants.

The *Moniteur* states, that this superiority of the English, in firing at the hull, was evinced in the combat with Lord Howe, and in that with Nelson, at the Nile: but here, in joining with the *Moniteur*, was to the incontrovertible superiority manifested by the British squadron upon the latter unparalleled day, I must dissent from him in affixing the glory of it to that cause to which he assigns it: to no defection on the part of his countrymen's tactics, to no indiscretion of firing at the rigging instead of the hull, was the event of that matchless transaction to be attributed. No, Mr. Editor, to the hail-storm alone must we apply for an explanation of that proud and unexampled manoeuvre.

As to Howe's renowned battle in the channel, be it remembered, that the ships of France were, on that occasion, better found and better fought than they had ever been under the old regime; every national, every republican, every pecuniary nerve was strained, to empower that formidable fleet to resist the English; every exertion was made to lay their ships close to the enemy; the old practice of firing at the rigging was completely abandoned. The prisoners in that well disputed combat unanimously declared, that the substituted system of firing at our hulls had been adopted, and executed with as much precision as the French seamen could be prevailed on to persevere in. But they did not, they could not persevere; the hail-storm totally defeated the design.

As to the fight of the Nile, be it recollected that the French ships were at anchor; that they had a three-decker of very heavy metal; that Nelson had two-deckers only; that the French purposely, declaredly, and universally pointed their whole numerous and ponderous artillery at our hulls, their broadsides at our hulls, end on: It was, at first, hundreds of shots to one, broadside to bow, point blank aim at ships necessarily less certain in their aim, because steering, and occasionally yawing; some length of time brought our ships hull to hull: then came on the aforesaid hail-storm: then might any Frenchman, advanced in the elegancies of the English tongue, have exclaimed, "From Hell, Hull, and Hail-storm, good Lord deliver us!"

In short, Sir, the *Moniteur* is correct in his data, but has erred in his conclusion, like Monsieur D'Areon, who suggested and superintended the floating batteries at Gibraltar. The able engineer pronounced his batteries (no doubt upon plausible data) to be impenetrable, incombustible, and insubmersible; whereas the batteries of Monsieur D'Areon were shot through, set on fire, and sunk.

I am, Sir, your humble servant,

HAIL-STORM

1809 - Difference Between French and English Gunpowder [XXI 23]

In the summer of 1808, a comparison was made at Bombay, of the quality of British and French powder, used in the late gallant action of his majesty's ship *San Fiorenzo* with the French frigate *la Piedmontaise*; and we are happy to exhibit a decisive proof of the superiority of the former, so essential an ingredient in British thunder. From a 7-inch brass mortar, with three ounces of powder, a 60lb. brass ball was projected, at an angle of 45 deg. and an average of three trials gave 595 feet to the *San Fiorenzo*, and 516 feet to *la Piedmontaise*, making a difference in favour of the British powder, of 79 feet. After such an experiment, it must appear singular that the French should be so partial to a *long* shot.

1809 - Flame-Thrower Demonstrated at Woolwich [XXI 349]

In addition to Shrapnell's shells and Congreve's rockets, another new, and, as is said, more destructive engine for the demolition of ships, was lately presented to the Ordnance Board by Captain Ouseley, of the foreign depôt. This thunder and lightning machine has been exhibited at Woolwich, to a vast number of general officers, officers of artillery, and engineers. The experiments were made on a flag-staff, rigged out by several ropes, and representing a mast and rigging. On the first trial the mast and rigging fell to the ground with an instant crash, involved in flames. The second trial was not so perfect owing to some irregularity in disposing the materials. The fire on the third trial clung to the mast and rigging, and burnt with the same astonishing fury as the first. The other trials were equally successful, in shewing the effect of the model of this engine, which is no larger than a couple of pint decanters united. Captain Ouseley was on the ground, and assisted in the management of it.

1809 - Congreve's Rockets
Letters to the Editor by "Brontes"

Letter 1, Sic itur ad astra. *XXII 100-102*

Having been long of opinion that there cannot be a more decisive test of merit than the confederacy of prejudice and ignorance against it, I have not been much surprised at seeing that improvement in warlike engines denominated the rocket system, become the object of vulgar abuse. I have been, however, somewhat surprised at finding in the NAVAL CHRONICLE, the lucubrations of a writer whose principles and style seem more calculated for the sphere of that self-created magistracy, calling itself the Society for the Suppression of Vice, than for a publication distinguished by liberality and knowledge. I can only attribute it to that scrupulous impartiality by which your conduct has been marked in the management of the N.C. and to your dislike to exercise your editorial powers in any way that might be liable to misinterpretation, or to the charge of shutting a door against fair discussion. As to Mr. Suppressor, I shall leave him to the censorship of your intelligent Correspondent H. who seems perfectly competent to vindicate the arts and sciences against sophistry and declamation, while I shall confine myself to the task of neutralising misrepresentation, by the dispassionate communication of certain facts concerning the origin and progress of those discoveries in pyrotechny, against which F.F.F. has declared war. [An extract from his letter appears above, p258.]

I am ignorant of the interior structure and combination upon which the powers of the rocket depend; and had it been otherwise, I should cautiously avoid any disclosure that might lead to the discovery thereof, for obvious reasons: but having acquired the knowledge of many particulars connected with its application to the purposes of war, and even witnessed some of the effects of it as a weapon, I feel emboldened to address you upon the subject, for the information of your scientific correspondents, and for the conviction of your *rational* readers: but I by no means hope or seek the conversion of enthusiasts or bigots. Should these lines therefore receive insertion, they will be followed by a few more letters under the different heads into which the subject naturally divides itself.

It was, as I understand, about the year 1804, that it first occurred to Mr. Congreve (son of a general officer in the artillery) that, as the projectile force of the rocket is exerted with little or no re-action upon the point from which it is discharged, it might be used with great convenience both afloat and ashore as a military engine, in many cases where, from the recoil produced by the explosion of gunpowder, the use of artillery is very circumscribed. But the *disideratum* as well as the difficulty was to obtain a force equal to render the projectile to be conveyed upon the rocket principle, of sufficient importance and efficacy. It was notorious that rockets were used in the wars of Hindostan: but it was understood that their magnitude was not considerable, and their utmost range not more than 1,000 yards. It was also known that the late General Desaguliers had turned his attention to the subject, and had tried some experiments at Woolwich far from successful. Mr. C. was, however, not discouraged from entering upon a fresh course of experiments, *at his own cost*, to ascertain the possibility of modifying the force of gunpowder in this way as well as in the ordinary mode.

The first point to be ascertained was the flight. He procured the largest rockets made by the trade in London: but upon trial none were found to exceed 600 yards in their actual state: although some of the same sort, treated according to the plan that suggested itself to his mind, were at length made to fly from 1,000 to 1,500 yards, according to their respective sizes and modes of construction. Our ingenious countryman thus found his perseverance rewarded in this early stage of the pursuit, by the demonstration that there did actually exist in this instrument a power capable of progressive extension in a very sensible degree. And it was not till this demonstration was obtained, that application was made to the Master General of the Ordnance for permission to have some trial rockets of large dimensions made in the artillery-laboratory at the public expense. It is only necessary to state concerning his first experiments at Woolwich, that the rocket was very shortly brought to range full 2,000 yards!

It was in this state of the discovery, that a plan was submitted to, and adopted by, government for employing this weapon against the invasion flotilla at Boulogne. Rear-admiral Sir Sidney Smith (then a captain) was appointed commodore of the squadron on that station for this particular service; and ten ship's launches were fitted for projecting rockets. Unfortunately it was so late in the year (1805) before arrangements were taken for this expedition that things were not in readiness before the middle of November. On the 18th the force destined for the attack was collected off Boulogne. The night of the 21st was fixed for the attempt. The weather had been favourable during the day, and the boats, &c. were already at their stations; when, about 8 P.M. the wind suddenly shifted to the N.W. with such violence, that the commodore was reluctantly constrained to recall the vessels without a single discharge having taken place. In fine, it was with difficulty the squadron got out of Boulogne bay, and it came on to blow to such a degree during the night, that five of the ten launches were swamped. So there was an end of the matter for that year.

In the spring of 1806, Mr. C. obtained permission to proceed in making still larger rockets, and forming them in metallic, instead of paper, cases. The event justified the idea. Rockets were constructed weighing 32 lbs. capable of conveying as much combustible composition as a 10-inch spherical carcass, and which would range 3,000 yards more or less. It was also discovered that the great length of the stick, given by the laboratory proportions, was not required in practice; but admitted of a reduction in length of not less than 10 feet from those proportions, making the new 32-pounder's even shorter than that of the old 8-pounder, thereby of course giving additional facility for service. These improvements formed the object of renewed experiments at Woolwich, in the presence of the Earl of Moira, then M.G. of the Ordnance, and of Viscount Howick, 1st Lord Commissioner of the Admiralty. It was wished that those ministers should decide upon the powers of this weapon by ocular demonstration - they did so; and the result was, (not such childish alarms as those felt or affected by M. Suppressor, F.F.F.) but on order for the immediate construction of a quantity like those just tried, and a warrant of Admiralty for the inventor to superintend such preparations as might be necessary (in this department) for a fresh attack against Boulogne, under the direction of Commodore E.W.C.R. Owen.

Here I shall take leave of the subject for the present; reserving the history of the second attempt at Boulogne, and the subsequent one at Copenhagen, for my next letter.

BRONTES

Shooter's Hill, 30th July, 1809

Letter 2, "Non est ad astra mollis à terris via." Seneca.[3] *XXII 201-203*

Mr. Editor, The attention you have been pleased to pay to my introductory letter on the origin and progress of Mr. Congreve's discoveries in pyrotechny, encourages me to proceed according to promise.

The decisive trial that was hoped to have been made in November, 1805, having been thwarted by the too advanced season of the year, the winter was employed in preparations for returning to the charge in the spring: but this attempt was almost as ill-fated as the first. No sooner was all in readiness at the proper season than negotiations for peace were set on foot, and the passage of our plenipotentiary was counted a sufficient reason for tacitly suspending hostilities against Boulognè, and the summer was consequently consumed in the journeys of messengers. Till at length, on the 8th of October, 1806, the Earl of Lauderdale being then known to have quitted Paris *ré infectá*, the commodore of our squadron (Captain Owen) was tempted not to lose a favourable coincidence of wind, weather, and tide, far from frequent on that station so late in the autumn. Accordingly, on the evening of that day (8th) boats, armed in the appropriate manner, took their stations in Boulogne Bay, to the number of 18.

Notwithstanding the want of expertness naturally attendant upon a first apprenticeship, not less than *two hundred* rockets were discharged in *half an hour*; and in about *ten minutes* the town appeared on fire: while such was the panic on shore that scarcely a shot was returned from the batteries.[4] The nature and extent of the mischief could never be thoroughly estimated: it was reported, however, that some vessels in the harbour were destroyed, and it is certain that a considerable range of buildings, apparently barracks or store-houses, were burnt - the fire could not, from its duration, have been trifling; having blazed from 2 A.M. till the evening. The ruins of eight buildings were discernible from the *Clyde* frigate; and from the extreme jealousy with which Lord L. and his retinue were guarded on passing through the town a few days afterwards,[5] there is reason to presume the ravages were serious, and more extensive than met the eye on board the squadron. It was only to be regretted that the conflagration had not taken effect more to the right, where the bulk of the flotilla lay: nevertheless, the efficiency of the weapon, and the vulnerability of Boulogne, were completely shewn; since it could not be doubted that what had destroyed houses of substantial masonry would have annihilated shipping, crowded in a sort of floating dock, had it fallen amongst them: besides, as the part of the town burnt was more remote from the boats than the basin, the range of the rockets was also demonstrated beyond a doubt; and lastly, the facility of using this weapon in small craft afloat was satisfactorily proved.

From this period till the expedition against Denmark, successive improvements were made, in the weapon itself, as well as in its accessory apparatus. It is not within the scope of this correspondence to detail these matters, but those at all conversant with gunnery can readily conceive the difficulty of attaining any thing like a state of early perfection with an invention so novel in most of its parts. Many of these mechanical details, though apparently of minor consideration, were in fact points of the first

---

3 "There is no easy way from the earth to the stars." It is not by common efforts immortality is attained.

4 In order to relieve the *compunctious visitings* of such cosmopolite patriots as reserve their philanthropic sympathies for our enemies, be it known that the destruction of the town formed no part of *that* project, nor was it wantonly attempted: but the precise situation of the flotilla basin not being visible from the cruising station, owing to the interposition of rising ground on the western side of the harbour (formed by the mouth of the river Lianne) the rockets were thrown by guess in the dark, rather too much to the left, or eastward.

5 Not one person having been suffered to leave their inn, nor to hold any external communication, and being conveyed through the streets in closed *cabriolets*.

importance, and consumed much time and attention. Considering that the system is still in its infancy, the construction is now reduced to a degree of uniformity and certainty, that promises entire success: while the effect universally acknowledged by the officers both of the navy and army to have been produced by it at Copenhagen, has operated a general conviction of its powers.

Indeed such a body of evidence, as to facts connected with the effects of the rockets on that occasion, has been collected by eye witnesses, as fully establishes, not only the certainty of their having contributed essentially to the conflagration of the place, but that of their powers of penetration, which many persons not fairly appreciating the effect of such a weight, pointed and solid as it is, falling from so great a height, were inclined to deny. But indeed had this testimony of facts been wanting, there is abundance of argument to induce the belief. - In the first place it may be stated that there never was an instance known of such a conflagration having been produced by mere bombardment in so short a time; and it is therefore fair to infer, that the addition of this weapon to the usual means contributed to such extraordinary effect: - but there is a stronger circumstance: the second night, when rockets were not discharged, although near 1,000 bomb-shells and carcasses were thrown, there was no conflagration; whereas on the other two nights, on which the rockets were used, the flames raged furiously; and yet from the first it is acknowledged by the artillery men, that the greater part of their spherical carcasses were well ignited on leaving the mortars from which they were fired. Consequently, it is no more offensive to sound reasoning than it is contradictory to public opinion to assert, that the rockets used at Copenhagen did very essentially contribute to the conflagration of that city; and if the weapon was able to accomplish any thing where only 300 were fired, and that only by the labour of 16 men, partly uninstructed, what more might not have been done by it, had it been previously adopted into our military system, and committed to the regiment of artillery, and to the navy, amongst their other implements of bombardment?

I repeat, therefore, that there are both fact and argument in abundance from the example at Copenhagen, to fix the credit of the rocket as a carcass; and *that*, without in the least undervaluing the execution produced by the *regular* bombardment; than which nothing could be more destructive, nor is it possible to say enough in praise of the professional skill manifested on that occasion.

Thus far I have merely given a cursory account of the origin and progress of the rocket system, detailing only as much as is necessary for the comprehension of the general extent of the improvements made in it, without attempting to investigate that art in point of construction, upon which the rocket's length of range or vigour of flight depends. I have already acknowledged the imperfection of my knowledge on this head: but I should ever feel it my duty to conceal even my conjectures thereon, inasmuch as if the weapon does contain any advantages superior to the common means of annoying an enemy at present used, it is important that we should possess it exclusively as long as possible, although it is a satisfaction for me to repeat a declaration the inventor has been often heard to make in the most distinct terms, that "*the principles of the Congreve rockets are widely different from those of ordinary sky-rockets, and are not discoverable by analysis or by inspection.*"

In my next letter I shall enter into the formation of the rocket-carcass, its principle of action, and the advantage it appears to possess, in conveniency of use, and in probability of effort, as an instrument of conflagration, when compared with the largest spherical carcasses and shells; shewing also its superior cheapness. But lest your tender-hearted correspondent F.F.F. should suffer disappointment at reading so far without finding any particular notice taken of his military ethics, I will just employ a few lines to remind him, that when a man employs his pen publicly, his readers have a right to expect he should know *something*, be it ever so little, of the subject matter on which he sits down to write. Had that writer observed this good rule, he would hardly have jumbled together in one sweeping anathema such heterogeneous articles as coffers, catamarans, *rockets*, infernals, fire-devils, water-worms, Shrapnell-shells, &c. for such are I think the items in his catalogue of *heterodox* implements of destruction, in contradistinction to "*orthodox* round and grape*"! And he would at least have escaped the unavoidable application of La Rochefoucault's maxim, that *"Les esprit Médiocres condemnent d'ordinaire tout ce qui posse leur portée."*[6]

BRONTES

Shooter's Hill, 24 September, 1809

Letter 3

"—: dolus, an virtus, quis in hoste requirat?" Virg. Aeneid L 2 V 389.
XXII 285-287

Mr. Editor, The 32-pound rocket carcass is the largest of the kind that has hitherto been constructed for use: but I am informed that it is proposed hereafter to try all the intermediate natures of rocket ammunition, such as 24 and 18-pounders, and even 42-pounders, to determine the *maximum* of the power and range of this weapon. The 32-pounder is completely cased in a stout iron cylinder, terminating in a conical head, and notwithstanding its weight (from which it receives its denomination) is not only fired without re-action, but is also unencumbered with the appendage of heavy apparatus to project it, as is the case with every other carcass. It is on these properties that depend its peculiar facilities for service. It is ammunition without ordnance; it is the soul of artillery without the body. It contains about 7 lbs of carcass composition, in which respect it equals the 10-inch spherical carcass in common use, while it is freed from the ponderous accompaniment of a 10-inch mortar. The 32-pounder will, by its inherent force, range between 2 and 3,000 yards; but it is doubtful whether the shell of the 10-inch carcass will suffer the charge requisite to project it the lesser of those distances. Should it therefore be wanted to increase its solidity, so as to allow of its ranging 3,000 yards, the 32-pounder rocket carcass will then convey considerably more composition than the 10-inch spherical carcass so thickened.

The next thing to be considered, in this comparison, is the probable difference of effect produced by each in falling either upon a house or ship; and here I cannot but conceive that the rocket carcass must have the advantage. The weight of the spherical carcass is so great, that with few exceptions, it goes completely through the building, and buries itself in the ground, nor can this be obviated by a reduction of its weight without a proportionate loss of power. On the other hand the rocket carcass, not weighing more than one-third of the other, will not pass quite through, but generally lodge somewhere in the body of the house, although its weight and penetration is sufficient always to pierce the roof and at least one floor. It may be presumed, therefore, that the combustible which lodges in the body of a house, in the midst of furniture and drapery, is more likely to set fire to it, than one which buries itself in the cellars.

---

6 Those of confined intellect in general find fault with every thing beyond the sphere of their knowledge.

But the very nature of the cone in which the combustible matter is contained, renders it more effective as a carcass, for the thin iron case absorbs no quantity of heat; on the contrary, it soon becomes red hot, calcines, and gives free issue to the ignited fluid, which soon becomes one extended blazing surface, while the massive shell of the spherical carcass greedily devours the caloric of its internal fire, without being itself completely heated, and suffers a comparatively feeble and lambent flame only to issue through a few confined apertures.

But it may be said that the rocket carcass should be compared with other natures of spherical besides the 10-inch. If then, it be compared with the 8-inch, I answer that it contains double the quantity of composition; if with the 13-inch, that the excessive penetration of the latter into the ground tells more against its setting fire to any building. Carcasses can seldom, if ever, be wanted against bomb-proofs; and it seems against those only that the spherical carcass would possess any superiority: but in almost every other case the rocket carcass must have the advantage. What I mean is, that in any given quantity, there is a greater probability of general success in the one than the other.

It has however been said, that "the enemy, when they discover that rockets are mere carcasses, will cease to fear them, and will extinguish them." Now, I must observe, that this assertion begins by begging the question - by presuming that the rockets are mere carcasses, which is not the case; for a certain number of them have a 6-pound grenade, or a cartridge of gunpowder enclosed in the body of the cylinder, which bursts during the combustion; and as these varieties are not distinguishable, the enemy must equally avoid all. In addition to this, every rocket contains smoak-ball composition, the suffocating quality of which is such, that no person can exist in a room where it has burnt but a few seconds. It has also been said, that "the rocket may easily be removed after it has fallen." This is, in a great measure, controverted by what has been said of the means taken to prevent approach: but farther to meet it, let it be considered how firmly such a body, and so shaped as is the head of the rocket, must fix itself into whatever substance receives it where it falls - it will in probability be found sticking in a floor or deck; and if a man cannot by his hand draw out a small nail driven but a little way into a board, how shall he extract a large spike, fixed a foot or 18 inches deep in plank, part of which moreover is during the time near red hot. In answer to this it has been objected that the rocket stick forms a lever at hand to prise it out. It is a fact, however, that when the rocket impinges on any solid substance, even on the ground, the stick is shattered into splinters, some of which fly to a considerable distance, and possess considerable powers of penetration: so that in effect the stick, instead of becoming useful to disarm the rocket, as has been supposed, greatly assists its mischievous powers.

Not to monopolize more of the space so valuable in a miscellaneous work, or exhaust the patience of your readers, to all of whom this subject may not be equally interesting, I shall not pursue this statement farther at present, but conclude by an explanatory list of the different species of rocket ammunition, which I conceive may prove gratifying to the curiosity of most persons into whose hands the NAVAL CHRONICLE is likely fallen.

Nature of Ammunition	Armed with		Extreme range
42-pounder Carcass Rockets	Carcasses	large, 18 lbs, small, 12 lbs	about 3,000 yds, but not yet
42-pounder Shell Rockets	Shells	5 1/2 inch 12-pound sphere	accurately ascertained.

32-pounder Carcass Rockets	*Carcasses*	large, 18 lbs	ext. range 2,000 yds
		medium, 12 lbs	ext. range 2,500 yds
		small, 8 lbs	ext. range 3,000 yds
32-pounder Shell Rockets	*Shells*	9-pdr spherical	3,000 yds
32-pounder Rocket Cast Shot	*Case Shot, which receives any increased velocity from the bursting powder*	large, contains 200 carbine balls	ext. range 2,500 yds
		small, 100 "	ext. range 3,000 yds
32-pounder Explosion Rockets	*Strong iron cones, containing from 5 to 12 lbs of powder, to burst by fuzees*		2,500 to 3,000 yds
42-pounder Rocket Case Shot	*Case Shot*	large, 72 carbine balls,	ext. range 2,000 yds
		small, 48 "	ext. range 2,500 yds
Rocket Light Balls	These Light Balls are projected into the air by Rockets of different natures at great elevations; and being liberated by bursting at the greatest height of the Rocket, they are sustained by a *parachute* so as to float with the wind, and give a strong and permanent light.		
Floating Rocket Carcasses	These Carcasses are contrived to be capable of extraordinary great ranges by means similar to those above described.		

I have been thus particular in describing the properties of the rocket carcass, feeling how necessary it is to meet the general objections in which men of vulgar minds and prejudiced understandings are apt to indulge against new inventions; and I trust I shall convince every candid reader, that far from being a diabolical contrivance in violation of the laws of war, it is only a legitimate extension of means already employed by hostile nations for mutual destruction, and a most ingenious improvement of machines at present in use.

BRONTES

Shooter's Hill, 29th September, 1809

Letter 4

"Est quoddam prodire tenus si non datur ultra." Horat. XXII 370-372

Mr. Editor, Since my last letter an article has appeared in some of the public prints, extracted from a foreign source, and pretending to be the analysis or detection of, what I shall henceforth term, our Congreves by Buonaparte's *servants*. I was prompted to have made that the subject of this letter: but I have seen (in the *Pilot* and other respectable newspapers) so satisfactory a *critique* of the French memoir that I need not digress farther from the historical task I have imposed upon myself, than to express the hope that F.F.F.'s philanthropy will urge him to address one of his homilies to the Parisian Institute, (for instance, through the medium of the *Argus*) upon the atrocity of pursuing such practical experiments as Citizen Gay Lusac's report announces. Because, although they may, and I devoutly hope will, not become masters of our secret, in such a case of *Lèze-Humanité*, *"Sat est voluisse."* In fact, had I not often witnessed the paralysing effects of fact opposed to declamation, I should be somewhat surprised at Mr. 3 F.'s fit of silence after his first display. However, much as one's vanity might find aliment in the retreat of an antagonist, I really could not help feeling some degree of self reproach for your sake, Mr. Editor, at being instrumental in checking the pen of one of those useful correspondents for a periodical work, who conscientiously give you in length what they want in depth. And, so saying, I shall resume the thread of the dry statement, broken off at the end of my last, hoping to wind it up in this, so as to permit me in my next to enter upon the use and advantages of the rocket system, as applicable to naval purposes in particular.

As an implement of conflagration there remains only to compare the Congreve-carcass with the *burning* power of the bomb-shell (with its terrors of *explosion* the Congreve does not pretend to measure). In the first place, the shell buries itself deeper in the ground than the spherical carcass; and consequently, though when it bursts the destruction is dreadful, still, except in the case of actually meeting with inflammable matter, the consequences are but momentary, and not continuous, as in the case of even the common spherical carcass. And supposing it otherwise, one cannot suppose that the scattering small lumps of the Valenciennes composition (none weighing more than 2 or 3 oz.) can accomplish more than a mass of 7lbs of the Congreve composition spreading itself like *lava*. I do not by any means assert, or wish to infer, that the laboratory composition does not occasionally succeed in producing conflagration; I only reason upon the probable and comparative effects of the two causes, under all the circumstances attaching to them.

But it may be said the explosion of a shell alone is sufficient to set fire to any house. Certainly it may do so: but a blast of powder must act upon something very inflammable indeed to be able to ignite it; even the V. composition will frequently be blown out of the shell uninflamed: nor is it to be supposed that such an addition would have been made, had the explosion alone been found sufficient: consequently the effect of the blast in any comparison is to be estimated at less than that composition. The fact is, however, that duration of time is required for the communication of fire; and by this rate therefore the general effect is to be calculated in both cases.

The expense of making a 32-pound Congreve, comprehending case complete, cone, stick, composition of the different kinds, paint, and labour, may be estimated at a fraction less than 22 shillings.[7] This calculation includes that of the projectile force, which conveys it 3,000 yards. Let us now see what spherical carcasses cost according to the actual prices paid by contract for the articles supplied:

A 10-inch carcass	£ 0/15/7
Charge of powder for 3,000 yards	0/6/0
Cartridge, tube, &c	0/1/0
[total]	£ 1/2/7

7 If the construction was more systematic, and elementary force used instead of manual labour, it is supposed that the expense might be lowered to less than £1 *per* rocket.

A 13-inch carcass	£ 1/12/7 1/2
Charge of powder as above	0/10/0
Cartridge, &c.	0/1/4
[Total]	£ 2/3/11 1/2

So that the Congreve, even in the present disadvantageous state of manufacture, costs less than the 10-inch, and not quite half so much as the 13-inch carcass; although from what has been already stated, it possesses more certain powers of conflagration than either. But the comparison does not end here - for to the charges already set down against the sphericals is to be added no trifling account for expense, and wear and tear of the mortar - mortar-bed - platform - and in certain cases of a ship of war expressly constructed for that service, with other almost endless *items* attached to the use of them: whereas for land service the Congreve literally requires hardly any apparatus - but of this more hereafter.

The next thing to be considered is durability. I do not pretend to say that in this respect it surpasses its spherical brethren: but I have seen reports from an officer who was sent out with a quantity of them to the Mediterranean station, stating the following facts: - Several boxes were penetrated by sea water during the passage; some of the cases had been so wetted as to become rusty: on a trial however at Malta, made by order, and in the presence of the admiral commanding there (Sir Sidney Smith), still the range was 2,500 yards, and the weapon pierced a stone wall of the customary thickness used for fences on that Island. This seems to prove that it is by no means subject to be easily damaged in service. But suppose the rocket even to have received so much injury as to be rendered unfit for service, it must be observed that it is not thereby destroyed, for most of all its concurring parts are in existence, and require only re-organization.

The rocket has also been called an unsafe weapon to keep in store. This, however, can only have been by persons whose knowledge in pyrotechny may not have reached beyond squibs and crackers: for where it is not conceived unsafe to keep barrels of gunpowder by hundreds and thousands, assuredly there can be no danger in storing a weapon hermetically sealed in a case, alike impervious to fire or water, and which it is impossible to ignite but by positive design.

One more point must be briefly mentioned - the accuracy of direction of which the rocket is susceptible. To assert that it is capable of the same precision of flight as a ball projected from a *long* cylinder, would indeed be exaggeration: nor is it necessary for the purpose that it should be so. In the present contemplation of the weapon, the object of comparison is the carcass fired from mortars; their use is thereby denoted to be confined to large objects, or to an extensive surface. To aim at a single house or ship a mile off, would not, I believe, be a much more successful attempt with one than with the other weapon. It is however extraordinary with what accuracy and steadiness the large rockets range, if the frame and stick be properly adjusted, and due allowance made (guided by practice) for the effect of wind; which after all does not affect its course so much as might be supposed.

The rocket is capable of a regulation of range as to distance, by increasing or diminishing the angles, as other projectiles; and I have understood such gradations to have been varied in practice from 1,500 to 3,000 yards: although I will not take upon me to affirm that such experiments have hitherto warranted the construction of tables in form, my conviction is, that from what has already been accomplished, it is capable of furnishing *data* with every requisite degree of nicety. It ought not, however, to be forgotten, that the Congreve is still in its infancy, and that if it had even more faults on its head, there is every ground for hope that time would produce the remedy. Let artillerists look back and contemplate the origin and progress of their system!

BRONTES

Shooter's Hill, 3d November, 1809

Letter 5 ^{XXII 461-463}

"Mobilitate viget; viresque acquirit eundo."
Virg. Aen. IV. 173

*"Swift from the first; and every moment brings New vigour to its flight,
new pinions to its wings."*

Mr. Editor, It is in the application of the Congreve to naval purposes that the advantages to be derived from the first principle of its flight are most conspicuous; for it is the power it possesses of projecting *itself* without re-action upon the point whence it departs, that not only renders the smallest boats in the navy as serviceable for the discharge of carcasses as the vessels of considerable tonnage hitherto employed for that service; but moreover enables us to project them by such means in vastly greater quantities and in much less time than by the ancient mode.

It is possible to equip a gun-brig so as to discharge twenty war-rockets of the largest calibre in one broadside, and as quick in succession as may be desired. Thus ten brigs so armed can, in a few minutes, discharge 200 rockets, each equal to a 10-inch spherical carcass, to say the least; whereas ten bomb-ketches would not throw the same number of the latter in less than two hours; during which time the brigs would send from 1,000 to 1,200 Congreves, conveying nearly four *tons* of combustible matter.

Therefore for a naval attack of any strongly fortified place or harbour, where the object is the conflagration of the town or shipping, it is not assuming too much to say, if the reasoning on the properties of this weapon, in my two former letters be admitted, that there is no other at present known possessing equal powers.

But a still stronger case may be put: if, for instance, it is desirable for the sake of security, or from want of time, to perform any such service by a *coup de main* absolutely - 20 brigs can discharge in a single volley 400 rockets, a shower that must make an impression on any place; and then, if required, immediately retire: nor is there any thing difficult in supposing the employment of such a force; whereas to accomplish the same thing in the old way, would require no less than 200 bomb-vessels, the having such a force as which in constant readiness, I leave the reader to judge the expediency and practicability of. For enterprises of this description, and the present moment is big with opportunities, I do not hesitate to affirm, that was this weapon put, *properly*, into the hands of the navy, its effect would be extremely important.

But in fact the advantages of it for naval purposes do not rest here; for such is the simplicity of the system of equipment, that the saving which would attach to this mode of throwing carcasses afloat in general, is incalculable, particularly when compared to the use, and that very limited, of vessels, constructed on purpose, at an *extra* expense, and fit for little else. Not that I would be misunderstood to mean that the use of mortars in the sea service should be entirely exploded. On the contrary, I think the improvement of that, as well as every other branch of marine artillery, it peculiarly behoves this naval nation to carry to its utmost *capability*; but I am also of opinion, that the present establishment of sea mortar service is excessively expensive, and extremely defective;

the latter I know was demonstrated at Copenhagen; where, moreover, a trial was made of marine 8-inch mortars in ten of the launches of Admiral Gambier's fleet, with a measure of success which went nigh to prove that the number of our men of war bombs may be diminished, if even their services might not be dispensed with altogether.

But it has been objected by F.F.F. and by others more versed in such matters than that writer, that was their arm added to the naval establishment, the facility of its application might cause an undue frequency in its use: indeed some are so fastidious as to question the lawfulness of it - the lawfulness of rendering our hostility in war burthensome to an enemy, and to such an enemy! But, independently of the substantial arguments afforded by the awful crisis to which the present contest has led this country, I beg leave to say, that the notorious existence of such an engine in the English navy, with that dominion of the seas, by which it can at all times approach any of the enemy's ports, would put much into our power without a struggle, that now sometimes costs us dear, and this without much of aggravated severity to the enemy, (if that must be taken into consideration to satisfy the philanthropic party) for was it once thoroughly well known to them that our cruisers were furnished with the means of burning any of their maritime towns; such for instance as distinguished themselves by privateering - what towns-people would, on a conditional threat of such destruction, refuse to surrender any vessels sheltered under its batteries? Would not such pernicious inmates be at once driven to take their chance in the offing, rather than be protected at the price of the place itself? Thus by bringing the realities of war home to their very doors, we might nearly dictate the terms of maritime warfare along the whole coast of France, where it is at present hardly felt in any other shape than the conscription, or the scarcity of certain foreign commodities. Terror might thus be excited in so large a portion of the population, that discontent without palliative would gradually extend its influence throughout the interior of the *Empire of the West*.

In this plan I find myself seconded, and in point of publicity anticipated, by another of your Correspondents (Ben Block) in page 374 of this Volume. I hope his useful hint may reach the knowledge of some of the *great* and *wise* at the helm of affairs, and be reduced to seasonable practice: for assuredly these are not times for inefficient theories, any more than for the nation to be amused by the contemptible cabals of selfish oligarchists.

It must be admitted that, in the single-handed contest we have now to maintain for our very existence as a nation, (since that, after all the vapouring of the borough-mongers, is the undisguised fact) some extraordinary addition, either to our means of defence or offence, seems as necessary as a change in the principles upon which our rulers since 1794 have carried on the war. The enemy naturally enough is very shy of meeting us at sea in the orthodox way. It is therefore a grand *desideratum* for our navy to be enabled to ferret him in his lurking places, and convince him of his vulnerability in his strongest holds. This was the opinion of Nelson; and one of his letters lately published,[8] written during the blockade of Cadiz, more particularly shows his sentiments on the then quite recent invention of the war-rocket.

BRONTES

Shooter's Hill, 2d December, 1809

---

8 Harrison's Life of Nelson, Vol. 1, page 425.

1811 – Improvements to the 42-pounder Carronade

From the 'Naval Biography of Rear-Admiral Thomas (Hoar) Bertie.' XXVI 9

It may here be proper to mention an improvement, which Captain Bertie effected on the 42-pounder carronades, belonging to the *Ardent*'s main-deck; particularly as the improvement was generally adopted, for some years afterwards, in all his Majesty's ships having that description of ordnance on board. – Observing, when he was first appointed to the *Ardent* [1797], that the inclined plane of the carriage was in a contrary direction to what, he conceived, it ought to be – being *within-board* instead of *without* – Captain Bertie communicated his ideas on the subject to the Board of Ordnance; and, in a correspondence which ensued, he had the satisfaction of convincing that Board of the utility of his proposed alteration. Orders were consequently given, for fitting up the carronades at Chatham, according to Captain Bertie's directions. The alteration consisted simply in depressing the stole of the carriage two inches. This not only imparted to it the good property of being worked, and run out, with a smaller number of men – (the 42-pounder being afterwards fought, and exercised, with only four men each, without any exertion or difficulty) – but it also checked the recoil, and necessarily added to the force of the shot. The simplicity of this improvement seems strongly to entitle it to attention.

1811 – Fulton's Torpedoes XXVI 234-238

Explosion machinery, particularly that of a sub-marine nature, has, at various times, been the subject of discussion and remark, in the *Naval Chronicle*. The invention of the coffers, or catamarans, rendered memorable in England by the expeditions against Boulogne in 1804-5-6, has generally been attributed to an American, of the name of Robert Fulton, who, in the year 1804, was patronised, to a certain extent, by the British government. His claim to the invention has been contested, and, we apprehend, with some justice. It is certain, however, that he has, at different periods, proffered his services successively to the American, British, and French governments; from each of which it has evidently been his wish to obtain pecuniary remuneration.

A partial exposure of the nefarious conduct of this man, has recently been made in an American paper; the Editor of which has addressed an article to Mr. Fulton, proving, that at the time he was receiving and expending sums of money for the perfection of his projects from his own government, to whom, of course, the secret ought, exclusively, to belong, he was making an offer of it to Buonaparte, through his minister, M. Marbois. "Congress," says the American Editor, "granted the petitioner, Fulton, (although the treasury was pennyless) the sum of 5,000 dollars, to enable him to 'proceed with ardour in an enterprise of such immense importance to *his country.*' This, it must be remembered, was just at the close of session, in the spring of 1809." 9

The proof that Fulton was, *at the same time,* offering to sell his discovery to France, is contained in the following letter of his, which is a singular one, and which, says the American Editor, "the reader may consider, without hesitation, as genuine, and peruse

---

9 Fulton had been in France prior to this period. He went thither, we apprehend, immediately on his departure from England. His sojourn in France, and return to New York, in July, 1807, are recorded in *The Pilot*, of August 27, 1807. [See above, p45.]

it as such; for, however it may have come into my hands, Mr. Fulton will never have the hardihood to deny it."

New York, March 22, 1809
Sir, You will recollect, while I was in France, I made some experiments on sub-marine navigation, and a new mode of attacking ships of war with sub-marine bombs; which I now call torpedoes, in consequence of the shock they give. Several years ago, I ascertained, by experiments on a sufficiently large scale, that if about one hundred pounds of powder could be exploded under the bottom of a first rate ship of the line, it would so wreck it, that it would immediately sink; to prove this, I have blown up two brigs, each of 200 tons.

My constant expectation has been to find a certain means, with least possible risk to the assailants, of getting the torpedo under the vessel, near the keel, where the shock would be perpendicular under her; with this view, I laboured three years at a sub-marine boat, which succeeded to navigate under water with ease and safety; but was of no use in fixing the torpedo under the vessel. I, therefore, abandoned the sub-marine boat, and sought for other means of supplying the torpedoes.

After five years of varied experiment, I have fortunately discovered an infallible mode of placing the torpedoes near the keel of any ship, however great her force may be; and it may be done while she is at anchor, or when sailing not more than five miles an hour. . . .

I therefore propose the following arrangement to his Majesty's Government:
"To such minister, or agent, as his Imperial and Royal Majesty will be pleased to name, I will send a complete torpedo, with such description and drawing as will enable any intelligent engineer to make them, and use them against the enemy. On the part of his Majesty, the minister or agent will agree, that I, my heirs, or assigns, shall be paid of out his Majesty's treasury, 1000 *francs* for each gun of each vessel of an enemy, which shall be destroyed by means of my sub-marine bombs or torpedoes . . . [etc.]

Being a citizen of a neutral nation, I felt free to act in any country where there was the best chance of getting my plan introduced into practice. In the infancy of my experiments, I made offers to France, but did not find the encouragement which was necessary to carry on the experiments to an useful result. Lord Sidmouth invited me to England. Mr. Pitt adopted my plan, in part; I knew if it succeeded against the Boulogne flotilla the ingenuity of the French engineers would be exerted; they would soon get possession of the engines, with the mode of using them, and the invention would recoil on England, to the destruction of her marine. A Carthaginian boat, you know, first gave the Romans the idea of constructing a fleet, which enabled them to destroy Carthage. - Mr. Pitt died. Lords Grenville and St. Vincent reproached the conduct of Mr. Pitt, in attempting to bring to perfection machines which might be turned against them, and destroy their superiority by sea. For this reason, the new ministry would not prosecute my plans. If the torpedoes did not succeed in the attack on the Boulogne flotilla, it was not, however, in consequence of any faults in principle, but from a defect in arrangement. I had not then discovered a certain mode of sending the torpedoes under the bottom, near the keel. This defect I have since remedied, and now the destruction of the vessel attacked is certain. His Royal and Imperial Majesty has too magnanimous a mind to be displeased with me, for acting first in France, and then in England; my whole object being to prove principles of so much importance. If you feel interested in the result of this invention; if you feel at liberty to communicate the contents of this letter to his Majesty, and he should order that my proposals be complied with, I will immediately send an agent to France, with such engines and details as I hope will satisfy his Majesty of their importance, and shew the power which he may have over the British marine. . . ."

To his Excellency Count Marbois

It is necessary to add but very little to the above. In VULCAN'S letter Vol. XX p. 452, mentioned in a preceding note, Mr. Fulton, *alias* Francis, is charged with obtaining money, on false pretences; and, upon research, we find it to appear distinctly, in the public accompts, that a grant to Robert Fulton, of £1,653 18s 8d in full satisfaction of all claims, received the sign manual on the 9th of September, 1806; and a grant was made to Cutler and Co. for clock-work furnished to Mr. Fulton, of £1,533 13s 7d per sign manual, September 19, 1806.

1811 - Vice-Admiral Hunter's Recoil System

[Vice-Admiral John Hunter's proposal to use counter-weights pulled up from below deck to check the recoil of the great guns is interesting, but his description lacked any solution to the engineering problems of encumbering ships with massive and apparently freely-swinging weights. Vol. XXVI, pp296-299.]

1811 - Improvement in the Discharge of Naval Ordnance XXVI 453

A recent letter from an officer of H.M.S. *Victory*, in the Baltic, presents the following important statement:

We lately had exhibited, on board of this ship, in the presence of Sir James Saumarez, Admirals Hope and Dixon, Sir Archibald Dickson, and several captains of the squadron, one of the most extraordinary, and for our service, one of the most useful inventions I ever beheld, *discharging guns without the use of fire*. It was produced by a pressure of the finger on a prepared tube, put into the vent of the gun; the effect was instantaneous and certain, and completely prevented the accidents that so frequently happen in action, from the loose powder that is spilt on the deck; it appears to do away [with] the use of locks and matches, and thereby removes not only the accidents that so often arise from them, but also their great uncertainty in stormy weather. It received from every one present very high and deserved approbation, and was said to be the invention of Captain Manby, of Yarmouth, who has bestowed so much attention on saving shipwrecked men.

1812 - Pyrotechny XXVII 102-103

A plan of a most destructive engine has been brought forward by a Mr. Fane, and exhibited before the Lords of the Admiralty. It is a four-pound shot, wrapped round with a prepared cotton, and made very hard; the moment it starts from the cannon's mouth, it presents one solid mass of fire; and whatever it hits, whether rigging or hull of a ship, will immediately take fire.

Vice-Admiral Hunter's Recoil System. Plate 14

Fig. 1.

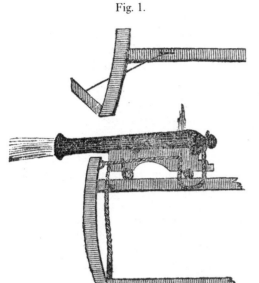

Fig. 2.

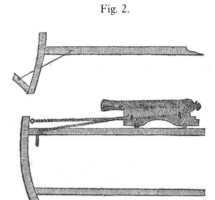

Fig. 2 is the gun after its discharge, and upon the recoil. Here the weight suspended is dragged up by the breast rope to the under side of the deck on which the gun stands. Whenever this gun is again loaded, the weight, in descending, facilitates the running out of the gun.

Scuttle, or Sheave-hole, in the deck.

Fig. 3.

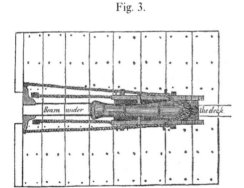

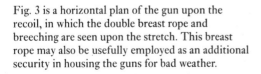

Fig. 3 is a horizontal plan of the gun upon the recoil, in which the double breast rope and breeching are seen upon the stretch. This breast rope may also be usefully employed as an additional security in housing the guns for bad weather.

1812 - Pyrotechny XXVIII 374

A Gentleman of Portsea, has submitted to government a shell, that at the immense distance of three miles, will explode 20 balls of combustible matter of three inches diameter, and upwards of 1000 musket and pistol balls; these will be scattered on the horizon within a circle whose diameter is 1,400 yards. - The weight of the shell will be upwards of 2 1/2 cwt.

1813 - Engineering Experiments, Penetration Power of Ordnance XXIX 111

In the last week of January, an experiment was made on board the *Venerable* and *Daedalus*, at Spithead, with a view to ascertain the efficiency and use of light 24-pounder guns (which those ships are fitted with), as a substitute for the guns in common use, carrying the same weight of shot. The desirable thing to effect is, to make ships of smaller rate throw as heavy a weight of shot as possible, without a heavy weight of metal, which is found to strain the ships in blowing weather. This experiment demonstrated that the light 24-pounder guns, weighing 33 cwt. each, when double-shotted, will not carry their shot beyond 450 yards; whilst the common 24-pounders, but which weigh nearly 50 cwt. will throw *three* shots from 1000 to 1200 yards. The consequence would be, that an English ship, fitted with these light guns, meeting with an enemy armed with the usual weight of metal, might, by distant firing, become disabled before the light guns would reach her adversary; and, consequently, the shot from the light guns, even at a closer distance, would lodge itself in the ship's side, while that of her enemy would go through both sides. In the experiment made on board the *Venerable*, 20 rounds were fired from the same guns, with first, 4 1/2, and then (as the guns heated) 4 lbs. of powder, in the short space of 19 minutes; but it was attended with very considerable recoil, much jumping of the gun towards the close, the fire from the muzzle (the gun being also shorter than the usual one) came in board, which is an inconvenience, attended with danger, particularly in a two-decked ship. The gun was elevated three degrees, when it carried about 450 yards; but once, by mistake, when elevated only one and a half degree, the shot dropped into the water at about 200 yards distance. The light 24-pounders are not on Grover's principle, not having any chamber. The experiment was conducted by Captain Milne (of the *Venerable*) and several officers of the navy, and Colonel Salmon, an officer of the royal artillery.

1813 - Use of Carronades at Extended Ranges XXIX 293-294

"Iron Gun" to the Editor, Bristol, 22d March, 1813

Mr. Editor, At page 111, you have given an account of an experiment lately tried on board of the *Daedalus* with a light 24-pounder iron gun, weighing 33 cwt.[10] with a view, it is said, of ascertaining the efficacy and use of substituting light 24-pounders for guns of this calibre that are in common use. The inference drawn is, that a ship fitted with light guns, meeting an enemy armed with guns of the usual weight of metal, might by distant firing, become disabled before the light guns could reach her adversary. This is

10 In all experiments, the length of the bore or cylinder of the gun should be inserted, as any little difference here, makes a great alteration in point of range, which the weight of the gun has nothing to do with; the weight being confined solely to its influence on the recoil.

a heavy complaint, and if correct, would be sufficient to reject these kind of guns from the service altogether.

I beg to differ in opinion from these premises, and, that this experiment ought, by no means, be adduced as a cause of rejecting short and light guns. Although these short guns were found unequal to range with two shot when loaded with only 4 1/2 and 4 pounds of powder[11] as far as common (or long) guns loaded with 8 pounds of powder, it is presumed single shot from these short guns would, even with these reduced charges,[12] be found to range with every effect to 1,200 yards, the assumed distance that a ship carrying short guns is said to be disabled at before she could reach her adversary. As this distance is, without a doubt, within range of these short guns, I cannot conceive what is to prevent a ship that is fitted with them, from having an equal chance of annoying her adversary with single shot, as there would be of her adversary disabling her by using two shot from long guns. The uncertainty of hitting an object at any designed point, being greater when using two shot each round, than with one shot; and this uncertainty increases as the distance becomes greater; therefore this mode of firing at 1,200 yards (or at any considerable distance), has not so great an advantage as is generally supposed; besides short guns from their lightness are easier worked than long guns in common use, and might be fired three rounds to the other's two.

This advantage of quickness of firing might be increased, by their being loaded with fixed ammunition (which will require sponges and rammers fixed to a staff instead of rope), this method of loading guns saves considerable time by requiring the rammer to be introduced only once into the cylinder of the gun; but when wads are used it requires the rammer to be introduced no less than three times before the gun can be loaded. The objection to using stave sponges has arisen from having the sponge head and rammer fixed to the same staff, by which means, when either the sponge or the rammer is about to be introduced into the cylinder of the gun, the other is necessarily projected to the distance of ten or eleven feet (according to the length of the gun) out of the port, which renders it from its weight, very difficult for one man to manage. To obviate this, the sponge head ought to be fixed on one staff, and the rammer on another; when they would be found easy and light to manage, far superior to sponges and rammers fastened to rope at present in use. Probably it is owing to this method of loading guns, and using these kind of sponges, that gave the Americans that advantage of quickness of firing, it is reported they were in possession of during their late action with the *Macedonian*; if so, its immediate adoption becomes imperative on our part.[13]

It is also further related, that their fire (in this action) was very conspicuous for its precision and destructive effect; this leads me to suggest the propriety of discontinuing that mode of firing designated a *broadside*, which ought to be but seldom or never used.

11 The charges used in the experiment.

12 One fifth the weight of shot is the proper charge of powder for single shot, for all light guns without chambers; with this charge these light 24-pounders will be found to carry single shot far beyond 1,200 yards.

13 At the distance of 1 1/2 to 2 cables' length, two shot are found to range within a yard of each other. At this distance an advantage would arise in point of quickness, by having cartridges fixed to two shot instead of one, which is effected by interposing a wood bottom between the shot, turned with concave ends, so as to receive a part of the convexity of both shot, which must be secured with straps of double tin in the usual manner; by this means no longer time is required in loading a gun with two shot than with one, by introducing the rammer but once into the gun. This mode of loading guns ought to be introduced when breaching a fortress or any other works, either from ships or *batteries*, particularly from the last, which are erected within half a cable's distance of the wall.

The firing of each gun should solely depend on the man that lays her, from the constant motion of the ship varying the direction of the gun. The falling off of the ship from the wind, and bringing her to, alters the line of fire; the rolling of the ship alters the elevation; either of these causes (and they are continually occurring) occasions a broadside, even at the distance of two cables' length (or 480 yards), to have little effect, and this is further diminished as the distance increases; from these causes it is impossible for a gun to carry her shot with any precision, if the word (fire) is given by any other person than the man that lays her: it is he alone that can discover the exact moment for discharging his gun to have the desired effect.

In my next letter (this being quite full) I shall submit to your consideration a mode for discharging guns in the shortest possible time after the word is given, far superior to the present practice, which occasions a delay (whilst the priming is burning in the vent) fatal to the direction of the gun. This mode will be found equal to the use of tubes and portfires, which articles are inadmissible on board.

P.S. Since writing the above, I am sorry to say, news has arrived of the taking of the *Java* frigate. It corroborates my assertion in a letter I addressed you in January last, that the Americans having a greater number of men was not the true cause of our inferiority, as more than the *Java*'s full complement remained, after sustaining a very heavy loss during the action. As long as our frigates carry guns of an inferior calibre to the Americans, we may always expect the same result. Our first class frigates might, for the present, carry 24-pounders of 18 calibres in length, which, on an average, weighs 47 cwt. 2 quarters each; this gives a difference [of] not quite 4 tons in substituting 24-pounders for the 14 18-pounders they now carry on a side. This difference of weight is too inconsiderable to merit any attention, when put in competition with the advantage that will arise from their being used.

1813 – Priming XXIX 396-398

Mr. Editor, The present mode of priming a gun on board a ship is with fine powder poured into the vent, previously pricking the cartridge with a priming wire; a small train of powder is then carried for two or three inches from the vent along the gun. On applying the match to the end of this train, the fire runs freely, till its arrival at the vent, where it keeps phizzing for some time before the gun is discharged. This delay destroys the intended effect of the best laid gun: for during the time the powder is burning in the vent, the motion of the ship has altered the direction of the gun, and in consequence the shot takes a direction as if the gun had never been laid.[14]

From this cause alone it is evident, that discharging a gun in the least possible time, after the word is given to fire, must be an advantage to firing with precision. To accomplish this, tubes and portfires have been adopted; but as these articles are inadmissible on board of a ship, gun-locks have been introduced. This certainly produces instant firing to the priming, but nearly the same delay occurs at the vent as in the common method.[15] I beg to submit a method for priming, which, *on trial*, will be found

---

14 This delay is liable to be further increased, by brushing this small train with the powder-horn (the man that primes being instructed to do so); in the performing of this, if care is not taken, the powder that is laid over the vent gets compressed, and forced into it, which in a manner plugs it up.

15 So long as powder is used for priming, this delay cannot be remedied, in consequence of the vents being vertical (or nearly so) to the bore of every species of ordnance; and the thicker of metal the gun is at the vent, the greater will be the delay.

to equal a tube in quickness of discharging either gun or mortar, and with a certainty far superior.[16]

The common slow or gun-match now in use, will be found to answer the purpose of firing the priming; equally as ready as a portfire, or red-hot iron. To effect this, it is essentially necessary to strictly forbid blowing the match previous to applying it to the priming (as the man that fires is now particularly instructed so to do); instead of which, on the word *fire* being given, the match ought to be smartly flipped with the finger a little above that part that is burning (this will cause the ashes to fall off, and disclose a bright coal of fire); and if it be that instant applied to the priming, will not fail to have immediate effect.

Instead of priming with powder, quick match[17] should be used, which, after loading the gun, is to be introduced into the vent, and suffered to fall down it, without using the least force, to prevent breaking the match, which would in a small degree choke or stop the vent, and probably impede the fire, turning the end of the match left sticking out of the vent[18] on that side of the gun next to the man that fires. On applying the gun or slow-match as above directed,[19] the quick-match will (if made agreeable to note 15 in

16 Tubes are known to miss firing the cartridge, and the defect cannot be discovered until it is fired: any defect or imperfection in quick match is immediately discovered.

17 The following composition for making quick match will be found superior to any now used: - Take three strands of equal lengths, either of *fine* cotton or worsted yarn; if the match is intended to be made of the former, let it weigh 2 lbs; if of the latter, 12 oz.; one gallon of *best* spirits of wine; 14 lbs. of mealed powder (that is, fine powder bruised and passed through a fine lawn or silk bottom sieve); and half a pint of thick starch, made in the usual manner; take the yarns, and lay them evenly in the bottom of a copper or earthen pan, leaving the last end of each strand hanging over the edge of the pan, which tie with a bit of thread to prevent their separating; dilute the starch with the spirits in another pan; add half of the mealed powder, which when well mixed with the spirits, pour over the yarns in the first pan; stir it up well with the hands, that the yarns may imbibe as much of the composition as possible; lay the ends of the yarns that were hanging out of the pan by themselves in the composition; let it soak for about 30 minutes; then take the ends of the yarns, and draw the whole of the yarns out of the first pan into the second pan; and as you draw them out, lay them evenly at bottom, as before directed; pour what composition remains in the first pan on the yarns that are now in the other pan, and let them soak for about 30 minutes longer; then take the ends that are at top, and fasten them to a wooden reel, and wind the match smoothly on it, leaving a small space between each round to prevent their touching each other; sprinkle as much of the remaining mealed powder from a dredging-box as will cover the match on one side of the reel; turn the reel and sprinkle the other side in the same manner; do this alternately as the mealed powder gets damped from the composition on the match, until no more will lay on it; then lay it to dry; proceed in this manner till the whole of the yarns is wound on reels; on the match being perfectly dry and stiff, it must be taken off the reels (by cutting each round of match in two with a pair of scissors), and packed up in dry port-fire paper for use.

To ensure having good match, it is necessary to have the best spirits of wine; to ascertain this, put a small quantity of powder (a quarter of an ounce will be sufficient) into a cup; pour on it as much spirits as will cover it; set fire to the spirits, and if the spirits is good, the whole will be consumed, and will ultimately fire the powder; but if the powder is not fired, the spirits is not good. When spirits of wine is not to be had, brandy, rum, &c. may be used; but the goodness of the match will depend on the quantity [quality?] of the spirits used.

18 The length of quick match, for priming a gun, will depend on the thickness of metal at the vent; whatever thickness this may be, and two inches more, will suffice. The length is given, rather to prevent the match from disappearing altogether in the vent, than from its being actually required to fire the cartridge; for if, only four inches be introduced into the vent, the discharge would be as certain as if the whole was introduced. Twenty lengths of quick match would be a sufficient quantity at one time for each gun, and which could be laid horizontally in a tin box with cover, and strapped round the waist of the vent's man.

19 The nearer the slow-match is applied to the vent, the quicker will be the discharge, taking care that the slow-match be not led immediately on the vent, as the explosion would break the coal of fire.

the preceding page) be found to take fire with equal facility as a tube, and the gun be instantly discharged.

Accidents that at times occur from using powder for priming, will be avoided by using of quick-match: as fire will not be found to remain about either the vent or carriage after the gun is discharged.

P.S. With regret, I observe, the mania for teak built ships has reached a department, the members of which have certainly been induced to adopt this measure, from the fallacious representations of interested individuals. However suitable teak may be for the building of merchant ships,[20] I am persuaded it is very unfit to be used in the construction of any of his Majesty's ships. No kind of plank or timber, that has hitherto been introduced into the service for ship building, will be found to splinter, and [be] shaken to pieces, in the manner teak will, from the effect of cannon shot. It would be doing the service a benefit, if they were to pause in giving orders for constructing any more ships of war in the east; previous to their causing an experiment to be made, under the superintendence of a committee of flag officers and post captains, by having two targets made of teak (8 or 9 feet square) and of the thickness commonly given to the side of a 38 gun frigate and a 74 gun ship (these targets to be framed and put together; to represent as near as possible, a portion of the side of each of these kind of vessels), and cause six rounds of round shot to be fired at each target at the distance of 5 or 600 yards: viz. 3 rounds perpendicular, and 3 rounds obliquely, at an angle of 15 or 20 degrees, with the usual service charge of powder, from an 18-pounder gun at the target, representing the side of a frigate; and from a 32-pounder at the other one. - Then let the committee in their report determine on the propriety of adopting teak in the construction of ships of war, or in making of masts or yards, &c.

The utility of making these experiments, is not only with regard to teak,[21] but it ought to be a standing rule, not to admit any new species of timber into the service, without previously subjecting it to an experiment, in order that its good or bad qualities may be discovered.

1813 - American Lead Cartridges
Editorial material from the Naval Chronicle for 1813. XXX 69

The partial victories of the American ships at the commencement of hostilities over the British frigates, are said to be attributable, in a great measure, to an improvement in their shot. The cartridge (instead of being made up in canvas) is ascertained to have been *cased* with *lead*. This enables them, it seems, to load with greater despatch, and to fire with additional effect; and hence the destructive havoc of their broadsides.

20 The rage for merchant ships built with teak plank and sissoo timbers, will assuredly fall into disrepute when the defect that sissoo is liable to, comes to be generally known; that is, its not being able to endure the confined warm damp air, which is in all ships' holds; from this cause, it soon gathers a white hoar or mould, which, in time, rots the timber to that degree, that handfuls may be pulled off. The first kind of prime sissoo is equally liable to this decay, as the kind that is generally used. Ships of this construction, will, in time, require repairs; and, on stripping the planks from off their bottoms, the shipwrights will discover what will agreeably surprise them [sic].
21 In order to prevent any delay in carrying this experiment into execution from the want of timber. As much teak as will be sufficient for making these targets, may be had from the upper works of —— frigate, arrived last year from the East Indies, (her name I do not immediately recollect) that there met with the same kind of accident, that has lately befallen the *Captain* at Plymouth.

1813 - Letter to the Editor, Bristol, 10 July 1813, urging the Establishment of a Board of Naval Artillery Officers, signed "Iron Gun" XXX 53-55

[On 12 August 1813 'Iron Gun' supplied the editor with a chart indicating the current practice and his proposed new grape shot for each calibre of gun in the sea service (Vol. XXX, p209).]

I beg to notice two kinds of fire capable of being greatly improved, and their effect rendered far superior to what is now adopted for sea service; viz. case and grape shot firing.

The Woolwich regulations (established 60 years ago) for making up case for sea service, are much too light. The case when filled with the allowed proportion of small iron shot, and made up complete, does not weigh for a gun of any calibre, so much as its round shot; and only 2/3 of this very small proportion of small shot is allowed for a carronade of the same calibre.

How such limited charges came first to be established, particularly that for a carronade, is surprising; and their being permitted to remain, when known to be too light, is unaccountably strange. It would be ridiculous to suppose that it proceeded from any apprehensions being entertained, that either guns or carronades when loaded with case shot, (equal in weight to that of its round shot) would recoil more than when loaded with a round shot; the fact is, that when they are loaded with case-shot, equal to double of the present allowances, the recoil will be less than when they are loaded with a round shot.

Case shot, made up agreeable to these old regulations, have been found to scatter too much, and [sic] which has been justly attributed to the lightness of the charge of shot contained in the cases. After many and various experiments, it has been ascertained, that, by increasing the weight of the case (by the addition of more shot) so as to be equal to 1 1/2 and twice the weight of the round shot, the effect of the case shot is *increased in the same proportion as the weight of the case used.* But as increasing the number must necessarily add to the length of the case, containing the shot, consequently it takes up more room than could be spared for stowing it away in carriages that accompany artillery in the field, this, has probably, been the reason, why only 1 1/2 in preference to twice the weight of the round shot has been fixed on at Woolwich for the land service. This may be a very good reason for adopting this charge for that service (though known not to produce so great an effect as the other), but the same objection cannot be applied against using the greater charge for sea service. There can be no difficulty experienced on board a ship, for want of room for stowage, on account of the increased length of the case. But how has it happened, that this improvement (whereby the effect is increased more than half as much again) has not been extended to the sea, as well as to the land service?

Grape, for all calibres, is made up with nine of the largest size shot (that will allow three shot of the same diameter to be stowed in a tier, round the iron spindle), each of which will be about 5-11 1/4 of the diameter of the round shot; this number of shot, with the iron bottom and spindle, weighs something more than the round shot for all calibres larger than an 18-pounder. This regulated proportion of only nine shot, partakes of the same defect as the common case shot; the remedy is the same for both; instead of the present limited number for making up of grape, they should be increased to 24 shot of the same dimensions for guns, and 15 shot for carronades, by which means their effect will be increased in the same proportion.

There are two kinds of small iron shot, supposed to be the best for filling cases, and are called tier shot, from their stowing in the cases in tiers of three or seven shot. The former being the largest and heaviest, are the same kind of shot as the grape is made with. The other kind is lighter and smaller, being only 1/3 the diameter of the round shot: although these are the lightest kind of shot (agreeable to the late regulations) used for medium and light guns for field service, they are, notwithstanding, twice as heavy as those used for the same calibres for sea service.

Guns on board of a ship should never be loaded with case or grape, containing a less number of shot than what are equal to twice the weight of the round shot, and with a charge of powder equal to 1/4 the weight of the round shot. For carronades, the number of small shot to be equal to 1 1/2 the weight of the round shot; and the charge of powder equal to 1/2 the weight of the round shot. These charges will be found to produce more than double the effect of those now in use, which is no trivial improvement, and merits attention.

Cases filled with three or four ounces iron shot, equal in weight to three times the weight of the round shot, for guns, and twice the weight of the round shot for carronades, should be used for *the last discharges* from guns or carronades, stationed on the quarter-deck, gangways, forecastle, and poop, preparatory to boarding, or for repelling of boarders, by which means a 32 pounder carronade, would, each round, discharge 256 four-ounce shot, instead of the present number of 40 8oz. shot; and a nine-pounder gun 144 3 oz. shot; instead of 44, the number now allowed.

1813 - A Reply From Jeoffrey Grape Shot [XXX 192-193]

Letter to the Editor by "Jeoffrey Grape Shot", 20th August 1813
It appears no less curious than inconsistent, that the "unaccountable neglect" complained of by the *Iron Gun*, in the equipment of our navy and in so vital a point, should have existed during the last twenty years of her exaltation and triumph; that Howe, St. Vincent, Duncan, Nelson, *and the innumerable galaxy of heroes in their immortal train*, should with transcendent genius for war, indefatigable zeal for the service of their King, and devoted patriotism as Britons, have *all* been insensible of these great neglects, now so publicly complained of; which many of them, when at the head of naval affairs, might have remedied, and which, it is well known, if properly stated to the Admiralty, and *authenticated*, would receive immediate attention and redress. On the contrary, it may be fairly inferred, that the above great and noble characters, as well as the majority of the officers of the British navy, not only approve, but admit the superiority of the equipments alluded to . .

1813 - Further Criticism of British Artillery Methods [XXX 414-416]

Letter to the Editor from "Iron Gun," 25th October 1813
. . . "The evils, as Jeffery is pleased to term them, have existed, and do now exist; and will remain so, until the existing regulations on these subjects are revised. That they have been suffered to remain so long, in my opinion, proceeds from their never having been brought under the notice of the illustrious characters he alludes to; consequently, they were not aware of their existence, or undoubtedly they would have been the means of correcting the errors pointed at. The same may be said of the recent affair at St. Sebastian's: it is reported, that the breaches in the walls of that fortress were made with

24 and 18-pounder guns. Had the Illustrious Personage who directed that siege been aware that the same number of 32-pounders would have effected more practicable breaches in less than half the time it necessarily took to accomplish what was done, with the description of ordnance that was sent him for this purpose, he certainly would have demanded 32-pounders in their stead. Not the least imputation is here meant to be attached to him, or even to those who sent him this description of ordnance. The blame lies in the regulation that prescribes only 24 and 18-pounders to be used in breaching, which ought to be revised, and larger calibres allowed for breaching of fortresses that may be situated near to or within an easy distance of water-carriage.

1813 - Pyrotechny

Editorial from the Naval Chronicle for 1813. ^{XXX} ₃₀₂

[See Vols XVIII, p281; XIX, p189 and XX, p452.]

The explosion machinery, for which the American adventurer, Fulton, obtained a premium from our government about six years ago, has been reproduced lately by the same industrious fire-worker in his own country, for the purpose of annoying our blockading squadrons. This apparatus can be brought in contact with the cable, by taking advantage of a strong tide, and a dark night, without much risk on the part of the persons in the boat necessarily employed on such an enterprise. The thing is to be done in this way: – When a-head of the vessel, and at some distance, the machine, with a rope attached to it, is to be thrown overboard, and so as to float on one side of the vessel, while the boat with the other end of the line is pulled to the other; by this means it catches the cable, which is to be dragged on till the machine is brought up, and it is so constructed, that the resistance of the cable to its further progress draws the trigger, when in an instant the vessel is adrift. Mr. Fulton has likewise invented what he calls his ground torpedoes, and these he proposes planting in the channel of the Narrows, *viz.* the entrance to the inner harbour of New York. It has been demonstrated, that if a torpedo can by any means be placed in contact, and directly under the keel of a vessel, she may be blown up, or rather, so shaken as to founder: he therefore proposes sinking, at given distances, in the Narrows, upright frames of wood, proportioned to the depth of water; and these frames are to present their sides to the stream; and on that facing the entrance of the harbour is to be placed a lever perpendicularly; to the lower end of which a torpedo is to be attached, while the other nearly reaches the surface of the water, and on any vessel's passing over, it gives way till it becomes horizontal: it turns on the upper and outer angle of the frame, so that the torpedo may be brought in contact with the keel, by the pressure of which on a spring it explodes. This is all very simple, no doubt, but by no means the less practicable on that account; – and as these two experiments were considered in that light by the most intelligent and disinterested members of the Committee directed to decide on the utility of Mr. Fulton's scheme for destroying the British navy, there can be no harm in exposing them, and putting our naval commanders on their guard. And the loss of the nine seamen, by the explosion of the *Eagle* schooner, three hours after she was taken possession of, may probably dispose them to pause before they treat the matter with contempt. In regard to Mr. F. sending out vessels in the way he did the *Eagle*, should that experiment be tried again, it would be very fair to convert such a prize into a cartel, and let her explode with American instead of British seamen.

1813 – New Incendiaries ^{XXX} 487-488

Letter to the Editor by "Vulcan", Dover, 20 December 1813
I beg Iron Gun, or any other contributing friend, to favour us with some information on the two following articles of intelligence extracted from the newspapers:

Captain Thomas Dundas, R.N. is said to have invented a new description of inflammable balls, applicable for besieging a town, and peculiar for its small weight, by which means it may be thrown to a great distance; and it takes fire on a very curious plan: it spreads a flame in three distinct openings, which is so strong that the fire extends a full yard in length from the ball itself; and is so powerful, that any thing under, over, or near, cannot escape its effects.

Another projectile of a most destructive nature is now in agitation, which has been brought forward by a Mr. Fane; and was, a few months since, exhibited before the Lords of the Admiralty. It is a four-pound shot, wrapped round with prepared cotton, and made very hard, so as to appear like a large cannon-ball - on firing of which it has the usual effect of a cannon-shot; but the moment it starts from the cannon's mouth, it presents one solid mass of fire - and whatever it hits, whether rigging or hull of a ship, will immediately take fire.

I will just seize this occasion to add, that the following warlike experiments are said to have been made at Woolwich about the month of September, 1767, by a Mr. Cross, and found to answer; but were not adopted, for reasons unknown: - 1. To fix gunpowder under the earth, to blow up when trodden upon. 2. The same under a gate, to blow up when the gate should open. 3. The same under the earth, to blow up when any thing laid thereon should be lifted up. 4. The same under the greatest building on the London side of the Thames, Mr. Cross to stand on the opposite side and blow it up without using match or train. 5. A moving battery, drawn by horses, to be made use of in battle, when 50 men would withstand 1000, firing cannon, small arms, hand-grenades, &c.[22]

1814 – Carronades ^{XXXI} 120-122

"Iron Gun" to the Editor, Bristol, 4th February 1814
Mr. Editor, I am sorry that it does not lie in my power to give your correspondent A.F.Y. the information he requires, to the extent of his wishes, or the importance the subject demands, regarding the intent, use, and construction of carronades. I have been informed, they were introduced into the service during the last American war, but by whom I never learnt. Probably, there are some of your readers that could favour both him and me with this information; also from what cause they derive their present appellation. Carronades, from the construction of their interior, appear to be an improvement on the principle of an howitzer; which has contributed to give to their fire, a degree of velocity and precision, far superior to that of an howitzer.[23] I apprehend it was part of the inventor's view, to supersede the use of guns, for which they seem well adapted, particularly when the object is at a close or near distance; their peculiar lightness renders them easier to work with fewer hands (being quicker loaded, readier pointed, &c.) than guns. These qualities will ever give them a decided preference, for arming the forecastle, poops, &c of all ships, where guns from their length and weight would be

22 *Quaere*: if some of these effects were not produced by means similar to those recently made use of by Mr. Congreve for the sub-marine bombs or torpedo.

too cumbersome. And were the decks of those ships that carry 12, 9 and 6-pounder guns, armed with 68, 42, and 32-pounder carronades instead of these guns, it would be adding considerably to the effect of their fire. The superior efficacy that large calibres have over small ones, having been generally known for a long time past, it surely is high time to banish from the decks of line of battle ships, all natures of ordnance, whose calibres are less than a 24-pounder, and from the naval service altogether, all that are less than an 18 pounder.

From the circumstance alluded to by A.F.Y. ships should never be wholly armed with carronades, without their being possessed, in a superior degree, of the qualities of closing with, or leaving their opponents. Instances have occurred, where the enemy have taken the advantage of these circumstances, and placed themselves out of range of their carronades, (without imputing any defect to their shot, from either holes or dents, or being below the proper gauge) whilst the shot from the enemy's long guns had every effect. To obviate in some measure this vexatious disadvantage, to which ships armed only with carronades are liable. The carronades ought to be elevated as high as their carriages will admit, and the charge of powder increased. Instead of using the allowed medium charge of one twelfth the weight of the round shot, the allowed highest charge ought to be used, *viz.* (one eighth the weight of the shot.) If this charge and high elevation should not produce the intended effect, the charge must be increased to one sixth the weight of the round shot; this I admit is an extraordinary high charge for carronades; but as it is indispensably necessary to return the enemy's fire with some chance of effect, and which has now become the first object to commanders of ships in this situation, the risk of dismounting one or more of the carronades, ought not to be adduced as a reason for not attempting the use of this charge. No apprehensions need be entertained of their bursting, as they already have been proved, by being fired twice, with a charge of powder equal to one fourth the weight of the shot.[24] Whenever an enemy, adopting this mode of attack, unexpectedly finds his fire returned, he will probably think himself very fortunate in having it in his power to give up the contest.

The great windage between the shot and carronade alluded to by A.F.Y., I cannot conceive how it could possibly occur; for in order to give carronades as great a velocity as possible, the allowed windage in them is less by one half than what are allowed in guns of the same calibre. The allowed windage for a 32-pounder gun is three inches, or the one twentieth part of the diameter of the shot; that of a 32-pounder carronade, being only fifteen inches, or the fortieth part of the diameter of the shot. [sic] Probably the shot alluded to, were French 26-pounders, which are fourteen inches less than our 32-pounders; if so, this will account for the great windage, and consequent shortness of

23 The first constructed carronades, when fired, were, from their shortness, attended with the disadvantage of not carrying the explosion clear of the ship; to remedy this defect, the diameter of the bore or cylinder at the muzzle has been increased, which simple alteration has, in a great measure, obviated this complaint. The same improvement would be of great utility to all short guns for sea service, as well as to long guns used in batteries; the frequent explosions from the latter, constantly prove destructive to the sole and facings of embrasures, and when faced with fascines frequently sets them on fire. This merits investigation.
   The interior construction of ordnance (of whatever description) is the part alone which affects their ranges. The exterior has no influence whatever, beyond determining its weight, and suitableness for mounting it on carriages. As to the external trappings and ornaments of rings, ogees, astragals, fillets, &c. they are useless. Guns would be found equally serviceable without them, as those that have them.
24 68 and 42-pounder carronades are an exception. The former being proved only with 13 lbs. and the latter with 9 lbs. of powder.

their ranges, better than ascribing it to a dent or two; which, if they are not of any depth, can have but little influence on their range. With respect to shot having holes in them, this proceeds from a defect in casting, and when such are tendered to the service by the contractor, they ought to be rejected. Dents likewise proceed from a defect in casting, but which are not discovered till after having been frequently moved: the collision attending their removal, breaks off the scaly part, and discloses those dents, which are commonly attributed to rust.[25]

1814 - Congreve's Rockets at the Siege of Flushing [XXXI 382]

A.B. to the Editor, London, 19th April, 1814
Mr. Editor, Having been lately at Middleburg, I was rather curious to learn every particular I could of the memorable siege of Flushing, where I used to go every day. Amongst other matters, I inquired whether or not Congreve's rockets were capable of being extinguished in water. To my great surprise, I was informed of many instances where those instruments of destruction had been extinguished. I was referred to an old woman named Leech, of whom I had been told that she took a burning rocket in her hand, and plunging it into a pail of water, at once extinguished it. "Curse your rockets," said she, "I thought it would have set fire to my house:" another was extinguished by the same means, by a tailor, named Louizon: a third by a bag of coffee, lodged in a warehouse belonging to old Mrs. Weeks. I send you these facts, knowing them to be genuine truths.

1816 - Copper Powder Barrels [XXXVI 70-72; 161-166]

From: Remarks &c. &c. on the Safe Conveyance and Preservation of Gunpowder. By James Walker, Inventor of the Improved Patent Copper Barrels for the effectual Preservation of Gunpowder and Cartridges in his Majesty's Royal Navy, &c. &c.

The great utility of Mr. Walker's Invention is too obvious to need any introductory comment from us. The purpose of our review is therefore rather to lay before our readers testimonies of the inventor's accomplishment of his object, than to prove the value of the invention. Almost as long as from the time when the composition of this powerful grain was first contrived, it has been the defence of nations; the importance of its preservation must therefore be commensurate with that of its employ; and in this point of view Mr. Walker thus considers the necessity and utility of his invention in his initiatory address:

"The capture of the British ships of war by those of the Americans, has been attributed by some to their ships being so superior in size - by others to their calibre; but the possibility of the American gunpowder being more effective than that with

25 The following composition will effectually guard iron from rust. Take equal parts of fine red ochre, and the dust of well burnt red brick, pass them through a fine hair sieve, mix and rub them together on a painter's stone, with as much Swedish tar as will thoroughly incorporate them (in the same manner as painters rub their paints); then add as much boiling hot tar, as will bring the composition to a proper consistence, and fit to lay on with a painter's brush, having previously freed the iron from all dirt, rust, &c. Two or three coats will be sufficient, observing to allow the first coat to be perfectly dry before the next is applied. This composition will effectually preserve all kind of timber or wood work that may be exposed to sun and weather, and will be found far superior to any kinds of prepared oils and paints, however manufactured.

which the British ships were defended, appears to have escaped all who have written on those events. The total destruction of the *Guerriere, Java*, and *Peacock*, while the American ships were so little injured, as well as the capture of the *Macedonian, Boxer,* and *Dominica*, are subjects, notwithstanding the victories obtained by the *Shannon* and *Pelican* by boarding, that demand serious consideration. These remarks are therefore written to shew, that the British gunpowder, although extremely well manufactured, is so soon deteriorated, as to leave no doubt that the ascendancy gained by the Americans is to be attributed in a very great degree to its defective state; and to the American powder being newly made, better preserved, and more immediately used, than that with which the British fought."

The advantages of Mr. Walker's Patent Copper Powder Barrels are thus stated:

"These barrels being calculated to prevent the deterioration of gunpowder, and to preserve its strength as well as the cartridges in all climates and situations, without which no ship can be properly equipped for battle, serious attention to the following remarks, setting forth the vast advantages to be obtained by the adoption of them, is requested.

First - The strength of the gunpowder will be preserved, its ignition will be instantaneous, and its effect will be complete.

Second - The dangerous operation of driving the hoops on and off, or coopering the powder-casks, will be done away.

Third - As it is proposed to fill the cartridges on shore ready for action, the dangerous operation of filling on shipboard will be remedied; nor will there be any necessity for shifting the gunpowder into fresh cartridges, which will cause an immense saving, as well in them as in powder.

Fourth - There will be no necessity for sending gunpowder on shore to be dried, at home or abroad, which is a circumstance of the greatest importance, as the service will not thereby be impeded.

Fifth - No more than one barrel need be opened at a time, as the operation is expeditious, and the cartridges can be so arranged in them as to be suited to the length of the action.

Sixth - The barrels are admirably suited to boat service, or to cases of invasion, as the water cannot get into them, although the boats be upset.

Seventh - There can be no scattering or waste of gunpowder, on board ships or elsewhere, which it is evident must produce great safety, as well as great saving.

Eighth - The barrels are constructed to prevent theft, as also the very common and pernicious attacks of vermin, which the present wooden barrels and their attendant articles are ever liable to.

Ninth - In case of a ship taking fire, the magazine may be filled with water, and the gunpowder cannot be injured.

Tenth - They will be particularly useful for the conveyance of combustibles for burning ships, or any purpose that may be required.

Eleventh - The patent barrels, from being cylindrical, contain, with ease, in cartridges, the quantity of gunpowder allowed by act of parliament to be conveyed loose in any package, namely, 100 lbs. The wooden barrels sent on board his Majesty's ships are filled with 90 lbs so as to allow the powder to be shook, to prevent its being set or lumpy; but notwithstanding every care, it is ever found to be the case, in consequence of the damp, which the patent barrels entirely exclude.

Twelfth - As the patent barrels contain more gunpowder than the wooden barrels, without occupying a greater space, the quantity required for a seventy-four gun ship will be held in three hundred, in place of three hundred and thirty barrels; so that there will be more spare room in the magazine, and no increased weight to impede the sailing of the ship, and all the following articles will not be required; viz.

Wooden Barrels, Copper Hoops, Copper Powder Measures, Copper Adzes, Copper Drivers, Copper Vices, Copper Sieves, Copper Funnels, Copper Shovels, Bouge Barrels, and Horse Hides, which are ever liable to be lost and pilfered, and are most expensive.

Thirteenth - Wooden barrels are a dangerous and useless conveyance for gunpowder; when returned to the magazines, they require repair and coopering: the breakage and loss of copper hoops is very great; and when the barrels are worn out, they are not of the least value: the patent barrels, on the contrary, are a perfectly safe conveyance for gunpowder; they require no repairs, and will last for a great many years.

Fourteenth - As gunpowder, when returned from on board ship in wooden barrels, is valued only at half-price, the saving which will be produced by the adoption of the patent barrels will be immense, as gentlemen of the highest chemical knowledge are of opinion they will keep it dry for any length of time; by which means they will render the drying-houses, and all the attendant expenses, unnecessary.

Fifteenth - The powder magazines of men of war occupy a large portion of the ship, and prevent, from their closeness, a proper circulation of air, which very frequently causes the dry rot underneath them; by the adoption of the patent barrels it may be avoided, as a greater circulation of air can be admitted.

Sixteenth - The recent occurrence on board H.M.S. *Tilbury*, (late *La Prudente*), stationed at Plymouth as a powder magazine, by which an immense number of barrels of gunpowder were spoiled, owing to that ship having fallen by the stern, so as to admit the water, could not have happened, had the powder been put into the patent, instead of wooden barrels; nor is there a possibility of a similar accident recurring, in the event of the patent barrels coming into general use, as they preserve the gunpowder even under water.

Seventeenth - It is presumed (including all the attendant expenses of drying houses, &c &c.) that gunpowder made by government costs infinitely more than it does at the private mills; but supposing each barrel of powder was to cost £8 exclusive of copper hoops, sixty thousand barrels, the quantity stated by the Honourable Wellesley Pole to be annually required, would amount to £480,000 per annum, one-fourth part of which, at the very lowest, may be annually saved by adopting the patent barrels.

Lastly - The patent barrels (being constructed of copper, and bound with hoops, to strengthen them, in conformity with the spirit of the act of parliament), will, at any period, produce three-fourths of the price of new copper; the expense of them, therefore, can be no obstacle to their being brought into use, particularly as they will do away the necessity of re-making gunpowder, and by that means will pay for themselves, with inconceivable rapidity. . . .

Ben Hallowell to Mr. James Walker, Blackheath Hill

H.M.S. Malta, in Tarragona Bay, February 4, 1814

I dare say you will have thought me very negligent, in having so long delayed making a report on your patent powder barrels; but as I was determined (in justice to yourself and government) to give them a fair and impartial trial, I deferred making any report until I was able, from experience, to decide on their merits; and having kept the barrels, which were packed in July 1811, unopened until the last month, I now feel confident in recommending them for general use in the navy, and particularly for all magazines in hot climates on shore.

The results of the different experiments made under my own observation, are such strong proofs of the superior strength of the powder contained in your barrels, after such a length of time, as cannot fail of being more satisfactory to you, than if I had given an opinion formed upon a shorter trial.

I beg leave to enclose the copy of a letter which I have written to the Secretary of the Admiralty on the subject; and I sincerely hope their Lordships may be induced to adopt them generally in the service.

To J.W. Croper, Esq. &c. &c.

H.M.S. Malta, in Tarragona Bay, February 1, 1814
Sir, I have deferred offering any report upon Mr. Walter's powder, brought out in the *Malta*, until it should have been long enough on board to admit of its real qualities and merit being ascertained. Having made several experiments last month at Tarragona, I beg to state the results, for the information of my Lords Commissioners of the Admiralty. The first experiment from a 4 2/5 inch howitzer, at an elevation of 45° with one ounce of powder, gave the following:

	Range of Powder	
	Walker's Barrels	Wooden Barrels
1st Discharge	205 1/2 yards	138 yards
2d	222	137
3rd	222	170

To render it a fair trial, the same shell was made use of in every discharge.

The powder taken from Mr. Walker's barrel was packed in July 1811 in paper cartridges, and had not been opened previous to this experiment.

A second experiment was made from the same barrel, with a 24-pounder long gun; the results were as follow:

			Range	
			Walker's	Wooden
1st Discharge	10 Eliv.	8lb Powder	1640	1164
2nd	50	7lb	1692	1612
3rd	60	6lb	1610	lost

Another barrel was opened a few days after, which came from England in the *Marlborough*, and had been filled in September 1812. The following are the results of an experiment made from a 12-pounder carronade, with one pound of powder:

		Range	
		Walker's	Wooden
1st Discharge, Point Blank		lost	534
2nd	10 Elevation	924	668
3d	10	762	536
4th	50	1062	982
5th	50	1018	922

I have since opened one of the barrels, No. 49, of loose priming powder, filled in July 1811, which is also in the most perfect order, without a single lump in it. Two barrels, one containing cartridges, flannel, and paper, for 24-pounder guns, the other flannel cartridges for 12-pounder carronades, have also been examined; both of which are in as good order as the day on which there were first packed.

The magazine of the *Malta* is frequently aired; and I do not believe there is one in the fleet more free from damp, or in more perfect order. The powder in cartridges is turned, one half one week, the remaining part the next, so that the whole undergoes this operation once a fortnight; the powder in barrels is turned and shaken once in three months; notwithstanding which, scarcely a week passes during the summer months, without finding many cartridges so bad, as to make it necessary to shift the powder into others; and the powder in barrels is frequently lumpy; which is not the case either with the loose powder or cartridges packed in Mr. Walker's copper barrels, although stowed in the same magazine, and in the same tiers with the others.

Most of the accidents which happen in action from explosions, are occasioned by the cartridges being damp, and breaking as they are taken out of the boxes, when handed up from the magazine. This danger, as well as that of filling powder in action, is avoided by the adoption of Mr. Walker's barrels; and they are admirably calculated for boat magazines, or for landing ammunition in a heavy surf, as there is no danger of the powder being damaged, if the boat should be filled with water.

Being satisfied, from experience, of the superiority of the powder kept in Mr. Walker's barrels over that kept in wooden ones, or in cartridges in the racks of a magazine, I do with confidence recommend them for general use in the navy; and in hot climates, where the magazines on shore are seldom perfectly dry, they would be particularly useful, and the saving to government would be immense.

Report made at Priddie's Hard, June 29, 1814
Pursuant to an order from Sir Richard Bickerton, Bart. Admiral of the White, &c. &c. we, the undersigned captains of his Majesty's ships *Magnificent, Valiant,* and *Norge,* have this day repaired to Priddie's Hard, and there carefully examined the comparative state of preservation of the powder in five of Walker's new invented copper barrels (as well as the condition of the cartridges and other contents), brought home in the *Stirling Castle,* and two of the common barrels of powder, taken out in her from England, sent by Captain Butterfield for that purpose; and we have to report our proceedings for their Lordships' information.

The powder was examined in the open air, and where the sun shone; and the whole process was performed in presence of Mr. Walker himself, who attended with the keys of the copper barrels.

1st, We proceeded to examine the common water-tight barrel, marked "K.P. February 1, 1812," and in chalk "Stirling Castle;" the barrel quite good, and hasps free from verdigris. It had no appearance of having been opened since it was shipped, nor of having suffered from bad stowage. The powder was in lumps, and various in colour; in several instances, the saltpetre apparent. The lumps came rather from the bottom than top of the barrel, but laid fairly, and without the least appearance of improper interference.

2d, Opened the common powder, marked "28LG Red, 90 Cyl." on one head, and on the other

$$\frac{B}{\text{June 8}}$$
$$R \mid S$$
1812

also in chalk, "Stirling Castle." This barrel was in the usual state of these into which restored powder is put, but appeared to have been opened since it was received from the magazine in England: the powder in lumps and damaged, considered as too bad to be manufactured.

3d, Mr. Walker unlocked the copper barrel marked "Sir S. Hood, No. 43;" removed first, the copper cover; second, a sheet of paper; third, a wooden plug, luted down with putty made of boiled linseed oil, which opened easily; fourth, a copper lid, luted in the same manner. The barrel contained three 42-pound cartridges, which had much room to play, and to this we attributed the bursting of the cartridges, the paper being good, and powder hard and dry, without lumps, or any appearance of saltpetre. Compared with new powder, it had a different colour, but that evidently proceeded from one being made with willow charcoal, and the other with alder. The paint had chipped off from the sides of the barrel, and mixed with the loose powder. There appeared to be a considerable quantity of dust, but Mr. Walker declared that he had made that objection in writing, when filled in June 1811, and sent to the *Owen Glendower*; and we conceive that it may also have been occasioned, in great measure, by the barrels not having been filled to the top, and frequently shifted.

4th, Examined the copper barrel marked "Sir S. Hood, No. 41;" secured as the last. On the wooden plug was this remark - "This did not hold the six cartridges without taking a little out of one cartridge;" contained flannel cartridges in a high state of preservation, free from moth, and the thread perfect; powder dry, but dusty. . . .

This volume is indexed in Volume V.